THE
unofficial GUIDE®
ᵀᴼDisneyland

2020

COME CHECK US OUT!

Supplement your valuable guidebook with tips, news, and deals by visiting our websites:

theunofficialguides.com

touringplans.com

Also, while there, sign up for The Unofficial Guide newsletter for even more travel tips and special offers.

Join the conversation on social media:

 @theUGSeries

 theUnofficialGuides

 theUGSeries

 theUGSeries

 TheUnofficialGuideSeries

Other Unofficial Guides

The Disneyland Story: The Unofficial Guide to the Evolution of Walt Disney's Dream

Universal vs. Disney: The Unofficial Guide to American Theme Parks' Greatest Rivalry

The Unofficial Guide to Disney Cruise Line

The Unofficial Guide to Las Vegas

The Unofficial Guide to Mall of America

The Unofficial Guide to Universal Orlando

The Unofficial Guide to Walt Disney World

The Unofficial Guide to Walt Disney World with Kids

The Unofficial Guide to Washington, D.C.

THE *unofficial* GUIDE®

TO Disneyland*

2020

SETH KUBERSKY *with* BOB SEHLINGER,
LEN TESTA, *and* GUY SELGA JR.

Please note that prices fluctuate in the course of time and that travel information changes under the impact of many factors that influence the travel industry. We therefore suggest that you write or call ahead for confirmation when making your travel plans. Every effort has been made to ensure the accuracy of information throughout this book, and the contents of this publication are believed to be correct at the time of printing. Nevertheless, the publishers cannot accept responsibility for errors or omissions, for changes in details given in this guide, or for the consequences of any reliance on the information provided by the same. Assessments of attractions and so forth are based upon the author's own experience; therefore, descriptions given in this guide necessarily contain an element of subjective opinion, which may not reflect the publisher's opinion or dictate a reader's own experience on another occasion. Readers are invited to write the publisher with ideas, comments, and suggestions for future editions.

Published by:
AdventureKEEN
2204 First Ave. S, Ste. 102
Birmingham. AL 35233

Cover design by Scott McGrew

Text design by Vertigo Design with updates by Annie Long

For information on our other products and services or to obtain technical support, please contact us from within the United States at 888-604-4537 or by fax at 205-326-1012.

AdventureKEEN also publishes its books in a variety of electronic formats. Some content that appears in print may not be available in electronic formats.

ISBN 978-1-62809-098-7 (pbk); ISBN 978-1-62809-099-4 (ebook)

Manufactured in the United States of America

5 4 3 2 1

CONTENTS

LIST of MAPS

ACKNOWLEDGMENTS

A BIG SALUTE to our whole Unofficial team, who rendered a Herculean effort in what must have seemed like a fantasy version of Jean-Paul Sartre's *No Exit* to the tune of "It's a Small World." We hope you all recover to tour another day.

Special thanks to cartoonist Tami Knight; child psychologist Karen Turnbow, PhD; Unofficial Guide statistician Fred Hazleton; "Unheralded Treasures" writer Lani Teshima; our Hollywood informer Eric Oh; and Unofficial research assistant Genevieve Bernard.

Amber Kaye Henderson, Annie Long, and Holly Cross all contributed energetically to shaping this latest edition. Much appreciation also goes to editorial-production manager Molly Merkle, cartographer Steve Jones, and indexer Rich Carlson.

—*Bob Sehlinger*

INTRODUCTION

▌█ WHY "UNOFFICIAL"?

DECLARATION OF INDEPENDENCE

THE AUTHORS AND RESEARCHERS OF THIS GUIDE specifically and categorically declare that they are and always have been totally independent of the Walt Disney Company, Inc., of Disneyland, Inc., of Walt Disney World Company, Inc., and of any and all other members of the Disney corporate family.

The material in this guide originated with the authors and researchers and has not been reviewed, edited, or in any way approved by Walt Disney Company, Inc., Disneyland, Inc., or Walt Disney World Company, Inc.

With no obligation to toe the Disney line, we represent and serve you, the reader. The contents were researched and compiled by a team of evaluators who are completely independent of the Walt Disney Company, Inc. If a restaurant serves bad food, if a gift item is overpriced, or if a ride isn't worth the wait, we say so. And in the process, we hope to make your visit more fun, efficient, and economical.

DANCE TO THE MUSIC

A DANCE HAS A BEGINNING AND AN END. But when you're dancing, you're not concerned about getting to the end or where on the dance floor you might wind up. You're totally in the moment. That's the way you should be on your Disneyland vacation.

You may feel a bit of pressure concerning your vacation. Vacations, after all, are very special events, and expensive ones to boot. So you work hard to make your vacation the best that it can be. Planning and organizing are essential to a successful Disneyland vacation, but if they become your focus, you won't be able to hear the music and enjoy the dance.

So think of us as your dancing coach. We'll teach you the steps to the dance in advance, so when you're on vacation and the music plays, you will dance with effortless grace and ease.

THE DEATH OF SPONTANEITY

ONE OF OUR ALL-TIME favorite letters is from a man in Chapel Hill, North Carolina. He writes:

Your book reads like the operations plan for an amphibious landing: Go here, do this, proceed to Step 15. You must think that everyone is a hyperactive, type-A theme park commando. What happened to the satisfaction of self-discovery or the joy of spontaneity? Next you will be telling us when to empty our bladders.

More recently, a reader from Seattle wrote online:

We skipped the touring plans and instead took our time to smell the flowers and truly take in the entire experience of Disney—isn't that what it is all about! Our friends decided to strictly follow the touring plans. We felt sorry for their 7-year-old daughter, who had a fever and was pumped up with Tylenol just so her parents could follow this plan. Their whole family was quite exhausted at the end.

Maximizing the number of rides/events one does is NOT the same as maximizing one's true enjoyment of Disney.

As it happens, we at The Unofficial Guides are a pretty existential crew. We are big on self-discovery when walking in the woods or watching birds. Some of us are able to improvise jazz without reading music, while others can whip up a mean pot of chili without a recipe. When it comes to Disneyland, however, we all agree that you either need a good plan or a frontal lobotomy. The operational definition of self-discovery and spontaneity at Disneyland is the "pleasure" of heat prostration and the "joy" of standing in line.

It's easy to spot the free spirits at Disneyland Park and Disney California Adventure, especially at opening time. While everyone else is stampeding to Space Mountain or Radiator Springs Racers, they're standing in a cloud of dust puzzling over the park map. Later, they're running around like chickens in a thunderstorm trying to find an attraction with less than a 40-minute wait. Face it: Disneyland Resort is not a very existential place. In many ways it's the ultimate in mass-produced entertainment, the most planned and programmed environment imaginable. Self-discovery and spontaneity work about as well at Disneyland as they do on your tax return. One mother of two young boys had this to say about our book:

Your book was invaluable in giving us the tools to plan a great day. We had a magical day thanks to being able to prioritize our goals. Thank you for the full descriptions of rides—with only one day, you really need to pick your battles.

We're not saying that you can't have a great time at Disneyland. Bowling isn't very spontaneous either, but lots of people love it. What we *are* saying is that you need a plan. You don't have to be inflexible. Just think about what you want to do—before you go. Don't delude yourself by rationalizing that the information in this book is only for the pathological and superorganized. For those who truly want to stop and smell the roses at Disneyland, we recommend our Anti-Touring Plan (see pages 280–283), which guarantees a day without stress, waiting in queues, or bouncing around the park. You won't actually get on many (if any) rides, but you can enjoy a full day of live entertainment and people-watching without sticking to a strict schedule. Just step out of the way when guests sprinting toward their next headliner rush by.

HOW *This* GUIDE WAS RESEARCHED *and* WRITTEN

WHILE MUCH HAS BEEN WRITTEN concerning Disneyland Resort, very little has been comparative or evaluative. In preparing this guide, nothing was taken for granted. The theme parks were visited at different times throughout the year by a team of trained observers who conducted detailed evaluations, rating the theme parks along with all of their component rides, shows, exhibits, services, and concessions according to formal, pretested rating criteria. Interviews with attraction patrons were conducted to determine what tourists of all age groups enjoyed most and least during their Disneyland visit.

Though our observers are independent and impartial, we do not claim special expertise or scientific backgrounds relative to the types of exhibits, performances, or attractions viewed. Like you, we visit the Disneyland parks as tourists, noting our satisfaction or dissatisfaction. Disneyland offerings are marketed to the touring public, and it is as the public that we have experienced them.

The primary difference between the average tourist and the trained evaluator is that the latter approaches attractions equipped with professional skills in organization, preparation, and observation. The trained evaluator is responsible for much more than simply observing and cataloging. While the tourist is being entertained and delighted by the *Enchanted Tiki Room*, the professional evaluator seated nearby is rating the performance in terms of theme, pace, continuity, and originality. The evaluator also checks out the physical arrangements: Is the sound system clear and audible without being overpowering; is the audience shielded from the sun or rain; is seating adequate; can everyone in the audience clearly see the stage? Similarly, detailed and relevant checklists are prepared by observer teams and applied to rides, exhibits, and concessions, as well as to the theme park in general. Finally, observations and evaluator ratings are integrated with audience reactions and the opinions of patrons to compile a comprehensive profile of each feature and service.

In compiling this guide, we recognize the fact that a tourist's age, gender, background, and interests will strongly influence his or her taste in Disneyland offerings and will account for his or her preference of one ride or feature over another. Given this fact, we make no attempt at comparing apples with oranges. How, indeed, could a meaningful comparison be made between the serenity and beauty of the Storybook Land Canal Boats and the wild roller coaster ride of the Incredicoaster? Instead, our objective is to provide the reader with a critical evaluation and enough pertinent data to make knowledgeable decisions according to individual tastes.

The essence of this guide, then, consists of individual critiques and descriptions of each feature of the Disneyland parks, supplemented with maps to help you get around and detailed touring plans to help you avoid bottlenecks and crowds. Because so many Disneyland guests also visit Universal Studios Hollywood to see The Wizarding World of Harry Potter, we have included comprehensive coverage and a touring plan for that park as well.

A WORD TO OUR READERS ABOUT ANNUAL REVISIONS

SOME OF YOU WHO PURCHASE EACH NEW EDITION of *The Unofficial Guide to Disneyland* have chastised us for retaining examples, comments, and descriptions from previous years' editions. This letter from a Grand Rapids, Michigan, reader is typical:

> *Your guidebook still has the same example stories. I expected a true update and new stuff, not the same old, same old!*

First, *The Unofficial Guide to Disneyland* is a reference work. Though we are flattered that some readers read the guide from cover to cover, and that some of you find it entertaining, our objective is fairly straightforward: to provide information that enables you to have the best possible Disneyland vacation.

Each year during our revision research, we check every attraction, restaurant, hotel, shop, and entertainment offering. Though there are many changes, much remains the same from year to year. When we profile and critique an attraction, we try to provide the reader with the most insightful, relevant, and useful information, written in the clearest possible language. It is our opinion that if an attraction does not change, then it makes little sense to risk clarity and content for the sake of freshening up the prose. Disneyland guests who try the Mad Tea Party or Pinocchio's Daring Journey today, for example, experience the same presentation as guests who visited Disneyland in 2013, 1995, or 1986. Moreover, according to our extensive patron surveys, today's guests still respond to these attractions in the same way as prior-year patrons.

The bottom line: We believe that our readers are better served if we devote our time to that which is changing and new as opposed to that which remains the same. The success or failure of this *Unofficial*

Guide is determined not by the style of the writing but by the accuracy of the information and, ultimately, whether you have a positive experience at Disneyland. Every change to the guide we make (or don't make) is evaluated in this context.

WE'VE GOT ATTITUDE

SOME READERS DISAGREE with our attitude toward Disney. A 30-something woman from Golden, Colorado, lambasts us, writing:

> *You were way too hard on Disney. It's disappointing, when you're all enthused about going, to be slammed with all these criticisms and possible pitfalls.*

A reader from Little Rock, Arkansas, also takes us to task:

> *Your book was quite complimentary of Disney, perhaps too complimentary. Maybe the free trips you travel writers get at Disneyland are chipping away at your objectivity.*

For the record, we've always paid our own way at Disneyland Resort: hotels, admissions, meals, the works. We don't dislike Disney, and we most definitely don't have an ax to grind. We're positive by nature and much prefer to praise than to criticize. We have enjoyed the Disney parks immensely over the years, both experiencing them and writing about them. Disney, however, as with all corporations, is better at some things than others. Because our readers shell out big bucks to go to Disneyland, we believe that they have the right to know in advance what's good and what's not. For those who think we're overly positive, please understand that *The Unofficial Guide to Disneyland* is a guidebook, not an exposé. Our overriding objective is for you to enjoy your visit. To that end we try to report fairly and objectively. When readers disagree with our opinions, we, in the interest of fairness and balance, publish their point of view right alongside ours. To the best of our knowledge, The Unofficial Guides are the only travel guides in print that do this.

THE UNOFFICIAL GUIDE PUBLISHING YEAR

WE RECEIVE MANY QUERIES each year asking when the next edition of *The Unofficial Guide to Disneyland* will be available. Usually our new editions are published and available in stores by late August or early September. Thus the 2021 edition will be on the shelves in fall 2020.

LETTERS, COMMENTS, AND QUESTIONS FROM READERS

MANY OF THOSE WHO USE *The Unofficial Guide to Disneyland* write to us, asking questions, making comments, or sharing their own strategies for visiting Disneyland. We appreciate all such input, both positive and critical, and encourage our readers to continue writing. Readers' comments and observations are frequently used in revised editions of *The Unofficial Guide to Disneyland* and have contributed immeasurably to its improvement.

Reader Survey

Please fill out our reader survey online by visiting touringplans.com /disneyland-resort/survey. You can rest assured that we won't release your name and address to any mailing-list companies, direct mail advertisers, or other third parties. Unless you instruct us otherwise, we will assume that you do not object to being quoted in a future edition.

How to Contact the Author

Write to Seth Kubersky at this address:

> *The Unofficial Guide to Disneyland*
> 2204 First Ave. S, Ste. 102
> Birmingham, AL 35233
> info@theunofficialguides.com

When you write, put your address on both your letter and envelope; sometimes the two get separated. It is also a good idea to include your phone number and email address. If you email us, please tell us where you're from. Remember, as travel writers, we're often out of the office for long periods of time, so forgive us if our response is slow. Unofficial Guide email is not forwarded to us when we're traveling, but we will respond as soon as possible when we return.

Questions from Readers

Questions frequently asked by readers are answered in an appendix at the back of this *Unofficial Guide.*

DISNEYLAND RESORT:
An OVERVIEW

IF YOU HAVEN'T BEEN TO DISNEYLAND in a while, you'll hardly know the place. First, of course, there is **Disneyland Park,** which in 2020 marks its 65th year as the original Disney theme park; it's also the only park that Walt Disney saw completed in his lifetime. Much more than the Magic Kingdom at Walt Disney World, Disneyland Park embodies the quiet, charming spirit of nostalgia that so characterized Walt himself. The park is vast yet intimate, steeped in the tradition of its creator yet continually changing.

Disneyland opened in 1955 on a 107-acre tract surrounded almost exclusively by orange groves, just west of the sleepy and little-known Southern California community of Anaheim. Constrained by finances and ultimately enveloped by the city it helped create, Disneyland operated on that same modest parcel of land until 2001.

Disneyland Park is a collection of adventures, rides, and shows symbolized by the Disney characters and Sleeping Beauty Castle. It's divided into nine subareas, or "lands," arranged around a central hub. First encountered is **Main Street, U.S.A.,** which connects the Disneyland entrance with the central hub. Moving clockwise around the hub, the other lands are **Adventureland, Frontierland, Fantasyland,** and **Tomorrowland.** Two major lands, **Critter Country** and **New Orleans Square,** are accessible via Adventureland and Frontierland but do not connect directly with the central hub. Another land, **Mickey's Toontown,** is accessed from Fantasyland. Finally, the huge **Star Wars: Galaxy's Edge** opened in 2019 on 14 acres of former backstage areas behind Critter Country and Frontierland, making it the biggest expansion in Disneyland Park's history. All nine lands will be described in detail later.

Growth and change at Disneyland (until 1996) had been internal, in marked contrast to the ever-enlarging development of Walt Disney World near Orlando, Florida. When something new was added at Disneyland, something old had to go. The Disney engineers, to their credit, however, have never been shy about disturbing the status quo. Patrons of the park's earlier, modest years are amazed by the transformation. Gone are the days of the "magical little park" with the Monsanto House of the Future, donkey rides, and Captain Hook's Pirate Ship. Substituted in a process of continuous evolution and modernization are state-of-the-art fourth-, fifth-, and sixth-generation attractions and entertainment. To paraphrase Walt Disney, Disneyland will never stop changing as long as there are new ideas to explore.

Disneyland Park was arguably Walt Disney's riskiest venture. It was developed on a shoestring budget and made possible only through Disney's relationship with ABC Television and other corporate sponsors. The capital available was barely sufficient to acquire the property and build the park; nothing was left over for the development of hotels or the acquisition and improvement of property adjoining the park. Even the Disneyland Hotel, connected to the theme park by monorail, was owned and operated by a third party until 1989.

Disneyland's success spawned a wave of development that rapidly surrounded the theme park with mom-and-pop motels, souvenir stands, and fast-food restaurants. The steady decline of the area encircling Disneyland continued to rankle Walt. After tolerating the blight for 30 years, the Walt Disney Company (finally flush with funds and ready for a good fight) set about putting Disneyland Park right. Quietly at first, then aggressively, Disney began buying up the mom-and-pop motels, as well as the few remaining orange and vegetable groves near the park.

In June 1993 the City of Anaheim adopted a Disney plan that called for the development of a new Disney destination resort, including a second theme park situated in what was once the Disneyland parking lot; a Disney-owned hotel district with 4,600 hotel rooms; two new parking facilities; and improvements, including extensive landscaping of the streets that provide access to the complex. Infrastructure changes required to support the expanded Disney presence included widening I-5, building new interchanges, moving a major power line, adding new sewer systems, and expanding utilities capacity.

By the end of 2000, all of the changes, modifications, and additions were finished, and Disneyland began the new century as a complete multi–theme park resort destination. The second and newest park, **Disney California Adventure** (or DCA to the initiated), celebrated its grand opening on February 8, 2001.

DCA is an oddly shaped park built around a lagoon on one side and the Grand Californian Hotel on the other, with one of Disney's trademark mountains, **Grizzly Peak,** plopped down in the middle. **Buena Vista Street,** an entranceway evoking 1920s Los Angeles, leads to six "lands." Inside the front gate and to the left is **Hollywood Land** (formerly Hollywood Pictures Backlot), a diminutive version of the Disney's Hollywood Studios theme park at Walt Disney World. Then there are **Grizzly Peak** (which absorbed the former Condor Flats area) and **Pacific Wharf,** a pair of lands (originally known collectively as Golden State) celebrating California's industry, cuisine, and natural resources. **Cars Land** is dedicated to the desert town of Radiator Springs from Disney-Pixar's *Cars.* A yet-unnamed home for Marvel superheroes is set to open in 2020 in the space between Cars Land and Hollywood Land that formerly featured attractions based on the Disney-Pixar film *A Bug's Life.* Finally, **Pixar Pier** incongruously integrates the grand old seaside amusement parks of the early 20th century with computer-animated characters from Toy Story and The Incredibles, while **Paradise Gardens Park** incorporates the viewing areas for the nighttime lagoon show, along with assorted non-Pixar attractions from the former Paradise Pier.

The entrances to Disneyland Park and DCA face each other across a palm-studded pedestrian plaza called the **Esplanade,** which begins at Harbor Boulevard and runs west, between the parks, passing into **Downtown Disney,** a dining, shopping, entertainment, and nightlife venue. From Downtown Disney, the Esplanade continues via an overpass across Downtown Drive and past the monorail station to the **Disneyland** and **Paradise Pier Hotels.**

Sandwiched between the Esplanade and Downtown Disney on the north and DCA on the south is the 1,019-room **Grand Californian Hotel,** which includes the 50-unit **Grand Californian Villas.** Designed in the image of rustic national park lodges, the Grand Californian supplanted the Disneyland Hotel as Disneyland's prestigious lodging property.

Future expansion at the Disneyland Resort is currently in question. After a political spat over tax incentives with the City of Anaheim, Disney abandoned plans for a new luxury hotel (after shutting down portions of Downtown Disney to build it) and has also halted a proposed parking hub to the east of the resort. The rumor mill has also been rumbling for many years about a third theme park, possibly to be built on an outlying parking lot, but Disney CEO Bob Iger has publicly downplayed any such plans.

North of the hotels and across West Street from Disneyland Park are two huge multistory parking garages—named Mickey & Friends and Pixar Pals—that can be accessed directly from I-5. With a combined total of over 15,000 parking spaces, this is where most Disneyland guests park. Tram transport is provided from the garages to the Esplanade, and buses ferry guests in from the outlying lots. Kennels are to the right of the Disneyland Park main entrance. Ticket booths are situated along the Esplanade.

SHOULD I GO TO DISNEYLAND PARK IF I'VE SEEN WALT DISNEY WORLD?

DISNEYLAND PARK IS ROUGHLY COMPARABLE to the Magic Kingdom theme park at Walt Disney World near Orlando, Florida. Both are arranged by "lands" accessible from a central hub and connected to the entrance by a main street. Both parks feature many rides and attractions of the same name: Space Mountain, Jungle Cruise, Pirates of the Caribbean, It's a Small World, and Dumbo the Flying Elephant, to name a few. Interestingly, however, the same name does not necessarily connote the same experience. Pirates of the Caribbean at Disneyland Park is much longer and more elaborate than its Walt Disney World counterpart. The Haunted Mansion is more elaborate in Florida, and the *Enchanted Tiki Room* is about the same in both places.

Disneyland Park is more intimate than the Magic Kingdom, not having the room for expansion enjoyed by the Florida park. Pedestrian thoroughfares are narrower, and everything from Big Thunder Mountain to the castle is scaled down somewhat. Large crowds are more taxing at Disneyland Park because there is less room for them to disperse. At Disneyland Park, however, there are dozens of little surprises, small unheralded attractions tucked away in crooks and corners of the park, which give Disneyland Park a special charm and variety that the Magic Kingdom lacks. And, of course, Disneyland Park has the stamp of Walt Disney's personal touch.

A Minnesota couple who have sampled Disney both east and west offered this observation:

> For parents with children 10 years of age and younger, I highly recommend Disneyland instead of WDW. Its size is much more manageable. You can stay within walking distance of the front gate. That makes it practical and easy to get to the gates early in the morning (imperative) and get away in the afternoon for a break (always helpful). The size and scale of WDW make this impractical.

A Salem, Massachusetts, family who had visited WDW three years prior to their Disneyland trip, agreed:

> We heard from many that Disneyland was small and that the castle was underwhelming. But the Disney magic was there, and we had a great time exploring what was unique about each park. We spent three days at the parks and wished that we had planned to be there longer. The parks may be smaller, but there is still plenty to see and do.

Another experienced WDW visitor who now lives in Oakland, California, wrote:

> We were amazed at how easy Disneyland is to navigate compared to WDW. I appreciated how Disneyland felt like Disney Lite. No one

was pushy about the vacation club, Visa card, or even the annual pass. It was great to experience the parks this way.

A woman from Chincoteague, Virginia, adds:

We found Disneyland to be much more relaxed than WDW. The WDW dining reservation and FastPass+ systems have really made trips much more difficult, whereas MaxPass was a great feature.

And these die-hard Disney veterans from Pleasantville, New York, praised the Anaheim resort's employees:

Disneyland is such a wonderful alternative to the traditional trip to Walt Disney World. We particularly were impressed with the cast members. The Disneyland cast members consistently went above and beyond for us, even compared to Orlando's cast members.

To allow for a meaningful comparison, we have provided a summary of those features found at Disneyland Park and not WDW's Magic Kingdom (listed alphabetically below), accompanied by a critical look at the attractions found at both parks on the facing page.

ATTRACTIONS FOUND ONLY AT DISNEYLAND PARK

ADVENTURELAND

- Indiana Jones Adventure • Tarzan's Treehouse

CRITTER COUNTRY

- Davy Crockett's Explorer Canoes

FANTASYLAND

- Alice in Wonderland • Casey Jr. Circus Train • Fantasyland Theatre
- Matterhorn Bobsleds • Mr. Toad's Wild Ride • Pinocchio's Daring Journey
- Royal Theatre at Fantasy Faire • Sleeping Beauty Castle Walk-Through
- Snow White's Scary Adventures • Storybook Land Canal Boats

FRONTIERLAND

- *Fantasmic!* (in WDW at Disney's Hollywood Studios) • The Golden Horseshoe
- Sailing Ship *Columbia*

MAIN STREET, U.S.A.

- *The Disneyland Story*, presenting *Great Moments with Mr. Lincoln*

MICKEY'S TOONTOWN

- Chip 'n Dale Treehouse • Gadget's Go Coaster • Goofy's Playhouse
- Mickey's House • Minnie's House • *Miss Daisy*, Donald's Boat
- Roger Rabbit's Car Toon Spin

STAR WARS: GALAXY'S EDGE

- *Millennium Falcon:* Smugglers Run (in WDW at Disney's Hollywood Studios)
- Star Wars: Rise of the Resistance (in WDW at Disney's Hollywood Studios)

TOMORROWLAND

- Disneyland Monorail System • Finding Nemo Submarine Voyage
- Star Tours—The Adventures Continue (in WDW at Disney's Hollywood Studios)
- Star Wars Launch Bay (in WDW at Disney's Hollywood Studios)
- Tomorrowland Theater

CRITICAL COMPARISON OF ATTRACTIONS FOUND AT BOTH PARKS

ADVENTURELAND

- *Enchanted Tiki Room* Similar at both parks; slightly longer show at Disneyland but more advanced rainstorm effects at Walt Disney World.
- **Jungle Cruise** Updated Audio-Animatronic (robotic) animals and funnier narrators at Disneyland but longer ride at Walt Disney World.

CRITTER COUNTRY

- **The Many Adventures of Winnie the Pooh** Longer and with more motion at the Magic Kingdom.
- **Splash Mountain** Longer ride and a bigger drop at the Magic Kingdom, but California has more animatronic animals.

FANTASYLAND

- **Carrousels** About the same at both parks.
- **Castles** Far larger and more beautiful at Magic Kingdom; Disneyland has walk-through display.
- **Dumbo the Flying Elephant** About the same, but WDW version has double the capacity and an interactive circus-themed queue.
- **It's a Small World** Disneyland version is longer with hidden Disney characters, and it gets a holiday overlay.
- **Mad Tea Party** Disneyland's is open-air; otherwise the same at both parks.
- **Peter Pan's Flight** Shorter but with upgraded special effects at Disneyland.
- **Royal Hall at Fantasy Faire/Princess Fairytale Hall** About the same, but Disneyland doesn't have FastPass.

FRONTIERLAND

- **Big Thunder Mountain Railroad** More monumental mountain and an interactive queue at Magic Kingdom; smoother track and explosive special effects at Disneyland.
- **Tom Sawyer Island** Comparable; pirate theme with more elaborate effects at Disneyland but more caves and play structures to explore at Magic Kingdom.
- **Various river cruises (canoes, boats, and such)** More interesting sights at Disneyland, and only Disneyland offers canoes.

MAIN STREET, U.S.A.

- **Railroads** The Disneyland Railroad is far more entertaining by virtue of the Grand Canyon Diorama and the Primeval World components not found at the Magic Kingdom.

NEW ORLEANS SQUARE

- **The Haunted Mansion** Longer ride and high-tech hitchhiking ghosts give Magic Kingdom the edge. Holiday version is offered only at Disneyland.
- **Pirates of the Caribbean** Far superior at Disneyland.

TOMORROWLAND

- **Astro Orbitor** About the same at both parks, but is much higher in the air at the Magic Kingdom.
- **Autopia/Tomorrowland Speedway** Disneyland version is superior.
- **Buzz Lightyear** More mobile guns and better game play at Disneyland.
- **Space Mountain** Much better effects and smoother track at Disneyland but a wilder ride with sharper drops at Magic Kingdom. Only Disneyland offers seasonal versions like Ghost Galaxy.

*It should be noted that some of the attractions at Disney California Adventure, such as Toy Story Midway Mania!, *Mickey's PhilharMagic,* and *Turtle Talk with Crush,* appeared first at one of the Walt Disney World theme parks. Versions of Ariel's Undersea Adventure and Soarin' Around the World have been exported to Walt Disney World. None of the remaining DCA attractions are found at Disney World.

PART ONE

PLANNING *Before* YOU LEAVE HOME

GATHERING INFORMATION

IN ADDITION TO THIS GUIDE, we recommend that you first visit our website, theunofficialguides.com, which is dedicated to news about our guidebooks, as well as a blog with posts from Unofficial Guide authors. You can also sign up for the Unofficial Guides Newsletter, containing even more travel tips and special offers.

Our sister website, touringplans.com, offers essential tools for planning your trip and saving you time and money. Its blog, blog.touringplans .com, lists breaking news for the Disneyland Resort and Disney theme parks worldwide. Touringplans.com also offers computer-optimized touring plans for Disneyland and Disney California Adventure (DCA), as well as searchable dining menus, including wine lists, for every food cart, stand, kiosk, counter-service restaurant, and sit-down restaurant in the Disneyland Resort.

Another really popular part of touringplans.com is its Crowd Calendar, which shows crowd projections for Disneyland and DCA for every day of the year. Look up the dates of your visit, and the calendar will not only show the projected wait times for each day but will also indicate for each day which theme park will be the least crowded. Historical wait times are also available, so you can see how crowded the parks were last year for your upcoming trip dates.

Much of the content on touringplans.com—including the menus, resort photos and videos, and errata for this book—is completely free for anyone to use. Access to parts of the site, most notably the Crowd Calendar, touring plans, and in-park wait times, requires a small annual subscription fee (current-book owners get a substantial discount). This nominal charge helps keep touringplans.com online and costs less than a souvenir bucket of popcorn at Disneyland. Plus touringplans.com offers a 45-day money-back guarantee.

A subscriber from Arvada, Colorado, wrote in to say:

I purchased a membership to your website approximately one month before we went to Disneyland in the summer. I would never go without it again. I knew what kind of crowds to expect in advance, and not having to ask nine people what they wanted to do or go on next was great. Lunch and dinner were planned at certain times, and we even made adjustments to your recommended plan, so my 4½-year-old niece got to ride a couple of the kids' rides right away.

We also recommend that you obtain copies of the following:

1. DISNEYLAND RESORT VACATION-PLANNING VIDEOS Disney has online videos that advertise the resort's offerings. To view them, you'll need to fill out a short survey at disneyplanning.com. You can also access videos about other Disney destinations from the same website.

2. *DISNEYLAND GUIDEBOOK FOR GUESTS WITH DISABILITIES* If members of your party are sight- or hearing-impaired or partially or wholly nonambulatory, you will find this small guide very helpful. Special guides are also available for guests with cognitive disabilities, including autism spectrum disorders. Disney does not mail them, but copies are readily available at the park. You can also download the guides at disneyland.disney.go.com/guest-services/guests-with-disabilities.

Disneyland Main Information Phone and Website

The following website and phone numbers provide general information. Inquiries may be expedited by using phone numbers specific to the nature of the inquiry (other phone numbers are listed elsewhere in this chapter, under their relevant topics, and in the table on page 14). If you don't mind interacting with artificial intelligence, you can call ☎ 714-520-7090 and Ask Otto, Disneyland's automated information hotline, about ride wait times and upcoming shows.

DISNEYLAND GUEST RELATIONS
☎ 714-781-4565 for recorded information
☎ 714-781-7290 for live operator
disneyland.com

The Phone from Hell

Sometimes it is virtually impossible to get through on the Disneyland information numbers listed above. When you get through, you will get a recording that offers various information options. If none of the recorded options answer your question, you will have to hold for a live person. Eat before you call—you may have a long wait. If, after repeated attempts, you get tired of a busy signal in your ear or, worse, 20 minutes' worth of singing mice warbling "Cinderelly" in alto falsettos while you are on hold, call the Disneyland Hotel at ☎ 714-778-6600.

RECOMMENDED WEBSITES

A NUMBER OF GOOD Disneyland information sources are online. The following are brief profiles of our favorites:

IMPORTANT DISNEYLAND RESORT PHONE NUMBERS	
Anaheim Travel Information	☎ 714-765-2800
Annual Passholder Member Services	☎ 714-781-4567
Ask Otto Automated Attraction Info	☎ 714-520-7090
Dining Reservations & Viewing Packages	☎ 714-781-3463, Option 2
Disability Services	☎ 407-560-2547
Disney Cruise Line	☎ 800-951-3532
Disney Guided Tours	☎ 714-781-8687
Disneyland Hotel	☎ 714-778-6600
Disneyland Resort Room Reservations	☎ 714-956-6425
Disneyland Vacation Packages	☎ 714-520-5060
Foreign Language Assistance	☎ 714-781-7290
Grand Californian Hotel	☎ 714-635-2300
Lost & Found	☎ 714-817-2166
Merchandise	☎ 877-560-6477
Paradise Pier Hotel	☎ 714-999-0990
PhotoPass Guest Support	☎ 714-520-7106

BEST OFFICIAL THEME PARK SITES At the official Disneyland website, disneyland.com, you must create an account before booking or log in with an existing My Disney Experience account. There's a ton of information, but it usually takes a lot of clicks to find what you're looking for.

The Universal Studios website is universalstudioshollywood.com. Like the Disneyland site, it has a lot of information, though there are no online dining reservations or registration process. Both sites are filled with photos and videos that can be slow to load, so as far as your internet connection is concerned, be high-speed or be gone.

BEST OFFICIAL AREA WEBSITE Visitanaheim.org is the official website of the Anaheim–Orange County Visitor & Convention Bureau. You'll find everything from hotels and restaurants to weather and driving directions on this site.

BEST GENERAL UNOFFICIAL WEBSITES We recommend the following websites for general information related to the Disneyland Resort.

Mouseplanet.com is a comprehensive resource for Disneyland data, offering features and reviews by guest writers, information on the Disney theme parks, discussion groups, and news. The site includes an interactive Disney restaurant and hotel review page, where users can voice opinions on their Disney dining and lodging experiences. We particularly enjoy the weekly Disneyland update column.

Disneytouristblog.com, run by park photographer extraordinaire and Touring Plans contributor Tom Bricker, hosts a comprehensive introduction to planning a Disneyland vacation, along with reporting on more exotic Disney destinations in France, China, and Japan.

Deb Wills, the founder of allears.net, has now retired, but the website still includes extensive information about the Disney resorts and attractions (including reader reviews), Disney restaurant menus, ticketing information, maps, and more.

Wdwinfo.com has a vibrant Disneyland section that includes up-to-date dining menus, attraction reviews, touring tips, and more. True to its name, DisneylandDaily.com features near-daily updates from Casey Starnes, a mom of three and frequent visitor to the park.

BEST DISNEYLAND HISTORY WEBSITE At yesterland.com you can visit the Disneyland of the past, where retired Disneyland attractions are brought back to life through vivid descriptions and historical photos. Yesterland attraction descriptions relate what it was once like to experience the Flying Saucers, the Mine Train through Nature's Wonderland, the *Tahitian Terrace,* and dozens of other rides, shows, and restaurants.

BEST WEBSITE FOR RUMORS AND THE INSIDE SCOOP Jimhillmedia .com is perfectly attuned to what's going on behind the scenes—Jim Hill always has good gossip.

BEST DISNEYLAND NEWS SITES Micechat.com, with a dedicated group of local editors, is the definitive on-the-ground coverage of the Disneyland Resort. Check out Dusty Sage's regular update columns that stay on the pulse of the parks, complete with photos. Mouseplanet.com and Robert Niles's themeparkinsider.com are other great sources for breaking Southern California theme park news, as are Brady McDonald (blooloop.com) and *The Orange County Register* (ocregister.com/things-to-do/amusement-parks). For official news, the Disney Parks Blog (disneyparks.com/blog) covers news from all Disney resorts. For Universal Studios Hollywood updates, visit insideuniversal.net and californiainformer.com.

BEST MONEY-SAVING SITE Mousesavers.com specializes in finding you the deepest discounts on hotels, park admissions, and rental cars. MouseSavers does not actually sell travel but rather unearths and publishes special discounts that you can use. It's the first place we look for deals when we go to Disneyland Resort.

BEST DISNEY DISCUSSION BOARDS The best online discussion of all things Disney can be found at micechat.com/forums, mousepad.mouse planet.com, and disboards.com. With tens of thousands of members and millions of posts, they are the most active and popular discussion boards online. There is also a rousing chat room inside the touringplans.com mobile application, Lines, where folks can ask questions and give travel tips. Hundreds of "Liners" interact every day in discussions that stay remarkably on-topic for an internet forum, and the group organizes regular in-park meets (learn more at touringplans.com/lines).

BEST DISNEY PODCASTS *Mousetalgia,* found at mousetalgia.com, covers Disneyland, DCA, and everything else Disney. The hosts appreciate the history of the resort while maintaining balanced coverage of new Disneyland developments. *The Sweep Spot* (thesweepspot.com) features Disney news from the irreverent perspective of two former Disneyland custodians.

Seasonpasspodcast.com has breaking news and in-depth interviews with theme park designers and executives from Disneyland and parks around the world. Hosted by industry veterans (and fans!), the show provides detailed discussions about how and why theme parks work. And if you want warts-and-all tales from behind the scenes of Mickey's kingdoms, don't miss *The Unofficial Guide Disney Dish Podcast with Jim Hill* (disneydish.bandcamp.com), hosted by coauthor Len Testa.

BEST DISNEY TWITTER FEEDS If you want your Disney news and rumors in 140 character bites, follow us at @TheUGseries, along with these prolific park Tweeters:

@datelinedisneyland @thedisneyblog @disneyland @disneylandcats
@disneylandtoday @disneyparks @micechat @ocregister
@touringplans @guyselga @skubersky

BEST DISNEYLAND YOUTUBE CHANNELS We don't necessarily advocate spoiling attractions you haven't yet experienced in person, but YouTube videos can be very useful for assuaging anxious children (see page 143) or reliving the magic once you return home. You can visit theugseries .com/youtube to subscribe to our YouTube channel and get automatically notified of all our new videos. The TouringPlans YouTube channel (you tube.com/touringplans) hosts a wealth of clips from every Disney park. Other good sources for Disney park videos are the official Disney Parks channel (youtube.com/disneyparks), *Attractions* Magazine (youtube .com/attractionsmagazine), and SoCal Attractions 360 (youtube.com /socalattractions360), which uploads 4K ultra-low-light footage of dark rides that look sharper and brighter than actually being there.

BEST DISNEYLAND MOBILE APPS Smartphone apps are a great way to stay up to date on Disneyland info inside and outside the parks. First and foremost, we suggest installing Disneyland's free app, which features official park hours, attraction wait times, show schedules, restaurant menus, and interactive maps. You can even use it to purchase or store admission tickets, retrieve MaxPass ride reservations, and link to all your PhotoPass pictures; you'll need to register for a free Disney online account to use these features. It's best to download this app in advance via Wi-Fi, so you don't waste time and bandwidth inside the park. Disneyland's Wi-Fi network is free to use but frustratingly flaky outside of the hot spots designated on the park map.

You'll also want to install and log into the official Play Disney Parks app ahead of time, especially if you want to explore the interactive experiences inside Star Wars: Galaxy's Edge. By playing with the app's simple time-killing games, you can unlock Apple Music playlists of theme park soundtracks or get free readings from the fortune-telling machines found at Disneyland. Be sure to enable Bluetooth, Push Notifications, and background Location services, and beware that this app is a battery hog.

We also recommend Lines, the mobile application of touringplans .com, available for the Apple iPhone and iPad at the iTunes Store (search for "TouringPlans") and for Android devices at the Google Play Store. Owners of other phones can use the web-based version at m.touringplans .com. The app is free to download, but you'll need to log in with a paid TouringPlans subscription to access most of its features.

Touringplans.com website's touring plans, menus, Crowd Calendar, and more are available in Lines, which provides continuous real-time updates on wait times at Disneyland. Using in-park staff and updates sent in by readers, Lines shows you the current wait and FastPass distribution times at every attraction in every park, as well as the estimated actual waits for these attractions for the rest of the day. For example, Lines will tell you that the posted wait time for Space Mountain is 60 minutes, and that based on what we know about how Disney manages Space Mountain's queue, the actual time you'll probably wait in line is 48 minutes. Lines is the only Disney app that shows you both posted and actual wait times.

As long as you have that smartphone handy while visiting the parks, we and your fellow *Unofficial Guide* readers would love it if you could report on the actual wait times you get while you're there. Run Lines, log in to your user account, and click +TIME in the upper right corner to help everyone out. We'll use that information to update the wait times for everyone in the park, and make everyone's lives just a little bit better.

A couple from Easton, Pennsylvania, found Lines especially useful:

I don't know what we would have done without The Unofficial Guide to Disneyland *and the Lines app. This was our first and possibly only trip to Disneyland. We were able to do everything we wanted and ride many big attractions like the Matterhorn several times. We also enjoyed using the menu feature on the site and app. I was able to plan all our meals before arriving at a restaurant instead of realizing later that there were no good vegetarian options.*

As did this family from Folsom, California:

The Lines app proved to be invaluable on our trip. Without Lines, we could not have accomplished nearly as much as we did. We used Lines to find out what was off-line and what had a reasonable wait time. For instance, we were going to give up on Radiator Springs Racers until we noticed that the single-rider line had a reasonable wait.

ADMISSION OPTIONS

THEME PARK ADMISSION OPTIONS can be a bit complicated at Disneyland Resort. For starters, you have three things to decide:

1. How many days admission you'll need.
2. What date you wish to attend, if only visiting for one day.
3. Whether you want to go to both Disneyland Park and DCA on the same day. This is known as park hopping.

Multiday tickets expire 13 days after the first use, so you don't want to buy more days than you'll need. Needless to say, tickets expire after you've used the number of days purchased even if 13 days haven't passed yet. Finally, all passes expire at the end of the year after they were purchased; passes purchased in 2020 expire December 31, 2021. That means you can't stockpile current tickets as a hedge against future inflation, but Guest Services will let you pay the difference and upgrade a wholly unused expired ticket to a new one at current prices, as long as it costs the same or more than you originally paid.

All admissions can be purchased at the park entrance, at Disneyland Resort hotels, on the Disneyland website and app, by calling ☎ 714-781-4565 or 800-854-3104, and at most Disney stores in the western United States. One- and 2-year-olds are exempt from admission fees.

Admission Costs and Available Discounts

You can learn about any special seasonal discounts offered directly from Disney at disneyland.disney.go.com/offers-discounts; some offers may only be available for purchase through the website and not on the app.

unofficial **TIP**
The money you can save makes researching Disney's dizzying array of ticket options worthwhile.

If you purchase tickets on the Disneyland website, you can choose between "hard" tickets, which will be shipped to you, or e-tickets, which can be downloaded as PDF files and printed at home or scanned from your mobile device. E-tickets normally arrive in your email inbox within minutes of purchase (and automatically attach to your app account if you're signed in while buying) but can take up to 24 hours for delivery. An e-ticket printed from your home computer will show two bar codes. A cast member will scan these at the turnstiles. Once the bar codes are read, the cast member can issue your actual ticket.

ADMISSION OPTIONS	ADULT (age 10 and UP)	CHILD (ages 3-9)
One-Day, One Park (depending on season)	$104-$149	$98-$141
One-Day Park Hopper (depending on season)	$154-$199	$148-$191
Two-Day, One Park Per Day	$225	$210
Two-Day Park Hopper	$280	$265
Three-Day, One Park Per Day with Magic Morning	$300	$280
Three-Day Park Hopper with Magic Morning	$355	$335
Four-Day, One Park Per Day with Magic Morning	$325	$305
Four-Day Park Hopper with Magic Morning	$380	$360
Five-Day, One Park Per Day with Magic Morning	$340	$320
Five-Day Park Hopper with Magic Morning	$395	$375
Southern California Select Annual Passport *(many blockout dates; only available to residents of certain zip codes)*	$399	$399
Flex Annual Passport *(limited blockout dates; reservations required at certain times)*	$599	$599
Deluxe Annual Passport *(some blockout dates)*	$799	$799
Signature Annual Passport *(a few blockout dates; parking included)*	$1,149	$1,149
Signature Plus Annual Passport *(no blockout dates; parking included)*	$1,399	$1,399
Disney Premier Passport *(no blockout dates; valid at all California and Florida parks)*	$2,099	$2,099

It's possible to obtain discounts on all multiday tickets, but only in the 4%–8% range. The deepest discounts we've found are from **ARES Travel** (arestravel.com). ARES usually beats the Disney advance purchase price by $5–$9 per day (up to $30 per ticket) and also includes the Magic Morning feature. Guests may print their tickets at home 2 hours after purchase; a $2-per-ticket convenience fee applies. You can order online or call ☎ 800-434-7894. You must provide the first date you intend to visit when purchasing the ticket. Another option is **The Cleaver Brothers' Discount Tickets & Tours** (discountticketsandtours. com), located at The Grand Legacy at the Park hotel on Harbor Boulevard. It sells legitimate multiday tickets that can be taken straight to the turnstiles for $5 under Disney's gate price. Whatever you do, never buy cheap Disney tickets on eBay, Craigslist, or off the street. The passes are probably partially used and not authorized for resale, and Mickey will not give you your money back if you are turned away at the turnstiles.

If you plan to visit other Southern California attractions in addition to Disneyland, you might want to consider a **CityPass**. CityPass includes between two and five days of admission to Disneyland Park and DCA (one park per day or park hopper), combined with your pick of tickets to Universal Studios Hollywood, SeaWorld San Diego, Legoland California, and/or the San Diego Zoo. By making full use of all the admissions you select for your personalized CityPass, you can save $3–$5 per day on the Disneyland portion and $10 or more per day on the other attractions. If you don't use all of the admissions, however, you will save little or nothing by purchasing the CityPass. The pass does not include dining or shopping discounts. Details concerning other CityPass destinations are available at citypass.com/southern-california.

Military discounts are available for all Disney theme parks, usually in the 25%–50% range; in 2019 a Three-Day Park Hopper was offered for roughly the regular price of a One-Day Park Hopper. Check with your base Morale, Welfare, & Recreation office for info. Be aware that one member of your party must show military ID at the park turnstiles to use the tickets, so you can't purchase them for friends or relatives you won't be traveling with. Learn about current military discount offers at disneyland.disney.go.com/offers-discounts.

Disneyland Resort and other area attractions sometimes offer discounted afternoon and evening tickets for conventioneers. See disney meetings.com.

Admission prices increase from time to time. For planning your budget, however, the table on the facing page provides a fair estimate. Note that Walt Disney World tickets are *not* valid for admission to Disneyland, with the sole exception of bicoastal Premier Annual Passports.

Single-Day Tickets with Variable Pricing

Disney has followed the lead of airline and ski resort industries by instituting three seasonal tiers—value, regular, and peak—for all single-day tickets, charging more money for tickets on the busiest days and offering a modest discount during periods of lower attendance.

The price difference between a value and peak single day is currently $45 for one-park tickets and Park Hoppers. That's probably not enough of a premium to dictate plans for most out-of-state visitors, whose vacation dates are mandated by school and work schedules, but it does encourage locals to shift their visits toward cheaper days, perversely pumping up crowds when the parks would otherwise be empty, without significantly shrinking them on peak days.

Because of the tiered pricing structure, you must be certain of which date you will visit Disneyland when buying your ticket, or risk buying a more expensive ticket than you need. A peak day ticket is valid on any day of the year, while a regular one is good during regular or value season. Value tickets are only accepted on those select days, but they (or any other admission) can be upgraded to any more expensive pass, presuming the park isn't sold out.

With a one-day ticket, you may exit and return to the park on the same day as many times as you like. Disneyland photographs every guest upon first entry for identification purposes; be prepared to have your pass (and face) scanned shortly before passing the turnstiles, with your picture replacing the old exit handstamps for readmission.

Multiday Tickets

These are good for two, three, four, or five days, respectively. Multiday tickets are not affected by the single-day pricing seasons and can be used on any day of the year. These multiday tickets do not have to be used on consecutive days, but they do expire 13 days after their first use, which must happen on or before the last day of the year after purchase (currently December 31, 2021, for tickets bought in 2020). If you mistakenly bought multiday tickets because you were not aware of the 13-day expiration, call ☎ 714-781-7290 or ☎ 714-781-4565 and ask to be connected to Guest Communications, which has the authority to issue you a voucher for the unused days on your ticket.

All three-, four-, and five-day Disneyland tickets also include one Magic Morning, which entitles you to enter Disneyland early on Tuesday, Thursday, or Saturday; see pages 27–29 for more details.

Any time before a pass expires, you can apply the full original amount you paid for the ticket toward the cost of a higher-priced ticket. If you buy a Four-Day Park Hopper ticket, for example, and then decide you'd rather have an annual passport, you can apply the full original cost of the former toward the purchase of the latter. (If your original tickets were discounted, you'll have to make up the difference when upgrading.) The maximum number of days you can purchase on a standard Disneyland ticket is five. After that you have to upgrade to an annual pass or buy another ticket, which makes a six- or seven-day visit extremely cost-ineffective. Upgraded passes expire on the same 13-day deadline date as the original ticket; annual passes expire one year from the first usage of the original ticket.

Park Hopper Tickets

By default, tickets without Park Hopper require you to choose one park or the other to visit each day. All single and multiday tickets may be purchased with the Park Hopper option, which allows you to visit both Disneyland Park and DCA during the same day. The Park Hopper premium on a single-day admission is quite pricey (currently $50), but on a five-day pass that drops to only $11 per day.

If you are spending more than two days at Disneyland Resort, we strongly encourage you to spring for the park-to-park access. The ease of walking from one park to the other makes the Park Hopper premium more than worth it. If you buy a multiday one-park-per-day pass, you can upgrade it to a Park Hopper before it expires, but you'll pay the premium based on the pass's original length, even if you are on its final day of admission.

Annual Passports

> **unofficial TIP**
> If you are a local who visits Disneyland five or more days each year, or a tourist making at least two five-day trips, an annual pass is a potential money saver.

The Signature Plus Passport is the only Disneyland annual pass that is good for an entire year with no blockout dates, and it includes self-parking in the theme park garages and lots. The pass costs $1,399 and is good for admission to both parks 365 days a year during normal operating hours, with use of all attractions (excluding arcades), up to 15% discounts at most resort dining locations, and 20% off most merchandise. Signature Passports ($1,149) are valid every day except for the weekend before Christmas through the weekend after New Year's Day; it includes the same free parking and discounts as Signature Plus. If you are a bicoastal Disneyphile for whom price is no object, the Disney Premier Passport ($2,099) permits unlimited access to any Disney theme park or water park in Anaheim or Orlando, along with free parking and 15%–20% discounts.

Disney Deluxe Annual Passports ($799) are valid 326 days of the year, with 39 blockout dates around Easter, Thanksgiving, Christmas, and most Saturdays. Deluxe pass holders get a 10% discount on most food and merchandise but have to pay full price for parking.

The Flex Passport ($599), introduced in 2019, is valid at both parks on 141 off-peak weekdays, with only 15 days around Christmas completely blocked out. For the remaining 210 days—including all off-peak weekends, plus summer and holiday periods—pass holders must make a reservation through the Disney Parks app up to 30 days in advance in order to enter the parks. Each pass holder can hold up to two reservations at a time, and reservations can be canceled but not modified; if you're a no-show for three reservations within 90 days, you won't be able to reserve again for a month.

A Southern California Select Annual Passport ($399) is valid 155 days per year to residents in qualifying zip codes. Locals can purchase any passport on an installment plan, paying $154 (the price of a one-day value park hopper ticket) up front and making interest-free payments starting at $20.40 a month.

Premier and Signature Plus passes include free unlimited usage of the MaxPass attraction reservation system (see pages 86–88 for details) and PhotoPass digital picture downloads (see pages 103–104 for details). All other tiers of pass holders can add MaxPass and PhotoPass for $100 per year.

In 2019 Disneyland Resort introduced additional park-specific blockout days during the summer, just in time for the debut of Star Wars: Galaxy's Edge. Deluxe and SoCal pass holders were permitted to enter DCA—but prohibited from Disneyland Park—during all of July, most of June and August, and on select days throughout the rest of the year. The blockout calendar at disneyland.disney.go.com /passes/blockout-dates is updated 13 months in advance; check it against your visitation dates before purchasing an annual pass.

Prices for children are the same as those for adults on all annual passports.

If you purchase your annual passport in July of this year and schedule your visit next year for June, you'll cover two years' vacations with a single pass.

Rides and Shows Closed for Repairs or Maintenance

Rides and shows at Disneyland parks are sometimes closed for maintenance or repairs. If a certain attraction is important to you, call ☎ 714-781-7290 or visit disneyland.disney.go.com/calendars before your visit to make sure that it will be operating. You'll also find an unofficial schedule of current and upcoming closures at touringplans.com/disney land-resort/closures. A mother from Dover, Massachusetts, lamented:

> We were disappointed to find Space Mountain and the riverboat closed for repairs. We felt that a large chunk [of the park] was not working, yet the tickets were still full price and expensive!

Even if an attraction isn't on the disabled list, unplanned outages may prevent you from riding, as a woman from Antioch, Illinois, discovered:

> The biggest drawback of the whole trip was the numerous breakdowns of the rides. We were aware of Big Thunder Mountain and a few other rides closed for long-term scheduled maintenance, but a lot of the rides broke down as soon as we headed to them! The only things that didn't have any breakdowns were the cash registers!

HOW MUCH DOES IT COST TO GO TO DISNEYLAND FOR A DAY?

LET'S SAY THAT we have a family of four—Mom, Dad, Tim (age 12), and Tami (age 8)—driving their own car. Because they plan to be in the area for a few days, they intend to buy the Three-Day Park Hopper tickets. A typical day would cost $771.94, excluding lodging and transportation. See the table on the facing page for a breakdown of expenses.

HOW MUCH DOES A DAY COST?	
Breakfast for 4 at Denny's with tax and tip	$48.00
Disneyland parking fee	$25.00
1 day's admission for 4 on a Three-Day Park Hopper Pass	$466.66
Dad: *Adult 3-day is $355 divided by 3 days* = $118.33	
Mom: *Adult 3-day is $355 divided by 3 days* = $118.33	
Tim: *Adult 3-day is $355 divided by 3 days* = $118.33	
Tami: *Child 3-day is $335 divided by 3 days* = $111.67	
Morning break (soda or coffee)	$17.20
Fast-food lunch (burger, fries, and soda), no tip	$58.65
Afternoon break (soda and popcorn)	$38.00
Dinner in park at counter-service restaurant with tax	$69.96
Souvenirs (Mickey T-shirts for Tim and Tami) with tax*	$48.47
One-day total (without lodging or transportation)	**$771.94**

* *Cheer up—you won't have to buy souvenirs every day.*

TIMING *Your* VISIT

SELECTING THE TIME OF YEAR FOR YOUR VISIT

unofficial **TIP**
You can't pick a less crowded time to visit Disneyland Resort than late August through September.

CROWDS ARE LARGEST AT DISNEYLAND during the summer (Memorial Day–Labor Day) and during specific holiday periods throughout the rest of the year. The busiest time of all is December 25–January 1. Thanksgiving weekend, the week of Presidents' Day, spring break for schools and colleges, and the two weeks around Easter are also extremely busy. To give you some idea of what *busy* means at Disneyland, more than 88,000 people have toured Disneyland Park in one day! While this level of attendance is far from typical, the possibility of its occurrence should prevent all but the ignorant and the foolish from challenging this mega-attraction at its busiest periods.

Historically, after Thanksgiving weekend until the week before Christmas was the least-busy time of all, but recently late August–September has taken that title. The next slowest times are January 8–early March (excepting Martin Luther King Jr. Day and Presidents' Day weekends) and the week following Easter to Memorial Day weekend. At the risk of being blasphemous, our research team was so impressed with the relative ease of touring in the fall and other off-season periods that we would rather take our children out of school for a few days than do battle with the summer crowds. Though we strongly recommend going to Disneyland in the fall or in the spring, it should be noted that there are certain trade-offs. The parks often close earlier on fall, winter, and spring days, sometimes early enough to eliminate evening parades, fireworks, and other live-entertainment

TOP 10 AMERICAN THEME PARKS		
THEME PARK	ANNUAL ATTENDANCE	AVERAGE DAILY ATTENDANCE
Walt Disney World's Magic Kingdom	20.9 million	57,148
Disneyland Park	18.7 million	51,140
Disney's Animal Kingdom	13.8 million	37,671
Walt Disney World's Epcot	12.4 million	34,093
Disney's Hollywood Studios	11.3 million	30,844
Universal Studios Florida	10.7 million	29,337
Disney California Adventure	9.9 million	27,016
Universal Orlando's Islands of Adventure	9.8 million	26,816
Universal Studios Hollywood	9.1 million	25,060
SeaWorld Orlando	4.6 million	12,586

Source: Themed Entertainment Association

offerings such as *Fantasmic!* Also, because these are slow times of the year at Disneyland, you can anticipate that some rides and attractions may be closed for maintenance or renovation. Finally, if the parks open late and close early, it's tough to see everything, even if the crowds are light.

Most readers who have tried Disney parks at varying times of the year concur. A wintertime visitor from Sacramento, California, agrees:

> *Though there was a torrential storm on two days of our four-day visit, I can safely say that I will never visit in high season again. Yes, we were wet. Yes, attractions and rides were closed for refurb. BUT the longest line we waited in was 25 minutes to see the princesses. Characters were EVERYWHERE, and access to them was easy as pie. There were no issues with heat or sunburn. And we saved a boatload of money.*

Not to overstate the case: We want to emphasize that you can have a great time at the Disneyland parks regardless of the time of year or crowd level. In fact, a primary objective of this guide is to make the parks fun and manageable for those readers who visit during the busier times of year.

unofficial **TIP**
In our opinion, the risk of encountering colder weather and closed attractions during an off-season visit to Disneyland is worth it.

The rule of thumb is that Disneyland is more crowded when school is out and less crowded when kids are in school. However, Disney has become increasingly adept at loading slow periods of the year with special events, conventions, food festivals, and the like. Discounts on rooms, variable pricing for single-day tickets, and annual pass holder blockouts also figure in. Other factors affecting crowding and long lines include a combination of closed rides and an improving US economy. As a result, we've added more data about ride closures and economic indicators to our crowd level forecasts. The increased attendance has not gone unnoticed by long-time visitors, like this family from Redmond, California:

For the first time, Disneyland felt like an amusement park—just a collection of rides—rather than a pleasant, away-from-reality, immersive environment. Most likely because it was so crowded, so consistently, that I couldn't see, hear, or smell much aside from a sea of people. So while I recommended Disneyland or DCA to others in the past, I'd now instead recommend that they consider Universal or a different park if there were a potential for smaller crowds.

From a La Center, Washington, family of frequent visitors:

Crowd levels in Disneyland continue to climb. Even on low attendance days you can barely walk with all the foot traffic . . . I would hate to attend on a day when crowd levels were at capacity.

A New Orleans couple describes their experience:

Everything we read led us to believe October after Columbus Day and before Halloween week would be relatively less crowded. Nothing prepared us for the crowds we experienced. I may not have understood the crowd estimates, but barely being able to move was not what I expected.

However, there are still some periods of more moderate attendance, such as late summer, as one family from Vancouver, Canada, found:

With many California schools starting in late August, we found a sweet spot to visit during the second-to-last week of August when our kids are still on vacation. The parks were still open late and all entertainment was still running, but the crowds were down from the summer peak.

The bottom line is that Disneyland can be packed at any time, and you need to dig a little deeper than merely the time of year to pinpoint the least-crowded periods. For a calendar of scheduled Disney events, see touringplans.com/disneyland-resort/events.

Of course, crowds are not the only consideration when deciding what time of year to visit Disneyland. Holidays are celebrated at Disneyland like nowhere else, and the festive decor is almost worth the price of admission. The parks are decked out for Halloween September–October. Be aware that after-hours extra-cost Halloween parties (tickets are $95–$130) cause one of the parks to close early to day guests on several evenings in the fall, as a Tucson, Arizona, family found:

The Halloween event changes the low season to a zoo. Every local with an annual pass showed up in the afternoon. The park closed early for this event, and [the other park] backed up because of the early closure.

Christmas trappings transform Disneyland Park from mid-November until after New Year's Day. There's also a Christmas parade, and several attractions such as The Haunted Mansion and It's a Small World offer a special holiday version.

unofficial **TIP**
If it's not your first trip to Disneyland and you must join the holiday-weekend crowds, you may have just as much fun enjoying Disney's fantastic array of shows, parades, and fireworks as you would riding the rides.

Disneyland's holiday entertainment, including the seasonal fireworks, are included in regular admission, as opposed to the extra-cost Very Merry Christmas Party held in Orlando. A reader from Union City, California, who visited during the second week of December, wrote:

> *The park was extremely crowded, but we knew what we were getting into and were ready to handle it. The holiday offerings are wonderful, but if you are not mentally prepared to deal with the massive crowds and congested walkways that plague the park throughout the entire month of December, it can be a very stressful vacation.*

A mom from McLean, Virginia, chimed in:

> *We were there over New Year's Eve, and Disneyland Park was crushingly crowded. We dared not leave for DCA or to go back to the hotel for a break for fear of not getting back in, and the younger ones really wanted to be in Disneyland Park for the fireworks. The weather was so horrible (COLD AND WINDY), they canceled the show anyway.*

Finally, beware of Grad Night late-night parties for high school seniors on select days each May and June. The kids have after-hours access to Disney California Adventure (DCA), but they also get admission to both parks during the daytime and make their presence known in the crowded queues starting midafternoon.

THE SPOILER

SO YOU CHOOSE YOUR OFF-SEASON DATES and then find it almost impossible to find a hotel room. What gives? In all probability you've been foiled by a mammoth convention or trade show at the Anaheim Convention Center. One of the largest and busiest convention venues in the country, the convention center hosts meetings with as many as 100,000 attendees and was recently expanded in a $190-million project that added 200,000 square feet to the center. The sheer numbers alone guarantee that hotel rooms will be hard to find. Compounding the problem is the fact that most business travelers don't have roommates. Thus a trade show with 8,000 people registered might suck up 13,000 rooms (including people who registered late)! The final straw, as you might expect, is that room rates climb into the stratosphere based on the high demand and scarcity of supply.

In regard to increased crowds at the theme parks, it's estimated that less than 10% of convention attendees will find time to enjoy the parks. It's also true, however, that business travelers are more likely to bring their spouse and even kids to a convention held in Anaheim, as this reader learned the hard way.

> *A music festival, with about 115,000 attendees, is held at the end of January every year at the Anaheim Convention Center. I am certain all of them extended their vacation and went to [Disneyland Resort] the week of January 28–February 2. It was unbelievably crowded! Previously, we went to Disneyland at the beginning of December and experienced about ¼ of the crowds.*

The bottom line is that you don't want to schedule your vacation while a major event is going on at the convention center. Visit anaheim.net /calendar.aspx?CID=26, to see what conventions are scheduled during your visit. In addition, the Disney parks can sometimes be overrun by events not associated with the convention center, such as unofficial fan gatherings like Dapper Day (April and November; dapperday.com). Schedules vary each year, so check the respective websites when planning your trip.

SELECTING THE DAY OF THE WEEK FOR YOUR VISIT

THE CROWDS AT WALT DISNEY WORLD in Florida are comprised mostly of out-of-state visitors. Not necessarily so at Disneyland Resort, which, along with Six Flags Magic Mountain, serves as an often-frequented recreational resource for the greater Los Angeles and San Diego communities. To many Southern Californians, Disneyland Park and DCA are their private theme parks. Yearly passes are available at less cost than a year's membership to the YMCA.

What all this means is that weekends are usually packed. If you have to go on a weekend, your best bet is to go on Sunday in the morning or after 5 p.m., or visit on a Saturday when most annual pass holders are blocked out from attending (visit disneyland.disney .go.com/passes/blockout-dates for details).

During the summer, Monday and Friday are very busy, Tuesday and Wednesday are usually less so, and Thursday is normally the slowest day of all. During the off-season (September–May, holiday periods excepted), Thursday is usually the least crowded day, followed by Friday and Wednesday.

Disneyland Park usually hosts crowds 50% larger than those at DCA, but because DCA is smaller, crowd conditions are comparable. Expressed differently, the most crowded and least crowded days are essentially the same for both Disneyland parks. However, if you are ineligible for early admission (see below), we advise visiting the park that does not offer early entry, as the other will be busy by the time ordinary guests arrive.

EARLY ENTRY

ANYONE WHO BUYS in advance a three-to-five-day ticket with Magic Morning admission may enter Disneyland Park 1 hour before the park is opened to the general public on one morning of their vacation. You can exercise your early-entry privilege on Tuesday, Thursday, or Saturday. Guests at the Paradise Pier, Grand Californian, and Disneyland Hotels can also enter on any early-entry day, as long as they have any valid ticket; this privilege is referred to as Extra Magic Hour. During this early-entry hour, most of the Fantasyland attractions and select rides in Tomorrowland will usually be open. The rest of the park's attractions—including all of Star Wars: Galaxy's Edge—will remain off-limits until the official opening time. DCA also offers its own Extra Magic Hour exclusively for hotel guests, offering access to all of Cars Land, along with select attractions in Hollywood Land, Paradise Gardens Park, Pixar Pier, and Grizzly Peak, on four mornings (Sunday, Monday, Wednesday, and Friday). Only the standby queues are in operation during early entry, though MaxPass users can make ride-reservation selections, with the first FastPass return windows beginning at the official park opening time for rides operating during early entry and 30–40 minutes after opening time for everything else (see page 87).

Security checkpoints can be painfully understaffed during Magic Mornings, so even on-site guests should plan on departing their hotel room a full 40 minutes before early entry begins to take full advantage of it. Also, so many guests are eligible for Magic Mornings at Disneyland that early-entry wait times in Fantasyland can exceed those during regular hours; if you can't be among the first through the turnstiles, you may want to avoid Disneyland Magic Mornings entirely, as this reader suggests:

> *Magic Morning was the absolute WORST! Even though we got [to Disneyland Park] an hour early, raced to be the first in line at the rope drop, and then ran to Peter Pan, the crowds were still insurmountable. Yes, we made it to Peter Pan as one of the first in line . . . but after that, every other ride in Fantasyland had over a 40-minute wait! We tried to stick to the itinerary, but we had to give up and just go to whatever line was shortest at the time. In the future, I think we will go to the opposite park of Magic Morning and enjoy an extra hour of sleep while everybody else deals with the atrocious Magic Morning crowds.*

Magic Mornings at DCA, on the other hand, are only available to hotel guests, so queues are far less crowded, making it one of the most valuable perks of staying on-site, as this San Francisco reader found:

MAGIC MORNING/EXTRA MAGIC HOUR ATTRACTIONS

DISNEYLAND PARK

• Alice in Wonderland	• Matterhorn Bobsleds
• Astro Orbitor	• Mr. Toad's Wild Ride
• Buzz Lightyear Astro Blasters	• Peter Pan's Flight
• Disneyland Monorail	• Pinocchio's Daring Journey
• Dumbo the Flying Elephant	• Snow White's Scary Adventures
• Finding Nemo Submarine Voyage	• Space Mountain
• King Arthur Carrousel	• Star Tours—The Adventures Continue
• Mad Tea Party	

DISNEY CALIFORNIA ADVENTURE

• Goofy's Sky School	• Mater's Junkyard Jamboree
• Guardians of the Galaxy—Mission: Breakout!	• Radiator Springs Racers
• Incredicoaster	• Soarin' Around the World
• The Little Mermaid: Ariel's Undersea Adventure	• Toy Story Midway Mania!
• Luigi's Rollickin' Roadsters	

Go. Early. It's hard to get up early to be there for a 7 a.m. opening, but it is totally worth it. In DCA, with an 8 a.m. early morning, we had ridden [Radiator Springs Racers] by 8:10, then Guardians of the Galaxy and Soarin', all before the 9 a.m. regular opening!

If you plan on driving to Disneyland, be advised that the Mickey & Friends and Pixar Pals parking structures open only 30 minutes before the park opens for Magic Morning. Due to this, we recommend arriving at the parking structures at least an hour before Magic Morning starts. You'll spend a bit of time waiting in your car for the parking structures to open, but it's necessary to get to Disneyland in time for the start of Magic Morning. It's also important to note that the Toy Story parking lot does not open early for Magic Morning. That means Mickey & Friends and Pixar Pals are your only options for parking that early in the day.

This reader from Tulsa, Oklahoma, wrote:

We tried to get to the turnstiles as you recommended on a Magic Morning 45 minutes before opening but were stuck in the Mickey & Friends parking structure waiting for it to open. It finally opened 30 minutes before Magic Morning. Needless to say, it ruined the touring plan, as we were well behind the mob at the turnstiles by the time we got a tram and went through security.

OPERATING HOURS

DISNEYLAND RESORT RUNS a dozen or more different operating schedules during the year, making it advisable to visit disneyland.disney .go.com/calendar or call ☎ 714-781-4565 the day before you arrive for exact hours of operation.

PACKED-PARK COMPENSATION PLAN

THE THOUGHT OF TEEMING, jostling throngs jockeying for position in endless lines under the baking Fourth of July sun is enough to wilt the will and ears of the most ardent Mouseketeer. Why would anyone go to Disneyland Park or DCA on a summer Saturday or during a major holiday period? The Disney folks, however, feel kind of bad about those interminably long lines and the basically impossible touring conditions on packed days and compensate patrons with an incredible array of first-rate live entertainment and happenings throughout the park.

Throughout the day, the party goes on with shows, parades, concerts, and pageantry. In the evening, there is so much going on that you have to make some tough choices. Musical acts sometimes perform on the Tomorrowland Terrace stage in Disneyland and in Hollywood Land at DCA. There are always parades and fireworks, and the Disney characters make frequent appearances. No question about it—you can go to the Disneyland parks on the Fourth of July (or any other crowded extended-hours day), never get on a ride, and still get your money's worth. Even on the busiest days, there are attractions at each park that rarely require more than a 15-minute wait: *Great Moments with Mr. Lincoln,* the *Enchanted Tiki Room,* the railroad and mono-rail, and Star Wars Launch Bay at Disneyland Park, as well as *Mickey's PhilharMagic,* Disney Animation, and the Bakery Tour at DCA.

If you decide to go on one of the parks' big days, we suggest that you arrive 1 hour and 20 minutes before the stated opening time. Use the touring plan of your choice until about 1 p.m., and then take the monorail to Downtown Disney for lunch and relaxation. Southern Californian visitors often chip in and rent a room for the group (make reservations well in advance) at one of the Disneyland Resort hotels, thus affording a place to meet, relax, have a drink, or change clothes before enjoying the pools at the hotel. A comparable arrangement can be made at other nearby hotels as long as they are within walking distance or furnish a shuttle service to and from the park. After an early dinner, return to the park for the evening's festivities, which really crank up at about 8 p.m.

 # GETTING THERE

WHILE MANY DISNEYLAND VISITORS hail from California and drive to the resort area, if you are flying in from across the country (or globe), you have three options for your arrival airport. With domestic and international service from nearly every airline known to man, **Los Angeles Airport** (LAX) is one of the largest and busiest in the world, and one of the more frustrating to navigate. LAX is also located 34 miles west of Anaheim, a 45-minute drive along the busy I-105 and I-55 freeways at the best of times, or an hour and a half or more in typical terrible traffic. Unless you are starting or ending your Disneyland vacation with a visit to Hollywood, we recommend looking at flights into **John Wayne Airport** (SNA) or **Long Beach Airport** (LGB), both of which are significantly calmer and closer to Disneyland. John Wayne (also known as Orange County Airport) is only 14 miles southeast of Disneyland on CA 55 and I-5 and is serviced by Alaska, American, Delta, Frontier, Southwest, United, and WestJet airlines. Long Beach (our personal favorite airport) is 24 miles west of Disneyland but can be reached using surface streets, making it the shortest drive when the highways are halted. Long Beach is only serviced by American, Delta, JetBlue, and Southwest, but it boasts the most painless on-site rental car return and security screening we've ever experienced; going from the airport parking lot to sitting at your departure gate usually takes about 15 minutes.

If you're arriving at LAX or John Wayne, Coach USA's official **Disneyland Resort Express** will take you and your luggage directly from the airport to your Disneyland-area hotel, then back to the airport when it's time for your flight home. Unlike Walt Disney World's Magical Express, this service is not free. Prices from LAX are $30 one-way, $48 round-trip for adults, and $9 one-way, $14 round-trip for children. Prices for John Wayne Airport are $20 one-way, $35 round-trip for adults and $7 one-way, $11 round-trip for children. Reservations

Southern California at a Glance

can be made in advance at dre.coachusa.com or by calling ☎ 800-828-6699. *Note:* The Disneyland Resort Express pickup is not well marked at LAX, so you may want to ask for directions.

Another transportation option is a third-party airport shuttle, such as **SuperShuttle** (supershuttle.com/disneyland), **PrimeTime** (primetime shuttle.com), or **Karmel Shuttle** (karmel.com). SuperShuttle charges $19 per person one-way, $36.10 per person round-trip from LAX; $37 per person one-way, $70.30 per person round-trip from Long Beach;

and $12.95 per person one-way, $24.70 per person round-trip from John Wayne. PrimeTime charges $17.95 per person one-way, $35.90 per person round-trip from LAX; $44.95 per person one-way, $89.90 per person round-trip from Long Beach; and $13 per person one-way, $25.90 per person round-trip from John Wayne. Karmel charges $30.45 per person each way from LAX, $27.60 per person each way from Long Beach, and $20.95 per person each way from John Wayne. None of the shuttle prices include tip (18% of the total or $5 per person each way is suggested), and all are for shared van service, so you may spend an extended time picking up or dropping off other passengers before arriving at your destination. The Disneyland Resort Express bus does not require child seats, but if you're riding a shuttle van, you'll need to provide your own.

Rental cars are also available at all local airports, as are taxis, but the price of a cab can become extremely expensive after sitting in Los Angeles traffic on the way to Disneyland Resort. We've heard reports from people who have paid almost $150 to get from LAX to their Anaheim hotel. Less expensive ride-share services (such as Uber and Lyft) are also readily available to and from Los Angeles International, John Wayne, and Long Beach Airports. At LAX, look for designated Ride Share Pickup locations on the upper Departures level. We've had great results using Lyft and Uber from the airports and Disney hotels.

Once in Anaheim, Disney patrons can drive directly into and out of parking facilities without becoming enmeshed in surface-street traffic. To avoid traffic problems, we recommend the following:

1. Stay as close to Disneyland as possible. If you are within walking distance, leave your car at the hotel and walk to the park using the pedestrian entrance on the east side of the resort, along Harbor Boulevard between Disney Way and Manchester Avenue, or through the security checkpoint between Downtown Disney and the Disneyland Hotel if walking from the west side along Disneyland Drive. If your hotel provides efficient shuttle service (that is, will get you to the parks at least 30 minutes before opening), use the shuttle.

2. If your hotel is more than 5 miles from Disneyland and you intend to drive your car, leave for the park extra early, say 1 hour or more.

3. If you must use the Santa Ana Freeway (I-5), give yourself lots of extra time.

4. Any time you leave the park just before, at, or just after closing time, you can expect considerable congestion in the parking lots and in the loading area for hotel shuttles. The easiest way to return to your hotel (if you do not have a car in the Disneyland Resort parking lot) is to take the monorail to the Disneyland Hotel or walk to the Grand Californian Hotel, and then take a cab to your own hotel. While cabs in Anaheim are a little pricey, they are usually available in ample numbers at the Disneyland hotels and at the taxi stand in Downtown Disney. When you consider the alternatives of fighting your way onto a hotel shuttle or trudging back to your hotel on worn-out feet, spending $10–$15 for a cab often sounds pretty reasonable. Ride-share services (such as **Uber** and **Lyft**) are an even cheaper option, costing about half the price of an equivalent taxi ride. The easiest places for ride-share drivers to access are the drop-off points on the west side behind Downtown Disney, and off Harbor Boulevard to the east, as well as the driveways outside the main lobbies of the Disneyland Hotel and Grand Californian.

5. The Orange County Transit District provides very efficient bus service to Disneyland with several different long-distance lines. Running about every 30 minutes during the day and evening, service runs 10 a.m.–midnight, depending on the season and your location. Buses drop off and pick up passengers at the east shuttle loop off Harbor Boulevard. From there, guests can walk to the park entrance. Bus fare is about $2 and children age 5 and under ride free; you can pay in cash (exact change required) or through the free OC Bus mobile app. A bus day pass is available for $5; 30-day passes are $69 for adults, $40 for children ages 6–18. For additional information, call ☎ 714-636-7433 or visit octa.net. For public transportation in the immediate area surrounding Disneyland, see our discussion of the Anaheim Resort Transit (ART) system on pages 36–37.

DISNEYLAND PARKING

DISNEYLAND HAS FOUR PARKING AREAS. The main parking facility, the Mickey & Friends and Pixar Pals parking garages, can be accessed directly from I-5, Disneyland Drive, or Ball Road. One of the largest parking structures in the world, the garages are connected to Downtown Disney and the theme parks by Disney tram. Noncollapsible strollers are permitted on trams only in the first or last car, where there are extralarge sections for strollers and wheelchairs. If you'd rather hoof it, the walking distance to the park gates is about a mile, cutting south to Downtown Disney; use the pedestrian bridge on the Pixar Pals garage's south side to cross over Magic Way and access the sidewalk past the parking lot. You'll have to pass through Disney's metal detectors and baggage screening on the ground floor of the garage if you want to ride the tram; if the checkpoint is overcrowded, there is sometimes a shorter wait outside Downtown Disney where walkers are inspected.

The secondary parking area is the Toy Story lot south of the corner of Katella Avenue and Harbor Boulevard, a favorite of local pass holders and our top pick for the most convenient place to park. Toy Story, which is the only lot that accommodates oversize vehicles like buses and RVs, offers shuttles to and from the bus loop east of the Esplanade, or you can walk (about 0.9 mile); a security checkpoint here before boarding the bus allows you to bypass the screening at the Esplanade. The Pumbaa lot off Disney Way across from the Anaheim GardenWalk is usually used as cast member or special event parking. Parking fees for all lots are $25 for cars and motorcycles, $30 for RVs and oversize vehicles without trailers, and $35 for buses and tractors with extended trailers. For $40 (or a $15 upgrade if prepaid) you can get Preferred Parking, which puts you in the first three rows of each level closest to the elevators and escalators; we'd rather spend the money on churros and use the extra yards to walk off the calories. After parking your car, save yourself a frantic search at the end of your day by taking a digital photo of the lot name and section number.

While the trams and buses to the parks operate fairly efficiently in the morning, at closing time they can become completely overwhelmed by exiting guests, as an unfortunate reader from Quincy, Massachusetts, found out:

Around Disneyland

The worst part of our vacation by far was taking the tram back to the parking garage at the end of the day. It is a complete free-for-all once the tram shows up. We waited through three trams boarding and leaving before we got to the front of the pack, and when the tram came, we still got split up into three different rows as a group of five adults. People were pushing and shoving their way on, and it was completely chaotic.

If you find yourself in a similar situation, it's possible to walk back to any of the parking facilities from the park.

You can park for free for up to 3 hours in the Downtown Disney parking lot with a $20 purchase at any Downtown Disney location, up to 5 free hours with validation from select table-service dining restaurants. Additional half hours cost $7 each up to a $56 daily maximum; there's a free 15-minute grace period for quick drop-offs. The Simba lot, located behind the Paradise Pier Hotel, is available only to guests with disability license plates and placards. From Simba you can walk through Downtown Disney to the parks or alternatively walk to the Downtown Disney monorail stop and take the monorail into Disneyland Park (not Disney California Adventure [DCA]). Valet parking is no longer offered at Downtown Disney but is available anytime at the resort hotels ($35 plus $10 per hour, up to $105 daily for nonguests). If you have money to burn, valet parking at the Grand Californian puts you closest to the parks. There are no annual pass discounts on parking at the hotels (though you can get 3–5 hours of complimentary parking by patronizing select restaurants or the spa), and overnight parking is not permitted in the theme park or Downtown Disney lots.

TAKING A TRAM OR SHUTTLE BUS FROM YOUR HOTEL

TRAMS AND SHUTTLE BUSES are provided by many hotels and motels in the vicinity of Disneyland. Usually without charge, they represent a fairly carefree means of getting to and from the theme parks, letting you off near the entrances and saving you the cost of parking. The rub is that they might not get you there as early as you desire (a critical point if you take our touring advice) or be available at the time you wish to return to your lodging. Also, some shuttles are direct to Disneyland, while others make stops at other motels and hotels in the vicinity. Each shuttle service is a little bit different, so check out the particulars before you book your hotel. If the shuttle provided by your hotel runs regularly throughout the day to and from Disneyland and if you have the flexibility to tour the parks over two or three days, the shuttle provides a wonderful opportunity to tour in the morning and return to your lodging for lunch, a swim, or perhaps a nap; then you can head back to Disneyland refreshed in the early evening for a little more fun.

unofficial **TIP**
Warning: Most shuttles don't add vehicles at park-opening or park-closing times. In the mornings, you may not get a seat.

Be forewarned that most hotel shuttle services do not add more vehicles at the parks' opening or closing times. In the mornings, your biggest problem is that you might not get a seat on the first shuttle. This occurs most frequently if your hotel is the last stop for a shuttle that serves several hotels. Because hotels that share a shuttle service are usually located close together, you can improve your chances of getting a seat by simply walking to the hotel preceding yours on the pickup route. At closing time, and sometimes following a hard rain, you can expect a mass exodus from the parks. The worst-case scenario in this event is that more people will be waiting for the shuttle to your hotel than the bus will hold and that some will be left. While most (but not all) hotel shuttles return for stranded guests, you may suffer a wait of 15 minutes–1 hour. Our suggestion, if you are depending on hotel shuttles, is to exit the park at least 45 minutes before closing. If you stay in a park until closing and lack the energy to deal with the shuttle or hike back to your hotel, go to the Disneyland Hotel and catch a cab or ride-share from there. A cab stand is also behind the monorail station in Downtown Disney and another is at the Grand Californian Hotel.

The shuttle-loading area is located on the Harbor Boulevard side of Disneyland Park's main entrances. The loading area connects to a pedestrian corridor that leads to the park entrances. Each hotel's shuttle bus is color-coded yellow, blue, red, silver, or white. Signs of like color designate where the shuttles load and unload. You'll also find a passenger drop-off loop (parking strictly prohibited) off Harbor; taxis and ride-shares may also pick up and drop off here. If you are staying south of the corner of Harbor and Katella, you can walk into the Toy Story parking lot and use its park shuttle for free.

Anaheim Resort Transit

Anaheim Resort Transit (ART) provides shuttle service to the Disneyland Resort, Anaheim GardenWalk, and the convention center. The service operates 19 routes designated 1–22 (excluding 13, 19, and 21). There are just three to nine well-marked stops on each route, so a complete circuit on any given route usually takes about 20 minutes, but some take up to 1 hour. All of the routes originate and terminate at Disneyland's bus loop east of the Esplanade near Harbor Boulevard. There is also service from Disneyland to Knott's Berry Farm, Discovery Cube Orange County, and Angel Stadium in case you want to catch an afternoon ballgame.

The colorful buses are wheelchair accessible. They ideally run every 10 minutes on peak days during morning and evening periods but can take up to 30 minutes when it's really busy, every 20 minutes during the less busy middle part of the day, and every 20 minutes all day long on off-peak days. Service begins 60 minutes before park opening and ends 30 minutes after park closing (may vary seasonally). If you commute to Disneyland on ART and then head to Downtown Disney after the parks close, you'll have to find your own way home if you stay at Downtown Disney more than 90 minutes. All shuttle vehicles and respective stops are clearly marked with the route designation. ART's service is usually pretty dependable but can have its bad days, according to this dad from Downs, Illinois:

> *ART has always been reliable in the past; this trip, not so much. We experienced 40-plus-minute waits for both routes 1 and 2 at Disneyland hub, and we even had a scheduled bus fly by a stop on Harbor without stopping. We ended up taking an Uber to make a dining reservation.*

Vending kiosks and hotels served by ART sell one-, three-, and five-day passes for $5.50 ($2 for kids), $14 ($3 for kids), and $23 ($5 for kids), respectively. Children age 2 years and under ride free with a paying adult. You'll also find an ART vending kiosk at the Disneyland bus loop, but you may not want to depend on them, as one Melbourne, Australia, reader discovered:

> *The ART buses around the Disneyland area were great; however, the ticket machine at Disneyland wasn't functioning well, and we couldn't find other machines easily.*

The most convenient option is to use the free smartphone app, which can be found by searching for "TokenTransit" on the Apple or Google Play app stores.

One-way cash fares are $3 for adults, $1 for children. Children must be taken out of strollers to ride. Passes cannot be purchased from the driver. For more information, call ☎ 888-364-ARTS (2787) or check rideart.org. Passes are also available at ART's website and can be delivered to your hotel for free with three days' notice.

∎ WHERE *to* STAY

TRAFFIC AROUND DISNEYLAND, and in the Anaheim–Los Angeles area in general, is so terrible that we advocate staying in accommodations within 2–3 miles of the park. Included in this radius are many expensive hotels as well as a considerable number of moderately priced establishments and a small number of bargain motels.

READERS' DISNEYLAND RESORT REPORT CARD

EACH YEAR OUR READERS grade their hotel in several categories (see table on the next page). Room quality indicates cleanliness, bed comfort, and room size. Check-in efficiency rates how quickly and accurately the hotel staff get you into your room. Quietness of room considers soundproofing from neighbors and exterior noise. The pool rating includes the size of the pool, how crowded it gets, and how clean the pool and pool area are. The staff category assesses how friendly and effective the hotel staff are at handling problems and special requests. Our hotel dining rating applies to any on-site counter-service dining, and the overall rating is the summary for every category.

Readers rate Disneyland hotels better than neighboring hotels, continuing a years-long trend. Much of the lodging around Disneyland consists of motels with aging rooms, many in need of refurbishment, content to trade on their proximity to the park rather than the quality of their rooms.

Readers indicate that Disneyland's top two hotels are substantially better than nearby hotels; however, the Anaheim Desert Inn & Suites (the off-site hotel that appears most often on our reader surveys) scores higher than the Paradise Pier in key categories. In this year's reader report card, Disney's highest grades are in room quality and staff friendliness—two things you'd expect to see, given the premium Disney charges for its lodging.

The Disneyland hotels fare poorly in the dining category, but some context is necessary. Each of the hotels offers decent choices for breakfast, from quick grab-and-go options to table-service meals. And the hotels' short walk to Downtown Disney and surrounding neighborhoods provides plenty of options for good lunches and dinners.

READERS' DISNEYLAND RESORT REPORT CARD

HOTEL	ROOM QUALITY	CHECK-IN EFFICIENCY	QUIETNESS OF ROOM	POOL	STAFF	HOTEL DINING	OVERALL RATING
Disneyland Hotel	A–	B	B	B+	A	C	B+
Grand Californian	A–	B–	B	A	A	C	A–
Paradise Pier	B	B	B	C	A	D	C+

WALKING TO DISNEYLAND FROM NEARBY HOTELS

WHILE IT IS TRUE THAT most Disneyland-area hotels provide shuttle service, or are on the ART routes, it is equally true that an ever-increasing number of guests walk to the parks from their hotels. Shuttles are not always available when needed, and parking in the Disneyland lot has become pretty expensive. A pedestrian walkway from Harbor Boulevard provides safe access to Disneyland for guests on foot. This pedestrian corridor extends from Harbor Boulevard west to the Disneyland Hotel, connecting Disneyland Park, Disney California Adventure (DCA), and Downtown Disney.

Close proximity to the theme parks figures prominently in the choice of a hotel. Harbor Boulevard borders Disneyland Resort on the east, and Katella Avenue runs along the resort's southern boundary. The closest non-Disney hotels, and the only ones really within walking distance, are on Harbor Boulevard from just south of I-5 to the north to just south of the intersection with Katella Avenue, and along Katella Avenue near Harbor. The eastern gateway, which leads between the guest drop-off and bus loops off Harbor Boulevard to a security checkpoint at the edge of the Esplanade, is the most popular entry point for pedestrians.

Farther south on Harbor are some of the best hotels in the area, but they are a little far removed for commuting to the parks on foot, although you can walk into the Toy Story parking lot and take a free bus to the parks. Additionally, these hotels are close to the Anaheim Convention Center and tend to cater, though certainly not exclusively, to business travelers.

While the hotels near Disneyland Drive appear close to Disney property on a map, pedestrian access to the parks from the west is a bit more circuitous. If staying along Katella Avenue to the west of the convention center, you can walk north on Disneyland Drive and cut through the hotel parking lot across from the Grand Californian to Downtown Disney's security checkpoint. A keycard-operated pedestrian gate on the Grand Californian's Disneyland Drive entrance prevents anyone not registered there from entering (including those staying at the other Disneyland Resort hotels). From West Ball Road, you can enter the Mickey & Friends garage from its north side through the employee gate on West Place, ascend to Level 2, and walk south about 6 minutes to reach the trams to the parks.

For families, a second important consideration is the quality of the hotel swimming pool. We mention this because, unfortunately, many of the non-Disney hotels closest to the theme parks have really crummy pools, sometimes just a tiny rectangle on a stark slab of concrete surrounded on four sides by a parking lot.

Our lodging reviews include the walking time from each hotel to the theme park entrances. The times provided are averages—a couple of fit adults might cover the distance in less time, and a family with small children will likely take longer. The walk times do not include the wait to pass through security screenings, which can be substantial. Note that several non-Disney hotels are closer than the Disneyland Resort hotels, except for the Grand Californian. Also in the reviews, we rate the swimming areas of the hotels listed on a scale of 1–5 stars, with 5 being best. As a rule of thumb, any pool with a rating less than 3 stars is not a place where most folks would want to spend much time.

The above discussion might lead you to wonder whether there's any real advantage to staying in a Disney-owned hotel. The Disney hotels, of course, are very expensive, but if you can handle the tariff, here are the primary benefits of staying in one:

1. You are eligible for early entry at Disneyland Park three days each week and DCA on the other four days.

2. Dozens of full- and counter-service restaurants are within walking distance.

3. The Disney hotels (especially the Grand Californian) offer some of the nicest rooms of any of the hotels within walking distance.

4. The Disney hotels offer the nicest swimming pools of any of the hotels within walking distance.

5. Numerous entertainment and shopping options are in Downtown Disney.

6. It's easy to retreat to your hotel for a meal, a nap, or a swim.

7. You don't need a car.

8. You can charge purchases at most Disney-owned shops and restaurants to your hotel account and have packages delivered to your room.

DISNEYLAND RESORT HOTELS

DISNEY OFFERS THREE ON-SITE HOTELS: the **Grand Californian Hotel,** the **Disneyland Hotel,** and the **Paradise Pier Hotel.** The Grand Californian, built in the rustic stone-and-timber style of the grand national park lodges, is the flagship property. Newer, more elaborately themed, and closer to the theme parks and Downtown Disney than the other two on-property hotels, the Grand Californian is without a doubt the best place to stay . . . if you can afford it.

The next most convenient is the sprawling Disneyland Hotel, the oldest of the three, though repeatedly renovated. Comprising three guest-room towers, the hotel is lushly landscaped with a new vintage Disneyana theme and offers large, luxurious guest rooms. Walking time to the monorail station, with transportation to Disneyland Park, is about 3–6 minutes. All three hotels offer club-level rooms with luxury amenities, such as nightly turndown service and access to a private club. One reader from Ontario, Canada, didn't feel that it was worth the extra money:

> The club lounge was open 6:30 a.m.–8:30 p.m. each day. The early-morning park hours began at 7 a.m., and one needs to be at the park at least 45 minutes before park opening, so breakfast in the lounge was not possible. The lounge also closed too early in the evening for us to stop and pick up a water or soda on our way back from the parks.

But another visitor from Oakland, California, managed to make good use of the club:

> We stayed at Paradise Pier club level, and it was SO NICE to have access to the club. We were able to get there when it opened at 6:30 a.m., divide and conquer between coffee and food, and make it to the 7 a.m. park opening. While I doubt I would ever pay rack rate for a club-level room, this perk was greatly appreciated and worthwhile.

The east side of the third Disney hotel overlooks the Paradise Gardens Park and Pixar Pier sections of DCA, hence the name Paradise Pier Hotel. Though guest rooms and public areas have a beach-and-boardwalk flavor, the hotel is not themed. Guest rooms here are large. Walking to the monorail station and Downtown Disney takes about 5–10 minutes.

Guests at all Disney-owned hotels can use their keys to charge dining and shopping within the resort to their room. Third-party vendors (including most Downtown Disney restaurants) are excluded, and you'll need to show photo ID along with your room key. Ask for a "pool key" when you check out if you want to use the amenities until closing on your departure day. Parking for registered resort guests at any of the Disney-owned hotels is $25 per night for self-parking (free for Disney Vacation Club members) or $35 per night for valet (☎ 714-635-2300). On the plus side, none of the hotels charge a resort fee, and all provide safes, mini-fridges, coffee makers, and free Wi-Fi (supposedly high-speed, but don't plan on streaming high-definition video) in rooms and public areas.

Disney's Grand Californian Hotel & Spa ★★★★½

Rate per night $626–$861. **Maximum occupants per room** 5. Pool ★★★★. **Fridge in room** Yes. **Breakfast** Paid. **Wi-Fi** Free. **Parking** $25 self/$35 valet. **Walk to Esplanade** 5 minutes (0.2 mile).

THE GRAND CALIFORNIAN HOTEL is the crown jewel of Disneyland Resort's hotels. With its shingle siding, rock foundations, cavernous hewn-beam lobby, polished hardwood floors, and cozy hearths, the hotel is a stately combination of elements from Western national park lodges. Designed by

1600 S. Disneyland Dr. Anaheim
☎ 714-635-2300
disneyland.com

architect Peter Dominick (who also designed the Wilderness Lodge at Walt Disney World), the Grand Californian is rendered in the Arts and Crafts style of the early 20th century, with such classic features as fly roofs, projecting beams, massive buttresses, and an earth-toned color palette. In 2017 Disney gave the Grand Californian a face-lift, refreshing the lobby and concierge Craftsman Club with new artisanal furnishings. We strongly encourage visitors with an interest in architecture to take the fascinating (and free) hour-long Art of the Craft walking tour of the resort, offered several times each week (currently Sunday, Monday, Thursday, and Friday at 1 p.m.) through the Guest Services desk; you don't have to stay on-site to sign up, but book in advance because tour groups are limited to 15 guests. Most reminiscent of The Majestic Yosemite Hotel (formerly The Ahwahnee) at Yosemite National Park, the Grand Californian combines rugged craftsmanship and grand scale with functional design and intimate spaces. Pull up a vintage rocker in front of a blazing fire, and the bustling lobby instantly becomes a snug cabin.

The hotel's main entrance off Downtown Drive is mainly for vehicular traffic. Two pedestrian-only entrances open into Downtown Disney and DCA; this last makes it easy to return to the hotel from DCA for a nap, a swim, or lunch.

The features we like in the 948 guest rooms include excellent light for reading in bed, more than adequate storage space, a two-sink vanity outside the toilet and bath, and, in some rooms, a balcony. All guest rooms were renovated in 2017 with new hardwood flooring, brighter carpets, white soft goods, orange tree–inspired wall art, and oak furnishings featuring headboards inlaid with Chip 'n' Dale (not Chippendale) designs. Lighting has been drastically improved, USB charging outlets are plentiful, and more storage space has been added. Views from the guest rooms overlook the swimming pool, Downtown Disney, or DCA theme park. Ranging $559 (for a standard view) to more than $2,613 (for a three-bedroom suite) per night, guest rooms are the most expensive at Disneyland Resort. A Houston, Texas, mother of two wrote to tell us:

> The Grand Californian's proximity to the parks is AMAZING! Still, it's not worth the exorbitant cost. I'm glad we did it, but I'd almost be embarrassed to recommend it to someone else because it's so expensive.

The Villas at Disney's Grand Californian, part of Disney's time-share condo enterprise, the Disney Vacation Club, consist of 48 two-bedroom equivalent villas and two Grand Villas. *Equivalent* is the term used to describe single units that can be sold (or rented) as studio suites or combined to make two- and three-bedroom villas. All villas except studio suites include kitchens, living rooms, and dining areas, as well as washers and dryers. Master bedrooms offer a king bed, while other bedrooms provide two queen beds. Studio suites have a single queen bed. All bedrooms have a flat-panel TV, private bath, and private balcony. Though studio suites don't have full kitchens, they do include a small fridge, a microwave, and a coffee maker. Two-bedroom villas consist of a one-bedroom villa joined to a studio suite. Three-bedroom Grand Villas are two-story affairs with the living area, kitchen, and master bedroom on the lower level and two bedrooms on the upper level. Rates for various villas range from $400 for a studio suite during the off-season to more than $6,000 for a three-bedroom Grand Villa on New Year's weekend. Other elements of the Grand Californian include a swimming pool for the villas and an underground parking garage.

The resort's beautiful High Sierra–themed pool complex, which gained an expansive new outdoor bar in 2019, features three pools surrounded by hand-laid stone, private cabanas that can be rented by the day or half-day, and a 90-foot waterslide that wraps around a redwood stump. Rounding out the Grand Californian's amenity mix are two clubby lounges.

GOOD (AND NOT-SO-GOOD) ROOMS AT GRAND CALIFORNIAN HOTEL
Grand Californian's rooms are large and attractive, but unless you're willing to pay extra, you'll be stuck looking at a parking lot or the backs of buildings. Standard rooms that don't have a great view but are close to the hotel's exclusive entrance into DCA are 2336, 2338–2346, 3334, 3336, and 3338.

Avoid even-numbered rooms X240–X260, as these are next to a loud roller coaster. Also avoid even-numbered rooms 3240–3252, as these are expensive, premium, theme-park-view rooms but don't offer a great view of the park.

For the best views of DCA we like even-numbered rooms 5424–5448 (which overlook the Grizzly Peak area of the park) or the ultra-expensive concierge-level rooms, which are even-numbered rooms 6402–6412 and 6416. Odd-numbered rooms 4419–4447 and 5419–5447 are the expensive Downtown Disney or deluxe view room types, but these offer views of Disneyland's fireworks show.

Disneyland Hotel   ★★★★

1150 W. Magic Way
Anaheim
☎ 714-778-6600
disneyland.com

Rate per night $475–$608. **Maximum occupants per room** 5. **Pool** ★★★★½. **Fridge in room** Yes. **Breakfast** Paid. **Wi-Fi** Free. **Parking** $25 self/$35 valet. **Walk to Esplanade** 9 minutes (0.5 mile).

WALT DISNEY BARELY managed to finance the construction of Disneyland Park. He certainly didn't have the funds to purchase adjacent property or build hotels, though on-site hotels were central to his overall concept. So he cut a deal with petroleum engineer and TV producer Jack Wrather to build and operate Disneyland Hotel. The deal not only gave Wrather the rights to Disneyland Hotel but also allowed him to build other Disneyland Hotels within the state of California until 2054. It always irked Walt that he didn't own the hotel that bore his name, but Wrather steadfastly refused to renegotiate the rights. After Jack Wrather died in 1984, the Walt Disney Company bought the entire Wrather Corporation, which among other things held the rights to the *Lone Ranger* and *Lassie* TV series and, improbably, the RMS *Queen Mary,* docked at Long Beach. By acquiring the whole corporation, the Walt Disney Company brought Disneyland Hotel under Disney ownership in 1988.

Disneyland Hotel consists of three towers facing each other across a verdant landscaped plaza, as well as a swimming complex, restaurants, and shops. Guest registration for all three towers is situated in the Fantasy Tower (previously called the Magic Tower, and the Marina Tower before that), which is connected to the Disneyland Convention Center and Disneyland Hotel's self-parking garage. Though all three towers share restaurants, shopping, and recreational amenities, the Fantasy Tower is most conveniently located. It and the Adventure Tower (formerly Dreams, née Sierra) are closest to Downtown Disney and the theme parks. The Frontier Tower (formerly Wonder, formerly Bonita) is the farthest from the action.

Rack rates for the Disneyland Hotel range from around $475 for a city view in the off-season to $762 for a theme park view during holiday periods (and more than $1,557 for a three-bedroom suite).

Disneyland Hotel embraces the retro-nostalgia of baby boomer Disneyland devotees with decorative elements evoking the park's early years; look for 1950s-style signage outside each tower and a tribute to Frontierland's long-gone Old Unfaithful geysers. The main lobby evokes Mary Blair's It's a Small World designs and features an enlarged fun map of the original park. The check-in area sports early attraction concept artwork and seating styled after the spinning teacups, whimsical touches that stand in stark contrast with the ultramodern sculpted steel behind the front desk. Peek inside the Frontier Tower lobby to see an amazingly detailed model of Big Thunder Mountain. Large windows, specially designed to filter outside noise, give the facade a glistening sky-blue tint. A family from Fort Collins, Colorado, wrote us in praise of the hotel's theme:

> We loved the ambience of the Disneyland Hotel. I was impressed with how the piped-in music changed from tropical around Adventure tower and Tangaroa Terrace to the Davy Crockett theme as you approached the Frontier tower.

The rooms have a sleek monochromatic contemporary look. Each room has one king or two queen beds, along with a pullout couch; one-bedroom suites with a wet bar and living room are also available. Features include a headboard with a carving of Sleeping Beauty Castle; fiber optics in the headboard create a skyline with fireworks (accompanied by a tinny rendition of "When You Wish Upon a Star") at the flick of a switch. Other decorative touches include black-and-white photography depicting the history of Disneyland and hidden Mickey designs in the carpet, though the overall feel is more business modern than Disney whimsy. Each room has a flat-panel HDTV, perfect for connecting a laptop or video game console. Other room amenities include mini-refrigerators; coffee makers; safes large enough for laptops; and high-tech phone, cable, and wireless internet connections.

If the standard rooms aren't pixie-dusted (or pricey) enough for you, five different elaborately themed Signature Suites allow big spenders to sleep in a pirate's lair, the Big Thunder mine, or Mickey's penthouse. A night in one of these rooms can easily run into the mid-four figures; if you have to ask how much, you probably can't afford it.

The bathrooms are small for an upscale hotel, but there is a sink and vanity outside the bathrooms. As in most family hotels built in the 1950s and '60s, a connecting door, situated by the closet and the aforementioned single sink, leads to an adjoining room. Soundproofing around the connecting doors is nonexistent, so be prepared to revel in the sounds of your neighbors brushing their teeth, coping with indigestion, and arguing over what to wear. Fortunately, these sounds don't carry into the sleeping area.

The swimming complex's centerpiece is a pair of waterslides (187 feet and 112 feet long, respectively) themed to resemble vintage monorail trains, topped by the classic Disneyland block letter logo. There's also a 19-foot kiddie slide and bubble jets for the little ones; family films are screened here in the evenings, and guests of the other on-site hotels may attend. A 4-foot-deep pool separates the 4,800-square-foot E-Ticket Pool and the waterslides, with a footbridge allowing easy passage from one side of the water to the other. On sunny days expect long inefficient lines for the slides, as well as a severe shortage of lounge chairs and elbow room.

Tangaroa Terrace and Trader Sam's, a casual restaurant and bar, bank on fond memories of Adventureland's 1960s-era *Tahitian Terrace* dinner show. Disneyland Hotel's other restaurants include Steakhouse 55 and Goofy's Kitchen, the hotel's character-meal headquarters. (All Disneyland Hotel restaurants are profiled in full in Part Four.)

As concerns practical matters, parking is a royal pain at the Disneyland Hotel. The self-parking garage is convenient only to the Fantasy Tower, and even there you'll probably have a long walk. To reach the other two towers, you must pass through the Fantasy Tower and navigate across the hotel's inner plaza and pool area. The Frontier Tower on the southern end of the property has a small parking lot to the rear, accessible via Downtown Drive and Paradise Way. Unfortunately, many of the already limited spaces are reserved for the adjacent Disney Vacation Club time-share sales office. Even so, if you're staying at the Frontier Tower, it's your best bet. If there's no room in the Frontier lot, you're better off parking in the Paradise Pier Hotel's lot than in the Disneyland Hotel parking garage. The only valet parking is at the Fantasy Tower, so even if you valet park, you'll still have to hoof it to the other towers.

While the monorail station in Downtown Disney is convenient, you can't always count on it for transportation into Disneyland Park, as this Buffalo, New York, woman discovered:

> *I found it annoying that the monorail closed with the rest of the park (or before!) and could not be used for transportation back to the hotel in the evening. It also shuts down if it's too hot in the afternoon because there is no AC.*

GOOD (AND NOT-SO-GOOD) ROOMS AT DISNEYLAND HOTEL There are three guest-room buildings at Disneyland Hotel: Fantasy, Adventure, and Frontier Towers. Each tower has three room view types: standard (of trees or parking lots), deluxe (of the resort's pool complex), and premium (facing Disneyland Park and Downtown Disney, or the pool). The best views can be had from the east-west-facing Adventure Tower, which overlooks the hotel's inner plaza and pool area on the west and Downtown Disney and the theme parks to the east. The most lackluster views are the north-facing vistas of the Fantasy Tower.

The Fantasy Tower's north side looks out onto several massive parking lots, but you can catch a glimpse of Disneyland Park if you crane your neck to the right. Rooms facing south in Fantasy Tower look out onto the pool and are categorized as deluxe view rooms. If you opt for standard view and want a slightly better view of Disneyland, go for odd-numbered rooms XX25–XX35 on floors 7–11. If you want to avoid views of parking lots but don't want to drop the extra cash on a room upgrade, even-numbered rooms XX00–XX34 on floors 2–3 on the tower's south side are categorized as standard.

Adventure Tower faces Disneyland and Downtown Disney on the east and the pool complex on the west. On Adventure Tower's east side, standard view rooms (odd-numbered rooms XX37–XX67 on floors 2–6) are better than the equivalently priced rooms in the other towers—instead of parking lots you'll mostly see trees. Almost all of the other rooms in Adventure are categorized as deluxe or premium and carry a hefty price tag. If you're willing to pay the extra money, go for odd-numbered rooms XX37–XX51 on floors 7–10 for the best views of Disneyland.

Rooms on Frontier Tower's north side face the hotel's pool, and most above the fourth floor are categorized as deluxe or premium views. Avoid any standard rooms facing south (odd-numbered rooms XX69–XX99, floors 2–14) in Frontier, as these are the worst views of any of the Disneyland Hotel's rooms.

Disney's Paradise Pier Hotel ★★★½

Rate per night $356–$436. **Maximum occupants per room** 5. **Pool** ★★★½. **Fridge in room** Yes. **Breakfast** Paid. **Wi-Fi** Free. **Parking** $25 self/$35 valet. **Walk to Esplanade** 12 minutes (0.6 mile).

1717 S. Disneyland Dr.
Anaheim
☎ 714-999-0990
disneyland.com

DISNEY ACQUIRED THE INDEPENDENT Pan Pacific Hotel just south of the Disneyland Hotel in 1995 and changed its name to the Disneyland Pacific Hotel. Just before DCA opened in 2001, the hotel was rechristened as the Paradise Pier Hotel in recognition of the Paradise Pier district (now known as Pixar Pier and Paradise Gardens Park) of DCA the hotel overlooks.

The 481-room property makes a mostly successful attempt to merge the hotel's original South Seas flavor with a vintage seaside amusement theme inspired by the attractions across the street. The sunny lobby sports a stunning glass-enclosed exterior elevator with high-tech touch screen controls (if it induces vertigo, interior elevators are available) and a statue of Goofy holding a surfboard. Guest rooms are furnished with blond wood furniture and the usual pastel soft goods, including bedspreads with a hidden Mickey pattern. Somewhat more whimsical than rooms at the Disneyland Hotel or the Grand Californian, Paradise Pier rooms include accents such as Mickey Mouse table lamps, beach ball pillows, and seashell-patterned carpets. Rates range $356–$1,189, depending on season and view.

For dining, the informal Disney's PCH Grill serves a breakfast (with characters) and dinner buffet daily. Next to the restaurant you'll find the Surfside Lounge, perfect for unwinding after an exhausting day of family fun. Amenities include a fitness center, conference rooms, a kids' game room, and an often breezy rooftop pool complete with a waterslide (the view from the top of the slide is killer). Self-parking in Paradise Pier's on-site garage is fast and convenient, and an Alamo rental car agency is located on the property. Somewhat isolated on the Disneyland Resort property, the hotel is a 12-minute hike to the theme park entrances, farther away than most non-Disney hotels lining Harbor Boulevard on the east side of the resort, since Paradise Pier guests must walk through the parking lot to the security check on the west side of Downtown Disney instead of cutting through the Grand Californian Hotel.

Many guests overlook the Paradise Pier, but this Superior, Colorado, family had a positive experience:

> *It was great with one exception: the tiny pool (especially compared to the other two Disney hotels). Staff was awesome, room was nice, restaurant was fun. We would definitely stay again.*

However, this reader from Kirkland, Washington, felt exactly the opposite:

> *The quality of the hotel for the cost is NOT worth it . . . PP had terrible beds, terrible walls, and was an incredibly long walk to the park. No thank you.*

GOOD (AND NOT-SO-GOOD) ROOMS AT PARADISE PIER HOTEL There are two guest-room buildings at Paradise Pier Hotel. Rooms facing east have excellent views of the Pixar Pier area of DCA. Rooms facing west look out onto parking lots and a nearby residential neighborhood. There are two room-view categories at Paradise Pier, standard and premium. All rooms facing west are tagged as standard, while all rooms facing east on the sixth floor and above are premium. Request rooms 300–318 and 326–345 if you want to be on the same floor as the pool. If you want to catch a small glimpse of DCA but don't want to pay the extra cost for a premium room, even-numbered rooms 502–518 are standard view rooms facing the park. Even-numbered rooms 1200–1218, 1300–1318, 1400–1418, 1500, and 1510 are premium rooms that offer the best views of DCA.

HOW TO GET DISCOUNTS ON LODGING AT DISNEYLAND RESORT HOTELS

unofficial **TIP**
For the best rates and least crowded conditions, try to avoid visiting Disneyland Resort when a major convention or trade show is in progress.

SO MANY GUEST ROOMS are in and around Disneyland Resort that competition is brisk, and everyone, including Disney, wheels and deals to keep them filled. Here are tips for getting price breaks:

1. DISNEYLAND RESORT WEBSITE Disney has become more aggressive about offering deals on its website. Go to disneyland.com and check the page for "Special Offers." When booking rooms on Disney's or any other site, be sure to click on "Terms and Conditions" and read the fine print *before* making reservations.

2. SEASONAL SAVINGS You can save $15 to more than $200 per night on a Disneyland Resort hotel room by visiting during the slower times of the year. Disney uses so many adjectives (regular, holiday, peak, value, and such) to describe its seasonal calendar, however, that it's hard to keep up without a scorecard. To confuse matters more, the dates for each season vary from hotel to hotel. Understand that Disney seasonal dates are not sequential like spring, summer, fall, and winter. For any specific resort, there are sometimes several seasonal changes in a month. This is important because your room rate per night is determined by the season prevailing when you check in. Let's say that you checked in to the Disneyland Hotel on April 20 for a five-night stay. April 20 is in the more expensive holiday season that ends April 21, followed by the less pricey regular season beginning April 23. Because you arrived during a holiday season, the holiday season rate will be applied for your entire stay, even though almost half of your stay will be in regular season. Your strategy, therefore, is to shift your dates (if possible) to arrive during a less expensive season.

3. ASK ABOUT SPECIALS When you talk to Disney reservationists, inquire specifically about special deals. Ask, for example, "What special rates or discounts are available at Disney hotels during the time of our visit?" Being specific and assertive paid off for an Illinois reader:

> I called Disney's reservations number and asked for availability and rates. [Because] of The Unofficial Guide *warning about Disney reservationists answering only the questions posed, I specifically asked, "Are there any special rates or discounts for that room during the month of October?" She replied, "Yes, we have that room available at a special price." [For] the price of one phone call, I saved $440.*

Along similar lines, a Warren Township, New Jersey, dad chimed in with this:

> *Your tip about asking Disney employees about discounts was invaluable. They will not volunteer this information, but by asking we saved almost $500 on our hotel room.*

4. LEARN ABOUT DEALS OFFERED TO SPECIFIC MARKETS The folks at mousesavers.com keep an updated list of discounts for use at Disney resorts. The discounts are separated into categories such as "for anyone," "for residents of certain states," "for annual passport holders," and so on. For example, the site once listed a deal targeted to residents of the San Diego area published in an ad in a San Diego newspaper. Dozens of discounts are usually listed on the site, covering almost all Disneyland Resort hotels. Usually anyone calling the Disneyland Resort Reservations Office (call ☎ 714-956-6425 and press 1 on the menu) can cite the referenced ad and get the discounted rate.

Disney has moved away from room discounts that anyone can use. Instead, Disney targets people with PIN codes in emails and direct mailings. PIN-code discounts are offered to specific individuals and are correlated with that person's name and address. PIN-code offers are nontransferable. When you try to make a reservation using the code, Disney will verify that the street or email address to which the PIN code was sent is yours.

To enhance your chances of receiving a PIN-code offer, you need to get your name and street or email address into the Disney system. One way is to call the Disney Resort Travel Sales Center at ☎ 714-520-5060

DISNEY LODGING FOR LESS

The people at mousesavers.com (see page 15) know more about Disney hotel packages than anyone on the planet. Here are their money-saving suggestions.

- **BOOK ROOM-ONLY.** It's frequently a better deal to book a room-only reservation instead of buying a vacation package. When you buy a package, you're typically paying a premium for convenience. You can often save money by putting together your own package—just book room-only at a resort and buy passes, meals, and extras separately.

  Disney prices its standard packages at the same rates as if you had purchased individual components separately, plus a few dollars a day extra. However, what Disney doesn't tell you is that components can usually be purchased separately at a discount. (Sometimes you can get special-offer packages that have exclusive discounts; see below.)

  Disney's packages often include extras you are unlikely to use. Also, packages require a $200 deposit and full payment 30 days in advance and have stringent change and cancellation policies. Generally, booking room-only requires a deposit of one night's room rate with the remainder due at check-in. Your reservation can be changed or canceled for any reason until five days before check-in.

  Whether you decide to book a Disney vacation package or create your own, there are a number of ways to save:

- **BE FLEXIBLE.** Buying a room or package with a discount is a little like shopping for clothes at a discount store: if you wear size XX-small or XXXX-large, or you like green when everyone else is wearing pink, you're a lot more likely to score a bargain. Likewise, resort discounts are available only when Disney has excess rooms. You're more likely to get a discount during less-popular times and at larger or less-popular resorts.

- **BE PERSISTENT.** This is the most important tip. Disney allots a certain number of rooms to each discount. Once the discounted rooms are gone, you won't get that rate unless someone cancels. Fortunately, people change and cancel reservations all the time. If you can't get your preferred dates or hotel with one discount, try another one (if available) or keep calling back first thing in the morning to check for cancellations; the system resets overnight, and any reservations with unpaid deposits are automatically released for resale.

and request that info be sent to you. Or go to disneyplanning.com and fill out the short survey to have offers and news sent automatically to your email address. If you've been to Disneyland previously, your name and address will already be on record, but you won't be as likely to receive a PIN-code offer as you would by calling and requesting to be sent information. The latter is regarded as new business. Or, expressed differently, if Disney smells blood, they're more likely to come after you.

Mousesavers.com also features a great links page with short descriptions and URLs of the best Disney-related websites and a current-year seasonal rates calendar.

5. ANNUAL PASSPORT HOLDER DISCOUNTS Annual pass holders are eligible for discounts on dining, shopping, and lodging. If you visit

Disneyland Resort once a year or more, or if you plan on a visit of five or more days, you might save money overall by purchasing an annual pass. We've seen resort discounts as deep as 30% offered to annual pass holders. It doesn't take long to recoup the extra bucks you spent on an annual pass when you're saving that kind of money on lodging. Discounts in the 10%–15% range are more the norm.

6. TRAVEL AGENTS Travel agents are active players in the market and are particularly good sources of information on time-limited special programs and discounts. In our opinion, a good travel agent is the best friend a traveler can have. And though we at The Unofficial Guides know a thing or two about the travel industry, we always give our agent a chance to beat any deal we find. If our agent can't beat the deal, we let her book it if she can receive commission from it. In other words, we create a relationship that gives her plenty of incentive to really roll up her sleeves and work on our behalf.

As you might expect, some travel agents and agencies specialize, sometimes exclusively, in selling Disneyland and Walt Disney World. These agents have spent an incredible amount of time at both resorts and have completed extensive Disney education programs. They are usually the most Disney-knowledgeable agents in the travel industry. Most of these specialists and their agencies display the Earmarked logo indicating that they are Authorized Disney Vacation Planners. These Disney specialists are so good that we use them ourselves. They save us time and money, sometimes lots of both. The best of the best include **Sue Pisaturo,** whom we've used many times and who is a contributor to this guide (sue@smallworldvacations.com), **Magical Vacations Travel** (magicalvacationstravel.com), **Mouse Fan Travel** (mousefantravel.com), and **The Magic for Less** (themagicforless.com).

7. ROOM UPGRADES Sometimes a room upgrade is as good as a discount. If you're visiting Disneyland Resort during a slower time, book the least expensive room your discounts will allow. Checking in, ask very politely about being upgraded to a pool view room. A fair percentage of the time, you will get one at no additional charge.

NON-DISNEY HOTELS

MANY OF THE HOTELS AND MOTELS near Disneyland were built in the early 1960s, and they are small and sometimes unattractive by today's standards. Quite a few motels adopted adventure or fantasy themes in emulation of Disneyland. As you might imagine, these themes from five decades ago seem hokey and irrelevant today. There is a disquieting (though rapidly diminishing) number of seedy hotels near Disneyland, and even some of the chain properties fail to live up to their national standards.

If you consider a non-Disney-owned hotel in Anaheim, check its quality as reported by a reliable independent rating system such as those offered by The Unofficial Guides, AAA Directories, Forbes Guides, or Frommer's guides. Also, before you book, ask how old the hotel is and when the guest rooms were last refurbished. Be aware that almost any hotel can be made to look good on a website, so don't depend on websites alone. Locate the hotel on our street map (see page 60) to verify its proximity to Disneyland. If you will not have a car, make sure that the hotel has a shuttle service that will satisfy your needs.

GOOD NEIGHBOR HOTELS

A GOOD NEIGHBOR HOTEL is a hotel that has paid Disney a marketing fee to display that designation. Usually a ticket shop in the lobby will sell full-price Disney tickets. Other than that, the Good Neighbor designation means little to nothing for the consumer. It does not guarantee quality or proximity to Disneyland. Unlike at Walt Disney World, Disneyland does not require Good Neighbor hotels to provide free shuttle service to the park, though many do. You can book Good Neighbor hotels in a package with park tickets through the Walt Disney Travel Co.; prices are the same as if booked à la carte, though they toss in a card for discounts at select Downtown Disney locations and a free collectible pin lanyard. In our opinion, you shouldn't let the presence or absence of the Good Neighbor designation influence your hotel choice.

GETTING A GOOD DEAL AT NON-DISNEY HOTELS

FOLLOWING ARE SOME TIPS and strategies for getting a good deal on a hotel room near Disneyland. Though the following list may seem a bit intimidating and may refer to players in the travel market that are unfamiliar to you, acquainting yourself with the strategies will serve you well in the long run. Simply put, the tips we provide for getting a good deal near Disneyland will work equally well at just about any other place where you need a hotel. Once you have invested a little time and have experimented with these strategies, you will be able to routinely obtain rooms at the best hotels and at the lowest possible rates.

Remember that Disneyland Resort is right across the street from the Anaheim Convention Center, one of the largest and busiest convention centers in the country. Room availability, as well as rates, are affected significantly by trade shows and other events at the convention center. To determine whether such an event will be going on during your projected dates, visit anaheim.net/calendar.aspx?CID=26, to view the convention calendar.

1. MOUSESAVERS.COM is a site dedicated to finding great deals on hotels, admissions, and more at Disneyland Resort and Walt Disney World. The site covers discounts on both Disney and non-Disney hotels and is especially effective at keeping track of time-limited deals and discounts offered in a select market—San Diego, for example. However, the site does not sell travel products.

2. KAYAK.COM AND MOBISSIMO.COM are travel search engines that search the better hotel-discount sites, as well as chain and individual hotel websites. (As an aside, Kayak used to be purely a search engine but now sells travel products, raising the issue of whether products not sold by Kayak are equally likely to come up in a search. Mobissimo, on the other hand, only links potential buyers to provider websites.)

3. EXPEDIA.COM AND TRAVELOCITY.COM sometimes offer good discounts on area hotels. We find that Expedia offers the best deals if you're booking within two weeks of your visit. In fact, some of Expedia's last-minute deals are amazing, really rock-bottom rates. Travelocity frequently beats Expedia, however, if you reserve two weeks to three months out. Neither site offers anything to get excited about if you book more than three months from the time of your visit. If you use either site, be sure to take into consideration the demand for rooms during the season of your visit, and check to see if any big conventions or trade shows are scheduled for the convention center.

4. PRICELINE.COM allows you to tender a bid for a room. You can't bid on a specific hotel, but you can specify location ("Disneyland Vicinity") and the quality rating expressed in stars. If your bid is accepted, you will be assigned to a hotel consistent with your location and quality requirements, and your credit card will be charged in a nonrefundable transaction for your entire stay. Notification of acceptance usually takes less than an hour. We recommend bidding $35–$55 per night for a three-star hotel and $55–$80 per night for a four-star property. To gauge your chances of success, check to see if any major conventions or trade shows are scheduled during your preferred dates.

5. SPECIAL WEEKEND RATES If you are not averse to about an hour's drive to Disneyland, you can get a great weekend rate on rooms in downtown Los Angeles. Most hotels that cater to business, government, and convention travelers offer special weekend discounts that range 15%–40% below normal weekday rates. You can find out about weekend specials by calling the hotel or by consulting your travel agent.

6. WHOLESALERS, CONSOLIDATORS, AND RESERVATION SERVICES Wholesalers and consolidators buy rooms, or options on rooms (room blocks), from hotels at a low negotiated rate. They then resell the rooms at a profit through travel agents, tour packagers, or directly to the public. Most wholesalers and consolidators have a provision for returning unsold rooms to participating hotels, but they are disinclined to do so. The wholesaler's or consolidator's relationship with any hotel is predicated on volume. If they return rooms unsold, the hotel might not make as many rooms available to them the next time around. Thus, wholesalers and consolidators often offer rooms at bargain rates, anywhere from 15%–50% off rack, occasionally sacrificing their profit margin to avoid returning the rooms to the hotel unsold.

When wholesalers and consolidators deal directly with the public, they frequently represent themselves as reservation services. When you call, you can ask for a rate quote for a particular hotel or, alternatively, ask for their best available deal in the area where you prefer to stay. If there is a maximum amount you are willing to pay, say so. Chances are that the service will find something that will work for you, even if they have to shave a dollar or two off their own profit. Sometimes you will have to prepay for your room with your credit card when you make your reservation. Most often, you will pay when you check out. Listed below are two services that frequently offer substantial discounts in the Anaheim area.

ANAHEIM AREA WHOLESALERS AND CONSOLIDATORS

HOTEL RESERVATIONS NETWORK ☎ 800-780-5733   cheap-discount-hotels.com
HOTELS.COM ☎ 800-246-8357   hotels.com

7. CLUBS AND ORGANIZATIONS If you belong to AAA, AARP, or a number of other organizations, you can obtain lodging discounts. Usually the discounts are modest, 5%–15%, but occasionally higher.

8. IF YOU MAKE YOUR OWN RESERVATION As you poke around trying to find a good deal, there are several things you should know. First, always call the hotel in question as opposed to the hotel chain's national toll-free number. Quite often, the reservationists at the national numbers are unaware of local specials. Always ask about specials before you inquire about corporate rates. Do not be reluctant to bargain. If you are buying a hotel's weekend package, for example, and want to extend your stay into the following week, you can often obtain at least the corporate rate for the extra days. Do your bargaining before you check in, however, preferably when you make your reservations. Work far enough in advance to receive a confirmation.

HOW TO GET THE ROOM YOU WANT

MOST HOTELS, INCLUDING DISNEY'S, won't guarantee a specific room when you book but will post your request on your reservations record and try to accommodate you. Our experience indicates that if you give them your first, second, and third choices, you'll probably get one of the three.

unofficial **TIP**
Request a renovated room at your hotel—these can be much nicer than the older rooms.

When speaking to the reservationist or your travel agent, be specific. If you want a room overlooking the pool, say so. Similarly, be sure to clearly state such preferences as a particular floor, a corner room, a room close to restaurants, a room away from elevators and ice machines, a nonsmoking room, a room with a balcony, or any other preference. If you have a list of preferences, type it up in order of importance, and email or fax it to the hotel or to your travel agent. Keep in mind that Disney's reservations computer is limited to storing a short block of text, so keep your request as brief and specific as possible. Be sure to include your own contact information and, if you've already booked, your reservation confirmation number. If it makes you feel better, call back in a few days to make sure that your preferences were posted to your reservations record.

About Hotel Renovations

Most hotels more than five years old refurbish 10%–20% of their guest rooms each year. This incremental approach minimizes disruption of business but makes your room assignment a crapshoot. You might luck into a newly renovated room or be assigned a threadbare room. Disney resorts will not guarantee a recently renovated room but will note your request and try to accommodate you. Non-Disney hotels will often guarantee an updated room when you book. Before you begin to shop for a hotel, take a hard look at this letter we received from a couple in Hot Springs, Arkansas:

> We canceled our room reservations to follow the advice in your book [and reserved a hotel highly rated by The Unofficial Guide]. We wanted inexpensive but clean and cheerful. We got inexpensive but dirty, grim, and depressing. I really felt disappointed in your advice and the room. It was the pits. That was the one real piece of information I needed from your book!

Needless to say, this letter was as unsettling to us as the bad room was to our reader. Our integrity as travel journalists, after all, is based on the quality of the information we provide to our readers. When we rechecked the hotel that our reader disliked so intensely, we discovered that our review was correctly representative but that he and his wife had unfortunately been assigned to one of a small number of threadbare rooms scheduled for renovation.

The key to avoiding disappointment is to do some snooping around in advance. We recommend that you check out the hotel's website to see a standard guest room photo before you book. Be forewarned, however, that some hotel chains use the same guest room photo for all hotels in the chain, and that the guest room in a specific property may not resemble the photo on the website. When you or your travel agent call, ask how old the property is and when the guest room you are being assigned was last renovated. If you arrive and are assigned a room inferior to that which you had been led to expect, demand to be moved to another room.

TRAVEL PACKAGES

PACKAGE TOURS THAT INCLUDE LODGING, park admission, and other features are routinely available. Some packages are very good deals if you make use of the features you are paying for.

How to Evaluate a Disneyland Travel Package

Hundreds of Disneyland package vacations are offered to the public each year. Some are created by the Disney Resort Travel Sales Center, others by airline touring companies, and some by independent travel agents and wholesalers. Almost all Disneyland packages include lodging at or near Disneyland and theme park admission. Packages offered by the airlines include air transportation.

Package prices vary seasonally, with mid-June–mid-August and holiday periods being the most expensive. During the off-season, forget packages; there are plenty of empty rooms, and you can negotiate great discounts (at non-Disney properties) yourself. Similarly, airfares and rental cars are cheaper at off-peak times.

When considering a package, choose one that includes features that you are sure to use. Whether you use all the features or not, you will most certainly pay for them. Second, if cost is of greater concern than convenience, make a few phone calls and see what the package would cost if you booked its individual components (such as airfare, rental car, and lodging) on your own. If the package price is less than the à la carte cost, the package is a good deal. If the costs are about the same, the package is probably worth it for the convenience.

If you buy a package from Disney, do not expect Disney reservationists to offer suggestions or help you sort out your options. As a rule they will not volunteer information but will only respond to specific questions you pose, adroitly ducking any query that calls for an opinion. A reader from North Riverside, Illinois, wrote to *The Unofficial Guide,* complaining:

> *I have received various pieces of literature from Disney, and it is very confusing to try and figure everything out. My wife made two phone calls, and the [Disney] representatives were very courteous. However, they answered only the questions posed and were not very eager to give advice on what might be most cost-effective. The reps would not say if we would be better off doing one thing over the other. I feel that a person could spend 8 hours on the phone with [Disney] reps and not have any more input than you get from reading the literature.*

If you cannot get the information you need from the Disney people, try a good travel agent. Chances are that the agent will be more forthcoming in helping you sort out your options.

Information Needed for Evaluation

For quick reference, visit disneyplanning.com and fill out a short survey to view video footage and descriptions for all Disneyland lodging properties. In addition, you can call the Disney Resort Travel Sales Center at ☎ 714-520-5060 and ask for a rate sheet listing admission options and prices for the theme parks. With this in hand, you are ready to evaluate any package that appeals to you. Remember that all packages are quoted on a per-person basis, two to a room (double occupancy). Good luck.

VISITING OTHER LOS ANGELES–AREA ATTRACTIONS

If your travel plans include a stay in the area of more than two or three days, lodge near Disneyland Resort only just before and on the days you visit the parks. The same traffic you avoid by staying close to the park will eat you alive when you begin branching out to other Los Angeles–area attractions. Also, the area immediately around Disneyland is uninspiring, and there is a marked scarcity of decent restaurants.

VACATION HOMES

SOME OF THE BEST LODGING DEALS in the Disneyland Resort area are vacation homes. Prices range from about $195 a night for two-bedroom condos and town homes to $200–$600 a night for three-to five-bedroom vacation homes.

Let's compare renting a vacation home with staying at a three-star hotel near Disneyland. A family of two parents, two teens, and two grandparents would need three hotel rooms at the Fairfield Inn Anaheim Resort. At the lowest rate obtainable, they'd be spending about $200 per night per room, or more than $600 total per night with tax and parking. Rooms are 228 square feet each, so they'd have a total of 684 square feet. Each room has a private bath, TV, and mini-fridge. The hotel has a pool and hot tub, but parking costs extra.

At the same time of year, they can rent a 1,400-square-foot, three-bedroom, two-bath vacation home with a private pool within easy walking distance of Disneyland for about $300 per night—a savings of about $300 per night over Fairfield Inn (a total savings of around $1,500 on a five-night stay). But that's not all: the home comes with a washer and dryer; an outdoor hot tub; a grill; an air hockey table; a family room with a 52-inch TV and surround sound; a dining room with seating for eight; and off-street parking. The only trade-off for our hypothetical family would be having two bathrooms instead of three.

You can find homes similar to the one described above at **Vacation Rental by Owner** (vrbo.com) and **Airbnb** (airbnb.com), listing services for owners of vacation properties worldwide. Both websites offer detailed information, including a good number of photos of each specific home. When you book, the home you've been looking at is the actual one you're reserving. On the other hand, some vacation-home rental companies, like rental car agencies, don't assign you a specific home until the day you arrive—these companies provide photos of a "typical" home instead of making information available on each of the individual homes in their inventory. In this case, you have to take the company's word that the typical home pictured is representative and that the property you'll be assigned will be just as nice.

Location is everything, especially in Southern California with its legendary traffic. Before renting a home, get the address. Then, using google.com/maps, obtain exact directions from the home to Disneyland. This will tell you how long and how complicated your commute will be. Avoid homes for which it's necessary to drive on a freeway for more than a couple of miles. Don't worry if the home isn't in Anaheim per se; it's the distance to Disneyland that counts.

The only practical way to shop for a rental home is online. Going online makes it relatively easy to compare different properties and rental companies. The best sites are easy to navigate, let you see what you're interested in without having to log in or divulge any personal information, and list memberships in such organizations as the Better Business Bureau. Before you book, ask about minimum stays, damage deposits, cleaning charges, and pets, as well as how any problems will be addressed once you're in the home.

In July 2016 the Anaheim City Council voted to impose a moratorium on new short-term rentals (including services like VRBO and

Airbnb) and begin an 18-month phaseout of existing rentals, terminating them all by February 2018. The city has extended the phaseout through 2021 for some owners, but if restrictions aren't ultimately overturned, area visitors may have fewer lodging options in the future. Thankfully, short-term rentals are still legal in neighboring towns like Buena Park, where we found a room near Knott's Berry Farm through Airbnb for about $100 a night.

THE BEST HOTELS *and* MOTELS NEAR DISNEYLAND

WHAT'S IN A ROOM?

EXCEPT FOR CLEANLINESS, STATE OF REPAIR, and decor, most travelers do not pay much attention to hotel rooms. There is, of course, a discernible standard of quality and luxury that differentiates Motel 6 from Holiday Inn, Holiday Inn from Marriott, and so on. In general, however, hotel guests fail to appreciate that some rooms are better engineered than others.

Contrary to what you might suppose, designing a hotel room is (or should be) a lot more complex than picking a bedspread to match the carpet and drapes. Making the room usable to its occupants is an art, a planning discipline that combines both form and function.

Decor and taste are important, certainly. No one wants to spend several days in a room where the decor is dated, garish, or even ugly. But beyond the decor, there are variables that determine how livable a hotel room is. In Anaheim, for example, we have seen some beautifully appointed rooms that are simply not well designed for human habitation. The next time you stay in a hotel, pay attention to the details and design elements of your room. Even more than decor, these are the things that will make you feel comfortable and at home.

ROOM RATINGS

ON PAGES 57–68, we provide a selective list of our preferred lodgings near Disneyland Resort. If you used an earlier edition of this guide, you will notice that we've revamped the way we review hotels. In the years since we began publishing, the internet has utterly upended the art of researching hotel rooms, with websites such as TripAdvisor now providing crowd-sourced ratings of hundreds more properties than our team could possibly properly investigate. Instead of attempting to appear comprehensive by filling pages with superficial statistics, we've focused on crafting a curated collection of properties across a range of price points, and supplied succinct details on what sets each one apart from its competition. Our recommendations take into consideration not only room quality but also location, services, recreation, and amenities.

Just because a hotel isn't listed here doesn't necessarily mean it's a bad bet for bedding down, but these properties are all places that we can personally vouch for. However, below is a short list of places near Disneyland where we do not recommend you stay, regardless of how tempting their room rates:

• Alamo Inn & Suites	• Anaheim Discovery Inn & Suites	• Anaheim Hotel
• Anaheim Maingate Inn	• Americas Best Value Inn & Suites	• Rodeway Inn & Suites

Special thanks to Tom Bricker of disneytouristblog.com for contributing to this section; hop over to his website for more in-depth vacation recommendations.

To separate properties according to the relative quality, tastefulness, state of repair, cleanliness, and size of their standard rooms, we have grouped the hotels and motels into classifications denoted by stars. Star ratings in this guide apply to Anaheim properties only and do not necessarily correspond to ratings awarded by Forbes, AAA, or other travel critics. Because stars have little relevance when awarded in the absence of commonly recognized standards of comparison, we have tied our ratings to expected levels of quality established by specific American hotel corporations.

OVERALL STAR RATINGS		
★★★★★	Superior rooms	Tasteful and luxurious by any standard
★★★★	Extremely nice rooms	What you'd expect at a Hyatt Regency or Marriott
★★★	Nice rooms	Holiday Inn or comparable quality
★★	Adequate rooms	Clean, comfortable, and functional without frills—like a Motel 6

DISNEYLAND AREA

Alpine Inn ★★½

Rate per night $135–$400. **Maximum occupants per room** 4. **Pool** ★½. **Fridge in room** Yes. **Breakfast** Free. **Wi-Fi** Free. **Parking** Free. **Walk to Esplanade** 15 minutes (0.8 mile).

715 W. Katella Ave. Anaheim
☎ 714-535-2186
alpineinnanaheim.com

ALPINE INN HAS MORE CURB APPEAL than the average cheap motel, with its cute chalet-style check-in building; however, none of this look is present anywhere else in the property. You can walk to the parks without having to cross busy Harbor Boulevard (a consideration if you have kids), but it's slightly farther from the parks and slightly more expensive than its closest competition. Rooms are clean and well kept but on the small side, with dated TVs. It's not a resort—just a place for sleeping and showering—and better bang-for-your-buck value accommodations are usually available, but there's absolutely nothing wrong with it for a budget motel.

Anaheim Camelot Inn & Suites ★★★

Rate per night $189–$279. **Maximum occupants per room** 4. **Pool** ★★½. **Fridge in room** Yes. **Breakfast** Free. **Wi-Fi** Free. **Parking** $15/day. **Walk to Esplanade** 6 minutes (0.3 mile).

1520 S. Harbor Blvd. Anaheim
☎ 714-635-7275
camelotinn-anaheim.com

HOW THE HOTELS COMPARE

HOTEL	OVERALL QUALITY RATING	WALKING DISTANCE TO PARKS	COST
DISNEYLAND AREA			
Disney's Grand Californian Hotel & Spa	★★★★½	0.2 mi.	$626–$861
Hyatt House at Anaheim Resort/Convention Center	★★★★½	0.6 mi.	$189–$279
Disneyland Hotel	★★★★	0.5 mi.	$475–$608
Courtyard Anaheim Theme Park Entrance	★★★★	0.5 mi.	$269–$386
Four Points by Sheraton Anaheim	★★★★	0.8 mi.	$194–$214
Homewood Suites by Hilton Anaheim Resort–Convention Center	★★★★	1 mi.	$239–$319
Hotel Indigo Anaheim	★★★★	0.7 mi.	$229–$309
Residence Inn at Anaheim Resort Convention Center	★★★★	1 mi.	$229–$329
Sheraton Park Hotel at the Anaheim Resort	★★★★	0.8 mi.	$116–$269
Springhill Suites at Anaheim Resort/Convention Center	★★★★	0.7 mi.	$218–$284
Anaheim Majestic Garden Hotel	★★★½	1.2 mi.	$124–$170
Best Western Plus Park Place Inn	★★★½	0.2 mi.	$229–$259
Desert Palms Hotel & Suites	★★★½	0.7 mi.	$168–$271
Disney's Paradise Pier Hotel	★★★½	0.6 mi.	$356–$436
Howard Johnson Anaheim	★★★½	0.6 mi.	$214–$243
Candy Cane Inn	★★★½	0.6 mi.	$189
Park Vue Inn	★★★½	0.3 mi.	$209–$259
Anaheim Camelot Inn & Suites	★★★	0.3 mi.	$189–$279
Anaheim Desert Inn & Suites	★★★	0.3 mi.	$159–$179
Best Western Plus Stovall's Inn	★★★	0.9 mi.	$144–$175
Fairfield Inn Anaheim Resort	★★★	0.5 mi.	$224–$450
Ramada Anaheim Maingate North	★★★	1 mi.	$129–$149
Tropicana Inn & Suites	★★★	0.3 mi.	$229–$249
Alpine Inn	★★½	0.8 mi.	$135–$400
Castle Inn & Suites	★★½	0.5 mi.	$159–$179
Eden Roc Inn and Suites	★★½	1 mi.	$117–$243
Grand Legacy at the Park	★★½	0.3 mi.	$184–$194
Kings Inn Anaheim	★★½	0.8 mi.	$132–$142
Del Sol Inn	★★	0.3 mi.	$129–$230
Riviera Motel	★★	0.8 mi.	$129–$152
UNIVERSAL AREA			
Sheraton Universal Hotel	★★★★	0.3 mi.	$259–$309
Tilt Hotel	★★★½	0.9 mi.	$$199–$241
BLVD Hotel & Spa	★★★	0.7 mi.	$209–$249

YOU CAN'T SPEND THE NIGHT inside the castle on Disney property, but you can sleep in one mere steps across the street. The catch is that the medieval theming at Camelot Inn & Suites is strictly skin deep; the rooms themselves sport dated, standard-issue motel decor. The top reasons to stay here are location, the 4th-floor terrace pool with a view of the fireworks, location, on-site ECV scooter rental, and location. Before booking, be sure to compare prices with its Harbor Boulevard neighbors such as Best Western Plus and Park Vue Inn, which are often somewhat better bargains.

Anaheim Desert Inn & Suites   ★★★

1600 S. Harbor Blvd.
Anaheim
☎ 714-772-5050
anaheimdesertinn.com

Rate per night $159-$179. **Maximum occupants per room** 4. **Pool** ★★½. **Fridge in room** Yes. **Breakfast** Free. **Wi-Fi** Free. **Parking** $13/day. **Walk to Esplanade** 6 minutes (0.3 mile). **Comments** $6/night resort fee.

DESERT INN IS THE ULTIMATE no-frills hotel. Suites sport small sitting rooms with charm-free furnishings, the indoor pool is basic, and your room view includes a parking lot and the back side of another hotel. With that out of the way, we recommend Desert Inn because the rooms are good enough, and it only takes a few minutes to walk to Disneyland. The hotel is directly across the street from the parks, and that more than makes up for its shortcomings. We've received more positive reader surveys about the Desert Inn than any other area motel, with 90% saying they'd stay again.

Anaheim Majestic Garden   ★★★½

900 S. Disneyland Dr.
Anaheim
☎ 714-778-1700
majesticgardenhotel.com

Rate per night $124-$170. **Maximum occupants per room** 4. **Pool** ★★★. **Fridge in room** Yes. **Breakfast** Paid. **Wi-Fi** Free. **Parking** $18/day. **Walk to Esplanade** 25 minutes (1.2 miles). **Comments** Pets allowed with $50 nonrefundable deposit; must notify the hotel in advance. Free shuttle to Disneyland.

ANAHEIM MAJESTIC GARDEN HOTEL'S Tudor facade is a touch tacky, but the medieval theming inside is subtly executed. We enjoyed the peaceful and beautifully landscaped hotel grounds. For those with children, the Legend of the Lair is told throughout the hotel on the carpet and walls, and Princess Corinne makes appearances during breakfast at the unexpectedly upscale on-site bistro. Guest rooms are modern and among the most spacious standard rooms in the area, with comfortable bedding. We usually see affordable prices at Majestic when comparing it to other local hotels, likely due to its slightly inconvenient location. We clocked the walk to the Mickey & Friends parking structure (where you can catch a tram to Disneyland Resort) at a little over 15 minutes. That, plus the time it takes to go through security and get on the tram, means it'll take over a half hour to be anywhere near the entrance of Disneyland. Luckily, a free shuttle is available, which takes about 5 minutes to drive to and from Disneyland, but we observed it filling up with guests quickly in the mornings and evenings.

Best Western Plus Park Place Inn   ★★★½

1554 S. Harbor Blvd.
Anaheim
☎ 714-776-4800
parkplaceinnand
minisuites.com

Rate per night $229-$259. **Maximum occupants per room** 4. **Pool** ★★. **Fridge in room** Yes. **Breakfast** Free. **Wi-Fi** Free. **Parking** $10/day. **Walk to Esplanade** 5 minutes (0.2 mile).

Disneyland-Area Hotels

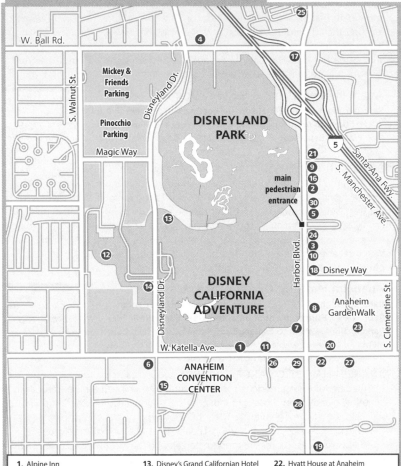

1. Alpine Inn
2. Anaheim Camelot Inn & Suites
3. Anaheim Desert Inn & Suites
4. Anaheim Majestic Garden
5. Best Western Plus Park Place Inn
6. Best Western Plus Stovall's Inn
7. Candy Cane Inn
8. Castle Inn & Suites
9. Courtyard Anaheim Theme Park
   Entrance
10. Del Sol Inn
11. Desert Palms Hotel & Suites
12. Disneyland Hotel
13. Disney's Grand Californian Hotel
    & Spa
14. Disney's Paradise
    Pier Hotel
15. Eden Roc Inn & Suites
16. Fairfield Inn Anaheim Resort
17. Four Points by Sheraton Anaheim
18. Grand Legacy at the Park
19. Homewood Suites by Hilton
    Anaheim Resort–
    Convention Center
20. Hotel Indigo Anaheim
21. Howard Johnson Anaheim
22. Hyatt House at Anaheim
    Resort/Convention Center
23. Kings Inn
24. Park Vue Inn
25. Ramada Anaheim
    Maingate North
26. Residence Inn at Anaheim
    Resort/Convention Center
27. Riviera Motel
28. Sheraton Park Hotel at Anaheim
29. SpringHill Suites Anaheim
    Resort/Convention Center
30. Tropicana Inn & Suites

BEST WESTERN PLUS PARK PLACE INN boasts that they are the closest hotel to Disneyland (even closer than Disney's own hotels). This is not hyperbole; it takes barely 5 minutes to walk from your room to the front gate. Besides the location, Park Place Inn has very nice and stylish rooms (including mini-suites that sleep 6) that feature comfortable beds, a desk and office chair, HDTV, a microwave, a mini-fridge, and a safe. Coffee makers weren't included during our stay, but instant coffee and tea are provided in the rooms. Also, a decent breakfast buffet is included in the price of the room, and served above the adjoining Captain Kidd's buffet restaurant. The only downside is the unappealing, undersized pool.

Best Western Plus Stovall's Inn ★★★

Rate per night $144–$175. **Maximum occupants per room** 4. **Pool** ★★★½. **Fridge in room** Yes. **Breakfast** Free. **Wi-Fi** Free. **Parking** $10/day. **Walk to Esplanade** 18 minutes (0.9 mile). **Comments** Room service available.

1110 W. Katella Ave. Anaheim
☎ 714-778-1880
stovallsinn.com

AS A FAMILY-OWNED MOTEL that has been across the street from Disneyland's southwest corner since the 1960s, Stovall's Inn (originally known as The Inn of Tomorrow) is showing its age but still rather comfortable thanks to repeated refurbishments that have honored its space-age origins. The glittering lobby offers a small business center, filtered water to refill your bottles, and a better-than-average free breakfast buffet with hot items such as waffles and bacon. The motel's centerpiece is an expansive pool complex, with hot tubs and a fitness room surrounded by painstakingly pruned animal topiaries. Coco's Bakery, a family restaurant with reasonable prices and excellent pastries, is located in the parking lot. Rooms are of average size for the era, and between the in-room air-conditioning units, thin walls, and exterior hallways, they can be noisy. Though it's a longer walk to the Esplanade than comparable properties on Harbor Boulevard, Stovall's Inn is convenient if you're stopping by the Disneyland Resort hotels for an après park cocktail.

Candy Cane Inn ★★★½

Rate per night $189. **Maximum occupants per room** 4. **Pool** ★★★. **Fridge in room** Yes. **Breakfast** Free. **Wi-Fi** Free. **Parking** Free. **Walk to Esplanade** 11 minutes (0.6 mile). **Comments** Free shuttle to Disneyland.

1747 S. Harbor Blvd. Anaheim
☎ 714-774-5284
candycaneinn.net

THIS FRIENDLY, FAMILY-RUN HOTEL has a charming homespun style, with grounds that are always lined with beautiful, flowering plants. The service here has given the place some seriously loyal customers. Guest rooms could use a renovation, but it's otherwise hard to fault this place; even the free continental breakfast is better than most on the block. This is a top pick for parties wanting California boutique hotel charm. It's a little longer walk than some hotels across Harbor Boulevard, but a free shuttle is available for anyone wanting to save their feet.

Castle Inn and Suites ★★½

Rate per night $159–$179. **Maximum occupants per room** 4. **Pool** ★½. **Fridge in room** Yes. **Breakfast** No. **Wi-Fi** Free. **Parking** Free. **Walk to Esplanade** 11 minutes (0.5 mile).

1734 S. Harbor Blvd. Anaheim
☎ 714-774-8111
castleinn.com

CASTLE INN, the other medieval fortress on Harbor Boulevard (not to be confused with the Camelot), goes even further with the kitschy facade, extending the theme into the lobby and guest rooms with heavy wooden furniture and artwork of European chateaus. Tackiness aside, this is a surprisingly pleasant place to stay, offering clean rooms with the essential amenities, if not many frills such as free breakfast. The biggest black mark is the bare-bones pool. Castle Inn is neither the cheapest, nor the closest, property near the parks, but it's an acceptable compromise when your first choices are all booked.

Courtyard Anaheim Theme Park Entrance ★★★★

1420 S. Harbor Blvd.
Anaheim
☎ 714-254-1442
marriott.com

Rate per night $269–$386. **Maximum occupants per room** 6. **Pool** ★★★★½. **Fridge in room** Yes. **Breakfast** Paid. **Wi-Fi** Free. **Parking** $24 valet only; no self-parking. **Walk to Esplanade** 10 minutes (0.5 mile).

IN TERMS OF QUALITY, the Courtyard Anaheim Theme Park Entrance sets a high bar for off-site Disneyland hotels, particularly for families with kids. The overall quality and the reasonably short walk to the park are the strong selling points here, with 530-square-foot standard rooms that are far larger than the area's average. Rooms feature two queen-size beds plus twin bunk beds, which are perfect for kids and serviceable for not-too-tall adults. The Surfside water park is significantly better than your average hotel pool, with a large splash playground and two short slides. Price is unquestionably the biggest negative, with rates around $100/night more expensive than some off-site alternatives; even comparable hotels can be significantly less expensive depending upon when you're traveling. This is our top pick for families wanting a short walk but who are not on a tight budget.

Del Sol Inn ★★

1604 S. Harbor Blvd.
Anaheim
☎ 714-234-3411
delsolinn.com

Rate per night $129–$230. **Maximum occupants per room** 4–6. **Pool** ★½. **Fridge in room** Yes. **Breakfast** Free. **Wi-Fi** Free. **Parking** $14/day. **Walk to Esplanade** 7 minutes (0.3 mile). **Comments** $7.59/night resort fee.

THIS MOTEL IS FINE for sleeping, showering, and spending all day in the parks. Rooms are dated and worn, but at least they're spacious, with decent beds and pillows. It's a fine option from a cleanliness and basic functionality perspective. The real reason to stay here is because it's often the cheapest hotel directly across the street from Disneyland. Request an upper floor near the front of the complex to avoid hearing stomping above you, and to save a couple minutes on your walk to the parks, as this is a fairly long hotel.

Desert Palms Hotel & Suites ★★★½

631 W. Katella Ave.
Anaheim
☎ 714-535-1133
desertpalmshotel.com

Rate per night $168–$271. **Maximum occupants per room** 4. **Pool** ★★. **Fridge in room** Yes. **Breakfast** Free. **Wi-Fi** Free. **Parking** $16/day. **Walk to Esplanade** 14 minutes (0.7 mile). **Comments** $9.95/night resort fee.

DESERT PALMS HOTEL & SUITES is a solid hotel overall, with some nice advantages like indoor hallways and an inviting lobby that make it seem superior to the hotels directly on Harbor Boulevard. The free breakfast buffet with make-your-own egg sandwiches is among the best in the neighborhood.

The location (right by 7-11 and the CVS Pharmacy) is convenient, and the rooms are fairly nice, but the high prices relative to other hotels in its class give us some pause with this one.

Disneyland Hotel *(see pages 42–45)*

Disney's Grand Californian Hotel & Spa *(see pages 41–42)*

Disney's Paradise Pier Hotel *(see pages 45–46)*

Eden Roc Inn & Suites ★★½

Rate per night $117–$243. **Maximum occupants per room** 4. **Pool** ★½. **Fridge in room** Yes. **Breakfast** No. **Wi-Fi** Free. **Parking** Free. **Walk to Esplanade** 20 minutes (1 mile). **Comments** $7/night resort fee.

1830 S. West St.
Anaheim
☎ 714-663-8700
edenrocanaheim.com

A TOP-TO-BOTTOM RENOVATION a couple of years ago gave the Eden Roc rooms a fresh, modern feel. In-room amenities include a microwave, a mini-fridge, a desk with chair, and a coffee maker. Rooms are a bit on the small side, but the previously mentioned offerings and the hotel's low price range make it a great option. Walking from your room to Disneyland (via the entrance at the western end of Downtown Disney, near Disneyland Hotel) can take over 20 minutes, but parking is free so you can make the short drive up Disneyland Drive and be at the park's parking structures in no time.

Fairfield Inn Anaheim Resort ★★★

Rate per night $224–$450. **Maximum occupants per room** 4. **Pool** ★★★. **Fridge in room** Yes. **Breakfast** Paid. **Wi-Fi** Free. **Parking** $21/day. **Walk to Esplanade** 9 minutes (0.5 mile). **Comments** Small on-site food court.

1460 S. Harbor Blvd.
Anaheim
☎ 714-772-6777
tinyurl.com/fairfieldinnana

FAIRFIELD INN ANAHEIM RESORT is a nice midtier name-brand hotel that offers close proximity to Disneyland, solid rooms, and a decent slate of amenities. It's not the nicest hotel near Disneyland, but it offers excellent balance. The rates are slightly higher than the hotels to which it's adjacent, and the parking is pricey, but it is arguably worth the slightly higher rates. Guests staying here can always recoup those higher prices by eating breakfast at McDonald's (right in front of the hotel) instead of in the parks.

Four Points by Sheraton Anaheim ★★★★

Rate per night $194–$214. **Maximum occupants per room** 4. **Pool** ★★★½. **Fridge in room** Yes. **Breakfast** Paid. **Wi-Fi** Free. **Parking** $16 self/$19 valet. **Walk to Esplanade** 16 minutes (0.8 mile).

1221 S. Harbor Blvd.
Anaheim
☎ 714-758-0900
fourpointsanaheim.com

THIS PROPERTY FILLS A NICHE at Disneyland occupied by few other hotels—let's call it adult fun spots. The only other hotels nearby that somewhat appeal to this same demographic are Disneyland Hotel and the major brand-name hotels near the convention center, all of which are considerably more expensive. All guest rooms have been recently refreshed with a contemporary sensibility and some of the most comfortable beds in all of Anaheim. Amenities and common areas are great, making this an excellent place to unwind after (or pregame before) a night in the parks. It's not for everyone, but for honeymooners and adult gatherings, it should not be overlooked. It's a top pick for adult fun on a budget thanks to its new restaurant and bar, with a focus on craft beers on tap. The only catch is that it's located right next to the interstate, and you must cross busy on and off ramps while walking to the parks.

Grand Legacy at the Park ★★½

1650 S. Harbor Blvd.
Anaheim
☎ 714-772-0440
grandlegacyhotel.com

Rate per night $184–$194. **Maximum occupants per room** 4. **Pool** ★★★½. **Fridge in room** Yes. **Breakfast** Free. **Wi-Fi** Free. **Parking** $17/day. **Walk to Esplanade** 7 minutes (0.3 mile).

THE LOFTILY NAMED Grand Legacy at the Park used to be a Ramada, and aside from a spiffed-up lobby, it still feels like a budget motel. As long as you know what you're getting into, the rooms are comfortable enough for the price, if not particularly roomy. The heated pool is impressively large and includes a small splash pad for the kids, and adults can enjoy the chic bar on the rooftop. There are also a handful of convenient shops and restaurants on the ground floor, including a pretty good pizza parlor and a ticket discounter. The best reason to book the Grand Legacy is because it's almost as close to Disneyland as the Park Vue Inn but costs even less.

Homewood Suites by Hilton Anaheim Resort–Convention Center ★★★★

2010 S. Harbor Blvd.
Anaheim
☎ 714-750-2010
tinyurl.com/home
woodanaconvctr

Rate per night $239–$319. **Maximum occupants per room** 6. **Pool** ★★★½. **Fridge in room** Yes. **Breakfast** Free. **Wi-Fi** Free. **Parking** $22/day. **Walk to Esplanade** 20 minutes (1 mile).

ALTHOUGH THE WALK from Homewood Suites to Disneyland can take 20 minutes, you can skip that thanks to its location next door to Disneyland Resort's Toy Story parking lot. From there, you can take a bus to the eastern entrance of the Esplanade between Disneyland and Disney California Adventure. Homewood Suites' large rooms and full kitchens (with full-size fridge, dishwasher, microwave, stove top, and dishes) are great for families or large groups. Breakfast is free, as are beer and wine at the hotel's evening social events. We really enjoyed relaxing at the large pool area, which also includes a hot tub.

Hotel Indigo Anaheim ★★★★

435 W. Katella Ave.
Anaheim
☎ 714-772-7755
tinyurl.com/hotelindigoana

Rate per night $229–$309. **Maximum occupants per room** 4. **Pool** ★★½. **Fridge in room** Yes. **Breakfast** Paid. **Wi-Fi** Free. **Parking** Free. **Walk to Esplanade** 14 minutes (0.7 mile). **Comments** Pets up to 40 pounds welcome with $100 nonrefundable fee; limit 2 pets.

INDIGO IS A BIT MORE EXPENSIVE than other local hotels, but the rooms are very nice and modern. The entire hotel has a chic and trendy vibe. Luckily, Indigo has more than just its looks going for it. Beds are comfortable, and on-site amenities include a pool, laundry room, fitness center, and café. A drawback for some families is there are no bathtubs, only walk-in showers. A huge benefit is the hotel's location—Disneyland is about a 10-minute walk north on Harbor Boulevard, while the Anaheim Convention Center is about the same distance to the south. Hotel Indigo is one of our favorite hotels in the Disneyland Resort area. Check out the dancing fountain show out front; it's like a pint-size World of Color.

Howard Johnson Anaheim   ★★★½

Rate per night $214–$243. **Maximum occupants per room** 4. **Pool** ★★★★. **Fridge in room** Yes. **Breakfast** No. **Wi-Fi** Free. **Parking** Free. **Walk to Esplanade** 11 minutes (0.6 mile).

1380 S. Harbor Blvd. Anaheim
☎ 714-776-6120
hojoanaheim.com

THIS HOJO HAS BEEN AROUND for a long time, and it's leaning into midcentury-modern nostalgia with its terrazzo-tiled lobby and retro-mod Shag artwork on the walls. The two main selling points of Howard Johnson Anaheim are its close location to Disneyland Resort (just over a 10-minute walk), and the hotel's elaborate water playground and pool area, which is slightly smaller than the one at Courtyard across the street. A laundry room and convenience store are also available on-site, and the sprawling grounds are well kept. We like the spacious rooms and bathrooms, but on the downside, the buildings are dated and have a few quirks, such as balconies that are only accessible through the closet. Another negative is the lack of free breakfast, or any on-site restaurant, although Mimi's Cafe is a short walk away. Be sure to check the hotel's website, as it frequently offers discounts.

Hyatt House at Anaheim Resort/ Convention Center   ★★★★½

Rate per night $189–$279. **Maximum occupants per room** 4. **Pool** ★★★½. **Fridge in room** Yes. **Breakfast** Free. **Wi-Fi** Free. **Parking** $20. **Walk to Esplanade** 13 minutes (0.6 mile).

1800 S. Harbor Blvd. Anaheim
☎ 714-971-1800
anaheimresort.house .hyatt.com

SIMPLY ONE OF THE BEST hotels near Disneyland, Hyatt House's rooms and public areas have a fresh, modern feel, with wonderfully comfortable beds and plenty of room for you and your family to relax. Rooms contain a king bed, two queens, or a queen and a bunk bed. Guest rooms also have a couch, desk with chair, microwave, coffee maker, HDTV, and safe. The pool features plenty of lounge chairs to relax in. Hyatt House's fitness center is especially large when compared to other Anaheim hotels. We've observed that Hyatt House's nightly rates are usually competitive with other hotels in the area, so we recommend it over many others.

Kings Inn   ★★½

Rate per night $132–$142. **Maximum occupants per room** 4. **Pool** ★★. **Fridge in room** Yes. **Breakfast** Free. **Wi-Fi** Free. **Parking** Free. **Walk to Esplanade** 15 minutes (0.8 mile). **Comments** $7.50/night resort fee.

415 W. Katella Ave. Anaheim
☎ 714-778-6900
kingsinnanaheim.com

KINGS INN, which used to be a Super 8, is a bargain-basement motel with virtually no exceptional amenities to boast about. The refurbished furnishings still aren't fancy, with queen beds in single rooms instead of kings, and the internet can be unreliable, but the continental breakfast is passable (assuming you can squeeze into the cramped serving room), and you can see fireworks from the second-story deck. The main reason we include it here is because it is often the cheapest room available within a 15-minute walk from Disneyland that we're comfortable staying in overnight. As long as you don't plan on spending much time lounging around your smaller-than-average room, or doing laps in the kidney-shaped pool, this is a safe spot for travelers on a tight budget to crash for a few hours between park visits.

Park Vue Inn ★★★½

1570 S. Harbor Blvd.
Anaheim
☎ 714-722-3691
parkvueinn.com

Rate per night $209–$259. **Maximum occupants per room 4. Pool** ★★★. **Fridge in room** Yes. **Breakfast** Free. **Wi-Fi** Free. **Parking** Free. **Walk to Esplanade** 5 minutes (0.3 mile). **Comments** Good fireworks viewing from rooftop terrace.

PARK VUE INN IS CLOSER to Disneyland than any of Disney's pricey hotels. It'll take you less than 10 minutes to walk from your room to the front gate of the park. That's hard to accomplish even at Disney's Grand Californian hotel. Park Vue's rooms are very modern with excellent bedding and contain the usual amenities you would expect—an HDTV, a desk, free Wi-Fi, a mini-fridge, a coffee maker, and a microwave. A small basic pool and exercise room are also available, as well as a Coldstone Creamery next to the lobby.

Ramada Anaheim Maingate North ★★★

921 S. Harobor Blvd.
Anaheim
☎ 714-999-0684
wyndhamhotels.com

Rate per night $129–$149. **Maximum occupants per room 4. Pool** ★★★. **Fridge in room** Yes. **Breakfast** Free. **Wi-Fi** Free. **Parking** Free. **Walk to Esplanade** 21 minutes (1 mile). **Comments** $7.50/night resort fee.

THIS BUDGET HOTEL is great for travelers who can't afford the hotels closer to Disneyland. Walking to the parks will take over 20 minutes, but a $5 shuttle is provided. Also, Uber and Lyft are decent options, with rides available for $3–$5. Ramada's rooms are clean and well maintained, and a decent continental breakfast is free for guests. Another good perk is the free parking, which is rare for hotels located near Disneyland.

Residence Inn Anaheim Resort Convention Center ★★★★

640 W. Katella Ave.
Anaheim
☎ 714-782-7500
tinyurl.com/resinnana
convctr

Rate per night $229–$329. **Maximum occupants per room 6. Pool** ★★★½. **Fridge in room** Yes. **Breakfast** Free. **Wi-Fi** Free. **Parking** $24/day. **Walk to Esplanade** 21 minutes (1 mile). **Comments** Pets up to 45 pounds welcome with $150 nonrefundable fee.

IF YOU'RE LOOKING FOR more spacious accommodations than a standard hotel room, this property offers exceptional bang for your buck. Technically an extended stay hotel brand, this Residence Inn was built with families visiting Disneyland in mind. High-quality, family suite–size rooms with fully equipped kitchens make it ideal for couples looking to spread out a bit and families with small children wanting to save money by cooking their own meals. The decor is sort of "meh," but that's a very minor quibble considering all you get for a relatively reasonable price point. This is a top pick for families on a budget or anyone needing more space but not wanting to get two separate rooms. The only drawback is the walk to Disneyland is significantly longer than some of our other favorites.

Riviera Motel ★★

410 W. Katella Ave.
Anaheim
☎ 714-776-9100
rivieramotelanaheim.com

Rate per night $129–$152. **Maximum occupants per room 4. Pool** ★½. **Fridge in room** Yes. **Breakfast** No. **Wi-Fi** Free. **Parking** Free. **Walk to Esplanade** 16 minutes (0.8 mile). **Comments** Bring your own soap and shampoo.

RIVIERA DOESN'T LOOK LIKE MUCH, but it's hard to not recommend it to budget-conscious visitors due to its cheap price and location to the parks (about a 15-minute walk). Rooms are a bit dated but clean and well maintained, plus they have mini-fridges, microwaves, and great air conditioners. Riviera even has a tiny pool tucked away in the corner of the parking lot.

Sheraton Park Hotel at Anaheim ★★★★

1855 S. Harbor Blvd.
Anaheim
☎ 714-750-1811
marriott.com

Rate per night $116–$269. **Maximum occupants per room** 4. **Pool** ★★★½. **Fridge in room** Yes. **Breakfast** Paid. **Wi-Fi** Paid. **Parking** $21 self/$26 valet. **Walk to Esplanade** 16 minutes (0.8 mile). **Comments** Pets welcome.

THE ROOMS AT SHERATON PARK HOTEL are huge, and most have balconies that either overlook Disney California Adventure or the Anaheim Convention Center. The beds are comfortable, and we especially liked the fluffy pillows. We also enjoyed the relaxing pool area, which is surrounded by trees and other vegetation. Overall, this is a fantastic hotel, especially if you're attending Disney's D23 Expo at the convention center. The walk to Disneyland from the hotel is over 15 minutes, but Sheraton does offer shuttle transportation for an extra fee. A big downside is that Wi-Fi costs a daily fee.

SpringHill Suites Anaheim Resort Area/ Convention Center ★★★★

1801 S. Harbor Blvd.
Anaheim
☎ 714-533-2101
springhillanaheim.com

Rate per night $218–$284. **Maximum occupants per room** 6. **Pool** ★★★. **Fridge in room** Yes. **Breakfast** Free. **Wi-Fi** Free. **Parking** $24/day. **Walk to Esplanade** 15 minutes (0.7 mile). **Comments** Pets up to 40 pounds welcome with $75 nonrefundable fee; limit 2 pets.

THE SPACIOUS SUITES HERE contain either a king or two queen beds plus a bunk bed or sofa sleeper. Mattresses were a bit firm, but that was one of the only negatives. A CVS located at the bottom level of the hotel allows you to easily stock up on groceries. Free breakfast, a gym, a rooftop pool with a view of Disneyland's fireworks, and close proximity to the parks make this one of the best hotel options in the area.

Tropicana Inn & Suites ★★★

1540 S. Harbor Blvd.
Anaheim
☎ 714-635-4082
tropicanainn-anaheim.com

Rate per night $229–$249. **Maximum occupants per room** 5. **Pool** ★★½. **Fridge in room** Yes. **Breakfast** Paid. **Wi-Fi** Free. **Parking** $15/day. **Walk to Esplanade** 6 minutes (0.3 mile).

TROPICANA INN IS another solid budget option for travelers who want to pay the least amount of money and stay as close as possible to Disneyland. Guest rooms aren't huge, but they offer plenty of space to sleep or relax thanks to each having one king or two queen beds, two cushioned chairs, and a desk with another chair. The usual HDTV, safe, microwave, coffee maker, and mini-fridge are included as well. Bathrooms are basic, but they do have plenty of counter space.

UNIVERSAL STUDIOS HOLLYWOOD AREA

BLVD Hotel & Spa ★★★

10730 Ventura Blvd.
Studio City
☎ 818-623-9100
blvdstudiocity.com

Rate per night $209–$249. **Maximum occupants per room** 4. **Pool** ★★. **Fridge in room** Yes. **Breakfast** No. **Wi-Fi** Free. **Parking** $31/day.

Walk to Universal 17 minutes (0.7 mile). **Comments** Viya Spa is open daily; treatments are by appointment only.

ONE OF THE CLOSEST affordable hotels to Universal Studios, BLVD's full-service bar and 24-hour grab and go café give it the appealing vibe of a hipster hangout. While the guest rooms were recently updated, they unfortunately exhibit some odd form-over-function design decisions—such as weirdly dark lighting—and are already showing wear, with loose faux-hardwood floorboards and wrinkled carpets. Rooms have lots of electrical outlets but no USB plugs, and the Wi-Fi is painfully slow. You can walk across the street to catch a free shuttle bus up to Universal, or spring for a $5 rideshare. There's nothing wrong with BLVD for a night or two, but for a similar price we'd stay at Tilt.

Sheraton Universal   ★★★★

333 Universal Hollywood Dr.
Universal City
☎ 818-980-1212
sheratonuniversal.com

Rate per night $259–$309. **Maximum occupants per room** 4. **Pool** ★★★½. **Fridge in room** Yes. **Breakfast** Paid. **Wi-Fi** Free. **Parking** $30 self/$45 valet. **Walk to Universal** 8 minutes (0.3 mile). **Comments** Pets up to 40 pounds welcome with $75 non-refundable fee; limit 1 pet.

A PERFECTLY ADEQUATE BUSINESS-CLASS HOTEL, Sheraton Universal has slightly small rooms with stylishly modern furnishings. The property got a major overhaul around the time the Wizarding World of Harry Potter opened, and aside from a few confounding trendy touches, such as a lack of drawer space, we find the facilities satisfactory. The problem is that, considering the steep price, we'd expect amenities equal to those afforded guests at the exceptional Loews-operated hotels at Universal Orlando. Sadly, there are practically zero in-park perks for guests staying here; you don't even get early park entry unless you buy admission online.

Tilt Hotel   ★★★½

3241 Cahuenga Blvd. W.
Los Angeles
☎ 323-845-1600
tilthotelhollywood.com

Rate per night $199–$241. **Maximum occupants per room** 4. **Pool** ★★½. **Fridge in room** Yes. **Breakfast** Free. **Wi-Fi** Free. **Parking** $15/day. **Walk to Universal** 19 minutes (0.9 mile).

INSPIRED BY THE ECLECTIC movie-star haunts of Hollywood's golden age, the Tilt Hotel is a charmingly chic property on the periphery of Universal and our favorite spot to stay when visiting the Studios. The high-end boutique furnishings—complete with quirky touches such as film-strip headboards and bordello-red curtains—belie a very reasonable rack rate. Standard rooms are adequate in size (if not enormous), and king suites with in-room hot tubs are available. An on-site Italian restaurant and tiny indoor pool round out the amenities. It's a longer walk to Universal's front gates from here than the BLVD, but you'll pass through CityWalk on the way, which is convenient for grabbing a bite before or after your adventures.

MAKING *the* MOST *of* YOUR TIME

ALLOCATING TIME

THE DISNEY PEOPLE RECOMMEND spending two to four full days at Disneyland Resort. While this may seem a little self-serving, it is not without basis. Disneyland Resort is *huge*, with something to see or do crammed into every conceivable space. In addition, there are two parks, and touring requires a lot of walking, and often a lot of waiting in line. Moving in and among large crowds all day is exhausting, and often the unrelenting Southern California sun zaps even the most hardy, making tempers short.

During our many visits to Disneyland, we observed, particularly on hot summer days, a dramatic transition from happy, enthusiastic touring on arrival to almost zombielike plodding along later in the day. Visitors who began their day enjoying the wonders of Disney imagination ultimately lapsed into an exhausted production mentality ("We have two more rides in Fantasyland; then we can go to the hotel").

If your schedule and budget permit, try building in a day of rest to break up your park visits, as a mom from Folsom, California, suggests:

You are SPOT ON when you emphasize how exhausting a Disney-land Resort trip is. If I could go back and do the trip again, I would spend one day at Disneyland, have a day of rest at the motel (with the kids swimming and me being in the shade and off my feet), and then go to California Adventure on our third day in Anaheim.

A family from Vancouver, Canada, concurs:

With a four- or five-day pass, I strongly recommend a day's break in between where you can sleep in, swim, read a book, and have a day off from theme parks. In hindsight I think this would have made the back end of our holiday that much more enjoyable.

Alternately, plan to spread your touring over additional days so that you can spend afternoons outside the park, as this Fort Collins, Colorado, family did:

We had a four-day park hopper ticket, which allowed for a much more leisurely pace compared to our previous visits. We were present each day at rope drop, which enabled us to complete our desired attractions and lunch by noon or 1 p.m., then head back to the hotel to rest or visit the pool, and then return to the parks later for parades, shows, or other events (DCA Food and Wine Festival). For the first time on a Disney vacation, I felt somewhat relaxed.

OPTIMUM TOURING SITUATION

WE DON'T BELIEVE THAT THERE IS ONE IDEAL ITINERARY. Tastes, energy levels, and perspectives on what constitutes entertainment and relaxation vary. This understood, here are some considerations for developing your own ideal itinerary.

Optimum touring at Disneyland requires a good game plan, a minimum of three to five days on-site (excluding travel time), and a fair amount of money. It also requires a fairly prodigious appetite for Disney entertainment. The essence of optimum touring is to see the attractions in a series of shorter, less-exhausting visits during the cooler, less-crowded times of day, with plenty of rest and relaxation between excursions.

Because optimum touring calls for leaving and returning to the theme parks, it makes sense to stay in one of the Disney hotels or in one of the non-Disney hotels within walking distance. If you visit Disneyland during busy times, you need to get up early to beat the crowds. Short lines and stress-free touring are incompatible with sleeping in. If you want to sleep in *and* enjoy your touring, visit Disneyland when attendance is lighter.

THE CARDINAL RULES FOR SUCCESSFUL TOURING

MANY VISITORS DON'T HAVE three days to devote to Disneyland Resort. For these visitors, efficient touring is a must. Even the most time-effective plan, however, won't allow you to cover both Disney theme parks in one day. Plan to allocate at least one day to each park. We provide a "best of" one-day park-hopper plan for those who insist on seeing the resort's highlights, but it's an expensive and exhausting option. Instead, if your schedule permits only one day of touring, we recommend that you concentrate on one theme park and save the other for another visit.

One-Day Touring

A comprehensive one-day tour of Disneyland Park or Disney California Adventure (DCA) is possible, but it requires knowledge of the parks, good planning, and plenty of energy and endurance. One-day touring doesn't leave much time for full-service meals, prolonged shopping, or lengthy breaks. One-day touring can be fun and rewarding, but allocating two days per park, especially for Disneyland Park, is always preferable if possible.

Successful touring of Disneyland Resort hinges on three rules:

1. DETERMINE IN ADVANCE WHAT YOU REALLY WANT TO SEE What rides and attractions most appeal to you? Which additional rides and attractions would you like to experience if you have any time left? What are you willing to forgo?

To help you establish your touring priorities, we describe every attraction in detail. We include the author's critical evaluation of the attraction as well as the opinions of Disneyland Resort guests expressed as star ratings. Five stars is the highest (best) rating possible.

Finally, because Disneyland Resort attractions range in scope from midway-type rides and horse-drawn trolleys to colossal, high-tech extravaganzas spanning the equivalent of whole city blocks, we have

developed a hierarchy of categories for attractions to give you some sense of their order of magnitude:

SUPER-HEADLINERS The best attractions that the theme park has to offer. They are mind-boggling in size, scope, and imagination and represent the cutting edge of modern attraction technology and design.

HEADLINERS Full-blown, full-scale, multimillion-dollar, themed adventure experiences and theater presentations. They are modern in their technology and design and employ a full range of special effects.

MAJOR ATTRACTIONS Themed adventure experiences on a more modest scale but incorporating state-of-the-art technologies, or larger-scale attractions of older design.

MINOR ATTRACTIONS Small-scale dark rides (spook house–type rides), Midway-type rides, minor theater presentations, transportation rides, and elaborate walk-through attractions.

DIVERSIONS Exhibits, both passive and interactive. Also include playgrounds, video arcades, and street theater.

Though not every attraction fits neatly into the above categories, the categories provide a relative comparison of attraction size and scope. Remember, however, that bigger and more elaborate does not always mean better. Peter Pan's Flight, a minor attraction, continues to be one of the park's most beloved rides. Likewise, for many small children, there is no attraction, regardless of size, that can surpass Dumbo the Flying Elephant.

2. ARRIVE EARLY! ARRIVE EARLY! ARRIVE EARLY! This is the single most important key to touring efficiently and avoiding long lines. With your admission pass in hand, be at the gate ready to go at least 30 minutes before the theme park's stated opening time. There are no lines and relatively few people first thing in the morning. The same four rides you can experience in 1 hour in the early morning will take more than 3 hours to see after 11 a.m. Have breakfast before you arrive, so you will not have to waste prime touring time sitting in a restaurant. This advice is especially important at Disneyland Resort, where locals arriving after work tend to swell queues in the afternoon and evening, the opposite of typical attendance patterns at Walt Disney World.

From a Cincinnati mom:

Arriving early made a tremendous difference. I'll admit that at 6:15 in the morning when I was dragging our children out of bed, I thought that we'd lost our minds. But we had so much fun that morning riding rides with no waiting in line. It was worth the early arrival.

A couple from Austin, Texas, waxed enthusiastic:

I tell everyone about your book. It saved my girlfriend and me hours and hours of waiting in line (during spring break no less!). We were first in line for the parks every morning, and boy was it worth it.

Be aware that all park guests must pass through a security checkpoint to enter Disneyland Resort. In addition to having their bags opened and manually inspected, guests must also empty their pockets and step through a metal detector or be scanned with a handheld wand. Security is set up in open tents to the east of the Esplanade between the two parks for guests entering from Harbor Boulevard and on the west end of Downtown Disney; additional checkpoints screen guests exiting the Mickey & Friends and Pixar Pals parking garages and Grand Californian Hotel. When entering the resort from the east, the far-left security line is often the shortest; feel free to "excuse me" your way through the long queue of folks snaking toward a central checkpoint while you beeline for the briefer wait. The checkpoint for guests from the Disneyland and Paradise Pier Hotels can get especially overwhelmed in the mornings; if the queue is backed up, look for a secondary screening area intended for guests walking from the parking garages. If you arrive before security screening begins and go straight to the turnstiles to await admittance, you will ultimately be directed to abandon your position to go through security. If this occurs, you'll find yourself behind people who arrived 20–30 minutes after you. Therefore, if you arrive before security is set up, wait in one of the open tents for the security folks to arrive. An expedited entrance for guests without bags or strollers is usually set up in the center of the security checkpoint.

3. AVOID BOTTLENECKS Helping you avoid bottlenecks is what this guide is all about. Bottlenecks occur as a result of crowd concentrations and/or less-than-optimal traffic engineering. Concentrations of hungry people create bottlenecks at restaurants during the lunch and dinner hours; concentrations of people moving toward the exit near closing time create bottlenecks in the gift shops en route to the gate; concentrations of visitors at new and unusually popular rides create bottlenecks and long waiting lines; rides slow to load and unload passengers create bottlenecks and long waiting lines. Avoiding bottlenecks involves being able to predict where, when, and why they occur. To this end, we provide field-tested touring plans to keep you ahead of the crowd or out of its way (see discussion following). In addition, we provide critical data on all rides and shows that helps you estimate how long you may have to wait in line, compares rides in terms of their capacity to accommodate large crowds, and rates the rides according to our opinions and the opinions of other Disneyland visitors.

WHAT'S A QUEUE?

THOUGH IT'S NOT COMMONLY used in the United States, *queue* (pronounced "cue") is the universal English word for a line, such as one in which you wait to cash a check at the bank or to board a ride at a theme park. There's a mathematical area of specialization within the field of operations research called queuing theory, which studies and models how lines work. Because The Unofficial Guides draw heavily on this discipline, we use some of its terminology. In addition to the noun, the verb *to queue* means "to get in line," and a queuing area is a waiting area that accommodates a line.

TOURING PLANS

Of Utmost Importance: Read This!

In analyzing reader surveys we were astonished by the percentage of readers who do not use our touring plans. Scientifically tested and proven, these plans can save you 4 entire hours or more of waiting in line. Four hours! Four fewer hours of standing, 4 hours freed up to do something fun. Our groundbreaking research that created the touring plans has been the subject of front-page articles in the *Dallas Morning News* and *The New York Times* and has been cited in numerous scholarly journals. So the question is, why would you not use them?

We get a ton of email from both our Disneyland and Walt Disney World readers—98% of it positive—commenting on our touring plans. First, from a family from Stockton, California, who descended on Disneyland Park over the Easter holiday:

> We're not much for plans and regimentation, so we winged it the first day. It was so awful that the next day we gave one of your itineraries a shot. It worked so well that I was telling strangers about it that night like [I was] some kind of Bible thumper.

From a Palo Alto, California, mother of three boys:

> My husband viewed my extensive planning with a great deal of amusement and humorously vowed to sabotage my plans by tempting the kids to go on an unplanned ride at the very start. I countered by involving the kids in crafting our touring plan, so they were as excited and committed to it as I was.
>
> My favorite part was when we rode the monorail in the late morning. By that time, we had already gone on a bunch of rides and never waited in a single line longer than 5–10 minutes. The monorail passed over the park entrance, which was mobbed with people. My 10-year-old exclaimed, "Wow! Look at the lines now!" My previously doubtful husband looked at me with a smile and said, "Thank you."

From a Chicago mom:

> I feel strongly that you have to go into a Disney trip with a firm plan or else all you will remember of your vacation will be the squabbles and the long lines! The daily touring plans not only allowed me to see

everything that I wanted but also allowed me time to revisit my favorite attractions multiple times! Those who complain that the touring plans are too rigid need a serious reality check. Yes, they are structured, but they save you mountains of time! RELAX and use the touring plans if you are going during a busy part of the year. Not only will it save you the time that you are spending complaining about the plans in the first place, but it will also save you the complaining you will be doing when you are in line for Space Mountain for 90 minutes!

From a Missoula, Montana, family:

My wife and I hadn't been to Disneyland in 40 years. I was a little cynical about the costs and the hassle of getting there, the crowds, etc. When we started reading your book, I really got excited. I thought, "Hey, we can do this and we have a friend with us telling us what to do the whole way!" In three days, we rode every ride you told us to (except Roger Rabbit—because it was broken), and we saw two parades, Fantasmic!, *and* World of Color *(don't miss these). We did 61 things in three days. Your book made it all come together for us.*

And finally, from a reader in Mililani, Hawaii:

With the personalized plans, we were able to hit every ride, show, and parade we wanted to see on the first day at both Disneyland and DCA without EVER waiting in a real line. As I walked by people standing in 70- to 120-minute lines, I felt so relieved that we used your process. It was an incredible, stress-free, and enjoyable experience, all thanks to you. Thank you.

Touring Plans: What They Are and How They Work

When we interviewed Disneyland visitors who toured the theme park(s) on slow days, they invariably waxed eloquent about the sheer delight of their experience. When we questioned visitors who toured on moderate or busy days, however, they talked at length about the jostling crowds and how much time they stood in line. What a shame, they said, that so much time and energy are spent fighting crowds in a place as special as Disneyland.

Given this complaint, our researchers descended on Disneyland to determine whether a touring plan could be devised that would liberate visitors from the traffic flow and allow them to see any theme park in one day with minimal waiting in line. On some of the busiest days of the year, our team monitored traffic into and through Disneyland Park, noting how it filled and how patrons were distributed among the attractions. We also observed which rides and attractions were most popular and where bottlenecks were most likely to occur.

After many years of collecting data, we devised preliminary touring plans, which we tested during one of the busiest weeks of the year. Each day, our researchers would tour the park using one of the preliminary plans, noting how long it took to walk from place to place and how long the wait in line was for each attraction. Combining the information gained on trial runs, we devised a master plan that we retested and fine-tuned. This plan, with very little variance from day to day, allowed us to experience all major rides and attractions and most lesser ones in one day, with an average wait in line of less than 10 minutes at each.

From this master plan, we developed alternative plans that took into account the varying tastes and personal requirements of different Disneyland patrons. Each plan operated with the same logic as the master plan but addressed the special needs and preferences of its intended users.

Finally, after all of the plans were tested by our staff, we selected (using convenience sampling) Disneyland visitors to test the plans. The only prerequisite for being chosen to test the plans was that the guests must have been visiting a Disney park for the first time. A second group of patrons was chosen for a control group. These were first-time visitors who would tour the park according to their own plans but who would make notes about what they did and how much time they spent in lines.

When the two groups were compared, the results were amazing. On days when major theme park attendance exceeded 42,000, visitors touring without our plans *averaged* 2 hours and 36 minutes more waiting in line per day than the patrons touring with our plans, and they experienced 33% fewer attractions. In 2004 the application of a cutting-edge algorithm to our touring plan software increased the waiting time saved to an average of 4 hours. Our latest advancement, introduced in 2012, gives subscribers to touringplans.com the ability to build personalized plans online, and then use the Lines smartphone app while inside the parks to optimize their itineraries with real-time wait-time data. We expect additional research to continue to improve the performance of the touring plans in future editions.

General Overview of the Touring Plans

Our touring plans are step-by-step guides for seeing as much as possible with a minimum of standing in line. They're designed to help you avoid crowds and bottlenecks on days of moderate to heavy attendance. On days of lighter attendance (see "Selecting the Time of Year for Your Visit," page 23), the plans still save time but aren't as critical to successful touring.

What You Can Realistically Expect from the Touring Plans

Though we present one-day touring plans for both parks, you should understand that Disneyland Park has more attractions than you can see in one day, even if you never wait in line. If you must cram your visit to Disneyland Park into a single day, the one-day touring plans will allow you to see as much as is humanly possible. Under certain circumstances you may not complete the plan, and you definitely won't be able to see everything. For Disneyland Park, the most comprehensive, efficient, and relaxing touring plans are the two-day plans. Though Disney California

Adventure (DCA) has grown, you should be able to see everything in one day by following our touring plans.

Variables That Will Affect the Success of the Touring Plans

How quickly you move from one ride to another; when and how many refreshment and restroom breaks you take; when, where, and how you eat meals; and your ability (or lack thereof) to find your way around will all have an impact on the success of the plans. Smaller groups almost always move faster than larger groups, and parties of adults generally can cover more ground than families with young children. Switching off (see page 147), among other things, prohibits families with little ones from moving expeditiously among attractions. Plus, some children simply cannot conform to the "early to rise" conditions of the touring plans. A mom from Nutley, New Jersey, writes:

> [Though] the touring plans all advise getting to parks at opening, we just couldn't burn the candle at both ends. Our kids (10, 7, and 4) would not go to sleep early and couldn't be up at dawn and still stay relatively sane. It worked well for us to let them sleep a little later, go out and bring breakfast back to the room while they slept, and still get a relatively early start by not spending time on eating breakfast out. We managed to avoid long lines with an early morning and by hitting popular attractions during parades, mealtimes, and late evenings.

And a family from Centerville, Ohio, says:

> The toughest thing about your touring plans was getting the rest of the family to stay with them, at least to some degree. Getting them to pass by attractions to hit something across the park was no easy task (sometimes impossible).

A multigenerational family wonders how to know if you are on track or not, writing:

> It seems like the touring plans were very time dependent, yet there were no specific times attached to the plan outside of the early morning. On more than one day, I often had to guess as to whether we were on track.

There is no objective measurement for being on track. Each group's experience will differ to some degree. Regardless of whether your group is large or small, fast or slow, the sequence of attractions in the touring plans will allow you to enjoy the greatest number of attractions in the least possible time. Two quickly moving adults will probably take in more attractions in a specific time period than will a large group comprised of children, parents, and grandparents. However, given the characteristics of the respective groups, each will maximize their touring time and experience as many attractions as possible. That said, if you really want specific times for each step of your touring plan, use the online versions and customize them for your specific day of travel.

Finally, if you have young children in your party, be prepared for character encounters. The appearance of a Disney character is usually sufficient to stop a touring plan dead in its tracks. What's more, while some characters continue to stroll the parks, it is becoming more the rule to assemble characters in a specific venue (such as at Mickey's Toontown), where families must queue for photos of and autographs from Mickey. Meeting characters, posing for photos, and collecting autographs can burn hours of touring time. If your kids are into character-autograph collecting, you will need to anticipate these interruptions to the touring plan and negotiate some understanding with your children about when you will follow the plan and when you will collect autographs. Our advice is to either go with the flow or alternatively set aside a certain morning or afternoon for photos and autographs. Be aware, however, that queues for autographs, especially in Fantasy Faire and Pixie Hollow at Disneyland Park, are as long as the queues for major attractions. The only time-efficient way to collect autographs is to line up at the character-greeting areas first thing in the morning. Because this is also the best time to experience the more popular attractions, you may have some tough decisions to make.

While we realize that following the touring plans is not always easy, we nevertheless recommend continuous, expeditious touring until around noon. After that hour, breaks and diversions won't affect the plans significantly.

Some variables that can profoundly affect the touring plans are beyond your control. Chief among these is the manner and timing of bringing a particular ride to capacity. For example, Big Thunder Mountain Railroad, a roller coaster in Disneyland Park, has five trains. On a given morning it may begin operation with two of the five, and then add the other three if and when they are needed. If the waiting line builds rapidly before operators decide to go to full capacity, you could have a long wait, even in early morning.

Another variable relates to the time you arrive for a show. Usually your wait will be the length of time from your arrival to the end of the presentation in progress. Thus, if the *Enchanted Tiki Room* show is 15 minutes long and you arrive 1 minute after a show has begun, your wait for the next show will be 14 minutes. Conversely, if you arrive as the show is wrapping up, your wait will be only 1 or 2 minutes.

What to Do If You Lose the Thread

Anything from a blister to a broken attraction can throw off a touring plan. If unforeseen events interrupt a plan:

1. If you're following a printed touring plan, skip one step on the plan for every 20 minutes' delay. If, for example, you lose your billfold and spend an hour hunting for it, skip three steps and pick up from there, or

2. Forget the plan; organize the remainder of your day using the standby wait times listed in Lines or the recommended attraction visitation times in each attraction profile.

3. If you're following a touring plan in the **Lines** app (touringplans.com/lines), just press the OPTIMIZE button when you're ready to start touring again. Lines will figure out the best possible plan for the remainder of your day.

Flexibility

The attractions included in the touring plans are the most popular attractions as determined by our reader surveys. Even so, your favorite attractions might be different. Fortunately, the touring plans are flexible. If the touring plan calls for an attraction that you don't wish to experience, simply skip it and move on to the next attraction on the plan. Additionally, you can substitute similar attractions in the same area of the park. If the plan calls for riding Dumbo, for example, and you're not interested but would enjoy the Mad Tea Party (which is not on the plan), then substitute the Mad Tea Party for Dumbo. As long as the substitution is a similar attraction (it won't work to substitute a show for a ride) and located pretty close to the attraction called for in the plan, you won't compromise the overall effectiveness of the touring plan.

For the ultimate in flexibility and efficiency, use the Lines smartphone app to check off steps on your plan as you complete them (or delete ones you decide to skip), and then let the optimizer get you back on track after any detours. For example, let's say that your touring plan calls for riding The Haunted Mansion next, but your family really needs an ice cream break and 30 minutes out of the sun. Get the ice cream and take the break. When you're done, click the OPTIMIZE button on your plan, and it will be updated with what to do next. The ability to redo your plan allows you to recover from any situation while still minimizing your waits for the rest of the day.

A family of four from South Slocan, British Columbia, found that they could easily tailor the touring plans to meet their needs:

We amended your touring plans by taking out the attractions we didn't want to do and just doing the remainder in order. It worked great, and by arriving before the parks opened, we saw everything we wanted, with virtually no waits! The best advice by far was to get there early!

A multigenerational family from South Jordan, Utah, found it helpful to use this book in conjunction with touringplans.com:

We didn't follow an exact touring plan, but I used the tips in your book and touring plans to make our own. We decided to do all the major attractions first before the crowds came. We arrived at about 8:05 a.m., and by 11 we were walking to our eighth attraction. We saw all we wanted and then took a more relaxed pace the rest of the day. A downside was that after getting on so many rides so quickly, we didn't want to wait in line for even 20 minutes the rest of the day.

Clip-Out Pocket Outlines of Touring Plans

Select the plan appropriate for your party, and then clip the pocket version from the back of this guide and carry it with you as a quick reference at the theme park. If you're feeling crafty, upgrade your clip-out plans like this lady from London, England:

I cut out the touring plan; wrote parade times, dining reservations, showtimes, etc., around the side; and then laminated it for our day.

Will the Plans Continue to Work Once the Secret Is Out?

Yes! First, all of the plans require that a patron be there when the theme parks open. Many Disneyland patrons simply refuse to get up early while on vacation. Second, less than 1% of any day's attendance has been exposed to the plans, too little to affect results. Last, most groups tailor the plans, skipping rides or shows according to personal taste.

How Frequently Are the Touring Plans Revised?

Because Disney is always adding new attractions and changing opera-tions, we revise the touring plans every year. Most complaints we receive about them come from readers who are using out-of-date editions of *The Unofficial Guide*. Be prepared, however, for surprises. Opening procedures and showtimes, for example, may change, and you never know when an attraction might break down. Touring plans inside our Lines app are updated even more often and can instantly adapt to any refurbishments or breakdowns during your visit.

Tour Groups from Hell

Tour groups of up to 200 people sometimes use our plans. Unless your party is as large as that tour group, this development shouldn't alarm you. Because tour groups are big, they move slowly and have to stop periodically to collect stragglers. The tour guide also has to accommo-date the unpredictability of five dozen or so bladders. In short, you should have no problem passing a group after the initial encounter.

Bouncing Around

Many readers object to crisscrossing a theme park, as our touring plans sometimes require. A woman from Decatur, Georgia, said she "got dizzy from all the bouncing around" and that the "running back and forth reminded [her] of a scavenger hunt." We empathize, but here's the rub.

In Disneyland Park, the most popular attractions are positioned across the park from one another. This is no accident. It's good plan-ning, a method of more equally distributing guests throughout the park. If you want to experience the most popular attractions in one day without long waits, you can arrive before the park fills and see those attractions first thing (which requires crisscrossing the park), or you can enjoy the main attractions on one side of the park first thing in the morning, and then use FastPass for the popular attractions on the other side. All other approaches will subject you to awesome waits at some attractions if you tour during busy times of the year.

The best way to minimize bouncing around at Disneyland Park is to use one of our two-day touring plans, which spread the more popular attractions over two mornings and work beautifully even when the park closes at 8 p.m. or earlier. Using FastPass will decrease your waiting time but will increase bouncing around because you must first go to the attraction to obtain your FastPass and then backtrack later to the same attraction to use your pass (unless you use MaxPass).

DCA is configured in a way that precludes an orderly approach to touring, or to a clockwise or counterclockwise rotation. Orderly touring is further frustrated by the limited guest capacity of the midway rides in the Paradise Gardens Park and Pixar Pier districts of the park. At DCA, therefore, you're stuck with bouncing around, whether you use the touring plan or not, if you want to avoid horrendous waits.

We suggest you follow the touring plans religiously, especially in the mornings, if you're visiting Disneyland during busy, more crowded times. The consequence of touring spontaneity in peak season is hours of otherwise avoidable standing in line. During quieter times of year, there's no need to be compulsive about following the plans.

Touring Plan Rejection

We've discovered that you can't implant a touring plan in certain personalities without vehement rejection. Some folks just do not respond well to regimentation. If you bump into this problem with someone in your party, it's best to roll with the punches, as did this couple:

> The rest of the group was not receptive to the use of the touring plans. They all thought I was being a little too regimented about planning this vacation. Rather than argue, I left the touring plans behind as we ventured off for the parks. You can guess the outcome. When we returned home, we watched the videos we took during our vacation. About every 5 minutes there is a shot of us all gathered around a park map trying to decide what to do next.

Finally, as a Connecticut woman alleges, the touring plans are incompatible with some readers' bladders as well as their personalities:

> When you write those day schedules next year, can you schedule bathroom breaks in there too? You expect us to be at a certain ride at a certain time and with no stops in between. The schedules are a problem if you are a laid-back, slow-moving, careful detail noticer. What were you thinking when you made these schedules?

Before you injure your urinary tract, feel free to deviate from the touring plan as necessary to heed the call of nature. If you are using a customized plan in Lines, you can build in as many breaks (bathroom or otherwise) as you like, and the optimizer will plan around them.

A Clamor for Customized Touring Plans

We're inundated by letters urging us to create additional touring plans. These include a plan for 9th- and 10th-graders, a plan for rainy days, a seniors' plan, a plan for folks who sleep late, a plan omitting rides that "bump, jerk, and clonk," a plan for gardening enthusiasts, and a plan for single women.

The touring plans in this book are intended to be flexible. Adapt them to your preferences. If you don't like rides that bump and jerk, skip them when they come up in a touring plan. If you want to sleep in and go to the park at noon, use the afternoon part of a plan. If you're a ninth-grader and want to ride Space Mountain three times in a row, do it. Will it decrease the touring plan's effectiveness? Sure, but the plan was created only to help you have fun. It's your day.

If you really want to tailor your itinerary, we highly recommend subscribing to touringplans.com, where you can customize your day's to-do list down to the last snack. Choose the date of your visit and the attractions you want to experience, including character greetings, parades, fireworks, meals, and midday breaks; the computer will generate an optimized step-by-step itinerary, showing you how to see everything with minimal waits in line. The touring plans can incorporate any FastPasses you retrieve and accommodate options like MaxPass and child swap. From a father of two teens from Superior, Colorado:

> We used a custom touring plan for our day at Disneyland and found it super useful. As always, arriving early was the key to success.

For a truly personalized experience, some of our team members (including this book's coauthor) offer professional tour-planning services; visit touringplans.com/disneyland-resort/touring-plans/faq or sethkubersky.com for details.

WHAT TO EXPECT WHEN YOU ARRIVE AT THE PARKS

BECAUSE EACH TOURING PLAN is based on being present when the theme park opens, you need to know a little about opening procedures. Disney trams to the parks, and the theme park parking lots, open 60–90 minutes before official opening time.

An entrance plaza is just outside the turnstiles of the parks. Usually you will be held outside the turnstiles until 15–30 minutes before official opening time. If you are admitted before the official opening time, you will usually be confined to a small section of the park until the official opening time. On early-entry mornings (Tuesday, Thursday, and Saturday at Disneyland; Monday, Wednesday, Friday, and Sunday at DCA), eligible guests are admitted through designated turnstiles 1 hour before official opening and may enjoy select attractions. All other guests will be admitted later in the hour through the remaining turnstiles and held at the central hub until official opening time. At Disneyland Park you might be admitted to Main Street, U.S.A.; at DCA to Buena Vista Street. If you proceed farther into a park, you will encounter a rope barrier manned by Disney cast members who will keep you from entering the remainder of the park. You will remain here until the rope drop, when the rope barrier is removed and the park and all (or most) of its attractions are opened at the official opening time.

A Word About the Rope Drop

Disney has a number of cast members supervising the rope drop in order to suppress the mayhem of anxiously waiting guests. A pleasantly parental prerecorded "Please walk; don't run" announcement seems to have a somewhat subduing effect on the straining crowds. In some cases, the rope is not even dropped. Instead, it's walked back. In other words, Disney cast members lead you with the rope at a fast walk toward the attraction you're straining to reach, forcing you (and everyone else) to maintain their pace. Not until they come within close proximity of the attraction do the cast members step aside.

So here's the scoop. If cast members persist in walking the rope back, the only way you can gain an advantage over the rest of the crowd is to arrive early enough to be one of those close to the rope. Be alert, though; sometimes the Disney folks will step out of the way after about 50 yards or so. If this happens, you can fire up the afterburners and speed the remaining distance to your destination.

FASTPASS AND MAXPASS

FASTPASS IS A FREE SYSTEM for moderating the waiting time for popular attractions. Here's how it works.

Your handout park map, as well as signs at respective attractions, will tell you which attractions are included. Attractions that use FastPass will have a regular line and a FastPass line. A sign at the entrance will tell you how long the wait is in the regular line. If the wait is acceptable, hop in line. If the wait seems too long, you can scan your park admission pass at a FastPass machine and receive an appointment (for a time later in the day) to come back and ride. (Also see pages 86–87 for information about MaxPass.) When you return at the appointed time, you will enter the FastPass line and proceed directly to the attraction's preshow or boarding area with minimal further wait. There is no extra charge to use FastPass, but you can get an

FASTPASS ATTRACTIONS	
DISNEYLAND PARK	**DISNEY CALIFORNIA ADVENTURE**
Big Thunder Mountain Railroad	Goofy's Sky School
Buzz Lightyear Astro Blasters	Grizzly River Run
Fantasmic!	Guardians of the Galaxy—Mission: Breakout!*
The Haunted Mansion	Incredicoaster
Indiana Jones Adventure*	Radiator Springs Racers*
It's a Small World	Soarin' Around the World*
Matterhorn Bobsleds*	Toy Story Midway Mania!
Roger Rabbit's Car Toon Spin	*World of Color*
Space Mountain*	
Splash Mountain*	
Star Tours—The Adventures Continue	

Denotes rides that routinely issue FastPasses for redemption 3–7 hours later.

appointment for only one attraction per park at a time (with a few exceptions, noted on pages 85–86).

FastPass works remarkably well, primarily because FastPass holders get amazingly preferential treatment. As a telling indication of their status, Disney (borrowing a term from the airlines) refers to those in the regular line as standby guests. Indeed, we watched guests in the regular line stand by and stand by, shifting despondently from foot to foot, while dozens and sometimes hundreds of FastPass holders were ushered into the boarding area ahead of them. Clearly Disney is sending a message here, to wit: FastPass is heaven; anything else is limbo at best and probably purgatory. In either event, you'll think you've been in purgatory if you get stuck in the regular line during the hot, crowded part of the day.

FastPass, however, doesn't eliminate the need to arrive at the theme park early. Because each park offers a dozen FastPass attractions at most, you still need to get an early start if you want to see as much as possible in a single day. Crucially, as of press time FastPass is not offered for the attractions inside Star Wars: Galaxy's Edge. Plus, as we'll discuss later, there's a limited supply of FastPasses available for each attraction on a given day. So if you don't show up until the middle of the afternoon, you might discover that all the FastPasses have been distributed to other guests. FastPass does, happily, make it possible to see more with less waiting than ever before, and it's a great benefit to those who like to sleep late or who enjoy an afternoon or evening at the theme parks on their arrival day. It also enables you to postpone wet rides such as the Grizzly River Run at DCA or Splash Mountain at Disneyland Park until the warmer part of the day.

Understanding the FastPass System

The purpose of the FastPass system is to reduce the waiting time for designated attractions by more equally distributing the arrival of guests at those attractions over the course of the day. This is accomplished by providing a shorter wait in line for guests who are willing to postpone experiencing the attraction until sometime later in the day. The system also, in effect, imposes a penalty—that is, being relegated to standby status—to those who opt not to use FastPass (though spreading guest arrivals more equally decreases waiting time for standby guests too).

When you scan your admission pass (physical or digital) at a FastPass machine, it spits out a small slip of paper about two-thirds the size of a credit card, small enough to fit in your wallet (but also small enough to lose easily). Printed on the paper will be the name of the attraction and a specific 1-hour time window—for example, 1:15–2:15 p.m. You can return to enjoy the ride any time from 1:15 to 2:15 p.m. Disneyland Resort strictly enforces the 1-hour FastPass windows, allowing an unpublicized 15-minute grace period and exceptions for ride breakdowns. Pay close attention to the time when you receive your FastPass, and plan your return accordingly. Each person in your party must have his or her own FastPass. Be aware that the printed FastPass tickets only serve as a reminder of your return time and cannot be traded or given away to another guest. Printed FastPass receipts may eventually be phased out entirely.

When you report back to the attraction later, you'll enter a line marked FASTPASS RETURN that will route you more or less directly to the boarding area or preshow area. Each person in your party must have his or her own FastPass and be ready to scan their admission pass or mobile device at the entrance of the FastPass return line.

You may show up at any time within your FastPass return window, and from our observation, no specific time is better or worse. This holds true because cast members are instructed to minimize waits for FastPass holders. Thus, if the FastPass return line is suddenly inundated (something that occurs more or less by chance), cast members rapidly intervene to reduce the FastPass line. This is done by admitting as many as 25 FastPass holders for each standby guest until the FastPass line is down to an acceptable length. Though FastPass will lop off as much as 80% of the wait you'd experience in the regular line, you can still expect a short wait, but usually less than 20 minutes.

unofficial **TIP**
Use FastPass if the wait in the regular line is more than 30 minutes.

You can obtain a FastPass any time after a park opens its turnstiles, with the first return windows beginning at the official park opening time (for early entry attractions only) or 30–40 minutes afterward (for all others). FastPass times can be retrieved during early entry, and MaxPass users may even reserve attractions that don't participate in Extra Magic Hour, but FastPass return queues don't open until regular operating hours start.

Whatever time you obtain a FastPass, you can usually be assured that there will be a period of time between when you receive your FastPass and the beginning of your return window. The interval can be as short as 30 minutes or as long as 7 hours depending on park attendance, the popularity of the attraction, and the attraction's hourly capacity. However, at certain times select attractions—including The Haunted Mansion, Buzz Lightyear Astro Blasters, Roger Rabbit's Cartoon Spin, and It's a Small World—may offer FastPasses with immediate return times or return times that are significantly quicker than waiting standby.

As a general rule, the earlier in the day you secure a FastPass, the shorter the interval between time of issue and the beginning of your return window. On a day that the park opens at 9 a.m., if you pick up a FastPass for Splash Mountain at, say, 9:25 a.m., your recommended window for returning to ride would be something like 10–11 a.m., or perhaps 10:10–11:10 a.m. The exact time will be determined by how many other guests have obtained FastPasses before you.

If an attraction is exceptionally popular and/or its hourly capacity is relatively small, the return window might be pushed back to park closing time. When this happens, the FastPass machines stop issuing return times. It would not be unusual, for example, for Radiator Springs Racers at DCA to distribute an entire day's allocation of FastPasses by noon. When this happens, the machines simply shut down and a sign is posted saying that FastPasses are all gone for the day.

FASTPASS GUIDELINES

- Park tickets must be activated at the park turnstiles (or Downtown Disney monorail station) before being used to obtain FastPasses, so you can't send one family member into the park while the others snooze. However, once everyone has entered, you can send one person across to the other park with everyone's tickets to retrieve FastPasses there (or use MaxPass).

- Don't use FastPass unless it can save you 30 minutes or more at an attraction or if the ride is distributing immediate FastPass return times.

- If you arrive after a park opens, obtain a FastPass for your preferred FastPass attraction first thing.

- Always check the FastPass return period before obtaining your FastPass. Keep an eye out for attractions whose FastPass return time is immediate, or at least sooner than the standby wait.

- Obtain FastPasses for Matterhorn Bobsleds, *Fantasmic!,* Space Mountain, and Splash Mountain at Disneyland Park and for Soarin' Around the World, Incredicoaster, Radiator Springs Racers, Guardians of the Galaxy—Mission: Breakout!, and *World of Color* at DCA as early in the day as practical.

- Try to obtain FastPasses for rides not mentioned above by 1 p.m.

- Don't depend on FastPasses being available for ride attractions after 2 p.m. during busier times of the year.

- Make sure everyone in your party has his or her own FastPass. FastPasses are tied to each individual admission pass and may not be transferred.

- You can obtain a second FastPass as soon as you enter the return period for your first FastPass or after 2 hours from issuance (90 minutes for MaxPass users), whichever comes first.

- Maximize efficiency by always obtaining a new FastPass for the next attraction before using the first FastPass you already hold.

- You must wait at least 30 minutes between getting FastPasses, so if you got a FastPass that has an immediate return time, you can't instantly request another one.

- Be mindful of your FastPass return time, and plan intervening activities accordingly. You may use your FastPass 5 minutes before its start time and up to 15 minutes after it expires. This unadvertised grace period is typically the only exception allowed to your assigned return window.

- Attractions may not dispense FastPasses while they are closed for technical difficulties or special events.

- You can retrieve FastPasses during the early entry hour, but they won't begin becoming valid until general admission begins. Don't panic if the FastPass kiosks aren't working immediately at rope drop; alert a cast member, and he or she can quickly activate them.

- If an attraction is temporarily unavailable due to technical difficulties during your FastPass return window, your FastPass automatically converts to a Replacement FastPass. Replacement FastPasses remain valid for use until closing time at that attraction (if it reopens) or at selected other FastPass attractions in the same park. If the original return window was near to closing time, the FastPass may be valid on the following day.

- You may hold only one FastPass at a time for a particular attraction. Thus, if your Space Mountain FastPass becomes valid at 1 p.m., you may retrieve another FastPass for any other attraction before riding Space Mountain, but you must use the first FastPass if you want to get a second FastPass in a row for Space Mountain. The only exception to this rule is a Replacement FastPass; there is no limit to the number of those you can simultaneously hold.

- If you've installed the official Disneyland app on your mobile device and linked it to your admission ticket, you can see your party's current FastPasses, delete any unwanted FastPasses, and see what other attractions are available around the parks. The free FastPass service provides most of the same information and features through the app as the paid MaxPass system (see below), with the exception of picking new return times.

- Each Disneyland ticket can only be controlled by one account at a time, so pick one member of your party to handle everyone's tickets and FastPasses on his or her phone. Alternatively, each person can create a personal account and attach it to the individual ticket, but you will not be able to see each other's FastPass selections within the app (unlike the "Friends and Family" feature found in Walt Disney World's app). If your group needs the option of splitting up but still wants access to each other's plans, create one account to handle everyone's admission passes, then have each party member log in to the app on their own phone using that same email and password.

MaxPass

After Walt Disney World rolled out FastPass+ in 2014, there was much speculation that the online ride-reservation system would eventually migrate west. As of yet, there's still no sign in Anaheim of RFID-based MagicBands or booking attraction appointments months in advance. However, Disneyland has implemented some aspects of FastPass+ in the form of MaxPass, an optional extra-cost service introduced in 2017.

While traditional FastPass remains free to all guests, MaxPass users pay an additional $15 per guest per day (included with Premier and Signature Plus annual passes; $100-per-year upgrade for other pass holders) for the privilege of retrieving FastPass return times using Disneyland's smartphone app. Instead of having to walk to an attraction and scan your admission at its FastPass kiosk, you retrieve a virtual return time from anywhere in the parks on your phone, which will be read by the scanners installed at FastPass queue entrances.

To use MaxPass, first download the Disneyland mobile app, and sign in with your existing disney.com credentials, or create a new account with an email and password. Next, purchase your admission tickets through the app, or scan the bar codes of any tickets you've already purchased to link them to your account. Finally, click on the MaxPass button to purchase the service for the day, if you didn't already pay for the MaxPass option when buying your tickets. Prepurchasing MaxPass is the easier option, but paying day by day allows you to test the service without committing for the full length of your ticket.

Make sure you get the app set up before arriving at the turnstiles, so you don't waste time upon entering the park. You'll need to keep your mobile device powered up and connected to the internet (on

Disney's unreliable free Wi-Fi or your own data plan) to take advantage of the service, which can be an issue for international visitors; see page 103 for additional smartphone advice.

MaxPass users are still subject to most of the usual FastPass restrictions: You can only hold one reservation per attraction at a time, reservations must be made the same day, and you must have entered a park for the day before reserving a time (though you can use MaxPass to pull a FastPass for a Disneyland ride while inside DCA, or vice versa). MaxPass is also available for nighttime spectaculars such as *Fantasmic!* and *World of Color*, which can be retrieved without interfering with your ride reservations.

Purchase of MaxPass also includes unlimited PhotoPass digital image downloads for the day (see pages 103–104), which may be as valuable as the shoe leather you'll save with the service.

Some important perks of using MaxPass include:

- You can book your first FastPass return time as soon as your admission is scanned at the park entrance (or monorail station), long before walkers reach the FastPass kiosks at the closest headliners.

- As soon as your return window arrives, you can immediately hop in the FastPass return queue and book your next attraction while waiting to ride, rather than first walking to your next attraction's FastPass kiosk.

- MaxPass users only have to wait 90 minutes after getting a FastPass before they're eligible for another, versus a 2-hour wait for traditional FastPass guests.

- Once you've entered the park for the day, you can use MaxPass to continue to retrieve FastPasses after you've exited, so you can reserve another ride while lunching in Downtown Disney or napping at your hotel.

- If you change your mind about a FastPass you selected, you can delete it through the app and replace it with a new attraction.

- When an attraction is temporarily unavailable, it may continue to dispense FastPasses through MaxPass, with a time buffer added to accommodate the anticipated downtime. If the attraction is closed for longer than expected, those FastPasses will become Replacement FastPasses valid at selected rides for the rest of the day, which are very desirable to have. This frequently happens at Radiator Springs Racers and Incredicoaster at DCA, and Splash Mountain and Big Thunder Mountain at Disneyland. Be aware that Replacement FastPasses may be divided into tiers based on demand; while you can use a replacement pass initially issued for the Matterhorn at Space Mountain, you can't swap Goofy's Sky School for Radiator Springs Racers.

Occasional cell service snafus aside, we've found the experience of using MaxPass to be eerily blissful; on a busy weekend, we used it to knock off a dozen headliners without ever queuing for more than 15 minutes. To be frank, it works so well that we're surprised Disney isn't charging twice as much for it; look for MaxPass's cost (and necessity) to skyrocket in the coming years.

We've received a flood of positive feedback about MaxPass since its debut, such as this rave from a reader in Woodinville, Washington:

The first visit we didn't use MaxPass and utilized 5 FastPasses with the manual system. I bought MaxPass for the second day to cut down on steps, but the real advantage turned out to be the number of Fast-Passes we could use. We utilized 11 FastPasses that day, more than double the FastPass efficiency. We hardly waited in lines with the MaxPass service. For us it was definitely worth the cost.

And from another in Madison, Wisconsin:

I saved so much time by not having to walk to the attractions to use the kiosks. (And the PhotoPass bonus was fantastic.)

A mom from Portland, Oregon, said:

We took full advantage of MaxPass, which was a game changer. It eliminated nearly all lines and gave us a bit of structure to help us with our last-minute decision to improvise.

A father of two teens from Vancouver, British Columbia, wrote:

MaxPass was absolutely worth the money. As the traditional "Fast-Pass runner," I was now able to spend the whole time with my family instead of going off to get the next FastPass. Moreover, we spent one afternoon lounging at our hotel pool while successively booking FastPasses for Radiator Springs Racers, Toy Story Midway Mania!, Guardians of the Galaxy, and Incredicoaster, all for later that evening. It definitely made our family holiday more enjoyable.

From a reader in Quincy, Massachusetts:

This was our first Disneyland trip using MaxPass, and I don't think we could ever go again without it. While we definitely felt the crowds, thanks to MaxPass we were still able to make back to back FastPasses for the rides we wanted.

Finally, here's the bottom line from an Atlanta, Georgia, mother of four boys:

Besides your book, the biggest advantage we had was MaxPass. We got 12 different sets of FastPasses. It was like we had secret knowledge. Sometimes I felt guilty strolling past people who had been waiting for Splash Mountain for 90 minutes.

Disconnected FastPass Attractions

Some attractions' FastPass kiosks are not hooked up to the park-wide FastPass system. Because a disconnected attraction has no way of knowing if you have a FastPass for another attraction, it will issue you a Fast-Pass at any time. There were no disconnected rides at Disneyland Resort at press time, though Buzz Lightyear Astro Blasters and Roger Rabbit's Car Toon Spin at Disneyland Park have been disconnected in the past. *World of Color*'s and *Fantasmic!*'s FastPasses are always disconnected from the other attractions. Disney can connect and disconnect FastPass attractions at will, so the disconnected lineup may vary somewhat during your visit. Finally, Disneyland Park's and DCA's FastPass systems *are* connected, so guests cannot obtain a FastPass at one park and then immediately hop to the other park and obtain another FastPass.

When to Use FastPass

Regardless of time of day, if the wait in the regular line at a FastPass attraction is 25–30 minutes or less, we recommend joining the regular line. The exception to this rule is if an attraction is distributing FastPasses that are valid immediately. In this circumstance, you can retrieve a Fast-Pass and use it with less wait than guests entering the standby queue.

Think about it. Using FastPass requires two trips to the same attraction: one to obtain the pass and one to use it (unless you use MaxPass). This means that you must invest time to secure the pass (by the way, sometimes there are lines at the FastPass machines!) and then later interrupt your touring and backtrack to use your FastPass. The additional time, effort, and touring modification required, therefore, are justified only if you can save more than 30 minutes. And don't forget: even in the FastPass line, you must endure some waiting.

Tricks of the Trade

Though Disney stipulates that you can hold a FastPass to only one attraction at a time, it's possible to acquire a second FastPass before using the first. Let's say you obtain a FastPass to Star Tours with a return time slot of 10:15–11:15 a.m. Any time after your FastPass window begins (anytime after 10:15 a.m.), you can obtain another FastPass, for Splash Mountain, for example. This is possible because the FastPass system monitors only the distribution of passes, ignoring whether or when a FastPass is used. Finally, don't forget that you can obtain a second FastPass 2 hours after the time of issuance of the first FastPass (90 minutes after for Max-Pass users) if that's sooner than the return time on your first FastPass.

When obtaining FastPasses, it's faster and more considerate of other guests if one person obtains passes for your entire party. This means entrusting one individual with both your valuable park admission passes and your FastPasses, so choose wisely.

FastPass Runners

This option may appeal to larger parties who don't want to pay the per-person MaxPass fee. First, choose a high-energy, inexhaustible member of your party who is quick on his feet and mature and responsible enough not to lose everyone's admission passes. Second, give him all the passes (after you enter the park) and dispatch him to the first attraction to obtain FastPasses for the whole group. Then, about once each hour, the FastPass runner will split from the group to get the next FastPasses. Rinse, repeat. In Disneyland Park, for example, he would speed off to Space Mountain. Because the return time is usually 1 hour or less, it won't be long until he can scoot off again to obtain FastPasses at Splash Mountain. And so it goes. You can even send the runner across the Esplanade to get FastPasses at the other park, provided you have Park Hopper tickets. Collecting Fast-Passes this way allows the group to spend the less-crowded early-morning time visiting popular slow-loading attractions that don't offer FastPass. A father from Petaluma, California, shares his technique:

The trick is to always be holding FastPasses for the next headliner ride. Sending a runner to get the FastPasses is easy to do, as a solo adult can quickly and easily make his/her way across the park and back to rejoin the group. A time-saving maneuver I call the FastPass Daddy Limbo works like this: The main group gets in line for a ride (the line must be at least 15–20 minutes long) while Dad takes off to get FastPasses for another ride. Dad returns 10–15 minutes later and rejoins his group in line by going under/over/through the railing (unclasping a chain if necessary). The dad may need to wait a few minutes to rejoin his group until they are positioned at an easily accessible point. This should be possible at other accessible lines such as Star Tours and Splash Mountain, provided that the line outside is long enough.

SAVING TIME IN LINE BY UNDERSTANDING THE RIDES

THERE ARE MANY TYPES OF RIDES IN DISNEYLAND. Some rides, such as It's a Small World, are engineered to carry several thousand people every hour. At the other extreme, rides such as Dumbo can accommodate only around 500 people an hour. Most rides fall somewhere in between, so we provide for each attraction an estimate (based on published information and our own observations) of its typical guest throughput, assuming normal operating conditions. Lots of factors figure into how long you will have to wait to experience a particular ride: the popularity of the ride, how it loads and unloads, how many people can ride at one time, how many units (cars, rockets, boats, flying elephants, or whatever) of those available are in service at a given time, and how many staff are available to operate the ride. Let's take them one by one:

1. HOW POPULAR IS THE RIDE? Newer rides such as Guardians of the Galaxy—Mission: Breakout! or *Millennium Falcon:* Smugglers Run attract a lot of people, as do longtime favorites such as Space Mountain. If you know a ride is popular, you need to learn a little more about how it operates to determine when might be the best time to ride.

2. HOW DOES THE RIDE LOAD AND UNLOAD? A ride need not be especially popular to form long lines. The lines can be the result of less-than-desirable traffic engineering; that is, it takes so long to load and unload that a line builds up. This is the situation at the Mad Tea Party and Dumbo. Only a small percentage of the visitors to Disneyland Park (mostly kids) ride Dumbo, for instance, but because it takes so long to load and unload, this ride can form long waiting lines.

Some rides never stop. They are like a circular conveyor belt that goes around and around. We call these continuous loaders. The Haunted Mansion is a continuous loader. The more cars or ships or whatever on the conveyor, the more people can be moved through in an hour. The Haunted Mansion has lots of cars on the conveyor belt and consequently can move more than 2,400 people an hour.

Other rides are interval loaders. This means that cars are unloaded, loaded, and dispatched at certain set intervals (sometimes controlled manually and sometimes by a computer). Matterhorn Bobsleds is an

CYCLE RIDES
AT DISNEYLAND PARK
FANTASYLAND • Casey Jr. Circus Train • Dumbo the Flying Elephant • King Arthur Carrousel • Mad Tea Party
MICKEY'S TOONTOWN • Gadget's Go Coaster
TOMORROWLAND • Astro Orbitor
AT DISNEY CALIFORNIA ADVENTURE
PARADISE GARDENS PARK • Golden Zephyr • Jumpin' Jellyfish • Silly Symphony Swings
PIXAR PIER • Inside Out Emotional Whirlwind • Jessie's Critter Carousel • Pixar Pal-A-Round
CARS LAND • Luigi's Rollickin' Roadsters • Mater's Junkyard Jamboree

interval loader. It has two separate tracks (in other words, the ride has been duplicated in the same facility). Each track can run up to 10 sleds, released at 23-second or greater intervals (the bigger the crowd, the shorter the interval). In another kind of interval loader, such as the Jungle Cruise, empty boats return to the starting point, where they line up waiting to be reloaded. In a third type of interval loader, one group of riders enters the vehicle while the last group of riders departs. We call these in-and-out interval loaders. Indiana Jones Adventure is a good example of an in-and-out interval loader. As a troop transport pulls up to the loading station, those who have just completed their ride exit to the left. At almost the same time, those waiting to ride enter the troop transport from the right. The troop transport is released to the dispatch point a few yards down the line where it is launched according to whatever time interval is being used. Interval loaders of all three types can be very efficient at moving people if (1) the release (launch) interval is relatively short and (2) the ride can accommodate a large number of vehicles in the system at one time. Because many boats can be floating through Pirates of the Caribbean at a given time and the release interval is short, almost 3,400 people an hour can see this attraction.

A third group of rides are cycle rides. Another name for these same rides is stop-and-go rides; those waiting to ride exchange places with those who have just ridden. The main difference between in-and-out interval rides and cycle rides is that with a cycle ride, the whole system shuts down when loading and unloading is in progress. While one boat is loading and unloading in It's a Small World, many other boats are proceeding through the ride. But when Dumbo touches down, the whole ride is at a standstill until the next flight is launched.

In discussing a cycle ride, the amount of time the ride is in motion is called ride time. The amount of time that the ride is idle while loading and unloading is called load time. Load time plus ride time equals cycle time, or the time expended from the start of one run of the ride until the start of the succeeding run. Cycle rides are the least efficient of all the Disneyland rides in terms of traffic engineering. Disneyland Park has six cycle rides, while DCA has eight, an astonishing number for a modern park.

3. HOW MANY PEOPLE CAN RIDE AT ONE TIME? This figure is defined in terms of per-ride capacity or system capacity. Either way, the figures refer to the number of people who can ride at the same time. Our discussion above illustrates that the greater a ride's carrying capacity (all other things being equal), the more visitors it can accommodate in an hour.

4. HOW MANY UNITS ARE IN SERVICE AT A GIVEN TIME? A unit is simply a term for the vehicle you sit in during your ride. At the Mad Tea Party the unit is a teacup, and at Alice in Wonderland it's a caterpillar. On some rides (mostly cycle rides), the number of units in operation at a given time is fixed. Thus, there are always 16 elephant units operating on the Dumbo ride, 72 horses on King Arthur Carrousel, and so on. What this fixed number of units means to you is that there is no way to increase the carrying capacity of the ride by adding more units. On a busy day, therefore, the only way to carry more people each hour on a fixed-unit cycle ride is to shorten the loading time (which, as we will see in number 5, is sometimes impossible) or by decreasing the riding time, the actual time the ride is in motion. The bottom line on a busy day for a cycle ride is that you will wait longer and be rewarded for your wait with a shorter ride. This is why we try to steer you clear of the cycle rides unless you are willing to ride them early in the morning or late at night.

Other rides at Disneyland can increase their carrying capacity by adding units to the system as the crowds build. Big Thunder Mountain Railroad is a good example. If attendance is very light, Big Thunder can start the day by running one of five available mine trains. When lines start to build, more mine trains can be placed into operation. At full capacity, a total of five trains can carry about 2,400 people an hour. Sometimes a long line will disappear almost instantly when new units are brought online. On the other hand, the queue may stop altogether for a few minutes while new units are added, extending the wait for guests who were about to board. When an interval-loading ride places more units into operation, it usually shortens the dispatch interval, so more units are being dispatched more often.

5. HOW MANY CAST MEMBERS ARE AVAILABLE TO OPERATE THE RIDE? Allocation of additional staff to a ride can allow extra units to be placed in operation, or additional loading areas or holding areas to be opened. Pirates of the Caribbean and It's a Small World can run two separate waiting lines and loading zones. The Haunted Mansion has a short preshow, which is staged in a "stretch room." On busy days a second stretch room can be activated, thus permitting a more continuous flow of visitors to the actual loading area. Additional staff make a world of difference on some cycle rides. Often, if not usually, one attendant will operate the Golden Zephyr. This single person must clear the visitors from the ride just completed, admit and seat visitors for the upcoming ride, check that all zephyrs are properly secured (which entails an inspection of each zephyr), return to the control panel, issue instructions to the riders, and finally, activate the ride (whew!). A second attendant allows for the division of these responsibilities and has the effect of cutting loading time by 25%–50%.

BEWARE OF THE DARK, WET, ROUGH, AND SCARY

OOPS, ALMOST FORGOT: There's a member of our team you need to meet. Called a Wuffo, she's our very own character. She'll warn you when rides are too scary, too dark, or too wet. You'll bump into her throughout the book doing, well, what characters do. Pay attention to her—she knows what she's talking about.

SAVING TIME IN LINE BY UNDERSTANDING THE SHOWS

MANY OF THE FEATURED ATTRACTIONS at Disneyland are theater presentations. While they're not as complex as rides from a traffic-engineering viewpoint, a little enlightenment concerning their operation may save some touring time.

Most Disneyland theater attractions operate in three distinct phases:

1. First, there are visitors who are in the theater viewing the presentation.
2. Next, there are visitors who have passed through the turnstile into a holding area or waiting lobby. These people will be admitted to the theater as soon as the current presentation is concluded. Several attractions offer a preshow in the waiting lobby to entertain the crowd until they are admitted to the main show.
3. Finally, there is the outside line. Visitors waiting here will enter the waiting lobby when there is room and then move into the theater when the audience turns over (is exchanged) between shows.

The theater capacity and popularity of the presentation, along with the level of attendance in the park, determine how long the lines will be at a given theater attraction. Except for holidays and other days of especially heavy attendance, the longest wait for a show usually does not exceed the length of one complete performance.

Because almost all Disneyland theater attractions run continually, only stopping long enough for the previous audience to leave and the waiting audience to enter, a performance will already be in progress when you arrive. If the *Enchanted Tiki Room* show lasts 15 minutes, the wait under normal circumstances should be 15 minutes if you were to arrive just after the show began.

All Disneyland theaters (except the Main Street Cinema and some amphitheater productions) are very strict when it comes to controlling access. Unlike at a regular movie theater, you can't just walk in during the middle of a performance; you will always have at least a short wait.

GUIDED TOURS AT DISNEYLAND PARK AND DCA

ONLY TWO GROUP TOURS are offered year-round, in addition to ultra-expensive private VIP tours. All require a valid park admission in addition to the price of the tour. Disneyland Resort tours can be booked up to 30 days in advance by calling ☎ 714-781-8687 for the standard tours or ☎ 714-300-7710 for the VIP treatment. Tours are subject to change without notice, and some tours are offered only on certain days, so call ahead. During the Halloween and Christmas seasons, tours highlighting holiday decorations may also be available. Disneyland Park tours begin at the Tour Gardens kiosk to the left of City Hall on Main Street, U.S.A. Annual pass holders, Disney Visa cardholders, and DVC members get a 15% discount on guided tours.

WALK IN WALT'S DISNEYLAND FOOTSTEPS This 3½-hour tour offers a historical perspective on both Disneyland Park and the man who created it. It covers Disney's vision and the challenges in bringing the theme park to life. You'll take a ride on a couple of vintage attractions; hear rare interviews and audio clips via a provided wireless earpiece; and visit Walt's private apartment above the Main Street firehouse (subject to availability), which is a bucket-list experience for any die-hard Disney devotee. The tour concludes with a boxed meal from Jolly Holiday

Bakery Cafe and a souvenir pin. Cost is $115 for all ages, and the tour is offered daily at 9:30 a.m. (regardless of the park's opening time), and at midday and midafternoon on weekends and during peak periods. (The tour is considered inappropriate for younger children, who will likely be bored; guests under age 18 must be accompanied by an adult.) We think the tour is a good introduction to Disney lore for fans of midcentury American culture, but a poor use of time for casual tourists. A reader from Superior, Colorado, gave it a mixed review:

> The tour was good, but I wouldn't do it more than once. Our guide was a little too rehearsed (read: memorization), and several people on the tour (including my husband and I) knew things she didn't know.

GRAND CIRCLE TOUR If you love steam trains as much as Walt did, this 2-hour early-morning tour is made for you. It begins with a brief breakfast snack and walking tour of Disneyland Park before the main event: a round-trip journey on the Disneyland Railroad inside the *Lilly Belle*, a private parlor car named for Mrs. Disney that isn't ordinarily open to the public. The $85 fee includes a collectible railroad map, and the tour is offered Friday–Monday, usually starting 15 minutes after park opening.

VIP TOURS Exclusive VIP tours are available for an eye-popping $425 per hour for up to 10 guests ($600 during peak season) with a 7-hour minimum. VIP guides will arrange special parade and show seating, make dining reservations, dispense Disneyland trivia, and (most crucially) "back door" you past the queues for unlimited expedited boarding at most attractions. You must make reservations 72 hours in advance and cancel at least 48 hours in advance or face a 2-hour cancellation fee.

PART TWO

ESSENTIALS

 The **BARE NECESSITIES**

CREDIT CARDS

AMERICAN EXPRESS, MASTERCARD, VISA, Discover, and Japan Credit Bureau credit cards are accepted for theme park admission. Disneyland shops, fast-food and counter-service restaurants, sit-down restaurants, and the Disneyland Resort hotels also accept all the cards listed above. Some vendor carts accept credit cards while others do not—ask before you order. Disney Visa cardholders can get a private character meet and greet in Disney California Adventure's Hollywood Land 10:30 a.m.–1:30 p.m., and an exclusive face-to-face with a *Star Wars* villain inside Disneyland's Star Wars Launch Bay 2–6 p.m. or 4–8 p.m. depending on the season. Cardholders also get a code to download all their private poses from disneyland.com/photopass or the Disneyland smartphone app. Disney Visa cardholders save 10% on merchandise ($50 minimum purchase) and dining at select resort locations and 15% on guided tours. Instant application kiosks can be found in Downtown Disney, with $100 or more in statement credits sometimes offered as an incentive to approved applicants.

Mobile payment or tap-to-pay, a wireless payment method on newer iPhones and NFC-equipped Android smartphones, is supported at most Disneyland Resort ticket booths, stores, quick-service restaurants, and outdoor vending carts. Locations that support tap-to-pay have a small black pad with a Contactless Indicator symbol (also known as an EMVCo symbol, which looks like a Wi-Fi symbol turned sideways). When it works, mobile payment is the swiftest way to pay, even quicker than swiping a hotel key.

RAIN

IF IT RAINS, GO ANYWAY; the bad weather will diminish the crowds. Additionally, most of the rides and attractions at the parks are under cover. Likewise, all but a few of the waiting areas are protected from inclement weather. Some outdoor attractions—such as Tom Sawyer's Island, Mad Tea Party, Alice in Wonderland, Tarzan's Treehouse, and Gadget's Go Coaster at Disneyland Park, and Radiator Springs Racers, Redwood Creek Challenge Trail, and Golden Zephyr at Disney California Adventure (DCA)—may close for safety reasons in inclement weather. Radiator Springs Racers may require hours of downtime after a storm before safely reopening. Roller coasters such as Big Thunder Mountain Railroad and the Incredicoaster can operate in a drizzle but will close down if lightning is nearby. Fireworks are rarely canceled solely due to rain but may be scuttled by strong winds, and parades may be shortened or modified for safety. A father from Petaluma, California, recommends some supplemental supplies for wet weather, writing:

> Ride operators make a token effort to use a shop vac or towels, but it's good to have your own towel even on sunny days for the water ride seats. For multiday park touring in the rain, have a second pair of shoes to switch off every night at the hotel, allowing 24 hours to dry. We used a small fan to dry shoes and jackets that got wet on rides.

If you get caught in an unexpected downpour, raingear can be purchased at a number of shops. Whatever you do, don't flee for the parking trams during a sudden thunderstorm, or you may find yourself in an unpleasant scene, like this mother of two from Los Angeles:

> It was pouring rain and the park rapidly emptied out. There was complete chaos by the tram loading area [with] hundreds of people pushing and shoving—desperate to get on a tram and get out of there. The trams were arriving very sporadically and tempers were rising.

Instead, wait out the storm inside a self-paced indoor attraction, such as *Great Moments with Mr. Lincoln,* Main Street Cinema, or Star Wars Launch Bay at Disneyland Park, and Boudin Bakery Tour or Disney Animation at DCA.

VISITORS WITH SPECIAL NEEDS

DISABLED VISITORS Rental wheelchairs are available just inside both parks' main gates. Daily wheelchair rentals are $12 (manual) or $50 (electric); a $20 refundable deposit is required. Note that wheelchairs and electric convenience vehicles rented inside the parks are not permitted beyond the Esplanade. A limited supply of manual wheelchairs, which may be taken through Downtown Disney, are available to rent at the Disneyland Resort hotels.

Close-in parking is available for the disabled; inquire when you pay your parking fee. Parking trams can accommodate guests who bring their own wheelchairs, and a special transportation van is also available (ask a parking lot cast member). Curbside drop-off is only available at the Harbor Boulevard entrance, near the stops for hotel shuttles and local buses. It may be challenging for disabled guests who don't bring their own wheelchairs to walk from there into the parks. If you don't think that you can travel the necessary distance, consider renting a chair or scooter for the length of your vacation from a third-party vendor who can deliver it to your hotel.

If you can afford the room rate, this North Wales, Pennsylvania, reader raved about the convenience of staying at the Grand Californian:

> *This was a once-in-a-lifetime trip, and I have some mobility issues. So staying at the Grand Californian for its location and renting an ECV from an off-site company were worth the cost. The Grand Californian is just gorgeous, and I was constantly finding new things to amaze me.*

Even with all of Disneyland's accommodations for disabled guests, one Claremont, California, woman says the resort still has a ways to go:

> *For disabled guests, restrooms are terrible. Usually there is only one handicapped stall, and it is OFTEN used by teens and even cast members, as well as moms taking strollers or multiple kids into the stall.*
>
> *There are only two companion restrooms in each park (outside of first aid). Other theme parks in Southern California have staff who assist and tell guests not to use these stalls, and other parks have added many more family and companion restroom facilities.*
>
> *There still are not enough handicapped parking spaces on more crowded days, nor adequate seating at many restaurants to accommodate the various types of need.*

Most rides, shows, attractions, restrooms, and restaurants are engineered to accommodate the disabled. For specific inquiries call ☎ 714-781-7290. If you have an impairment that makes it difficult for you to stand in line and navigate stairs, or otherwise need special assistance, go to City Hall on Main Street in Disneyland Park or Guest Relations in the entrance plaza at DCA and ask to register for Disability Access Service (DAS), which will be electronically attached to your admission ticket. This program is free and available for the disabled visitor and up to five additional guests. You should not have to show a doctor's note or proof of disability, but you will need to discuss your (or your family member's) limitations and requested accommodations with a cast member; it may help to describe difficulties handling things such as the stress of waiting in queues and crisscrossing the park.

Guests in wheelchairs who do not have additional cognitive or sensory issues do not need to sign up for DAS because all attraction standby queues in Disney California Adventure, and most in Disneyland, are fully wheelchair accessible. At those in Disneyland that are not fully accessible, guests in wheelchairs will go to the ride's main entrance and be issued a return time based on the current wait time (minus 10 minutes), at which point they can report to an alternate accessible entrance. Though similar to DAS, this program is independent of it and does not require preregistration.

With DAS, instead of being immediately admitted to an attraction's entrance, users are issued return times based on the current standby wait (minus 10 minutes) from designated kiosks strategically scattered around the parks. In effect, DAS is a special FastPass for disabled guests and can be used in conjunction with the regular FastPass service; you can even view (though not make) DAS reservations inside the Disneyland app, whether or not you've paid for MaxPass. A DAS enrollment is valid for 60 days, after which it must be renewed in person, which should be fine for most visitors but can be annoying for local annual pass holders. The current system was intended to reduce rampant abuse of the system, which sometimes had hundreds of able-bodied guests skipping the standby line for limited-capacity attractions, but it has proven controversial among autism activists whose children may have meltdowns when told they must wait for their ride. Additional services, such as rider switch and break areas, are available for guests with cognitive disabilities. If you feel you may need the DAS program or other accommodations, be sure to read up on your options in advance at disneyland.disney.go.com/guest-services /guests-with-disabilities. A Southern California mom with an autistic daughter had this suggestion:

> *Anyone staying any length of time should go to DCA to get their DAS card—the lines are always shorter there, unless you are in the gates of Disneyland at opening.*

For guests with visual or auditory impairments, digital audio and Braille guides, assistive listening devices, captioning, and sign language services are available through City Hall and Guest Relations. Trained service animals are welcome but must be kept on a leash at all times. Note the special symbol on park maps designating service animal relief areas in both parks.

VISITORS WITH DIETARY RESTRICTIONS Guests on special or restricted diets, including those requiring kosher meals, can arrange for assistance at City Hall at Disneyland Park or at Guest Relations at DCA. These locations can also provide information on gluten-free menu options at restaurants in the resort. For special service at Disneyland Resort restaurants, call the restaurant one day in advance for assistance. See page 162 for more details on allergies and dietary restrictions at Disneyland Resort.

FOREIGN-LANGUAGE ASSISTANCE Translation services are available to guests who do not speak English. Inquire by calling ☎ 714-781-7290 or visiting City Hall at Disneyland Park or Guest Relations at DCA.

LOST ADULTS Arrange a plan for regrouping with those in your party should you become separated. Failing this, you can leave a message at City Hall or Guest Relations for your missing person. For information concerning lost children, see pages 149–151.

MESSAGES Messages for your fellow group members can be left at City Hall in Disneyland Park or at DCA Guest Relations.

CAR TROUBLE If you elected to decrease the chance of losing your keys by locking them in your car, or decided that your car might be easier to find if you left your lights on, you may have a little problem to deal with when you return to the parking lot. Fortunately, the security patrols that continually cruise the parking lots are equipped to handle these types of situations and can quickly put you back in business.

LOST AND FOUND The lost-and-found office, which services both theme parks and Downtown Disney, is located in the Guest Services building in the Esplanade to the west of the park entrances. If you don't discover your loss until after you have left the parks, call ☎ 714-817-2166 8 a.m.–8 p.m. daily. If you lose your park ticket, Guest Services may be able to retrieve it using the credit card with which it was purchased, but it's far easier for them to reprint if you take a digital photo of the bar code when you first get your pass.

EXCUSE ME, BUT WHERE CAN I FIND . . .

SOME PLACE TO PUT ALL THESE PACKAGES? Lockers are available both outside the entrance of each park, for $7–$15 per day, and inside each park, for $7–$10. Pricing depends on size and includes unlimited in-and-out access throughout the day. Disneyland Resort will deliver purchases to on-site hotels but has discontinued free package pickup at the front of the parks; however, you can check your souvenirs at most major stores and retrieve them later in the day.

GROCERIES? Several convenience stores are on Harbor Boulevard near Disneyland, but no supermarkets are within easy walking distance. The closest stores with a good selection are **Food-4-Less** at 1616 W. Katella Ave. and the **Walmart Neighborhood Market** at 10912 Katella Ave., both about a mile west of Disneyland Resort. **Target** is about a 5-minute drive south of Disneyland on Harbor. The adjacent **Viva Bargain Center** is a good place for cheap supplies. If you don't have a car, **Vons Grocery Delivery** (shop.vons.com) will bring food directly to your hotel with a $49 minimum order. You must be present to receive the delivery but can select a 1- to 4-hour time window when placing your order.

A MIXED DRINK OR BEER? At Disneyland Park, you will have to exit the park and try one of the hotels or Downtown Disney unless you have a reservation at Galaxy's Edge's cantina or an ultraexpensive membership to the exclusive Club 33 hidden in New Orleans Square. At DCA alcoholic beverages are readily available.

SOME RAINGEAR? At Disneyland, raingear is available at most shops but is not always displayed. You have to ask for it. Ponchos are $12 for adults and $10 for kids, and umbrellas are $20 and up.

A CURE FOR THIS HEADACHE? Aspirin and various sundries can be purchased on Main Street at the Emporium in Disneyland Park and at Elias and Company at the DCA entrance plaza (they're behind the counter, so you have to ask). Basic medical supplies are in each hotel's gift shop.

A PHARMACY? Unfortunately, there is no place in Disneyland Resort to have a prescription filled. The nearest full-service pharmacies are the **Walgreens** and **CVS** on the corner of Harbor Boulevard at Katella Avenue, about a block south of Disneyland.

A DOCTOR? HouseCall Physicians (☎ 800-362-7911) will make house calls to your hotel room 24-7. The fee varies depending on the reason for the visit and the insurance you have, and the fee is payable at the time of the visit. The closest hospital to Disneyland is the **University California Irvine Medical Center,** which is about 2 miles distant at Chapman Avenue and City Drive. For dental emergencies, there is **7 Day Dental** at 637 N. Euclid St. in Anaheim, ☎ 866-989-1335.

If you are staying at a Disneyland on-site hotel, dial 911 on the in-house phone to connect with the resort's medical services, who can send a registered nurse to your room free of charge.

SUNTAN LOTION? Suntan lotion and various sundries can be purchased in Disneyland Park on Main Street at the Emporium and at Elias and Company at the DCA entrance plaza (they're behind the counter, so you have to ask).

A SMOKE? You won't find cigarettes for sale at Disneyland parks, and as of May 1, 2019, smoking (and vaporizing) is prohibited inside the Disney parks and Downtown Disney. There are designated locations at the resort hotels where you may still inhale, but if you need a puff while inside the parks, you'll have to exit the Esplanade and pass through security again after you're done. And even though recreational and medical marijuana are now legal in California, it's explicitly prohibited on Disney property.

FEMININE-HYGIENE PRODUCTS? These are available in most women's restrooms at Disneyland Resort.

CASH? Basic banking services and foreign currency exchange are provided at City Hall in Disneyland Park, Guest Relations at DCA, Travelex in Downtown Disney, and the front desks of Disneyland hotels. ATMs can be found in the following places:

AT DISNEYLAND PARK

- Outside the main entrance   • At the entrance to Frontierland on the left
- On Main Street, next to the *Disneyland Story* at the Town Square end
- Near Fantasyland Theatre   • In Tomorrowland, near the Space Mountain exit

AT DOWNTOWN DISNEY

- Next to Salt & Straw   • At the Lego Store

AT DISNEY CALIFORNIA ADVENTURE

- Outside the main entrance   • Near the restrooms at Hollywood Land
- At the locker complex just inside the main entrance and to the right
- Near the restrooms on Pacific Wharf   • Near Pixar Pal-A-Round at Pixar Pier
- Near the restrooms behind Flo's V8 Cafe in Cars Land
- Near the restrooms across from The Little Mermaid: Ariel's Undersea Adventure entrance
- Outside the restrooms near Paradise Garden Grill

A PLACE TO LEAVE MY PET? Pets (except for service dogs) are not allowed in the parks. Kennels and holding facilities are provided for the temporary care of your pets. If you are adamant, the folks at the kennels will accept custody of just about any type of animal. Owners of pets, exotic or otherwise, must themselves place their charge in the assigned cage. Small pets (mice, hamsters, birds, snakes, turtles, alligators, and the like) must arrive in their own escape-proof quarters. Kennels cost $20 per pet, per day and are located to the right of the Disneyland Park main entrance. For more information, call ☎ 714-781-7662. There are several other details you may need to know:

- Advance reservations for animals are not accepted.
- Kennel employees are not permitted to handle your pet, so you will need to transfer your pet to and from its enclosure and return during the day to walk him or her.
- Cash or credit is accepted.
- Kennels open 30 minutes before and close 30 minutes after theme park operating hours.
- Pets may not be boarded overnight, and none of the on-site Disneyland hotels accept pets.
- Guests leaving exotic pets should supply food for their pet.
- On busy days, there is a 1- to 2-hour bottleneck at the kennel, beginning 30 minutes before the park opens. If you need to use the kennels on such a day, arrive at least 1 hour before the park's stated opening time.
- Pets are fed on request only (yours, not your pet's), and there is no additional charge for food.
- All pets must be at least 4 months old and fully immunized. For dogs, proof of current rabies, distemper, hepatitis, parvovirus, parainfluenza, and Bordetella vaccines is required. For cats, proof of rabies, panleukopenia, rhinotracheitis, and calicivirus vaccines is required. Documentation must include contact info for the owner and veterinarian, a description of the pet, and dates for each type of vaccination.
- Pets are allowed to ride on the Mickey & Friends and Pixar Pals parking structure tram but are NOT allowed on the Toy Story parking lot buses.

A PLACE TO CHARGE MY CELL PHONE? A few free accessible power outlets can be found around the parks (our favorites are along the stage in *Great Moments with Mr. Lincoln,* inside the Main Street train station, at Royal Street Veranda, and in the balcony in the Golden Horseshoe). Be sure not to block traffic or remove any installed plugs or covers, and even then you may still be ushered away by an employee.

Another energy option is the FuelRod, a precharged battery pack sold from a dozen-odd automated kiosks around the parks and inside each on-site hotel. You can find higher-capacity batteries online for less than the $30 FuelRod, but FuelRod's advantage is that, whenever it's drained, you can simply stop at any kiosk on Disney property and swap it for a full one free of charge. FuelRods can also be found online and in airports and malls for about $20, and all are compatible with Disneyland's kiosks, so save yourself some money by buying them outside the resort. You'll also find FuelRods at Walt Disney World, so bicoastal Mouse fans may get double mileage out of them. Google for a discount code to get $3 off your initial purchase, and sign into the FuelRod smartphone app for five free swaps at kiosks outside Disney.

Incidentally, cell phone coverage inside Disneyland can be a crap-shoot at best, especially on crowded days. We've watched our AT&T LTE service drop down to an antiquated 3G data stream when transmission towers become overloaded by Instagramming guests.

Disneyland offers free Wi-Fi access inside its parks. No password is required to join the "Disney Guest" Wi-Fi network, but you will need to open a browser and agree to the terms and conditions before accessing the internet. Connections can be inconsistent, especially inside attraction queues; find one of the hot spot locations marked on the park map and in the official app for your best shot at a stable signal.

Disney's spotty Wi-Fi coverage ensures that your phone will constantly be seeking a signal, thereby draining the battery, which quickly becomes a Catch-22 for MaxPass users who have paid for the internet-dependent service. This can be especially aggravating for international guests without data plans who use the Disneyland app to store their tickets, since the parks' turnstile plazas have patchy Wi-Fi coverage. Here are a few hints for helping your smartphone survive a Disney day:

- Take a screenshot of your admission bar code as a backup; you can even make it your phone's lock screen for easy access.
- Only turn on your Wi-Fi when you know you're near a hot spot.
- Switch your cell phone into low power mode as soon as you arrive.
- Turn your screen brightness up to full whenever approaching a turnstile or FastPass scanner, so that your code can be read, then lower it to save power.

CELEBRATION PINS? Disneyland first-timers (along with honeymooners and birthday or anniversary celebrants) are rewarded with a special pin, as this Oregon mom relates:

City Hall on Main Street had pins to proudly announce it was a first visit to DL. I didn't know about this during my older son's first visit. Fortunately, there is no date on it, so I got one for each son.

Another reader, who celebrated her 50th birthday there, reports:

I recommend getting birthday buttons. Not a single cast member failed to see them and make a big deal about it! And you don't have to show proof or anything; just go ask for one.

You can pick up free celebration buttons from Guest Services inside either park or at any on-site hotel. They're also kept behind the counter at most park shops, so don't waste time in a long Guest Services line just to get one.

CAMERAS AND PHOTO SERVICES? You can buy a disposable camera, with or without a flash, as well as digital memory cards and batteries, throughout the parks. If you'd rather let professionals take the pictures, Disney PhotoPass photographers are stationed at scenic spots around the parks. You'll find them located at key landmarks, such as Sleeping Beauty Castle and Carthay Circle, as well as accompanying most character meet and greets; some even offer Magic Shots that superimpose an animated character into your family's pose; ask a photographer outside

Star Wars: Rise of the Resistance for a priceless Porg picture. They'll take your snapshot with their camera (and yours, if you request) for free, and then hand you a PhotoPass identification card, which you can continue using during your vacation. Later, stop by Main Street Photo Supply Co. in Disneyland Park or Kingswell Camera Shop in DCA (go at midafternoon to avoid long lines), or log onto disneyland.com/photopass within 45 days of your visit to preview and purchase all your pictures. You can download photos individually for $14.95 each, or get a digital copy and a glossy print for $16.95 and up each. Alternatively, purchase a one-week PhotoPass+ package from disneyland.com/memories for $78 and get unlimited digital downloads of an entire week's worth of photos. Better yet, purchase MaxPass (see page 87) for at least one member of your party, and he or she can download unlimited PhotoPass images from the day for only $15. Unlimited PhotoPass downloads are also included with the two most expensive tiers of annual passes, and lower-level pass holders can add it to their tickets with MaxPass for $100 per year.

All PhotoPass packages also include your pictures taken at character meals in the parks and hotels, as well as on-ride snapshots from select attractions, including Space Mountain and Splash Mountain at Disneyland, and Radiator Springs Racers, the Incredicoaster, and Guardians of the Galaxy—Mission: Breakout! at DCA. Find a complete list of locations at disneyland.disney.go.com/guest-services/photo-pass-service or inside the official Disneyland app under the "PhotoPass" tab.

Be sure to use the Disneyland app to secure your MaxPass upgrade and attach it to your admission ticket before leaving the park, as a mom from St. Louis learned the hard way:

> We couldn't figure out how to purchase the MaxPass upgrade on the day of our visit to download the park photos for our one-day visit. I decided to wait until I had more time to figure it out, but by that time customer service was closed. I called the next morning but was told that it had to be purchased on the day of the visit and was not available after the fact. The only option at that point was the one-week photo package, so it ended up costing much more than it should have.

Finally, if you want up to 45 days worth of photos, along with physical prints of your character-meal pictures and a disc full of stock photos of the resort, you can purchase a Disney PhotoPass Collection package, in person only, from either park's camera center for $99, or $119 including a disc of your personal pictures; activate the package online immediately after your vacation to ensure all your images are included.

All PhotoPass photos expire 45 days after the photo was taken, so remember to download and archive your purchases; a one-time 15-day extension on the expiration date can be purchased for $19.95. Signature Plus and Premier Passport holders (and lower-level pass holders who paid for MaxPass upgrades) get unlimited free PhotoPass downloads while their passport is valid, and their pictures don't expire until 365 days after they're snapped.

PART THREE

DISNEYLAND *with* KIDS

I am very grateful for the help your book gave me. The best part was that there were no surprises that spoiled the fun. I was ready for rain, wind, cold, expensive food, small-child meltdowns, and 40-minute potty stops for the grandparents (well, maybe not quite ready for the 40-minute potty stops). I did need an hour alone in the Grand Californian bar after the third day.

—Mom from Lompoc, California

The **BRUTAL TRUTH** *About* **FAMILY VACATIONS**

IT HAS BEEN SUGGESTED that the phrase *family vacation* is a bit of an oxymoron because you can never take a vacation from the responsibilities of parenting if your children are traveling with you. Though you leave work and normal routine far behind, your children require as much attention, if not more, when traveling as they do at home.

Parenting on the road requires imagination and organization. You have to do all the usual stuff (feed, dress, bathe, supervise, comfort, discipline, and so on) in an atmosphere where your children are hyperstimulated, without the familiarity of place and the resources available at home. Though not impossible—and possibly even fun—parenting on the road is not something you want to learn on the fly.

The point is that preparation, or the lack thereof, can make or break your Disneyland vacation. Believe us: you don't want to leave the success of your expensive Disney vacation to chance. Your preparation can be organized into several categories: mental, emotional, physical, organizational, and logistical. You also need a basic understanding of the two theme parks and a well-considered plan for how to go about seeing them.

MENTAL *and* EMOTIONAL PREPARATION

MENTAL PREPARATION BEGINS with realistic expectations about your Disney vacation and consideration of what each adult and child in your party most wants and needs from his or her Disneyland experience. Getting in touch with this aspect of planning requires a lot of introspection and good, open family communication.

DIVISION OF LABOR

TALK ABOUT WHAT you and your partner need and what you expect to happen on the vacation. This discussion alone can preempt some unpleasant surprises mid-trip. If you are a two-parent family, do you have a clear understanding of how the parenting workload will be distributed? We've seen some disruptive misunderstandings in two-parent households in which one parent is (pardon the legalese) the primary caregiver. Often, the other parent expects the primary caregiver to function on vacation as she (or he) does at home. The primary caregiver, on the other hand, is ready for a break. She expects her partner to either shoulder the load equally or perhaps even assume the lion's share, so she can have a real vacation. However you divide the responsibility is up to you. Just make sure that you negotiate a clear understanding before you leave home.

TOGETHERNESS

ANOTHER DIMENSION TO CONSIDER is how much togetherness seems appropriate to you. For some parents, a vacation represents a rare opportunity to really connect with their children, to talk, exchange ideas, and get reacquainted. For others, a vacation affords the time to get a little distance, to enjoy a round of golf while the kids are enjoying the theme park. The point here is to think about your and your children's preferences and needs concerning your time together. A typical day at a Disney theme park provides the structure of experiencing attractions together, punctuated by periods of waiting in line, eating, and so on, which facilitate conversation and sharing. Most attractions can be enjoyed together by the whole family, regardless of age ranges. This allows for more consensus and less dissent when it comes to deciding what to see and do. For many parents and children, however, the rhythms of a Disneyland day seem to consist of passive entertainment experiences alternated with endless discussions of where to go and what to do next.

Two observations: First, fighting the crowds and keeping the family moving along can easily escalate into a pressure-driven outing. Having a plan or itinerary eliminates moment-to-moment guesswork and decision-making, thus creating more time for savoring and connecting. Second, external variables such as crowd size, noise, and weather, among others, can be so distracting as to preclude any meaningful togetherness. These negative impacts can be moderated, as previously discussed in Part One, by being selective concerning the time of year, day of the week, and the time of day you visit the theme parks, as well as the number of days of your visit. The bottom line is that you can achieve the degree of connection and togetherness you desire with a little advance planning and a realistic awareness of the distractions you will encounter.

LIGHTEN UP

PREPARE YOURSELF MENTALLY to be a little less compulsive on vacation about correcting small behavioral deviations and pounding home the lessons of life. So what if Matt eats hamburgers for breakfast, lunch, and dinner every day? You can make him eat peas and broccoli when you get home. Roll with the little stuff, and remember when your children act out that they are wired to the max. At least some of that adrenaline is bound to spill out in undesirable ways. Coming down hard will send an already frayed little nervous system into orbit.

SOMETHING FOR EVERYONE

unofficial TIP
Try to schedule some time alone with each of your children—if not each day, then at least a couple of times during the trip.

IF YOU TRAVEL WITH AN INFANT, toddler, or any child who requires a lot of special attention, make sure that you have some energy and time remaining for the rest of your brood. While planning, invite each child to name something special to do or see at Disneyland with Mom or Dad alone. Work these special activities into your trip itinerary. Whatever else, if you commit, write it down so that you don't forget. Remember that a casually expressed willingness to do this or that may be perceived as a promise.

WHOSE IDEA WAS THIS, ANYWAY?

THE DISCORD THAT many vacationing families experience arises from the kids being on a completely different wavelength from Mom and Dad. Parents and grandparents are often worse than children when it comes to conjuring fantasy scenarios of what a Disneyland vacation will be like. It can be many things, but believe us when we tell you that there's a lot more to it than just riding Dumbo and seeing Mickey.

In our experience, most parents and nearly all grandparents expect children to enter a state of rapture at Disneyland, bouncing from attraction to attraction in wide-eyed wonder, appreciative beyond words to their adult benefactors. What they get, more often than not, is not even in the same ballpark. Preschoolers will, without a doubt, be wide-eyed, often with delight but also with a general sense of being overwhelmed by noise, crowds, and Disney characters as big as toolsheds. We've substantiated through thousands of interviews and surveys that the best part of a Disney vacation for a preschooler is the hotel swimming pool. With some grade-schoolers and pre-driving-age teens, you get near-manic hyperactivity coupled with periods of studied nonchalance. This last phenomenon, which relates to the importance of being cool at all costs, translates into a maddening display of boredom and a "been there, done that" attitude. Older teens are frequently the exponential version of younger teens and grade-schoolers, but without the manic behavior.

For preschoolers, you can keep things light and happy by limiting the time you spend in the theme parks. Most critical is that the overstimulation of the parks must be balanced by adequate rest and more-mellow activities. For grade-schoolers and early teens, you can moderate the hyperactivity and false ennui by enlisting their help in planning the vacation, especially by allowing them to take a leading role in determining the itinerary for days at the theme parks. Putting them in charge of specific responsibilities that focus on the happiness of other family members also works well. For example, one reader turned a 12-year-old liability into an asset by asking him to help guard against attractions that might frighten his 5-year-old sister. Knowledge enhances anticipation and at the same time affords a level of comfort and control that helps kids understand the big picture. The more they feel in control, the less they will act out of control.

BASIC CONSIDERATIONS:
Is Disneyland for Everyone?

ALMOST ALL VISITORS enjoy Disneyland on some level and find things to see and do that they like. The more salient question, then (since this is a family vacation), is whether the members of your family basically like the same things. If you do, fine. If not, how will you handle the differing agendas?

A mother from Toronto described her husband's aversion to Disney's (in his terms) "phony, plastic, and idealized version of life." Touring the theme parks, he was a real cynic and managed to diminish the experience for the rest of the family. As it happened, however, Dad's pejorative point of view didn't extend to the area golf courses. So Mom packed him up and sent him golfing while the family enjoyed the theme parks.

If you have someone in your family who doesn't like theme parks or, for whatever reason, doesn't care for Disney's brand of entertainment, it helps to get the attitude out in the open. We recommend dealing with the person up front. Glossing over or ignoring the contrary opinion and hoping that "Tom will like it once he gets there" is naive and unrealistic. Either leave Tom at home or help him discover and plan activities that he will enjoy, resigning yourself in the process to the fact that the family won't be together at all times.

THE NATURE OF THE BEAST

THOUGH MANY PARENTS don't realize it, there is no law that says you must take your kids to Disneyland. Likewise, there's no law that says you will enjoy Disneyland. And though we will help you make the most of any visit, we can't change the basic nature of the beast—er, mouse. A Disneyland vacation is an active and physically demanding undertaking. Regimentation, getting up early, lots of walking, waiting in lines, fighting crowds, and (often) enduring the hot California sun are as intrinsic to a Disneyland vacation as stripes are to a zebra. Especially if you're traveling with children, you'll need a sense of humor, more than a modicum of patience, and the ability to roll with the punches.

KNOW THYSELF AND NOTHING TO EXCESS

FIRST, CONCERNING THE "know thyself" part, do some serious thinking about what you want in a vacation. Entertain the notion that having fun and deriving pleasure from your vacation may be very different from doing and seeing as much as possible.

Because Disneyland Resort is expensive, many families confuse seeing everything to get your money's worth with having a great time. Sometimes the two are compatible, but more often they're not. So if sleeping in, relaxing with a cup of coffee, sunbathing by the pool, or taking a nap rank high on your vacation hit parade, you need to give them due emphasis on your Disney visit, even if it means that you see less of the theme parks.

Which brings us to the "nothing to excess" part. At the Disneyland parks, especially if you're touring with children, less is definitely more. Trust us: it's tough to go full tilt from dawn to dusk in the theme parks. First you'll get tired, then you'll get cranky, and then you'll adopt a production mentality ("We have three more rides, and then we can go back to the hotel"). Finally, you'll hit the wall because you just can't maintain the pace.

This mom had a great vacation, but not exactly the vacation she had been expecting:

unofficial **TIP**
Get a grip on your needs and preferences before you leave home, and develop an itinerary that incorporates all the things that make you happiest.

I was unprepared for traveling with a 2-year-old. All the indoor rides were deemed too dark and scary, and all she wanted to do was see the characters (which I thought she'd be petrified of!). We had a great trip once I threw all my plans out the window and just went with the flow! We all would have appreciated more pool time. Think twice before bringing a 2-year-old. It is one exhausting trip!

Plan on seeing the Disneyland parks in bite-size chunks with plenty of swimming, napping, and relaxing in between. Most Disneyland vacations are short. Even if you have to stay an extra day to build in some relaxation, you'll be happier while you're there and more rested when you get home, as this Palo Alto, California, parent found:

I recommend that families—especially those with young children—put regular buffers in their plans. Having open buffer time made it easier to slow down periodically during the day and smell the roses. While we loved doing all the rides, we also enjoyed soaking up the atmosphere, having an ice cream cone, and so on.

Ask yourself over and over in both the planning stage and while you are at Disneyland: what will contribute the greatest contentedness, satisfaction, and harmony? Trust your instincts. If stopping for ice cream or returning to the hotel for a dip feels like more fun than seeing another attraction, do it—even if it means wasting the remaining hours of an expensive admission pass.

The AGE THING

THERE'S A LOT OF SERIOUS COGITATION among parents and grandparents regarding how old a child should be before embarking on a trip to Disneyland. The answer, not always obvious, stems from the personalities and maturity of the children, and the personalities and parenting style of the adults.

Disneyland for Infants and Toddlers

unofficial **TIP**
Traveling with infants and toddlers sharpens parenting skills and makes the entire family more mobile and flexible, resulting in a richer, fuller life for all.

We believe that traveling with infants and toddlers is a great idea. Developmentally, travel is a stimulating learning experience for even the youngest of children. Infants, of course, won't know Mickey Mouse from a draft horse but will respond to sun and shade, music, bright colors, and the extra attention they receive from you.

From first steps to full mobility, toddlers respond to the excitement and spectacle of the Disneyland parks, though of course in a much different way than you do. Your toddler will prefer splashing in fountains and clambering over curbs and benches to experiencing most attractions, but no matter: he or she will still have a great time.

An Iowa City, Iowa, mother of three says, "Get over it!":

> *Get over it! In my opinion, people think too much about the age thing. If taking your 3-year-old would make you happy, that's all that counts. It doesn't matter if the trip is really for you or your child. You shouldn't have to jump through hoops to give yourself permission to go.*

unofficial **TIP**
Baby supplies—including disposable diapers, formula, and baby food—are for sale, and rockers and special chairs are available for nursing mothers at each park's Baby Care Center.

Somewhere between 4 and 6 years of age, your child will experience the first vacation that he or she will remember as an adult. Though more likely to remember the coziness of the hotel room than the theme parks, the child will be able to experience and comprehend many attractions. Even so, his or her favorite activity is likely to be swimming in the hotel pool.

As concerns infants and toddlers, there are good reasons and bad reasons for vacationing at Disneyland. A good reason for taking your little one to Disneyland Resort is that you want to go and there's no one available to care for your child during your absence. Philosophically, we are very much against putting your life (including your vacation) on hold until your children are older.

Especially if you have children of varying ages (or plan to, for that matter), it's better to take the show on the road than to wait until the youngest reaches the perceived ideal age. If your family includes a toddler or infant, you will find everything from private facilities for breastfeeding to changing tables in both men's and women's restrooms to facilitate baby's care.

An illogical reason, however, for taking an infant or toddler to Disneyland Resort is that you think Disneyland is the perfect vacation destination for babies. It's not, so think again if you are contemplating Disneyland Resort primarily for your child's enjoyment. For starters, attractions are geared more toward older children and adults. Even designer play areas such as the Pirate's Lair on Tom Sawyer Island in Disneyland Park are developed with older children in mind.

That said, let us stress that, for the well prepared, taking a toddler to Disneyland Resort can be a totally glorious experience. There's truly nothing like watching your child respond to the color, the sound, the festivity, and, most of all, the characters. You'll return home with photos that you will treasure forever. Your little one won't remember much, but your memories will be unforgettable.

If you elect to take your infant or toddler to Disneyland Resort, rest assured that their needs have been anticipated. The theme parks have centralized facilities for infant and toddler care. Everything necessary for changing diapers, preparing formula, and warming bottles and food is available. At the Disneyland Park, the Baby Care Center is next to the Plaza Inn at the end of Main Street and to the right. At Disney California Adventure (DCA) the Baby Care Center is tucked out of the way next to the Ghirardelli Chocolate Factory in the Pacific Wharf area of the park. Dads in charge of little ones are welcome at the centers and can use most services offered. In addition, men's restrooms in the parks have changing tables.

Infants and toddlers are allowed to experience any attraction that doesn't have minimum height or age restrictions. A mother of three from Utah wrote to us, saying:

We traveled with my 9-month-old, so we did the switching-off option a lot. However, I would appreciate it if you listed a complete list of all the rides that babies can be carried on. I was there alone with all three kids, and it would've been really nice to just look at a list of all the rides that we could've gone on with a baby.

*un*official **TIP**
Infants are easy travelers. As long as they are fed and comfortable, there is really no limit to what you can do when on the road with little ones. Food plus adequate rest are the perfect formula for happy babies.

It's actually far easier to list the attractions that you *can't* take a baby on at Disneyland. Unless a minimum height or age requirement is explicitly posted, children of any size—even handheld infants—are welcome on any ride. That includes all the family dark rides, kiddie carnival attractions, and slow-moving boats. On the following page is a table of all the rides that impose a height restriction; if a ride isn't listed, you can bring the

ATTRACTION MINIMUM HEIGHT REQUIREMENTS

DISNEYLAND PARK

Autopia 32" *(54" to drive unassisted)*

Big Thunder Mountain Railroad 40"

Gadget's Go Coaster 35"

Indiana Jones Adventure 46"

Matterhorn Bobsleds 42"

Millennium Falcon: **Smugglers Run** 38"

Space Mountain 40"

Splash Mountain 40"

Star Tours—The Adventures Continue 40"

Star Wars: Rise of the Resistance 40"

DISNEY CALIFORNIA ADVENTURE

Goofy's Sky School 42"

Grizzly River Run 42"

Guardians of the Galaxy—Mission: Breakout! 40"

Incredicoaster 48"

Jumpin' Jellyfish 40"

Luigi's Rollickin' Roadsters 32"

Mater's Junkyard Jamboree 32"

Radiator Springs Racers 40"

Redwood Creek Challenge Trail 42" **(rock wall and zip line only)**

Silly Symphony Springs 40" *(tandem swing)*   48" *(single swing)*

Soarin' around the world 40"

young 'uns along. But as a Minneapolis mother reports, some attractions are better for babies than others:

> *Shows and boat rides are easier for babies (ours was almost 1 year old, not yet walking). Rides where a bar comes down are doable but harder. Peter Pan's Flight was our first encounter with this type, and we had barely gotten situated when I realized that he might fall out of my grasp. The 3-D films are too intense; the noise level is deafening and the images inescapable.*
>
> *I thought you might want to know what a baby thought (based on his reactions). At Disneyland Park: Jungle Cruise: didn't get into it. Pirates of the Caribbean: slept through it. Mark Twain Riverboat: the horn made him cry. It's a Small World: wide-eyed, took it all in. Peter Pan's Flight: couldn't really sit on the seat. A bit dangerous. He didn't get into it. Disneyland Railroad: liked the motion and scenery.* Enchanted Tiki Room: *loved it. Danced, clapped, sang along.*

The same mom also advises:

> *We used a baby sling on our trip and thought it was great when standing in the lines—much better than a stroller, which you have to park before getting in line and navigate through crowds. It is impractical to go to the Baby Care Center every time your baby needs to nurse, so moms should be comfortable nursing in public situations.*

The rental strollers at the parks are designed for toddlers and children up to 4 and 5 years old but definitely not for infants. Still, if you bring pillows and padding, the strollers can be made to work. You can alternatively bring your own stroller, but only a limited number of non-collapsible strollers fit on each parking tram, and only collapsible strollers are allowed on Toy Story lot's shuttle buses.

Even if you opt for a stroller (your own or a rental), we recommend that you bring a baby sling or baby/child backpack. Simply put, there will be many times in the theme parks when you will have to park the stroller and carry your child.

Many nursing moms recommend breastfeeding during a dark Disney theater presentation. This only works, however, if the presentation is long enough for the baby to finish nursing. Shows at the Hyperion Theater at DCA are long enough (at least 45 minutes long), but the theater is not as dark as those that show films. Tomorrowland Theater at Disneyland Park is way too loud, as is the 3-D movie in Hollywood Land at DCA.

unofficial **TIP**
In addition to providing an alternative to carrying your child, a stroller serves as a handy cart for diaper bags, water bottles, and other necessary items.

Many Disney shows run back-to-back with only 1 or 2 minutes in between to change the audience. If you want to breastfeed and require more time than the length of the show, tell the cast member on entering that you want to breastfeed and ask if you can remain in the theater while your baby finishes.

If you can adjust to nursing in more public places with your breast and the baby's head covered with a shawl or some such, nursing will not be a problem at all. Even on the most crowded days, you can always find a back corner of a restaurant or a comparatively secluded park bench or garden spot to nurse.

A mom from Georgia writes:

> *Many women have no problem nursing uncovered, and they have the right to do so in public without being criticized. Even women who want to cover up may have a baby who won't cooperate and flings off the cover; plus, it's not necessary to sit through an entire show to feed your child. Babies will eat almost anywhere, and mothers shouldn't feel pressured to sneak off when a baby is hungry. Breastfeeding is normal and not something that needs to be hidden or covered.*

Disneyland for 4-, 5-, and 6-Year-Olds

Kids in this age group vary immensely in their capacity to comprehend and enjoy Disneyland Resort. With this age group, the go-no-go decision is a judgment call. If your child is sturdy, easygoing, and fairly adventuresome and demonstrates a high degree of independence, the trip will probably work. On the other hand, if your child tires easily, is temperamental, or is a bit timid or reticent in embracing new experiences, you're much better off waiting a few years. Whereas the travel and sensory-overload problems of infants and toddlers can be addressed and (usually) remedied on the go, discontented 4- to 6-year-olds have the ability to stop a family dead in its tracks, as this mother of three from Cape May, New Jersey, attests:

> *My 5-year-old was scared pretty badly on Snow White's Scary Adventures our first day. For the rest of the trip, we had to coax and reassure her before each and every ride before she would go.*

If you have a retiring, clinging, and/or difficult 4- to 6-year-old who, for whatever circumstances, will be part of your group, you can sidestep or diminish potential problems with a bit of preparation. Even if your preschooler is plucky and game, the same prep measures (described later in this section) will enhance his or her experience and make life easier for the rest of the family.

Parents who understand that a visit with 4- to 6-year-old children is going to be more about the cumulative experience than about seeing it all will have wonderful memories of their children's amazement.

The Ideal Age

Though our readers report successful trips as well as disasters with children of all ages, the consensus is that children's ages ideal for family compatibility and togetherness at Disneyland are 8–12 years. This age group is old enough, tall enough, and sufficiently stalwart to experience, understand, and appreciate practically all Disney attractions. Moreover, they are developed to the extent that they can get around the parks on their own steam without being carried or collapsing. Best of all, they are still young enough to enjoy being with Mom and Dad. From our experience, ages 10–12 are better than 8–9, though what you gain in maturity is at the cost of that irrepressible, wide-eyed wonder so prevalent in the 8- and 9-year-olds. A reader from Folsom, California, strongly agrees:

> *I recommend other families consider waiting until your kids are past the preschooler stage to go. My kids were 12, 10, and 6 (almost 7). These were the perfect ages for them to appreciate most of the attractions and also, generally, have the patience to wait in line and the stamina to tour the parks. They were also tall enough to go on anything.*

Disneyland for Teens

Teens love Disneyland, and for parents of teens, Disneyland Resort is a nearly perfect, albeit expensive, vacation choice. Though your teens might not be as wide-eyed and impressionable as their younger sibs, they are at an age where they can sample, understand, and enjoy practically everything Disneyland Resort has to offer.

For parents Disneyland Resort is a vacation destination where you can permit your teens an extraordinary amount of freedom. The entertainment is wholesome, the venues are safe, and the entire complex of hotels, theme parks, restaurants, and shopping is easily accessible on foot. Because most adolescents relish freedom, you may have difficulty keeping your teens with the rest of the family. Thus, if one of your objectives is to spend time with your teenage children during your Disneyland vacation, you will need to establish some clear-cut guidelines regarding togetherness and separateness before you leave home. Make your teens part of the discussion and try to meet them halfway in crafting a decision with which everyone can live. For your teens, touring on their own at Disneyland is tantamount to being independent in an exotic city. In any event, we're not suggesting that you just turn them loose. Rather, we are just attempting to sensitize you to the fact that, for your teens, some transcendent issues are involved. (Children must be at least 14 years old to enter a Disneyland Resort park without an accompanying parent or guardian.)

Most teens crave the company of other teens. If you have a solitary teen in your family, do not be surprised if he or she wants to invite a friend on your vacation. If you are invested in sharing intimate, quality time with your solitary teen, the presence of a friend will make this more difficult, if not impossible. However, if you turn down the request to bring a friend, be prepared to go the extra mile to be a companion to your teen at Disneyland. If you're a teen, it's not much fun to ride Space Mountain by yourself.

One specific issue that absolutely should be addressed before you leave home is what assistance (if any) you expect from your teen in regard to helping with younger children in the family. Once again, try to carve out a win-win compromise. Consider the case of the mother from Indiana who had a teenage daughter from an earlier marriage and two children under age 10 from a second marriage. After a couple of vacations where she thrust the unwilling teen into the position of being a surrogate parent to her half sisters, the teen declined henceforth to participate in family vacations.

Some parents have asked if there are unsafe places at Disneyland Resort or places where teens simply should not be allowed to go. Though the answer depends more on your family values and the relative maturity of your teens than on Disneyland Resort, the basic answer is no. Though it's true that teens who are looking for trouble can find it anywhere, there is absolutely nothing at Disneyland Resort that could be construed as a precipitant or a catalyst. Be advised, however, that adults consume alcohol at most Disneyland Resort restaurants outside of Disneyland Park. Also, be aware that some of the movies available at the cinemas at Downtown Disney demand the same discretion you exercise when allowing your kids to see movies at home.

About INVITING *Your* CHILDREN'S FRIENDS

IF YOUR CHILDREN WANT TO INVITE FRIENDS on your Disneyland vacation, give your decision careful thought. First, consider the logistics. Is there room in the car? Will you have to leave something at home that you had planned on taking to make room in the trunk for the friend's luggage? Will additional hotel rooms or a larger suite be required? Will the increased number of people in your group make it hard to get a table at a restaurant?

If you determine that you can logistically accommodate one or more friends, the next step is to consider how the inclusion of the friend will affect your group's dynamics. Generally speaking, the presence of a friend will make it harder to really connect with your own children. So if one of your vacation goals is an intimate bonding experience with your children, the addition of friends will possibly frustrate your attempts to realize that objective.

If family relationship building is not necessarily a primary objective of your vacation, it's quite possible that the inclusion of a friend will make life easier for you. This is especially true in the case of only children, who may otherwise depend exclusively on you to keep them happy and occupied. Having a friend along can take the pressure off and give you some much-needed breathing room.

If you allow a friend to accompany you, limit the selection to children you know really well and whose parents you also know. Your children's friends who have spent time in your home will have a sense of your parenting style, and you will have a sense of their personality, behavior, and compatibility with your family. Assess the prospective child's potential to fit in well on a long trip. Is he or she polite, personable, fun to be with, and reasonably mature? Does he or she relate well to you and to the other members of your family?

A trip to the mall including a meal in a sit-down restaurant will tell you volumes about the friend. Likewise, inviting the friend to share dinner with the family and then spend the night will provide a lot of relevant information. Ideally this type of evaluation should take place early on in the normal course of family events, before you discuss the possibility of a friend joining you on your vacation. This will allow you to size things up without your child (or the friend) realizing that an evaluation is taking place.

By seizing the initiative, you can guide the outcome. For example, Ann, a Redding, California, mom, anticipated that her 12-year-old son would ask to take a friend on their vacation. As she pondered the various friends her son might propose, she came up with four names. One, an otherwise sweet child, had a medical condition that Ann felt unqualified to monitor or treat. A second friend was overly aggressive with younger children and was often socially inappropriate for his age. Two other friends, Chuck and Marty, with whom she had had a generally positive experience, were good candidates for the trip. After orchestrating some opportunities to spend time with each of the boys, she made her decision and asked her son, "Would you like to take Marty with us to Disneyland?" Her son was delighted, and Ann had diplomatically preempted having to turn down friends her son might have proposed.

We recommend that you do the inviting, instead of your child, and that the invitation be extended parent to parent (to avoid disappointment, you might want to sound out the friend's parent before broaching the issue with your child). Observing this recommendation will allow you to query the friend's parents concerning food preferences, any medical conditions, how discipline is administered in the friend's family, and how the friend's parents feel about the way you administer discipline.

Before you extend the invitation, give some serious thought to who pays for what. Make a specific proposal for financing the trip a part of your invitation; for example: "There's room for Marty in the hotel room, and transportation's no problem because we're driving. So we'll just need you to pick up Marty's meals, theme park admissions, and spending money."

unofficial **TIP**
We suggest that you arrange for the friend's parents to reimburse you after the trip for things such as restaurant meals and admissions. This is much easier than trying to balance the books after every expenditure.

"HE WHO HESITATES IS LAUNCHED!" *Tips and Warnings for Grandparents*

SENIORS OFTEN GET INTO PREDICAMENTS caused by touring with grandchildren. Run ragged and pressured to endure a blistering pace, many seniors just concentrate on surviving Disneyland rather than enjoying it. The theme parks have as much to offer older visitors as they do children, and seniors must either set the pace or dispatch the young folks to tour on their own. An older reader writes:

> Being a senior is not for wusses. At Disney [parks] particularly, it requires courage and pluck. . . . Half the time, your grandchildren treat you like a crumbling ruin, and then turn around and trick you into getting on a roller coaster in the dark. Seniors have to be alert and not trust anyone. Not their children or even the Disney people, and especially not their grandchildren. When your grandchildren want you to go on a ride, don't follow along blindly like a lamb to the slaughter. Make sure you know what the ride is all about. Stand your ground and do not waffle. He who hesitates is launched!

If you don't get to see much of your grandchildren, you might think that Disneyland is the perfect place for a little bonding and togetherness. Wrong! Disneyland can potentially send children into system overload and precipitates behaviors that pose a challenge even to adoring parents, never mind grandparents. You don't take your grandchildren straight to Disneyland for the same reason you don't buy your 16-year-old son a Ferrari: handling it safely and well requires some experience.

Begin by spending time with your grandchildren in an environment that you can control. Have them over one at a time for dinner and to spend the night. Check out how they respond to your oversight and discipline. Most of all, zero in on whether you are compatible, enjoy each other's company, and have fun together. Determine that you can set limits and that they will accept those limits. When you reach this stage, you can contemplate some outings to the zoo, the mall, or the state fair. Gauge how demanding your grandchildren are when you are out of the house. Eat a meal or two in a full-service restaurant to get a sense of their social skills and their ability to behave appropriately. Don't expect perfection, and be prepared to modify your behavior a little too.

If you have a good relationship with your grandchildren and have had a positive one-on-one experience taking care of them, you might consider a trip to Disneyland. If you do, we recommend visiting Disneyland without them to get an idea of what you're getting into. A scouting trip will also allow you to enjoy some of the attractions that won't be on the itinerary when you return with the grandkids.

Tips for Grandparents

1. It's best to take one grandchild at a time, two at the most. Cousins can be better than siblings because they don't fight as much. To preclude sibling jealousy, try connecting the trip to a child's milestone, such as finishing the sixth grade.

2. Let your grandchildren help plan the vacation, and keep the first one short. Be flexible, and don't overplan.

3. Discuss mealtimes and bedtime. Fortunately, many grandparents are on an early dinner schedule, which works nicely with younger children.

4. Gear plans to your grandchildren's age levels, because if they're not happy, you won't be happy.

5. Create an itinerary that offers some supervised activities for children in case you need a rest.

6. If you're traveling by car, this is the one time we highly recommend earbuds. It's simply more enjoyable when everyone can listen to his or her own preferred style of music, at least for some portion of the trip.

7. Take along a night-light.

8. Carry a notarized statement from parents for permission for medical care in case of an emergency. Also be sure that you have insurance information and copies of any prescriptions for medicines the kids may take. Ditto for eyeglass prescriptions.

9. Tell your grandchildren about any medical problems you may have, so they can be prepared if there's an emergency.

10. Many attractions and hotels offer discounts for seniors, so be sure to check ahead of time for bargains.

11. Plan your evening meal early to avoid long waits. And make reservations if you're dining in a popular spot, even if it's early. Take some crayons and paper to keep kids occupied. If planning a family-friendly trip seems overwhelming, try a tour operator–travel agent aimed at kids and their grandparents.

A FEW WORDS *for* SINGLE PARENTS

BECAUSE SINGLE PARENTS are generally also working parents, planning a special getaway with your children can be the best way to spend some quality time together. But remember, the vacation is not just for your child—it's for you too. You might invite a grandparent or a favorite aunt or uncle along; the other adult provides nice company for you, and your child will benefit from the time with family members. You might likewise consider inviting an adult friend.

Though bringing along another adult is the best option, the reality is that many single parents don't have friends, grandparents, or favorite aunts or uncles who can make the trip. And while spending time with your child is wonderful, it is very difficult to match the energy level of your child if you are the sole focus of his or her world.

One alternative: Try to meet other single parents at Disneyland. It may seem odd, but most of them are in the same boat as you; besides, all you have to do is ask. Another option, albeit expensive, is to take along a trustworthy babysitter (18 or up) to travel with you.

The easiest way to meet other single parents is to hang out at the hotel pool. Make your way there on the day you arrive, after traveling by car or plane and without enough time to blow a full admission ticket at a theme park. In any event, a couple of hours spent poolside is a relaxing way to start your vacation.

If you visit Disneyland Resort with another single parent, get adjoining rooms; take turns watching all the kids; and, on at least one night, get a sitter and enjoy an evening out.

Throughout this book we mention the importance of good planning and touring. For a single parent, this is an absolute must. In addition, make sure that you set aside downtime each day back at the hotel.

Finally, don't try to spend every moment with your children on vacation. Instead, plan some activities for your children with other children. Then take advantage of your free time to do what you want to do: Read a book, have a massage, take a long walk, or enjoy a catnap.

HOW *to* CHILDPROOF *a* HOTEL ROOM

TODDLERS AND SMALL CHILDREN up to 3 years of age (and sometimes older) can wreak mayhem if not outright disaster in a hotel room. They're mobile, curious, and amazingly fast, and they have a penchant for turning the most seemingly innocuous furnishing or decoration into a lethal weapon. Here's what to look for.

Begin by checking the room for hazards that you cannot neutralize, such as balconies, chipping paint, cracked walls, sharp surfaces, and windows that can't be secured shut. If you encounter anything that you don't like or is too much of a hassle to fix, ask for another room.

If you use a crib supplied by the hotel, make sure the mattress is firm and covers the entire bottom of the crib. If there is a mattress cover, it should fit tightly. Slats should be $2\frac{3}{8}$ inches (about the width of a soda can) or less apart. Test the drop sides to ensure that they work properly and that your child cannot release them accidentally. Examine the crib from all angles (including from underneath) to make sure that it has been assembled correctly and that there are no sharp edges. Check for potentially toxic substances that your child might ingest. Wipe down surfaces that your child might touch to diminish the potential of infection transmitted from a previous occupant. Finally, position the crib away from drape cords, heaters, wall sockets, and air conditioners.

If your infant can turn over, we recommend changing him or her on a pad on the floor. Likewise, if you have a child seat of any sort, place it where it cannot be knocked over, and always strap your child in.

If your child can roll, crawl, or walk, you should bring about eight electrical outlet covers and some cord to tie cabinets shut and to bind drape cords and the like out of reach. Check for appliances, lamps, ashtrays, ice buckets, and anything else that your child might pull down on him- or herself. Have the hotel remove coffee tables with sharp edges and both real and artificial plants that are within your child's reach. Round up items from tables and countertops such as matchbooks, courtesy toiletries, and drinking glasses and store them out of reach.

If the bathroom door can be accidentally locked, cover the locking mechanism with duct tape or a doorknob cover. Use the security chain or upper latch on the room's entrance door to ensure that your child doesn't open it without your knowledge.

Inspect the floor and remove pins, coins, and other foreign objects that your child might find. Don't forget to check under beds and furniture. One of the best tips we've heard came from a Fort Lauderdale, Florida, mother who crawls around the room on her hands and knees to see possible hazards from her child's perspective.

If you rent a suite, you'll have more territory to childproof and will have to deal with the possible presence of a stove, a refrigerator, cooking utensils, and low cabinet doors, among other things. Sometimes the best option is to seal off the kitchen with a safety gate.

PHYSICAL PREPARATION

YOU'LL FIND THAT some physical conditioning, coupled with a realistic sense of the toll that Disneyland takes on your body, will preclude falling apart in the middle of your vacation. As one of our readers put it, "If you pay attention to eat, heat, feet, and sleep, you'll be OK."

As you contemplate the stamina of your family, it's important to understand that somebody is going to run out of steam first, and when they do, the whole family will be affected. Sometimes a cold drink or a snack will revive the flagging member. Sometimes, however, no amount of cajoling or treats will work. In this situation it's crucial that you recognize that the child, grandparent, or spouse is at the end of his or her rope. The correct decision is to get them back to the hotel. Pushing the exhausted beyond their capacity will spoil the day for them—and you. Accept that stamina and energy levels vary, and be prepared to administer to members of your family who poop out. One more thing: no guilt trips. "We've driven 300 miles to take you to Disneyland, and now you're going to ruin everything!" is not an appropriate response.

THE AGONY OF THE FEET

IF YOU SPEND A DAY at Disneyland Park, you will walk 3–6 miles! If you walk to the park from your hotel, you can add 1–2 miles, and another couple of miles if you park-hop to DCA. The walking, however, will be nothing like a 5-mile hike in the woods. At Disneyland Park and DCA, you will be in direct sunlight most of the time, navigate through huge jostling crowds, walk on hot pavement, and endure waits in line between bursts of walking. The bottom line, if you haven't figured it out, is that Disney theme parks (especially in the summer) are not for wimps, as this step-tracking reader from Phoenix, Arizona, was surprised to discover:

> We walked more than the equivalent of two marathons in four days. When I consider that people train for marathons for months in advance, I feel a little bit better about needing a few days post-vacation to recover!

Prevent Blisters In Five Easy Steps

1. PREPARE As mentioned above, you can easily cover 5–10 miles a day at the parks, so get your feet and legs into shape before you leave home. Though most children are active, their normal play usually doesn't condition them for the exertion of touring a Disney theme park. We recommend starting a program of family walks 6 weeks or more before your trip. A Pennsylvania mom who did just that offers the following:

> We had our 6-year-old begin walking with us a bit every day one month before leaving—when we arrived [at Walt Disney World], her little legs could carry her and she had a lot of stamina.

Start with short walks around the neighborhood. Increase your distance gradually until you can do 6 miles without needing CPR. As you begin, remember that little people have little strides, and though your 6-year-old may create the appearance of running circles around you, consider that (1) he won't have the stamina to go at that pace very long, and (2) more to the point, he probably has to take two strides or so to every one of yours to keep up when you walk together.

2. PAY ATTENTION During your training program, your feet will tell you if you're wearing the right shoes. Choose well-constructed, broken-in running or hiking shoes. If you feel a "hot spot" coming on, chances are a blister isn't far behind. The most common sites for blisters are heels, toes, and balls of feet. If you develop a hot spot in the same place every time you walk, cover it with a blister bandage (such as Johnson & Johnson) or cushion before you set out.

Don't wear sandals, flip-flops, or slip-ons in the theme parks. Even if your feet don't blister, they'll get stepped on by other guests or run over by strollers.

3. SOCK IT UP Good socks are as important as good shoes. When you walk, your feet sweat like a mule in a peat bog, and the moisture only increases friction. To counteract friction, wear socks made from material such as Smartwool or CoolMax, which wicks perspiration away from your feet (Smartwool socks come in varying thicknesses). To further combat moisture, dust your feet with antifungal powder.

4. DON'T BE A HERO Take care of foot problems the minute you notice them. Carry a small foot-emergency kit with gauze, antibiotic ointment, disinfectant, and moleskin or blister bandages. Extra socks and foot powder are optional.

If carrying all of that sounds like too much, stop by a park First Aid Center as soon as you notice a hot spot forming on your foot.

5. CHECK THE KIDS Young children might not say anything about blisters forming until it's too late. Stop several times a day and check their feet. If you find a blister, either treat it using the kit you're carrying, or stop by a First Aid Center.

Finally, a stroller will provide your child the option of walking or riding, and if he poops out, you won't have to carry him. Even if your child hardly uses the stroller, it serves as a convenient place for water bottles and other stuff you may not feel like carrying. Strollers at Disneyland are covered in detail beginning on page 134.

REST AND RELAXATION

PHYSICAL CONDITIONING is important but is not a substitute for rest. Even marathon runners need recovery time. If you push too hard and try to do too much, you'll either crash or, at a minimum, turn what should be fun into an ordeal. Rest means plenty of sleep at night and, if possible, naps during the afternoon and planned breaks in your vacation itinerary. And don't forget that the brain, as well as the body, needs rest and relaxation. The stimulation inherent in touring a Disney theme park is enough to put many children and some adults into system overload. It is imperative that you remove your family from this unremitting assault on the senses and do something relaxing and quiet such as swimming or reading.

The theme parks are pretty big, so don't try to see everything in one day. Even during the off-season, when the crowds are smaller and the temperatures more pleasant, the size of the theme parks will exhaust most children under age 8 by lunchtime. A Texas family underscores the importance of naps and rest:

> Despite not following any of your touring plans, we did follow the theme of visiting a specific park in the morning, leaving midafternoon for either a nap back at the room or a trip to the pool, and then returning to one of the parks in the evening. On the few occasions we skipped your advice, I was muttering to myself by dinner. I can't tell you what I was muttering.

When it comes to naps, this mom does not mince words:

One last thing for parents of small kids—take the book's advice and get out of the park and take the nap, take the nap, TAKE THE NAP! Never in my life have I seen so many parents screaming at, ridiculing, or slapping their kids. (What a vacation!) Disney [parks are] overwhelming for kids and adults.

A mom from Rochester, New York, was equally adamant:

You absolutely must rest during the day. Kids went 8 a.m.–9 p.m. in the park. Kids did great that day, but we were all completely worthless the next day. Definitely must pace yourself.

If you plan to return to your hotel at midday and would like your room made up, let housekeeping know before you leave in the morning. If the location of your hotel room makes returning to the room impractical, you should still find alternative ways to take an afternoon break, as this California family advises:

We found it to be less tiring to just get off our feet within a park, have a cool drink, and sit in some shade than to add in an extra trip to and from the hotel.

The Main Street Opera House and old motorboat landing at Disneyland, Disney Animation and the Boudin Bakery Tour at DCA, and the lobby of the Grand Californian Hotel are all great places to pause and recharge without leaving the resort.

Routines That Travel

If when at home you observe certain routines—for example, reading a book before bed or having a bath first thing in the morning—try to incorporate these familiar activities into your vacation schedule. They will provide your children with a sense of security and normalcy.

Maintaining a normal routine is especially important with toddlers, as a mother of two from Lawrenceville, Georgia, relates:

The first day, we tried an early start, so we woke the children (ages 2 and 4) and hurried them to get going. BAD IDEA with toddlers. This put them off schedule for naps and meals the rest of the day. It is best to let young ones stay on their regular schedule and see Disney at their own pace, and you'll have much more fun.

DEVELOPING *a* GOOD PLAN

ALLOW YOUR CHILDREN to participate in the planning of your time at Disneyland. Guide them diplomatically through the options, establishing advance decisions about what to do each

unofficial **TIP**
To keep your thinking fresh and to adequately cover all bases, develop your plan in two or three family meetings no longer than 40 minutes each. You'll discover that all members of the family will devote a lot of thought to the plan both in and between meetings. Don't try to anticipate every conceivable contingency, or you'll end up with something as detailed and unworkable as the tax code.

day. Begin with your trip to Disneyland, deciding what time to depart, who sits by the window, whether to stop for meals or eat in the car, and so on. For the Disneyland part of your vacation, build consensus for wake-up call, bedtime, and naps into the itinerary, and establish ground rules for eating, buying refreshments, and shopping. Determine the order for visiting the two theme parks and make a list of must-see attractions. To help you fill in the blanks of your days, and especially to prevent you from spending most of your time standing in line, we offer a number of field-tested touring plans. The plans are designed to minimize your waiting time at each park by providing step-by-step itineraries that route you counter to the flow of traffic. The plans are explained in greater detail starting on page 73.

Generally, it's better to just sketch in the broad strokes on the master plan. The detail of what to do when you actually arrive at the park can be decided the night before you go, or with the help of one of our touring plans once you get there. Above all, be flexible. One important caveat: Make sure that you keep any promises or agreements that you make when planning. They may not seem important to you, but they will to your children, who will remember for a long, long time if you let them down.

The more you can agree to and nail down in advance, the less potential you'll have for disagreement and confrontation once you arrive. Because children are more comfortable with the tangible than the conceptual, and also because they sometimes have short memories, we recommend typing up all of your decisions and agreements and providing a copy to each child. Create a fun document, not a legalistic one. You'll find that your children will review it in anticipation of all the things they will see and do, will consult it often, and will even read it to their younger siblings.

Your itinerary should provide minimum structure and maximum flexibility, specifying which park the family will tour each day without attempting to nail down exactly what the family will do there. No matter how detailed your itinerary is, be prepared for surprises at Disneyland, both good and bad. If an unforeseen event renders part of the plan useless or impractical, just roll with it. And always remember that it's your itinerary; you created it, and you can change it. Just try to make any changes the result of family discussion and be especially careful not to scrap an element of the plan that your children perceive as something you promised them.

LOGISTIC PREPARATION

WHEN WE WERE DISCUSSING good logistic preparation for a Disneyland vacation, a friend from Phoenix said, "Wait, what's the big deal? You pack clothes, a few games for the car, and go!" So OK, we confess, that will work, but life can be sweeter and the vacation smoother (as well as less expensive) with the right gear.

CLOTHING

LET'S START WITH CLOTHES. We recommend springing for vacation uniforms. Buy for each child several sets of jeans (or shorts) and T-shirts, all matching, and all the same. For a one-week trip, for example, get each child three pairs of khaki shorts, three light-yellow T-shirts, and three pairs of Smartwool or Coolmax hiking socks. What's the point? First, you don't have to play fashion designer, coordinating a week's worth of stylish combos. It's simple, it saves time, and there are no decisions to make or arguments about what to wear. Second, uniforms make your children easier to spot and keep together in the theme parks. Third, the uniforms give your family, as well as the vacation itself, some added identity. If you're like an ever-increasing number of families we see in the parks, you might go so far as to create a logo for the trip to be printed on the shirts.

unofficial **TIP** Give your teens the job of coming up with the logo for your shirts. They will love being the family designers.

Buy short-sleeved shirts in light colors for warm weather, or long-sleeved, darker-colored T-shirts for cooler weather. All-cotton shirts are a little cooler and more comfortable in hot, humid weather. Polyester-cotton blend shirts are more wrinkle-resistant and dry a bit faster if they get wet.

unofficial **TIP** Equip each child with a big bandanna. These come in handy for wiping noses, scouring ice cream from chins and mouths, and dabbing sweat from the forehead and can also be tied around the neck to protect from sunburn.

LABELS A great idea, especially for younger children, is to attach labels with your family name, hometown, the name of your hotel, the dates of your stay, and your cell phone number inside the shirt—for example:

**HODDER FAMILY OF DENVER, CO.;
CAMELOT INN; MAY 5–12; 303-555-2108**

Instruct your smaller children to show the label to an adult if they get separated from you. Elimination of the child's first name (which most children of talking age can articulate in any event) allows you to order labels that are all the same, that can be used by anyone in the family, and that can also be affixed to such easily lost items as hats, jackets, hip packs, ponchos, and umbrellas. If fooling with labels sounds like too much of a hassle, check out "Lost Children" (pages 149–151) for some alternatives.

unofficial **TIP** If your kids are little and don't mind a hairdo change, consider getting them a short haircut before you leave home. Not only will they be cooler and more comfortable, but— especially with your girls— you'll save them (and yourselves) the hassle of tangles and about 20 minutes of foo-fooing a day.

DRESSING FOR COOLER WEATHER Southern California experiences temperatures all over the scale November–March, so it could be a bit chilly if you visit during those months. Our suggestion is to layer: for example, a breathable, waterproof or water-resistant windbreaker over a light, long-sleeved polypropylene shirt over a long-sleeved T-shirt. As with the baffles of a sleeping bag or down coat, the air trapped between the layers is what keeps you warm. If all the layers are thin, you won't be left with something bulky to cart around if you want to pull off one or more. Later in this section, we'll advocate wearing a hip pack. Each layer should be sufficiently compactible to fit easily in that hip pack along with whatever else is in it.

ACCESSORIES

FOR YOUR CHILDREN we recommend pants with elastic waistbands; this eliminates the need to wear a belt (one less thing to find when you're trying to leave). If your children like belts or want to carry an item suspended from their belts, buy them military-style 1½-inch-wide web belts at any Army–Navy surplus or camping equipment store. The belts weigh less than half as much as leather, are cooler, and are washable.

SUNGLASSES Smog notwithstanding, the California sun is so bright and the glare so blinding that we recommend sunglasses for each family member. For children and adults of all ages, a good accessory item is an eyeglass strap for spectacles or sunglasses. The best models have a little device for adjusting the amount of slack in the strap. This allows your child to comfortably hang sunglasses from his or her neck when indoors or, alternately, to secure them fast to his or her head while experiencing a fast ride outdoors.

HIP PACKS AND WALLETS Unless you are touring with an infant or toddler, the largest thing anyone in your family should carry is a hip pack or fanny pack. Each person should have one. The pack should be large enough to carry at least a half-day's worth of snacks and other items deemed necessary (lip balm, bandanna, antibacterial hand gel, and so on) and still have enough room left to stash a hat, poncho, or light windbreaker. We recommend buying full-size hip packs at outdoor retailers as opposed to small, child-size hip packs. The packs are light; can be made to fit any child large enough to tote a hip pack; have slip-resistant, comfortable, wide belting; and will last for years.

Do not carry billfolds or wallets, car keys, Disney Resort IDs, or room keys in your hip packs because children tend to inadvertently drop their wallet in the process of rummaging around in their hip packs for snacks and other items.

You should weed through your billfold and remove to a safe place anything that you will not need on your vacation (photos, library card, department store credit cards, business cards, and so on). In addition to having a lighter wallet to lug around, you will decrease your exposure in the event that your wallet is lost or stolen. When we are working at Disneyland, we carry a small profile billfold with a driver's license, a credit card, our room key, and a small amount of cash. You don't need anything else.

DAY PACKS We see a lot of folks at Disneyland carrying day packs (that is, small, frameless backpacks) and/or water bottle belts that strap around your waist. Day packs might be a good choice if you plan to carry a lot of camera equipment or if you need to carry baby supplies on your person. Otherwise, try to travel as light as possible. Packs are hot, cumbersome, and not very secure, and they must be removed every time you get on a ride or sit down for a show. Hip packs, by way of contrast, can simply be rotated around the waist from your back to your abdomen if you need to sit down. Additionally, our observation has been that the contents of one day pack can usually be redistributed to two or so hip packs (except in the case of camera equipment).

CAPS Kids pull caps on and off as they enter and exit attractions, restrooms, and restaurants, and—big surprise—they lose them. If your children are partial to caps, purchase a short, light cord with little alligator clips on both ends, sold at ski and camping supply stores. Hook one clip to the shirt collar and the other to the hat.

RAINGEAR Rain is a fact of life, though persistent rain day after day is unusual. Check out the Weather Channel or weather forecasts online for three or so days before you leave home to see if any major storm systems are heading for Southern California. Weather predictions concerning systems and fronts four to seven days out are pretty reliable. If it appears that you might see some rough weather during your visit, you're better off bringing raingear from home. If, however, nothing big is on the horizon weather wise, you can take your chances.

Ponchos sell for about $12 adults, $10 child, and are available in seemingly every retail shop; they're even cheaper at local discount stores (such as Target). If you do find yourself in a big storm, you'll want to have both a poncho and an umbrella. As one Unofficial reader puts it, "Umbrellas make the rain much more bearable. When rain isn't beating down on your ponchoed head, it's easier to ignore."

And consider this tip from a Memphis, Tennessee, mom:

Scotchgard your shoes. The difference is unbelievable.

MISCELLANEOUS ITEMS

MEDICATION Some parents of hyperactive children on medication discontinue or decrease the child's normal dosage at the end of the school year. Be aware that the Disneyland parks might overly stimulate such a child. Consult your physician before altering your child's medication regimen. Also, if your child has attention deficit disorder, remember that especially loud sounds can drive him or her right up the wall. Unfortunately, some Disney theater attractions are almost unbearably loud.

unofficial **TIP**
Several companies, such as Neutrogena and California Baby, make sunscreens that won't burn your eyes. Look for a product *without* the active ingredient avobenzone, which is usually the culprit when it comes to stinging and burning.

SUNSCREEN Overheating and sunburn are among the most common problems of younger children at Disneyland. Carry and use sunscreen of SPF 30 or higher. Be sure to put some on kids in strollers, even if the stroller has a canopy. Some of the worst cases of sunburn we've seen were on the exposed foreheads and feet of toddlers and infants in

RESPECT FOR THE SUN

Health and science writer **Avery Hurt** sheds some light on the often confusing products and methods for avoiding sunburn. Here's the basic advice from the medical experts.

• **Choose a sunscreen that is convenient for you to use.** Some prefer sprays, others lotions. The form of sunscreen doesn't matter as much as the technique of applying it.

• **Apply sunscreen a half hour before going out,** and be sure to get enough on you. One ounce per application is recommended—that means a full shot glass worth each time you apply. The 1-ounce amount was calculated for average adults in swimsuits; an average 7-year-old will probably take two-thirds of an ounce (20 cc). It's a good idea to measure that ounce in your hands at home, so you'll be familiar with what an ounce looks like in your palms. It's far more sunscreen than you tend to think.

• **Get a generous covering on all exposed skin.** Then reapply (another full shot glass) every 2 hours or after swimming or sweating. No matter what it says on the label, water resistance of sunscreen is limited. And none of them last all day.

• **There is very little difference in protection** between 30 or so SPF and 45 or 50 or greater. There is no need to spend more for higher SPF numbers. In fact, it is much safer to choose a lower (and typically less expensive) SPF (as long as it is at least 30) and apply it more often. However, do be sure to choose a product that has broad-spectrum coverage, meaning that it filters out both UVA and UVB rays. As long as the SPF is at least 30 and offers broad-spectrum protection, one brand can serve the whole family. There's no need to pay extra for special formulas made for children.

• **It is best to keep babies under 6 months old covered** and out of the sun. However, the American Academy of Pediatrics condones a small amount of sunscreen on vulnerable areas, such as the nose and chin, when you have your baby out. Be very careful to monitor your baby even if he is wearing a hat and sitting under an umbrella.

• **Use a lip balm** with an SPF of 15 and reapply often to your own lips and those of your kids. Again, the brand is less important than choosing something that you will use—and remembering to use it.

• **Sunglasses are also a must.** Too much sun exposure can contribute to age-related macular degeneration (among other things). Not all sunglasses filter out damaging rays. Be sure to choose shades (for adults and kids) that have 99% UV protection. Large lenses and wraparound styles might not look as cool, but they offer much better protection. You may have to spend a little more to be sure you are getting adequate protection, but you don't want to skimp on this.

• **If you do get a burn,** cool baths, aloe gels, and ibuprofen usually help ease the suffering. Occasionally sunburns can be as dangerous in the short term as they are in the long term. If you or your child experience nausea, vomiting, high fever, severe pain, confusion, or fainting, seek medical care immediately.

strollers. Protect skin from overexposure. To avoid overheating, rest regularly in the shade or in an air-conditioned restaurant or show.

WATER BOTTLES Don't count on keeping young children hydrated with soft drinks and water fountains. Long lines may impede buying refreshments, and fountains may not be handy. Furthermore, excited children may not realize or tell you that they're thirsty or hot. We recommend carrying bottles of water and sports drinks. Bottled water is about $4 in all major parks, or bring your own water bottle and strap from home.

COOLERS AND MINI-FRIDGES If you drive to Disneyland, bring two coolers: a small one for drinks in the car and a large one for the hotel room. If you fly and rent a car, stop and purchase a large biodegradable cooler, which can be discarded at the end of the trip. If you will be without a car, book a hotel with mini-fridges in each room. All on-site Disneyland hotels provide free mini-fridges and coffee makers. If mini-fridges aren't provided, rent one from the hotel.

Coolers and mini-fridges allow you to have breakfast in your hotel room, store snacks and lunch supplies to take to the theme parks, and supplant expensive vending machines for snacks and beverages at the hotel. To keep the contents of your cooler cold, freeze a 2-gallon milk jug full of water before you head out. In a good cooler, it will take the jug five or more days to thaw. If you buy a biodegradable cooler, you can use bagged ice and ice from the ice machine at your hotel. Even if you have to rent a mini-fridge, you will save a bundle of cash as well as significant time by reducing dependence on restaurant meals and expensive snacks and drinks purchased from vendors.

unofficial **TIP**
About two weeks before arriving, ship a box to your hotel containing food, plastic cutlery, and toiletries, plus pretty much any other consumables that might come in handy during your stay. If you fly, this helps avoid overweight baggage fees and problems with liquid restrictions for carry-on luggage.

FOOD-PREP KIT If you plan to make sandwiches, bring along condiments and seasonings from home. A typical travel kit will include mayonnaise, ketchup, mustard, salt and pepper, and packets of artificial sweetener or sugar. Also throw in some plastic knives and spoons, napkins, plastic cups, and plastic zip-top bags. For breakfast you will need some plastic bowls for cereal. Of course, you can buy this stuff in Anaheim, but you probably won't consume it all, so why waste the money? If you drink bottled beer or wine, bring a bottle opener and corkscrew.

ENERGY BOOSTERS Kids get cranky when they're hungry, and when that happens, your entire group has a problem. Like many parents you might, for nutritional reasons, keep a tight rein on snacks available to your children at home. At Disneyland, however, maintaining energy and equanimity trumps snack discipline. For maximum zip and contentedness, give your kids snacks containing complex carbohydrates (fruits, crackers, nonfat energy bars, and the like) before they get hungry or show signs of exhaustion. You should avoid snacks that are high in fats and proteins because these foods take a long time to digest and will tend to unsettle your stomach if it's a hot day.

An experienced and wise grandma underscores the point:

> Children who get cranky during a visit often do so from all that time and energy expended without food. Feed them! A snack at any price goes a long way to keeping the little kids happy and enjoying the parks, and keeping parents sane. The security people are very nice about you taking snacks or drinks in, but DO NOT bring glass containers. That is apparently what they are really looking for.

ELECTRONICS Regardless of your kid's ages, always bring a night-light. Flashlights are handy for finding stuff in a room after the kids are asleep.

Tablets, iPods, and handheld video games are often controversial gear for a family outing. We recommend compromise. Earbuds allow kids to create their own space even when they're with others, and that can be a safety valve. That said, try to agree before the trip on some parameters, so you don't begin to feel as if they're being used to keep other family members and the trip itself at a distance. If you're traveling by car, take turns choosing the radio station or playlist for part of the trip.

Likewise, cell phones are a mixed blessing. On the one hand, they can be invaluable in an emergency or if your party wants to split up, and if you have a smartphone, you can use Disneyland's app to see current wait times in the parks. Unfortunately, they also lead to guests missing out on what's around them and bumping into each other because they're glued to a tiny screen. Disneyland's free Wi-Fi is still somewhat unreliable, and local cell towers become overloaded on busy days, so posting social media from the parks may drain your phone in a matter of hours. Put your device in airplane mode when you aren't using it, and see page 103 for more power-saving tips.

Be especially cautious about taking expensive iPads or other tablets into the parks, and for Mickey's sake, beware while using them as cameras during shows and parades, lest you blind or block everyone behind you. Also, selfie sticks are not allowed in Disney parks, though collapsible monopods and tripods are OK. Any friendly cast member will be happy to take your photo for you the old-fashioned way.

DON'T FORGET THE TENT When Bob's daughter was preschool age, he almost went crazy trying to get her to sleep in a shared hotel room. She was accustomed to having her own room at home and was hyperstimulated whenever she traveled. Bob tried makeshift curtains and room dividers and even rearranged the furniture in a few hotel rooms to create the illusion of a more private, separate space for her. It was all for naught. It wasn't until she was around 4 years old and Bob took her camping that he seized on an idea that had some promise. She liked the cozy, secure, womblike feel of a backpacking tent and quieted down much more readily than she ever had in hotel rooms. So the next time the family stayed in a hotel, he pitched his backpacking tent in the corner of the room. In she went, nested for a bit, and fell asleep.

Modern tents are self-contained with floors and an entrance that can be zipped up for privacy but cannot be locked. Affordable and sturdy, many are as simple to put up as opening an umbrella. Some tents are even specifically made to turn a bed into a fort. Kids appreciate having their own space and enjoy the adventure of being in a tent, even one set up in the corner of a hotel room. Sizes range from children's play tents with a 2- to 3-foot base to models large enough to sleep two or three husky teens. Light and compact when stored, a two-adult-size tent in its own storage bag (called a stuff sack) will take up about one-tenth or less of a standard overhead bin on a commercial airliner. Another option for infants and toddlers is to drape a sheet over a portable crib or playpen to make a tent.

THE BOX Bob here: On one memorable Disneyland excursion when my children were younger, we began each morning with an immensely annoying, involuntary scavenger hunt. Invariably, seconds before our scheduled departure to the theme park, we discovered that some combination of shoes, billfolds, sunglasses, hip packs, or other necessities were missing. For the next 15 minutes we would root through the room like pigs hunting truffles in an attempt to locate the absent items. I finally swung by a local store and mooched a big empty box. From then on, every time we returned to the room, I had the kids deposit shoes, hip packs, and other potentially wayward items in the box. After that the box was off-limits until the next morning, when I doled out the contents.

PLASTIC GARBAGE BAGS At the Grizzly River Run raft ride at DCA and at Splash Mountain in Disneyland Park, you are certain to get wet and possibly soaked. If it's really hot and you don't care, then fine. But if it's cool or you're just not up for a soaking, bring a large plastic trash bag or a cheap poncho to the park. By cutting holes in the top and on the sides of a trash bag, you can fashion a sack poncho that will keep your clothes from getting wet. On the raft ride, you will also get your feet wet. If you're not up for walking around in squishing, soaked shoes, bring a second, smaller plastic bag to wear over your feet while riding. Even if you don't mind getting wet yourself, a small zip-top bag (or free plastic bag from a gift shop) is handy for saving your cell phone and wallet from a fatal soaking.

SUPPLIES FOR INFANTS AND TODDLERS

BASED ON RECOMMENDATIONS from hundreds of Unofficial Guide readers, here's what we suggest that you carry with you when touring with infants and toddlers:

- A disposable diaper for every hour you plan to be away from your hotel
- A cloth diaper or kitchen towel to put over your shoulder for burping
- Two receiving blankets: one to wrap the baby and one to lay the baby on or to drape over you when you nurse
- Ointment for diaper rash
- A package of wipes

- Prepared formula in bottles if you are not breastfeeding
- A washable bib, baby spoon, and baby food if your infant is eating solids
- For toddlers, a small toy for comfort and to keep them occupied during attractions

Baby Care Centers at the theme parks will sell you just about anything that you forget or run out of. Like all things Disney, prices will be higher than elsewhere, but at least you won't need to detour to a drugstore in the middle of your touring day.

REMEMBERING *Your* TRIP

1. Purchase a notebook for each child and spend time each evening recording the day's events. If your children have trouble getting motivated or don't know what to write about, start a discussion; otherwise, let them write or draw whatever they want to remember from the day.

2. Collect mementos along the way and create a treasure box in a small tin or cigar box. Months or years later, it's fun to look at postcards, pins, or ticket stubs to jump-start a memory.

3. Add inexpensive postcards to your photographs to create an album; then write a few words on each page to accompany the images.

4. Give each child a disposable camera to record his or her version of the trip. One 5-year-old snapped an entire series of photos that never showed anyone above the waist—his view of Disneyland (and the photos were priceless).

5. Many families travel with a digital camera or camera phone, though we recommend using one sparingly—parents end up viewing the trip through the lens rather than being in the moment. If you must, take it along, but only record a few moments of major sights (too much is boring anyway). And let the kids record and narrate. On the topic of narration, speak loudly so as to be heard over the not-insignificant background noise of the parks. Make use of lockers at the parks when the equipment becomes a burden or when you're going to experience an attraction that might damage it or get it wet. Unless you have a camera designed for underwater shots or a waterproof carrying case, leave it behind on Splash Mountain, the Grizzly River Run, and any other ride where water is involved. Don't forget extra batteries or external battery chargers.

6. Consider using Disney's PhotoPass service for some professional-quality pictures; it's free to use and you only pay for the images you want to keep (see pages 103–104 for details).

Finally, when it comes to taking photos and collecting mementos, don't let the tail wag the dog. You are not going to Disneyland to build the biggest scrapbook in history. Or as this Houston mom put it:

Tell your readers to get a grip on the photography thing. We were so busy shooting pictures that we kind of lost the thread. We had to look at our pictures when we got home to see what all we did [while on vacation].

TRIAL RUN

IF YOU GIVE THOUGHTFUL CONSIDERATION to all areas of mental, physical, organizational, and logistical preparation discussed in this chapter, what remains is to familiarize yourself with the Disneyland parks and, of course, to conduct your field test. Yep, that's right, we want you to take the whole platoon on the road for a day to see if you are combat ready. No joke—this is important. You'll learn who tuckers out first, who's prone to developing blisters, who has to pee every 11 seconds, who keeps losing her cap, and, given the proper forum, how compatible your family is in terms of what you like to see and do.

For the most informative trial run, choose a local venue that requires lots of walking, dealing with crowds, and making decisions on how to spend your time. Regional theme parks and state fairs are your best bets, followed by large zoos and museums. Devote the whole day. Kick off the morning with an early start, just like you will at Disneyland, paying attention to who's organized and ready to go and who's dragging his or her butt and holding up the group. If you have to drive 1 or 2 hours to get to your test venue, no big deal. You may have to do some commuting at Disneyland too. Spend the whole day, eat a couple of meals, and stay late.

Don't mess with the outcome by telling everyone that you are practicing for Disneyland. Everyone behaves differently when they know that they are being tested or evaluated. Your objective is to find out as much as you can about how the individuals in your family, as well as the family as a group, respond to and deal with everything they experience during the day. Pay attention to who moves quickly and who is slow; who is adventuresome and who is reticent; who keeps going and who needs frequent rest breaks; who sets the agenda and who is content to follow; who is easily agitated and who stays cool; who tends to dawdle or wander off; who is curious and who is bored; who is demanding and who is accepting. You get the idea.

Discuss the findings of the test run with your spouse the next day. Don't be discouraged if your test day wasn't perfect; few (if any) are. Distinguish between problems that are remediable and problems that are intrinsic to your family's emotional or physical makeup (no amount of hiking, for example, will toughen up some people's feet).

Establish a plan for addressing remediable problems (further conditioning, setting limits before you go, trying harder to achieve family consensus) and develop strategies for minimizing or working around problems that are a fact of life (waking sleepyheads 15 minutes early, placing moleskin on likely blister sites before setting out, or packing familiar food for the toddler who balks at restaurant fare). If you are an attentive observer, a fair diagnostician, and a creative problem solver, you'll be able to work out many of the problems you're likely to encounter at Disneyland before you leave home.

ABOUT THE UNOFFICIAL GUIDE TOURING PLANS   Parents who embark on one of our touring plans are often frustrated by the various interruptions and delays occasioned by their small children. In case you haven't given the subject much thought, here is what to expect:

1.   Many small children will stop dead in their tracks whenever they see a Disney character. Our advice: Live with it. An attempt to haul your children away before they have satisfied their curiosity is likely to precipitate anything from whining to a full-scale revolt.

2.   The touring plans call for visiting attractions in a specified sequence, often skipping certain attractions along the way. Children do not like skipping anything! If they see something that attracts them, they want to experience it now. Some children can be persuaded to skip attractions if parents explain things in advance. Other kids severely flip out at the threat of skipping something, particularly something in Fantasyland. A mom from Charleston, South Carolina, had this to say:

    Following the touring plans turned out to be a train wreck. The main problem is that the plan starts in Fantasyland. When we were on Dumbo, my 5-year-old saw eight dozen other things in Fantasyland she wanted to see. After Dumbo, there was no getting her out of there.

3.   Children seem to have a genetic instinct when it comes to finding restrooms. We have seen perfectly functional adults equipped with all manner of maps search interminably for a restroom. Small children, on the other hand, including those who cannot read, will head for the nearest restroom with the certainty of a homing pigeon. While you may skip certain attractions, you can be sure that your children will ferret out (and want to use) every restroom in the park.

STROLLERS

STROLLERS MAY BE RENTED for $15 per day for a single, $35 per day for a double; the rental covers the entire day and is good at both parks. If you rent a stroller and later decide to go back to your hotel for lunch, a swim, or a nap, turn in your stroller but keep your rental receipt. When you return to either park later in the day, present your receipt. You will be issued another stroller at no additional charge. The rental procedure is fast and efficient, and a central stroller rental facility is in the Esplanade between Disneyland and DCA, to the right of the Disneyland Park entrance. Likewise, returning the stroller is a breeze. Even in the evening, when several hundred strollers are turned in following the fireworks or water show, there is no wait or hassle. *Note:* Rented strollers are not permitted in Downtown Disney.

unofficial **TIP**
Strollers are also great for older kids who tire easily.

The strollers come with sun canopies and small cargo compartments under the seat. For infants and toddlers, strollers are a must, and we recommend a small pillow or blanket to help make the stroller more comfortable for your child during what may be long periods in the seat. We have also observed many sharp parents renting strollers for somewhat older children. Strollers prevent parents from having to carry

children when they run out of steam and provide an easy, convenient way to carry water, snacks, diaper bags, and the like.

When you enter a show or board a ride, you will have to park your stroller, usually in an open, unprotected area. If it rains before you return, you'll need a cloth, towel, or spare diaper to dry off the stroller.

Bringing Your Own Stroller

You are allowed to bring your own stroller to the theme parks, provided it is no larger than 31 inches wide by 52 inches long, and is not a wagon or stroller wagon (such as a Keenz 7s). However, only collapsible strollers are allowed on the monorail and Toy Story parking lot buses. Your stroller is unlikely to be stolen, but mark it with your name. We strongly recommend bringing your own stroller. In addition to the parks, there is the walk from and to your hotel, the parking lot bus, or the bus/hotel-shuttle boarding area, not to mention many other occasions at your hotel or during shopping when you will be happy to have a stroller handy.

If you do not want to bring your own stroller, you may consider buying one of the umbrella-style collapsible strollers. The on-site hotel gift shops sell them for less than $50. You may even consider ordering online and shipping it right to your hotel, or consider renting a stroller from a third party. Make sure you leave enough time between your order and arrival dates.

Having her own stroller was indispensable to this mother of two toddlers:

unofficial **TIP**
Often little ones fall asleep in their strollers (hallelujah!). Bring a large lightweight cloth to drape over the stroller to cover your child from the sun. A few clothespins will keep it in place.

How I was going to manage to get the kids from the parking lot to the park was a big worry for me before I made the trip. I found that, for me personally, since I have two kids ages 1 and 2, it was easier to walk to the entrance of the park from the parking lot with the kids in my own stroller than to take the kids out of the stroller, fold the stroller (while trying to control the two kids and associated gear), load the stroller and the kids onto the bus, etc. No matter where I was parked, I could always just walk to the entrance. It sometimes took a while, but it was easier for me.

An Oklahoma mom, however, reports a bad experience with bringing her own stroller:

The first time we took our kids we had a large stroller (big mistake). It is so much easier to rent one in the park. The large [personally owned] strollers are nearly impossible to get on [airport shuttle] buses and are a hassle at the airport. I remember feeling dread when a bus pulled up that was even semifull of people. People look at you like you have a cage full of live chickens when you drag heavy strollers onto the bus.

Stroller Wars

Sometimes strollers disappear while you are enjoying a ride or a show. Do not be alarmed. You won't have to buy the missing stroller, and you will be issued a new stroller for your continued use. Lost strollers can be replaced at the main rental facility near the park entrances.

While replacing a ripped-off stroller is not a big deal, it is an inconvenience. One family complained that their stroller had been taken six times in one day. Even with free replacements, larceny on this scale represents a lot of wasted time. Through our own experiments and suggestions from readers, we have developed several techniques for hanging on to your rented stroller:

1. Write your name in permanent marker on a 6-by-9-inch card, put the card in a transparent freezer bag, and secure the bag to the handle of the stroller with masking or duct tape.

2. Affix something personal (but expendable) to the handle of the stroller. Evidently most strollers are pirated by mistake (because they all look the same) or because it's easier to swipe someone else's stroller (when yours disappears) than to troop off to the replacement center. Because most stroller theft is a function of confusion, laziness, or revenge, the average pram-pincher will balk at hauling off a stroller bearing another person's property. After trying several items, we concluded that a bright, inexpensive scarf or bandanna tied to the handle works well, and a sock partially stuffed with rags or paper works even better (the weirder and more personal the object, the greater the deterrent).

A multigenerational family tried this:

We decorated our stroller with electrical tape to make it stand out. We also zip-tied an unused, small, insulated diaper bag to the handle to make carrying things easier. One of your readers mentioned using a bike chain or cable lock to insure their stroller was not stolen but said the Disney cast members were a little disturbed. So I took an extra firearm lock (looks like a mini-bike lock) to lock a wheel to the frame while parked. My son added a small cowbell to make it clang if moved. The stroller could then be moved easily for short distances by lifting the back, but trying to go farther would be uncomfortable and noisy.

We receive quite a few letters from readers debating the pros and cons of bringing your own stroller versus renting one of Disney's. A mother with two small children opted for her own pram:

I took my own stroller because the rented strollers aren't appropriate for infants (we had a 5-year-old and a 5-month-old). No one said anything about me using a bike lock to secure our brand-new Aprica stroller. However, an attendant came over and told us not to lock it *anywhere because it's a fire hazard! (Outside?) When I politely asked the attendant if she wanted to be responsible for my $300 stroller, she told me to go ahead and lock it but not tell anyone! I observed the attendants constantly moving the strollers. This seems very confusing— no wonder people think their strollers are getting ripped off!*

As the reader mentioned, Disney cast members often rearrange strollers parked outside an attraction. Sometimes this is done simply to tidy up. At other times the strollers are moved to make additional room along a walkway. In any event, do not assume that your stroller is stolen because it is missing from the exact place you left it. Check around. Chances are that it will be neatly arranged just a few feet away.

BABYSITTING

CHILDCARE SERVICES ARE UNAVAILABLE in the Disney parks. The childcare facility in the Grand Californian Hotel was removed during the 2017 renovation with no plans to replace it. You can ask the hotel concierge to recommend a third-party babysitting service.

DISNEY, KIDS, *and* SCARY STUFF

DISNEYLAND PARK and Disney California Adventure (DCA) are family theme parks. Yet some of the Disney adventure rides can be intimidating to small children. On certain rides, such as Splash Mountain and the roller coasters (Incredicoaster, Space Mountain, Matterhorn Bobsleds, and Big Thunder Mountain Railroad), the ride itself may be frightening. On other rides, such as The Haunted Mansion and Snow White's Scary Adventures, it is the special effects. We recommend a little parent-child dialogue coupled with a "testing the water" approach. A child who is frightened by Peter Pan's Flight should not have to sit through The Haunted Mansion. Likewise, if Big Thunder Mountain Railroad is too much, don't try Space Mountain or the Incredicoaster. Just because a child in your party isn't ready for a ride doesn't mean that the grown-ups have to miss out; learn about Disney's Rider Switch system on page 147.

Disney rides and shows are adventures. They focus on the substance and themes of all adventure, and indeed of life itself: good and evil, beauty and the grotesque, fellowship and enmity, quest, and death. Though the endings are all happy, the impact of the adventures, with Disney's gift for special effects, is often intimidating and occasionally frightening to small children.

There are rides with menacing witches, rides with burning towns, and rides with ghouls popping out of their graves, all done tongue in cheek and with a sense of humor, provided you are old enough

continued on page 141

SMALL-CHILD FRIGHT-POTENTIAL TABLE

As a quick reference, we provide this table to warn you which attractions to be wary of and why. The table represents a generalization, and all kids are different. It relates specifically to kids 3–7 years of age. On average, as you would expect, children at the younger end of the age range are more likely to be frightened than children in their 6th or 7th year.

Disneyland Park

MAIN STREET, U.S.A.

- **Disneyland Railroad** Tunnel with dinosaur display frightens some small children.
- *The Disneyland Story,* **presenting** *Great Moments with Mr. Lincoln* Brief battle sound effects may surprise small children.
- **Main Street Cinema** Not frightening in any respect.

ADVENTURELAND

- *Enchanted Tiki Room* A small thunderstorm momentarily surprises very young children.
- **Indiana Jones Adventure** Visually intimidating, with intense effects and a jerky ride. Switching-off option (see p. 147).
- **Jungle Cruise** Moderately intense, with some macabre sights; a good test attraction for little ones.
- **Tarzan's Treehouse** Not frightening in any respect.

NEW ORLEANS SQUARE

- **The Haunted Mansion** Name of attraction raises anxiety, as do sights and sounds of waiting area. An intense attraction with humorously presented macabre sights. The ride itself is gentle.
- **Pirates of the Caribbean** Slightly intimidating queuing area; an intense boat ride with gruesome (though humorously presented) sights and two short, unexpected slides down flumes.

CRITTER COUNTRY

- **Davy Crockett's Explorer Canoes** Not frightening in any respect.
- **The Many Adventures of Winnie the Pooh** Not frightening in any respect.
- **Splash Mountain** Visually intimidating from the outside. Moderately intense visual effects. The ride itself, culminating in a 52-foot plunge down a steep chute, is somewhat hair-raising for all ages. Switching-off option (see p. 147).

STAR WARS: GALAXY'S EDGE

- *Millennium Falcon:* **Smugglers Run** Simulated space flight with intense visual effects may discombobulate droids (and guests) of all ages. Switching-off option (see p. 147).
- **Rise of the Resistance** Intense visual effects, close encounters with sci-fi villains, and one big drop that can scare kids and sensitive adults. Switching-off option (see p. 147).

FRONTIERLAND

- **Big Thunder Mountain Railroad** Visually intimidating from the outside; moderately intense visual effects. The roller coaster may frighten many adults, particularly seniors. Switching-off option (see p. 147).
- *Fantasmic!* Loud and intense with fireworks and some scary villains, but most young children like it.
- **Frontierland Shootin' Exposition** Frightening to children scared of guns.
- **The Golden Horseshoe—Laughing Stock Co.** Not frightening in any respect.
- *Mark Twain* **Riverboat** Not frightening in any respect.
- **Pirate's Lair on Tom Sawyer Island** Some very small children are intimidated by dark walk-through tunnels that can be easily avoided.
- **Sailing Ship** *Columbia* Not frightening in any respect, aside from a single loud cannon blast that is announced well in advance.

SMALL-CHILD FRIGHT-POTENTIAL TABLE (continued)

FANTASYLAND

- **Alice in Wonderland** Pretty benign but frightens a small percentage of preschoolers.
- **Casey Jr. Circus Train** Not frightening in any respect.
- **Dumbo the Flying Elephant** A tame midway ride; a great favorite of most small children.
- **Fantasyland Theatre** Not frightening in any respect.
- **It's a Small World** Not frightening in any respect.
- **King Arthur Carrousel** Not frightening in any respect.
- **Mad Tea Party** Midway-type ride can induce motion sickness in all ages.
- **Matterhorn Bobsleds** The ride itself is wilder than Big Thunder Mountain Railroad but not as wild as Space Mountain. Switching-off option (see p. 147).
- **Mr. Toad's Wild Ride** Name of ride intimidates some. Moderately intense spook house–genre attraction with jerky ride. Frightens only a small percentage of preschoolers.
- **Peter Pan's Flight** Not frightening in any respect.
- **Pinocchio's Daring Journey** Less frightening than Snow White's Scary Adventures but scares a few very young preschoolers.
- **Pixie Hollow** Not frightening in any respect.
- **Royal Hall at Fantasy Faire** Not frightening in any respect.
- **Royal Theatre at Fantasy Faire** Not frightening in any respect.
- **Sleeping Beauty Castle** Not frightening in any respect.
- **Snow White's Scary Adventures** Moderately intense spook house–genre attraction with some grim characters. Absolutely terrifying to many preschoolers.
- **Storybook Land Canal Boats** Not frightening in any respect.

MICKEY'S TOONTOWN

- **Chip 'n Dale Treehouse** Not frightening in any respect.
- **Gadget's Go Coaster** Tame as far as coasters go; frightens some small children.
- **Goofy's Playhouse** Not frightening in any respect.
- **Mickey's House and Meet Mickey** Not frightening in any respect.
- **Minnie's House** Not frightening in any respect.
- *Miss Daisy,* **Donald's Boat** Not frightening in any respect.
- **Roger Rabbit's Car Toon Spin** Intense special effects, coupled with a dark environment and wild ride; frightens many preschoolers.

TOMORROWLAND

- **Astro Orbitor** Waiting area is visually intimidating to preschoolers. The ride is a lot higher, but just a bit wilder, than Dumbo.
- **Autopia** The noise in the waiting area slightly intimidates preschoolers; otherwise, not frightening.
- **Buzz Lightyear Astro Blasters** Intense special effects plus a dark environment frighten some preschoolers.
- **Disneyland Monorail System** Not frightening in any respect.
- **Finding Nemo Submarine Voyage** Being enclosed, as well as certain ride effects, may frighten preschoolers.
- **Space Mountain** Very intense roller coaster in the dark; Disneyland's wildest ride and a scary roller coaster by anyone's standards. Switching-off option (see p. 147).
- **Star Tours—The Adventures Continue** Extremely intense visually for all ages; one of the wildest in Disney's repertoire. Switching-off option (see p. 147).
- **Tomorrowland Theater** Intense visuals and loud sound effects may scare some preschoolers, depending on what's playing.

SMALL-CHILD FRIGHT-POTENTIAL TABLE (continued)
Disney California Adventure

BUENA VISTA STREET

- **Red Car Trolley** Not frightening in any respect.

GRIZZLY PEAK

- **Grizzly River Run** Frightening to guests of all ages. Wet too! Switching-off option (see p. 147).
- **Redwood Creek Challenge Trail and Wilderness Explorer Camp** Trail is a bit overwhelming to preschoolers but not frightening.
- **Soarin' Around the World** Frightens some children 7 years and under, especially anyone afraid of heights. Really a very sweet ride. Switching-off option (see p. 147).

HOLLYWOOD LAND

- **Anna & Elsa's Royal Welcome** Not frightening in any respect.
- **Disney Animation** Not frightening in any respect.
- *Disney Junior Dance Party* Not frightening in any respect.
- *Frozen—Live at the Hyperion* Very intense and loud; otherwise not frightening.
- **Guardians of the Galaxy—Mission: Breakout!** Frightening to guests of all ages. Switching-off option (see p. 147).
- *Mickey's PhilharMagic* Loud with intense 3-D effects. Frightens some preschoolers.
- **Monsters, Inc. Mike & Sulley to the Rescue** May frighten children under 7 years of age.
- *Turtle Talk With Crush* Not frightening in any respect.

PACIFIC WHARF

- **Bakery Tour** Not frightening in any respect.

PARADISE GARDENS PARK

- **Golden Zephyr** Frightening to a small percentage of preschoolers.
- **Goofy's Sky School** Frightening to the under-8 crowd. Switching-off option (see p. 147).
- **Jumpin' Jellyfish** The ride's appearance frightens some younger children. The ride itself is exceedingly tame.
- **The Little Mermaid: Ariel's Undersea Adventure** Moderately intense effects; Ursula may frighten children under 7 years of age.
- **Silly Symphony Swings** Height requirement keeps preschoolers from riding. Moderately intimidating to younger grade-schoolers.
- *World of Color Nighttime Spectacular* Not frightening for most children, but it is very loud with bursts of flame and a chance of getting wet.

PIXAR PIER

- **Incredicoaster** A launched looping roller coaster that's potentially terrifying for guests of all ages. Switching-off option (see p. 147).
- **Inside Out Emotional Whirlwind** Not frightening in any respect.
- **Jessie's Critter Carousel** Not frightening in any respect.
- **Pixar Pal-A-Round** The ride in the stationary cars is exceedingly tame. The ride in the swinging cars is frightening to guests of all ages.
- **Toy Story Midway Mania!** Loud and intense but not frightening.

CARS LAND

- **Luigi's Rollickin' Roadsters** Not frightening, aside from some brief moderate spinning at the end.
- **Mater's Junkyard Jamboree** Can induce motion sickness in all ages.
- **Radiator Springs Racers** Moderately intense effects, with high-speed sections that may frighten younger children. Switching-off option (see p. 147).

continued from page 137

to understand the joke. And there are bones, lots of bones—human bones, cattle bones, and whole skeletons are everywhere you look. There have to be more bones at Disneyland Park than at the Smithsonian and the School of Medicine at UCLA combined. A stack of skulls is at the headhunter's camp on the Jungle Cruise; a veritable platoon of skeletons sails ghost ships in Pirates of the Caribbean; a macabre assemblage of skulls and skeletons are in The Haunted Mansion; and more skulls, skeletons, and bones punctuate Snow White's Scary Adventures, Peter Pan's Flight, and Big Thunder Mountain Railroad.

One reader wrote us after taking his preschoolers on Star Tours:

We took a 4- and 5-year-old, and they had the *#%! scared out of them at Star Tours. We did it in the morning, and it took hours of Tom Sawyer Island and It's a Small World to get back to normal.

Preschoolers should start with Dumbo and work up to the Jungle Cruise in the late morning, after being revved up and before getting hungry, thirsty, or tired. Pirates of the Caribbean is out for preschoolers. You get the idea.

The reaction of young children to the inevitable system overload of Disney parks should be anticipated. Be sensitive, alert, and prepared for almost anything, even behavior that is out of character for your child at home. Most small children take Disney's variety of macabre trappings in stride, and others are quickly comforted by an arm around the shoulder or a little squeeze of the hand. For parents who have observed a tendency in their kids to become upset, we recommend taking it slowly and easily by sampling more benign adventures such as the Jungle Cruise, gauging reactions, and discussing with children how they felt about the things they saw. A mother of two reported this:

We pressured our kids into going on Pirates of the Caribbean because my husband and I wanted us all to ride as a family. Big mistake! I had not read enough about what the ride would be like. My 12-year-old (who is very sensitive) balked when we were in the queue, but still we pressured her to go on. Well, both she and her 6-year-old sister ended up sobbing through the whole ride.

Sometimes, small children will rise above their anxiety in an effort to please their parents or siblings. This behavior, however, does not necessarily indicate a mastery of fear, much less enjoyment. If children come off a ride in ostensibly good shape, we recommend asking if they would like to go on the ride again (not necessarily right now, but sometime). The response to this question will usually give you a clue as to how much they actually enjoyed the experience. There is a big difference between having a good time and mustering the courage to get through something.

Evaluating a child's capacity to handle the visual and tactile effects of the Disney parks requires patience, understanding, and experimentation.

Each of us, after all, has his own demons. If a child balks at or is frightened by a ride, respond constructively. Let your children know that lots of people, adults as well as children, are scared by what they see and feel. Help them understand that it is OK if they get frightened. Take pains not to compound the discomfort by making a child feel inadequate; try not to undermine self-esteem, impugn courage, or subject a child to ridicule. Most of all, do not induce guilt, as if your child's trepidation is ruining the family's fun. When older siblings are present, it is sometimes necessary to restrain their taunting and teasing.

A visit to a Disney park is more than an outing or an adventure for a small child. It is a testing experience, a sort of controlled rite of passage. If you help your little one work through the challenges, the time can be immeasurably rewarding and a bonding experience for both of you.

The Fright Factor

While each youngster is different, there are essentially seven attraction elements that alone or combined can push a child's buttons:

1. THE NAME OF THE ATTRACTION Small children will naturally be apprehensive about something called The Haunted Mansion or Snow White's Scary Adventures.

2. THE VISUAL IMPACT OF THE ATTRACTION FROM OUTSIDE Splash Mountain, Guardians of the Galaxy—Mission: Breakout!, and Big Thunder Mountain Railroad look scary enough to give even adults second thoughts. To many small kids, the rides are visually terrifying.

3. THE VISUAL IMPACT OF THE INDOOR QUEUING AREA Pirates of the Caribbean with its dark bayou scene and The Haunted Mansion with its "stretch rooms" are capable of frightening small children before they even board the ride.

4. THE INTENSITY OF THE ATTRACTION Some attractions are so intense as to be overwhelming; they inundate the senses with sights, sounds, movement, and even smell. *Mickey's PhilharMagic* in DCA, for instance, combines loud music, tactile effects, lights, and 3-D cinematography to create a total sensory experience. For some preschoolers, this is two or three senses too many.

5. THE VISUAL IMPACT OF THE ATTRACTION ITSELF As previously discussed, the sights in various attractions range from falling boulders to lurking buzzards, from underwater volcanoes to attacking hippos. What one child calmly absorbs may scare the owl poop out of another child the same age.

6. DARK Many Disneyland attractions are dark rides—that is, they operate indoors in a dark environment. For some children, this fact alone is sufficient to trigger significant apprehension. A child who is frightened on one dark ride, for example Snow White's Scary Adventures, may be unwilling to try other indoor rides.

7. THE RIDE ITSELF; THE PHYSICAL EXPERIENCE Some Disney rides are downright wild—wild enough to induce motion sickness, wrench backs, and generally discombobulate patrons of any age.

A Bit of Preparation

We receive many tips from parents relating how they prepared their children for the Disneyland experience. A common strategy is to acquaint kids with the characters and the stories behind the attractions by reading Disney books and watching Disney movies at home.

You can view a clip of every attraction and show on youtube.com. Videos of dark rides aren't stellar but are good enough to get a sense of what you're in for. The mom of a 7-year-old found YouTube quite effective:

> We watched every ride and show on YouTube before going, so my timid 7-year-old daughter would be prepared, and we cut out all the ones that looked too scary to her.

A mother from Gloucester, Massachusetts, handled her son's preparation a bit more extemporaneously:

> The 3½-year-old was afraid of The Haunted Mansion. We pulled his hat over his face and quietly talked to him while we enjoyed the ride.

A Word About Height Requirements

Many attractions require children to meet minimum height and age requirements, usually 32 inches tall to ride with an adult, or at least 40 inches and 7 years of age to ride alone. If you have children too short or too young to ride, you have several options, including switching off (described on page 147). Though the alternatives may resolve some practical and logistical issues, be forewarned that your smaller children might nonetheless be resentful of their older (or taller) siblings who qualify to ride. A mom from Virginia bumped into this situation, writing:

> You mention height requirements for rides but not the intense sibling jealousy this can generate. Frontierland was a real problem in that respect. Our very petite 5-year-old, to her outrage, was stuck hanging around while our 8-year-old went on Splash Mountain and Big Thunder Mountain with Grandma and Granddad, and the nearby alternatives weren't helpful [too long a line for rafts to Tom Sawyer Island, and so on]. If we had thought ahead, we would have left the younger kid back in Mickey's Toontown with one of the grown-ups for another roller coaster or two and then met up later at a designated point. The best areas had a playground or other quick attractions for short people near the rides with height requirements.

The reader makes a valid point, though splitting the group and then meeting later can be more complicated in practical terms than she might imagine. If you choose to split up, ask the Disney greeter at the entrance to the height-restricted attraction(s) how long the wait is. If you tack 5 minutes for riding onto the anticipated wait, and then add 5 or so minutes to exit and reach the meeting point, you'll have an approximate sense of how long the younger kids (and their supervising adult) will have to do other stuff. Our guess is that even with a long

line for the rafts, the reader would have had more than sufficient time to take her daughter to Tom Sawyer Island while the sibs rode Splash Mountain and Big Thunder Mountain with the grandparents. For sure she had time to tour Tarzan's Treehouse in adjacent Adventureland.

Additionally, children under age 7 must be accompanied on all attractions by another guest age 14 or older, who must sit in the same ride vehicle in the same row or an adjacent one. While this shouldn't pose a problem on most attractions, some with small vehicles (such as Gadget's Go Coaster) may require use of a Rider Switch (see page 147) if your party has an uneven ratio of little members to big ones; ask a cast member at the ride entrance for assistance if you have questions.

Attractions that Eat Adults

You may spend so much energy worrying about Junior's welfare that you forget to take care of yourself. Several attractions likely to cause motion sickness or other problems for older children and adults are listed in the table below. Fast, jerky rides are also noted with icons in the attraction profiles.

POTENTIALLY PROBLEMATIC ATTRACTIONS FOR ADULTS
DISNEYLAND PARK
• **ADVENTURELAND**   Indiana Jones Adventure
• **CRITTER COUNTRY**   Splash Mountain
• **FANTASYLAND**   Mad Tea Party | Matterhorn Bobsleds
• **FRONTIERLAND**   Big Thunder Mountain Railroad
• **STAR WARS: GALAXY'S EDGE**   *Millennium Falcon:* Smugglers Run | Star Wars: Rise of the Resistance
• **TOMORROWLAND**   Space Mountain | Star Tours—The Adventures Continue
DISNEY CALIFORNIA ADVENTURE
• **CARS LAND**   Mater's Junkyard Jamboree | Radiator Springs Racers
• **GRIZZLY PEAK**   Grizzly River Run
• **HOLLYWOOD LAND**   Guardians of the Galaxy—Mission: Breakout!
• **PARADISE GARDENS PARK**   Goofy's Sky School
• **PIXAR PIER**   Incredicoaster | Pixar Pal-A-Round (swinging)

WAITING-LINE STRATEGIES *for* ADULTS *with* SMALL CHILDREN

CHILDREN HOLD UP BETTER through the day if you minimize the time they spend in lines. Arriving early and using the touring plans in this guide will reduce waiting time immensely. There are, however, additional measures that you can employ to reduce stress on little ones.

1. LINE GAMES Smart parents know that a little structured activity can relieve the stress and boredom of waiting in line. In the morning, kids handle the inactivity of waiting in line by discussing what they want to see and do during the course of the day. Later, however, as events wear on, they need a little help. Watching for, and counting, Disney characters is a good diversion. Simple guessing games such as 20 Questions also work well. Lines for rides move so continuously that games requiring pen and paper are cumbersome and impractical. Waiting in the holding area of a theater attraction, however, is a different story. Here, tic-tac-toe, hangman, drawing, and coloring can really make the time go by.

For Apple and Android smartphone users, our favorite queue distraction is Ellen DeGeneres's Heads Up, a Taboo-style game where one player holds a phone against his or her forehead, and the others help him or her guess the phrase displayed before the timer counts down. The app costs 99¢ and includes several starter "decks" of clues to play. If you're inside Disneyland Resort, you can unlock a deck featuring Disney characters and attractions for free. Don't be surprised if you see several shouting families playing Heads Up in any given line. There's also a free official Play Disney Parks app with simple games that unlock inside select attraction queues and all around the Star Wars area; beware that this power-hungry program doesn't drain your battery before you board.

2. LAST-MINUTE ENTRY If a ride or show can accommodate an unusually large number of people at one time, it is often unnecessary to stand in line. The *Mark Twain* Riverboat in Frontierland is a good example. The boat holds about 450 people, usually more than are waiting in line to ride. Instead of standing uncomfortably in a crowd with dozens of other guests, grab a snack and sit in the shade until the boat arrives and loading is under way. After the line has all but disappeared, go ahead and board.

In large-capacity theaters, such as Tomorrowland Theater, ask the entrance greeter how long it will be until guests are admitted to the theater for the next show. If the answer is 15 minutes or more, use the time for a restroom break or to get a snack; you can return to the attraction just a few minutes before the show starts. You will not be permitted to carry any food or drink into the attraction, so make sure you have time to finish your snack before entering.

To help you determine which attractions to target for last-minute entry, we provide the following table.

ATTRACTIONS YOU CAN USUALLY ENTER AT THE LAST MINUTE
DISNEYLAND PARK
• **ADVENTURELAND** *Enchanted Tiki Room*
• **FANTASYLAND** Fantasyland Theatre
• **FRONTIERLAND** *Mark Twain* Riverboat | Sailing Ship *Columbia*
• **MAIN STREET, U.S.A.** *Disneyland Story,* presenting *Great Moments with Mr. Lincoln*
• **TOMORROWLAND** Tomorrowland Theater
DISNEY CALIFORNIA ADVENTURE
• **HOLLYWOOD LAND** Disney Animation | *Mickey's PhilharMagic*

3. THE HAIL MARY PASS Certain waiting lines are configured in such a way that you and your smaller children can pass under the rail to join your partner just before boarding or entry. This technique allows the kids and one adult to rest, snack, cool off, or tinkle, while another adult or older sibling does the waiting. Other guests are understanding when it comes to using this strategy to keep small children content. You are likely to meet hostile opposition, however, if you try to pass older children or more than one adult under the rail. Attractions where it is usually possible to complete a Hail Mary pass are listed in the table below.

ATTRACTIONS WHERE YOU CAN USUALLY COMPLETE A HAIL MARY PASS
DISNEYLAND PARK
• **FANTASYLAND** Casey Jr. Circus Train | Dumbo the Flying Elephant | King Arthur Carrousel | Mad Tea Party | Mr. Toad's Wild Ride | Peter Pan's Flight | Snow White's Scary Adventures | Storybook Land Canal Boats
• **TOMORROWLAND** Autopia

**ATTRACTIONS WHERE YOU CAN USUALLY COMPLETE
A HAIL MARY PASS** (*continued*)

DISNEY CALIFORNIA ADVENTURE

- **PARADISE GARDENS PARK** Golden Zephyr | Jumpin' Jellyfish
- **PIXAR PIER** Jessie's Critter Carousel
- **CARS LAND**   Luigi's Rollickin' Roadsters | Mater's Junkyard Jamboree

**4. SWITCHING OFF (ALSO KNOWN AS RIDER SWITCH, BABY SWAP, OR
CHILD SWAP)** Several attractions have minimum height and/or age
requirements (see the table on page 112). In addition, all children must
be at least 7 years old and 40 inches tall to ride any attraction without
an accompanying adult. Some couples with children too short or too
young forgo these attractions, while others take turns riding. Missing
some of Disneyland's best rides is an unnecessary sacrifice, and waiting
in line twice for the same ride is a tremendous waste of time.

Instead, take advantage of switching off. To switch off, there must
be at least two adults. When you approach the queue, tell the first ride
attendant you see (known as a greeter) that you want to switch off.

The cast member will ask your party to split into two groups, with
up to three people selected to stay outside the attraction and supervise
the kids while the rest ride first. Those remaining behind will have their
admission passes (or apps) scanned to receive a Rider Switch entitle-
ment on their account, which functions just like an immediate FastPass.
Once the first group exits the ride, the second set of guests have up to an
hour to redeem their Rider Switch passes by entering through the ride's
FastPass queue. You can only hold one Rider Switch pass at a time, but
it will not interfere with any other FastPasses. This system eliminates
confusion and congestion at the boarding area while sparing the nonriding adult and child the tedium and physical exertion of waiting in
line. While this system usually works fairly well, using Rider Switch can
become frustrating when FastPass return lines grow long, especially if,
like this La Center, Washington, mom, you've previously experienced
the child swap waiting rooms at Universal's park.

> *Disney does a terrible job with rider swaps. The process is ridiculous
> and confusing. Why would I want to wait in the FastPass line twice
> just to do a rider swap? Universal Studios does it right by letting you
> swap when you are getting ready to load. They also give you a nice
> place to sit and rest while you wait for your party to disembark. Dis-
> ney makes you wait at the back of the line!*

There is no cost to use the switching-off option. The attractions
where switching off is routinely practiced, often oriented to more
mature guests, are listed below. Sometimes children suddenly fear
abandonment when one parent leaves to ride. Prepare your children
for switching off, or you might have an emotional crisis on your
hands. A mom from Edison, New Jersey, writes:

> *Once my son understood that the switch off would not leave him
> abandoned, he did not seem to mind. I would recommend practicing*

the switch off at home, so your child is not concerned that he will be left behind. At the very least, explain the procedure in advance, so little ones know what to expect.

ATTRACTIONS WHERE SWITCHING OFF IS COMMON
DISNEYLAND PARK
• **ADVENTURELAND**   Indiana Jones Adventure
• **CRITTER COUNTRY**   Splash Mountain
• **FANTASYLAND**   Matterhorn Bobsleds
• **FRONTIERLAND**   Big Thunder Mountain Railroad
• **STAR WARS: GALAXY'S EDGE**   *Millennium Falcon:* Smugglers Run | Star Wars: Rise of the Resistance
• **TOMORROWLAND**   Space Mountain | Star Tours—The Adventures Continue
DISNEY CALIFORNIA ADVENTURE
• **CARS LAND**   Radiator Springs Racers
• **GRIZZLY PEAK**   Grizzly River Run | Soarin' Around the World
• **HOLLYWOOD LAND**   Guardians of the Galaxy—Mission: Breakout!
• **PARADISE GARDENS PARK**   Goofy's Sky School
• **PIXAR PIER**   Incredicoaster

5. HOW TO RIDE TWICE IN A ROW WITHOUT WAITING Many small children like to ride a favorite attraction two or more times in succession. Riding the second time often gives the child a feeling of mastery and accomplishment. Unfortunately, repeat rides can be time-consuming, even in the early morning. If you ride Dumbo as soon as Disneyland Park opens, for instance, you will only have a 1- or 2-minute wait for your first ride. When you come back for your second ride, your wait will be about 12 minutes. If you want to ride a third time, count on a 20-minute or longer wait. The best way for getting your child on the ride twice (or more) without blowing your whole morning is by using the Chuck-Bubba Relay (named in honor of a reader from Kentucky):

1. Mom and little Bubba enter the waiting line.
2. Dad lets a certain number of people go in front of him (32 in the case of Dumbo) and then gets in line.
3. As soon as the ride stops, Mom exits with little Bubba and passes him to Dad to ride the second time.
4. If everybody is really getting into this, Mom can hop in line again, no less than 32 people behind Dad.

The Chuck-Bubba Relay will not work on every ride because of differences in the way the waiting areas are configured (that is, it is impossible in some cases to exit the ride and make the pass). The rides where the Chuck-Bubba Relay does work, along with the number of people to count off, appear in the table on the facing page.

When practicing the Chuck-Bubba Relay, if you are the second adult in line, you will reach a point in the waiting area that is obviously the easiest place to make the handoff. Sometimes this point is where those exiting the ride pass closest to those waiting to board. In any event, you will know it when you see it. Once there, if the first parent has not arrived with little Bubba, just let those behind you slip past until Bubba shows up.

ATTRACTIONS WHERE THE CHUCK-BUBBA RELAY USUALLY WORKS
DISNEYLAND PARK   *Number of people between adults*
• **ALICE IN WONDERLAND** (tough, but possible) 38 • **CASEY JR. CIRCUS TRAIN** 34, if 2 trains are operating • **DAVY CROCKETT'S EXPLORER CANOES** 94, if 6 canoes are operating • **DUMBO THE FLYING ELEPHANT** 32 • **KING ARTHUR CARROUSEL** 70 • **MAD TEA PARTY** 53 • **MR. TOAD'S WILD RIDE** 32 • **PETER PAN'S FLIGHT** 25 • **SNOW WHITE'S SCARY ADVENTURES** 30
DISNEY CALIFORNIA ADVENTURE   *Number of people between adults*
• **GOLDEN ZEPHYR** 64 • **JESSIE'S CRITTER CAROUSEL** 64 • **JUMPIN' JELLYFISH** 16 • **LUIGI'S ROLLICKIN' ROADSTERS** 40

6. LAST-MINUTE COLD FEET If your small child gets cold feet at the last minute after waiting for a ride (where there is no age or height requirement), you can usually arrange with the loading attendant for a switch-off; see the table on the opposite page. This situation arises frequently at Pirates of the Caribbean—small children lose their courage en route to the loading area.

There is no law that says you have to ride. If you get to the boarding area and someone is unhappy, just tell a Disney attendant that you have changed your mind, and one will show you the way out. Older children and adults who are unable or unwilling to ride an attraction may also experience the queue with their party and exit before boarding without embarrassment.

LOST CHILDREN

unofficial **TIP**
We suggest that children younger than 8 years old be color-coded by dressing them in purple T-shirts or equally distinctive clothes.

LOST CHILDREN NORMALLY do not present much of a problem at Disneyland Resort. All Disney employees are schooled in handling such situations. If you lose a child while touring, report the situation to a Disney employee; then check in at City Hall (Disneyland Park) or Guest Relations (DCA) where lost-children logs are maintained. In an emergency, an alert can be issued throughout the park through internal communications. If a Disney cast member encounters a lost child, the cast member will escort the child to the Baby Care Center located at the central-hub end of Main Street in Disneyland Park and at the entrance plaza in DCA. Guests age 11 or under are taken to the Baby Care Center in the Pacific Wharf area at DCA. Guests age 12 and older may leave a written message at City Hall or the Guest Relations lobby or wait there.

It is amazingly easy to lose a child (or two) at a Disney park. It is a good idea to sew a label into each child's shirt that states his or her name, your name, and the name of your hotel. The same task can be accomplished by writing the information on a strip of masking tape; hotel security professionals suggest that the information be printed in small letters, and that the tape be affixed to the outside of the child's shirt 5 inches or so below the armpit.

HOW KIDS GET LOST

CHILDREN GET SEPARATED from parents every day at the Disney parks under remarkably similar (and predictable) circumstances.

1. PREOCCUPIED SOLO PARENT In this scenario the only adult in the party is preoccupied with something such as buying refreshments or using the restroom. Junior is there one moment and gone the next.

2. THE HIDDEN EXIT Sometimes parents wait on the sidelines while allowing two or more young children to experience a ride together. As it usually happens, the parents expect the kids to exit the attraction in one place, and lo and behold, the young ones pop out somewhere else. The exits of some Disney attractions are considerably distant from the entrances. Make sure that you know exactly where your children will emerge before letting them ride by themselves.

3. AFTER THE SHOW At the completion of many shows and rides, a Disney staffer will announce, "Check for personal belongings and take small children by the hand." When dozens, if not hundreds, of people leave an attraction at the same time, it is easy for parents to temporarily lose contact with their children unless they have them directly in tow.

4. RESTROOM PROBLEMS Mom tells 6-year-old Tommy, "I'll be sitting on this bench when you come out of the restroom." Three situations: One, Tommy exits through a different door and becomes disoriented (Mom may not know there is another door). Two, Mom belatedly decides that she will also use the restroom, and Tommy emerges to find her absent. Three, Mom pokes around in a shop while keeping an eye on the bench but misses Tommy when he comes out. A restroom adjacent to Rancho del Zocalo Restaurante in Frontierland accounts for many lost children. Because it's located in a passageway connecting Frontierland and Fantasy Faire, children can wander into a totally different area of the park from where they came by simply making a wrong turn out of the restroom.

If you can't be with your child in the restroom, make sure that there is only one exit. Designate a meeting spot more distinctive than a bench, and be specific in your instructions: "I'll meet you by this flagpole. If you get out first, stay right here." Have your child repeat the directions back to you.

5. PARADES There are many special parades and shows at the theme park during which the audience stands. Children, because they are small, tend to jockey around for a better view. By moving a little this way and a little that way, it is amazing how much distance kids can put between themselves and you before anyone notices.

6. MASS MOVEMENTS Another situation to guard against is when huge crowds disperse after shows, fireworks, or parades, or at park closing. With 5,000–12,000 people suddenly moving at once, it is very easy to get separated from a small child or others in your party. Extra caution is recommended following the evening parades, fireworks, and *Fantasmic!* Families should develop specific plans for what to do and where to meet in the event they are separated.

TIPS FOR KEEPING TRACK OF YOUR BROOD

• Same-colored T-shirts for the whole family will help you gather your troops in an easy and fun way. Opt for just a uniform color or have the T-shirts printed with a logo, such as The Brown Family's Assault on the Mouse. You might also include the date or the year of your visit. Light-colored T-shirts can even be autographed by the Disney characters.

• Clothing labels are great. If you don't sew, buy labels that you can iron on the garment. Include your cell phone number or the number of the hotel where you'll be staying on the label.

• An easier option is a temporary tattoo with your child's name and your phone number. Unlike other methods, the tattoos cannot fall off or be lost. Temporary tattoos last about two weeks, won't wash or sweat off, and are not irritating to the skin. They can be purchased online at safetytat.com or tattooswithapurpose.com. Special tattoos are available for children with food allergies or cognitive impairment such as autism.

• In pet stores you can have name tags printed for a very reasonable price. These are great to add to necklaces and bracelets, or attach them to your child's shoelaces or a belt loop.

• When you check into the hotel, take a business card of the hotel for each member in your party, especially those old enough to carry wallets and purses.

• Always agree on a meeting point before you see a parade, fireworks, or nighttime spectacles. Make sure the meeting place is in the park (as opposed to the car or some place outside the front gate).

• If you have a digital camera or camera phone, take a picture of your kids every morning. If they get lost, the picture will show what they look like and what they are wearing.

• If all members of your party have cell phones, it's easy to locate each other. However, the noise in the parks is so loud that you probably won't hear your cell phone ring. Carry your phone in a front pants pocket and program the phone to vibrate. Or communicate via text message. If any of your younger kids carry cell phones, secure the phones with a strap.

• Save key tags and luggage tags for use on items you bring to the parks, including your stroller, diaper bag, and backpack or hip pack.

• Don't underestimate permanent markers. They are great for labeling pretty much anything. Mini-Sharpies are useful for collecting character autographs.

7. CHARACTER GREETINGS A fair amount of activity and confusion is commonplace when the Disney characters are on the scene. See the next section on meeting the Disney characters.

The DISNEY CHARACTERS

FOR YEARS THE COSTUMED, walking versions of Mickey, Minnie, Donald, Goofy, and others have been a colorful supporting cast at Disneyland and Walt Disney World. Known unpretentiously as the Disney characters, these large and friendly figures help provide a link between Disney animated films and the Disney theme parks.

About 250 of the Disney animated-film characters have been brought to life in costume. Of these, a relatively small number (about 50) are greeters (the Disney term for characters who mix with the patrons). The remaining characters are relegated exclusively to performing in shows or participating in parades. Some appear only once or twice a year, usually in holiday parades.

CHARACTER ENCOUNTERS

CHARACTER WATCHING has developed into a pastime. Where families were once content to stumble across a character occasionally, they now pursue them armed with autograph books and cameras. For those who pay attention, some characters are more frequently encountered than others. Mickey, Minnie, and Goofy, for example, are seemingly everywhere, while Thumper rarely appears. Other characters are seen regularly but limit themselves to a specific location.

The fact that some characters are seldom seen has turned character watching into character collecting. Mickey Mouse may be the best-known and most-loved character, but from a collector's perspective, he is also the most common. To get an autograph from Mickey is no big deal, but Daisy Duck's signature is a real coup. Commercially tapping into the character-collecting movement, Disney sells autograph books throughout the parks. One *Unofficial Guide* reader offers this suggestion regarding character autographs:

> *Young children learn very quickly! If they see another child get an autograph, they will want an autograph book as well. I recommend buying an autograph book right away. My 4-year-old daughter saw a child get Goofy's autograph, and right away she wanted to join the fun.*

PREPARING YOUR CHILDREN TO MEET THE CHARACTERS Because most small children are not expecting Minnie Mouse to be the size of a fork-lift, it's best to discuss the characters with your kids before you go. Almost all of the characters are quite large, and several, such as Br'er Bear, are huge! All of them can be extremely intimidating to a preschooler.

unofficial **TIP**
Don't underestimate your child's excitement at meeting the Disney characters—but also be aware that very small kids may find the large, costumed characters a little frightening.

On first encounter, it is important not to thrust your child upon the character. Allow the little one to come to terms with this big thing from whatever distance the child feels safe. If two adults are present, one should stay close to the youngster while the other approaches the character and demonstrates that the character is safe and friendly. Some kids warm to the characters immediately, while some never do. Most take a little time and often require several different encounters.

There are two kinds of characters: those whose costume includes a face-covering headpiece (animal characters plus some human characters such as Captain Hook), and face characters, or actors who

resemble the cartoon characters to such an extent that no mask or headpiece is necessary. Face characters include Mary Poppins, Ariel, Jasmine, Aladdin, Cinderella, Mulan, Tarzan, Jane, Belle, Snow White, and Prince Charming, to name a few.

Only the face characters are allowed to speak. Headpiece characters, called furs in Disney-speak, do not talk or make noises of any kind. Because the cast members could not possibly imitate the distinctive voice of the characters, the Disney folks have determined that it is more effective to keep them silent. Lack of speech notwithstanding, the headpiece characters are extremely warm and responsive, and they communicate very effectively with gestures. As with the characters' size, children need to be forewarned that the characters do not talk. The only exceptions are the costumed stars of some newer shows and parades, who boast articulated facial features that blink and flap in sync with the soundtracks, and select *Star Wars* characters (like Darth Vader and Kylo Ren) who use prerecorded dialogue clips to converse with guests.

unofficial **TIP**
Explain to your children that the headpiece characters do not talk. Keep in mind, too, that the characters are clumsy and have a limited field of vision.

Parents need to understand that some of the character costumes are very cumbersome and that cast members often suffer from very poor visibility. You have to look closely, but the eyeholes are frequently in the mouth of the costume or even down on the neck. What this means in practical terms is that the characters are sort of clumsy and have a limited field of vision. Children who approach the character from the back or the side may not be noticed, even if the child is touching the character. It is perfectly possible in this situation for the character to accidentally step on the child or knock him or her down. The best way for a child to approach a character is from the front, and occasionally not even this works. For example, the various duck characters (Donald, Daisy, Uncle Scrooge, and so on) have to peer around their bills. If it appears that the character is ignoring your child, pick your child up and hold her in front of the character until the character responds.

It is OK to touch, pat, or hug the character if your child is so inclined. Understanding the unpredictability of children, the characters will keep their feet very still, particularly refraining from moving backward or to the side. Most of the characters will sign autographs (except for *Star Wars* characters) or pose for pictures. Once again, be sure to approach from the front so that the character will understand your intentions. If your child collects autographs, it is a good idea to carry a big, fat pen about the size of a Magic Marker. The costumes make it exceedingly difficult for the characters to wield a smaller pen, so the bigger the better.

THE BIG HURT Many children expect to bump into Mickey the minute they enter a park and are disappointed when he is not around. If your children are unable to settle down and enjoy things until they see Mickey, simply ask a Disney cast member where to find him. If the cast member does not know Mickey's whereabouts, he or she can find out for you in short order.

"THEN SOME CONFUSION HAPPENED" Be forewarned that character encounters give rise to a situation during which small children sometimes get lost. There is usually a lot of activity around a character, with both adults and children touching the character or posing for pictures. In the most common scenario, the parents stay in the crowd while their child marches up to get acquainted. With the excitement of the encounter, all the milling people, and the character moving around, a child may get turned around and head off in the wrong direction. In the words of a Salt Lake City mom:

> Milo was shaking hands with Dopey one moment, then some confusion happened, and he [Milo] was gone.

Families with several small children, and parents who are busy fooling around with cameras, can lose track of a youngster in a heartbeat. Our recommendation for parents of preschoolers is to stay with the kids when they meet the characters, stepping back only long enough to take a picture, if necessary.

MEETING CHARACTERS You can *see* the Disney characters in live shows and in parades. For times, consult your app or *Times Guide*. If you have the time and money, you can share a meal with the characters (more about this later). But if you want to *meet* the characters, get autographs, and take photos, it's helpful to know where the characters hang out.

unofficial **TIP**
Characters make appearances in all the "lands" but are especially thick in Fantasyland, Mickey's Toontown, and Town Square on Main Street.

Disneyland Resort includes information about characters in its mobile app, handout park maps, and entertainment *Times Guide*. A listing specifies where and when certain characters will be available and also provides information on character dining. On the maps of the parks themselves, Mickey's gloved hand is used to denote locations where characters can be found.

At Disneyland Park, Mickey and Minnie have all-day tours of duty in their Toontown homes. All of the "fab five" (including Goofy, Pluto, and Donald), along with Chip 'n' Dale and Cruella De Vil, also make morning appearances in Main Street, U.S.A.'s Town Square. Likewise, Pooh, Tigger, and Eeyore can usually be found in Critter Country. The Fantasy Faire plaza adjacent to Sleeping Beauty Castle is the prime place to meet Ariel, Aurora, Cinderella, Belle, Princess Elena of Avalor, Merida, and Rapunzel with Flynn Rider. Tinker Bell and her fairy friends draw long lines at their Pixie Hollow area off the central hub between Tomorrowland and the Matterhorn. *Star Wars* celebrities can be spotted in and around Tomorrowland's Star Wars Launch Bay and roam the alleyways of Batuu's Black Spire Outpost in Galaxy's Edge. Tiana and Dr. Facilier (occasionally accompanied by Louis and Prince Naveen) from *The Princess and the Frog* appear in New Orleans Square or at Frontierland's riverboat dock.

At DCA, the fab five—plus Daisy Duck and throwback characters such as Horace Horsecollar and Clarabelle Cow—can be found on Buena Vista Street and around Carthay Circle (the central hub) dressed in Depression-era duds. Also look for characters in Hollywood Land near the Animation Building, in parades, and in shows at the Hyperion Theater. In Cars Land, you'll find interactive incarnations of the series' automotive stars. Anna and Elsa from *Frozen* hold court inside the Disney Animation attraction, sometimes accompanied by Olaf the Snowman, while current Disney Junior stars such as Fancy Nancy greet guests right outside the building. Marvel's Captain America and Spider-Man also appear in Hollywood Land, near the entrance to the Hyperion Theater, and Captain Marvel and Black Panther prowl just around the corner; Thor and Black Widow can sometimes be spotted patrolling the neighborhood. Nick and Judy from *Zootopia* stake out the San Francisco street near Ariel's ride, Chip 'n' Dale camp out at Redwood Creek Challenge Trail, and The Incredibles stand guard outside their coaster as their plastic *Toy Story* pals play on Pixar Pier.

While making the characters routinely available has taken the guesswork out of finding them, it has likewise robbed character encounters of much of their surprise and spontaneity. Instead of chancing on a character as you turn a corner, it is much more common now to wait in a queue to meet the character. However, you are still far more likely to encounter free-range characters in Disneyland than at Walt Disney World, especially in the slower morning hours when they are given a longer leash to roam. Be aware that lines for face characters move much more slowly than lines for nonspeaking characters do, as you might surmise. Because face characters are allowed to talk, they do, often engaging children in lengthy conversations, much to the consternation of the families stuck in the queue.

If you believe that Disneyland Park already has quite enough lines, and furthermore, if you prefer to bump into your characters on the run, here's a quick rundown of where the bears and chipmunks roam. In the morning, there is almost always a princess or two posing in front of the Mickey flower bed just inside the park entrance. There will almost always be a character in Town Square on Main Street and often at the central hub; for example, Mary Poppins and Bert are frequently found near Coke Corner. Snow White's Wicked Queen hangs out near the wishing well in the courtyard of the castle, occasionally accompanied by Aladdin and Jasmine. Alice and her Wonderland friends, as well as Peter Pan and Captain Hook, wander around Fantasyland. And Redd, the female rumrunner from Pirates of the Caribbean, and Jack Sparrow sometimes roam New Orleans Square. Any characters whom we haven't specifically mentioned generally continue to turn up randomly throughout the park. Character selection can vary seasonally, with some (such as Jack Skellington) appearing only around Halloween or Christmas.

Characters are also featured in the afternoon and evening parades, *Fantasmic!,* and Fantasy Faire. Performance times for all of the shows and parades are listed in the app and daily *Times Guide.* After the shows, characters will sometimes stick around to greet the audience.

Mickey Mouse is available to meet guests and pose for photos all day long in his dressing room at Mickey's Movie Barn in Mickey's Toontown. To reach the Movie Barn, proceed through the front door of Mickey's House and follow the crowd. If the line extends back to the entrance of Mickey's House, it will take you about 25–30 minutes to actually reach Mickey. When you finally get to his dressing room, a few families at a time are admitted for a short personal audience with Mickey.

Many children are so excited about meeting Mickey that they can't relax to enjoy the other attractions. If Mickey looms large in your child's day, board the Disneyland Railroad at the Main Street Station as soon as Toontown opens for the day (usually 1 hour after the rest of the park), and proceed directly to Mickey's Toontown (half a circuit). If you visit Mickey within an hour of Toontown's opening, your wait will be short.

Minnie receives guests at her house in Toontown, but only until midafternoon. Also, be aware that the characters bug out for parades and certain other special performances. Check the app or daily *Times Guide* for performance times and plan your visit to Toontown accordingly.

CHARACTER DINING

FRATERNIZING WITH DISNEY CHARACTERS has become so popular that Disney offers character breakfasts, brunches, and dinners where families can dine in the presence of Minnie, Goofy, and other costumed versions of animated celebrities. Character meals provide a familiar, controlled setting in which young children can warm gradually to the characters. All meals are attended by several characters. Adult prices apply to persons age 10 or older, children's prices to

unofficial **TIP**
Arrange dining reservations as far in advance as possible. Your wait for a table will usually be less than 15 minutes.

ages 3–9. Little ones under age 3 eat free. Because character dining is very popular, we recommend that you arrange reservations as far in advance (up to 60 days) as possible.

CHARACTER DINING: WHAT TO EXPECT   Character meals are bustling affairs, held in hotels' or theme parks' largest table-service or "buffeteria" restaurants. Character breakfasts (there are four) offer a fixed menu served family-style or as a buffet. The typical family-style breakfast includes scrambled eggs; bacon, sausage, and ham; hash browns; waffles, pancakes, or French toast; biscuits, rolls, or pastries; and fruit. The meal is served in large skillets or platters at your table. If you run out of something, you can order seconds (or thirds) at no additional charge. Buffets offer much the same fare, but you have to fetch it yourself.

Whatever the meal, characters circulate around the room while you eat. During your meal, each of the three to five characters present will visit your table, arriving one at a time to cuddle the kids (and sometimes the adults), pose for photos, and sign autographs. Keep autograph books (with pens) and cameras handy. For the best photos, adults should sit across the table from their children. Always seat the children where characters can reach them most easily. If a table is against a wall, for example, adults should sit with their backs to the wall and children should sit nearest the aisle.

Usually, there's also a character with a PhotoPass photographer stationed at the entrance, but prints are not included in the price of your meal, so you'll want to use MaxPass or a PhotoPass+ package rather than paying à la carte for your poses.

You will not be rushed to leave after you've eaten. Remember, however, lots of eager children and adults might be waiting not so patiently to be admitted.

You can dine with Disney characters at the restaurants listed below. For information about character meals and to make dining reservations up to 60 days in advance, call ☎ 714-781-DINE (3463). *Note:* The following prices don't include tax or gratuities.

DISNEY'S PCH (PACIFIC COAST HIGHWAY) GRILL   PCH Grill at the Paradise Pier Hotel serves Donald Duck's Seaside Breakfast buffet (Monday–Thursday, 7–11 a.m.; Friday–Sunday, 7–11:30 a.m.), which features traditional Mexican breakfast items such as chilaquiles in addition to the usual American fare. Prices are $39 for adults ($23 kids). Donald, along with Daisy and Stitch, entertains you. This is usually the least crowded of the hotel character meals.

GOOFY'S KITCHEN   Located at the Disneyland Hotel, Goofy's Kitchen serves a character breakfast buffet 7–11:30 a.m. (until 1:15 p.m. Saturday–Sunday) and a character dinner buffet 5–8:45 p.m. Breakfast is $44 for adults ($26 kids). Dinners run $48 and $28, respectively. Goofy, of course, is the head character, but he's usually joined by Minnie, Pluto, and others.

NAPA ROSE Disneyland Resort's latest and most luxurious character meal is the Disney Princess Breakfast Adventure, held Thursday–Monday, 8 a.m.–noon, at the Grand Californian Hotel's toniest table, Napa Rose. The three-course meal includes upscale starters such as mini lobster salad and caramel beignets, plus a buffet of brunch standards. After eating, Belle, Mulan, Rapunzel, and friends invite guests onto the outdoor patio for interactive storytelling. A private photo session and souvenirs are included in the $125 price (adults and kids cost the same).

PLAZA INN Located in Disneyland Park at the end of Main Street and to the right, the Plaza Inn character buffet is usually packed because it hosts character breakfasts that are included in vacation packages sold by the Disney Resort Travel Sales Center. Served from park opening until 11 a.m., the buffet costs $34 for adults ($19 kids). Characters present usually include Minnie, Goofy, Pluto, and Chip 'n' Dale.

STORYTELLERS CAFÉ Storytellers Café, at the Grand Californian Hotel, is the setting for the only meal featuring both Mickey and Minnie. A breakfast buffet is served daily, 7–11:30 a.m., and brunch is available Friday–Sunday until 2 p.m. The buffet costs $44 for adults ($26 kids) at breakfast; adults pay an extra $2 during brunch. The meal is periodically punctuated by interactive parades around the dining room, led by the Mouse power couple and a few of their closest friends.

PART FOUR

DINING *and* SHOPPING *In and Around* DISNEYLAND

▌ DINING *in* DISNEYLAND RESORT

IN THIS SECTION, we aim to help you find good food without going broke or tripping over one of Disneyland Resort's many culinary land mines. More than 50 restaurants operate in Disneyland Resort, including about 20 full-service restaurants, several of which are inside the theme parks. Collectively, Disney restaurants offer reasonable variety, serving everything from Louisiana Creole to California fusion, but sadly, international cuisines other than Mexican, Asian, Mediterranean, and Italian are not well represented.

On the upside, Disneyland Resort restaurant quality is much better now than it was a decade ago, though the gains have leveled off lately. Ingredients are fresher, preparation is more careful, and even steam tables and buffets are under almost constant supervision. As a whole, the culinary team has definitely stepped up its game, and we are the winners. Many establishments have undergone complete menu makeovers, with terrific results. On the downside, we've seen repeated portion reductions and price increases at some of our former favorite eateries. Unlike other attractions and shops inside the resort, the food and beverage operation remains in constant flux. Venues open and close, add and delete menu items, and change decor throughout the year. We strive to provide you with the most accurate information possible; however, we do eventually have to go to press with the most current information we have at the time. Keep this in mind when using the guide. You can find up-to-date Disneyland Resort menu information in the Lines app and the official Disneyland app.

You can expect to pay hefty prices for food within Disneyland Resort. Nearly every entrée, snack, and drink purchased inside the theme parks and resort hotels will cost anywhere from 50% to 300% more than similar items at your hometown eateries. On the concession markup scale, Disneyland falls just behind airports and sports stadiums. As a Vancouver, Washington, reader observed:

After visiting the park several times in the last couple years, I've finally come to accept that the price charged for food, souvenirs, and lodging is probably double what they are actually worth. Sort of like getting charged $10 for a Bud Light at an NBA game.

However, its food is a bargain compared to some regional theme parks, and you can find munchies at more moderate (or at least mall-like) prices in Downtown Disney. To prepare your belly and budget, Disneyland's official app lets you browse the menu (including prices) for every eatery in the resort, from fine dining to the churro carts.

With fine dining offered at Disney California Adventure (DCA), you can enjoy a glass of wine, a mug of beer, or even a cocktail without having to exit the park. Downtown Disney offers a wide variety of dining options, from mediocre to awesome, from intimate and adult to wild and kid-friendly. The Grand Californian Hotel is home to **Napa Rose,** one of the finest dining spots in all of Southern California, and even character meals at eateries such as **Storytellers Cafe** and **Disney's PCH Grill** offer better, healthier food than ever before.

DISNEY DINING 101

DISNEYLAND RESORT RESTAURANT RESERVATIONS: WHAT'S IN A NAME

DISNEY TINKERS CEASELESSLY with its restaurant-reservations policy. Disney Dining issues reservations that aren't exactly reservations. When you call Disney Dining at ☎ 714-781-3463, your name and essential information are taken, well, as if you were making a reservation. The Disney rep then tells you that you have dining reservations for the restaurant on the date and time you requested, usually explaining that you will be seated ahead of walk-ins—that is, those guests without reservations. Frequent eaters who hate talking on the phone will be thrilled to find that Disneyland's online dining reservations system allows you to book a table without any pesky human interaction. On your computer or smartphone, visit disneyland.disney.go.com/dining, or tap "Dining" in the Disneyland app, to see restaurant availability; most tables may be reserved through either method, but dining packages for

unofficial **TIP**
Dining reservations are available to all Disneyland visitors—not just guests of the resort hotels. In the theme parks, you can make reservations for later in the day at the door of the restaurant.

shows and parades must be booked via a web browser rather than the mobile app. You will need to create a Disney login account (if you don't already have one) and supply a credit card and phone number to secure a booking (see the discussion below). Reservations can be booked 60 days in advance for Disneyland Resort hotel guests and off-site visitors alike, starting at midnight PST online or 7 a.m. PST over the phone.

Travelers who have experienced Walt Disney World's dining reservations system will be relieved to discover that Disneyland's dining reservations scheme is far less stress-inducing, largely because the Disney Dining Plan is not nearly as popular in Anaheim. Except during the busiest season, most restaurants in the park offer same-week (and often same-day) availability, especially if you are flexible with your mealtimes. If your preferred seatings are unavailable at first, keep checking back, because cancellations are common.

BEHIND THE SCENES AT DISNEYLAND RESORT DINING

DISNEY RESTAURANTS OPERATE on what they call a template system. Instead of scheduling reservations for actual tables, reservationists fill time slots. The number of slots available is based on the average observed length of time that guests occupy a table at a particular restaurant. Disneyland Resort Dining (DRD) tries to fill every time slot for every seat in the restaurant, or come as close to filling every slot as possible. No seats—repeat, none—are *reserved* for walk-ins, though all restaurants accommodate such customers on a space-available basis.

With dining reservations, your waiting time will almost always be less than 20 minutes during peak hours, and often less than 10 minutes. If you just walk in, especially during busier seasons, expect to wait 40–75 minutes.

Note: Disneyland dining reservations are the Disney-restaurant equivalent of FastPass. This feature, available where noted, gives you the option of picking a time and cutting to the head of the line. You may still have to wait, but it's from the front of the line instead of the back.

GETTING YOUR ACT TOGETHER

DRD HANDLES reservations for both Disney-owned and independent restaurants at the theme parks, Disney hotels, and Downtown Disney.

If you fail to make dining reservations before you leave home, or if you want to make your dining decisions spontaneously, your chances of getting a table at the restaurant of your choice are good. Blue Bayou at Disneyland Park, Carthay Circle at DCA, Napa Rose at the Grand Californian Hotel, and the various character-meal venues are the most likely to sell out. If, however, you visit Disneyland during a busy time of year, it's to your advantage to make dining reservations.

Disneyland collects a credit card number with every dining reservation. If you poop out in the park and are a no-show for your meal, you will be charged $10 per person. Your reservation will be voided 15 minutes after the scheduled time, and the penalty will apply unless you call DRD at least 24 hours before your seating (some restaurants or events require more notice). This same cancellation policy applies to appointments at Bibbidi Bobbidi Boutique, as well as cabanas at the hotel pools. If you've lined up many seatings, it's a good idea to phone DRD a few days before you arrive to make sure that everything is in order. If you stay at a Disney resort, Guest Services can print out a summary of all your dining reservations. If you have a seating for a theme park restaurant at a time before park opening, as is sometimes the case for a character breakfast, simply proceed to the turnstiles and inform a cast member, who will admit you to the park.

DRESS

DRESS IS INFORMAL at all theme park restaurants, but dressy casual is appropriate for resort restaurants such as Napa Rose. That means dress slacks (or dress shorts) with a collared shirt for men and slacks, skirts, or dress shorts with a blouse or sweater (or a dress) for women.

FOOD ALLERGIES AND SPECIAL REQUESTS

WITH MILLIONS OF AMERICANS now reporting sensitivity to certain foods or following specific diets, the restaurants at Disneyland Resort are receiving a record number of special dietary requests. Happily, Disney has responded to this trend and is now able to accommodate most guests' gustatory needs. If you have dietary concerns, call ☎ 714-781-3463 to discuss any special requests when making dining reservations, and ask to speak with a chef or manager before your meal whenever arriving at a restaurant to confirm that your needs can be met.

Disneyland provides allergy-friendly menus upon request at many of its table- and quick-service restaurants, both inside and outside the theme parks. These menus explicitly call out dishes without ingredients such as gluten, dairy, peanuts, tree nuts, eggs, soy, or shellfish. If you have one of these common allergies or are vegetarian, you can be confident of finding something to eat almost anywhere without needing to make special arrangements ahead of time. However, if you have an uncommon or complicated allergy or a metabolic disorder, email special.diets@disneyland.com with your needs at least two weeks before your visit.

Kosher meals are available on request at Plaza Inn, Rancho del Zocalo, and Galactic Grill at Disneyland Park, and at Smokejumpers Grill at DCA. Kosher meals can also be delivered to table-service locations with 24 hours' notice (call the above number). About the only diet that can still be challenging to accommodate is vegan. While all locations have vegetarian dishes, they often don't alert you to incidental animal products in things such as cooking oil.

The Disney folks do their best to meet guests' needs, but they don't have separate allergen-free kitchen facilities or dining areas, so inadvertent cross contamination is always a possibility. Large coolers are prohibited unless your dietary issue is a matter of life or death. However, you are allowed to bring your own food and medication into the parks in small soft-sided coolers; loose ice cubes and dry ice are prohibited, but you can bring reusable ice packs or frozen bottled water. Medication can be refrigerated at First Aid. Glass containers are still prohibited, but snacks and EpiPens are OK; just know that Disney employees aren't allowed to hold or heat up your personal food.

Do Disney's attempts at dietary accommodation work? Well, a Phillipsburg, New Jersey, mom reports her family's experience:

My 6-year-old has many food allergies, and we often have to bring food with us to restaurants when we go out to eat. I was able to make reservations at the Disney restaurants in advance and indicate these allergies to the reservation clerk. When we arrived at the restaurants, the staff was already aware of my child's allergies and assigned our table a chef who double-checked the list of allergies with us. Each member of the waitstaff was also informed of the allergies. The chefs were very nice and made my son feel very special (to the point where my other family members felt a little jealous).

However, employees at outdoor food carts, as well as at the temporary kitchen kiosks used during special events, may not be as well educated about allergies, as a reader from Salt Spring Island, British Columbia, discovered:

We were there for the start of Festival of Holidays, and it was impossible to get anything gluten-free. Cast members did not have answers to dietary restrictions.

A FEW CAVEATS

BEFORE YOU BEGIN EATING YOUR WAY through Disneyland, take our advice:

1. However creative and enticing the menu descriptions, avoid fancy food at full-service restaurants in the theme parks. Order dishes that the kitchen is unlikely to botch. Stick with what's familiar in most cases and you won't be disappointed.

2. Don't order baked, broiled, poached, or grilled seafood unless the restaurant specializes in seafood or rates at least ★★★½ in our dining profiles.

3. Theme park restaurants rush their customers to make room for the next group of diners. Eating at high speed may appeal to a family with young, restless children, but for people wanting to relax, it's more like dining in a pressure chamber. The exceptions to this rule may be Wine Country Trattoria and Carthay Circle Restaurant inside DCA, upscale venues that encourage a respite over a glass or bottle of premium wine. But, sadly, you may feel pressure even there in peak season.

   If you want to linger over your expensive meal, don't order your entire dinner at once. Order drinks, study the menu while you sip, and then order appetizers. Tell the waiter you need more time to decide among entrées. Order your main course only after appetizers have been served. Dawdle over coffee and dessert.

DISNEYLAND RESORT RESTAURANT CATEGORIES

IN GENERAL, food and beverage offerings at Disneyland Resort are defined by service, price, and convenience:

FULL-SERVICE RESTAURANTS Full-service restaurants are in all Disneyland Resort hotels, both parks, and Downtown Disney. Disney operates most of the restaurants in the theme parks and its hotels; contractors or franchisees operate those at Downtown Disney. The restaurants accept Visa, MasterCard, American Express, Discover, and Diners Club.

BUFFETS AND FIXED-PRICE MEALS With set-price character meals, you can choose one item each from a limited selection of appetizers, salads, main courses, and desserts. Character buffets, such as the one at Goofy's Kitchen in the Disneyland Hotel, have a separate children's menu featuring kid favorites such as hot dogs, burgers, chicken nuggets, pizza, macaroni and cheese, and spaghetti and meatballs, as well as healthier options such as sliced fruit, yogurt, and whole-grain baked goods. Dining reservations are highly recommended for all character meals.

COUNTER SERVICE Counter-service fast food is available at both theme parks and Downtown Disney. The food compares in quality with McDonald's, Long John Silver's, Pizza Hut, or Taco Bell but is more expensive, though it's often served in larger portions.

HARD CHOICES

DINING DECISIONS will definitely affect your Disneyland Resort experience. If you're short on time and you want to see the theme parks, avoid full service. Ditto if you're short on funds. If you want to try a Disney full-service restaurant, arrange dining reservations—this won't reserve you a table, but it will minimize your wait.

Integrating Meals into the Unofficial Guide Touring Plans

Arrive before the park of your choice opens. Tour expeditiously, using your chosen plan (taking as few breaks as possible) until about 11–11:30 a.m. Once the park becomes crowded around midday, meals and other breaks won't affect the plan's efficiency. If you intend to stay in the park for evening parades, fireworks, or other events, eat dinner early enough to be finished in time for the festivities.

Character Dining

A number of restaurants, primarily those that serve all-you-can-eat buffets or family-style meals, offer character dining. At character meals, you pay a fixed price and dine in the presence of one to five Disney characters who circulate throughout the restaurant, hugging children, posing for photos, and signing autographs. Character breakfasts, lunches, and dinners are served at restaurants in and out of the theme parks. For an extensive discussion of character dining, see pages 156–158.

FULL-SERVICE DINING FOR FAMILIES WITH YOUNG CHILDREN

unofficial **TIP**
Bottom line: Young children are the rule, not the exception, at Disney restaurants.

NO MATTER HOW FORMAL A RESTAURANT appears, the staff is accustomed to impatient and often boisterous children. In Disneyland Resort's finest dining rooms, it's not unusual to find at least two dozen young diners attired in basic black . . . mouse ears.

Almost all Disney restaurants offer children's menus, and all have booster seats and high chairs. Waiters will supply little ones with crackers and rolls and serve your dinner much faster than in comparable restaurants elsewhere. In fact, letters from readers suggest that being served too quickly is much more common than having a long wait.

QUIET, ROMANTIC PLACES TO EAT

RESTAURANTS WITH GOOD FOOD *and* a couple-friendly ambience are rare in the theme parks. **Blue Bayou** at Disneyland Park satisfies both requirements. In DCA, **Wine Country Trattoria** offers one of the quietest and more relaxed environments, along with a California wine country–inspired menu, while the elegant **Carthay Circle Restaurant** ranks as one of the best restaurants in any theme park. Among the hotels at the resort, **Napa Rose** at the Grand Californian Hotel is the leading candidate for a romantic adult dining experience. At Downtown Disney, try **Ralph Brennan's Jazz Kitchen**; ask for a quiet table, though, if you're not interested in the jazz music. **Catal** in Downtown Disney also offers a quiet ambience and an ambitious gourmet menu geared mostly to adults.

Eating later in the evening and choosing a restaurant we've mentioned will improve your chances for intimate dining; nevertheless, know that children, well behaved or otherwise, are everywhere at Disneyland, and you can't escape them.

FAST FOOD IN THE THEME PARKS

BECAUSE MOST MEALS during a Disneyland vacation are consumed on the run while touring, we'll tackle counter-service and vendor foods first. Plentiful at all theme parks are hot dogs, hamburgers, chicken sandwiches, salads, and pizza. They're augmented by special items that relate to the park's theme or the part of the park you're touring. In the alpine village setting of Fantasyland, for example, counter-service bratwurst is sold; in New Orleans Square, Cajun and Creole dishes are available. Counter-service prices are fairly consistent from park to park. Expect to pay the same amount for your coffee or hot dog at DCA that you would at Disneyland Park.

If you are used to counter-service food at Walt Disney World, the quality and variety in Anaheim may catch you off guard, as it did a Cottleville, Missouri, reader:

> *I was surprised that the counter-service food was so excellent. Plaza Inn, Flo's V8 Cafe, and French Market were superb. Selection and quality were clearly better than even table service at WDW.*

Getting your act together in regard to counter service is more a matter of courtesy than necessity. Rude guests rank fifth among reader complaints. A mother from Fort Wayne, Indiana, points out that indecision can be as maddening as outright discourtesy, especially when you're hungry:

> *Every fast-food restaurant has menus the size of billboards, but do you think anybody reads them? People waiting in line spend enough time in front of these menus to memorize them and still don't have a clue what they want when they finally get to the order taker. Tell your readers to PULEEEZ get their orders together ahead of time!*

Another reader offers a tip about counter-service food lines:

Many counter-service registers serve two queues each, one to the left and one to the right of each register. People are not used to this and will instinctively line up in one queue per register. We had register operators wave us up to the front several times to start a left queue instead of waiting behind others on the right.

Healthful Food at Disneyland Resort

*un*official **TIP**
Restaurants with a **Disney Check** logo on their menus (Mickey's head with a check mark) offer special meals for kids ages 3–9. Menu items (including turkey meatballs, chicken skewers, and PB&J sandwiches) are designed to meet balanced nutritional guidelines with zero saturated and trans fats, less sugar, and reduced sodium.

One of the most commendable developments in food service at Disneyland has been the introduction of healthier foods and snacks. Diabetics, vegetarians, weight watchers, those requiring kosher meals, and guests on restricted diets should be able to find something to eat. The same goes for anyone seeking wholesome, nutritious food. Health-conscious choices (including gluten-free bread) are available at most fast-food counters and even from select vendors. A simple request is likely to get you what you need even if it doesn't always appear on the menu.

Cutting Your Dining Time at the Theme Parks

Even if you confine your meals to vendor and counter-service fast food, you lose a lot of time getting sustenance in the theme parks. At Disneyland Park and DCA, everything begins with a line and ends with a cash register. When it comes to fast food, *fast* may apply to the time you spend eating it, not the time invested in obtaining it.

Here are suggestions for minimizing the time you spend hunting and gathering food:

1. Don't waste touring time on breakfast at the parks. Restaurants outside Disneyland offer some outstanding breakfast specials. Many hotels furnish small refrigerators in guest rooms, or you can rent one. If you can get by on cold cereal, rolls, fruit, and juice, having a fridge in your room will save a ton of time. If you can't get a fridge, bring a cooler.

2. After a good breakfast, buy snacks from vendors in the parks as you tour, or stuff some snacks in a hip pack. This is very important if you're on a tight schedule and can't spend a lot of time waiting in line for food.

3. All theme park restaurants are busiest 11:30 a.m.–2:15 p.m. for lunch and 6–9 p.m. for dinner. For shorter lines and faster service, don't eat during these hours, especially 12:30–1:30 p.m.

4. Many counter-service restaurants sell cold sandwiches. Buy a cold lunch (except for drinks) before 11:30 a.m., and carry it until you're ready to eat. Ditto for dinner. Bring small plastic bags in which to pack the food; purchase drinks at the appropriate time from any convenient vendor.

5. Most fast-food eateries have more than one service window. Regardless of the time of day, check the lines at all windows before queuing. Sometimes a window that's staffed but out of the way will have a much shorter line or none at all. Note, however, that some windows may offer only certain items.

6. If you're short on time and the park closes early, stay until closing and eat dinner outside Disneyland before returning to your hotel. If the park stays open late, eat dinner about 4 or 4:30 p.m. at the restaurant of your choice. You should miss the last wave of lunchers and sneak in just ahead of the dinner crowd. Be warned, however, that most eateries at Downtown Disney and the Disneyland Resort hotels stop serving at 10 p.m., even when the parks are open until midnight.

7. Crowds pack nearby eateries before, during, and immediately after special events, parades, and shows such as Disneyland's *Fantasmic!* and *World of Color* in DCA. Conversely, dining venues far from the action are almost empty during their run times, and you can typically walk right up to the counter without any wait at all.

Mobile Ordering

Disneyland Resort has rolled out Mobile Ordering to a growing number of counter-service restaurants and snack windows inside both parks. If you have a Disney online account (with an associated credit card), you can use the mobile app to make your family's meal selections before arriving at the restaurant. Once you're ready to dine, alert the app to your presence, and your food will soon be ready to pick up from a designated window, without ever needing to engage with a human cashier. Mobile Ordering even automatically applies annual pass discounts and allows limited customization of entrées and side dishes, along with options for specific allergy requirements. We are huge fans of using Mobile Ordering, which has saved us up to 30 minutes of standing in line for a register, though you'll still wait a few minutes for your order to be assembled.

Beyond Counter Service: Tips for Saving Money on Food

Though buying food from counter-service restaurants and vendors will save you time and money compared with full-service dining, additional strategies can bolster your budget and maintain your waistline. Over the years, our readers have offered the following suggestions:

1. Go to Disneyland during a period of fasting and abstinence. You can save a fortune *and* save your soul!

2. Wear clothes that are slightly too small and make you feel like dieting. (No spandex!)

3. Whenever you're feeling hungry, ride the Mad Tea Party, the Incredicoaster, or other attractions that can induce motion sickness.

4. Leave your cash and credit cards at your hotel. Buy food only with money your children fish out of fountains and wishing wells.

5. There's no official limit on sourdough bread slices and sample chocolate squares from Boudin Bakery and Ghirardelli at DCA. Test that theory by bouncing back and forth between them until you're sufficiently carb-loaded, or security leads you away.

Cost-conscious readers also have volunteered ideas for stretching food dollars. A Missouri mom writes:

We stocked our cooler with milk and sandwich fixings. I froze water in a milk jug, and we replenished it daily from the resort ice machine.

I also froze small packages of deli meats for later in the week. We ate cereal, milk, and fruit each morning, with boxed juices. I also had a hot pot to boil water for instant coffee, oatmeal, and soup.

Each child had a hip pack, which he filled from a box of goodies each day. The box included actual food, such as packages of crackers and cheese or peanuts and raisins, and worthless junk, such as candy and gum. They grazed from their packs throughout the day, with no interference from Mom and Dad. Each also had a small, rectangular plastic water bottle that could hang on the belt. We filled these at water fountains before getting into lines and were the envy of many.

We left the park before noon; ate sandwiches, chips, and soda in the room; and napped. We purchased our evening meal in the park at a counter-service eatery. We budgeted for morning and evening snacks from a vendor but often did not need them. It made the occasional treat all the more special.

The top budget-trimming tip we can offer is to skip the soft drinks and instead order free ice water with every meal. It's far healthier and more hydrating than soda (sugared or artificially sweetened), and at $4 per large fountain drink, you'll be shocked how swiftly the savings add up. The park's drinking fountains are potable in a pinch, but the filtered water that all counter-service restaurants (excluding vending carts) give away tastes as good as the bottled Dasani they sell for $4.

A mom from Whiteland, Indiana, who purchases drinks in the parks, offers this suggestion:

One must-take item if you're traveling with younger kids is a supply of small cups to split drinks, which are both huge and expensive.

We interviewed one woman who brought a huge picnic for her family of five packed in a large diaper–baby paraphernalia bag. She stowed the bag in a locker on Main Street and retrieved it when the family was hungry.

Note: Disney prohibits loose or dry ice, glass containers, and alcoholic beverages, as well as coolers larger than a six-pack and backpacks larger than 18 by 25 by 37 inches (the maximum dimensions that will fit inside the parks' lockers).

THEME PARK COUNTER-SERVICE RESTAURANT
Mini-Profiles

TO HELP YOU FIND PALATABLE fast-service foods that suit your taste, we have developed mini-profiles of Disneyland Park and DCA counter-service restaurants. The restaurants are listed alphabetically by park. Detailed profiles of all Disneyland full-service restaurants follow this section, beginning on page 181.

The restaurants profiled in the following pages are rated for quality and portion size as well as value. The value rating ranges from A to F as follows:

A = Exceptional value, a real bargain **B** = Good value	
C = Fair value, you get exactly what you pay for	
D = Somewhat overpriced **F** = Significantly overpriced	

Note: Because they offer special or unusual dishes, the following counter-service restaurants are profiled in full and are listed with the full-service restaurants:

- Docking Bay 7 Food and Cargo *Disneyland Park*
- French Market Restaurant *Disneyland Park*
- Plaza Inn *Disneyland Park*
- Rancho del Zocalo Restaurante *Disneyland Park*
- Tangaroa Terrace *Disneyland Hotel*

DISNEYLAND PARK

Alien Pizza Planet

QUALITY Fair-Good   **VALUE** C   **PORTION** Medium-Large   **LOCATION** Tomorrowland
Reader-Survey Responses 81% 👍

Selections Large slices of pizza; pasta with meatballs or chicken; Caesar, Asian chicken, or antipasto salads.

Comments Alien Pizza Planet (formerly known as Redd Rockett's Pizza Port) is loosely themed after the arcade eatery from the Toy Story movies. The restaurant is set up cafeteria-style, so all hot items sit under heat lamps until someone grabs them, but servers will be happy to mix up a fresh bowl of pasta or a pizza on request (a much better choice). The Asian chicken noodle salad is topped with edamame and a tangy citrus sauce, and seasonal pizza toppings such as buffalo chicken are offered. Free drink refills are available. The cafeteria-style setup usually means less waiting. The AC system is on steroids, making it a really cool place on a hot day. Even on the busiest days, there's ample room to sit on the outdoor patio.

Bengal Barbecue

QUALITY Good-Excellent   **VALUE** B-   **PORTION** Small   **LOCATION** Adventureland
READER-SURVEY RESPONSES 92% 👍

Selections Beef, chicken, pork, or veggie skewers; breadsticks; spring rolls.

Comments Skewers are small, but most items cost less than $7. The bacon-wrapped asparagus and pork belly skewers are best, proving the old adage that everything tastes better on a stick. Portions have shrunk noticeably over the years, but this is still a good and relatively healthy fast-food alternative to the dine-in options inside the park. A couple dozen tables are inside the covered bazaar behind the food stand.

Daisy's Diner

QUALITY Fair   **VALUE** C-   **PORTION** Medium   **LOCATION** Mickey's Toontown
Reader-Survey Responses 85% 👍

BEST SNACKS AT DISNEYLAND RESORT

We share our snacking insights on keeping your tummy happy at The Happiest Place on Earth. Call ☎ 714-781-0112 for a recorded message that reveals what candy will be made that week.

DISNEYLAND PARK

- Frozen lemonade *(vending cart)* • Ronto Wrap *(Star Wars: Galaxy's Edge)*
- Mustafarian Lava Roll *(Star Wars: Galaxy's Edge)* • Turkey legs *(vending cart)*
- Stuffed baked potatoes *(Troubadour Tavern)* • Honey-pot krispie *(Pooh Corner)*
- DL Tigger tails *(Pooh Corner)* • Pommes frites *(Café Orléans)* • Taffy *(Candy Palace)*
- Pickles *(Critter Country Fruit Cart)* • English toffee *(Candy Palace)*
- New Orleans fritters *(Royal Street Veranda)* • Peanut brittle *(Candy Palace)*
- Apple pie apple *(Pooh Corner)* • Mickey-shaped crispy rice treat *(Candy Palace)*
- Pork belly skewer *(Bengal Barbecue)* • Snickerdoodles *(Pooh Corner)*
- Mint juleps *(nonalcoholic; Mint Julep Bar)* • Bratwurst *(Troubadour Tavern)*
- Chocolate-dipped Oreos *(Pooh Corner)* • Side of chili with cheese *(Golden Horseshoe)*
- Bacon-wrapped asparagus *(Bengal Barbecue)* • Corn dog *(Little Red Wagon)*
- Mickey-shaped pancakes *(breakfast at Red Rose Taverne)*
- Mickey-shaped waffles *(breakfast at Carnation Café)*
- Chili-lime corn on the cob *(Edelweiss Snacks)*
- Raspberry Dole whip and pineapple *lumpia (Tropical Hideaway)*
- Coconut macaroons shaped like the Matterhorn *(Jolly Holiday Bakery Café)*
- Ice cream in a freshly made, chocolate-dipped waffle cone *(Gibson Girl Ice Cream Parlor)*
- Pretzels stuffed with jalapeño cheese *(Refreshment Corner)*
- Pineapple—Dole whips, Dole whip floats, pineapple spears *(Tiki Juice Bar)*

DISNEY CALIFORNIA ADVENTURE

- Red's Apple Freeze *(Cozy Cone Motel)* • Charcuterie board *(Alfresco Tasting Terrace)*
- Hand-dipped ice cream bars *(Clarabelle's)* • Corn dog *(Corn Dog Castle)*
- Character-inspired candy apples *(Trolley Treats)* • Seasonal doughnuts *(Schmoozies)*
- Funky flavored popcorn *(Cozy Cone Motel)* • Saltwater taffy *(Bing Bong's Sweet Stuff)*
- Milkshakes with cookie "road gravel" *(Flo's V8 Cafe)*
- Edamame with sriracha *(Lucky Fortune Cookery)*
- Chocolate-covered pineapple skewer *(Trolley Treats)*
- Freshly made caramel popcorn *(cart near Carthay Circle)*

DOWNTOWN DISNEY

- Fried shrimp po'boy *(Ralph Brennan's Jazz Kitchen Express)*
- Candy unique to Disneyland *(Marceline's Confectionery)*
- Churro ice cream sandwich *(vending cart)*
- Beignets and chicory coffee *(Ralph Brennan's Jazz Kitchen Express)*
- Milkshakes *(Black Tap Craft Burgers & Shakes)*

RESORT RESTAURANTS

- Tuna poke *(GCH Craftsman Grill at Grand Californian Hotel)*
- Panko-crusted long beans *(Trader Sam's Enchanted Tiki Bar at Disneyland Hotel)*
- Caramel French toast *(character breakfast at Storytellers Café at Grand Californian Hotel)*

Selections Pepperoni and cheese pizzas.

Comments Subpar pizza for eating on the run, with no convenient place to sit.

Galactic Grill

QUALITY Fair   **VALUE** C+   **PORTION** Large   **LOCATION** Tomorrowland
Reader-Survey Responses 80% 👍

Selections Breakfast burrito, egg-and-bacon sandwich, or French toast sticks; Angus burger, chicken sandwich, chopped salad with chicken, or veggie wrap; kids' meals of chicken nuggets, turkey sandwich, burger, or smoothie with fruit and crackers.

Comments The food isn't anything special, though the bread is fresh. Seating is available outdoors overlooking the Tomorrowland Terrace stage, which hosts live music.

The Golden Horseshoe

QUALITY Fair   **VALUE** C   **PORTION** Medium   **LOCATION** Frontierland
Reader-Survey Responses 83% 👍

Selections Chicken wings, fish-and-chips, grilled chicken salad, chili, and ice cream sundaes.

Comments The Golden Horseshoe hosts live interactive entertainment and fair fried food. Meaty chili is a tribute to Walt and available atop loaded potato skins or pepper jack mac and cheese (or in an unadvertised side portion perfect for snacking). Service can be slow. Opera box–style seating next to the stage is best.

Harbour Galley

QUALITY Good   **VALUE** B   **PORTION** Medium   **LOCATION** Critter Country
Reader-Survey Responses 86% 👍

Selections Clam chowder, broccoli Cheddar soup, or seasonal soup, all served in a sourdough bread bowl; tuna or shrimp salad; lobster roll with house-made potato chips; lobster mac and cheese.

Comments The soup-filled bread bowls are always a reliable choice, especially the lobster bisque (when in season). Limited seating, but other seats are available along the dock around the back of the restaurant. The lobster roll is skimpy and overseasoned with Old Bay.

Hungry Bear Restaurant

QUALITY Fair-Good   **VALUE** B   **PORTION** Medium–Large   **LOCATION** Critter Country
Reader-Survey Responses 90% 👍

Selections Barbecue double cheeseburger, a fried fish sandwich with spicy-sweet slaw, and a fried chicken sandwich with honey mustard. Healthier choices include barbecue chicken salad and Messy Melvin's vegan burger.

Comments Popular and crowded during busier times of the year. During slower times, grab a snack and sit on the deck overlooking the Rivers of America. The barbecue salad is a good lighter choice; balance it out with a funnel cake for dessert. On nights when *Fantasmic!* is shown, Hungry Bear offers a dining package for $29.99 per adult ($19.99 for kids 3–9), plus tax, that includes an entrée, drink, and a FastPass to *Fantasmic!* (see page 264 for details).

Jolly Holiday Bakery Café

QUALITY Good–Excellent **VALUE** B **PORTION** Medium **LOCATION** Main Street, U.S.A.
Reader-Survey Responses 94% 👍

Selections Egg and bacon croissants for breakfast; chicken and sun-dried tomato Caesar salad; mixed greens with pecans and Feta; toasted cheese sandwich with tomato soup; turkey, tuna salad, roast beef, or caprese sandwich; grilled vegetable salad; assorted pastries and coffees.

Comments Themed to *Mary Poppins,* with stained glass windows featuring penguin waiters, this is a good spot for a light breakfast or lunch, though lines can grow long at peak mealtimes. Seating is outdoors only, and soup portions are small, but the salads and sandwiches are substantial and savory. The caprese sandwich and grilled veggie salad are among the park's best quick-service entrées for vegetarians. Don't miss the massive Matterhorn coconut macaroons, and be sure to ask about the tasty yet affordable seasonal items.

Kat Saka's Kettle

QUALITY Good **VALUE** B- **PORTION** Medium **LOCATION** Galaxy's Edge
Reader-Survey Responses Too new to rate

Selections Kettle-cooked popcorn with sweet, spicy, and savory seasoning.

Comments A local grain farmer runs this small stand, serving red and purple kernels coated in exotic spices collected from across the galaxy. Outpost Mix combines three different flavors; you can't order them individually. Soda is sold in collectible spherical bottles that make affordable souvenirs.

Market House

QUALITY Good **VALUE** B- **PORTION** Medium **LOCATION** Main Street, U.S.A.
Reader-Survey Responses 97% 👍

Selections Starbucks coffee, cocoa, tea, pastries, and breakfast sandwiches.

Comments Starbucks's usual vast array of blended beverages is available (including seasonal flavors), accompanied by its trademark long lines. You can also get a selection of hot breakfast sandwiches in the morning and sweets all day. Starbucks loyalty cards are valid for payment, and you'll earn stars for your purchase, but you can only redeem rewards at the Downtown Disney location. The coffee shop features a seating area themed after a vintage bookshop. Look for the potbellied stove, checkerboard, and antique party line phones, all holdovers from the former decor.

Milk Stand

QUALITY Fair–Poor **VALUE** C- **PORTION** Small **LOCATION** Galaxy's Edge
Reader-Survey Responses Too new to rate

Selections Frozen nondairy "milk" drinks.

Comments Direct from the Bubo Wamba Family Farms comes Disney's ill-fated attempt at a Butterbeer-style must-try beverage. Luckily, guests don't have to suckle this vegan coconut and rice milk frozen slushie straight from a sea cow's nipple. Green (as seen in *The Last Jedi*) has tropical flavors like orange blossom and tangerine; the blue beverage from *A New Hope* tastes of berry and melon. Both have the cloying mouth-feel of fruit-scented shampoo, and it's debatable which is more undrinkable; we advise splitting one with a group or skipping it altogether.

Oga's Cantina

QUALITY Good-Excellent   **VALUE** B-   **PORTION** Medium   **LOCATION** Galaxy's Edge
Reader-Survey Responses   Too new to rate

Selections Alcoholic and non-alcoholic cocktails; exclusive wines and beer; Japanese-style snack mix.

Comments This cantina, overseen by alien proprietor Oga Garra, will instantly remind fans of the Mos Eisley watering hole seen in *A New Hope*. DJ R-3X (better known as Captain Rex, the former Star Tours droid pilot voiced by Paul "Pee Wee Herman" Rubens), spins an original 80s-style synth-pop soundtrack. Bartenders dispense drinks from a tangle of tubes and bubbling tubs behind the bar; all beverages here are premixed and *Star Wars* themed, so you can't order a gin and tonic or other terrestrial tipple. Ten signature alcoholic cocktails are on the menu, including Bespin Fizz (a bubbly Cosmopolitan), Fuzzy Tauntaun (foam-topped citrus), Jedi Mind Trick (botanicals and bitter grapefruit), and Yub Nub (passion fruit rum punch). Our favorites are the Outer Rim margarita with black salt and the spicy bourbon Jet Juice. Draft craft beers and private-label wines—such as Toniray, a teal-colored cuvée from Princess Leia's doomed home planet Alderaan—are also served, as are nonalcoholic drinks (such as the frozen cookie-crowned Blue Bantha) and an addictive snack mix with seaweed crackers and wasabi peas. At breakfast, you can get a Bloody Rancor (Bloody Mary with "bone" garnish) and spiked Spiran coffee with a decadent Mustafarian Lava Roll (cinnamon roll topped with crumbled Oreo cookies) or a refreshing cup of Rising Moons Overnight Oats with yogurt and exotic fruit.

As the first (and so far only) place to drink alcohol inside Disneyland Park, Oga's is packed from rope drop to last call, so you must have a reservation to enter. Use the Disneyland app or visit disneyland.com/cantina at 7 a.m. on the morning of your visit to book your bar time; be prepared for a 15- to 30-minute wait once you check in, and beware of a $10 per person penalty for no-shows. There are only a few booths, so most patrons must stand along the bar. Service can be brusque at best, and if you linger too long over your libation, you may be asked to exit after two drinks or 45 minutes.

Pluto's Dog House

QUALITY Fair-Good   **VALUE** C   **PORTION** Medium   **LOCATION** Mickey's Toontown
Reader-Survey Responses   81% 👍

Selections Hot dog basket, kids' turkey dog, and mac and cheese.
Comments The food's not bad, but there's really no place to sit and eat it.

Red Rose Taverne

QUALITY Excellent-Good   **VALUE** B-   **PORTION** Medium   **LOCATION** Fantasyland
Reader-Survey Responses   90% 👍

Selections The vaguely French-influenced menu includes smoked salmon flatbread and Mickey-shaped pancakes for breakfast, and *pommes frites* and chicken à la Lumière for lunch and dinner, along with hamburgers and chopped salads. Kids can pick a carved turkey sandwich or power pack with carrots and crackers.

Comments Red Rose Taverne replaced the Pinocchio-themed Village Haus, with the release of the 2017 live-action *Beauty and the Beast* remake. The signature Beast's Forbidden Burger is topped with a slice of upscale

Wagyu steak and carmelized onions; it's probably the best burger in the parks. Vegetarians will rejoice over the roasted cauliflower samosa sandwich. Movie-themed desserts include Grey Stuff (tastes better than it sounds) and crispy treats shaped like Chip and Mrs. Potts.

Refreshment Corner

QUALITY Fair–Good **VALUE** C **PORTION** Medium **LOCATION** Main Street, U.S.A.
Reader-Survey Responses 92% 👍

Selections Hot dogs, chili-cheese dogs, and chili in a bread bowl.

Comments Some of the topping selections sound strange (mac and cheese? bacon and avocado mayo?!?), but the dogs are good. Limited seating; time it right to catch the ragtime pianist or Dapper Dans performing on the patio. Ask for your Coke with a shot of raspberry and/or vanilla syrup.

Ronto Roasters

QUALITY Good–Excellent **VALUE** B+ **PORTION** Medium–Large **LOCATION** Galaxy's Edge
Reader-Survey Responses Too new to rate

Selections Flatbread sandwich filled with roast pork and grilled Portuguese sausage, turkey jerky, non-alcoholic fruit punch.

Comments A disgruntled smelting droid named 8D-J8 does the cooking here, turning alien meats on a rotating spit as they roast underneath a recycled podracing engine. The pita sandwiches, dressed with tangy slaw and spicy szechuan peppercorn "clutch sauce," are our favorite snack in Batuu, but the hand-cut jerky (in sweet teriyaki or spicy herb flavors) is painfully dry. Wash it down with a tart Sour Sarlacc raspberry limeade.

Royal Street Veranda

QUALITY Good **VALUE** B **PORTION** Medium **LOCATION** New Orleans Square
Reader-Survey Responses 89% 👍

Selections Steak or vegetarian gumbo and clam chowder, all served in a sourdough bread bowl; coffee, espresso, cappuccino; fritters for dessert.

Comments It can get quite crowded, especially around *Fantasmic!* showings, but usually worth the wait. Veggie gumbo and clam chowder are the best, though all are seasoned well. You have to look hard to find any steak in the steak gumbo. Don't miss the fritters with fruit dipping sauce, which now feature a rotating roster of seasonal varieties, including sweet potato, apple, and banana.

Stage Door Café

QUALITY Fair **VALUE** C– **PORTION** Medium **LOCATION** Frontierland
Reader-Survey Responses 90% 👍

Selections Chicken nuggets, fish-and-chips, corn dogs, and funnel cakes.

Comments The corn dogs are nearly as good as those from the Main Street cart, with a shorter line. The grilled chicken spinach wrap is surprisingly tasty, and the fried fish is edible (albeit previously frozen), but the fries and nuggets are bland. Try the funnel cakes, but avoid the chicken fried steak sandwich at all costs.

Tropical Hideaway

QUALITY Good-Excellent   **VALUE** C+   **PORTION** Small   **LOCATION** Adventureland
Reader-Survey Responses   100% 👍

Selections Pineapple, orange, and raspberry Dole whip soft serve in cups, floats, or sundaes; bao steamed buns stuffed with beef, chicken, or veggies; pineapple-and-cheese-stuffed *lumpia* pastries; cold ramen noodle salad.

Comments Formerly Aladdin's Oasis, and before that the Tahitian Terrace, this outdoor eating area alongside the Jungle Cruise shoreline is a thematic extension of both that ride and the neighboring *Enchanted Tiki Room;* look for Rosita, an animatronic bird mentioned in the show who cracks corny jokes at passing boats. The bao are savory but insanely overpriced. The pineapple *lumpia* is a must-try, as is the loaded Dole whip with fruit chunks, coconut flakes, crystallized hibiscus, and Pocky "spears"; try requesting it with raspberry.

Troubadour Tavern

QUALITY Fair-Good   **VALUE** C+   **PORTION** Medium   **LOCATION** Fantasyland
Reader-Survey Responses   91% 👍

Selections Bratwurst with sauerkraut, jumbo pretzels with cheese sauce, stuffed baked potatoes (with bacon and sour cream or broccoli and cheese), turkey legs, and ice cream bites.

Comments Built as a concession stand for Fantasyland Theatre, Troubadour Tavern is overwhelmed during shows but often overlooked the rest of the day. This is the only quick-service sausage vendor that serves spicy brown mustard.

Vendor Treats

LOCATIONS Throughout the park   **READER-SURVEY RESPONSES**   90% 👍

Selections Popcorn, fries, smoked turkey legs, ice cream, churros, chimichangas, and more.

Comments There's something undeniably primal about tucking into a huge, meaty smoked turkey leg. For a quick snack, try Maurice's Treats, close to Fantasy Faire; it serves sweet (if overpriced) pastries, as well as a boysenberry apple freeze. Its Cheddar garlic bagel twist is tough and tasteless.

DISNEY CALIFORNIA ADVENTURE

Award Wieners

QUALITY Fair-Good   **VALUE** C   **PORTION** Medium   **LOCATION** Hollywood Land
Reader-Survey Responses   91% 👍

Selections Chili-cheese dogs, grilled sausages, and hot dogs; grilled mushroom, onion, and pepper sandwich.

Comments Street dogs are topped with bacon, fried onions, or pico de gallo and served on a potato roll. Check out the rotating seasonal specialty sausages for some seriously strange condiments. The film strip fries are great with the optional chili cheese.

Boardwalk Pizza & Pasta

QUALITY Good **VALUE** B **PORTION** Medium–Large **LOCATION** Paradise Gardens Park
Reader-Survey Responses 86% 👍

Selections Pizzas run the gamut from a traditional cheese or pepperoni to a vegetarian with roasted seasonal veggies. Pasta offerings include spaghetti and meatballs, chicken pasta in a sun-dried tomato cream sauce, or pesto ravioli. Freshly tossed salads include a chicken Caesar and a Mediterranean chef salad with salami, fresh mozzarella, roasted peppers, and olives in a red-wine vinaigrette.

Comments Part of Paradise Garden, a Victorian-era outdoor courtyard with freestanding beer and corn dog stands outside the plaza. Salads are large enough to split three ways; say "hold the olives" (or another ingredient) for a fresh-mixed serving. The pesto pasta with pine nuts is our top pick. The uncompelling conventional slices come with steep prices.

Cocina Cucamonga Mexican Grill

QUALITY Good-Excellent **VALUE** A- **PORTION** Large **LOCATION** Pacific Wharf
Reader-Survey Responses 88% 👍

Selections Street tacos or rice-and-bean bowls with beef, pork, or chicken; grilled half chicken; chicken salad with corn and avocado dressing; torta ahogada sandwich with pork al pastor. Kids' choices include arroz con pollo (chicken with rice), taco or rice bowl, and chicken quesadillas.

Comments The chicken is marinated with garlic, cilantro, and citrus, and it comes with corn tortillas. Very tasty. The torta is one of the best Disney quick-service entrées in Guy's opinion. If you're looking for something light, try the Cocina Bowls, which include choice of meat, beans, rice, and salsa.

Corn Dog Castle

QUALITY Good **VALUE** B **PORTION** Medium **LOCATION** Paradise Gardens Park
Reader-Survey Responses 92% 👍

Selections Corn dogs, Cheddar cheese sticks, fountain beverages.

Comments The corn dogs served here and at the Little Red Wagon on Main Street, U.S.A. have gained a cult following, and deservedly so: they're the freshest, lightest version of the deep-fried fair favorite you'll ever find. This location can draw long lines but is capable of serving more swiftly than its Disneyland cousin, and it offers additional sausage styles, like hot link. All the dogs are priced to include sliced apples or a small bag of chips, but you can save a few dollars by requesting they hold the side. Skip the cheese stick, which quickly turns cold.

Cozy Cone Motel

QUALITY Fair-Good **VALUE** B- **PORTION** Small-Medium **LOCATION** Cars Land
Reader-Survey Responses 93% 👍

Selections Bread cones stuffed with chili, mac and cheese, or chicken; ice cream; churros; and pretzel bites. Cone #5 coats popcorn in unusual favors such as dill pickle and sriracha, with multiple rotating varieties offered daily. Signature beverages include a syrupy pomegranate limeade (available with or without vodka) and Red's Apple Freeze, a curiously addictive blend of tart frozen apple juice and sweet toasted marshmallow.

Comments Each conical commissary in this food court, based on Sally's construction-cone motel from the film, serves different snacks and drinks with punny names such as "chili cone queso" and "route beer floats." A limited number of picnic tables are behind the motel office, whose interior features a number of hidden Pixar references.

Fiddler, Fifer & Practical Café

QUALITY Good   **VALUE** B-   **PORTION** Medium   **LOCATION** Buena Vista Street
Reader-Survey Responses 92% 👍

Selections Starbucks coffee, hot breakfast sandwiches, cinnamon rolls with cream cheese icing, premade cold sandwiches, and salads.

Comments This quick-service eatery, named after both the Three Little Pigs and an imaginary songstress trio whose manufactured mementos hang inside, boasts a large open dining area in the Arts and Crafts style. You can get your morning jolt of Starbucks-brand joe and grab-and-go breakfast pastries here, but expect long waits around opening. Starbucks loyalty cards can be used for payment but not for free refills or other rewards.

Flo's V8 Cafe

QUALITY Good   **VALUE** B-   **PORTION** Medium–Large   **LOCATION** Cars Land
Reader-Survey Responses 92% 👍

Selections At breakfast, try the French toast, which is more like caramel bread pudding. Lunch and dinner offer fried chicken, cheeseburgers, tuna or club sandwiches, Cobb salad, vegetarian pot pie, and milkshakes.

Comments Cars Land's largest eatery sadly switched its menu from classic American comfort food with a Southwestern twist to standard roadside diner fare. Your best bets are the fried chicken blue plate special and the club sandwich with steak fries. Kids' meals come in a Lightning McQueen car. Memorabilia from proprietor Flo's past as a famous Motown singer is featured in the decor. Sit on the back patio for a spectacular view of Radiator Springs Racers' high-speed finale.

Lucky Fortune Cookery

QUALITY Good   **VALUE** B   **PORTION** Medium   **LOCATION** Pacific Wharf
Reader-Survey Responses 82% 👍

Selections Steamed rice bowls with vegetables and your choice of chicken, beef, or tofu, all with your pick from a variety of pan-Asian sauces, including a popular teriyaki and a spicy, tangy Korean sauce; edamame; mango slices; teriyaki chicken and rice for kids.

Comments The tofu bowl is good, the chicken and beef are average, and the coconut curry sauce is bland. Edamame makes a nice side to share, especially dipped in spicy sriracha sauce. Ingredient quality has been on the upswing here, making the rice bowls a good value.

Pacific Wharf Café

QUALITY Good–Excellent   **VALUE** A   **PORTION** Medium   **LOCATION** Pacific Wharf
Reader-Survey Responses 98% 👍

Selections Fresh salads and soups served in hollowed-out sourdough loaves from San Francisco's famous Boudin bakery, plus turkey sandwiches and macaroni for the kids. The Chinese chicken salad and broccoli-and-cheese soup are both good, as is the clam chowder, with heaps of clams.

Comments Adults will appreciate the food and ambience as well as the very kid-friendly menu (yogurt smoothie, sliced apples, and whole-grain fish crackers). For dessert, try the seasonal bread pudding, or step across the street to Ghirardelli Soda Fountain & Chocolate Shop for candy, hot cocoa, ice cream sundaes, or milkshakes.

Paradise Garden Grill

QUALITY Good–Excellent **VALUE** B- **PORTION** Medium **LOCATION** Paradise Gardens Park
Reader-Survey Responses 92% 👍

Selections This takeout window's excellent standard menu, featuring Mediterranean meats grilled on skewers, beef gyros, and Greek salad, is frequently preempted. During Hispanic festivals such as ¡Viva Navidad! and Asian events like Lunar New Year, the menu offers some excellent ethnic entrées. During the Festival of Holidays and Food & Wine Festival, the fare runs to fried fish and meatless meatballs. The grill may serve a less-interesting menu of hamburgers during peak periods or shutter altogether on slow days.

Comments This open-air venue, with a Victorian beer garden theme, shares seating with Boardwalk Pizza. It usually changes its offerings with the season to tie in with whatever event is currently being promoted.

Pixar Pier Snack Vendors

QUALITY Fair–Good **VALUE** C- **PORTION** Small–Medium **LOCATION** Pixar Pier
Reader-Survey Responses 94% 👍

Selections Soft-serve ice cream, cookies, churros, fried chicken, hot dogs.

Comments When transforming Paradise Pier into Pixar Pier, Disney handed the reigns of several snack stands around the area to second-string CGI characters. The hit menu item at Adorable Snowman Frosted Treats is "It's Snow-Capped Lemon," a nondairy lemon dessert topped with white chocolate, but the line here moves very slowly. Jack-Jack Cookie Num Nums also attracts crowds in front of the Incredicoaster with its ginormous chocolate chip cookies. Señor Buzz Churro is the only spot to get the popular pastry with caliente chili powder. Poultry Palace, which looks like an oversize happy meal box, and Angry Dogs, featuring a statue of the hot-tempered *Inside Out* character, both make more memorable photo ops than eateries.

Smokejumpers Grill

QUALITY Fair–Good **VALUE** C **PORTION** Medium–Large **LOCATION** Grizzly Peak
Reader-Survey Responses 87% 👍

Selections Chili cheeseburger with onion rings or waffle fries, spicy Buffalo chicken sandwich, grilled chicken salad, s'mores, and milkshakes.

Comments The burgers come with a variety of toppings and sauces, and a separate toppings bar is available in case you need to stack on more. The onion rings are decent, and this is the only place in DCA that serves them. Adventurous vegetarians can conquer the barbecue jackfruit sandwich with "bear paw" slaw. The handsome location, inspired by "brave men and women who fight wildfires in our California forests," features ample seating surrounded by lush pine trees.

DISNEYLAND RESORT RESTAURANTS:
Rated and Ranked

TO HELP YOU make your dining choices, we've developed profiles of full-service restaurants at Disneyland Resort. Each profile lets you quickly check the restaurant's cuisine, location, star rating, cost range, quality rating, and value rating. Profiles are listed alphabetically by restaurant. In addition to all full-service restaurants, we also list and profile a couple of counter-service restaurants in the theme parks that transcend basic burgers, hot dogs, and pizza. All restaurants listed here have disabled access.

PAYMENT All Disney restaurants accept American Express, MasterCard, Visa, Diners Club, Discover, and Japanese Credit Bureau.

STAR RATING The star rating represents the entire dining experience: style, service, and ambience, in addition to taste, presentation, and food quality. Five stars, the highest rating, indicates that the restaurant offers the best of everything. Four-star restaurants are above average, and three-star restaurants offer good, though not necessarily memorable, meals. Two-star restaurants serve mediocre fare, and one-star restaurants are below average. Our star ratings don't correspond to ratings awarded by AAA, Forbes, Zagat, or other restaurant reviewers.

COST RANGE The next rating tells how much an entrée (or, depending on the restaurant, an entrée and side dish) will cost. Appetizers, desserts, drinks, and tips aren't included. We've rated the cost as inexpensive, moderate, or expensive.

INEXPENSIVE	$15 or less per person
MODERATE	$15–$35 per person
EXPENSIVE	More than $35 per person

QUALITY RATING The food quality is rated on a scale of one to five stars, five being the best. The quality rating is based on the taste, freshness of ingredients, preparation, presentation, and creativity of food. There is no consideration of price. If you want the best food available and cost is no issue, look no further than the quality ratings.

VALUE RATING If, on the other hand, you are looking for both quality and value, check the value rating, also expressed as stars.

★★★★★	Exceptional value; a real bargain
★★★★	Good value
★★★	Fair value; you get exactly what you pay for
★★	Somewhat overpriced
★	Significantly overpriced

continued on page 181

DISNEYLAND RESORT RESTAURANTS BY CUISINE

CUISINE	LOCATION	OVERALL RATING	COST	QUALITY RATING	VALUE RATING
AMERICAN					
LAMPLIGHT LOUNGE	DCA	★★★½	Exp	★★★★	★★★
THE RIVER BELLE TERRACE	Disneyland Park	★★★	Mod	★★★½	★★½
PLAZA INN*	Disneyland Park	★★★	Mod	★★★	★★★½
TANGAROA TERRACE*	Disneyland Hotel	★★★	Inexp	★★★	★★★½
BLACK TAP CRAFT BURGERS & SHAKES	Downtown Disney	★★★	Mod	★★★	★★★
CARNATION CAFÉ*	Disneyland Park	★★★	Mod	★★★	★★★
SPLITSVILLE LUXURY LANES	Downtown Disney	★★★	Mod	★★★	★★★
DISNEY'S PCH GRILL*	Paradise Pier Hotel	★★★	Mod/Exp	★★★	★★½
GOOFY'S KITCHEN*	Disneyland Hotel	★★	Exp	★★	★★½
CALIFORNIAN/FUSION					
NAPA ROSE	Grand Californian	★★★★★	V. Exp	★★★★★	★★★½
CARTHAY CIRCLE RESTAURANT	DCA	★★★★½	Exp	★★★★½	★★★½
WINE COUNTRY TRATTORIA	DCA	★★★★	Mod	★★★★	★★★
STORYTELLERS CAFÉ*	Grand Californian	★★★½	Exp	★★★★	★★★
DOCKING BAY 7 FOOD AND CARGO	Disneyland Park	★★★½	Inexp	★★★½	★★★
BALLAST POINT	Downtown Disney	★★½	Mod	★★½	★★½
CAJUN/CREOLE					
FRENCH MARKET RESTAURANT	Disneyland Park	★★★½	Inexp	★★★½	★★★★
CAFÉ ORLÉANS	Disneyland Park	★★★½	Mod	★★★½	★★★
BLUE BAYOU	Disneyland Park	★★★½	V. Exp	★★★½	★★½
RALPH BRENNAN'S JAZZ KITCHEN*	Downtown Disney	★★★½	Mod	★★★½	★★½
CHARACTER DINING					
STORYTELLERS CAFÉ*	Grand Californian	★★★½	Exp	★★★★	★★★
PLAZA INN*	Disneyland Park	★★★	Mod	★★★	★★★½
DISNEY'S PCH GRILL*	Paradise Pier Hotel	★★★	Mod/Exp	★★★	★★½
GOOFY'S KITCHEN*	Disneyland Hotel	★★	Exp	★★	★★½
DELI/BAKERY					
NAPOLINI*	Downtown Disney	★★★	Inexp	★★★½	★★★★
LA BREA BAKERY CAFÉ*	Downtown Disney	★★★	Inexp	★★½	★★★

DISNEYLAND RESORT RESTAURANTS BY CUISINE
(continued)

CUISINE	LOCATION	OVERALL RATING	COST	QUALITY RATING	VALUE RATING
ITALIAN					
NAPOLINI*	Downtown Disney	★★★	Inexp	★★★½	★★★★
NAPLES RISTORANTE E PIZZERIA	Downtown Disney	★★★	Mod	★★★	★★★
MEDITERRANEAN					
CATAL RESTAURANT & UVA BAR*	Downtown Disney	★★★½	Mod/Exp	★★★½	★★★
MEXICAN					
TORTILLA JO'S	Downtown Disney	★★★	Mod/Exp	★★½	★★½
RANCHO DEL ZOCALO RESTAURANTE	Disneyland Park	★★½	Inexp	★★½	★★½
POLYNESIAN					
TANGAROA TERRACE*	Disneyland Hotel	★★★	Inexp	★★★	★★★½
STEAK HOUSE					
STEAKHOUSE 55*	Disneyland Hotel	★★★★	V. Exp	★★★★½	★★★

Serves breakfast

continued from page 179

Ballast Point ★★½

CALIFORNIAN   **MODERATE**   **QUALITY** ★★½ **VALUE** ★★½
READER-SURVEY RESPONSES 93% 👍

Downtown Disney; ☎ 714-781-DINE (3463)

Reservations Available. **When to go** Lunch or dinner. **Entrée range** $12–$24. **Service** ★★. **Friendliness** ★★. **Bar** Beer. **Dress** Casual. **Hours** Daily, 11 a.m.–midnight.

SETTING AND ATMOSPHERE Ballast Point, a popular San Diego–based brewer, has brought the Disneyland Resort its first-ever on-site brewery, just as Walt would have wanted. The boatwright-inspired restaurant boasts 4,000 square feet of interior space, including a tasting room and an open kitchen, plus a 3,000-square-foot outdoor beer garden in which to imbibe.

HOUSE SPECIALTIES Southern California–style flatbreads, burgers, salads, and small plates, focusing on sustainable seasonal ingredients.

OTHER RECOMMENDATIONS Beer, beer, and more beer.

SUMMARY AND COMMENTS We had great expectations for the menu here, but despite the impressive ingredient lists, the food turned out like ESPN Zone's sports bar fare, only at a higher price point. Stick with the award-winning craft brews (available in flight-friendly sampling sizes), perhaps paired with a Bavarian pretzel, and enjoy the second-story view over Downtown Disney, but save your appetite for dinner elsewhere.

Black Tap Craft Burgers & Shakes ★★★

AMERICAN **MODERATE** **QUALITY ★★★ VALUE ★★★**
READER-SURVEY RESPONSES Too new to rate

Downtown Disney; ☎ 714-781-DINE (3463)

Reservations Available. **When to go** Lunch or dinner. **Entrée range** $15–$26. **Service**
★★★. **Friendliness** ★★★. **Bar** Beer, wine, and cocktails. **Dress** Casual. **Hours** Daily,
11 a.m.–midnight.

SETTING AND ATMOSPHERE A classic New York–style luncheonette, done
on a Disney scale with indoor and outdoor seating. Think subway tile,
street art, and neon signage.

HOUSE SPECIALTIES Burgers, both beef-based and vegan. For dessert, signature CrazyShakes with over-the-top toppings like cotton candy.

OTHER RECOMMENDATIONS Craft beers from around the country, on draft
and in bottles. Burger-topped salads for those avoiding carbs, Korean barbecue chicken sandwiches, onion rings, and sweet potato fries.

SUMMARY AND COMMENTS Stick to the burgers and you won't be disappointed. The menu offers about a dozen different topping combinations,
from the basic All-American (lettuce, tomato, pickles, American cheese,
and "special sauce") to the fancy-pants Greg Norman (Wagyu beef
topped with blue cheese and arugula). Prime beef is the primary offering, but patties made of bison, turkey, black bean, and falafel are available. Expect to pay $16–$20 for a burger with fries; shakes cost $9–$15
but are big enough to share.

Blue Bayou ★★★½

CAJUN/CREOLE **VERY EXPENSIVE** **QUALITY ★★★½ VALUE ★★½**
READER-SURVEY RESPONSES 87% 👍

Disneyland Park; ☎ 714-781-DINE (3463)

Reservations Required. **When to go** Early or late lunch, early evening. **Entrée range**
$30–$50. **Service** ★★★. **Friendliness** ★★★. **Dress** Casual. **Hours** Daily, 11 a.m.–
10:15 p.m.

SETTING AND ATMOSPHERE Blue Bayou overlooks Pirates of the Caribbean and maintains an appropriately dark, damp ambience. The best
tables ring the perimeter and afford a view of the faux bayou, replete with
fireflies flickering among the weeping willows and mangroves, dilapidated
houseboats, and soft lantern lights. If you're not lucky enough to get a
table bayou-side, there's still enough wrought iron, uneven lighting, and
twilight allure to soften the most hardened soul.

HOUSE SPECIALTIES Lobster tail, filet mignon, and (at lunch) the Monte
Cristo sandwich.

OTHER RECOMMENDATIONS Jambalaya or roasted chicken. Spring for the
saffron-infused bouillabaisse if offered as a seasonal special. Entrées
include a cup of mild gumbo or a superb side salad with candied pecans
and dried cranberries.

SUMMARY AND COMMENTS Easily the fanciest restaurant in Disneyland
Park, Blue Bayou is as close to fine dining as you'll get here. The restaurant
fills quickly and stays busy, so make reservations before you leave home
(up to 60 days in advance) or obtain a same-day reservation at the restaurant door as soon as you get to the park. Though there's a children's menu,

this isn't the place to bring wound-up or tired kids for a leisurely meal; they'll be bored. Tables are tightly packed, and nothing disrupts the busy servers more than wild kids up and out of their seats. Blue Bayou is more of a place where adults can escape the noise and happy chaos in the rest of the park without having to exit the gates. For lunch, we love the Monte Cristo sandwich, a deep-fried turkey, ham, and cheese creation that you don't find on many menus these days. Side dishes—including the Blue Bayou au gratin potatoes and fresh vegetables—are quite good as well. The crème brûlée is also a crowd-pleaser. Servers are Disney-pleasant, if a tad harried, but they're more than happy to accommodate the random request. And the dinner rolls are great! If seated at an unromantically overlit table near the kitchen, don't be shy about requesting a relocation. On days when *Fantasmic!* is shown, Blue Bayou offers a lunch package for $62 per adult ($29 for kids 3–9), plus tax, 11:30 a.m.–4 p.m., and a dinner package after 4 p.m. for $72 per adult ($29 for kids 3–9). Both packages include a starter, entrée, and dessert, as well as a FastPass to *Fantasmic!*'s center viewing section. Unless you order the most expensive items on the prix fixe menu (rib eye or surf and turf), you'll be paying a lot for that FastPass.

La Brea Bakery Café ★★★

DELI/BAKERY	INEXPENSIVE	QUALITY ★★½ VALUE ★★★
READER-SURVEY RESPONSES 92% 👍		

Downtown Disney; ☎ 714-490-0233 or 714-781-DINE; labreabakery.com

Reservations Available. **When to go** Breakfast. **Entrée range** $10–$27. **Service** ★★★. **Friendliness** ★★★. **Bar** Limited. **Dress** Casual. **Hours** Sunday–Thursday, 8 a.m.–9 p.m., Friday–Saturday, 8 a.m.–10 p.m. Open 1 hour later in summer.

SETTING AND ATMOSPHERE This indoor-outdoor space is rich with the yeasty aromas of breads and cakes, plus whiffs of herbs and spices. Hardwood floors and large glass display counters distinguish the dining room. A pleasant patio with colorful umbrellas fronting the café is the perfect perch for a quick cappuccino and pastry while you people-watch.

HOUSE SPECIALTIES For brunch, eggs Benedict, short rib hash, or the BELT sandwich, with eggs over easy, bacon, lettuce, and heirloom tomatoes. For lunch and dinner, entrée salads with shrimp, chicken, or fish; pastas and flatbread pizzas; and sandwiches like the spicy barbecue bacon chicken, with sriracha barbecue bacon jam.

OTHER RECOMMENDATIONS Take home one or more loaves of the artisanal breads. If you just want a quick soup or salad, you can get it slightly cheaper from La Brea's express counter.

SUMMARY AND COMMENTS It's all about the bread . . . and the muffins, pastries, desserts, and anything else containing flour and yeast. Breakfast is the obvious time to enjoy La Brea, and if you must supplement your carbohydrate fix, add some smoked salmon or pecan-smoked bacon. At lunch and dinner, the salads, sandwiches, and flatbread pizzas take over. Service has improved markedly in recent years; servers are more attentive and pleasant. Get there early—it's the first eatery at the east end of the resort entrance, and a popular starting (and ending) place for tourists and locals alike. The express counter serves Silverback Coffee, which supports the people and gorillas of Rwanda, with much less waiting than at Starbucks.

Café Orléans ★★★½

CAJUN/CREOLE	MODERATE	QUALITY ★★★½	VALUE ★★★

READER-SURVEY RESPONSES 92% 👍

Disneyland Park; ☎ 714-781-DINE (3463)

Reservations Recommended. **When to go** Early or late lunch, early evening. **Entrée range** $20–$24. **Service** ★★★★. **Friendliness** ★★★★. **Dress** Casual. **Hours** Daily, 11:30 a.m.–park closing.

SETTING AND ATMOSPHERE Across the alley from Blue Bayou, Café Orléans overlooks the Rivers of America. There's a small patio and limited inside seating, but the table-side service offers a nice break from the serve-yourself and buffet options in the same price range. It's nice to kick back amid the wrought iron and scrolled-wood accents.

HOUSE SPECIALTIES The *pommes frites* have to be among the best sides in the park: traditional thick-cut fries tossed with Parmesan and garlic and served with a mildly spicy Cajun rémoulade sauce. If they aren't served piping hot, send them back. Mickey-shaped beignets are also a treat.

OTHER RECOMMENDATIONS A seafood gratin with crab, shrimp, and spinach; an artery-clogging Monte Cristo sandwich in two versions, traditional and three-cheese; and a lobster Cobb salad.

SUMMARY AND COMMENTS The *pommes frites* are worth the price of admission. If you don't eat anything else in the park your entire visit, try these. We like to hit Café Orléans for a midafternoon break, kick our feet up with a soda or sweet tea, and pick through a plate of fries while we people-watch. The small menu makes ordering easy, provided you bring a big appetite and aren't afraid of a little cholesterol. The Monte Cristo sandwiches are as good as Blue Bayou's but several bucks cheaper, and they're easily large enough to share. Kids love the three-cheese version: Swiss, mozzarella, and double-cream Brie between thick slices of deep-fried, egg-battered bread. A Dixieland jazz band periodically provides lively entertainment.

Carnation Café ★★★

AMERICAN	MODERATE	QUALITY ★★★	VALUE ★★★

READER-SURVEY RESPONSES 92% 👍

Disneyland Park; ☎ 714-781-DINE (3463)

Reservations Recommended. **When to go** Breakfast or late lunch. **Entrée range** $12–$23. **Service** ★★★★. **Friendliness** ★★★★. **Dress** Casual. **Hours** Daily, 8 a.m.–9 p.m.

SETTING AND ATMOSPHERE A Main Street staple since the park opened in 1955, Carnation Café serves up an American menu heavy with traditional favorites—hamburgers and meat loaf, eggs Benedict and Mickey-shaped waffles, and fried chicken—in a parlor circa 1890.

HOUSE SPECIALTIES The loaded baked potato soup (a hot, creamy concoction with Cheddar cheese, chives, and large chunks of baked potato) is a favorite. Other specialties include a spinach-and-tomato frittata at breakfast and a sourdough bacon melt (with pepper Jack, grilled onions, and spicy sauce) for lunch. Chef Oscar Martinez (the park's longest-tenured employee at 60-plus years) has retired, but he's memorialized as a breakfast combo. Guy thinks the meat loaf is one of the best entrées in the park.

OTHER RECOMMENDATIONS For starters, try the deep-fried dill pickle spears, dipped in a rémoulade-style sauce. The menu features a TV dinner–style pot roast, roasted turkey sandwich on a multigrain roll, and warm spinach salad topped with grilled chicken and portobello mushrooms.

SUMMARY AND COMMENTS Here, adults can find a decent plate, the kids can choose from their favorites, and it's easy on the wallet. Because of its location on Main Street, close to restrooms and across from the lockers, it gets busy—expect to see lines stretching down the street. Service is friendly and unusually patient; someone's briefed these cast members on how an hour's wait and low blood sugar can quickly erode a diner's mood. Once you're seated, the order comes quickly and with a smile.

Carthay Circle Restaurant ★★★★½

CALIFORNIA   **EXPENSIVE**   **QUALITY** ★★★★½ **VALUE** ★★★½
READER-SURVEY RESPONSES 90% 👍

Disney California Adventure; ☎ 714-781-DINE (3463)

Reservations Recommended. **When to go** Lunch or dinner. **Entrée range** $24–$52. **Service** ★★★. **Friendliness** ★★★★. **Bar** Full bar. **Dress** Dressy casual. **Hours** Daily, noon–9 p.m.

SETTING AND ATMOSPHERE Intimate booths, wood paneling, and candle sconces evoke the setting of the opening night in 1937 of *Snow White and the Seven Dwarfs*.

HOUSE SPECIALTIES Crispy firecracker duck wings with chili sauce, grilled Angus steak, sustainable fish with seasonal vegetables, and fried biscuits with Cheddar, bacon, and jalapeño.

OTHER RECOMMENDATIONS The menu here is revamped too frequently to recommend any particular item, but the fish ceviche appetizers and fresh ravioli entrées are reliably delicious. Skuna Bay salmon, Wagyu beef, and truffles are among the upscale ingredients that make frequent appearances on the menu. The signature biscuits (more like cheese-filled fritters) are heavy but have built a fanatical cult following, as have the surprisingly meaty sriracha-laced duck wings. The kids' menu offers fresh fish with veggies, mini crispy tacos, or pasta.

SUMMARY AND COMMENTS The chefs of Napa Rose developed the Southern Californian menu. A downstairs lounge serves appetizers and quick meals, while the larger upstairs restaurant takes reservations. A three-course fixed-price *World of Color* menu is also offered (lunch: $56 adults, $25 kids ages 3–9; dinner: $74 adults, $25 kids ages 3–9; all plus tax and gratuity), which includes access to the prime center-stage viewing section. Terrace seating is available. Though service is sometimes unexpectedly inattentive, this is among the finest restaurants found inside the gates of any American theme park (including the vaunted Club 33) and one of the best dining experiences at Disneyland Resort outside of its sibling at the Grand Californian, at a slightly less astronomical price point. If you don't want an entire meal, stop in the downstairs lounge for a classic craft cocktail and Vietnamese tacos or cheese board; it's just a shame that the duck wings aren't served downstairs.

Catal Restaurant & Uva Bar ★★★½

**MEDITERRANEAN   MODERATE-EXPENSIVE   QUALITY ★★★½ VALUE ★★★
READER-SURVEY RESPONSES 88% 👍**

Downtown Disney; ☎ 714-774-4442; patinagroup.com/catal

Reservations Recommended. **When to go** Anytime. **Entrée range** $14–$46. **Service**
★★★. **Friendliness** ★★★. **Bar** Full bar and extensive wine list. **Dress** Dressy casual.
Hours Sunday–Thursday, 8 a.m.–9 p.m.; Friday–Saturday, 8 a.m.–10 p.m. Bar is open 2
hours later; happy hour 3–5 p.m. daily.

SETTING AND ATMOSPHERE Uva Bar, a circular open-air lounge, sits immediately outside the restaurant and is a good place for a quick bite (sans
line) or cocktail while you watch the crowds go by. The outside bistro features a menu focused on Cal-Mediterranean gastropub cuisine. Inside is an
elegant Art Deco–inspired restaurant with hardwood floors and spacious
dining areas. There are two fireplaces and a large central bar; a narrow balcony with tables wraps around the entire top floor.

HOUSE SPECIALTIES French toast or chilaquiles for breakfast; braised
oxtail, lamb chops, slow-roasted prime rib, and diver scallops with roasted
cauliflower for dinner. At Uva, sample the lamb burger with roasted peppers, arugula, and red onion aioli.

OTHER RECOMMENDATIONS Try a huge and very tasty plate of paella with
chicken, chorizo Bilbao, and saffron rice, or the classic Uva garlic fries with
flank steak, chipotle crema, avocado salsa, and cotija cheese.

SUMMARY AND COMMENTS Catal & Uva Bar are a Patina Group pairing, one
in a chain of eateries operated by celebrity chef Joachim Splichal. Despite
overblown descriptions, the menu is pretty straightforward. The appetizers and salads are better than the rest of the menu and a real value for the
money. When the weather cooperates, Uva is the better of the two venues.
Be cautious when ordering some of the more complex or unusual offerings; they can be very inconsistent. Side dishes shine though. Price notwithstanding, this is a very adult experience.

Disney's PCH Grill ★★★

**CHARACTER DINING/AMERICAN   MOD-EXP   QUALITY ★★★   VALUE ★★½
Reader-Survey Responses 85% 👍**

Disney's Paradise Pier Hotel; ☎ 714-781-DINE (3463)

Reservations Accepted. **When to go** Breakfast and dinner. **Entrée range** $25–$39.
Service ★★★★. **Friendliness** ★★★★. **Bar** Wine and beer. **Dress** Casual. **Hours** Daily,
7–11:30 a.m. and 5:30–9 p.m.

SETTING AND ATMOSPHERE A taste of Southern California beach life:
bright primary colors, potted palms, and decorative elements such as surf-
boards and beach chairs.

HOUSE SPECIALTIES Breakfast: chilaquiles, Mickey-shaped waffles, smoked
salmon. Dinner: grilled salmon, made-to-order pasta, lamb osso bucco,
and the s'mores bar.

OTHER RECOMMENDATIONS Donald Duck's Seaside Breakfast is your best
bet, with an omelet station for grown-ups and a kids' buffet. The Calitalian
dinner buffet has some surprisingly decent Italian dishes and desserts.

SUMMARY AND COMMENTS If you can take one more character breakfast, this time with Donald Duck and friends, get the kids up early and hit the beach.

Docking Bay 7 Food and Cargo ★★★½

INTERGALACTIC/FUSION   INEXPENSIVE   QUALITY ★★★½   VALUE ★★★
READER-SURVEY RESPONSES Too new to rate

Disneyland Park; ☎ 714-781-DINE (3463)

Reservations Not accepted. **When to go** Lunch and dinner. **Entrée range** $14–$19. **Service ★★★. Friendliness ★★★. Dress** Jedi-casual. **Hours** Daily, 8 a.m.–10 p.m.

SETTING AND ATMOSPHERE Chef Strono "Cookie" Tuggs (a blink-and-you-missed-him background character from *Episode VII*) has moved his "Tugg's Grub" mobile kitchen to Black Spire's ramshackle shipping station, converting a cluttered cargo depot into a futuristic food hall inspired by Japan's legendary Tsukiji fish market.

HOUSE SPECIALTIES Meat, seafood, and vegan entrées featuring Mediterranean and Asian flavors with a sci-fi flair. Non-alcoholic drinks and desserts.

OTHER RECOMMENDATIONS Our favorites are the smoked Kaadu Ribs (named after the creature Jar Jar rode in *Episode I*), which are cut vertically to give them an alien appearance and served with homey corn muffins, and the fork-tender Shaak roast, served only at dinner. Endorian Tip-Yip (actually chicken) is served roasted on a quinoa-curry salad, or compressed into cubes and deep-fried with herbaceous gravy. Vegans will rejoice at meatless menu items featuring Impossible Foods; the garden loaf will even win over hardened carnivores.

SUMMARY AND COMMENTS To find Batuu's biggest restaurant, look for Cookie's Sienar-Chall Utilipede-Transport ship parked on the roof. Place your order at the cashier station (or in the mobile app), pick up your food from one of the windows in the rear, and eat it on the patio or inside an abandoned cargo crate, each with its own theme; look for the seafood vendor's stall and a tiny carbonite freezing chamber.

All of the food here is named after unpronounceable otherworldly species, but rest assured that it's really made of earthbound ingredients, many of which are sustainably sourced. The food here is a cut above typical theme park fare, and approaches the resort's sit-down restaurants in quality and price; the braised pot roast with cavatelli and kale is white tablecloth worthy. No alcohol is served here, but you can sip a Phattro (iced tea and lemonade) or Moof Juice (fruit punch).

French Market Restaurant ★★★½

CAJUN/CREOLE   INEXPENSIVE   QUALITY ★★★½ VALUE ★★★★
Reader-Survey Responses 93% 👍

Disneyland Park; ☎ 714-781-DINE (3463)

Reservations Not accepted. **When to go** Lunch or dinner. **Entrée range** $11–$15. **Service ★★★. Friendliness ★★★. Dress** Casual. **Hours** Daily, 11 a.m.–10 p.m.

SETTING AND ATMOSPHERE In the heart of New Orleans Square, French Market Restaurant suggests a laid-back Southern vibe with lots of wrought iron under the shade of large, mature ficus trees. There's a small indoor dining area, but the best seating is outdoors on a large patio, covered with umbrellas and shadowed further by the trees.

HOUSE SPECIALTIES The menu features a roasted half chicken with citrus and Cajun spices, French dip sandwich, and shrimp po'boy. The jambalaya is a savory alternative that hits the spot on cooler winter days. Most meals come with a side of rice or mashed potatoes and corn bread.

OTHER RECOMMENDATIONS Hearty soups; a few fresh and flavorful salads (including a roasted potato and bacon salad).

SUMMARY AND COMMENTS French Market Restaurant features comfort food with a Cajun-Creole flair and periodic entertainment from one or more of the roving park musicians or groups. The cafeteria-style service line becomes bottlenecked at the beverage station; see if you can skip to an open cashier at the end if you don't need drinks.

Goofy's Kitchen ★★

CHARACTER DINING/AMERICAN   EXPENSIVE   QUALITY ★★   VALUE ★★½
Reader-Survey Responses 90% 👍

Disneyland Hotel; ☎ 714-781-DINE (3463)

Reservations Available. **When to go** Breakfast. **Entrée range** $26–$48. **Service** ★★★★. **Friendliness** ★★★★. **Bar** Wine, beer, and cocktails. **Dress** Casual. **Hours** Daily, 7–11:30 a.m. and 4–8:45 p.m.

SETTING AND ATMOSPHERE Bright, fun, and modern, but also very loud. Goofy, Pluto, and other characters always put a smile to kids' faces.

HOUSE SPECIALTIES It's a buffet and your chef is Goofy, which should tell you everything you need to know. Breakfast features Mickey-shaped waffles, sausages, pancakes, bacon, scrambled eggs, and other traditional breakfast items. Dinner offers everything from prime rib to salads.

OTHER RECOMMENDATIONS Kids love Goofy's peanut butter pizza.

SUMMARY AND COMMENTS You come for two reasons: 1) It's convenient, especially if you're staying at the resort, and 2) the youngsters haven't yet had their fill of dining with a rotating cast of Disney characters. Breakfast is your best option for both food and wait times. Goofy's Kitchen has many fans, including this Alpine, Utah, grandmother:

Goofy's Kitchen, even at the staggering price, was well worth it. The food was really good, a lot of the menu is designed for children, and the character visits are worth the price. What a thrill to see my grandchildren's delight at being visited by Minnie, Pluto, Chip, and Snow White (with whom my 2-year-old grandson flirted brazenly!).

Lamplight Lounge ★★★½

AMERICAN   EXPENSIVE   QUALITY ★★★★   VALUE ★★★
READER-SURVEY RESPONSES 89% 👍

Disney California Adventure; ☎ 714-781-DINE (3463)

Reservations Recommended. **When to go** Anytime. **Entrée range** $19–$23. **Service** ★★★★. **Friendliness** ★★★★. **Bar** Wine, beer, and cocktails. **Dress** Casual. **Hours** Daily, 11 a.m.–9 p.m.; brunch on Saturday and Sunday, park opening–noon.

SETTING AND ATMOSPHERE This seaside hangout has a backstory as a wharf warehouse, with exposed steel and reclaimed wood attesting to its faux history. Look for a hanging sculpture of concept sketches and knick-knacks left behind by the Pixar artists who allegedly loiter here.

HOUSE SPECIALTIES Gastropub appetizers and sandwiches with signature cocktails. Lobster nachos, salmon PLT (pancetta, romaine, and plum tomato), sushi rolls with stone crab or New York strip, doughnuts with dipping sauces.

OTHER RECOMMENDATIONS Tuna poke, deviled eggs, and a rustic ratatouille with fresh burrata cheese.

SUMMARY AND COMMENTS Ariel's Grotto, DCA's popular princesses dining venue, was converted into the Lamplight Lounge during the Pixar Pier makeover, resulting in a much more mature mealtime experience. Adults (with or without their children) can escape upstairs to the alfresco bar for a glass of wine, a cocktail, or a bottle of beer. The bar also serves a selection of appetizers, including the overrated lobster nachos that were a cult favorite at the former Cove Bar. Bigger Bites and kids' meals are only available in the downstairs dining room, where some open-air tables sport built-in fire pits. This is a good spot to catch *World of Color* without a Fast-Pass; views of the fountains from here are great, but the oblique angle to the projection screens isn't ideal.

Napa Rose ★★★★★

CALIFORNIAN/FUSION   VERY EXPENSIVE   QUALITY ★★★★★   VALUE ★★★½
READER-SURVEY RESPONSES 95% 👍

Grand Californian Hotel; ☎ 714-781-DINE (3463)

Reservations Recommended. **When to go** Dinner. **Entrée range** $38-$54; $100 for four courses. **Service** ★★★★★. **Friendliness** ★★★★. **Bar** Impressive wine list. **Dress** Dressy casual. **Hours** Daily, 5:30-9:30 p.m.

SETTING AND ATMOSPHERE Napa Rose is Disneyland Resort's flagship fine-dining experience. The Grand Californian's Craftsman theme is carried into this premier room with sweeping views of DCA from virtually every table. A large, open demonstration kitchen lets you watch the magic happen, and wine, in all its glory, is displayed at every turn. Fine linens and china are the norm. This is an absolutely gorgeous room, with food and service to match.

HOUSE SPECIALTIES The menu, rotated seasonally, focuses on the cuisine of California's wine region, ranchlands, farm belts, and coastline. Wine finds its way onto most of the menu in sauces, reductions, infusions, and dressings. Dishes may include warm bone marrow custard, roasted pheasant roulade, truffle mac and cheese, and American bison "pot roast," as well as warm butterscotch bread pudding for dessert.

OTHER RECOMMENDATIONS Game meat, ranch and free-range beef and poultry, and the chef's prix fixe Vintner's Table are constantly changing and always exciting. On select mornings, the restaurant hosts a brunch with the Disney princesses (see page 158).

SUMMARY AND COMMENTS Napa Rose may be the best restaurant in Orange County and has been at the top of most critics' lists since its debut. Top talent in the kitchen (award-winning chef Andrew Sutton leads the charge) and in the dining room make this an incomparable gustatory experience. Every server has earned sommelier status, a designation that takes years of study and practical experience with wine and winemaking, easing the chore of choosing a wine from its cellar of more than 16,000 bottles. The waitstaff brings the whole experience, from wine rookies to experts, to match your level of knowledge and tastes. Look for unusual ingredients (Tahitian vanilla, smoked sturgeon, truffled quail eggs, lemongrass, almond oil) married to top-notch staples (Colorado lamb, Berkshire pork, pheasant breast, sustainable fresh fish), all deftly handled by a world-class kitchen crew. And though staff are very accommodating in the usual Disney manner, this is definitely not an adventure for the kids. Napa Rose should be on every adult's Disney bucket list, a must-do at least once. If the full menu is too rich for your blood, sit in the cozy lounge and order appetizers. An Albuquerque, New Mexico, woman tried both Napa Rose and Steakhouse 55 (in the Disneyland Hotel) and offers this comparison:

Prices were quite high, but we had a very good time. Napa Rose was the high-light of the trip, and our waiter was very good. Steakhouse 55 was the big-gest letdown. We were expecting to repeat our experience at Napa Rose, but the staff and food didn't come close.

A Suffern, New York, reader with good taste advises:

If you're doing the Napa Rose Chef's Counter, get the tasting menu.

Naples Ristorante e Pizzeria ★★★

ITALIAN	MODERATE	QUALITY ★★★ VALUE ★★★
READER-SURVEY RESPONSES 88% 👍		

Downtown Disney; ☎ 714-776-6200 or 714-781-DINE (3463); patinagroup.com/naples

Reservations Recommended. **When to go** Late lunch or early dinner. **Entrée range** $18–$28. **Service** ★★. **Friendliness** ★★★. **Bar** Extensive wine list and full bar. **Dress** Casual. **Hours** Daily, 11 a.m.–10 p.m.

SETTING AND ATMOSPHERE Food aside, this is a really fun restaurant: modern, colorful, and spacious, with tile floors, an open demonstration kitchen, and whimsical design touches that mirror nearby Disneyland. It's also noisy and crowded, typically filled with families. During peak hours, it's difficult to hear yourself think, let alone carry on a meaningful conversation. Nonetheless, it's a great gathering place, and there's something to appeal to everyone from small children to adults.

HOUSE SPECIALTIES Wood-fired Neapolitan-style pizzas: thin, crispy crusts with a hearty, almost spicy red sauce; handmade mozzarella cheese; and fresh toppings of choice.

OTHER RECOMMENDATIONS Some of the non-pasta entrées, such as pan-seared salmon with roasted tomatoes and spinach, are the real highlights.

SUMMARY AND COMMENTS A major renovation gave this Patina–Joachim Splichal venture a big boost to its outdoor dining and bar area, along with some appreciated tweaks to its extensive but somewhat uninspired menu. The kids will enjoy the colorful decor and activities; adults can get a good glass of wine or a cocktail and feed the entire crew for less than $100.

Napolini ★★★

ITALIAN/DELI   INEXPENSIVE   QUALITY ★★★½ VALUE ★★★★
READER-SURVEY RESPONSES 88% 👍

Downtown Disney; ☎ 714-781-DINE (3463)

Reservations Not accepted. **When to go** Lunch or a quick dinner. **Entrée range** $6–$8. **Service ★★**. **Friendliness ★★★**. **Bar** Wine and beer only. **Dress** Casual. **Hours** Daily, 10 a.m.–11 p.m.

SETTING AND ATMOSPHERE This is next-door Naples's cousin—a quick-in, quick-out deli with grab-and-go salads and sandwiches, plus made-to-order pizzas at remarkably reasonable prices.

HOUSE SPECIALTIES Wood-fired Neapolitan-style pizzas, cold sandwiches, and salads for lunch and dinner.

OTHER RECOMMENDATIONS Customize a personal-size pie with your pick of toppings. If you're overwhelmed by the choices, go for one of the signature combos, like California barbecue chicken or Capri lemon-pesto shrimp.

SUMMARY AND COMMENTS A 2018 renovation transformed Napolini from an acceptable fallback option to one of the best dining deals in all of Downtown Disney. If you like Blaze Pizza or Pizza Press, you should be very satisfied with a pie from here.

Plaza Inn ★★★

CHARACTER DINING/AMERICAN   MODERATE   QUALITY ★★★   VALUE ★★★½
READER-SURVEY RESPONSES 93% 👍

Disneyland Park; ☎ 714-781-DINE (3463)

Reservations Recommended (breakfast only). **When to go** When you need a compromise, the kids insist, or you arrive right at the meal switch. **Entrée range** $13–$19. **Service ★★★**. **Friendliness ★★★**. **Dress** Casual. **Hours** Daily, 7 a.m.–park closing.

SETTING AND ATMOSPHERE Probably the high point of your meal at Plaza Inn is the gorgeous Victorian B&B ambience—comfortable, widely spaced tables in a spacious dining room with lots of brocade and brass. The large patio commands a great view of Main Street, where parades, strolling musicians, and the massive variety of visitors endlessly entertain us.

HOUSE SPECIALTIES This buffeteria can be hit-or-miss; see if you can catch something being freshly delivered. Timing is everything. Best bets are the pot roast or the fried chicken (which some claim is better than Knott's famous birds), two items that rarely suffer from sitting on the steam table.

OTHER RECOMMENDATIONS Kids love the daily character breakfast (reservations strongly suggested) hosted by Minnie Mouse and two to four other characters. Adults will suffer through rubbery pancakes and soggy bacon.

SUMMARY AND COMMENTS Don't expect fine dining when you eat at the Plaza Inn, but strides have been made in the quality of the food and the steam table's maintenance, and portions are very generous. Hit this place right when everything comes fresh, during the transitions from breakfast to lunch and from lunch to dinner, but it's still your basic been-in-the-steam-table-too-long scenario.

Ralph Brennan's Jazz Kitchen ★★★½

CAJUN/CREOLE	MODERATE	QUALITY ★★★½ VALUE ★★½
READER-SURVEY RESPONSES 90% 👍		

Downtown Disney; ☎ 714-776-5200; rbjazzkitchen.com

Reservations Available. **When to go** Lunch or dinner. **Entrée range** $15–$38. **Service** ★★★. **Friendliness** ★★½. **Bar** Full bar. **Dress** Casual. **Hours** Sunday, 10 a.m.–10 p.m.; Monday–Thursday, 11 a.m.–10 p.m., Friday–Saturday, 11 a.m.–11 p.m. (*Jazz Kitchen Express:* Daily, 8 a.m.–10 p.m.)

SETTING AND ATMOSPHERE Take a step back in time and space to the 19th-century French Quarter of New Orleans. Almost half the seating area is an open-air courtyard surrounded by wrought iron, hanging ferns, and milled hardwood. Above a small stage where live jazz plays daily, there's a pounded-copper ceiling; to stage left is a beautiful enamel-finished grand piano. You can people-watch from a balcony dining area, but no matter where you sit, you're going to enjoy the ambience and music.

HOUSE SPECIALTIES Gumbo Ya-Ya, blackened fish, and New York steak with brandy-peppercorn sauce.

OTHER RECOMMENDATIONS Barbecue shrimp and grits, grilled filet mignon medallions, and pasta jambalaya are all good.

SUMMARY AND COMMENTS This used to be one of our favorite restaurants in or immediately around the resort, but it seems to have declined a little over the past decade. The Brennan family is still intimately involved with every aspect of the menu, but both quality and presentation decline between visits from the New Orleans crew. Servers, including actual Southerners and even a smattering of Louisiana natives, exude a laid-back (sometimes too laid-back), gracious attitude most of the time but have been known to get a little testy and impatient during the restaurant's busy times. This is a dining experience best suited to adults. Add live jazz to the mix (the zydeco brunch is especially fun), and, all things considered, you have one of Disneyland's better dining experiences. For a quick breakfast after 8 a.m., the sugar-dusted beignets and chicory coffee from the adjoining quick-service counter can't be beat. The Sunday Brunch Fest menu (featuring bananas Foster French toast and Cajun omelets) is offered every Sunday morning 10 a.m.–3 p.m., accompanied by a made-to-order Bloody Mary bar and table-side card tricks.

Rancho del Zocalo Restaurante ★★½

MEXICAN	INEXPENSIVE	QUALITY ★★½ VALUE ★★½
READER-SURVEY RESPONSES 92% 👍		

Disneyland Park; ☎ 714-781-DINE (3463)

Reservations Not accepted. **When to go** Early lunch or early dinner. **Entrée range** $12–$15. **Service** ★★★. **Friendliness** ★★★. **Dress** Casual. **Hours** Daily, 10:30 a.m.–9 p.m.

SETTING AND ATMOSPHERE Welcome to the hacienda! Faux adobe, wooden beams, and Mexican tile ring a dark interior and covered outdoor patio. Tucked away from the throngs in the northeast area of Frontierland, this can be a nice, quiet place for a meal.

HOUSE SPECIALTIES The enchiladas are your best bet, probably because they lend themselves to the buffet-style dining here.

OTHER RECOMMENDATIONS Hit-or-miss: If you can catch a tray of soft tacos, burritos, or grilled chicken fresh from the commissary, you score. The salad is a good size, and the carne asada has improved in recent years. The frosty horchata beverage is *muy bueno.*

SUMMARY AND COMMENTS Three words sum up the Zocalo: Mexican, cafeteria style. On the bright side, most of the cuisine holds up well under the heat lamps and over the steam tables, the enchiladas and grilled chicken in particular. The rest of the menu—typical tacos, burritos, Mexican rice, and refried beans—is resolutely average, except at opening or right before the dinner rush, when the food is fresh and uncorrupted. Tortillas, both corn and flour, are consistently good. Anyone not intimately familiar with really good Mexican cuisine may rate this place higher. Zocalo is also a great choice when you can't possibly choke down another hot dog, burger, or pizza slice.

The River Belle Terrace ★★★

AMERICAN	MODERATE	QUALITY	★★★½	VALUE	★★½
READER-SURVEY RESPONSES 77% 👍					

Disneyland Park; ☎ 714-781-DINE (3463)

Reservations Not accepted. **When to go** Lunch or dinner. **Entrée range** $19–$27. **Service** ★★★. **Friendliness** ★★★. **Dress** Casual. **Hours** Daily, 8 a.m.–10:45 a.m. and 11:30 a.m.–9 p.m.

SETTING AND ATMOSPHERE Situated between New Orleans Square and Frontierland, The River Belle Terrace has an Old South–style exterior replete with wrought iron and wood siding. Large shuttered windows belie a small indoor-dining area; most of the seating is outdoors on a large patio covered with colorful umbrellas.

HOUSE SPECIALTIES For breakfast, skillet with short rib and sunny-side up eggs or pecan-maple monkey bread. Pork spareribs, pulled-pork sandwich, barbecue half chicken, and beef brisket sandwich.

OTHER RECOMMENDATIONS Sustainable fish of the day or barbecue tofu.

SUMMARY AND COMMENTS This 1955 Disneyland original, now a table-service venue, offers homey Southern dishes at lunch and dinner. For fans of the former Big Thunder Ranch Barbecue, River Belle's ribs are the closest they'll find to that all-you-could-eat favorite at the resort, albeit at a much higher cost. While the food quality is acceptable (the pan-seared arctic char we ate was even excellent), entrée pricing places it close behind Blue Bayou on the list of most expensive theme park restaurants, above the average cost at Carnation Café and even Café Orléans, both of which we prefer. The outdoor seating area is good to people-watch or just take in the view of Rivers of America from the patio, but the value proposition is too poor for such uncomplicated fare. On nights when *Fantasmic!* is shown, River Belle Terrace offers a dining package for $45 per adult ($25 for kids 3–9), plus tax, that includes a starter, entrée, and dessert, as well as a FastPass to *Fantasmic!*'s center viewing section.

Splitsville Luxury Lanes ★★★

AMERICAN	MODERATE	QUALITY ★★★	VALUE ★★★
READER-SURVEY RESPONSES 89% 👍			

Downtown Disney; ☎ 714-781-DINE (3463)

Reservations Accepted. **When to go** Lunch or dinner. **Entrée range** $12–$30. **Service** ★★★½. **Friendliness** ★★★½. **Bar** Full service. **Dress** Casual. **Hours** Daily, 11 a.m.–11 p.m.

SETTING AND ATMOSPHERE Splitsville is part of a multistate chain of hybrid bowling alleys–restaurants. The two-story Anaheim branch looks like a mid-century movie star's mansion, with rich hardwood surfaces, space-age lighting fixtures, and faux-vintage billboards referencing the region's history. It isn't nearly as loud as the Orlando location, and the 20 bowling lanes are split up and secluded among the various dining rooms, making eating here feel like less of an afterthought.

HOUSE SPECIALTIES The sushi—salmon, shrimp, tuna, crab, and various combinations thereof—is the best thing on the menu.

OTHER RECOMMENDATIONS Steak sliders, short ribs, and chicken wings. Giant cake slices for dessert.

SUMMARY AND COMMENTS The menu is more spread out than a 7/10 split: burgers, sushi, pizza, seafood, barbecue, Mexican, and Italian are represented, plus nachos and other bar food. It would be a stretch for any kitchen to make half of these things well, let alone a kitchen in a bowling alley, but this California venue makes a better effort at it than its Floridian cousin. Ingredients taste fresh and are of consistent quality, but the flavor profiles are unbalanced, often overwhelming savory dishes with sweet sauces. Stick with the potent cocktails and appetizers. Bowling costs $24 per person ($19 before 4 p.m., Monday–Friday) for shoe rental and 60–105 minutes of lane time, depending on party size; to reserve Priority Bowling for $10 per person or to book a private lane for $120–$175 an hour, visit splitsvillelanes.com/wp-content/reserve/anaheim.html.

Steakhouse 55 ★★★★

STEAK HOUSE	VERY EXPENSIVE	QUALITY ★★★★½	VALUE ★★★
READER-SURVEY RESPONSES 89% 👍			

Disneyland Hotel; ☎ 714-781-DINE (3463)

Reservations Recommended. **When to go** Breakfast, afternoon tea, or dinner. **Entrée range** $36–$58. **Service** ★★★★. **Friendliness** ★★★★. **Bar** Wine list and full bar. **Dress** Business casual. **Hours** Daily, 7–10:30 a.m. and 5–10 p.m. *High tea:* Friday–Sunday, noon–3 p.m.

SETTING AND ATMOSPHERE Stylishly Art Deco–inspired hardwood tables, sleek leather chairs, and smaller banquettes decorate this updated classic American steak house. The indirect lighting casts a warm glow over everything, including an impressive collection of black-and-white photographs from Disney's storied past.

HOUSE SPECIALTIES Breakfast is a good value and features eggs Benedict and New York steak and eggs. At dinner it's all about the meat—grilled certified Angus beef seasoned with the restaurant's signature rub—but you can also order one of the fresh seafood choices or delectable lamb, pork, or chicken. Choose a bottle of wine from an impressive wine cellar, or engage one of the many sommeliers to choose a wine to complement your meal.

OTHER RECOMMENDATIONS The lobster and steak combination is actually very good, but the price can catch you by surprise; always ask before ordering unless you have very deep pockets. The side of lobster mac and cheese is good enough to be an entrée.

SUMMARY AND COMMENTS This underrated eatery has been a well-kept secret for years and matches many of the more well-known steak houses in the area (Morton's and Ruth's Chris) steak for steak. It's alluring and comfortable, a perfect place to spend a grown-up evening over a leisurely meal matched to premium wines. Best to leave the kids behind for this experience; they'll bore easily and may disrupt what could be one of the best adult nights of your stay. The children may enjoy the classic English high tea held three afternoons each week. Traditional scones and finger sandwiches are on the menu, as are adult aperitifs and more kid-friendly items like hot chocolate. However, there are no characters.

Storytellers Café ★★★½

CHARACTER DINING/CALIFORNIAN   EXPENSIVE   QUALITY ★★★★   VALUE ★★★
READER-SURVEY RESPONSES 92% 👍

Grand Californian Hotel; ☎ 714-781-DINE (3463)

Reservations Recommended. **When to go** Breakfast or dinner. **Entrée range** $26–$44. **Service ★★★★★. Friendliness ★★★★. Bar** Extensive wine list and full bar. **Dress** Casual. **Hours** Daily, 7 a.m.–9:45 p.m.

SETTING AND ATMOSPHERE Storytellers Café carries the Grand Californian Hotel's Arts and Crafts theme throughout with large, open beams; natural wood and wood carvings; milled stone; and stained glass. The walls are adorned with impressive murals depicting the state's rich literary history, from Mark Twain's "The Celebrated Jumping Frog of Calaveras County" to Scott O'Dell's *Island of the Blue Dolphins.*

HOUSE SPECIALTIES Children under age 10 will love the character breakfast buffet. Hosted by Mickey Mouse, the meal features a complement of cartoon friends who visit the tables, sing songs, and pose for photos between bites of omelets, waffles, and caramel French toast. The dinner buffet features a meat-carving station and rotating selections of seafood and pasta.

OTHER RECOMMENDATIONS The *chilaquiles* with fresh eggs and tomatillo salsa is the best item on the breakfast buffet. The charred corn chowder with rotisserie chicken at dinner is filling. Kids can make their own pizzas.

SUMMARY AND COMMENTS You may experience a little sticker shock at first, but there's real value here. It's not quite on par with Napa Rose across the way, but the same dedication to quality and originality is evident from the menu to the service. Kids will find lots to like about the food, while adults will enjoy the California wine country–inspired menu options (from smoked salmon to seasonal flatbreads) and a leisurely cocktail or glass of wine. You'll want to save some room for dessert too—who could pass up warm bread pudding with vanilla sauce? A Manitowoc, Wisconsin, reader recommends the café as an alternative to dining inside DCA, writing:

We ended up eating at Storytellers Café on a spur-of-the-moment decision, and it was one of the best places at which we ate at the park, as far as food, price, and atmosphere. The lemonade with the foam on top was AMAZING!

Tangaroa Terrace Tropical Bar and Grill ★★★

**AMERICAN/POLYNESIAN   INEXPENSIVE   QUALITY ★★★ VALUE ★★★½
READER-SURVEY RESPONSES 88% 👍**

Disneyland Hotel; ☎ 714-781-DINE (3463)

Reservations Not accepted. **When to go** Anytime. **Entrée range** $7–$13. **Service**
★★★★. **Friendliness** ★★★★. **Bar** Beer, wine, and cocktails. **Dress** Casual. **Hours**
Daily, 6:30 a.m.–11 p.m.

SETTING AND ATMOSPHERE This is Disneyland Hotel's poolside tropical
retreat. Tiki torches and South Seas music are a dead giveaway that they
want to evoke that island feeling. It was expanded in 2018 with additional
outdoor seating and bar service.

HOUSE SPECIALTIES Breakfast has French toast with banana-caramel
sauce and pineapple upside-down pancakes. Lunch and dinner feature a
one-third-pound Hawaiian cheeseburger with teriyaki sauce, bacon, and
caramelized pineapple on a brioche bun, or try the shrimp salad with
romaine, radicchio, and arugula in a tropical vinaigrette.

OTHER RECOMMENDATIONS Hawaiian-style specialties get a little more
exotic with fried spam musubi and pork-topped poutine. Tangaroa Terrace
serves the same bar snacks as Trader Sam's next door, including the exquisite long beans.

SUMMARY AND COMMENTS This eatery has something for everyone, as
long as everyone enjoys food with an Asian-Polynesian flare. Adults can
enjoy a cocktail (maybe something a little exotic with a fruit garnish and
little pink umbrellas) while kids frolic in the nearby pool in between bites.
The adjoining Trader Sam's Enchanted Tiki Bar serves exotic cocktails and
Asian-inspired appetizers in an intimate and elaborately decorated environment reminiscent of Walt Disney World's extinct Adventurers Club.
Order an Uh Oa, Krakatoa Punch, or Shipwreck on the Rocks to see some
explosive special effects. The best bet for late-night snacks are Sam's
panko-crusted long beans or sweet and spicy Asian wings. If the interior is
at capacity (a frequent occurrence on weekends), try the patio, which has
live music and a cozy fireplace.

Tortilla Jo's ★★★

**MEXICAN   MODERATE-EXPENSIVE   QUALITY ★★½ VALUE ★★½
READER-SURVEY RESPONSES 90% 👍**

Downtown Disney; ☎ 714-535-5000; patinagroup.com/tortilla-jos

Reservations Available. **When to go** Lunch or dinner. **Entrée range** $12–$28. **Service**
★★★. **Friendliness** ★★★. **Bar** Full bar. **Dress** Casual. **Hours** Sunday, 9 a.m.–10 p.m.;
Monday–Thursday, 11 a.m.–10 p.m.; Friday, 11 a.m.–11 p.m.; Saturday, 9 a.m.–11 p.m. *Taque-
ria:* Daily, 8 a.m.–11 p.m.

SETTING AND ATMOSPHERE Old Mexico meets California modern. Mexican
touchstones such as glazed tiles; thick, crude glass; and wrought iron
accent an open dining room with modern, eclectic touches. You can grab
a quick bite at the taqueria, and the bartender pours from a huge selection of more than 100 premium and super-premium tequilas at an outdoor

cantina. The place goes crazy on the weekends, so gird yourself for a rau-cous, booze-shooting, beer-chasing good time.

HOUSE SPECIALTIES Start with guacamole made fresh at your table. For an entrée, any one of the gigantic burritos, especially the signature Fajita Bur-rito, are good.

OTHER RECOMMENDATIONS Enchiladas or the beer-battered fish taco.

SUMMARY AND COMMENTS Another Patina Group eatery from überchef Joachim Splichal, Tortilla Jo's is upscale Mexican with a culinary twist. You can customize any taco or burrito. The eclectic, hybrid menu (and the loosey-goosey crowd) may be too much for the kids, but adults will appre-ciate a shot of Sauza Silver tequila and a tall glass of Corona beer, com-plete with a lime wedge. Strolling mariachi musicians fill the dining room and bar with foot-stomping traditional Mexican music.

Wine Country Trattoria ★★★★

CALIFORNIA NOUVELLE   **MODERATE**   **QUALITY ★★★★ VALUE ★★★**
READER-SURVEY RESPONSES 85% 👍

Disney California Adventure; ☎ 714-781-DINE (3463)

Reservations Recommended. **When to go** Lunch or dinner. **Entrée range** $18–$36. **Service ★★★. Friendliness ★★. Bar** Wine, beer, and cocktails. **Dress** Casual. **Hours** Daily, 11:30 a.m.–9 p.m.

SETTING AND ATMOSPHERE Arguably one of the better dining options at either park, the trattoria is a leisurely place to park yourself and family away from the frenetic crowds. Whether you choose one of three themed patios outside or the "patio" inside, this spacious bistro captures the California-casual mood with plenty of tile, wood, and trellised greenery, whisking you away from downtown Anaheim and positing you in the mid-dle of California wine country.

HOUSE SPECIALTIES Try the pasta: spaghetti Bolognese or spaghetti with vegetables, lasagna, fettuccine shrimp Alfredo, or linguine with clams.

OTHER RECOMMENDATIONS Salmon with dill-butter sauce, braised lamb shank, or Tuscan salad with shrimp. And to finish: seasonal *panna cotta.*

SUMMARY AND COMMENTS Wine Country Trattoria is a popular spot for a Mediterranean-style or California-inspired meal, paired with a glass of wine from its extensive cellar. The trattoria appeals more to adults without chil-dren, though an improved kids' menu and *World of Color* fixed-price dining packages have made this a more attractive option for families ($49 adults, $25 kids ages 3–9; all plus tax and gratuity). Note that viewing package lunch and dinner patrons each receive a ticket for a reserved viewing area but do not watch the show from the restaurant itself. The soup or salad and desserts included in the viewing package are all excellent, and the entrées are now equal to the à la carte selections; the rib eye is one of the best steaks on property, and well worth the upcharge. For a refreshing late-afternoon break, order a glass of wine and plate of charcuterie at the Alfresco Tasting Terrace on the upstairs patio or at the Sonoma Terrace around the corner. From a Richfield, Ohio, mom:

One place we all agreed on was the Wine Country Trattoria at DCA. The ser-vice was a bit on the slow side, but the food was delicious and fresh.

DINING *Outside*
DISNEYLAND RESORT

UNOFFICIAL GUIDE RESEARCHERS LOVE GOOD FOOD and invest a fair amount of time scouting new places to eat. And because food at Disneyland Resort (all of the Disney complex, including the theme parks, hotels, and Downtown Disney) is so expensive, we (like you) have an economic incentive for finding palatable meals off campus. Redevelopment of the surrounding real estate has attracted a whole new glut of fine-dining and fast-casual options. Choices range from the familiar (**Tony Roma's, Denny's, Ruth's Chris Steak House**) to local favorites (**Umami Burger, The Catch**). Unique dining experiences are also prevalent. While the average Disneyland visitor stays for only two to four nights, there are more than enough fine-dining and fast-casual venues outside Disneyland Resort to keep you happy, if not confused, for that amount of time. Good ethnic dining, however, is woefully underrepresented. Especially hard to find are high-quality Thai, Chinese, Mexican, Japanese, Korean, and Greek restaurants. We've confined our coverage to restaurants that you can reach by car in 15 minutes or less. If you're willing to range farther afield, your choices increase exponentially.

Among restaurants in and out of Disneyland Resort, location and price will determine your choice. For example, a decent Italian restaurant is in Downtown Disney, and several independent Italian eateries are within 5 miles of the Disney complex. Which one you select depends on how much you want to spend and how convenient the restaurant is.

Better restaurants outside Disneyland Resort cater primarily to adults and aren't as well equipped to deal with children. This is a plus, however, if you're looking to escape children and eat in peace and quiet.

The Anaheim GardenWalk retail and entertainment complex is east of the park. Popular chains such as **The Cheesecake Factory, Roy's Restaurant, California Pizza Kitchen,** and **Bubba Gump Shrimp Co.** are doing brisk business. The best of the lot is probably **McCormick & Schmick's Grille,** which serves well-prepared fresh seafood at outrageous prices.

The **Anaheim Packing House** (440 S. Anaheim Blvd., ☎ 714-533-7225, anaheimpackingdistrict.com; open daily, 11 a.m.–9 p.m.) is a century-old Sunkist citrus warehouse that has been reborn as a trendy urban food hall, not unlike New York's Chelsea Market, filled with more than two dozen independent eateries and bars. We like the kebabs and naan at **Adya Fresh Indian Flavors,** salmon poke at **Orange Tei,** and the shaved snow dessert from **i am.** On weekends, locals pack the house, as well as the neighboring Packing District's farmers' park and breweries, jockeying for scarce parking spots. Instead, park for free at the City Hall garage and hail a FRAN (ridefran.com) electric micro-van for a free ride around the block.

BUFFETS AND MEAL DEALS
OUTSIDE DISNEYLAND RESORT

BUFFETS, RESTAURANT SPECIALS, and discount dining abound in the area surrounding Disneyland Resort, especially on Harbor Boulevard and Katella Avenue. The local visitor magazines, which are distributed free at non-Disney hotels, among other places, are packed with advertisements and discount coupons for seafood feasts, buffets (Asian, Indian, and the like), and a host of combination specials for everything from lobster to barbecue. For a family trying to economize on meals, some of the come-ons are mighty attractive. But are these places any good? Is the food fresh, tasty, and appealing? Are the restaurants clean and inviting? Armed with little more than a roll of Tums, the Unofficial research team tried all the eateries that advertise heavily in the tourist publications. Here's what we discovered.

Asian Super Buffets

Talk about an oxymoron. If you've ever cooked Asian food, especially a stir-fry, you know that split-second timing is required to avoid overcooking. So it should come as no big surprise that Asian dishes languishing on a buffet lose their freshness, texture, and flavor in a hurry. On the bright side, however, super buffets are so cheap that you really can't go wrong. So what if it's not the best food you've ever had if you can scarf down all you want for $16? All the Asian buffets serve chicken prepared a dozen different ways but also offer such goodies as peel-and-eat shrimp, various fish and shellfish, the occasional carved meat, salads, soups, and sometimes sushi. Desserts are usually lackluster, but most folks are too stuffed to eat them anyway. The best Asian buffet within a 15-minute drive of Disneyland Resort is as follows:

TEPPANYAKI GRILL SUPREME BUFFET 1630 W. Katella Ave., Anaheim; ☎ 714-530-9699. Dinner: $14.99 adults, Monday–Thursday; $15.99 adults, Friday–Sunday; $9.99 for children ages 7–10, $5.99 for children ages 3–6, free for children under age 2. Features made-to-order Japanese hibachi and sushi in addition to Chinese dishes, including excellent soup and dim sum.

Indian Buffets

Indian food survives the ravages of heat lamps and steam tables much better on a buffet than Chinese food does. The mainstays of Indian buffets are curries. *Curry,* you may be surprised to know, is essentially the Indian word for "stew." In India each curry is prepared with a different combination of spices (dominated by cumin and turmeric). The salient point about Indian buffets is that curries, unlike stir-fries, actually improve with a little aging. If you've ever reheated a leftover stew at home and noticed that it tasted better the second time, it's because the flavors and ingredients continued to marry during the storage period, making the stew richer and tastier.

In the Disneyland Resort area, most Indian restaurants offer buffets at lunch only—not too convenient if you plan on spending your day at the theme parks. If you're out shopping or taking a day off, here are a couple of Indian buffets worth trying:

GANDHI PALACE 1188 W. Katella Ave., Anaheim; ☎ 714-808-6777; gandhipalaceanaheim.com. Lunch buffet: Monday–Saturday, $12. Discount coupons available.

MASALACRAFT 575 W. Chapman Ave., Anaheim; ☎ 714-406-4314; masalacraft.us. Lunch buffet: daily, 11 a.m.–2:30 p.m., $11.99.

Salad Buffets

The most popular of these in the Disneyland Resort area is **Souplantation** (1901 W. Malvern Ave., Fullerton; ☎ 714-446-0566; souplantation .com). The buffet features prepared salads and an extensive array of ingredients to build your own. Souplantation also offers a variety of soups, a modest pasta bar, a baked potato bar, an assortment of fresh fruit, and ice cream sundaes. Dinner runs $12.49 for adults, $5.99 for children ages 7–12, and $3.99 for children ages 3–6. Lunch is $10.49 for adults; kids eat for the same price as at dinner.

ANAHEIM-AREA FULL-SERVICE RESTAURANTS

SOUTHERN CALIFORNIA is a mother lode of wonderful dining, and if we directed you to Newport Beach, La Jolla, or LA, we could guarantee you a fantastic eating experience every night. In that you've chosen Disneyland as your destination, however, we've elected to profile only solid restaurants that you can reach by car or cab in 15 minutes or less. That said, here are our picks; all of them offer disabled access.

Bierstube German Pub at the Phoenix Club ★★★½

GERMAN	INEXPENSIVE-MODERATE	QUALITY ★★★½	VALUE ★★★★

1340 S. Sanderson Ave., behind Honda Center, Anaheim;
☎ 714-563-4166; thephoenixclub.com

Reservations Recommended. **When to go** Lunch or dinner. **Entrée range** $12–$19. **Service** ★★★. **Friendliness** ★★★★. **Bar** Wine list, extensive draft beer offerings, and full bar. **Dress** Casual. **Hours** Sunday and Tuesday–Thursday, 11 a.m.–10 p.m.; Friday–Saturday, 11 a.m.–11 p.m.; kitchen closes at 9 p.m.

SETTING AND ATMOSPHERE Once a private club reserved for family members of the original German settlers of Anaheim and more recent émigrés, this landmark is now open to the public (members enjoy a few extra privileges). It has more than a half dozen German beers on tap. Its menu is somewhat limited, trending toward less-fancy preparations, but it's these basic dishes that keep folks coming back. The pub is conducive to raucous eating, drinking, and carousing. Live music seems omnipresent, from local and guest polka bands to renowned accordion artists.

GREAT EATS IN AND AROUND ANAHEIM

BEST BOBA TEA

Bobatopia 1650 S. Harbor Blvd. Ste. B, Anaheim; ☎ 714-829-4504; instagram.com
/bobatopia. The closest place to the Disneyland Resort to get boba, taiyaki, and acai and
pitaya bowls. If you like your desserts a little less exotic, they also have smoothies,
slushies, and ice cream by the scoop.

BEST BURGER

Umami Burger 338 S. Anaheim Blvd., Anaheim; ☎ 714-991-8626; umamiburger.com.
Juicy house-ground burgers served mid-rare and topped with truffle cheese, shiitake
mushrooms, fried eggs, or other fancy fixin's. Try the homemade pickles.

BEST CHINESE

Panda Kitchen 1770 S. Harbor Blvd., Ste. 120, Anaheim; ☎ 714-999-6888; panda
kitchentogo.com. For so-bad-it's-good, greasy, late-night lo mein.

BEST INDIAN

Punjabi Tandoor 327 S. Anaheim Blvd., Ste. A, Anaheim; ☎ 714-635-3155; punjabi
tandoor.com. The fresh tandoori in the evening is exceptional. Offers original dishes and
excellent naan.

BEST JAPANESE

Sushi Pop 1105 S. Euclid St., Fullerton; ☎ 714-278-1062; www.sushipopus.com. An
unpretentious strip mall eatery offering all-you-can-eat nigiri and unusual maki rolls at
reasonable prices.

BEST MEDITERRANEAN

Zankou Chicken 2424 W. Ball Road, Anaheim; ☎ 714-229-2060; zankouchicken.com.
Forget that this place is a chain, disregard the cheesy ambience, and go for the spit-
roasted chicken, hummus, and shawarma beef. Inexpensive and delicious.

BEST MEXICAN

La Casa Garcia 531 W. Chapman Ave., Anaheim; ☎ 714-740-1108; lacasagarcia.com.
Carnitas, *barbacoa* (beef slow-cooked in a red-chile sauce), and three-flavor chimichangas,
all with a Tex-Mex twist, are not to be missed.

Los Sanchez 11906 Garden Grove Blvd., Garden Grove; ☎ 714-590-9300; lossanchez
.com. This locals-only gem serves authentic Sonoran cuisine at reasonable prices. Fish
ceviche, *lengua* (tongue) tacos, seafood soup, and the best chicken mole you've ever had.

BEST PIZZA

Pizza Press 1700 S. Harbor Blvd., Anaheim; ☎ 714-323-7134; thepizzapress.com.
Excellent artisanal thin-crust pies with upscale toppings for a very reasonable $10.25—
plus tossed-to-order salads, craft beers, and a 1 a.m. closing time—make this tiny
independent pizzeria across from Disneyland a perfect post-park pit stop.

HOUSE SPECIALTIES Wursts, kraut, pork roast, mixed platters, and sauer-
braten are the best in a 100-mile radius.

OTHER RECOMMENDATIONS Pork in a creamy mushroom sauce.

SUMMARY AND COMMENTS The bastion of Anaheim's founding families
and subsequent waves of German immigrants, The Phoenix Club offers a
little taste of the *Mutterland* far from home. The food is good, occasionally
great; the beer is always cold; and the help is always ready to show you a
good time, German or not. During Oktoberfest, the place rocks. Kids will
love the early reminders of a rough and rural Anaheim and the oompah
bands, Mom and Dad will love the German beers, and everyone will love
the sweet-and-sour flavors of German cuisine.

ANAHEIM-AREA RESTAURANTS BY CUISINE

CUISINE/LOCATION	OVERALL RATING	COST	QUALITY RATING	VALUE RATING
AMERICAN				
ROSCOE'S HOUSE OF CHICKEN & WAFFLES S. Harbor Blvd.	★★★★	Inexp	★★★★	★★★½
CAJUN/CREOLE				
HOUSE OF BLUES RESTAURANT & BAR W. Katella Ave.	★★★	Mod	★★★½	★★½
CHINESE				
MAS' CHINESE ISLAMIC RESTAURANT E. Orangethorpe Ave.	★★★½	Mod	★★★	★★★½
GASTROPUB				
HAVEN CRAFT KITCHEN + BAR S. Glassell St.	★★★	Mod	★★★★	★★★½
GERMAN				
BIERSTUBE GERMAN PUB AT THE PHOENIX CLUB S. Sanderson Ave.	★★★½	Inexp/ Mod	★★★½	★★★★
JÄGERHAUS E. Ball Road	★★★	Inexp	★★★½	★★★
ITALIAN				
CAROLINA'S ITALIAN RESTAURANT Chapman Ave.	★★★	Inexp	★★★	★★★½
MEXICAN				
GABBI'S MEXICAN KITCHEN S. Glassell St.	★★★	Mod	★★★★	★★★½
SEAFOOD				
THE CATCH E. Katella Ave.	★★★½	Exp	★★★★	★★★½
MCCORMICK & SCHMICK'S GRILLE W. Katella Ave.	★★★	Mod/ Exp	★★★	★★★
STEAK				
PARK AVE STEAKS & CHOPS Beach Blvd.	★★★★½	Exp	★★★★	★★★★
MORTON'S S. Harbor Blvd.	★★★★	Exp	★★★½	★★★½
THE CATCH E. Katella Ave.	★★★½	Exp	★★★★	★★★½
PRIME CUT CAFÉ & WINE BAR W. Katella Ave.	★★★	Mod/ Exp	★★★	★★★½

Carolina's Italian Restaurant ★★★

SOUTHERN ITALIAN   INEXPENSIVE   QUALITY ★★★   VALUE ★★★½

915 S. Harbor Blvd., Anaheim, and 12045 Chapman Ave., Garden Grove;
☎ 714-971-5551; carolinasitalianrestaurant.com

Reservations Recommended. **When to go** Dinner. **Entrée range** $10–$23. **Service**
★★½. **Friendliness** ★★★½. **Bar** Extensive beer and wine lists. **Dress** Casual. **Hours**
Daily, 11 a.m.–midnight.

SETTING AND ATMOSPHERE A classic Italian family restaurant replete with
wall murals of the motherland, comfortable seating, and the overwhelming
aroma of garlic and olive oil. It's like walking through a time warp.

HOUSE SPECIALTIES You can't go wrong with any one of more than three
dozen hearty pasta dishes, from a very traditional meat sauce to an outstanding lasagna. Try the Atlantic salmon salad.

OTHER RECOMMENDATIONS The Taste of Italy features the colors of Italy's flag with a combination of chicken penne pesto, shrimp fettuccine Alfredo, and spaghetti with meatballs. The house-made tiramisu, if you can manage more food after the large plates, is a treat.

SUMMARY AND COMMENTS Family owned and operated for three generations, Carolina's also features more than 200 beers from around the globe and a rather well-selected wine list for such a place. Portions tend toward the gigantic, so bring your appetite.

The Catch ★★★½

SEAFOOD/STEAK   EXPENSIVE   QUALITY ★★★★ VALUE ★★★½

2100 E. Katella Ave., Ste. 104, Anaheim; ☎ 714-935-0101; catchanaheim.com

Reservations Recommended. **When to go** Lunch or dinner. **Entrée range** $16–$86. **Service** ★★★. **Friendliness** ★★★½. **Bar** Full bar. **Dress** Business casual. **Hours** Sunday, 5–9 p.m.; Monday–Friday, 11:30 a.m.–10 p.m.; Saturday, 5–10 p.m.

SETTING AND ATMOSPHERE Clean, contemporary take on a steak house classic, The Catch exudes urban chic with a comfortable blend of hardwood, glass, and tile. Expect to see dozens of young urban professionals; old, die-hard loyalists; and even a smattering of professional athletes who play for the local Angels baseball or Anaheim Ducks hockey teams dallying at the bar and/or enjoying dinner with friends and family.

HOUSE SPECIALTIES Grilled fresh fish, premium meats, and chops. The top sirloin may be the best cut you're likely to sample anywhere.

OTHER RECOMMENDATIONS Lunch features butcher-block sandwiches: piles of thinly sliced meats or fish piled high on fresh slabs of bread, accompanied by all the usual condiments and some not-so-common spreads such as lemon aioli. For dinner, try the terrific bone-in rib eye.

SUMMARY AND COMMENTS Yes, the place is very expensive, but you're not likely to find a more beautiful yet comfortable room, attentive service, or high-quality food prepared with love and care anywhere close by. It has a vibrant bar scene favored by local luminaries, a beautiful dining room, and even a nicely appointed patio.

Gabbi's Mexican Kitchen ★★★

GOURMET MEXICAN   MODERATE   QUALITY ★★★★ VALUE ★★★½

141 S. Glassell St., Orange; ☎ 714-633-3038; gabbipatrick.com

Reservations Recommended. **When to go** Lunch or dinner. **Entrée range** $11–$28. **Service** ★★★. **Friendliness** ★★★. **Bar** Full bar. **Dress** Casual. **Hours** Sunday–Thursday, 11 a.m.–10 p.m.; Friday–Saturday, 11 a.m.–11 p.m.

SETTING AND ATMOSPHERE Locals flock to Gabbi's vintage storefront that has no sign (look for the *poquito* patio next door to the Army surplus store). Just steps south of Orange's beloved plaza in charming Old Town, Gabbi's adds style to the narrow space with tall ceilings, exposed brick, and giant, colorful Mexican urns.

HOUSE SPECIALTIES Braised achiote Kurobuta pork with habañero salsa or carne asada tacos.

OTHER RECOMMENDATIONS Chicken enchiladas and signature margaritas made from a tequila collection that would make a desperado blush.

SUMMARY AND COMMENTS In this county teeming with taco stands and burrito counters, chef-owner Gabbi Patrick stands apart with her more refined, regional takes on Mexican food that reflect both her Napa training and her Latino family's roots in the restaurant business.

Haven Craft Kitchen + Bar ★★★

GASTROPUB	MODERATE	QUALITY ★★★★	VALUE ★★★½

190 S. Glassell St., Orange; ☎ 714-221-0680; havencraftkitchen.com

Reservations Recommended. **When to go** Lunch or dinner. **Entrée range** $14–$30. **Service** ★★★. **Friendliness** ★★★½. **Bar** Beer and wine. **Dress** Casual. **Hours** Monday–Friday, 11 a.m.–2 a.m.; Saturday–Sunday, 9 a.m.–2 a.m.

SETTING AND ATMOSPHERE The restaurant is in Old Town Orange, a historic area of preserved homes and businesses, including this little gem. Like its neighbor, Gabbi's, Haven is housed in a restored brick building. Inside, you'll find a large open dining room packed with tables and booths, framed by a massive bar on one side and an open kitchen on the other.

HOUSE SPECIALTIES Try the burger with aged goat cheese and tomato marmalade at lunch, or the Ora king salmon with sunchoke puree for dinner.

OTHER RECOMMENDATIONS Braised beef served poutine style with jalapeño cheddar cheese foam; locally raised roasted chicken served with carrots cooked in duck fat.

SUMMARY AND COMMENTS Think beer, anything made with beer, and all the food that goes with beer, and you have a grasp of what executive chef Craig Brady has put together here. Combine more than 200 craft beers on tap and in a bottle—and a service crew who knows every one of them intimately—with an adventurous menu of faux familiar and exotic foods, and you have Haven. The place is a favorite for the local college students and fills quickly on weekends but stays open late every night until 2 a.m.

House of Blues Restaurant & Bar ★★★

CAJUN/CREOLE	MODERATE	QUALITY ★★★½	VALUE ★★½

321 W. Katella Ave., Anaheim GardenWalk; ☎ 714-520-2334; houseofblues.com/anaheim

Reservations Recommended. **When to go** Dinner. **Entrée range** $10–$27. **Service** ★★★. **Friendliness** ★★★. **Bar** Wine list and full bar. **Dress** Casual. **Hours** Daily, 11 a.m.–9 p.m.

SETTING AND ATMOSPHERE The House of Blues closed up shop at Downtown Disney in May 2016 and reopened early 2017 in a larger space at the Anaheim GardenWalk a few blocks away. Think rustic-but-trendy blues club somewhere along the Mississippi River, maybe St. Louis. The restaurant has a more open feel than the previous location, as well as a built-in stage with live music almost every night. The walls feature a fantastic collection of American folk artists, including artworks created especially for the venue.

HOUSE SPECIALTIES Jambalaya, St. Louis–style ribs, pulled pork sandwich, and barbecue bacon burgers.

OTHER RECOMMENDATIONS Nashville hot chicken wings and barbecue brisket tacos.

SUMMARY AND COMMENTS House of Blues is first and foremost a major concert site, with marquee names, up-and-comers, and strong local talent taking the stage every night. Unless stated otherwise, the separately ticketed concert hall is strictly an adult venue (18 and older), but children are always welcome in the restaurant. Happy hour (Monday–Friday, 3–6 p.m.) offers discounted drinks and cut-rate appetizers. You can experience everything the venue has to offer by attending the family-friendly Gospel Brunch, a Sunday-morning event that showcases local gospel singers and features an all-you-can-eat Southern-influenced buffet.

Jägerhaus ★★★

GERMAN	INEXPENSIVE	QUALITY ★★★½	VALUE ★★★

2525 E. Ball Road, Anaheim; ☎ 714-520-9500; jagerhaus.net

Reservations Recommended only for large parties. **When to go** Breakfast. **Entrée range** $9–$24. **Service** ★★½. **Friendliness** ★★★★. **Bar** Wine list and extensive imported draft beer offerings. **Dress** Casual. **Hours** Monday–Friday, 7 a.m.–9 p.m.; Saturday–Sunday, 8 a.m.–9 p.m.

SETTING AND ATMOSPHERE We don't think that anything has changed since this restaurant opened decades ago. Wood paneling dominates. Pictures of alpine meadows and picturesque old-world villages hang beneath shelves of kitschy accoutrements, from delicate porcelain teapots to hearty beer steins—but it's clean and neat.

HOUSE SPECIALTIES The German pancakes, dense, doughy, platter-size egg cakes flavored with everything from lemon and powdered sugar to fruit jams and even fresh fruit; fat, juicy bratwursts.

OTHER RECOMMENDATIONS Omelets, corned beef hash, and house-made sausage patties.

SUMMARY AND COMMENTS Everyone from recent German émigrés and tourists to descendants of the original German settlers gather here to eat fat, fluffy German pancakes and sausage and gossip over coffee. The huge menu offers something for everyone, from burgers to bratwurst and Wiener schnitzel.

Mas' Chinese Islamic Restaurant ★★★½

NORTHERN CHINESE	MODERATE	QUALITY ★★★	VALUE ★★★½

601 E. Orangethorpe Ave., Anaheim; ☎ 714-446-9553; masislamic.com

Reservations Recommended. **When to go** Lunch or dinner. **Entrée range** $11–$28. **Service** ★★★. **Friendliness** ★★★½. **Dress** Casual but modest (no shorts). **Hours** Monday–Thursday, 11 a.m.–3 p.m. and 5–9 p.m.; Friday–Sunday, 11 a.m.–3 p.m. and 5–9:30 p.m.

SETTING AND ATMOSPHERE One of a small chain of Islamic Chinese restaurants, this is the real deal. Mas's dining room is spacious, with comfortable booths and large tables. The decor blends Middle Eastern and Chinese motifs with lots of tile, repetitive patterned mosaics, and lofty arches.

HOUSE SPECIALTIES Get the thick sesame bread with green onions as a starter. Any lamb dish is a sure bet, especially the one served with *sha cha*, a spicy brown sauce.

OTHER RECOMMENDATIONS The warm pots—northern-Chinese stews—are great, as is the beef with green onions.

SUMMARY AND COMMENTS This is a veritable institution among local Muslims (Arabs and East and Southeast Asians), so expect to see women in veils and burkas and men dressed very conservatively; also, note that no alcohol is served. Service is gracious, if a bit English-challenged. Stick to the northern-Chinese specialties—the more familiar Chinese side of the menu is less exciting.

McCormick & Schmick's Grille ★★★

SEAFOOD	MODERATE-EXPENSIVE	QUALITY ★★★	VALUE ★★★

321 W. Katella Ave., Anaheim GardenWalk; ☎ 714-535-9000; mccormickandschmicks.com

Reservations Recommended. **When to go** Lunch or dinner. **Entrée range** $13–$50. **Service** ★★★. **Friendliness** ★★★★. **Bar** Full bar and extensive wine list. **Dress** Business casual. **Hours** Sunday–Thursday, 11:30 a.m.–10 p.m.; Friday–Saturday, 11:30 a.m.–11 p.m.

SETTING AND ATMOSPHERE This large chain of seafood eateries designs each of its units differently to match its local surroundings. In addition to lots of dark hardwoods and spacious booths, the decor here takes its cues from the rich agricultural history of the area.

HOUSE SPECIALTIES Fish is fresh and infinitely variable. The menu changes daily; each chef is free to choose from among 80 different preparations. You can't miss with king crab, lobster, salmon, or killer fresh swordfish.

SUMMARY AND COMMENTS This is a very popular spot with local business types, and waits without reservations can be long. The menu can be overwhelming; on the other hand, there's something for everyone, even folks who don't eat fish. Happy hour specials (daily, 4–7 p.m.) somewhat soften the sting of expensive entrées, but you must sit at the bar or patio and order a drink.

Morton's ★★★★

STEAK HOUSE	EXPENSIVE	QUALITY ★★★½	VALUE ★★★½

1895 S. Harbor Blvd., Anaheim; ☎ 714-621-0101; mortons.com/anaheim

Reservations Recommended. **When to go** Dinner. **Entrée range** $24–$99. **Service** ★★★★. **Friendliness** ★★★★. **Bar** Extensive wine list and full bar. **Dress** Dressy casual. **Hours** Sunday, 5–10 p.m.; Monday–Saturday, 5:30–11 p.m.

SETTING AND ATMOSPHERE Classic steak house with overstuffed booths, soft lighting, and dark hardwoods.

HOUSE SPECIALTIES Try the center-cut filet mignon Oscar-style (with lump crab, asparagus, and béarnaise sauce).

OTHER RECOMMENDATIONS The bone-in rib eye is a Chicago staple and beef-eater's dream: 22 ounces of prime steak, grilled to order.

SUMMARY AND COMMENTS Morton's is a carnivore's delight—beef, lamb, and chicken dominate the menu. Of course, there's a smattering of fish options, including shrimp in several different iterations, but this place is really about the beef.

Park Ave Steaks & Chops ★★★★½

STEAK HOUSE	EXPENSIVE	QUALITY ★★★★	VALUE ★★★★

11200 Beach Blvd., Stanton; ☎ 714-901-4400; parkavedining.com

Reservations Recommended. **When to go** Dinner. **Entrée range** $14–$50. **Service** ★★★. **Friendliness** ★★★½. **Bar** Full bar. **Dress** Dressy casual/business. **Hours** Sunday, 4–9 p.m.; Tuesday–Thursday, 11 a.m.–9 p.m.; Friday, 11 a.m.–10 p.m.; Saturday, 4–10 p.m.

SETTING AND ATMOSPHERE From the flagstone walls and Sputnik-like lighting to red leather booths, this place exudes 1950s modern chic. There's also an expansive terrace and meticulously maintained grounds, where the chef grows his own herbs, vegetables, and fruit.

HOUSE SPECIALTIES Bone-in rib eye and the five-spiced baked salmon drizzled with honey mustard.

OTHER RECOMMENDATIONS The chef does a marvelous job with a salad featuring marinated skirt steak with a ginger, molasses, and soy sauce.

SUMMARY AND COMMENTS Park Ave is a throwback to all things mid-20th century—except the menu. The proprietors have managed to avoid the kitsch and concentrate on things that evoke a simpler, less complicated era—down to a friendly bar shaking up some of the meanest martinis in Orange County. The food is exceptionally good (award winning), but service gets a little sloppy, especially on slower nights. A more casual garden restaurant on the same grounds offers a compact menu of Italian classics.

Prime Cut Café & Wine Bar ★★★

STEAK HOUSE	MODERATE-EXPENSIVE	QUALITY ★★★	VALUE ★★★½

1547 W. Katella Ave., Ste. 101, Stadium Promenade, Orange;
☎ 714-532-4300; primecutcafe.com

Reservations Recommended. **When to go** Lunch or dinner. **Entrée range** $15–$40. **Service** ★★★. **Friendliness** ★★★. **Bar** Wine and cocktails. **Dress** Casual. **Hours** Sunday–Thursday, 11 a.m.–9:30 p.m.; Friday–Saturday, 11 a.m.–10:30 p.m.

SETTING AND ATMOSPHERE Polished but laid-back, this dapper café is a welcome independent in a sea of chain operations. A massive granite bar anchors the attractive space that also offers a roomy patio overlooking the shopping center's water fountain.

HOUSE SPECIALTIES Slow-roasted prime rib is offered in two sizes, both partnered with good Yorkshire pudding. A huge pork chop is another winner, paired with butter-braised bacon and apple cider reduction.

OTHER RECOMMENDATIONS Prime rib may hog the spotlight, but steaks, burgers, and entrée salads often outshine the showy star of the menu. Sides such as potato gratin are scene-stealers, as are from-scratch desserts.

SUMMARY AND COMMENTS Prime Cut Café does a good job of making first-rate dining affordable and approachable. Sixty-plus wines sold by the glass or bottle are an attraction for wine lovers, though wine snobs might find the list a bit lowbrow. The menu offers lots of appetizers and snacks that pair well with wine, making this a great option for a quick bite or grown-up get-together. The central location means that crowds swell or recede according to events at nearby Anaheim Stadium, Honda Center, or even what's hot at the adjacent multiplex cinema.

Roscoe's House of Chicken & Waffles ★★★★

AMERICAN	INEXPENSIVE	QUALITY ★★★★	VALUE ★★★½

2110 S. Harbor Blvd., Anaheim; ☎ 714-823-4130;
roscoeschickenandwaffles.com

Reservations Not accepted. **When to go** Anytime. **Entrée range** $6–$21. **Service** ★★★. **Friendliness** ★★★. **Dress** Casual. **Hours** Sunday–Thursday, 8 a.m.–11 p.m.; Friday–Saturday, 8 a.m.–1 a.m.

SETTING AND ATMOSPHERE The plain, almost featureless, exterior is surrounded by palm trees. The decorations inside are also sparse, save for the occasional cheap painting or neon sign. Going on only looks, you'll wonder why there's a huge line to get in, especially on nights and weekends.

HOUSE SPECIALTIES It's right there in the name: chicken and waffles.

OTHER RECOMMENDATIONS We love the Jeanne Jones Omelette and the macaroni and cheese side dish.

SUMMARY AND COMMENTS Roscoe's is a longtime Los Angeles institution that finally made its way to Orange County in 2014. Like all the other locations, locals flock to Roscoe's for its delicious Southern-style comfort food, including the signature chicken and waffles. While the fried chicken is good, it may not be the best you'll ever have. But the waffles are excellent, and the macaroni and cheese is a must-try.

SHOPPING *at* DISNEYLAND

SHOPS ADD REALISM and atmosphere to the various theme settings and offer souvenirs, clothing, novelties, jewelry, decorator items, and more. Much of the merchandise displayed (with the exception of Disney trademark souvenir items), though, is available back home and elsewhere, so we recommend bypassing the shops on a one-day visit. If you have two or more days to spend at Disneyland Resort, browse in the early afternoon, when many attractions are crowded.

Our recommendations notwithstanding, we realize that for many guests, Disney souvenirs and memorabilia are irresistible. One of our readers writes:

> *People have a compelling need to buy Disney stuff at Disneyland. When you get home, you wonder why you ever got a cashmere sweater with Mickey Mouse embroidered on the breast, or a tie with tiny Goofys all over it. Maybe they put something in the food?*

If you don't want to lug your packages around, you can leave them at the shop where you made your purchase and pick them up before you exit the park. If you're staying at a Disneyland Resort hotel, your loot will be delivered directly to your resort's bellhop desk (by 7 a.m. the following day) on request. If you have a problem with your purchases or need to make a return, call Disneyland Exclusive Merchandise at ☎ 877-560-6477. If you return home and realize that you forgot to buy those Rastafarian mouse ears or some similarly essential tchotchke, a large selection of park-exclusive merchandise is available at shopdisney.com/parks. To reduce the resort's use of single-use plastic, Disneyland Resort now offers reusable themed bags with your purchases for $2–$3; free disposable bags are still available upon request for now.

DOWNTOWN DISNEY

VERDANT AND LANDSCAPED BY DAY, Downtown Disney pops alive with neon and glitter at night. The complex offers more than 300,000 square feet of specialty shopping, restaurants, and entertainment. Most of the western end of Downtown Disney between the monorail station and the Disneyland Hotel, including the AMC Movieplex, ESPN Zone, and Rainforest Cafe, was closed for the construction of a now-canceled luxury hotel. The popular Earl of Sandwich has since reopened, and a temporary Mickey Mouse art exhibit was installed, but no permanent plans have been announced for the storefronts that are still shuttered.

Many of the restaurants offer entertainment in addition to dining, including **Ralph Brennan's Jazz Kitchen** and **Splitsville Luxury Lanes,** an improbably but surprisingly successful mash-up of bowling alley and sushi bar. Other restaurant options include **Naples Ristorante e Pizzeria, Tortilla Jo's** Mexican restaurant, **Catal Restaurant, Ballast Point,** and **Black Tap Craft Burgers & Shakes.** An elegant **Starbucks,** across from the parking tram stop, serves all the chain's beverages and sandwiches (including beer and wine in the evenings) and offers free Wi-Fi, phone-charging stations, and full loyalty card benefits (though it doesn't accept Disney gift cards or annual pass discounts). If you have a sweet tooth, **Marceline's Confectionery** makes the same character candy apple found inside the parks, and **Salt & Straw** offers one-of-a-kind ice cream flavors like honey lavender, roasted strawberry coconut, and (for real) black olive brittle and Humboldt fog goat cheese.

If you're not hungry, a 40,000-square-foot **World of Disney** store anchors the shopping scene; watch for Tinker Bell in the paint jars behind the main checkout area and animated artwork on the walls. Other retailers include **Sanuk,** specializing in comfy flip-flops; **Disney Dress Shop,** a boutique of vintage-style apparel inspired by old-school Disney icons like the Orange Bird; **Sephora,** featuring cosmetics; **Pandora,** which carries jewelry; and **Disney Home,** where you can stock up on Mickey towels and utensils for your bath and kitchen. If expensive designer sunglasses are your thing, head to **Sunglass Icon** for a large variety of shades. For an artistic memento, **WonderGround Gallery** showcases edgy (and expensive) reinterpretations of classic Disney images, often signed by their creators. **LEGO Store** features interactive play tables with LEGO bricks and life-size statues of Disney characters made entirely of LEGOs.

A virtual reality experience called **The Void** opened in late 2017, featuring **Star Wars: Secrets of the Empire.** Created in partnership with ILMxLAB, this 30-minute high-tech adventure turns you and three friends into spies for the Rebellion, tasked by *Rogue One*'s Captain Cassian with breaking in to an Imperial base disguised as Stormtroopers and retrieving a top-secret artifact. A new Marvel Super Hero virtual reality experience is scheduled to be introduced in summer 2019. The 3-D headsets you wear for both are a bit awkward (especially if you wear prescription eyeglasses), but the visuals are sharp, tracking your head and hand movements with no nauseating lag. Physical effects like heat and wind, and tactile feedback from your vibrating vest, all greatly enhance the immersion; you can even reach out and touch a friendly droid. The VR portion of the attraction lasts under 15 minutes, and replay value is limited, but even at $32.95 per player ($34.95 Friday–Sunday and holiday weeks), this is a must-do for hard-core gamers and uberfans of the respective franchises. Operating hours are Sunday–Thursday, 9 a.m.–11 p.m.; Friday–Saturday, 9 a.m.–midnight; book your time slot in advance at thevoid.com/locations/anaheim.

Our map of Downtown Disney, listing storefronts and restaurants, appears on the facing page.

ANAHEIM GARDENWALK

BUILT ON THREE LEVELS AND NICELY LANDSCAPED, Anaheim GardenWalk is a shopping, dining, and entertainment venue that stretches from West Katella Avenue to Disney Way. It effectively doubles the restaurant, lounge, and shopping choices for Disneyland Resort visitors and attendees of conventions at nearby Anaheim Convention Center. Restaurants include **Bubba Gump Shrimp Co., California Pizza Kitchen, The Cheesecake Factory, House of Blues, Fire + Ice, McCormick & Schmick's Grille, P.F. Chang's Chinese Bistro,** and **Roy's Restaurant.**

For entertainment, there's an escape-room game, a 41-lane bowling complex and nightspot combo, a 24-hour fitness center, a virtual reality arcade, and a tiny cabaret hosting magic shows (kipbarryscabaret.com). The GardenWalk, which changed hands yet again in early 2019, has long struggled to retain tenants, and several plans that the previous owners had to resuscitate the venue—such as a Toby Keith restaurant that never opened and a giant escalator that was constructed but then demolished—sputtered out. The complex's latest hopeful saviors are **House of Blues,** which relocated to GardenWalk from Downtown Disney in early 2017, and a new AMC movie theater that lacks modern IMAX or Dolby amenities. A handful of venues, such as an indoor family-entertainment center, are still hanging on, but there are more shuttered storefronts than open ones, giving the entire venue a depressing *Dawn of the Dead* vibe. For additional information, see anaheimgardenwalk.com.

Downtown Disney

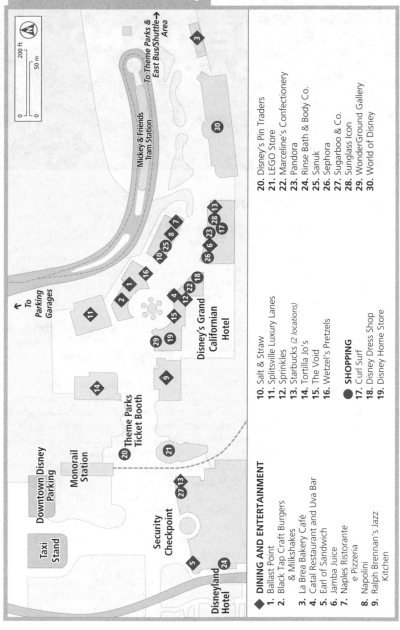

♦ DINING AND ENTERTAINMENT

1. Ballast Point
2. Black Tap Craft Burgers & Milkshakes
3. La Brea Bakery Café
4. Catal Restaurant and Uva Bar
5. Earl of Sandwich
6. Jamba Juice
7. Naples Ristorante e Pizzeria
8. Napolini
9. Ralph Brennan's Jazz Kitchen
10. Salt & Straw
11. Splitsville Luxury Lanes
12. Sprinkles
13. Starbucks (2 locations)
14. Tortilla Jo's
15. The Void
16. Wetzel's Pretzels

● SHOPPING

17. Curl Surf
18. Disney Dress Shop
19. Disney Home Store
20. Disney's Pin Traders
21. LEGO Store
22. Marceline's Confectionery
23. Pandora
24. Rinse Bath & Body Co.
25. Sanuk
26. Sephora
27. Sugarboo & Co.
28. Sunglass Icon
29. WonderGround Gallery
30. World of Disney

PART FIVE

DISNEYLAND PARK

ARRIVING *and* GETTING ORIENTED

AFTER PARKING AT OR WALKING into the resort, guests pass through security screenings before entering the Esplanade to approach Disneyland's front turnstiles. Two entrance gates, 14 and 19, are blocked by trees situated in the entrance plaza about 10 feet from the security checkpoint. The trees sometimes inhibit the formation of a line in front of both the obstructed gates. Gates 14 and 19 are staffed nonetheless and draw guests from adjacent lines 13 or 15 and 18 or 20. When this happens, it significantly speeds up the entry process for guests waiting in lines 13 and 20. Our advice on arriving, therefore, is to inspect the lines leading to gates 14 and 19 and join whichever looks to be shortest. Later in the day, the outside gates (1 and 32) tend to be fastest for reentry. Stroller and wheelchair rentals are available in the Esplanade between Disneyland and Disney California Adventure. As you enter Main Street, City Hall is to your left, serving as the center for general information, lost and found, and entertainment information.

To combat rampant resales of unexpired tickets, Disneyland Resort has implemented a policy of photographing all guests upon their first park entry. Have your ticket ready for scanning by a cast member just before you enter the turnstiles; if your mug isn't yet in Mickey's mainframe, you'll be asked to pose before proceeding. These added steps can sometimes slow the line at the start of the day, and there's no express lane for returning guests or annual pass holders.

Be sure to pick up a park map as you pass through the turnstiles. Maps are also available in the passages connecting the park entrance to Main Street, U.S.A.; at City Hall; and at a number of shops throughout the park. Printed *Times Guide* pamphlets, which detail daily entertainment schedules for live shows, parades, fireworks, and character greetings, are being phased out in favor of the Disneyland smartphone app; if you want one, look on the racks of foreign-language maps near the tunnels under the train station, or outside City Hall. If you are attending a special hard-ticket event, the daily entertainment schedule may be included in the park map. The park map lists all the attractions, shops, and eateries and provides helpful information about first aid, baby care, assistance for the disabled, and more.

Notice on your map that Main Street ends at a central hub from which branch the entrances to four other sections of Disneyland: **Adventureland, Frontierland, Fantasyland,** and **Tomorrowland.** Two other "lands," **New Orleans Square** and **Critter Country,** can be reached through Adventureland and Frontierland, and **Star Wars: Galaxy's Edge** connects to Critter Country and Frontierland. **Mickey's Toontown** is located on the far side of the railroad tracks from It's a Small World in Fantasyland. **Sleeping Beauty Castle,** the entrance to Fantasyland, is a focal landmark and the visual center of the park. The castle is a great place to meet if your group decides to split up during the day, and it can serve as an emergency meeting place if you are accidentally separated. Keep in mind, however, that the castle covers a lot of territory, so be specific about *where* to meet at the castle. Also be forewarned that parades and live shows sometimes make it difficult to access the entrance of the castle fronting the central hub. Another good meeting spot is the *Partners* statue of Mickey and Walt in the central hub.

STARTING THE TOUR

EVERYONE WILL SOON FIND their own favorite and not-so-favorite attractions in Disneyland Park. Be open-minded and adventuresome. Don't dismiss a ride or show as not being for you until *after* you have tried it. Our personal experience and our research indicate that each visitor is different in terms of which Disney offerings he or she most enjoys. So don't miss seeing an attraction because a friend from home didn't like it; that attraction may turn out to be your favorite.

We do recommend that you take advantage of what Disney does best—the fantasy adventures such as Indiana Jones Adventure and The Haunted Mansion and the Audio-Animatronics (talking robots, that is) attractions such as Pirates of the Caribbean. Unless you have almost unlimited time, don't burn a lot of daylight browsing through the shops. Except for some special Disney souvenirs, you can find much of the same merchandise elsewhere. Try to minimize the time you spend on midway-type rides, as you probably have an amusement park, carnival, or state fair close to your hometown. Don't, however, mistake rides such as Splash Mountain and the Big Thunder Mountain Railroad for amusement park rides. They may be of the flume ride or roller coaster genre, but they represent pure Disney genius. Similarly, do not devote a lot of time to waiting in line for meals. Eat a good early breakfast before you come, snack on vendor-sold foods during the touring day, or follow the suggestions for meals incorporated into the various touring plans presented.

continued on page 216

Disneyland Park

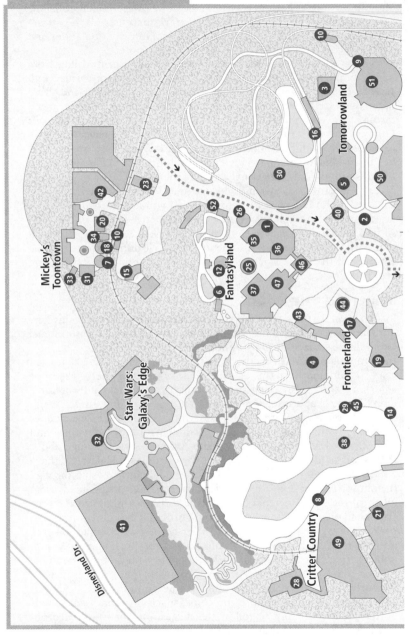

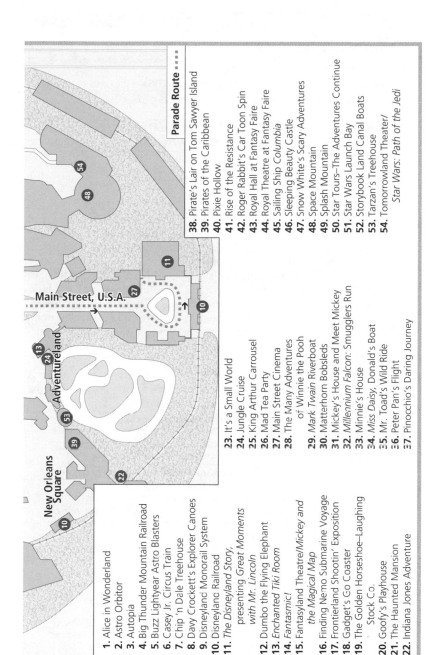

Parade Route ▪▪▪▪

Main Street, U.S.A.

New Orleans Square

Adventureland

1. Alice in Wonderland
2. Astro Orbitor
3. Autopia
4. Big Thunder Mountain Railroad
5. Buzz Lightyear Astro Blasters
6. Casey Jr. Circus Train
7. Chip 'n Dale Treehouse
8. Davy Crockett's Explorer Canoes
9. Disneyland Monorail System
10. Disneyland Railroad
11. *The Disneyland Story,*
    presenting Great Moments
    with Mr. Lincoln
12. Dumbo the Flying Elephant
13. *Enchanted Tiki Room*
14. *Fantasmic!*
15. Fantasyland Theatre/*Mickey and*
    the Magical Map
16. Finding Nemo Submarine Voyage
17. Frontierland Shootin' Exposition
18. Gadget's Go Coaster
19. The Golden Horseshoe—Laughing
    Stock Co.
20. Goofy's Playhouse
21. The Haunted Mansion
22. Indiana Jones Adventure

23. It's a Small World
24. Jungle Cruise
25. King Arthur Carrousel
26. Mad Tea Party
27. Main Street Cinema
28. The Many Adventures
    of Winnie the Pooh
29. *Mark Twain Riverboat*
30. Matterhorn Bobsleds
31. Mickey's House and Meet Mickey
32. *Millennium Falcon:* Smugglers Run
33. Minnie's House
34. *Miss Daisy,* Donald's Boat
35. Mr. Toad's Wild Ride
36. Peter Pan's Flight
37. Pinocchio's Daring Journey

38. Pirate's Lair on Tom Sawyer Island
39. Pirates of the Caribbean
40. Pixie Hollow
41. Rise of the Resistance
42. Roger Rabbit's Car Toon Spin
43. Royal Hall at Fantasy Faire
44. Royal Theatre at Fantasy Faire
45. Sailing Ship *Columbia*
46. Sleeping Beauty Castle
47. Snow White's Scary Adventures
48. Space Mountain
49. Splash Mountain
50. Star Tours—The Adventures Continue
51. Star Wars Launch Bay
52. Storybook Land Canal Boats
53. Tarzan's Treehouse
54. Tomorrowland Theater/
    Star Wars: Path of the Jedi

NOT TO BE MISSED AT DISNEYLAND PARK
ADVENTURELAND Indiana Jones Adventure
CRITTER COUNTRY Splash Mountain
FRONTIERLAND Big Thunder Mountain Railroad
NEW ORLEANS SQUARE The Haunted Mansion | Pirates of the Caribbean
STAR WARS: GALAXY'S EDGE *Millennium Falcon:* Smugglers Run | Star Wars: Rise of the Resistance
TOMORROWLAND Space Mountain | Star Tours—The Adventures Continue
LIVE ENTERTAINMENT *Fantasmic!* | *Disneyland Forever*

continued from page 213

SINGLE-RIDER LINES

YOU CAN OFTEN SAVE TIME waiting in line by taking advantage of single-rider lines, a separate line for people who don't mind riding alone or with a stranger. The objective of single-rider lines is to fill odd spaces left by groups who don't fill the entire ride vehicle. Because there aren't many singles and most groups aren't willing to split up, single-rider lines are usually much shorter than the regular line. In Disneyland Park, Indiana Jones Adventure, Matterhorn Bobsleds, *Millennium Falcon:* Smugglers Run, Rise of the Resistance, Space Mountain, and Splash Mountain have single-rider lines. Ask an attraction employee how to enter the single-rider queue; you may be given a paper pass and directed up the exit.

PARK-OPENING PROCEDURES

YOUR PROGRESS AND SUCCESS during your first hour of touring will be affected by the opening procedure used that day.

A. All guests are held at the turnstiles until the park opens (which may or may not be at the official opening time). On admittance, all "lands" are open. If this is the case on the day you visit, blow right past Main Street and head for the first attraction on whatever touring plan you are following.

B. Guests are admitted to Main Street 15–60 minutes before the remaining "lands" open. Rope barriers block access to the various lands from the central hub. On admittance, move to the rope barrier and stake out a position as follows:

(1) If you are going to Star Wars: Galaxy's Edge, line up on the left side of the central hub outside Frontierland and wait for cast members to walk you into Batuu through the Critter Country entrance.

(2) If you are going to Indiana Jones Adventure or Splash Mountain first, take up a position in front of Jolly Holiday Bakery at the central-hub end of Main Street on the left. Wait next to the rope barrier blocking the walkway to Adventureland. When the rest of the park opens, proceed quickly to Adventureland for Indiana Jones, or Critter Country by way of Adventureland and New Orleans Square for Splash Mountain.

(3) If you are going to Finding Nemo Submarine Voyage, Star Tours, or Space Mountain first, wait on the right side of the central hub. When the rope drops at opening time, bear right and zip into Tomorrowland.

(4) If you are going to Fantasyland or Frontierland first, proceed as far forward in the central hub as allowed and line up at the rope, to the left of Walt and Mickey's central statue.

DISNEYLAND PARK SERVICES
BABY CARE CENTER At the central-hub end of Main Street
BANKING SERVICES/CURRENCY EXCHANGE At City Hall at the railroad station end of Main Street
DISNEYLAND AND LOCAL ATTRACTION INFORMATION At City Hall
FIRST AID Two doors down from Plaza Inn at the central-hub end of Main Street
LIVE ENTERTAINMENT AND PARADE INFORMATION At City Hall
LOST ADULTS AND MESSAGES At City Hall
LOST AND FOUND Lost and Found for the entire resort is located west of the entrance to Disneyland Park.
LOST CHILDREN At the central-hub end of Main Street
STORAGE LOCKERS Down Main Street one block (as you walk toward the castle) and to the right

MAIN STREET, U.S.A.

THIS SECTION OF DISNEYLAND PARK is where you'll begin and end your visit. The Disneyland Railroad stops at the Main Street Station, and you can board here for a grand circle tour of the park, or you can get off the train in New Orleans Square, Mickey's Toontown/Fantasyland, or Tomorrowland.

Main Street is an idealized version of a turn-of-the-20th-century American small-town street. Many visitors are surprised to discover that all the buildings are real, not elaborate props. Attention to detail is exceptional—interiors, furnishings, and fixtures conform to the period. As with any real Main Street, the Disney version is essentially a collection of shops and eating places, with a city hall, a fire station, and an old-time cinema. A mixed-media attraction combines static exhibits recalling the life of Walt Disney with a patriotic remembrance of Abraham Lincoln. Horse-drawn trolleys, fire engines, and horseless carriages give rides along Main Street and transport visitors to the central hub.

Disneyland Railroad ★★★½

APPEAL BY AGE	PRESCHOOL ★★★★	GRADE SCHOOL ★★★★	TEENS ★★★★
YOUNG ADULTS ★★★★		OVER 30 ★★★★	SENIORS ★★★★

What it is Scenic railroad ride around the park's perimeter; also transportation to New Orleans Square, Mickey's Toontown, Fantasyland, and Tomorrowland. **Scope and scale** Major attraction. **When to go** After 11 a.m. or when you need transportation. **Comment** The Main Street and Tomorrowland Stations are usually the least-congested boarding points. **Duration of ride** About 22 minutes for a full circuit. **Average wait in line per 100 people ahead of you** 7 minutes; assumes 3 trains operating. **Loading speed** Fast.

DESCRIPTION AND COMMENTS This transportation ride blends an eclectic variety of sights and experiences with an energy-saving way of getting around the park. In addition to providing a glimpse of all the lands except Adventureland and Galaxy's Edge, the train passes through the Grand Canyon Diorama (between Tomorrowland and

Thumbs Up for the Whole Family

Main Street), a three-dimensional replica of the canyon, complete with wild-life, as it appears from the southern rim. Another sight on the train circuit is Primeval World, a depiction of a prehistoric peat bog and rain forest populated by Audio-Animatronic (robotic) dinosaurs. Opened in 1966 Primeval World uses animatronics recycled from the Disney-designed Ford's Magic Skyway pavilion for the 1964 World's Fair, and it was a precursor to a similar presentation at Epcot's former Universe of Energy.

The train's path has shifted south over what was once a portion of the Rivers of America to accommodate Galaxy's Edge. Passengers' views of the new land are blocked by a mountain range, complete with elevated train trestles and waterfalls that recall the park's original Nature's Wonderland.

TOURING TIPS Save the train ride until after you've seen the featured attractions, or use it when you need transportation. It can also be a way to relax during the peak times of the day when the crowds are swelling. You can get a good estimate of how long you'll wait for the next train by using the posted wait time sign outside each station. It will either list 5 minutes (three trains operating), 10 minutes (two trains), or 20 minutes (only one train). If you have small children who are hell-bent on seeing Mickey first thing in the morning, you might consider taking the train to Mickey's Toontown (a half circuit) and visiting Mickey in his dressing room as soon as you enter the park (note that Toontown opens 1 hour later than the rest of the park). Many families find that this tactic puts the kids in a more receptive frame of mind for the other attractions. On busy days, lines form at the New Orleans Square and Mickey's Toontown/Fantasyland Stations but rarely at the Main Street or Tomorrowland Stations.

The Disneyland Story, presenting Great Moments with Mr. Lincoln ★★★½

APPEAL BY AGE	PRESCHOOL ★★	GRADE SCHOOL ★★★	TEENS ★★★
YOUNG ADULTS ★★★		OVER 30 ★★★	SENIORS ★★★

What it is Nostalgic exhibits documenting the Disney success story, followed by an Audio-Animatronics patriotic presentation. **Scope and scale** Minor attraction. **When to go** During the hot, crowded period of day. **Duration of show** 15 minutes including preshow of Disney exhibits. **Probable waiting time** Usually none.

Thumbs Up for the Whole Family

DESCRIPTION AND COMMENTS A warm and well-presented remembrance of the man who started it all. Well worth seeing. The attraction lobby consists of a museum of Disney memorabilia. Especially interesting are rotating Disney Gallery displays of concept art and historical artifacts, most recently featuring a tribute to the Haunted Mansion's 50th anniversary, with original sculptures and paintings from the beloved attraction. Beyond the Disney memorabilia, guests are admitted to a large theater where *Great Moments with Mr. Lincoln* is presented. The patriotic performance stars an extremely lifelike and sophisticated Audio-Animatronic Abraham Lincoln delivering an amalgamation of his notable speeches (though the overfamiliar "Gettysburg Address" is not recited in full) as originally recorded by actor Royal Dano for the 1964 World's Fair. Lincoln's head is stunningly emotive, capable of wrinkling his brow and pursing his lips with unrivaled realism. Surround sound effects and songs borrowed from Epcot's

American Adventure add to this brief but inspiring biography of America's 16th president. The show is periodically preempted for previews of Disney's upcoming feature films.

TOURING TIPS You usually do not have to wait long for this show, so see it during the busy times of day when lines are long elsewhere or as you are leaving the park. Sit up close to best see the detail on the Lincoln figure, or sit a few rows back for a more comfortable view of the screen. For crowd-control reasons, *The Disneyland Story* shuts down during evening parades, a fact often not noted in the entertainment schedule.

Main Street Cinema   ★★

APPEAL BY AGE	PRESCHOOL ★★½	GRADE SCHOOL ★★★½	TEENS ★★½
YOUNG ADULTS ★★★½	OVER 30 ★★★½		SENIORS ★★★★½

What it is Vintage Disney cartoons. **Scope and scale** Diversion. **When to go** Whenever you want. **Comments** Wonderful selection of old-time flicks; audience stands. **Duration of show** Runs continuously. **Probable waiting time** None.

DESCRIPTION AND COMMENTS An opening-day attraction, this small theater shows six classic Disney cartoons simultaneously. Early black-and-white Mickey Mouse shorts such as "Steamboat Willie" and "Plane Crazy" are screened, along with the celebrity caricature–stocked oddity "Mickey's Polo Team." The films are played at a low enough volume that the theater remains a quiet respite from the rest of the park.

TOURING TIPS Good place to get out of the sun or rain or to kill time while others in your group shop on Main Street. Fun, but not something you can't afford to miss. Audience stands.

Transportation Rides

DESCRIPTION AND COMMENTS Trolleys, buses, and the like add color to Main Street. One-way only.

TOURING TIPS The rides will save you a walk to the central hub. Not worth waiting in line. If you catch the first trolley of the morning, you may be serenaded onboard by the Dapper Dans.

▌▊ ADVENTURELAND

ADVENTURELAND IS THE FIRST "LAND" to the left of Main Street and somehow manages to seamlessly combine South Pacific island, Middle Eastern bazaar, and African safari themes. Transitions from one part of Adventureland to another feel quite natural, and the identity crisis inherent in the mixed-theme cocktail never registers in the minds of most guests. Before Galaxy's Edge opened, Adventureland's stroller parking and seating areas were rearranged to relieve what was among the worst pedestrian bottlenecks in any Disney theme park, but space is still tight. If you're just passing through Adventureland, say on your way to Splash Mountain, you can avoid the congestion by transiting Frontierland instead.

Enchanted Tiki Room ★★★½

What it is Audio-Animatronic Pacific island musical show. **Scope and scale** Minor attraction. **When to go** Anytime. **Duration of show** 14½ minutes plus preshow of talking totem poles. **Probable waiting time** 11 minutes.

  DESCRIPTION AND COMMENTS An unusual sit-down theater performance in which more than 200 birds, flowers, and tiki-god statues sing and whistle through a Polynesian-style musical program. One of Walt's first large-scale uses of Audio-Animatronics, *Tiki Room* might be more impressive for the technology it took to get the show (ahem) flying in 1963. Beloved by Disneyland fans for its detail and immersive setting, the current version of the show is only slightly altered from the original.

TOURING TIPS One of the most bizarre (yet endearing) of the Disneyland Park entertainments and rarely crowded. We like it in the late afternoon, when we can especially appreciate sitting for a bit in an air-conditioned theater. Back row seats provide the broadest view with the least neck strain.

The Tiki Juice Bar that straddles the *Tiki Room* entrance dispenses Dole Whip, a delectable blend of pineapple slush and vanilla soft-serve ice cream, one of the park's most popular snacks. Dole sponsors the attraction, so you can enjoy your Tiki Juice Bar treats while watching the show. There are service windows both inside and outside the attraction's waiting area. The line inside is reserved for mobile order pickup, which is highly recommended here; the outside cashier queue (or even the entire stand) may close on busy days to alleviate crowding on the Adventureland bridge.

Indiana Jones Adventure *(FastPass)* ★★★★★

What it is Motion-simulator dark ride. **Scope and scale** Super-headliner. **When to go** Before 9:30 a.m. or use FastPass. **Comments** Not to be missed. Must be 46" tall to ride; switching-off option (see page 147). **Duration of ride** 3⅓ minutes. **Average wait in line per 100 people ahead of you** 3 minutes. **Loading speed** Fast.

      DESCRIPTION AND COMMENTS This is a combination track ride and motion simulator. In addition to moving along its path, the military troop–transport vehicle bucks and pitches (the simulator part) in sync with the visuals and special effects. Though the plot is complicated and not altogether clear, the bottom line is that if you look into the Forbidden Eye, you're in big trouble. The Forbidden Eye, of course, stands out like Rush Limbaugh in a diaper, and *everybody* stares at it. The rest of the ride consists of a mad race to escape the temple as it collapses around you. In the process, you encounter snakes, spiders, lava pits, rats, swinging bridges, and the house-size granite bowling ball that everyone remembers from *Raiders of the Lost Ark*.

The Indiana Jones ride is a Disney masterpiece—nonstop action from beginning to end with brilliant visual effects. Elaborate even by Disney standards, the attraction provides a level of detail and variety of action that make use of the entire Imagineering arsenal of high-tech gimmickry. In recent years, the ride was upgraded with dazzling digital projections that bring the Chamber of Destiny doors and idol to life, but a few long-malfunctioning effects are still in need of refurbishment.

Sophisticated in its electronic and computer applications, Indiana Jones purports to offer a different experience on each ride. According to the designers, there are veritable menus of special effects that the computer can mix and match. In practice, however, we could not see much difference from ride to ride. There are, no doubt, subtle variations, but the ride is so wild and frenetic that it's hard to apprehend subtlety.

The adventure begins in the queue, which sometimes extends out the entrance of the attraction and over the bridge leading to Adventureland! When you ultimately work your way into the attraction area, you find yourself at the site of an archaeology expedition with the Temple of the Forbidden Eye entrance beckoning only 50 feet away. After crossing a wooden bridge, you finally step into the temple. The good news is that you are out of the California sun. The bad news is that you have just entered Indiana Jones's indoor queuing area, a system of tunnels and passageways extending to within 50 yards of the Santa Monica Pier.

Fortunately, the queuing area is interesting. You wind through caves, down the interior corridors of the temple, and into subterranean rotundas where the archaeologists have been hard at work. Along the way there are various surprises (be sure to disregard any DO NOT TOUCH signs you see on supporting poles or safety ropes), as well as a succession of homilies etched in an "ancient" language on the temple walls. You will eventually stumble into a chamber where a short movie will explain the plot. From there it's back into the maze and finally on to the loading area.

TOURING TIPS Indiana Jones stays fairly mobbed all day. Try to ride during the first hour the park is open or use FastPass. Another alternative, if you don't mind riding alone, is to take advantage of the single-rider line, where the wait is generally about one-third that of guests in the regular queue. Be forewarned that the single-rider line at Indiana Jones is a bit of a maze, requiring you to negotiate your way up the exit ramp, up one elevator, across a walkway over the track, and then down another elevator to the loading area.

If you miss Indiana Jones in the early morning and the FastPasses are all gone, try again during a parade or *Fantasmic!,* or during the hour before the park closes. Regarding the latter, the Disney folks will usually admit to the attraction anyone in line at closing time. During one visit to Indiana Jones, Disneyland Park closed at 8 p.m. We hopped in the line for Indiana Jones at 7:45 p.m. and actually got on the ride at 8:30 p.m.

Though the Indiana Jones ride is wild and jerky, the motion has been somewhat toned down since its debut, and it is primarily distinguished by its visual impact and realistic special effects. Thus, we encourage the over-50 crowd to give it a chance; we think you'll like it. As for children, most find the ride extremely intense and action-packed but not particularly frightening. We encountered very few children who met the 46-inch minimum-height requirement who were in any way intimidated.

Jungle Cruise ★★★

What it is A Disney outdoor-adventure boat ride. **Scope and scale** Major attraction. **When to go** Before 10 a.m. or after 6 p.m. **Comment** A Disney standard. **Duration of ride** 7½ minutes. **Average wait in line per 100 people ahead of you** 3½ minutes; assumes 10 boats operating. **Loading speed** Moderate–slow.

Thumbs Up for the Whole Family

DESCRIPTION AND COMMENTS On this boat ride through jungle waterways, passengers encounter elephants, lions, hostile natives, and a menacing hippo. It's a long-enduring Disney favorite, with the boatman's spiel adding measurably to the fun.

As more technologically advanced attractions have been added to the park over the years, the Jungle Cruise has, by comparison, lost some of its luster. Though still a good attraction, it offers few thrills and no surprises for Disneyland Park veterans, many of whom can rattle off the ride's narration right along with the guide. For park first-timers, however, the Jungle Cruise continues to delight.

Though dated, the Jungle Cruise can still draw long waits, as this Anacortes, Washington, family found out:

Jungle Cruise's line can be insanity-inducing long. If the line goes upstairs, expect a very long wait through the grandfather of switchback queues. Nearly every time you expect the queue to turn around back to the ride, it continues into another room.

TOURING TIPS This ride loads slowly, and long lines form as the park fills. To compound problems, guests exiting Indiana Jones tend to head for the Jungle Cruise. Go early, or during a parade or *Fantasmic!* Be forewarned that the Jungle Cruise has an especially deceptive line: just when you think that you are about to board, you are shunted into yet another queuing maze (not visible outside the ride). Regardless of how short the line *looks* when you approach the Jungle Cruise, inquire about the length of the wait—at least you will know what you are getting into. If the second floor of the queue building is in use, you're in for at least a 20-minute wait. When the queue splits before the loading dock, the left lane is often quicker. Finally, many readers consider the Jungle Cruise much better at night. If the Jungle Cruise is closed for refurbishment during your visit, the "Skipper School" and "Land Tour" comedy skits that cast members perform in front of the construction walls are nearly as entertaining as the actual ride (without any waiting required).

Tarzan's Treehouse ★★★

Thumbs Up for the Whole Family

What it is Walk-through tree house exhibit. **Scope and scale** Minor attraction. **When to go** Anytime. **Comments** Requires climbing a lot of stairs; a very creative exhibit. **Duration of tour** 8–12 minutes. **Average wait in line per 100 people ahead of you** 7½ minutes.

DESCRIPTION AND COMMENTS Inspired by Disney's 1999 animated film *Tarzan*, Tarzan's Treehouse replaced the venerable Swiss Family Treehouse that had been an Adventureland icon for 37 years. To enter the attraction, you climb a rustic staircase and cross a suspension bridge. From there, as they say, it's all downhill. Pages from Jane's sketchbook scattered about tell the story of Tarzan and provide insights into the various rooms and levels of the tree house. At the base of the tree is an interactive play area.

TOURING TIPS This self-guided, walk-through tour involves a lot of climbing up and down stairs but with no ropes or ladders or anything fancy. People who stop to look extra-long or to rest sometimes create bottlenecks that slow crowd flow. We recommend visiting this attraction in the late afternoon or early evening if you are on a one-day tour schedule.

NEW ORLEANS SQUARE

ACCESSIBLE VIA ADVENTURELAND AND FRONTIERLAND, New Orleans Square is one of four "lands" that don't emanate from the central hub. The architecture and setting are Caribbean Colonial, like New Orleans itself, with exceptional attention to detail.

Disneyland Railroad

DESCRIPTION AND COMMENTS The Disneyland Railroad stops in New Orleans Square on its circle tour around the park. See the description beginning on page 217 for additional details regarding the sights en route. This is a pleasant and feet-saving way to commute to Mickey's Toontown/Fantasyland, Tomorrowland, or Main Street. Be advised, however, that the New Orleans Square Station is usually the most congested.

The Haunted Mansion *(FastPass)* ★★★★

APPEAL BY AGE	PRESCHOOL ★★★	GRADE SCHOOL ★★★★	TEENS ★★★★
YOUNG ADULTS ★★★★		OVER 30 ★★★★	SENIORS ★★★★

What it Is Indoor haunted-house ride. **Scope and scale** Major attraction. **When to go** Before 11:30 a.m. or after 6:30 p.m. **Comments** Not to be missed; some of Disneyland's best special effects. Frightens some small children. **Duration of ride** 5½-minute ride plus a 2-minute preshow. **Average wait in line per 100 people ahead of you** 2½ minutes; assumes both "stretch rooms" operating. **Loading speed** Fast.

Dark   Scary

DESCRIPTION AND COMMENTS The Haunted Mansion is a fun attraction more than it is a scary one. An ingenious preshow serves as a vehicle to deliver guests to the ride's boarding area, where they board "doom buggies" for a ride through the mansion's parlor, dining room, library, halls, and attic before descending to an uncommonly active graveyard. Disney employs almost every special effect in its repertoire in The Haunted Mansion, making it one of the most inventive and different of all Disney attractions. Be warned that some youngsters build a lot of anxiety concerning what they think they will see. The actual attraction scares almost nobody. Though this mansion is the original, the ride is somewhat shorter and lacks the interactive queue and some high-tech upgrades that the Walt Disney World version has; however, Disneyland does have the infamous Hat Box Ghost, an impressive new animatronic that "rematerialized" in the mansion's attic in 2015, nearly 45 years after appearing briefly during the attraction's opening days and sparking generations of urban legends. The reimagined figure employs digital projection trickery to make his leering skull vanish from his shoulders and reappear hanging from his outstretched hand, adding an effectively eerie punctuation to the ride's second act.

The Haunted Mansion is one of veteran Unofficial Guide writer Eve Zibart's favorite attractions. She warns:

Don't let the childishness of the old-fashioned Haunted Mansion put you off: this is one of the best attractions in the park. It's jam-packed with visual puns, special effects, hidden Mickeys, and really lovely Victorian-spooky sets. It's not scary, except in the sweetest of ways, but it will remind you of the days before ghost stories gave way to slasher flicks.

Each September, The Haunted Mansion substitutes a special holiday version of the attraction that runs through early January. Inspired by Tim Burton's 1993 stop-motion musical *The Nightmare Before Christmas,* the overlay features characters such as Jack Skellington and Oogie Boogie cavorting among the familiar mansion haunts to songs from Danny Elfman's classic score. *Note:* The attraction closes for several weeks before and after the holiday season to install and remove the overlay.

TOURING TIPS This attraction would be more at home in Fantasyland, but no matter—it's Disney at its best: another not-to-be-missed attraction. Because The Haunted Mansion is in an especially high-traffic corridor (located between Pirates of the Caribbean and Splash Mountain), it stays busy all day. Try to see The Haunted Mansion before 11:30 a.m., after 6:30 p.m., or during a parade. In the evening, crowds for *Fantasmic!* gather in front of The Haunted Mansion, making it very difficult to access. Fast-Pass is offered year-round but is usually only necessary for the holiday version of this attraction, which is very popular and draws quite a queue.

Pirates of the Caribbean ★★★★★

APPEAL BY AGE	PRESCHOOL ★★★½	GRADE SCHOOL ★★★★½	TEENS ★★★★½
YOUNG ADULTS ★★★★½		OVER 30 ★★★★½	SENIORS ★★★★½

What it is A Disney indoor-adventure boat ride. **Scope and scale** Major attraction. **When to go** Before 11:30 a.m. or after 4:30 p.m. **Comments** Our pick as one of Disneyland's very best; not to be missed. Frightens some small children. **Duration of ride** Approximately 14 minutes. **Average wait in line per 100 people ahead of you** 2 minutes; assumes 42 boats operating. **Loading speed** Fast.

 DESCRIPTION AND COMMENTS Another boat ride, this time indoors, Pirates of the Caribbean takes you through a series of sets depicting a pirate raid on an island settlement, from the bombardment of the fortress to the debauchery that follows the victory. The attraction includes characters Jack Sparrow and Barbossa from the Pirates of the Caribbean movies in animatronic form. In 2018 the infamous "take a wench for a bride" scene was reworked, transforming the auction of women into a sale of looted goods and upgrading the fan-favorite Redhead into Redd, a rum-rustling pirate queen.

TOURING TIPS Undoubtedly one of the most elaborate and imaginative attractions in Disneyland Park. Though engineered to move large crowds, this ride sometimes gets overwhelmingly busy in the early and midafternoon. Try to ride before noon or while a parade or *Fantasmic!* is in progress. If you have only experienced the Walt Disney World version of Pirates, don't bypass Disneyland's version thinking that it's more of the same: the original ride is far longer, more detailed, and better maintained than its Floridian cousin. Fans of Redd can sometimes find the sassy swashbuckler interacting with guests around New Orleans Square. A reader from Sacramento, California, shares this important safety tip:

You CAN get wet on Pirates of the Caribbean! That had never happened to me before, but we sat in the very front one time, and we got absolutely drenched and had to walk around with wet butts for a few hours.

CRITTER COUNTRY

SITUATED BETWEEN New Orleans Square and a meandering pathway to Galaxy's Edge, Critter Country sports a pioneer appearance not unlike that of Frontierland.

Davy Crockett's Explorer Canoes *(seasonal)* ★★★

APPEAL BY AGE	PRESCHOOL ★★	GRADE SCHOOL ★★★★	TEENS ★★★★
YOUNG ADULTS ★★½		OVER 30 ★★★	SENIORS ★

What it is Scenic canoe ride. **Scope and scale** Minor attraction. **When to go** As soon as it opens, usually 11 a.m. **Comments** Skip if the lines are long; closes at sunset. Most fun way to see Rivers of America. **Duration of ride** 8–10 minutes, depending on how fast you paddle. **Average wait in line per 100 people ahead of you** 12½ minutes; assumes 6 canoes operating. **Loading speed** Slow.

DESCRIPTION AND COMMENTS This paddle-powered ride around Tom Sawyer Island and Fort Wilderness runs the same route with the same sights as the steamboat and sailing ship. The canoes operate only on busier days and close at sunset. The sights are fun, and the ride is a little different in that patrons paddle the canoe. Those with tender rotator cuffs be warned: the trip can give your shoulders quite a workout, unless you slack off and let your fellow passengers handle the hard rowing.

TOURING TIPS The canoes represent one of three ways to see the same waterways. Because the canoes are slower in loading, we usually opt for the larger steamboat or sailing ship. If you're not up for a boat ride, a different view of the same sights can be had by hoofing around Tom Sawyer Island. Try to ride at 11 a.m. or shortly thereafter. The canoes operate on selected days during seasonal periods only. If the canoes are a big deal to you, call ahead to make sure that they are operating.

The Many Adventures of Winnie the Pooh ★★★½

APPEAL BY AGE	PRESCHOOL ★★★★	GRADE SCHOOL ★★★★	TEENS ★★★★
YOUNG ADULTS ★★★★		OVER 30 ★★★★	SENIORS ★★★★

What it is Indoor track ride. **Scope and scale** Minor attraction. **When to go** Before 11 a.m. or late afternoon or evening. **Duration of ride** About 3 minutes. **Average wait in line per 100 people ahead of you** 5 minutes. **Loading speed** Moderate.

DESCRIPTION AND COMMENTS Pooh is sunny, upbeat, and fun—more in the image of Peter Pan's Flight or Splash Mountain. You ride a "hunny pot" through the pages of a huge picture book into the Hundred Acre Wood, where you encounter Pooh, Eeyore, Owl, Rabbit, Tigger, Kanga, Roo, and Piglet too as they contend with a blustery day. There's even a dream sequence with Heffalumps and Woozles, a favorite

Thumbs Up for the Whole Family

of this 30-something couple from Lexington, Massachusetts, who think Pooh has plenty to offer adults:

The attention to detail and special effects make this ride worth seeing even if you don't have children in your party. The Pooh dream sequence was great!

TOURING TIPS Though well done, The Many Adventures of Winnie the Pooh is not wildly popular. The wait is rarely more than 15 minutes and is typically less than 5. The only exceptions are on supercrowded days or when Splash Mountain is temporarily closed, which then causes crowds to swarm Winnie the Pooh.

Splash Mountain *(FastPass)*   ★★★★½

APPEAL BY AGE	PRESCHOOL ★★★★†	GRADE SCHOOL ★★★★½	TEENS ★★★★½
YOUNG ADULTS ★★★★½		OVER 30 ★★★★½	SENIORS ★★★★½

†*Many preschoolers are too short to meet the height requirement, while others are intimidated by watching the ride while standing in line. Of those preschoolers who actually ride, most give the attraction high marks.*

What it is Water-flume adventure boat ride. **Scope and scale** Headliner. **When to go** Before 11 a.m. or use FastPass or the single-rider line. **Comments** A wet winner; not to be missed. Must be 40″ tall to ride; those age 7 or younger must ride with an adult; switching-off option (see page 147). **Duration of ride** About 10 minutes. **Average wait in line per 100 people ahead of you** 3½ minutes. **Loading speed** Moderate.

Scary   Lose Things   Queasy   Muss Your 'Do

DESCRIPTION AND COMMENTS Splash Mountain is a Disney-style amusement park flume ride. The ride combines steep chutes with a variety of Disney's best special effects. Covering more than 0.5 mile, the ride splashes through swamps, caves, and backwoodsy bayous before climaxing in a 52-foot plunge and Br'er Rabbit's triumphant return home. The entire ride is populated by more than 100 Audio-Animatronics, including Br'er Rabbit, Br'er Bear, and Br'er Fox, all regaling riders with songs, including "Zip-A-Dee-Doo-Dah."

TOURING TIPS This is the among the most popular rides in Disneyland Park for patrons of all ages—happy, exciting, and adventuresome all at once. Though eclipsed somewhat by newer attractions, Splash Mountain nevertheless builds crowds quickly during the morning, and waits of more than 70 minutes are not uncommon once the park fills up on a busy day. Lines persist throughout the day until a few minutes before closing. This is particularly true on hotter days, as weather affects the wait times significantly.

A Disneyland veteran from Layton, Utah, offers this suggestion:

Use FastPass to experience Splash. This lets you visit non-FastPass, slow-loading attractions in the golden early morning. Also, who wants to get wet first thing in the morning?

A Suffolk, Virginia, mom contends that there are more important considerations than beating crowds:

Definitely wait to do Splash Mountain at the end of the day. We were seated in the front of the ride, and we were drenched to the bone. If we had ridden first thing in the morning, I personally would have been miserable for the rest of the day. Parents, beware! It says you will get wet, not drowned.

It is almost a certainty that you will get wet, though probably not drenched, riding Splash Mountain. During the summer months, the water jets are cranked up to 11, practically guaranteeing that you'll get soaked. If you visit on a cool day, you may want to carry a plastic garbage bag. By tearing holes in the bottom and sides, you can fashion a sort of raincoat. Be sure to tuck the bag under your bottom. Though you can get splashed regardless of where you sit, riders in the front seat generally get the worst of it. If you have a camera, either leave it with a nonriding member of your party or wrap it in a plastic bag.

One final word: This is not just a fancy flume ride—it is a full-blown Disney adventure. The scariest part by far is the big drop into the pool (visible from the sidewalk in front of Splash Mountain), and even this plunge looks worse than it really is. Despite reassurances, however, many children wig out after watching it from the sidewalk. A Grand Rapids, Michigan, mother recalls her kids' rather unique reaction:

We discovered after the fact that our children thought they would go underwater after the five-story drop and tried to hold their breath throughout the ride in preparation. They were really too preoccupied to enjoy the clever Br'er Rabbit story.

STAR WARS: *Galaxy's Edge*

STAR WARS HAS BEEN ASSOCIATED with Disneyland ever since Star Tours opened in 1987, but once the Walt Disney Company acquired Lucasfilm in 2012 for the Death Star–size sum of $4 billion, fans of George Lucas's sci-fi saga seriously began salivating for a Disney theme park land dedicated to that galaxy far, far away. Disneyland broke ground in early 2016 on its most ambitious and expansive expansion ever, dedicating 14 acres of backstage areas to a new land called Star Wars: Galaxy's Edge, which opened to the public in summer 2019.

The new Star Wars land is carefully concealed from the rest of the park by a mountainous berm built along the north edge of Frontierland's rerouted Rivers of America. Guests access the area either via two rocky tunnels branching off from Frontierland's Big Thunder Trail (one of which may be restricted to exit only) or along a forested path winding north from Critter Country. There, they find themselves at the Black Spire Outpost on the planet Batuu, an exotic Outer Rim spaceport on the fringe of the Galactic Empire frontier that was once a hub of commerce, before being bypassed by the hyperspace highways and becoming a haven for outcasts. (Sounds suspiciously like the backstory of Cars Land's Radiator Springs to us.)

This location—which hasn't yet been seen on the big screen but is referenced in *Solo: A Star Wars Story,* the Star Tours attraction, and various tie-in novels—incorporates design elements similar to iconic

Star Wars locales such as Naboo, Yavin 4, Mos Eisley, and Maz Kanata's hideaway, without re-creating any single familiar setting. Massive attraction buildings reaching as high as 150 feet are camouflaged by towering petrified trees, lush landscaping, and alien architecture, creating a bustling bazaar teeming with extraterrestrial life.

The Imagineers, who collaborated closely with Lucasfilm's story group on integrating the land's backstory into official *Star Wars* lore, claim they created this new locale so that guests could feel like the heroes of their own journey, rather than simply retracing Anakin and Luke's footsteps, and also so that old fans and newcomers alike would be on equal footing. The righteous Resistance, still reeling from their close shave on Crait in *Episode VIII,* have established a temporary hideout on this remote planet, but the fascist First Order's 709th Stormtrooper battalion (aka the Red Fury) has recently arrived to root out the rebel scum. Chronologically speaking, Galaxy's Edge is set during the most recent *Star Wars* sequel trilogy in the gap between *The Last Jedi* and *The Rise of Skywalker,* so you won't see Darth Vader or Obi-Wan Kenobi, but you might bump into Kylo Ren or Chewbacca.

GALAXY'S EDGE IN DETAIL

DEPENDING ON WHICH PATH you take into Galaxy's Edge, you'll experience a different cinematic reveal of the land. The Frontierland entrance, which is used by most guests, opens straight onto the center of the bustling Black Spire Outpost, which is built around a mysterious onyx monolith embedded in the town square. The path from Critter Country, which is where early arrivals enter, leads to ancient ruins concealing the Resistance's secret encampment, which doubles as the entrance of **Star Wars: Rise of the Resistance,** one of the land's two rides. The tunnel closest to Fantasyland, which is typically restricted to exit-only and VIPs if the land reaches capacity, leads to the iconic *Millennium Falcon:* **Smugglers Run,** the expansion's other attraction.

No matter which route you travel to Batuu, you'll be completely isolated from the rest of Disneyland, and utterly immersed in the authentic detail lavished on every inch of the land. It's essentially the exact same formula that Universal used to great acclaim in building their Wizarding Worlds of Harry Potter, but bulked up to a level never before seen. In addition to visiting Morocco and Istanbul for inspiration, Disney's designers did a deep dive into the *Star Wars* archives, going so far as to model the original R2-D2's treads for droid tracks imprinted in the cement. Disney's dedication to maintaining the *Star Wars* theme extends from the audible (John Williams composed new music heard as you enter and exit the land, and Frank Oz recorded new dialogue as Yoda) to the ineffable (appropriate scents are piped into the air) to the downright prosaic: restrooms are called "refreshers," and you may detect a Dianoga swimming in the drinking fountain.

Outside of the area's two headliner rides (detailed on pages 232–234), Batuu boasts a Marrakech-esque marketplace of shops selling unique in-universe merchandise, some of which are practically attractions in themselves. Note how none of the packaging being sold bears the standard *Star Wars* or Disney parks logos, in order to maintain the illusion that all the souvenirs for sale were actually crafted by and for the Black Spire villagers themselves.

At **Savi's Workshop,** 14 guests at a time are led by "Gatherers" through the ritual-like process of building their own lightsabers, from picking a colorful kyber crystal, to selecting customizable handles from a range of eras and alignments. Lightsabers come with a price tag of $200, including a carrying sling. It's ludicrously expensive and time-consuming, but the experience at Savi's Workshop is pure Disney magic, and holding our lightsaber as it turned on for the first time was an emotional moment. It's fun picking out the components and building the lightsaber you've always wanted, and the custom hilts with removable light-up blades don't feel like cheap theme park toys; they feel solid in the hand, thanks to high-quality metal parts with great paint jobs. Sound emits from the bottom of each lightsaber, so every time you wave it around or clash against another one you'll hear the satisfying noises as heard in the *Star Wars* films. Same-day reservations are required (see below), and you must arrive 20–60 minutes prior to your appointment, or you forfeit your turn.

You can proudly pair your lightsaber with a screen-accurate Jedi tunic ensemble from **Black Spire Outfitters,** but only wear it outside the park (costumes are still forbidden for guests 14 and older).

Dok-Ondar's Den of Antiquities is overseen by a surly hammerheaded Ithorian who's the local godfather of black market goods; if you want to buy a historical character's lightsaber or Sith holocron, you may need to barter with the animatronic bi-mouthed bigwig, who haggles with guests through his human helpers. Sharp-eyed fans will spot Easter eggs from practically every *Star Wars* film and television show, including a 12-foot-tall taxidermy Wampa from *The Empire Strikes Back*.

Two shops allow guests to take an interactive pal back to their home planet. At Mubo's **Droid Depot,** you can pick robot parts off of conveyor belts to build your own pint-size R-series or BB-series droid for $100 (and up), which will then communicate with its full-scale counterparts around the land. We didn't expect much going in to the Droid Depot building experience, but it ended up being a lot of fun to sift through the parts, really making the droid your own. You're then taken to a station where you can assemble the droid with actual tools. The experience wraps up with a delightful little moment where you activate the droid and it begins beeping and booping. The droids themselves are sturdy and made of good-quality components, and each includes a remote control. Preassembled droids, such as a chatty C-3PO, a DJ Rex bluetooth speaker, and even a $25,000 life-size R2-D2, are also available.

Bina's Creature Stall allows guests to adopt a plush Porg puppet, an adorably disgusting writhing baby Rathtar, or a shoulder-sitting Kowakian monkey-lizard like Salacious Crumb. All the animals react to your touch with sound and movement, and the stall is stuffed with additional animatronic aliens that unfortunately can't be taken home.

For kids young and old, Zabaka the **Toydarian Toymaker** has plush dolls of legendary characters that look handcrafted from upcycled scraps of fabric, alien musical instruments, and other unconventional playthings. For more typical T-shirts, hats, pins, and the like, you can either report to **First Order Cargo,** a spaceport hangar selling Dark Side propaganda, or sign up at the makeshift **Resistance Supply** stall and show your support for the freedom fighters. Finally, **Jewels of Bith** has pins, patches, and trinkets from across the Outer Rim.

When you get hungry, you'll find that just as much attention has gone into the food and drink of Galaxy's Edge as everything else; even the Coca-Cola sodas come in unique spherical bottles emblazoned in Aurebesh, the *Star Wars* alphabet. There is no sit-down table service inside the land, but you can rustle up galactic food-truck grub from **Docking Bay 7** or grab a sausage that's been grilled under a podracer engine at **Ronto Roasters.** More importantly, **Oga's Cantina** introduced publicly available alcohol to Disneyland Park, pouring exclusive drinks from Spice Runner cider to Jet Juice shooters. See Part Four pages 172–175 and 187 for more dining details.

INTERACTIVITY IN GALAXY'S EDGE

PERHAPS THE MOST INTRIGUING ELEMENTS of Galaxy's Edge are its experiments in live interaction, both digital and analog. The streets swarm with live performers, including First Order officers and Resistance spy Vi Moradi, who can engage with guests and selected souvenirs. Even the shopkeepers and street sweepers have customized costumes and personal histories; feel free to chat them up about their jobs, or their opinions on the warring factions.

Guests who install the Play Disney Parks app will find their smartphones turning into *Star Wars* datapads upon entering Galaxy's Edge. Embark on your personalized adventure by aligning yourself with either the Resistance heroes, First Order evildoers, or a shady gang of Scoundrels. Then you can check the app's jobs board to select a mission, such as recovering a missing shipment or recruiting new forces. The quests are completed through four touchscreen puzzle games, disguised as "tools": the **hack** tool lets slicers interact with droids, the **scan** tool uses your camera to decode cargo shipping labels, **translate** helps interpret alien languages, and **tune** intercepts coded radio communications. It all ties together with a land-wide outpost control meta-game, where opposing teams compete to claim the First Order's surveillance system control panels secreted in doorways around the outpost. The game continues until one side secures a majority of stations, and then resets for further play, with the winners receiving Galactic Credits good for digital collectibles that upgrade their avatars.

In addition, visitors can complete two different challenges inside the Rise of the Resistance ride queue, and can play a third while waiting to fly the *Millennium Falcon.* Your experiences on those attractions also have a lasting impact; survive an encounter with Kylo Ren, and you'll be hailed as a hero of the Resistance, but bang up the *Millennium Falcon* and the local residents may ridicule you later.

GALAXY'S EDGE TOURING TIPS

THANKS TO A STRICT RESERVATIONS-ONLY admission policy and extensive blockouts of pass holders and cast members, the opening of Star Wars: Galaxy's Edge brought surprisingly small crowds to Disneyland, but we expect the expansion to be a mob scene during peak attendance periods once all restrictions on access are lifted. The good news is that Disney built Galaxy's Edge with more elbow room than both Wizarding Worlds and Pandora—The World of Avatar all put together. The other good news is that there is no extra cost to enter the Star Wars section beyond your park admission, and no paid or advance reservations are required to visit Batuu.

The bad news is that the land may fill to capacity shortly after park opening. To handle this situation, Disney has stolen another page from Universal's Harry Potter playbook and implemented a virtual queue to control the flow of guests into Galaxy's Edge. The first wave of guests to enter the park each morning will be walked straight into Galaxy's Edge via the Critter Country entrance. However, once the area approaches its maximum capacity—which is determined by how many riders the attractions inside can process—direct entry to the land is shut off. At this point, guests must use their smartphone's Disneyland app or visit a designated FastPass kiosk (located at the Haunted Mansion, Indiana Jones Adventure, Matterhorn Bobsleds, Space Mountain, and Splash Mountain) to secure a free "boarding pass," which holds their place in a virtual queue.

This system works similarly to a FastPass, but there's no set time at which you schedule your return; rather, you'll receive a push notification on your phone when your turn has arrived, and you will then have up to 2 hours to use your boarding pass and enter Black Spire Outpost through the Big Thunder Trail entrance near Frontierland. (Those without a phone can periodically check their status at a kiosk.)

Like FastPasses, you must have scanned your admission at a park entrance before retrieving a Galaxy's Edge boarding pass. If the virtual queue is full for the day, check back an hour or two before closing, when crowds may disperse enough to allow unrestricted access.

At press time, Galaxy's Edge does not participate in Magic Morning early entry, and neither of its attractions offer FastPass or MaxPass. However, guaranteed entry into Galaxy's Edge may periodically be offered with on-site hotel stays as an incentive. Down the road we expect that Disney may offer paid opportunities to get into Galaxy's Edge before the park opens or after it closes.

If you are among the first guests of the day entering the park, we suggest heading straight to Rise of the Resistance, because it is a complicated ride that's susceptible to breakdowns and has a modest hourly capacity under ideal conditions. *Millennium Falcon:* Smugglers

Run has redundant systems capable of running at reduced capacity rather than shutting down entirely, plus it offers a time-saving single-rider option. Since Savi's Workshop can only handle around 42 builders per hour, and Oga's Cantina is always elbow-to-elbow, if you want a customized lightsaber or alien cocktail, you must make a reservation at 7 a.m. on the morning of your visit, either through the Disneyland app, or at disneyland.com/savisworkshop or disneyland.com/cantina. Reservations include entry to the land at the appropriate hour, so you won't need to also secure a boarding pass, but Oga's charges $10 a head for cancellations, and Savi's bills no-shows a staggering $200.

Operating procedures for Galaxy's Edge were still in flux at press time, so visit theugseries.com/SWGE for the latest updates.

Millennium Falcon: Smugglers Run ★★★★½

What it is Interactive simulator ride. **Scope and scale** Super-headliner. **When to go** As soon as it opens, in the last hour of the day, or use the single-rider line. **Comments** Not to be missed. Must be 38" tall to ride; switching-off option (see page 147). **Duration of ride** 4½ minutes. **Average wait in line per 100 people ahead of you** 3½ minutes. **Loading speed** Moderate–fast.

Queasy

DESCRIPTION AND COMMENTS The first attraction to open inside Galaxy's Edge lets guests fulfill their childhood fantasy of flying at the helm of Han Solo's *Millennium Falcon,* the "fastest hunk of junk in the galaxy" that made the Kessel Run in less than 12 parsecs.

Guests approaching the attraction will see all 110 feet of the *Falcon* parked outside the spaceport, periodically venting gas as technicians tinker with the temperamental craft. (You can look at the full-sized *Falcon,* but not walk under or touch it.)

Before boarding the bird, you must first be recruited by Hondo Ohnaka, a pirate familiar to viewers of the *Clone Wars* and *Rebels* cartoons, who has cut a deal with Chewbacca for use of the *Falcon* in his sketchy Ohnaka Transport Solutions company. After ascending to a second-story catwalk with wraparound views of the ship, visitors enter Ohnaka's command center, where Hondo and his astromech assistant R5-P8 explain the setup, while the *Falcon* can be seen through the video screen "windows" behind them preparing for launch. Ohnaka is one of Disney's most advanced A-1000 animatronics, with electric motors capable of 50 functions, and his movements are eerily fluid.

At this point, riders enter the *Falcon* through an umbilical bridge and are handed boarding cards that assign them to a six-person flight crew. While awaiting your turn, you can relax in the ship's instantly recognizable main hold, complete with a holographic chess board to pose behind (though not play) and a plethora of familiar props.

When the time arrives, your group of six guests walks down the ship's curving corridors and appears to enter the *Falcon*'s one and only cockpit, thanks to a patented carousel system that keeps the small simulator cabins hidden from each other. Each rider is assigned his or her own station—a pilot and copilot up front to steer around obstacles and activate the hyperdrive; two gunners in the middle to shoot down enemy fighters; and a pair of engineers in the rear to repair the ship when the pilots and gunners mess up—and computer-generated scenery is projected on an ultra-high-definition dome outside the windshield.

What separates this ride from other simulators (like Star Tours) is that its graphics are generated in real time by an array of bleeding-edge Nvidia processors, creating cinema-quality images that react instantly to the guests' actions. There are 200 buttons, switches, and levers in the cockpit, and every one does something when activated; watch for indicator rings to illuminate around certain controls, cluing you into the correct moment to punch them. Your randomly selected mission (there are reportedly three, but only one was working when the ride debuted) may see you running guns to the resistance, escaping the maw of an interstellar leviathan, or hijacking a trainload of Coaxium on Corellia, Han Solo's homeworld.

Smugglers Run's queue and preshow represent some of Disney's best work, and simply walking into the cockpit is a not-to-be-missed experience for any fan. But some members of our team were let down by the ride itself, reckoning it a marginal improvement over older simulators despite the time and technology that went into it. Everyone loves being one of the pilots, who have the most say over how successful—or motion sick—their team ends up (Pro Tip: go easy on the oversensitive steering). Gunners can pick "automatic targeting" to make it easier on themselves, while Engineers just bash blinking buttons and get blasted with air. The latter two positions must use controls mounted 90 degrees to their side, making it awkward to focus on the screen, and although the ship will never destruct due to your incompetence, there's no way to opt out entirely from the interactivity.

If you have a team who can communicate and coordinate, flying the *Falcon* can truly feel like the Force is with you; if not, it often ends in fighting and frustration. However, even if the simulator finale is somewhat of a D-Ticket disappointment, the attraction as a whole marks a milestone in themed entertainment.

TOURING TIPS The mere sight of the *Falcon* in all her glory is enough to make grown fanboys weep, and you can expect Smugglers Run to be mobbed from the moment the park opens. The full queue and preshow are well worth experiencing your first time through, but the single-rider queue (which skips the preshow and goes straight to the holochess room) can save you significant time on follow-up flights, as long as you don't mind being assigned to engineer. There are seven six-passenger cabins on each of the four carousels, plus two stationary simulators that allow disabled guests to experience the attraction without interrupting operations for other guests.

Be careful how you fly because your flight team's collective success or failure will be remembered by characters you encounter later around the land. If you badly bruise the ship, you'll see the results in the wrecked exit corridor as you disembark, and the cantina's barkeep may give you the cold shoulder when you stop in for a cold one. Make sure your Play Disney app is open as you exit in order to receive credit for your mission.

Star Wars: Rise of the Resistance

What it is Next-generation dark ride. **Scope and scale** Super-headliner. **When to go** As soon as it opens or in the last hour of the day. **Comments** Not to be missed. Must be 40″ tall to ride; switching-off option (see page 147). **Duration of ride** About 25 minutes with all preshows; about 5 minutes for ride. **Average wait in line per 100 people ahead of you** 4 minutes. **Loading speed** Moderate–fast.

Dark   Queasy   Loud   Scary

DESCRIPTION AND COMMENTS A mobile Resistance gun turret tucked into a scrubland forest marks the entrance to the most epic indoor dark ride in Disney theme park history. Rise of the Resistance is an innovative attempt to integrate at least four different ride experiences—including trackless vehicles, a motion simulator, walk-through environments, and even an elevator drop—into Disney's longest attraction ever.

The adventure begins as you are exploring the Resistance military outpost that has been laser-carved out of ancient stone. An animatronic BB-8 rolls in, accompanied by a hologram of Rey (Daisy Ridley), who recruits you to strike a blow against the First Order. Fifty guests at a time exit the briefing room to board a standing-room-only shuttlecraft piloted by Nien Nunb from *Return of the Jedi;* you can feel the rumble as the ship breaks orbit and see Poe Dameron (Oscar Issac) accompanying you in his X-wing, until a Star Destroyer snags you in its tractor beam and sucks you into its belly.

When the doors to your shuttlecraft reopen, you've been convincingly transported into an enormous hangar, complete with 50 Stormtroopers, TIE Fighters, and a 100-foot-wide bay window looking into outer space. Cast members clad as First Order officers brusquely herd captive guests into holding rooms to await their interrogation by helmet-headed baddie Kylo Ren (Adam Driver).

Before long, you're making a break for it in an eight-passenger (two four-seat rows) troop transport with an animatronic astromech droid as your driver; the car is capable of traveling without a fixed track (like Luigi's Rollickin' Roadsters) and simulating movement. The ride blends dozens of robotic characters and enormous sets with video projections to create some of the most overwhelming environments ever seen in an indoor ride. One sequence sends you in between the legs of two towering AT-ATs while dodging laser fire from legions of Stormtroopers, while another puts you face-to-face with the Solo-slaying Ren. In the epic finale (spoiler alert), you'll survive an escape pod's dramatic crash back to Batuu, a heart-stopping multistory plunge enhanced by digital projections.

TOURING TIPS Rise of the Resistance was not open at press time but is scheduled to debut in early 2020. We expect it to become the second most popular ride in the park, right behind *Millennium Falcon:* Smugglers Run. If it's operating, make it your first destination of the day, or your very last. The drop at the end isn't quite as intense as Mission: Breakout! at DCA, but don't underestimate it's ability to loosen your lunch.

FRONTIERLAND

FRONTIERLAND ADJOINS NEW ORLEANS SQUARE as you move clockwise around the park. The focus here is on the Old West, with log stockades and pioneer trappings. Along the Big Thunder Trail to Fantasyland, where a petting zoo and barbecue restaurant once stood, you'll now find two tunnels leading to Star Wars: Galaxy's Edge. Don't feel baa-d for the goats that lived there; they've gone to live on a farm in Murrieta, California, with other four-legged former theme park employees.

Big Thunder Mountain Railroad *(FastPass)* ★★★★

APPEAL BY AGE	PRESCHOOL ★★★★	GRADE SCHOOL ★★★★½	TEENS ★★★★½
YOUNG ADULTS ★★★★½		OVER 30 ★★★★½	SENIORS ★★★★½

What it is Tame roller coaster with exciting special effects. **Scope and scale** Headliner. **When to go** Before 10:30 a.m., after 6:30 p.m., or use FastPass. **Comments** Great effects, though a relatively tame ride. Not to be missed. Must be 40" tall to ride; switching-off option (see page 147). **Duration of ride** 3½ minutes. **Average wait in line per 100 people ahead of you** 3 minutes; assumes 5 trains operating. **Loading speed** Moderate-fast.

Scary   Lose Things   Queasy   Rough   Muss Your 'Do

DESCRIPTION AND COMMENTS On this coaster through and around a Disney "mountain," the idea is that you're on a runaway mine train during gold rush days. Along with the usual thrills of a roller coaster (about a 5 on a scary scale of 10), the ride showcases some first-rate examples of Disney creativity: lifelike scenes depicting a mining town, colorful caverns, and a dynamite-chewing goat, all humorously animated.

The train ride's ramshackle exterior (featuring reconstructions of the Rainbow Ridge storefronts from 1956) belies a remarkably smooth track and impressive special effects, which include a fog-fueled explosion inside the final lift hill.

TOURING TIPS A superb Disney experience but not too wild a roller coaster. The emphasis here is much more on the sights than on the thrill of the ride itself. Regardless, it's a not-to-be-missed attraction. Finally, give Big Thunder a try after dark. The lighting gives the attraction a whole new feel.

As an example of how differently guests experience Disney attractions, consider this letter from a reader in Brookline, Massachusetts:

As senior citizens with limited time, my friend and I confined our activities to those attractions rated as 4 or 5 stars for seniors. Because you listed it as not to be missed, we waited an hour to board Big Thunder Mountain Railroad, which you rated a 5 on a scary scale of 10. After living through 3½ minutes of pure terror, I rate that attraction a 15 on a scary scale of 10. We were so busy holding on and screaming and even praying for our safety that we did not see any falling rocks or a mining town. In our opinion it should not be recommended for seniors or preschool children.

A woman from New England discovered that there's more to consider about Big Thunder than being scared:

I won't say it warranted a higher scare rating, but it was much higher on the lose-your-lunch meter. One more sharp turn and the kids in front of me would have needed a dip in Splash Mountain!

Frontierland Shootin' Exposition ★★

APPEAL BY AGE	PRESCHOOL ★★★★★	GRADE SCHOOL ★★★★	TEENS ★★★★
YOUNG ADULTS ★★★★		OVER 30 ★★★★	SENIORS ★★★★★

What it is Electronic shooting gallery. **Scope and scale** Diversion. **When to go** Whenever convenient. **Comments** Costs extra; a nifty shooting gallery.

DESCRIPTION AND COMMENTS A very elaborate electronic shooting gallery that costs $1 to play. One of the few attractions in Disneyland Park not included in the admission pass.

TOURING TIPS Good fun for those who like to shoot, but definitely not a place to blow time if you are on a tight schedule. You get about 25 infrared bullets for your buck. Try it on your second day if time allows.

Thumbs Up for the Whole Family

The Golden Horseshoe—Laughing Stock Co. ★★★

APPEAL BY AGE	PRESCHOOL ★★★★★	GRADE SCHOOL ★★★★½	TEENS ★★½
YOUNG ADULTS ★★★½		OVER 30 ★★★★	SENIORS ★★★½

What it is Western dance hall with improvisation comedy show. **Scope and scale** Minor attraction. **When to go** Catch a show and lunch at the same time; check the app or *Times Guide* for schedule. **Comment** Zany show. **Duration of show** 12 minutes.

DESCRIPTION AND COMMENTS The Golden Horseshoe has always offered a decent show, hearty snacks, and a nice air-conditioned respite from the sun. Today, the stage originally headlined by Steve Martin's mentor Wally Boag, and later Billy Hill and the Hillbillies (who currently perform at nearby Knott's Berry Farm under a slightly different name), is now commanded by the Laughing Stock Co. comedy troupe.

Each interactive, semi-improvised Laughing Stock Co. show is different and includes a set of zany Wild West–style characters. A particular favorite is "find a suitor," where unsuspecting members of the crowd are selected to answer questions from the Mayor of Frontierland's less-than-handsome daughter (played by a man). It's an amusing diversion when you want a break from big rides, but it isn't a must-see like some of its predecessors.

TOURING TIPS The Golden Horseshoe has first-come, first-served seating. We recommend arriving 30 minutes early if you want to find a table and grab some grub. Food service can be slow; look for the shortest of the open service lines, usually on the far left. Absurdly oversize safety railings now ruin sight lines from the balcony (curse you, OSHA!), so the best view is from the floor, front and center, but Walt liked the opera box seats best.

Mark Twain Riverboat ★★★

APPEAL BY AGE	PRESCHOOL ★★★★	GRADE SCHOOL ★★★½	TEENS ★★★½
YOUNG ADULTS ★★★½		OVER 30 ★★★½	SENIORS ★★★½

What it is Scenic boat ride. **Scope and scale** Minor attraction. **When to go** 11 a.m.–5 p.m. **Comments** Provides an excellent vantage point. **Duration of ride** About 14 minutes. **Average wait to board** 10 minutes. **Loading speed** Fast—en masse.

DESCRIPTION AND COMMENTS This large-capacity paddle wheel riverboat navigates the waters around Tom Sawyer Island and Fort Wilderness. A beautiful craft, the riverboat provides a lofty perch from which to see Frontierland and New Orleans Square. The *Mark Twain*, Sailing Ship *Columbia*, and Davy Crockett's Explorer Canoes travel through the Rivers of America. The show scenes include a home for Mike Fink (and one of his keelboats, a former Disneyland attraction) and 26 Audio-Animatronic animals; the audio spiel includes a musical nod to the New Orleans–set *The Princess and the Frog*. The river's path was shortened to accommodate the new land Star Wars: Galaxy's Edge, as well as to provide an impressive new mountain range to admire as you steam by. The *Mark Twain*'s speed has been slowed accordingly, so your total travel time remains about the same.

TOURING TIPS One of three boat rides that survey the same real estate. Because the Explorer Canoes are slower in loading and the *Columbia* operates seasonally, we think the riverboat makes more efficient use of touring time. If you're not in the mood for a boat ride, many of the same sights can be seen by hiking around Tom Sawyer Island. The riverboat typically operates until 75 minutes before the park closes, except on *Fantasmic!* performance nights, when the voyages end at 5:45 p.m. If you're looking for a new experience aboard the *Mark Twain,* try asking a cast member if you can enjoy the trip from the pilothouse.

Pirate's Lair on Tom Sawyer Island   ★★★

APPEAL BY AGE	PRESCHOOL ★★★★	GRADE SCHOOL ★★★★½	TEENS ★★★★½
YOUNG ADULTS ★★★★½		OVER 30 ★★★½	SENIORS ★★★½

What it is Walk-through exhibit and rustic playground. **Scope and scale** Minor attraction. **When to go** Midmorning–late afternoon. **Comments** The place for rambunctious kids; closes at sunset. **Duration of experience** For the raft, a little more than 1 minute one-way. As long as you want on the island. **Average wait in line per 100 people ahead of you** For raft, 4½ minutes; assumes 3 rafts operating. **Loading speed** For raft, moderate.

DESCRIPTION AND COMMENTS Pirate's Lair on Tom Sawyer Island manages to impart a sense of isolation from the rest of the park. It has hills to climb, tipsy bridges to cross, paths to follow, and a "rock climbing" play area. It's a delight for adults but a godsend for children who have been in tow all day. The realignment of Rivers of America removed a sliver of the island's northern tip, and the tree house and fort are permanently off-limits, but for the most part, this is the same oasis that's been entertaining kids for more than 60 years.

As an aside, a mother of four from Duncan, South Carolina, found Tom Sawyer Island as much a refuge as an attraction, writing:

In the afternoon, when the crowds were at their peak, the weather was hottest, and the kids started lagging behind, our organization began to suffer. We then retreated over to Tom Sawyer Island, which proved to be a true haven. My husband and I found a secluded bench and regrouped. Meanwhile, the kids were able to run freely in the shade. Afterward, we were ready to tackle the park again, refreshed and with direction once more.

The island has sets from the Pirates of the Caribbean films, such as William Turner's blacksmith shop, tucked into every nook and cranny. Kids exploring the caverns of Dead Man's Grotto will encounter spooky voices, ghostly apparitions, and buried treasure. Elsewhere, a sunken chest can be discovered by operating a hoist.

Evidently, you can't have a pirate's lair without a bunch of gore. A pop-up head and moving skeletal arm are just the beginning. There's also a "bone cage" and, our favorite, a treasure chest containing Davy Jones's beating heart. The Bootstrappers pirate band occasionally rides the rafts over to administer pirate oaths and lead sing-alongs, and Captain Jack Sparrow can sometimes be spotted stumbling along the island's shoreline.

TOURING TIPS Pirate's Lair is not one of Disneyland Park's more celebrated attractions, but it's certainly one of the most well-done. Attention to detail is excellent, and kids particularly revel in its adventuresome atmosphere. We think it's a must for families with children ages 5–15. If your party has only adults, visit the island on your second day, or stop by on your first day if you have seen the attractions you most wanted to see. We like the island from about noon until the island closes at sunset. Access is by raft from Frontierland, and you may have to stand in line to board both coming and going. Two or three rafts operate simultaneously, however, and the round-trip is usually pretty time efficient. Tom Sawyer Island takes about 30 minutes or so to see, but many children could spend a whole day there.

Sailing Ship *Columbia (seasonal)*   ★★★½

APPEAL BY AGE	PRESCHOOL ★★½	GRADE SCHOOL ★★★★	TEENS ★★★★
YOUNG ADULTS ★★★★		OVER 30 ★★★★	SENIORS ★★★★

What it is Scenic boat ride. **Scope and scale** Minor attraction. **When to go** 11 a.m.–5 p.m. **Comments** Pirates on extremely busy days; a stunning piece of workmanship. **Duration of ride** About 14 minutes. **Average wait to board** 10 minutes. **Loading speed** Fast—en masse.

Thumbs Up for the Whole Family

DESCRIPTION AND COMMENTS The *Columbia* is a stunning replica of a three-masted 18th-century merchant ship. Both its above- and belowdecks are open to visitors, with belowdecks outfitted to depict the life and work environment of the ship's crew in 1787. The *Columbia* operates only on busier days and runs the same route as the canoes and the riverboat. As with the other rivercraft, the *Columbia* suspends operations at sunset.

TOURING TIPS The *Columbia,* along with the *Mark Twain* Riverboat, provides a short-wait, high-carrying-capacity alternative for cruising the Rivers of America. We found the beautifully crafted *Columbia* by far the most aesthetically pleasing and historically interesting of any of the three choices of boat rides on the Rivers of America. If you have time to be choosy, ride aboard the *Columbia.* After boarding, while waiting for the cruise to begin, tour below. Once the ride begins, come topside and stroll the deck, taking in the beauty and complexity of the rigging.

The *Columbia* does not usually require a long wait, which makes it a good bet during the crowded afternoon hours. Like the other attractions on the river, the *Columbia* closes early on *Fantasmic!* performance evenings.

❚▮ FANTASYLAND

TRULY AN ENCHANTING PLACE, spread gracefully like a miniature alpine village beneath the towers of Sleeping Beauty Castle, Fantasyland is the heart of the park. Fantasyland is the backbone of the Magic Mornings early-entry program, with nine rides open. If your group consists of older kids and adults, ride Peter Pan's Flight first during the early-entry period, followed by Alice in Wonderland and Matterhorn Bobsleds. If you have younger children in your group, start with Peter Pan's Flight and Alice in Wonderland and then ride Mr. Toad's Wild Ride and Dumbo. Certain Fantasyland attractions close for fireworks and may not reopen until the fire marshal gives the all clear, as this Calgary, Alberta, dad discovered:

> A significant number of Disneyland's Fantasyland attractions close before fireworks, and of these, some reopen several minutes later while others remain closed for the night. We arrived at Fantasyland immediately after the fireworks and found very little open.

Alice in Wonderland ★★★½

APPEAL BY AGE	PRESCHOOL ★★★★	GRADE SCHOOL ★★★★	TEENS ★★★★
YOUNG ADULTS ★★★★		OVER 30 ★★★★	SENIORS ★★★★

What it is Track ride in the dark. **Scope and scale** Minor attraction. **When to go** Before 11 a.m. or after 5 p.m. **Comment** Good characterization and story line. **Duration of ride** Almost 4 minutes. **Average wait in line per 100 people ahead of you** 12 minutes; assumes 16 cars operating. **Loading speed** Slow.

DESCRIPTION AND COMMENTS This attraction recalls the story of *Alice in Wonderland* with some nice surprises and colorful effects. Guests ride nifty caterpillar cars in this Disney spook-house adaptation. Though not a spring chicken, Alice is a third-generation Disney dark ride with more vibrant, evocative, and three-dimensional sets and characters than Pinocchio's Daring Journey or Mr. Toad's Wild Ride. This is also the only two-story Disney dark ride with an outdoor section. The ride turned 60 in 2018, but its classic charms still remain relevant with the aid of advanced projection effects, which utilize original hand-drawn animation to bring the static sets to life.

TOURING TIPS This is a well-done ride in the best Disney tradition, with familiar characters, good effects, and a theme you can follow—too bad it loads very slowly. Do not confuse it with the Mad Tea Party ride. This very popular attraction can build a lengthy line as the morning progresses, so we like to ride as early in the day as possible, usually right after Peter Pan's Flight.

Bibbidi Bobbidi Boutique

This pricey beauty salon for little ones is located next to Sleeping Beauty Castle. Here, Fairy Godmothers–in-training make would-be princesses look like prom queens (or vice versa). A range of packages is offered, including everything from hair styling and makeup to princess gowns and accessories. The top-of-the-line package includes skip-the-line VIP access to the nearby Royal Hall princess meet and greet, which may be worth its *wait* in gold. If you have the bucks, the girls love it. For reservations, call ☎ 714-781-7895 up to 60 days in advance. A Winston, Oregon, mom thinks highly of Bibbidi Bobbidi:

> Bibbidi Bobbidi Boutique is a must if traveling with little girls. Our party had three girls ages 4, 4, and 6, and this was their favorite and most memorable event of the trip. Even though we traveled during the off-season, it was hectic and a little unorganized. We made reservations and still had to wait 30 minutes, but once the girls were matched with their Fairy Godmother–in-training, we were absolutely pleased with the service. It is a little spendy, but it was completely worth it. The hair survived the rest of the day and looked perfect when they put their princess gowns on at night for the fireworks.

Casey Jr. Circus Train ★★½

APPEAL BY AGE PRESCHOOL ★★★★ GRADE SCHOOL ★★★★ TEENS ★★★
YOUNG ADULTS ★★★★ OVER 30 ★★★★ SENIORS ★★★★

What it is Miniature train ride. **Scope and scale** Minor attraction. **When to go** Before 11 a.m. or after 5 p.m. **Comment** A quiet, scenic ride. **Duration of ride** A little under 4 minutes. **Average wait in line per 100 people ahead of you** 12 minutes; assumes 2 trains operating. **Loading speed** Slow.

DESCRIPTION AND COMMENTS A long-standing attraction and a pet project of Walt Disney, Casey Jr. circulates through a landscape of miniature towns, farms, and lakes. Visible from this ride are some stunning bonsai specimens, as well as some of the most manicured landscaping you are ever likely to see.

TOURING TIPS This ride covers the same sights as the Storybook Land Canal Boats but does it faster and with less of a wait. Accommodations for adults, however, are less than optimal on this ride, with some passengers having to squeeze into diminutive caged cars (after all, it is a circus train). If you do not have children in your party, you can enjoy the same sights more comfortably by riding the Storybook Land Canal Boats, which also benefit from live narration instead of Casey Jr.'s canned soundtrack.

A father of two toddlers from Menlo Park, California, explains that issues of redundancy were not uppermost in his children's minds.

Contrary to your advice, the Casey Jr. Circus Train and Storybook Land Canal Boats are totally different experiences—if you are 4 or younger. Hey, one is a boat, and one is a train! Seems obvious to the mind of a 4-year-old. We did both, and the kids loved both.

Disneyland Railroad

DESCRIPTION AND COMMENTS The Disneyland Railroad stops in Fantasyland/Mickey's Toontown on its circuit around the park. The station is located to the left of It's a Small World, next to the Fantasyland Theatre. From this often-crowded boarding point, transportation is available to Tomorrowland, Main Street, and New Orleans Square. See the description beginning on page 217 for additional details regarding the sights en route.

Dumbo the Flying Elephant ★★½

APPEAL BY AGE PRESCHOOL ★★★★ GRADE SCHOOL ★★★★ TEENS ★★★★
YOUNG ADULTS ★★★★ OVER 30 ★★★★ SENIORS ★★★★

What it is Disneyfied midway ride. **Scope and scale** Minor attraction. **When to go** Before 10 a.m. or during late evening parades, fireworks, or *Fantasmic!* performances. **Duration of ride** 1⅔ minutes. **Average wait in line per 100 people ahead of you** 12 minutes. **Loading speed** Slow.

DESCRIPTION AND COMMENTS A nice, tame, happy children's ride based on the lovable Disney flying elephant, this is an upgraded rendition of a ride that can be found at state fairs and amusement parks across the country. Shortcomings notwithstanding, Dumbo is the favorite Disneyland Park attraction of most preschoolers. A lot of readers take us to task for lumping Dumbo in with state-fair midway rides. These comments from a reader in Armdale, Nova Scotia, are representative:

I think you have acquired a jaded attitude. I know Dumbo is not for every-body, but when we took our oldest child (then just 4), the sign at the end of the line said there would be a 90-minute wait. He knew and he didn't care, and he and I stood in the hot afternoon sun for 90 blissful minutes waiting for his 90-second flight. Anything that a 4-year-old would wait for that long and that patiently must be pretty special.

TOURING TIPS This is a slow-loading ride that we recommend you bypass unless you are on a very relaxed touring schedule. On the plus side, a much-needed shaded queue was added in 2018. If your kids are excited about Dumbo, try to get them on the ride before 10 a.m., during the parades or *Fantasmic!*, or just before the park closes. Also, consider this advice from an Arlington, Virginia, mom:

Grown-ups, beware! Dumbo is really a tight fit with one adult and two kids. My kids threw me out of their Dumbo, and I had to sit in a Dumbo all by myself. Pretty embarrassing, and my husband got lots of pictures.

Fantasyland Theatre / *Mickey and the Magical Map* ★★★½

APPEAL BY AGE PRESCHOOL ★★★★   GRADE SCHOOL ★★★★½ TEENS ★★★★½
YOUNG ADULTS ★★★★½   OVER 30 ★★★★½   SENIORS ★★★★½

What it is Musical stage show. **Scope and scale** Major attraction. **When to go** Check the app or *Times Guide* for schedule; arrive at least 15 minutes before showtime for the best seats. **Duration of show** 22 minutes. **Probable waiting time** 15 minutes.

DESCRIPTION AND COMMENTS This venue is a sophisticated amphitheater where concerts and elaborate stage shows are performed according to the daily entertainment schedule. Better productions that have played here include *Beauty and the Beast Live, Snow White,* and *The Spirit of Pocahontas,* all musical stage adaptations of the respective Disney-animated features.

Mickey and the Magical Map involves apprentice Mickey's accidental adventure into sorcerer Yen Sid's mysterious dream-controlling map. This 22-minute musical adventure combines new songs and classic tunes in a score that skips from India to Hawaii, with a stopover under the sea. Rapunzel, Pocahontas, Mulan, King Louie, Sebastian, and Stitch are among the Disney icons who appear, along with a platoon of dancing paintpots and brushes, but the show is stolen by a mischievous animated paint splotch (brought to life through high-tech video effects).

The opening song is less than memorable, and the computer-generated animation of Yen Sid is disappointingly chunky, but on the whole this is among the park's more entertaining musical productions. Live singing and energetic choreography influenced by drum corps enliven the somewhat overfamiliar songs, and a gospel-flavored riverboat finale (complete with streamers shot over the audience) brings down the house. Well worth watching once you've experienced the headliners, or on your second day.

TOURING TIPS Performance times are listed in the app and *Times Guide.* Arrive at least 15 minutes early for optimal seating. Though it's a stage show, the performances are complemented by three giant video screens, each of which spans almost the entire width of the stage, that form a raised platform on which much of the action takes place. For that reason, the best seats are the ones farther back and slightly raised, in the center of the theater. Avoid the seats up front or too far on the sides, where the images on the slanted screen will look distorted.

It's a Small World *(FastPass)* ★★★★

What it is World brotherhood–themed indoor boat ride. **Scope and scale** Major attraction. **When to go** Anytime except after a parade. **Duration of ride** 14 minutes. **Average wait in line per 100 people ahead of you** 2½ minutes; assumes busy conditions with 56 boats operating. **Loading speed** Fast.

Thumbs Up for the Whole Family

DESCRIPTION AND COMMENTS A happy and upbeat attraction with a world-brotherhood theme and a catchy tune that will stick in your head for weeks. Small boats convey visitors on a tour around the world, with singing and dancing dolls showcasing the dress and culture of each nation. Almost everyone enjoys It's a Small World (well, there are those jaded folks who are put off by the dolls' homogeneous appearance, especially in light of the diversity theme), but it stands, along with the *Enchanted Tiki Room,* as an attraction that some could take or leave but that others consider one of the real masterpieces of Disneyland Park. More than 20 Disney and Pixar characters have been integrated into the classic attraction; tastefully crafted in the style of original artist Mary Blair, the additions don't detract from the ride, except in the tacky U.S.A. tribute added to the end. A mom from Castleton, Vermont, commented:

It's a Small World was like a pit stop in The Twilight Zone. *They were very slow unloading the boats, and we were stuck in a line of about six boats waiting to get out while the endless chanting of that song grated on my nerves. I told my husband that I was going to swim for it just to escape one more chorus.*

From November through New Year's, the attraction receives an annual holiday overlay inside the attraction as well as outside, featuring "Jingle

Bells" and "Deck the Halls" instead of the usual earworm soundtrack. We particularly enjoy the light show and projection effects outside the attraction that happen every 15 minutes.

A dad from New Brunswick, Canada, gives this advice for surviving the Happiest Cruise That Ever Sailed:

Ask to sit at the back of the boat. Pull out your earbuds once you're in the building, and blast some heavy metal. You'd be amazed how different and deceptively funny the ride becomes!

TOURING TIPS This fast-loading ride is usually a good bet during the busier times of the day. The boats are moved along by water pressure, which increases as boats are added. Thus, the more boats in service when you ride (up to a maximum total of 60), the shorter the duration of the ride (and wait). Small World is taken off-line in mid-October and reopened in November with a special Christmas holiday theme. Removal of the overlay also keeps the ride closed for several weeks after the holiday season. Two notes: While the loading can be very quick when many boats are running, the unloading can be very slow. Second, the FastPasses (highly recommended for the holiday version) are distributed from kiosks located across from the Matterhorn Bobsleds entrance.

King Arthur Carrousel ★★★

APPEAL BY AGE **PRESCHOOL** ★★★★ **GRADE SCHOOL** ★★★★ **TEENS** ★★★★
YOUNG ADULTS ★★★★ **OVER 30** ★★★★ **SENIORS** ★★★★

What it is Merry-go-round. **Scope and scale** Minor attraction. **When to go** Before 11:30 a.m. or after 5 p.m. **Comments** A showpiece carousel; adults enjoy the beauty and nostalgia of this ride. **Duration of ride** A little more than 2 minutes. **Average wait in line per 100 people ahead of you** 7½ minutes. **Loading speed** Slow.

DESCRIPTION AND COMMENTS A merry-go-round to be sure, but certainly one of the most elaborate and beautiful you will ever see, especially when lit at night. A white horse named Jingles (with bells all over) pays tribute to Julie Andrews and her iconic role in *Mary Poppins*. She's the horse closest to the handicapped ramp.

TOURING TIPS Unless you have small children in your party, we suggest that you appreciate this ride from the sidelines. If your children want to ride, try to get them on before 11:30 a.m. or after 5 p.m. While nice to look at, the carousel loads and unloads very slowly.

Mad Tea Party ★★

APPEAL BY AGE **PRESCHOOL** ★★★★ **GRADE SCHOOL** ★★★★½ **TEENS** ★★★★½
YOUNG ADULTS ★★★★½ **OVER 30** ★★★★½ **SENIORS** ★★★★

What it is Midway-type spinning ride. **Scope and scale** Minor attraction. **When to go** Before 11 a.m. or after 5 p.m. **Comments** You can make the teacups spin faster by turning the wheel in the center of the cup; fun but not worth the wait. **Duration of ride** 1½ minutes. **Average wait in line per 100 people ahead of you** 5½ minutes. **Loading speed** Slow.

Queasy   Muss Your 'Do

DESCRIPTION AND COMMENTS Well done in the Disney style, but still just an amusement park ride. *Alice in Wonderland*'s Mad Hatter provides the theme, and patrons whirl around feverishly in big teacups. A rendition of this ride, sans Disney characters, can be found at every local carnival and fair. Colorful LED lighting makes the ride especially attractive after dark.

TOURING TIPS This ride, besides not being particularly special, loads notoriously slowly. Skip it on a busy schedule if the kids will let you. Ride in the morning of your second day if your schedule is more relaxed. A warning for parents: Teenagers like to lure adults onto the teacups and then turn the wheel in the middle (which makes the cup spin faster) until the adults are plastered against the side of the cup and on the verge of throwing up.

Matterhorn Bobsleds *(FastPass)* ★★★½

†*Some preschoolers love Matterhorn Bobsleds; others are frightened.*

What it is Roller coaster. **Scope and scale** Major attraction. **When to go** During the first 90 minutes the park is open or during the hour before it closes. **Comments** Fun ride but not too scary. Must be 42" tall to ride. **Duration of ride** 2½ minutes. **Average wait in line per 100 people ahead of you** 3½ minutes; assumes both tracks operating with 10 sleds per track with 23-second dispatch intervals. **Loading speed** Moderate.

Scary Lose Things Queasy Rough Muss Your 'Do

DESCRIPTION AND COMMENTS The Matterhorn is the most distinctive landmark on the Disneyland scene, visible from almost anywhere in the park. Open since 1959, the Matterhorn maintains its popularity and long lines year in and year out. Matterhorn Bobsleds is a roller coaster with an alpine motif. On the scary scale, the ride ranks about 6 on a scale of 10. The special effects don't compare to Space Mountain's, but they do afford a few surprises. Riders first glimpse the mysterious yeti during the initial uphill climb as a menacing silhouette distorted by ice and then cruise past an ominous collection of old ride vehicles (including vintage bobsleds and an antique Skyway bucket) that the beast has hoarded. Finally, you'll come face-to-face with the furry legend not once but twice; the encounters are brief, but he moves with a fluid ferocity that his frozen cousin in Disney World's Expedition Everest can only dream of. Added padding has made the ride marginally less murderous on tailbones, but the three-passenger cars with individual seats are unfriendly to the long-legged. Tall riders are advised to ask for the middle or back rows, which have marginally more room, and slide their feet forward into the snug footwells on either side of the seat ahead. For the short-limbed, the front seat is usually the smoothest. But be warned that, wherever you sit, this is the bumpiest coaster in Disneyland's inventory. As a visitor from San Francisco, California, puts it:

The Matterhorn is really just a fast, jarring roller coaster. The [bobsleds] don't have much legroom, and my husband was very uncomfortable the whole ride!

A Richboro, Pennsylvania, dad disagrees with our scary rating of the Matterhorn:

My biggest disappointment was the Matterhorn. I understand it's iconic, but the notion that it could rate a 6 out of 10 on the scare factor is pure insanity. I'd rate it a 1! After the steep climb in the dark, you basically just go down in circles until you are left baffled that the "roller coaster" ride is over.

TOURING TIPS Lines for the Matterhorn form as soon as the gates open and persist throughout the day. Disneyland added FastPass to the Matterhorn as part of the rollout of MaxPass, resulting in an even slower standby queue. The FastPass kiosks are located across from the ride's entrance, near the old motorboat docks. If you don't grab a return time, ride first thing in the morning or just before the park closes. If you are a roller coaster person, ride Space Mountain and then hurry over and hop on the Matterhorn. If roller coasters are not the end-all for you, we recommend choosing one of the other coasters or saving this one for a second day. The Matterhorn's poorly marked single-rider line, which can save you an hour in the queue, is currently one of the park's best-kept secrets. Ask an employee at the entrance how to take advantage of it.

The Matterhorn is actually made up of two separate coasters. Though the two sides are similar, they are not identical; veterans say the left-hand Tomorrowland track is faster with steeper drops, while the Fantasyland side on the right side is slightly longer with sharper turns.

Mr. Toad's Wild Ride ★★½

APPEAL BY AGE **PRESCHOOL** ★★★½ **GRADE SCHOOL** ★★★½ **TEENS** ★★★½ **YOUNG ADULTS** ★★★½ **OVER 30** ★★★½ **SENIORS** ★★★½

What it is Track ride in the dark. **Scope and scale** Minor attraction. **When to go** Before 11 a.m. **Comment** Past its prime. **Duration of ride** Almost 2 minutes. **Average wait in line per 100 people ahead of you** 9 minutes; assumes 12 cars operating. **Loading speed** Slow.

DESCRIPTION AND COMMENTS Mr. Toad's Wild Ride is a twisting, curving ride in the dark that passes two-dimensional sets and props. There are a couple of clever effects, but basically it's at the technological basement of the Disney attraction mix. Though Mr. Toad doesn't compare well with newer high-tech attractions, many Disneyland veterans appreciate it because it's one of a handful of attractions remaining from the park's beginning. Hannah, an official Touring Plans Stunt Kid™, summed the ride's appeal up perfectly:

Mr. Toad's Wild Ride is awesome, and everyone should go on it because it's about a toad who goes to hell. I feel like that's a neglected topic in theme parks these days.

TOURING TIPS Not a great but certainly a popular attraction. Lines build early in the day and never let up. Catch Mr. Toad before 11 a.m. Parents beware: There are some loud sound effects as well as a spooky "hell" scene at the end of the attraction.

Peter Pan's Flight ★★★★

APPEAL BY AGE **PRESCHOOL** ★★★★ **GRADE SCHOOL** ★★★★½ **TEENS** ★★★★½ **YOUNG ADULTS** ★★★★½ **OVER 30** ★★★★½ **SENIORS** ★★★★½

What it is Indoor fantasy-adventure ride. **Scope and scale** Minor attraction. **When to go** Immediately at park opening or after 6 p.m. **Duration of ride** Just over 2 minutes. **Average wait in line per 100 people ahead of you** 10 minutes; assumes 13 ships operating. **Loading speed** Slow.

Thumbs Up for the Whole Family

DESCRIPTION AND COMMENTS Though it is not considered one of Disneyland Park's major attractions, Peter Pan's Flight is superbly designed and absolutely delightful, with a happy theme, a reunion with some unforgettable Disney characters, beautiful effects, and charming music. Tiny pirate ships suspended from an overhead track launch you from Wendy's window to fly over nighttime London and on to Never Land and an encounter with Captain Hook, Mr. Smee, and the ubiquitous crocodile. In 2015 Peter Pan celebrated the park's 60th anniversary with a refreshed exterior and brand-new special effects inside, including digital pixie dust projections and floating figures of Wendy and the Darling boys in the nursery scene. The colorful London flyover and rippling water effects are especially lovely. We think Peter Pan's Flight is the best attraction in Fantasyland.

TOURING TIPS This attraction has a consistent wait of at least 20 minutes within the first few minutes of park operation. On the busiest of days, we've seen the wait go up to more than 60 minutes at the extreme. Try to ride right at rope drop (especially on Magic Mornings) or after 6 p.m., during the afternoon or evening parade(s), or during a performance of *Fantasmic!*

Pinocchio's Daring Journey ★★½

APPEAL BY AGE PRESCHOOL ★★★½ GRADE SCHOOL ★★★½ TEENS ★★★½
YOUNG ADULTS ★★★½ OVER 30 ★★★½ SENIORS ★★★½

What it is Track ride in the dark. **Scope and scale** Minor attraction. **When to go** Before noon or after 3:30 p.m. **Comment** A big letdown. **Duration of ride** Almost 3 minutes. **Average wait in line per 100 people ahead of you** 8 minutes; assumes 15 cars operating. **Loading speed** Slow.

DESCRIPTION AND COMMENTS This is another twisting, curving track ride in the dark, this time tracing the adventures of Pinocchio as he tries to find his way home. The action is hard to follow, and it lacks continuity. Though the sets are three-dimensional and more visually compelling than, say, Mr. Toad, the story line is dull and fails to engage the guest. In the ride's defense, it features some deliciously trippy Pleasure Island imagery, a clever vanishing Blue Fairy effect, and almost always an empty queue.

TOURING TIPS The word must be out about Pinocchio because the lines are seldom very long. Still, the longest waits occur 11:30 a.m.–4:30 p.m. While most small children seem to handle this ride better than Snow White, a Manhattan mom warns:

Pinocchio is quite scary; it seems to feature one nightmare after another, particularly if a child is not familiar with the story/movie. Our son refused to ride any other rides for an hour or two after it, and it was our first one!

Pixie Hollow ★★

APPEAL BY AGE PRESCHOOL ★★★★½ GRADE SCHOOL ★★★★ TEENS ★★½
YOUNG ADULTS ★★½ OVER 30 ★★★½ SENIORS ★★★★

What it is Character-greeting opportunity. **Scope and scale** Minor attraction. **When to go** Before 10 a.m. **Comment** Closes at 4 p.m. **Duration of experience** About 10 minutes. **Probable waiting time** 40 minutes or less.

DESCRIPTION AND COMMENTS An elaborate character-greeting area situated on the path connecting Matterhorn Bobsleds to the central hub, Pixie Hollow features Tinker Bell (or one of her fairy friends) in a standard character meet and greet. The line can be deceivingly long.

TOURING TIPS Pixie Hollow accumulates substantial wait times just after opening in the morning that last throughout the day until early evening, when it closes. It also closes temporarily during parades. The best way to visit Tink is to line up near the entrance to Tomorrowland about 15 minutes before the park officially opens.

Royal Hall at Fantasy Faire ★★★

APPEAL BY AGE   PRESCHOOL ★★★★★   GRADE SCHOOL ★★★★½   TEENS ★★★½
YOUNG ADULTS ★★★★★   OVER 30 ★★★★   SENIORS ★★★★★

What it is Princess meet and greet. **Scope and scale** Major attraction. **When to go** If meeting the princesses is important to your little ones, try to arrive 15 minutes before opening. **Comment** Note that Royal Hall doesn't stay open late, even if the park does. **Duration of experience** 5 minutes. **Probable waiting time** 35–60 minutes.

DESCRIPTION AND COMMENTS Once a sleepy corner off the central hub, mainly known since the 1950s for weekend swing-dancing parties, Carnation Plaza Gardens was given a pink-and-purple princess makeover in 2013 and emerged as the Fantasy Faire, which is comprised of Royal Hall and Royal Theatre (see the next profile). Even if you aren't enamored of the princess marketing craze, you can't help but admire the loving details applied throughout this mini-land, from a snoozing animatronic Figaro kitty and crank-operated Clopin's music box to the twinkling hair on the courtyard's *Tangled*-inspired tower.

This indoor meet and greet features three princesses always on duty (usually Ariel, Cinderella, and Snow White). The usual Disneyland queue (mercifully mostly shaded) must be endured to meet and be photographed, but this current incarnation typically sees somewhat shorter waits than the former Fantasy Faire location. The trick is that the Royal Hall's intimate wood-paneled interior actually houses two identical meeting areas with duplicate trios of princesses (perhaps the product of an Epcot cloning experiment?) for double the greeting capacity.

TOURING TIPS Little girls love the Royal Hall, as do boys age 6 and younger. Incidentally, you won't believe how many of the kids come in costume. If you do everything, you'll spend about an hour, not counting shopping time. On busy days, you may be barred from bringing your stroller into Fantasy Faire, unless your child is asleep in it, so teach your kid to play possum on command if you don't want to park.

Royal Theatre at Fantasy Faire ★★★★

APPEAL BY AGE   PRESCHOOL ★★★★½   GRADE SCHOOL ★★★½   TEENS ★★½
YOUNG ADULTS ★★★★   OVER 30 ★★★★   SENIORS ★★★★★

What it is Interactive storytelling show. **Scope and scale** Minor attraction. **When to go** Check the app or *Times Guide* for showtimes. **Duration of show** 20 minutes. **Probable waiting time** 30 minutes.

DESCRIPTION AND COMMENTS Royal Theatre, which once hosted jazz greats such as Dizzy Gillespie, now houses a rotating repertory of 20-minute stage shows dramatizing the tales of popular Disney royalty. (Boogie and jive fans, don't get jumpy: the weekend swing-dancing parties return to Disneyland, on its original dance floor, on select Saturday nights; see tinyurl.com/disneydanceband for the schedule.) *Tangled* and *Beauty and the Beast* are the featured fables, with Rapunzel and Flynn Rider or Belle joining in their respective reenactments, accompanied by narrators

Mr. Smythe and Mr. Jones, milkmaid stagehands, and a live pianist. Rather than straightforward retellings, these fast-paced comic condensations capture the anarchic slapstick of a Renaissance fair trunk show. Witty enough to keep adults far outside the target demographic awake, the Royal Theatre's shows are the sleeper hits of Fantasy Faire. Stick around after the curtain falls for an autograph session with the stars.

The *Beauty and the Beast* show is usually performed at the first three showtimes of the day, with *Tangled* typically taking the stage for the remainder. If you must pick between those two, *Tangled* has the better script.

TOURING TIPS The theater only seats a little more than 200 people (with room for 50 kids on the floor up front), so you may want to line up 30 or more minutes before showtime or simply settle for standing right outside the theater.

Sleeping Beauty Castle ★★★

APPEAL BY AGE	PRESCHOOL ★★★★	GRADE SCHOOL ★★★½	TEENS ★★★½
YOUNG ADULTS ★★★½		OVER 30 ★★★½	SENIORS ★★★½

What it is Walk-through exhibit. **Scope and scale** Minor attraction. **When to go** Anytime. **Comment** Must be able to climb up and down two flights of stairs. **Duration of exhibit** Varies; about 10 minutes. **Probable waiting time** Usually none.

DESCRIPTION AND COMMENTS Disneyland Park's most famous icon, Sleeping Beauty Castle is at the heart of Disneyland and serves as a stage for shows and special events. For the non-claustrophobic, the Sleeping Beauty Castle walk-through exhibit is a miniature 3-D series, arranged along a narrow passage inside the castle, that tells the story of Sleeping Beauty. Originally opened on April 29, 1957, to preview the upcoming 1959 movie *Sleeping Beauty*, and then closed for most of a decade after 9/11, the attraction reopened in 2008 with new dioramas reflecting the style of artist Eyvind Earle, who gave *Sleeping Beauty* its distinctive design. In this version there are animated scenes, interactive elements, and Pepper's Ghost projection effects (as also seen in The Haunted Mansion).

TOURING TIPS The entrance is on the Fantasyland side of the castle near the passageway to Fantasy Faire and Frontierland. The exhibit allows for one-way traffic only. It can get a bit crowded inside, but there should rarely be a line outside the attraction. For guests unable to handle stairs, a small alcove to the left of the bridge to Tomorrowland contains a collection of the animations, as well as music, allowing you to experience the attraction's elements without walking. The viewing location runs on a loop, so you might have to watch it out of order.

Snow White's Scary Adventures ★★★

APPEAL BY AGE	PRESCHOOL ★★★	GRADE SCHOOL ★★★½	TEENS ★★★½
YOUNG ADULTS ★★★½		OVER 30 ★★★½	SENIORS ★★★½

What it is Track ride in the dark. **Scope and scale** Minor attraction. **When to go** Before 11 a.m. or after 5 p.m. **Comments** Quite intimidating for preschoolers; worth seeing if the wait is not long. **Duration of ride** Almost 2 minutes. **Average wait in line per 100 people ahead of you** 9 minutes; assumes 10 cars operating. **Loading speed** Slow.

Dark   Scary

DESCRIPTION AND COMMENTS Here, you ride in a mining car in the dark through a series of sets drawn from *Snow White and the Seven Dwarfs*. The attraction has a *Perils of*

Pauline flavor and features Snow White as she narrowly escapes harm at the hands of the wicked witch. The action and effects are a cut above Mr. Toad's Wild Ride but not as good as Peter Pan's Flight. High-tech projection effects enhance the magic mirror and rainstorm scenes.

TOURING TIPS Enjoyable but not particularly compelling. Experience it if the lines are not too long or on a second-day visit. Ride before 11 a.m. or after 5 p.m. if possible. Also, don't take the "scary" part too seriously. The witch looks mean, but most kids take her in stride. Or maybe not. A mother from Knoxville, Tennessee, commented:

The outside looks cute and fluffy, but inside, the evil witch just keeps coming at you. My 5-year-old, who rode Space Mountain three times [and took other scary rides] right in stride, was near panic when our car stopped unexpectedly twice during Snow White. After Snow White, my 6-year-old niece spent a lot of time asking, "Will a witch jump out at you?" before other rides. So I suggest that you explain a little more what this ride is about. It's tough on preschoolers who are expecting forest animals and dwarfs.

It really punches the buttons of the 6-and-under crowd, when other more traditionally scary rides don't. Many kids, once frightened by Snow White's Scary Adventures, balk at trying any other attractions that go into the dark, regardless of how benign they are.

Storybook Land Canal Boats ★★★

APPEAL BY AGE	PRESCHOOL ★★★★	GRADE SCHOOL ★★★½	TEENS ★★★½
YOUNG ADULTS ★★★½	OVER 30 ★★★½		SENIORS ★★★½

What it is Scenic boat ride. **Scope and scale** Minor attraction. **When to go** Before 10:30 a.m. or after 5:30 p.m. **Comment** Pretty, tranquil, and serene. **Duration of ride** 6½ minutes. **Average wait in line per 100 people ahead of you** 15 minutes; assumes 7 boats operating. **Loading speed** Slow.

Thumbs Up for the Whole Family

DESCRIPTION AND COMMENTS Guide-operated boats wind along canals situated beneath the same miniature landscapes visible from the Casey Jr. Circus Train. This ride—offering stellar examples of bonsai cultivation, selective pruning, and miniaturization—is a must for landscape-gardening enthusiasts. The landscapes include scenes from more recent Disney features—such as the kingdom of Arendelle and Elsa's ice palace from *Frozen*—in addition to those from such classics as *The Wind in the Willows* and *The Three Little Pigs*. We find Storybook Land to be a charming respite from the surrounding overstimulation, but not every guest gets the attraction, as this California reader will attest:

I thought there would be beautiful flowers to see or interesting dioramas, but you just sail past small buildings meant to look like cottages, castles, and so on. There aren't even any little figurines or characters in it.

TOURING TIPS The boats are much more comfortable than the train, the view of the miniatures is better, and the pace is more leisurely. On the downside, the lines are long and, if not long, definitely slow moving. The ride itself also takes a lot of time. Our recommendation is to ride Casey Jr. if you have children or are in a hurry. Take the boat if your party is all adults or your pace is more leisurely. Best of all, the boats' pilots deliver live narration that (depending on the driver) can be delightfully droll. If you ride the boats, try to get on before 10:30 a.m. If the queue isn't prohibitive, this ride is especially appealing after sunset, when the creative lighting adds a whole new dimension.

MICKEY'S TOONTOWN

MICKEY'S TOONTOWN IS SITUATED across the Disneyland Railroad tracks from Fantasyland. Its entrance is a tunnel that opens into Fantasyland just to the left of It's a Small World. Mickey's Toontown was inspired by the Disney animated feature *Who Framed Roger Rabbit?*, in which humans were able to enter the world of cartoon characters.

If you want to see characters, Mickey's Toontown is the place to go. In addition to Mickey, who receives guests all day (except during parades) in his dressing room, and Minnie, who entertains in her house, you are likely to bump into such august personages as Goofy and Pluto lurking around the streets.

Mickey's Toontown is rendered with masterful attention to artistic humor and detail. The businesses around the Fireworks Factory have interactive doorbells that elicit audible responses from their occupants. Across the street, the sidewalk is littered with crates containing strange contents addressed to exotic destinations. If you pry open the top of one of the crates (which is easy to do), the crate will emit a noise consistent with its contents. A box of "train parts," for example, broadcasts the sound of a racing locomotive when you lift the top. And next to Goofy's Playhouse is a Goofy-shaped impact crater that marks the spot where he missed his swimming pool while high diving.

Be forewarned that Mickey's Toontown is not very large, especially in comparison to neighboring Fantasyland. A tolerable crowd in most of the other lands will seem like Times Square on New Year's Eve in Mickey's Toontown. In 2022, Toontown will welcome Mickey and Minnie's Runaway Railway, a next-generation dark ride that's scheduled to debut at Walt Disney World in 2020. The new attraction, which will displace the gift shop and some backstage offices but not evict any existing rides, will surely make Toontown even more congested than before.

Mickey's Toontown opens 1 hour after the rest of the park. If you're touring with younger children, hit the Fantasyland attractions during the first hour the park is open, and then head for Toontown.

Finally, be aware that all of Toontown, including Roger Rabbit's Car Toon Spin, will close early before every nighttime fireworks show. It seems that rockets are launched from a building behind the land, showering Mickey's city with fiery embers, which might prove inconvenient for anyone standing below.

Chip 'n Dale Treehouse   ★★

APPEAL BY AGE	PRESCHOOL ★★★★	GRADE SCHOOL ★★★½	TEENS ★★★½
YOUNG ADULTS ★★		OVER 30 ★★★½	SENIORS ★★½

What it is Imaginative children's play area. **Scope and scale** Diversion. **When to go** Anytime. **Comment** Good exercise for the small fry.

DESCRIPTION AND COMMENTS Play area consisting of a tree house with slides.

TOURING TIPS Located in the most remote corner of Mickey's Toontown and obscured by the crowd waiting to ride the roller coaster next door, the tree house is frequently overlooked. Of all the attractions in Mickey's Toontown, this is the easiest one to get the kids into without much of a wait. Most any child who can fit is allowed to rummage around in the tree house.

Disneyland Railroad

DESCRIPTION AND COMMENTS Mickey's Toontown and Fantasyland share a station on Disneyland Railroad's route around the perimeter of the park. This station becomes fairly crowded on busy days. If you are interested primarily in getting there, it may be quicker to walk. See the description beginning on page 217 for additional details regarding the sights en route.

Gadget's Go Coaster ★★

APPEAL BY AGE	PRESCHOOL ★★★★	GRADE SCHOOL ★★★★	TEENS ★★★★
YOUNG ADULTS ★★★★		OVER 30 ★★★★	SENIORS ★★★★

  What it is Small roller coaster. **Scope and scale** Minor attraction. **When to go** Before 10:30 a.m., during the parades or *Fantasmic!* in the evening, or just before the park closes. **Comments** Great for little ones but not worth the wait for adults. Must be 35" to ride; expectant moms shouldn't ride. **Duration of ride** About 50 seconds. **Average wait in line per 100 people ahead of you** 10 minutes. **Loading speed** Slow.

Rough   Lose Things

DESCRIPTION AND COMMENTS Gadget's Go Coaster is a very small roller coaster; the idea is that you are miniaturized and riding around in an acorn shell. The zippy ride is over so quickly that you hardly know that you've been anywhere. In fact, of the 52 seconds the ride is in motion, 32 seconds are consumed in exiting the loading area, being ratcheted up the first hill, and braking into the off-loading area. The actual time you spend careening around the track is a whopping 20 seconds.

TOURING TIPS Gadget's Go Coaster, a beginner roller coaster for young children, is the perfect attraction to gauge the pluckiness of your little ones before tossing them to the coyotes on Big Thunder Mountain Railroad. The coaster cars are not very comfortable for adults, and you can expect a fair amount of whiplash, but as noted, the ride takes less than a minute. The coaster is both slow-loading and visually attractive, so you can expect long waits except during the first 30 minutes that Toontown is open.

Goofy's Playhouse ★★½

APPEAL BY AGE	PRESCHOOL ★★★★	GRADE SCHOOL ★★★½	TEENS ★★★½
YOUNG ADULTS ★★★		OVER 30 ★★★	SENIORS ★★★½

What it is A whimsical children's play area. **Scope and scale** Diversion. **When to go** Anytime.

DESCRIPTION AND COMMENTS Goofy's Playhouse is a small but nicely themed play area for the under-6 set. Usually not crowded, the playhouse is a pleasant place to let preschoolers ramble and parents relax while older sibs enjoy more adventurous attractions.

TOURING TIPS There's not a lot of shade, so visit early or late in the day.

Mickey's House and Meet Mickey ★★★

APPEAL BY AGE	PRESCHOOL ★★★★	GRADE SCHOOL ★★★★	TEENS ★★★★
YOUNG ADULTS ★★★★		OVER 30 ★★★★	SENIORS ★★★★

What it is Walk-through tour of Mickey's House and Movie Barn, ending with a personal visit with Mickey. **Scope and scale** Minor attraction. **When to go** Before 10:30 a.m. or after 5:30 p.m. **Duration of tour** 15–30 minutes (depending on the crowd). **Average wait in line per 100 people ahead of you** 10 minutes.

DESCRIPTION AND COMMENTS Mickey's House is the starting point of a self-guided tour that winds through the famous mouse's house, into his backyard, past Pluto's doghouse, and then into Mickey's Movie Barn. This last stop harks back to the so-called "barn" studio where Walt Disney created a number of the earlier Mickey Mouse cartoons. Once in the Movie Barn, guests are entertained by the Disney Channel's current series of retro-styled Mickey Mouse shorts while awaiting admittance to Mickey's Dressing Room.

In small groups of one or two families, guests are ultimately conducted into the dressing room where Mickey awaits to pose for photos and sign autographs. The visit is not lengthy (2–4 minutes), but there is adequate time for all of the children to hug, poke, and admire the star.

TOURING TIPS The cynical observer will discern immediately that Mickey's House, backyard, Movie Barn, and so on are no more than a cleverly devised queuing area to deliver guests to Mickey's Dressing Room for the mouse encounter. For those with some vestige of child in their personalities, however, the preamble serves to heighten anticipation while providing the opportunity to get to know the corporate symbol on a more personal level. Mickey's House is well conceived and contains a lot of Disney memorabilia. You will notice that children touch everything as they proceed through the house, hoping to find some artifact that is not welded or riveted into the set (an especially tenacious child during one of our visits was actually able to rip a couple of books from a bookcase).

Meeting Mickey and touring his house are best done during the first 2 hours that Toontown is open or in the evening during *Fantasmic!* If meeting Mickey is at the top of your child's list, consider taking the Disneyland Railroad from Main Street to the Toontown/Fantasyland Station as soon as you enter the park (note that Toontown opens 1 hour after the rest of the park). Some children are so obsessed with seeing Mickey that they cannot enjoy anything else until they get Mickey in the rearview mirror. (Mickey is not available during parades.)

Minnie's House ★★½

APPEAL BY AGE	PRESCHOOL ★★★★	GRADE SCHOOL ★★★★½	TEENS ★★★★½
YOUNG ADULTS ★★★★½		OVER 30 ★★★★½	SENIORS ★★★★½

What it is Walk-through exhibit and character-greeting opportunity. **Scope and scale** Minor attraction. **When to go** Before 10:30 a.m. **Duration of tour** About 10 minutes. **Average wait in line per 100 people ahead of you** 12 minutes.

DESCRIPTION AND COMMENTS Minnie's House consists of a self-guided tour through the various rooms and backyard of Mickey Mouse's main squeeze. Similar to Mickey's House, only predictably more feminine, Minnie's House likewise showcases some fun Disney memorabilia. Among the highlights of the short tour are the fanciful appliances in Minnie's kitchen. Like Mickey, Minnie is usually present to receive guests.

TOURING TIPS Minnie's House can't accommodate as many guests as Mickey's House can. See Minnie early and before Mickey to avoid waiting outdoors in a long queue. Minnie is not available during parades and normally knocks off for the day by midafternoon; check the app or *Times Guide* for her appearance schedule.

Miss Daisy, Donald's Boat ★★

APPEAL BY AGE	PRESCHOOL ★★★★	GRADE SCHOOL ★★★½	TEENS ★★½
YOUNG ADULTS ★★½	OVER 30 ★★★		SENIORS ★★★

What it is Creative play area with a boat theme. **Scope and scale** Diversion. **When to go** Before 10:30 a.m. or after 4:30 p.m.

DESCRIPTION AND COMMENTS Another children's play area, this time with a tugboat theme. Children can climb nets, ring bells, survey Toontown from the captain's bridge, and scoot down slides. The idea is that Donald Duck (who, as everyone knows, lives in Duckburg) is visiting Toontown.

TOURING TIPS Kids more or less wander on and off the *Miss Daisy,* and usually there isn't any sort of organized line or queuing area. Enjoy this play area at your leisure and stay as long as you like.

Roger Rabbit's Car Toon Spin *(FastPass)* ★★★½

APPEAL BY AGE	PRESCHOOL ★★★★	GRADE SCHOOL ★★★½	TEENS ★★★½
YOUNG ADULTS ★★★½	OVER 30 ★★★½		SENIORS ★★★½

What it is Track ride in the dark. **Scope and scale** Major attraction. **When to go** Before 10:30 a.m. or after 6:30 p.m. **Comment** Ride with your kids, if you can stomach it. **Duration of ride** A little more than 3 minutes. **Average wait in line per 100 people ahead of you** 9 minutes. **Loading speed** Slow.

 DESCRIPTION AND COMMENTS In this so-called dark ride, guests become part of a cartoon plot. The concept is that you are renting a cab for a tour of Toontown. As soon as your cab gets under way, however, weasels throw a slippery glop (known as dip) on the road, which sends the cab into a more or less uncontrollable spin. This spinning continues as the cab passes through a variety of sets populated by cartoon and Audio-Animatronic characters and punctuated by simulated explosions. As a child of the 1960s put it, "It was like combining Mr. Toad's Wild Ride with the Mad Tea Party while tripping on LSD." The ride features an elaborate indoor queue and some of the best effects of any Disneyland cartoon dark ride, climaxing in a head-scratchingly effective "portable hole" gag that holds up under repeated viewing.

The main problem with the Car Toon Spin is that, because of the spinning, you are often pointed in the wrong direction to appreciate (or even see) many of the better visual effects. Furthermore, the story line is loose. The attraction lacks the continuity and humor of Splash Mountain or the suspense of The Haunted Mansion or Snow White's Scary Adventures.

The spinning, incidentally, can be controlled by the guests. If you don't want to spin, you don't have to. If you do elect to spin, you still will not be able to approach the eye-popping speed attainable on the teacups at the

Mad Tea Party. Sluggish spinning aside, our advice for those who are at all susceptible to motion sickness is not to get near this ride if you are touring with anyone under 21 years of age.

A reader from Milford, Michigan, echoed our sentiments, lamenting:

The most disappointing ride to me was Roger Rabbit's Car Toon Spin. I stood in line for 45 minutes for a fun house ride, and the wheel was so difficult to operate that I spent most of my time trying to steer the bloody car and missed the point of the ride.

TOURING TIPS The ride is popular for its novelty, and it is one of the few Mickey's Toontown attractions that parents (with strong stomachs) can enjoy with their children. Because the ride stays fairly thronged with people all day long, ride in the first 90 minutes that Toontown is open, during parades or *Fantasmic!,* or in the hour before the park closes. The best move is to obtain FastPasses before 10:30 a.m., when the return time is an hour or less away, and then let your children enjoy the other Toontown attractions until it's time to ride.

▮ TOMORROWLAND

LOCATED DIRECTLY TO THE RIGHT of the central hub is Tomorrowland. This themed area is a futuristic mix of rides and experiences that relates to technological development and what life will be like in the years to come.

Tomorrowland's design reflects a nostalgic vision of the future as imagined by dreamers and scientists in the 1920s and 1930s. Frozen in time, Tomorrowland conjures up visions of Buck Rogers (whom nobody under age 60 remembers), fanciful mechanical rockets, and metallic cities spread beneath towering obelisks. Disney refers to Tomorrowland as the "Future That Never Was." *Newsweek* dubbed it "retro-future."

Astro Orbitor ★★

APPEAL BY AGE	PRESCHOOL ★★★★	GRADE SCHOOL ★★★★	TEENS ★★★★
YOUNG ADULTS ★★★★		OVER 30 ★★★★	SENIORS ★★★★

What it is Very mild midway-type thrill ride. **Scope and scale** Minor attraction. **When to go** Before 10 a.m. or during the hour before the park closes. **Comment** Not worth the wait. **Duration of ride** 1½ minutes. **Average wait in line per 100 people ahead of you** 12½ minutes. **Loading speed** Slow.

Thumbs Up for the Whole Family

Queasy

DESCRIPTION AND COMMENTS The Astro Orbitor is a visually appealing midway-type ride involving small rockets that rotate on arms around a central axis. Be aware that the Astro Orbitor flies higher and faster than Dumbo, and it frightens some small children.

TOURING TIPS Astro Orbitor is slow to load and expendable on any schedule. If you want to take a preschooler on this ride, place your child in the seat first and then sit down yourself.

Autopia ★★½

What it is Drive-'em-yourself miniature cars. **Scope and scale** Minor attraction. **When to go** Before 10 a.m. or after 5 p.m. **Comments** Boring for adults; great for preschoolers. Must be at least 54″ tall to drive unassisted; must be at least 32″ tall to ride (and one guest in car must be at least 54″ tall). **Duration of ride** Approximately 4½ minutes. **Average wait in line per 100 people ahead of you** 3½ minutes; assumes 35 cars operating on each track. **Loading speed** Moderate.

DESCRIPTION AND COMMENTS An elaborate miniature freeway with gasoline-powered cars that travel at speeds of up to 7 miles per hour. In 2016 Autopia was updated with new preshow displays (look for clips from the 1958 educational cartoon "Magic Highway USA") and minimally moving roadside tableaus featuring ASIMO (Honda's humanoid robot that used to perform in Innoventions before it became Star Wars Launch Bay) and his robo-bird buddy, but it still has the same basic appeal it's held for decades. The attraction design—with its sleek cars, auto noises, highway signs, and even an "off-road" section—is quite alluring. In actuality, the cars poke along on a track that leaves the driver with little to do. Pretty ho-hum for most adults and teenagers, but at least it's much more visually stimulating than the unthemed Magic Kingdom version.

TOURING TIPS This ride is appealing to the eye but definitely expendable on a schedule for adults. Preschoolers, however, love it. If your preschooler is too short to drive, place the child behind the wheel and allow him or her to steer (the car runs on a guide rail) while you work the foot pedal.

A mom from North Billerica, Massachusetts, writes:

I was amazed by the number of adults in line. Please emphasize to your readers that these cars travel on a guided path and are not a whole lot of fun. The only reason I could think of for adults to be in line was an insane desire to go on absolutely every ride. The cars tend to pile up at the end, so it takes almost as long to get off as it did to get on. Parents riding with their preschoolers should keep the car going as slow as it can without stalling. This prolongs the preschooler's joy and decreases the time you have to wait at the end.

FastPass was previously offered at Autopia. If it returns, don't bother; it doesn't work very well, with FastPass return lines typically exceeding 20 minutes. Ride early or late in the day instead.

Buzz Lightyear Astro Blasters *(FastPass)* ★★★★

What it is Space-travel interactive dark ride. **Scope and scale** Major attraction. **When to go** Before 10:30 a.m. or after 6 p.m. **Comment** A real winner! **Duration of ride** About 4½ minutes. **Average wait in line per 100 people ahead of you** 3½ minutes. **Loading speed** Fast.

DESCRIPTION AND COMMENTS Based on the space-commando character Buzz Lightyear from *Toy Story,* the marginal story line has you and Buzz trying to save the universe from the evil Emperor Zurg. The indoor ride is interactive—you can spin your car and shoot simulated laser cannons at Zurg and his minions.

A similar attraction at the Magic Kingdom at Walt Disney World is one of the most popular attractions in the park. The Disneyland version, situated across from Star Tours, is much the same except mobile guns allow more accurate aiming. Don't forget to smile! You can email an on-ride photo to yourself for free from kiosks at the exit; these pictures are not connected to PhotoPass.

Praise for Buzz Lightyear is almost universal. This comment from a Massachusetts couple is typical:

Buzz Lightyear was the surprise hit of our trip! My husband and I enjoyed competing for the best score so much that we went on this ride several times during our stay. Definitely a must.

Each car is equipped with two laser cannons and a score-keeping display. Each score-keeping display is independent, so you can compete with your riding partner. A joystick allows you to spin the car to line up the various targets. Each time you pull the trigger, you'll release a red laser beam that you can see hitting or missing the target.

TOURING TIPS Most folks' first ride is occupied with learning how to use the equipment (fire off individual shots as opposed to keeping the trigger depressed) and figuring out how the targets work. The next ride (as with certain potato chips, one is not enough), you'll surprise yourself by how much better you do. *Unofficial Guide* readers are unanimous in their praise of Buzz Lightyear. Some guests, in fact, spend several hours on the attraction, riding again and again. See Buzz Lightyear early in the morning after riding Peter Pan's Flight, Matterhorn Bobsleds, and Star Tours. Buzz Lightyear's FastPasses are dispensed from the two kiosks at the far end of Star Tours' distribution area and are often available for immediate use.

Disneyland Monorail System   ★★★

APPEAL BY AGE   PRESCHOOL ★★★★   GRADE SCHOOL ★★★★   TEENS ★★★★
YOUNG ADULTS   ★★★★   OVER 30   ★★★★   SENIORS   ★★★★

What it is Scenic transportation. **Scope and scale** Major attraction. **When to go** During the hot, crowded period of the day (11:30 a.m.–5 p.m.). **Comments** Nice, relaxing ride with some interesting views of the park; take the monorail to Downtown Disney for lunch. **Duration of ride** 3 minutes one-way to Downtown Disney; 5½ minutes to return. **Average wait in line per 100 people ahead of you** 5 minutes; assumes 3 monorails operating. **Loading speed** Moderate–fast.

Thumbs Up for the Whole Family

DESCRIPTION AND COMMENTS The monorail is a futuristic transportation ride that affords the only practical opportunity for escaping the park during the crowded lunch period and early afternoon. Boarding at the Tomorrowland monorail station, you can commute to the Disneyland Resort hotels and Downtown Disney. The monorail provides a tranquil trip with a nice view of Downtown Disney, Disney California Adventure, Fantasyland, and Tomorrowland. The Mark VII monorails have a sleek, retro look but can get quite hot inside during the summer (no air-conditioning!) and may shut down entirely on very warm days.

TOURING TIPS We recommend using the monorail to commute to Downtown Disney for a quiet, relaxing lunch away from the crowds and the heat. If you only want to experience the ride, go whenever you wish; the wait to board is usually 15–25 minutes except in the 2 hours before closing when everyone tries to leave at once. On afternoons when round-trip riders are not required to disembark and requeue at Downtown Disney, inbound guests may wait through multiple monorails for an empty seat. The monorail may suspend services from 1 hour before Disneyland Park's evening fireworks until 45 minutes afterward, and it ceases to bring guests into the park 30 minutes before closing, though you can exit the park on it as long as you've entered the queue by 5 minutes before closing. Also, you must be staying at a Disney hotel to enter Disneyland via monorail during Magic Morning hours. For a treat, ask a cast member on the platform about riding up front with the pilot.

Disneyland Railroad

DESCRIPTION AND COMMENTS The Disneyland Railroad makes a regular stop at the Tomorrowland Station. The wait to board here is usually short. See pages 217–218 for additional details regarding the sights en route.

Finding Nemo Submarine Voyage ★★★★

APPEAL BY AGE PRESCHOOL ★★★★ GRADE SCHOOL ★★★★ TEENS ★★★★
YOUNG ADULTS ★★★★ OVER 30 ★★★★ SENIORS ★★★★

What it is Simulated submarine ride. **Scope and scale** Headliner. **When to go** Before 10 a.m. or during evening parades or fireworks. **Duration of ride** 11½ minutes. **Average wait in line per 100 people ahead of you** 7 minutes; assumes 8 subs operating. **Loading speed** Slow-moderate.

DESCRIPTION AND COMMENTS The Finding Nemo Submarine Voyage ride is based on the story line of the hit Disney-Pixar animated feature *Finding Nemo*. Here you board a submarine in a loading area situated below the Disneyland monorail station in Tomorrowland. After a quick lap of the open-air lagoon, the sub passes through a waterfall and inside to follow the general *Finding Nemo* story. Special effects center on a combination of traditional Audio-Animatronics and, once you're inside the dark interior of the building, what appear to be rear-projection screens, underwater, at a distance of 3–10 feet from the sub's windows. Encased in rock and shipwrecks, the screens are natural looking and allow the animated characters to appear three-dimensionally in the undersea world. Other elements include traveling through a minefield and a sea of jellyfish (very cool) and entering the mouth of a whale. The onboard sound system allows the story to "travel" from front to back of the sub, and the visual experience is different depending on what seat you're in.

The attraction is well done, though time and water are taking their toll on the scenery. You don't have to be a Nemo fan to be impressed by the scale and effects. It's not fast-paced but, rather, leisurely in the way that Pirates of the Caribbean is.

TOURING TIPS The attraction's capacity is only about 900 guests per hour, a shockingly small capacity for a headliner attraction. We've determined that, taking the day as a whole, you make much better use of your time enjoying Space Mountain, Splash Mountain, Peter Pan's Flight, and other popular attractions during the first hour the park is open and saving the subs for later, when a parade, fireworks show, or *Fantasmic!* has siphoned a large number of guests from the line. The last 30 minutes before park closing is another good time to get in line.

Claustrophobes may not be comfortable with the experience, even though the sub doesn't actually submerge (we saw one 30-ish woman who started hyperventilating before the sub left the dock). Children may be scared of the same thing, or of the encounter with sharks (they keep their distance). The sharks here are a bit less menacing than in the movie too.

The bright-yellow subs use electric power to minimize noise and pollution. The subs fit 40 people. It's not easy to get 40 aboard, however, because the seats are narrow and a few guests take up two. Ideally, large guests should aim to be in one of the four seats at the front or back, but this may be difficult to negotiate.

Wheelchair-bound guests or those who can't get down the spiral staircase into the sub can view the experience from a special topside viewing room (seats about six able-bodied persons plus two wheelchairs). With the exception of one small animated effect, the visual is identical (perhaps faster), but despite a large monitor, the creatures appear smaller than when viewing them through a real porthole. The wait for the alternate viewing area is usually brief (ask a cast member how to bypass the standby line), and there are Mickeys hidden in the dive lockers inside.

A reader from Sydney, Australia, disagrees with our Finding Nemo rating, writing:

Finding Nemo was the most overrated ride. Perhaps it would rate high for those younger than 8 years old, but for our group it was one of the worst rides. It was boring, had rushing water, and moved slowly. What made it worse was that it had a high rating, and this raised expectations.

Space Mountain *(FastPass)* ★★★★½

**APPEAL BY AGE   PRESCHOOL ★★½   GRADE SCHOOL ★★★★½   TEENS ★★★★½
YOUNG ADULTS ★★★★½   OVER 30 ★★★★½   SENIORS ★★★★½**

What it is Roller coaster in the dark. **Scope and scale** Super-headliner. **When to go** Right after the park opens or use FastPass. **Comments** Not to be missed. Must be 40" tall to ride. **Duration of ride** 2¾ minutes. **Average wait in line per 100 people ahead of you** 3½ minutes. **Loading speed** Moderate.

DESCRIPTION AND COMMENTS Space Mountain is an indoor roller coaster with a theme of high-speed interstellar travel. It's a designer version of the Wild Mouse, a midway ride that's been around for at least 50 years. There are no long drops or swooping hills as there are on a traditional roller coaster—only quick, unexpected turns and small drops. Disney's contribution essentially was to add a space theme to the Wild Mouse and put it in the dark. And this does indeed make the Mouse seem wilder.

The most surprising thing about Space Mountain is its aesthetic beauty. The vistas of the solar system and the stars, the distant galaxies, and passing comets are intoxicating and very realistic. Because you can't see the track or anticipate where your vehicle will go, your eyes are free to feast on the rich visuals, as your ears enjoy Michael Giacchino's groovy synchronized score behind your screams.

Disney transforms Space Mountain into Ghost Galaxy for Halloween, adding atmospheric audio and video projections of an angry space ghost (no, not that Space Ghost) chasing you through the cosmos. The interstellar specter is more goofy than genuinely scary, but it makes a fun novelty for the spooky season. Nighttime video projections, which make the iconic conical building look like it's crumbling to dust or crackling with electricity, are the most impressive element of the overlay.

TOURING TIPS Space Mountain is one of the park's most popular attractions. Experience it immediately after the park opens, use FastPass, or use the single-rider line, which is accessed through the ride's exit and frequently has little to no wait.

Star Tours—The Adventures Continue *(FastPass)* ★★★★

APPEAL BY AGE	PRESCHOOL ★★★½		GRADE SCHOOL ★★★★½	TEENS ★★★★½
YOUNG ADULTS ★★★★½		OVER 30 ★★★★½		SENIORS ★★★★

What it is Space-flight simulation ride. **Scope and scale** Headliner. **When to go** Before 11 a.m. or use FastPass. **Comments** A blast; not to be missed. Frightens many small children; expectant mothers advised against riding; must be 40″ tall to ride. Switching-off option (see page 147). **Duration of ride** Approximately 7 minutes. **Average wait in line per 100 people ahead of you** 4½ minutes; assumes 4 simulators operating. **Loading speed** Moderate.

Scary   Queasy   Rough

DESCRIPTION AND COMMENTS Star Tours is a flight simulator that features crystal-clear digital 3-D screens and in-cabin Audio-Animatronic figures of C-3PO, your golden droid pilot. During your inevitably turbulent travels, you'll bump, twist, and dive into a Who's Who of *Star Wars* icons, with heroes Master Yoda and Admiral "It's A Trap!" Ackbar on your side, and villains Darth Vader and Boba Fett on your back. You'll either be visiting planets from both the classic trilogy—such as icy Hoth and arid Tatooine—and the not-so-classic prequels, including Geonosis (home of the dreaded Death Star) and Naboo (home of the equally dreaded Jar Jar Binks), or taking a perilous tour of Jakku's starship graveyard and the mineral planet Crait from the recent sequels, with cameos from BB-8 and Maz Kanata; another new scene should be added for *Episode IX*'s debut. The big twist is that the various possible cosmic destinations and multiple celebrity cameos (look for Han Solo and Chewbacca in the background) are randomly combined into hundreds of different story variations, giving the attraction unprecedented reridability. A wealth of references to the original Star Tours ride (along with hidden Disney characters and *Star Wars* inside jokes) can be found inside the detailed queue, and the ride is quite smooth and well synchronized.

TOURING TIPS Star Tours sees hour-plus waits on busy days, so ride as early in the day as possible or grab a FastPass. The ride's long-term future is uncertain now that Galaxy's Edge has arrived. A single-rider queue has been tested here, but it involves a confusing trek up the exit ramp inside Star Traders.

Star Wars Launch Bay　★★½

What it is Movie exhibits and character greetings. **Scope and scale** Minor attraction.
When to go Anytime; open 10 a.m.–8 p.m. **Duration of exhibit** Varies. 30 minutes to
examine all exhibits; 30 minutes or more for each meet and greet. **Probable waiting
time** 30 minutes for each meet and greet.

Loud　　Scary

DESCRIPTION AND COMMENTS Star Wars Launch Bay is
a walk-through exhibit housed inside the former Innoventions building (originally the *Carousel of Progress*) that pays
homage to the entire *Star Wars* cinematic series.

A 9-minute introductory film featuring interview snippets with some of
the creators of the new *Star Wars* films—including Lucasfilm president
Kathleen Kennedy and *Rise of Skywalker* director J. J. Abrams—runs on an
endless loop to the right of the exhibit entrance, next to a small sliver of
the model for Star Wars: Galaxy's Edge.

The central display area is devoted to the most recent *Star Wars* films.
The room showcases weapons, vehicles, and costumes as seen on-screen,
though all are exacting re-creations as opposed to authentic movie props.

Another area displays replica props and models representing the vehicles and weapons of the Rebel Alliance and Galactic Empire, as seen in
Episodes IV–VI. The highlight of this area is a detailed scale reproduction
of Boba Fett's *Slave I,* with a tiny figure of the infamous bounty hunter visible inside the cockpit.

The back portion of the Star Wars Launch Bay building is dominated
by two elaborate meet and greets: one leads to a Rebel base where Chewbacca, the world's favorite Wookiee, makes appearances; the other to an
Imperial bunker occupied by Darth Vader, the iconic Dark Lord of the Sith.
Whichever side you select, you'll find a couple cases of replica helmets and
light sabers to look at. The line moves slowly, but the wait is well worth it
because both meet and greets use Disney's latest interactive technology
to bring these iconic characters to life. Chewbacca can move his mouth
and growl in response to your questions, while Vader has a full vocabulary
of sinister phrases to taunt you with. The queue is also carefully managed
to prevent guests from seeing the encounter ahead of them, so your face-
to-face really feels like an intimate experience.

In addition to the public meet and greets, a private meet and greet with
Darth (or another Dark Side villain) is reserved for Disney Visa credit card
holders. It's open for 4 hours every afternoon and always has a shorter wait
than the public line, in addition to providing free PhotoPass downloads.

Beyond the meet and greets, Launch Bay includes a small mock-up of
the Mos Eisley cantina—where you may snap a selfie at the holochess
table—and a corner full of video game consoles and Lego toys to test drive.

To exit, guests pass through the Launch Bay Cargo Shop, stocked with
high-end memorabilia aimed at well-heeled collectors. If you simply want
mass-market *Star Wars* clothes and toys, head over to The Star Trader in
Tomorrowland. If, on the other hand, you want to spend $4,000 on an

authentically detailed Darth Vader costume (perfect for wearing to any wedding or bar mitzvah) or $3,050 on a life-size Kenner Boba Fett action figure, this is the place.

TOURING TIPS Lines can get long for the meet and greets, so be sure to set aside at least 30 minutes each to meet one of the heroes or baddies; note that there is a separate queue for each character. Star Wars Launch Bay doesn't open until 10 a.m., and now that Galaxy's Edge has opened, Launch Bay's days are likely numbered.

Tomorrowland Theater / *Star Wars: Path of the Jedi* ★★½

APPEAL BY AGE	PRESCHOOL ★★★★	GRADE SCHOOL ★★★★½	TEENS ★★★½
YOUNG ADULTS ★★★½		OVER 30 ★★★★	SENIORS ★★★★★

What it is Film clips with special effects. **Scope and scale** Minor attraction. **When to go** Anytime. **Comment** The loud, intense show with tactile effects frightens some young children. **Duration of show** Approximately 10 minutes. **Probable waiting time** 15 minutes.

Loud

Scary

DESCRIPTION AND COMMENTS The Tomorrowland Theater, located directly in front of Space Mountain, featured *Captain EO,* a 3-D sci-fi music video starring Michael Jackson, 1986–1987 and 2009–2014, and *Honey, I Shrunk the Audience,* based on the Rick Moranis comedy franchise, 1987–2009.

The theater now promotes Disney's upcoming or recent theatrical releases or hosts limited-time film festivals. When not showing movie trailers, the theater is home to *Path of the Jedi,* a 10-minute montage of memorable moments from every episode in the Skywalker saga.

Rather than try to recap the plot of the first six films, *Path of the Jedi* takes iconic images and dialogue from the saga and stitches them together thematically instead of chronologically. If you haven't already seen all the movies, the result will be visually dazzling but incoherent; for the rest of us, it makes a great memory jog. The classic footage culminates in the death of Darth Vader, which then segues into a montage of moments from the newest sequels. Footage from the recent films includes glimpses of an aged Han Solo, Luke Skywalker, and Princess Leia, alongside the youthful new heroes.

Path of the Jedi is not presented in 3-D (a shame since 3-D conversions of all the films exist), but it does use in-theater lighting, wind effects, and powerful subwoofers to give the visuals an added punch.

TOURING TIPS The Tomorrowland Theater isn't on our must-do list. But if you are interested in the featured film, it makes a fine air-conditioned distraction, either on your second day in the park or when everything else has too long a line.

Shows usually begin on the hour and continue about every 15 minutes throughout the day. Even during busier times, you should be able to get into the next show without issue.

The sound level can be earsplitting, frightening some young children. Some adults report that the loud soundtrack is distracting, even uncomfortable. Avoid seats in the first several rows to avoid a stiff neck.

LIVE ENTERTAINMENT *and* SPECIAL EVENTS

BANDS, DISNEY CHARACTER APPEARANCES, parades, singing and dancing, and ceremonies further enliven and add color to Disneyland Park on a daily basis. During the off-season, certain evening spectaculars (such as the fireworks and *Fantasmic!*) may be performed only on weekends. For specific information about what's happening on the day you visit, check the daily entertainment schedule in the app or *Times Guide*. Be forewarned, however, that if you are on a tight schedule, it is impossible to both see the park's featured attractions and take in the numerous and varied live performances offered. In our one-day touring plans, starting on page 369, we exclude the live performances in favor of seeing as much of the park as time permits. This is a tactical decision based on the fact that the parades and *Fantasmic!*, Disneyland Park's river spectacular, siphon crowds away from the more popular rides, shortening waiting lines.

The color and pageantry of live events around the park are an integral part of the Disneyland Park entertainment mix and a persuasive argument for second-day touring. Though live entertainment is varied, plentiful, and nearly continuous throughout the day, several productions are preeminent.

Fantasmic! (FastPass) ★★★★★

| APPEAL BY AGE | PRESCHOOL ★★★★ | GRADE SCHOOL ★★★★½ | TEENS ★★★★½ |
| YOUNG ADULTS ★★★★½ | OVER 30 ★★★★½ | | SENIORS ★★★★½ |

What it is Multimedia water pageant with live characters. **Scope and scale** Superheadliner. **When to go** Check the app or *Times Guide* for showtimes; FastPass only. If there's only one show, get a FastPass the first hour the park is open. **Comment** Not to be missed. **Duration of show** 23 minutes. **Probable waiting time** 30–60 minutes for best view.

DESCRIPTION AND COMMENTS *Fantasmic!* is a mixed-media show presented one or more times each evening the park is open 10 p.m. or later. Staged at the end of Tom Sawyer Island opposite the Frontierland and New Orleans Square waterfronts, *Fantasmic!* stars Mickey Mouse in his role as the sorcerer's apprentice from *Fantasia*. The production uses lasers, images projected on a shroud of mist, fireworks, lighting effects, and music in combinations so stunning that you can scarcely believe what you have seen.

The plot is simple: good versus evil. The story gets lost in all the special effects at times, but no matter—it is the spectacle, not the story line, that is so overpowering. While *beautiful, stunning,* and *powerful* are words that immediately come to mind, they fail to convey the uniqueness of this presentation, which includes a 45-foot-tall full-bodied fire-breathing dragon (nicknamed Murphy) for the finale. It could be argued, with some validity, that *Fantasmic!* alone is worth the price of Disneyland Park admission. Needless to say, we rate *Fantasmic!* as not to be missed.

TOURING TIPS After years of watching guests stake out prime viewing spots along the edge of the New Orleans Square and Frontierland waterfronts as much as 4 hours in advance, Disney implemented a FastPass-only policy for *Fantasmic!* that is very similar to the one enforced at DCA's *World of Color.* There are now a few ways to see *Fantasmic!,* none of which should require showing up more than an hour before showtime.

The easiest method is to grab a FastPass early in the day. Distribution of *Fantasmic!* FastPasses takes place between the petrified tree and the riverboat dock in Frontierland, or through Disney's app for MaxPass users. FastPasses are distributed until 1 hour before showtime or until they run out, whichever comes first. Historically, tickets for the first show can sell out within an hour after park opening; the second show (when scheduled) may run out before noon but can sometimes be snagged until just an hour or so before showtime.

Fantasmic! general FastPass return windows begin 1 hour before showtime and end when the show begins. If you need to stand right at the railing in the heart of the splash zone, you'll want to be the first inside the viewing pen when it opens. Otherwise, you're best off arriving about 20–30 minutes before curtain and watching from the rear, taking advantage of any available elevation. Entry can be a bit confusing, so pay careful attention to your kids; look for the entrance near the riverboat landing, and follow the flashlight-wielding cast members' directions.

Fantasmic! FastPasses are disconnected from the rest of Disneyland's FastPass system, meaning that if you obtain a *Fantasmic!* FastPass, you can also immediately get one for another attraction.

Fantasmic! dining packages are available at Blue Bayou ($62 adults, $29 kids for lunch; $10 more for adults at dinner) and River Belle Terrace ($45 adults, $25 kids), both plus tax and tip. Dining packages include a three-course meal and a FastPass for a special preferred viewing area. Most free FastPass viewing areas are standing room only, but guests in the table service dining package sections sit on the ground. River Belle Terrace diners can pay an extra $25 per adult ($15 per child) for premium 8 p.m. patio seating, allowing them to stay and watch the 9 p.m. show from the restaurant. Lunch service starts at 11:30 a.m., and the dinner packages begin at 4 p.m. While the meals are certainly overpriced, especially in comparison to the similar *World of Color* packages next door, the ease of entry and expansive elbow room afforded by preferred FastPasses are almost worth the expense, according to this St. Louis, Missouri, reader:

I highly recommend a Fantasmic! *dining package. It took so long to just move around the park that it was nice not to have to stake out a place for the show. We did Blue Bayou, which was expensive, but everyone enjoyed the food.*

Another reader who tried River Belle's upgraded seating agreed:

The River Belle Terrace Fantasmic! *premium dining package is a great (but expensive) way to avoid the crowds for the show. Very relaxing, with plenty of space during dinner and the show rather than standing (or hopefully sitting) on the pavement in the other dining package areas. We went on a day without the 10 p.m.* Fantasmic! *show and were allowed to stay at our table for the fireworks show.*

But one visitor from Hometown, Connecticut, wrote us about their disappointment with the River Belle patio package:

The people walking by and the cast members flashing their flashlights was so distracting. The table next to us even complained about how bad it was. Plus the food was terrible.

For a little less money, there is also the *Fantasmic!* On-the-Go Dining Package ($29.99 adults, $19.99 kids) at Hungry Bear Restaurant. This package includes an entrée (salmon, barbecue chicken, pork ribs, or vegetarian frittata), a green salad, a can of natural soda, and a reserved FastPass for the standing-room viewing section to the left of Blue Bayou's center area. We found the food quality considerably better than Hungry Bear's regular fare (though you can substitute any standard entrée for the same price), making this the best value of the resort's viewing upgrades. On-the-Go Dining Packages can be reserved in advance and may be picked up 3–8 p.m. (varies with show schedule). Reservations for all *Fantasmic!* dining packages can be made online at disneyland.disney.go.com/dining/disneyland /fantasmic-dinner-packages or by calling ☎ 714-781-3463.

Fantasmic! viewing spots are first come, first served for all guests, including those in the FastPass dining-experience viewing section, which is located along the waterfront from center stage to the raft landing for Tom Sawyer Island. You can enter the dining section near the Harbour Galley restaurant beginning 1 hour before each showtime, and the earlier you get in, the better spot you will obtain, as this Australian reader discovered:

Even with the FastPass, people were lining up an hour beforehand to get prime position, and the ground is cold and very hard on your butt when you have to sit there for an hour waiting for the action to start!

Disney also offers limited standby viewing for all showings. The standby viewing areas are along the far left waterfront between the Harbour Galley restaurant and the Tom Sawyer Island raft dock, as well as in front of the French Market, and on the bridge over Pirates of the Caribbean's entrance. You may be looking at the side of the show rather than the front of it. The standby viewing section along the waterfront doesn't open until 30–60 minutes before showtime, but the other standby areas begin filling up 2 hours beforehand. If you do not have a FastPass, you will be aggressively shooed away from every available vantage point outside the designated standby sections.

No matter which method you use, you'll probably spend some time sitting around waiting. A mom from Lummi Island, Washington, dismantled her Disney stroller to make a nest:

We used the snap-off cover on the rental stroller to sit on during Fantasmic! *since the ground was really cold.*

Along similar lines, a middle-aged New York man wrote, saying:

Your excellent guidebook also served as a seat cushion while seated on the ground waiting for the show. Make future editions thicker for greater comfort.

Rain and wind conditions sometimes cause *Fantasmic!* to be canceled. Unfortunately, Disney officials usually do not make a final decision about whether to proceed or cancel until just before showtime. Note that if you purchased a *Fantasmic!* dining package earlier in the day, you will not be refunded if a show is canceled.

If you see the first *Fantasmic!* showing, stay in place afterward for the nightly fireworks (if scheduled), which should start a few minutes later; following the fireworks, you will be forced to exit Frontierland into Adventureland to make room for the next audience. If attending the second performance, you'll be prevented from entering the New Orleans waterfront until all the earlier guests have exited the viewing areas.

Finally, make sure to hang on to children during *Fantasmic!* and to give them explicit instructions for regrouping in the event that you become separated. Be especially vigilant when the crowd disperses after the show.

Incidentally, if you invested in the Made with Magic light-up ears and other glowing accessories that synchronize with DCA's *World of Color* show (see page 313), you'll find that they interact with *Fantasmic!* as well.

PARADES

DISNEY THEME PARKS are famous the world over for their parades. Typically, there is a parade every day in late afternoon or early evening. On days when the park closes late (10 p.m.–midnight), the parade may run twice. The parades are full-blown productions with some combination of floats, huge balloons of the characters, marching bands, old-time vehicles, dancers, and costumed Disney characters. Themes for the parades vary from time to time, and a special holiday parade is always produced for Christmas. Disneyland retired its long-running daytime processional **Mickey's Soundsational Parade** shortly before press time, with an all-new parade scheduled to debut in 2020. The vintage **Main Street Electrical Parade** also made a brief encore appearance in summer 2019.

Parades always draw thousands of guests from the attraction lines. We recommend, therefore, watching from the departure point. With this strategy you can enjoy the parade and then, while the parade is continuing on its route, take advantage of the diminished lines at the attractions. Watching a parade that begins in Fantasyland from Small World Mall affords the greatest mobility in terms of accessing other areas of the park when the parade has passed. On days with two scheduled parades, the first performance will start at It's a Small World, travel past the west side of Matterhorn Bobsleds, go around the Tomorrowland side of Central Plaza, head down Main Street, and then circle Town Square counterclockwise. The second performance will begin at Town Square and run the route in the opposite direction.

The upper platform of the Main Street Station affords the best viewing perspective along the route. The best time to get a position on the platform is when the parade begins in Fantasyland. When this happens, good spots on the platform are available right up to the time the parade begins. When you are at the end of the parade route, you can assume that it will take the parade 15–18 minutes to get to you.

Most guests watch from Central Plaza or Main Street, and on busy days people begin camping out on the curbs there an hour or more before step-off time. The viewing area in front of It's a Small World will fill up last, so we recommend checking there if you need a spot.

Any spot along the parade route will offer the same experience, so you shouldn't worry if you can't see the parade on Main Street. Once the parade has started, count on gridlock all along the route, especially on Main Street. Due to aggressive crowd-control restrictions on the sidewalks, you're best off entering or exiting the park via the backstage breezeways (if open) or Emporium shops.

Keep an eye on your children during parades and give them explicit instructions for regrouping in the event that you get separated. Children constantly jockey for better viewing positions. A few wiggles this way and a few wiggles the other, and presto, they are lost in the crowd. Finally, be especially vigilant when the crowd starts dispersing after the parade. Thousands of people suddenly strike out in different directions, creating a perfect situation for losing a child or two.

LIVE ENTERTAINMENT THROUGHOUT THE PARK

PARADES AND FANTASMIC! make up only a part of the daily live-entertainment offerings at Disneyland Park. The following is an incomplete list of other performances and events that are scheduled with some regularity and that require no reservations.

DISNEY CHARACTER APPEARANCES Disney characters appear at random throughout the park but are routinely present in Mickey's Toontown, in Fantasyland, and on Main Street. Disney princesses are on call daily at the Royal Hall at Fantasy Faire (see page 247). An elaborate character-greeting area, Pixie Hollow (see page 246) offers a chance to meet Tinker Bell.

DISNEY CHARACTER MEALS Disney characters join guests for breakfast each morning until 11 a.m. at the **Plaza Inn** on Main Street, **Disney's PCH Grill** at Paradise Pier Hotel, and **Storytellers Café** at the Grand Californian Hotel. Disney characters also join guests for breakfast and dinner at **Goofy's Kitchen** at the Disneyland Hotel, and the princesses host brunch at the Grand Californian Hotel's **Napa Rose** on select mornings.

DISNEYLAND FOREVER ★★★★½ Several years after its supposed retirement, Disneyland has resurrected this acclaimed show, which originally debuted during the resort's Diamond Anniversary celebration. Created by extravaganza expert Steve Davison, who designed *Wishes* and *World of Color,* this production runs the full gamut of special effects: a rousing score, castle lighting, lasers, and an impressive flight from Tinker Bell— not to mention spectacular fireworks effects. After an introduction evoking the orange groves that originally covered Anaheim, the show sails through memorable musical vignettes from beloved Disney movies.

The immersive projections mapped onto Sleeping Beauty Castle, the Main Street buildings, the facade of It's a Small World, and mist screens on the Rivers of America create amazing visual effects and are a major feature of this fireworks show. Digital imagery paints landmarks around the park, transforming them into coral reefs, jungle forests, or an African savanna. Via the projections, Main Street buildings may be covered in honey during the Winnie the Pooh segment or look like they're submerged in water during the Little Mermaid segment. It's a beautiful effect that works well.

This pyrotechnic tribute to Disney's films also features a flyby from Nemo the fish as he "swims" his way toward the Matterhorn, which appears as the smoldering volcano known as Mount Wannahockaloogie. Of course, *Disneyland Forever* features an obligatory upbeat theme song, "Live the Magic."

Disneyland Forever is a fantastic finale to your day in the park, particularly if you can see it from the proper perspective (see discussion following). It doesn't have quite the same resonance for lifelong Disneyland fans as the beloved *Remember . . . Dreams Come True* 50th-anniversary spectacular, and a number of the featured songs are already overused around the resort. But, if an eye-popping aerial extravaganza of Disney standards is what you seek, *Disneyland Forever* more than fits the bill.

We rate this show as not to be missed, but seeing it poses some challenges of which you should be aware. Without a doubt, the area around the central hub is the best vantage point for watching the show; stand too far down Main Street or at the train station and the castle projections will be just postage stamps. For the most immersive impression from the projection mapping effects, you'll want to stand in the middle of Main Street, from the Carnation Café up to Coke Corner.

Unfortunately, every guest in the park won't fit in that sweet spot at the same time. Fortunately, the show was specifically designed to look good from multiple locations throughout the park.

The same projections seen on the castle are also projected on the surface of It's a Small World. You'll be missing out on the bevy of effects and lasers that shoot out of Sleeping Beauty Castle, but It's a Small World will be your best option if Main Street is full. The fireworks are off-center from here, but the video looks sharper here than on the castle, and there's often space to sit on or in front of the mall stairs.

Your third option is viewing from the Rivers of America. Fountains and lighting fixtures come to life around Tom Sawyer Island, and video is projected onto the mist screens used in *Fantasmic!*, but they're not as sharp as the ones projected on the other two locations. You'll also miss most or all of the flames and flying figures around the castle. The benefit of viewing from Rivers of America is that, if you have a FastPass for the first showing of *Fantasmic!*, you can stay in your spot through the fireworks. Though you get the least impressive view from here, it's the least stressful way to experience the show and can be very enjoyable if you haven't already seen it from a better location.

Finally, be forewarned that the fireworks may be canceled for safety reasons with only a few minutes' notice if there are stiff winds at upper altitudes, even if the air at ground level seems calm. During one of our weeklong visits, the fireworks were nixed a full 40% of the time, which is a fairly frustrating percentage; you've never heard a collective groan like 50,000 people learning they've waited for nothing. For this reason, we don't recommend that you build your night around the fireworks—as wondrous as they are—if you only have one night at the resort.

On nights when pyro is planned, Disneyland offers the Tomorrowland Skyline Lounge Experience, which bundles a boxed snack and beverage with access to the upstairs balcony of the Star Wars Launch Bay building, which affords a fine vantage for the fireworks but no view of the castle projections. Admission is $50 per person (age 3 and up) including tax, and there are no refunds if the fireworks are canceled; visit disneyland.disney.go.com/dining/disneyland/tomorrowland-skyline-lounge or call ☎ 714-781-3463 to make reservations.

To celebrate Mickey Mouse's 90th birthday, Disneyland launched *Mickey's Mix Magic* (★★★★), a short-lived evening spectacular that relied on modern music and video projections more than pyrotechnics. DJ Mickey spun a techno-heavy soundtrack featuring catchy dubstep remixes of classic cuts like "Everybody Wants to Be a Cat" and "Grim Grinning Ghosts." Fireworks were only used during select performances, and even when pryrotechnics were employed, they weren't quite as impressive as in past productions, with no dramatic launches from the castle itself. On the plus side, that means Fantasyland's attractions didn't need to close down during the show, which didn't have to cancel during windy weather. While the limited-time run of *Mix Magic* ended with Mickey's birthday party, it can still be shown as a substitute if *Disneyland Forever* is canceled due to technical difficulties, and we wouldn't be surprised if it (or a similarly pyro-less spectacular) were to return to the schedule on off-peak weekday evenings instead of the more explosive (and expensive) fireworks show.

Believe . . . in Holiday Magic is performed seasonally. Tinker Bell does not appear in the winter show, and the soundtrack selections focus on traditional holiday tunes, making *Holiday Magic* the most dignified and least Disneyfied of the fireworks spectaculars.

DISNEY ROCK GROUPS High-energy Disney rock groups perform seasonally in Tomorrowland according to the entertainment schedule.

FLAG RETREAT CEREMONY Every day at around sunset in Town Square, an honor guard lowers the flag as the Disneyland marching band plays patriotic tunes. Members of the armed forces are encouraged to participate in this respectful ceremony and are called up to be honored by branch.

STREET ENTERTAINMENT Various bands, singers, comics, and strolling musicians entertain in spontaneous (that is, unscheduled) street performances throughout the park. Musical styles include banjo, Dixieland, steel drum, marching, and fife and drum. The Disneyland Band, now with younger musicians, accompanies its repertoire of Disney tunes with more contemporary orchestrations and some drum corps–style choreography. You'll often find the Bootstrappers, a roving band of musical pirates, roaming the waterfront near New Orleans Square. For a respite from the rides, grab a snack and listen to the ragtime piano player outside the Refreshment Corner on Main Street. You don't want to miss the Dapper Dans, a slapstick barbershop quartet that has been performing on Main Street, U.S.A. in Disneyland since 1959. While the cast changes on a regular basis, the Dans really liven up the street.

UNHERALDED TREASURES
at DISNEYLAND PARK

THESE SPECIAL FEATURES found in all of the Disney theme parks add texture, context, beauty, depth, and subtlety to your visit. Generally speaking, unheralded treasures are nice surprises that should be accorded a little time. Lani Teshima, Unofficial Guide friend and writer for mouseplanet.com, knows them all. Her list follows.

TREASURE Snow White's Grotto and Wishing Well | **LOCATION** The front right of Sleeping Beauty Castle

A SLOW STROLL around the Sleeping Beauty Castle can be romantic, but sitting quietly to its right is Snow White's Grotto and Wishing Well. If you stop for a few moments, you can hear the voice of Snow White singing "I'm Wishing" in the area. The grotto includes a trickling waterfall framing statues of Snow White and the Seven Dwarfs, placed on three tiers to make Snow White appear to be off in the distance in an optical illusion that masks the fact that her statue is the same height as those of the dwarfs. Next to the grotto is a wishing well, where you can toss a coin and make a wish. This area is a popular place for Snow White or other characters to appear for photos, so don't be surprised to see a group of people milling around.

TREASURE Disneyland Railroad | **LOCATION** Stations in Main Street, U.S.A.; New Orleans Square; Mickey's Toontown/Fantasyland; and Tomorrowland

AFTER A LONG DAY, the Disneyland Railroad offers a nice way to get from one end of the park to another. But trains held a special place in Walt Disney's heart, and the railroad offers much more than just a ride back to the park gates. Pause and turn around before you enter Main Street Station for a beautiful view of the entire length of Main Street, U.S.A. Inside the station, you can enjoy looking at model trains and other little exhibits. If you get off at the New Orleans Square Station, stop and listen—that beeping sound you hear is Walt Disney's 1955 Disneyland Park opening speech in telegraphic code. And don't forget to ride from Tomorrowland back to Main Street, so you can enjoy an unexpected treat: two large indoor dioramas inside the train tunnel, one depicting the Grand Canyon and another depicting a primeval world, complete with large-scale dinosaurs!

TREASURE Windows on Main Street | **LOCATION** Main Street, U.S.A.

THE NAMES ON THE MAIN STREET WINDOWS represent very special people who have had a profound influence on the park in some way, like guardian angels looking over park guests. The names are also often associated with "professions" related to what the person used to do when he or she worked for Disney. For example, the inscription for a window dedicated to the person who modeled Disneyland's waterways reads, DECORATIVE FOUNTAINS AND WATERCOLOR BY FRED JOERGER. Disneyland still occasionally bestows this window honor in official dedication ceremonies in the park.

TREASURE Frontierland Shootin' Exposition | **LOCATION** Frontierland
SMACK IN THE MIDDLE OF FRONTIERLAND is the shooting gallery where cowpokes can close an eye and squeeze the trigger to try to get their target to ping, ting, move, or light up. Don't discount the Frontierland Shootin' Exposition as just another arcade gimmick. Everything about this well-themed attraction is dusty and rustic—except the laser-powered guns, which are both safe and cause little wear on the targets. About the only things missing are blowing tumbleweeds.

TREASURE Edible Plants | **LOCATION** Tomorrowland
THE DISNEY THEME PARKS are known for their magnificent landscaping, but did you know that many of the plants in Tomorrowland are edible, emphasizing the practicality of a future where the garden plants do double-duty as your vegetable garden? For example, the entryway to Tomorrowland is lined with orange trees, and the bushes along the walkways are planted with leafy vegetables such as lettuce, kale, and rhubarb, as well as herbs such as sage, chives, rosemary, and basil.

TREASURE Flag Retreat Ceremony | **LOCATION** Main Street Square
EVERY DAY IN THE AFTERNOON, the Disneyland Band or Dapper Dans vocal group marches to the front of Main Street to perform a number of Americana tunes. Park security guards then lower the American flag as the band plays "The Star-Spangled Banner" in this very respectful ceremony.

TREASURE *Partners* statue | **LOCATION** Central Plaza
AT THE CASTLE END of Main Street, in the center of the circular hub, is a bronze statue of Walt Disney holding the hand of Mickey Mouse. The statue, simply called *Partners*, pays homage to the two original ambassadors of Disneyland. If you stand in front of the statue, you can get a nice shot of it with Sleeping Beauty Castle in the background. The spot is encircled by a bench, and it's a great place to meet should your family decide to split up to visit different lands. Smaller statues of other popular Disney figures such as Dumbo, Goofy, and Pluto form a ring around this garden oasis in the middle of the park.

QUIET PLACES AT DISNEYLAND PARK

PEACE AND QUIET are anything but the norm at Disneyland. Yet sometimes when you're overwhelmed by it all, a place to decompress is worth a lot, as a reader from Culver City, California, points out:

> I can't tolerate the hyperstimulation as well as my husband and kids do. Sometimes when I'm on my ninth nerve, I'd give anything to put myself in time-out and just collapse for a while. Are there any nice out-of-the-way places in the park where this is possible?

Actually, there are a few. A **pier** with a canopy and benches, opposite the Matterhorn Bobsleds loading area, overlooks a quiet pool. There's still ambient noise, of course, but the pier is far enough removed from the action to afford both tranquility and a lovely setting. The **Hungry Bear Restaurant** in Critter Country offers upper and lower covered outdoor decks overlooking the Rivers of America. In between major feeding periods, the decks are decidedly low-key. **Snow White's Grotto and Wishing Well** (see page 269) is also very pleasant, though it does have a modest but continuous flow of pedestrian traffic. Finally, the alfresco dining area of **Troubadour Tavern,** adjacent to Fantasyland Theatre, is relaxing between shows.

TRAFFIC PATTERNS
at DISNEYLAND PARK

1. WHAT ATTRACTIONS AND WHICH SECTIONS OF THE PARK DO VISITORS HEAD FOR WHEN THEY FIRST ARRIVE? When guests are admitted, the flow of people to Star Wars: Galaxy's Edge is heaviest, followed by Tomorrowland (Space Mountain, Buzz Lightyear Astro Blasters, Star Tours, and Finding Nemo Submarine Voyage). The next most crowded land is Fantasyland, though the crowds are distributed over a larger number of attractions. Critter Country is likewise crowded with its small area and only two attractions (Splash Mountain and The Many Adventures of Winnie the Pooh). Adventureland, Frontierland, and New Orleans Square fill more slowly, with Mickey's Toontown not really coming alive until later in the morning. As the park fills, visitors appear to head for specific favored attractions that they wish to ride before the lines get long. This, more than any other factor, determines traffic patterns in the mornings and accounts for the relatively equal distribution of visitors throughout Disneyland, though Galaxy's Edge is currently drawing the lion's share of guests, with the overflow impacting the adjacent areas of Frontierland, Fantasyland, and Critter Country; former top draws in Adventureland and Tomorrowland have seen corresponding drops in their crowds.

ATTRACTIONS HEAVILY ATTENDED IN EARLY MORNING
ADVENTURELAND Indiana Jones Adventure | Jungle Cruise
CRITTER COUNTRY Splash Mountain
FANTASYLAND Alice in Wonderland | Dumbo the Flying Elephant | Matterhorn Bobsleds | Peter Pan's Flight
STAR WARS: GALAXY'S EDGE *Millennium Falcon:* Smugglers Run | Star Wars: Rise of the Resistance
TOMORROWLAND Buzz Lightyear Astro Blasters | Finding Nemo Submarine VoyageSpace Mountain | Star Tours—The Adventures Continue

2. HOW LONG DOES IT TAKE FOR THE PARK TO REACH PEAK CAPACITY FOR A GIVEN DAY? HOW ARE THE VISITORS DISPERSED THROUGHOUT THE PARK? A surge of early birds arrives before or around opening time but is quickly dispersed throughout the empty park. After the initial onslaught is absorbed, there is a bit of a lull that lasts until about an hour after opening. Following the lull, the park is inundated with arriving guests for about 2 hours, peaking 10–11 a.m. Guests continue to arrive in a steady but diminishing stream until around 2 p.m.

Sampled lines reached their longest length noon–3 p.m., indicating more arrivals than departures in the early afternoon. For general touring purposes, most attractions develop substantial lines 9:30–11 a.m.

In the early morning, Star Wars: Galaxy's Edge, Tomorrowland, Critter Country, and Fantasyland fill up first. By late morning and into early afternoon, attendance is fairly equally distributed throughout all of the "lands" except Galaxy's Edge. Mickey's Toontown, because it is comparatively small, stays mobbed from about 11:30 a.m. on. By midafternoon, however, we noted a concentration of visitors in Fantasyland, New Orleans Square, and Adventureland, and a slight decrease of visitors in Tomorrowland.

In the late afternoon and early evening, attendance continues to be more heavily distributed in Galaxy's Edge, Tomorrowland, Critter Country, and Fantasyland. Though Space Mountain, Buzz Lightyear Astro Blasters, Splash Mountain, and Star Tours remain inundated throughout the day, most of the other attractions in Tomorrowland and Critter Country have reasonable lines. In New Orleans Square, The Haunted Mansion, Pirates of the Caribbean, and the multitudes returning from nearby Critter Country keep traffic brisk. Frontierland (except Big Thunder Mountain Railroad) and Adventureland (except Indiana Jones Adventure) become less congested as the afternoon and evening progress.

3. HOW DO MOST VISITORS GO ABOUT TOURING THE PARK? IS THERE A DIFFERENCE IN THE TOURING BEHAVIOR OF FIRST-TIME VISITORS AND REPEAT VISITORS? Many first-time visitors accompany relatives or friends who are familiar with Disneyland and who guide their tour. These tours sometimes proceed in an orderly (clockwise or counterclockwise) sequence. First-time visitors without personal touring guidance tend to be more orderly in their touring. Many first-time visitors, however, are drawn to Sleeping Beauty Castle on entering the park and thus commence their rotation from Fantasyland. Repeat visitors usually proceed directly to their favorite attractions or to whatever is new. And, of course, *Star Wars* fans are sprinting en masse straight toward Galaxy's Edge.

4. WHAT EFFECT DO SPECIAL EVENTS HAVE ON TRAFFIC PATTERNS? Special events such as parades, fireworks, and *Fantasmic!* pull substantial numbers of visitors from the lines for rides. Unfortunately, however, the left hand taketh what the right hand giveth. A parade or *Fantasmic!* snarls traffic flow throughout Disneyland so much that guests find themselves captive wherever they are. Attraction lines in Tomorrowland and Adventureland diminish dramatically, making Space Mountain, Finding Nemo Submarine Voyage, Buzz Lightyear Astro Blasters, Star Tours, Jungle Cruise, and Indiana Jones Adventure particularly good choices during the evening festivities. Crowds in Mickey's Toontown and Fantasyland (behind the castle) also wane at night, but the rides there close prior to the fireworks for safety reasons. Critter Country, New Orleans Square, Frontierland, Main Street, and Small World Mall in Fantasyland are so congested with guests viewing the parade or *Fantasmic!* that it's almost impossible to move. Conversely, when *Fantasmic!* is on hiatus, the crowds that would otherwise be watching it must go elsewhere, chiefly toward the parade route and attraction queues. Because it's relatively isolated from the other lands, Galaxy's Edge crowds aren't greatly impacted by special performances.

5. WHAT ARE THE TRAFFIC PATTERNS NEAR TO AND AT CLOSING TIME? On our sample days, which were recorded in and out of season, park departures outnumbered arrivals beginning in midafternoon, with a substantial number of guests leaving after the afternoon parade. Additional numbers of visitors departed during the late afternoon as the dinner hour approached. When the park closed early, there were steady departures during the 2 hours preceding closing, with a mass exodus of remaining visitors at closing time.

When the park closed late, departures were distributed throughout the evening hours, with waves of departures following the evening parade(s), fireworks, and *Fantasmic!* Though departures increased exponentially as closing time approached, a huge throng was still on hand when the park finally shut down. The balloon effect of this last throng at the end of the day generally overwhelmed the shops on Main Street, the parking lot, trams, and the hotel shuttles, as well as the exits onto adjoining Anaheim streets. In the hour before closing in the lands other than Main Street, touring conditions were normally uncrowded except inside Galaxy's Edge and at Indiana Jones Adventure in Adventureland, Space Mountain in Tomorrowland, and Splash Mountain in Critter Country.

DISNEYLAND PARK TOURING PLANS

THE GOAL OF OUR STEP-BY-STEP TOURING PLANS is to help you see as much as possible with a minimum of time wasted standing in line. They are designed to avoid crowds and bottlenecks on days of moderate to heavy attendance. On days of lighter attendance (see "Selecting the Time of Year for Your Visit," page 23), the plans will still save you time but will not be as critical to successful touring.

Rest assured that there will be an army of cast members directing the way to Star Wars: Galaxy's Edge. Simply seeing its two headliner attractions could consume a significant chunk of your day. Arriving an hour before rope drop may no longer be enough; some eager fans have attempted to camp out overnight, or at least arrive before dawn.

Choosing the Right Touring Plan

If you have two days to spend at Disneyland Park, the two-day touring plans are by far the most relaxed and efficient. The Two-Day Touring Plan A takes advantage of early-morning touring, when lines are short and the park has not yet filled with guests. This plan works well all year and is particularly recommended for days when Disneyland Park closes before 8 p.m. On the other hand, Two-Day Touring Plan B combines the efficiencies of early-morning touring on the first day with the splendor of Disneyland Park at night on the second day. This plan is perfect for guests who wish to sample both the attractions and the special magic of Disneyland Park after dark, including *Fantasmic!*, parades, and fireworks. The Two-Day Touring Plan for Adults with Small Children spreads the experience over two more-relaxed days and incorporates more attractions that both children and parents will enjoy.

For readers who have requested a Three-Day Park-Hopper Touring Plan, we recommend using the Two-Day Disneyland Park Touring Plan of your choice and mixing it with the One-Day Disney California Adventure Touring Plan as you see fit. Enter Disneyland Park first, and then send a runner across the Esplanade to DCA with your entire group's tickets (or use MaxPass) to collect FastPasses for *World of Color*. Just keep an eye on your return windows when juggling cross-park FastPasses, as attendants enforce the expiration times.

If you have only one day but wish to see as much as possible, use the One-Day Touring Plan for Adults. This plan will pack as much into a single day as is humanly possible, but it is pretty exhausting. If you prefer a more relaxed visit, try the Author's Select One-Day Touring Plan. This plan features the best that Disneyland Park has to offer (in the authors' opinion), eliminating some of the less impressive attractions.

If you have small children, you may want to use the Dumbo-or-Die-in-a-Day Touring Plan for Adults with Small Children. This plan includes most of the children's rides in Fantasyland and Mickey's Toontown and omits roller coasters and other attractions that small children cannot ride (because of Disney's age and height requirements), as well as rides and shows that are frightening for small children. Because this plan calls for adults to sacrifice many of the better Disney attractions, it is not recommended unless you are touring Disneyland Park primarily for the benefit of your children. In essence, you pretty much stand around, sweat, wipe noses, pay for stuff, and watch the children have fun. It's great.

An alternative to the Dumbo plan is the One-Day Touring Plan for Adults or the Galaxy's Edge and Best of Disneyland One-Day Plan, taking advantage of switching off (see page 147). Switching off allows adults to enjoy the wilder rides while keeping the whole group together.

For guests who really want to burn the candle at both ends (as well as a bunch of money) by buying a single-day Park Hopper, we offer a one-day/two-park touring plan that touches on the highlights of Disney California Adventure in the morning and Disneyland in the afternoon.

PRELIMINARY INSTRUCTIONS FOR ALL DISNEYLAND PARK TOURING PLANS

ON DAYS OF MODERATE to heavy attendance, follow the touring plans exactly, deviating only when you do not wish to experience a listed show or ride. For instance, the touring plan may direct you to go next to Big Thunder Mountain Railroad, a roller coaster. If you do not like roller coasters, simply skip that step and proceed to the next activity.

1. Buy your admission in advance (see "Admission Options" on page 17).

2. Call ☎ 714-781-7290 the day before you go for the official opening time.

3. Become familiar with the park-opening procedures (described on page 216) and read over the touring plan of your choice, so you will have a basic understanding of what you are likely to encounter as you enter the park.

THE BEST OF DISNEYLAND RESORT IN ONE DAY
(pages 369–370)

FOR Guests who really want to burn the candle at both ends (and a bunch of money) by buying a single-day Park Hopper.

ASSUMES Willingness to experience all major rides (including roller coasters) and shows in both parks and to walk a lot.

This plan is for groups who wish to visit both Disneyland and DCA in one day. Most of the major, must-see attractions are included for each park. The plan starts in DCA with Guardians of the Galaxy—Mission: Breakout! and switches over to Disneyland in the afternoon, finishing the night with Space Mountain. This plan is only recommended on days when the parks open early and stay open late. Try to finish up the DCA portion of this plan by 1 p.m., so you have enough time to ride everything in Disneyland.

ABOUT EARLY ENTRY If you are eligible for early entry, experience (1) Guardians of the Galaxy—Mission: Breakout!, (2) Luigi's Rollickin' Roadsters, (3) Mater's Junkyard Jamboree, and (4) Toy Story Midway Mania!, in that order, followed by (5) Soarin' Around the World (time permitting). Pick up FastPasses for (6) Radiator Springs Racers before official park opening. Begin the touring plan after getting your FastPasses, skipping any attractions you've already seen, and return to ride Radiator Springs Racers once your FastPass window starts.

DCA normally hosts early entry on Sunday, Monday, Wednesday, and Friday. Unlike Disneyland, DCA's early entry is for hotel guests only; Magic Morning ticket holders may not enter early. If you are not eligible for early entry, try not to use the plan on an early-entry day. Cars Land may be busy with early-entry guests before you even get past the turnstiles.

AUTHORS' SELECT ONE-DAY PLAN WITH
STAR WARS: GALAXY'S EDGE *(page 371)*

FOR Adults without small children who want to experience Star Wars: Galaxy's Edge.

ASSUMES Willingness to experience all major rides (including roller coasters) and shows.

Be forewarned that this plan requires a lot of walking and some backtracking; this is necessary to avoid long waits in line. A little extra walking coupled with some hustle in the morning will save you 2–3 hours of standing in line. Note that you might not complete this tour. How far you get will depend on the size of your group, how quickly you move from ride to ride, how many times you pause for rest or food, how quickly the park fills, and what time the park closes.

STAR WARS: GALAXY'S EDGE AND BEST OF DISNEYLAND ONE-DAY PLAN FOR ADULTS WITH SMALL CHILDREN *(page 372)*

FOR Parents with children under age 7 who want to experience Star Wars: Galaxy's Edge.

ASSUMES Periodic stops for rest, restrooms, and refreshment.

We expect that riding one ride in Star Wars: Galaxy's Edge and experiencing the land will take about half a day (up to 5 hours). After leaving Galaxy's Edge, this plan hits most of the highest-rated Disneyland rides for children, such as Peter Pan's Flight, Alice in Wonderland, and Dumbo.

STAR WARS: GALAXY'S EDGE COMPLETE TOURING PLAN *(page 373)*

FOR Those who want to experience everything Star Wars: Galaxy's Edge has to offer.

ASSUMES Periodic stops for rest, restrooms, and refreshment.

This plan starts with rides on Rise of the Resistance and *Millennium Falcon:* Smugglers Run, then moves on to drinks at Oga's Cantina, the very popular lightsaber presentation at Savi's Workshop, shopping and general exploration of the land, and wraps up with viewing the evening fireworks near the *Millennium Falcon.* Also be sure to try the interactive games in the Play Disney Parks app as you wait in the attraction queues and wander around the land. At 7 a.m. on the morning of your visit, make reservations for Savi's Workshop and Oga's Cantina by using the Disneyland app or visiting disneyland.com/savisworkshop and disneyland.com/cantina. Try to schedule Savi's for late morning and Oga's for midafternoon.

DISNEYLAND PARK ONE-DAY TOURING PLAN FOR ADULTS *(page 374)*

FOR Adults without small children.

ASSUMES Willingness to experience all major rides (including roller coasters) and shows.

If you have only one day and wish to see the "classic" Disneyland outside of Galaxy's Edge, use this touring plan. It packs as much into a single day as is humanly possible, but it is pretty exhausting. Be forewarned that this plan requires a lot of walking and some backtracking; this is necessary to avoid long waits in line. A little extra walking coupled with some hustle in the morning will save you 2–3 hours of standing in line. Note that you might not complete this tour. How far you get will depend on the size of your group, how quickly you move from ride to ride, how many times you pause for rest or food, how quickly the park fills, and what time the park closes.

ABOUT EARLY ENTRY If you are eligible for early entry, arrive at the turnstiles 45–60 minutes before the early-entry period begins on Tuesday, Thursday, or Saturday (days subject to change) with admission in hand. Upon admission to the park, experience (1) Peter Pan's Flight, (2) Alice in Wonderland, (3) Matterhorn Bobsleds, (4) Star Tours, and (5) Buzz Lightyear Astro Blasters, and then obtain FastPasses for Space Mountain, in that order. If you're not able to enjoy all of the above during the early-entry hour, see as many as you can. When the park opens to the general public, begin the touring plan, skipping any attractions you've already seen.

If you wish to tour on an early-entry day but are not eligible for early entry, visit Disney California Adventure and save Disneyland Park for a non-early-entry day (currently Sunday, Monday, Wednesday, or Friday). Do not attempt to use the plan on an early-entry day—Disneyland Park will be packed with early-entry guests before you even make it past the turnstiles.

Note: The success of this touring plan hinges on you being among the first to enter the park when it opens. Arrive at the entrance at least 40 minutes before official opening time.

DISNEYLAND PARK TWO-DAY TOURING PLAN FOR ADULTS WITH SMALL CHILDREN *(pages 375–376)*

FOR Parents with children under age 7 who wish to spread their Disneyland Park visit over two days.

ASSUMES Frequent stops for rest, restrooms, and refreshments.

This touring plan represents a compromise between the observed tastes of adults and the observed tastes of younger children. Included in this touring plan are many of the midway-type rides that your children may have the opportunity to experience at local fairs and amusement parks. These rides at Disneyland Park often require long waits in line, and they consume valuable touring time that could be better spent experiencing the many rides and shows found only at a Disney theme park and which best demonstrate the Disney genius. This touring plan is heavily weighted toward the tastes of younger children. If you want to balance it a bit, try working out a compromise with your kids to forgo some of the carnival-type rides (such as Mad Tea Party, Dumbo, King Arthur Carrousel, and Gadget's Go Coaster) or such rides as Autopia. All of the attractions are appropriate for children 40 inches and shorter.

Another alternative is to use one of the other two-day touring plans and take advantage of the switching-off option (see page 147). This technique allows parents of small children to take turns enjoying rides such as Space Mountain, Indiana Jones Adventure, Big Thunder Mountain Railroad, Star Tours, and Splash Mountain.

TIMING This two-day touring plan takes advantage of early-morning touring. On each day you should complete the structured part of the plan by 3 p.m. or so. We highly recommend returning to your hotel by midafternoon for a nap and an early dinner. If the park is open in the evening, come back to the park by 7:30 or 8 p.m. for the evening parade, fireworks, and *Fantasmic!*

ABOUT EARLY ENTRY If you are eligible for early entry, experience (1) Peter Pan's Flight, (2) Alice in Wonderland, (3) Mr. Toad's Wild Ride, and (4) Dumbo, in that order, followed by the other Fantasyland attractions. At the end of the early-entry hour, begin day two of the touring plan, skipping any attractions you've already seen.

Do not attempt to use day two of the touring plan on early-entry days if you are not eligible for early entry—Fantasyland will be packed with early-entry guests before you even make it past the turnstiles. Day one of the plan begins in Adventureland, which is not affected by early entry. Come back to Disneyland Park on the following non-early-entry day and proceed with day two. You can do day two first (the order makes no difference) as your travel plans dictate.

Note: Because the needs of small children are so varied, we have not built specific instructions for eating into the touring plan. Simply stop for refreshments or a meal when you feel the urge. For best results, however, try to keep moving in the morning. In the afternoon, you can eat, rest often, and adjust the pace to your liking.

DISNEYLAND PARK TWO-DAY TOURING PLAN A, FOR DAYTIME TOURING OR FOR WHEN THE PARK CLOSES EARLY *(pages 377–378)*

FOR Parties wishing to spread their Disneyland Park visit over two days and parties preferring to tour in the morning.

ASSUMES Willingness to experience all major rides (including roller coasters) and shows.

TIMING This two-day touring plan takes advantage of early-morning touring and is the most efficient of all the touring plans for comprehensive touring with the least time lost waiting in line. On each day you should complete the structured part of the plan by 3 p.m. or so. If you are visiting Disneyland Park during a period of the year when the park is open late (after 8 p.m.), you might prefer our Two-Day Touring Plan B, which offers morning touring on one day and late afternoon and evening touring on the other day. Another highly recommended option is to return to your hotel around midafternoon for a well-deserved nap and an early dinner and to come back to the park by 7:30 or 8 p.m. for the evening parade, fireworks, and live entertainment.

ABOUT EARLY ENTRY If you're eligible for early entry, experience (1) Peter Pan's Flight, (2) Alice in Wonderland, (3) Mr. Toad's Wild Ride, and (4) Matterhorn Bobsleds, in that order. If you're not able to enjoy all of the above during the early-entry hour, ride as many as you can. When the park opens to the general public, begin day one of the touring plan, skipping any attractions you've already seen.

Do not attempt to use the plan on early-entry days if you are not eligible for early entry—Disneyland Park will be packed with early-entry guests before you even make it past the turnstiles. Do day one of the plan on a non-early-entry day. The next day will be an early-entry day, so visit Disney California Adventure on that day. Come back to Disneyland Park on the following non-early-entry day and proceed with day two.

DISNEYLAND PARK TWO-DAY TOURING PLAN B, FOR MORNING AND EVENING TOURING OR FOR WHEN THE PARK IS OPEN LATE *(pages 379–380)*

FOR Parties who want to enjoy Disneyland Park at different times of day, including evenings and early mornings.

ASSUMES Willingness to experience all major rides (including roller coasters) and shows.

TIMING This two-day touring plan is for those visiting Disneyland Park on days when the park is open late (after 8 p.m.). The plan offers morning touring on the first day and late afternoon and evening touring on the other day. If the park closes early, or if you prefer to do all of your touring during the morning and early afternoon, use the Two-Day Touring Plan A.

ABOUT EARLY ENTRY If you are eligible for early entry, experience (1) Peter Pan's Flight, (2) Alice in Wonderland, (3) Matterhorn Bobsleds, (4) Space Mountain, and (5) Finding Nemo Submarine Voyage, in that order. If you're not able to enjoy all of the above during the early-entry hour, ride as many as you can. When the park opens to the general public, begin day one of the touring plan, skipping any attractions you've already seen.

If you are not eligible for early entry, do not try to use day one of the plan on an early-entry day. Disneyland Park will be packed with early-entry guests before you even get past the turnstiles.

DUMBO-OR-DIE-IN-A-DAY TOURING PLAN FOR ADULTS WITH SMALL CHILDREN *(page 381)*

FOR Parents with children under age 7 who feel compelled to devote every waking moment to the pleasure and entertainment of their small children.

ASSUMES Periodic stops for rest, restrooms, and refreshment.

The name of this touring plan notwithstanding, this itinerary is not a joke. Regardless of whether you are loving, guilty, masochistic, truly selfless, insane, or saintly, this touring plan will provide a small child with about as perfect a day as possible at Disneyland Park.

If this description has intimidated you somewhat or if you have concluded that your day at Disneyland Park is as important as your children's, use the One-Day Touring Plan for Adults, making use of the switching-off option (see page 147) at those attractions that impose height or age restrictions.

Because the children's attractions in Disneyland Park are the most poorly engineered in terms of handling large crowds, this touring plan is the least efficient of our touring plans. It does represent the best way to experience most of the child-oriented attractions in one day, if that is what you hope to do. We do not make recommendations in this plan for meals. If you can, try to hustle along as quickly as is comfortable until about noon. After noon, it won't make much difference if you stop to eat or take it a little easier.

ABOUT EARLY ENTRY If you are eligible for early entry, experience (1) Peter Pan's Flight, (2) Dumbo, and (3) Alice in Wonderland, in that order, and then begin the touring plan, skipping any attractions you've already seen.

If you wish to tour on an early-entry day but are not eligible for early entry, visit Disney California Adventure and save Disneyland Park for a non-early-entry day (currently Sunday, Monday, Wednesday, or Friday). Do not attempt to use the plan on an early-entry day—Disneyland Park will be packed with early-entry guests before you even make it past the turnstiles.

Note: The success of this touring plan hinges on you being among the first to enter the park when it opens. Arrive at the entrance 40 minutes before official opening time.

THE DISNEYLAND NO RIDES, NO QUEUES, NO STRESS ANTI-TOURING PLAN

MOST OF OUR READERS are interested in touring plans to get them through as many attractions as possible in the most efficient manner. But, like the authors, some of you may have siblings, spouses, or other companions who are congenitally opposed to queuing for anything clanking or claustrophobic. What can Disney do to occupy your Aunt Gertie, who is dead set against standing in a line, or sitting in anything with a lap bar?

Disneyland Park is one of the few places where you can experience a full day of entertainment without getting on a ride faster than the railroad, and without waiting more than 15 minutes or so, even during the busiest season.

Yes, you can get your money's worth at Disneyland without sprinting to Space Mountain or spinning in a teacup. You just have to adjust your expectation of what constitutes an attraction. (A handful of sedate activities are available at Disney California Adventure, such as Disney Animation, the winery, and the bakery tour, but not enough to justify a full-price pass.)

Because this "anti-touring" plan is designed to eliminate stress, there is no strict order to follow the steps in, nor instructions to arrive before rope drop (though it doesn't hurt). Simply tour the park as your feet take you, skipping any suggested experiences that don't interest you. If there is more than a 15- to 20-minute wait for anything you want to do, simply move along and check back later. Most important, take a break after 4 or 5 hours and leave the park for a nap, meal, or swim. The key is to take your time and (literally) stop to smell the roses.

Main Street, U.S.A.

- Ride one of the vintage vehicles up Main Street to the hub, and then take a different one back.

- Look at the memorabilia in the Main Street Station, and then ride the rails for a round-trip or two around the park.

- Explore the Disneyana shop's collectible artwork inside the old Bank of Main Street.

- Peer in the Emporium's high-tech animated window displays.

- See *Great Moments with Mr. Lincoln,* arriving early enough to see the lobby's Disney Gallery historical displays.

- Watch the classic short films inside the Main Street Cinema.

- Snoop on the antique party line telephones inside the Market House, and then sit outside at a table on Center Street, listening to the amusing sounds emanating from the windows above.

- Check out the primitive 3-D movie viewers in the Penny Arcade.

- Watch the chefs in the candy store whip up a batch of sweets. On select days during the holidays, the handmade supersize candy canes are a can't-miss. They are in short supply, so you'll need to line up early and receive a numbered wristband to buy one, but anyone can watch them being made.

- Catch a performance or three of the Dapper Dans, Main Street Marching Band, or Coke Corner ragtime pianist. The daily flag retreat ceremony is not to be missed.

- Try to identify the names of Disney Legends and Imagineers honored on Main Street's windows.

- Stop and watch some artisans—such as the silhouette cutters and glass sculptors—work.

- Ask the prestidigitators at the Magic Shop to demonstrate some tricks for you, and stare at the creepy optical illusion in the window.

- On the right side of the street next to the silhouette shop, sit in the chairs on the porch.

- Take a picture with the *Partners* statue in the central hub, and appreciate the surrounding flora and fauna.

Adventureland

- See the *Enchanted Tiki Room,* arriving in time to buy a Dole Whip and watch the preshow. After exiting the show, visit with Rosita at the neighboring Tropical Hideaway.

- Jungle Cruise is gentle fun if the line isn't long.
- If stairs aren't an issue, climb Tarzan's Treehouse, or at least enter through the exit and watch the kids going wild on the playground.
- Consider walking through the Indiana Jones Adventure queue at least once, even if you aren't interested in riding; it's an impressive (if exhausting) example of scenic design. When the posted wait time is more than 15 minutes, get a FastPass to skip the boring exterior line. Before you climb the stairs near the loading bay, simply tell a cast member that you want to exit. If you are brave but impatient, Indy's single-rider line often has little to no wait.

New Orleans Square

- Haunted Mansion and Pirates of the Caribbean both move guests through quickly even on busy days, and neither is likely to disturb any but the most delicate constitutions.
- Seek out the jazz and pirate bands that play in the area.
- Poke around the lovingly detailed alleyways around the Pirates of the Caribbean exit.
- Sit outside Café Orléans with a plate of *pommes frites* and watch the crowds go by.

Critter Country

- Stand on the bridge near Splash Mountain and watch riders take the plunge. If you dare to get damp, the single-rider wait is usually bearable.
- Observe the ducks from the porch behind the Hungry Bear Restaurant.

Star Wars: Galaxy's Edge

- Explore the environs of Black Spire Outpost, admiring the imaginative architecture and realistic rockwork and interacting with the droids and aliens that roam the area.
- Use the Play Disney Parks app on your smartphone to decode alien languages and discover other hidden features around Batuu.
- Browse for unique *Star Wars* souvenirs in Galaxy Edge's bazaar.
- Grab some galactic grub from the vendor stalls.

Frontierland

- Take a raft to Tom Sawyer Island, and explore the island.
- Sail on the Sailing Ship *Columbia, Mark Twain* Riverboat, or both. You can usually step on board just before departure time without standing in line, or board early for the best seat at the top front.
- Grab some chili and a box seat for the show in The Golden Horseshoe.
- Look for the petrified tree that was an anniversary gift from Walt to his wife; she donated it to the park. Also try to spot railroad tunnel remains from Mine Train Through Nature's Wonderland, across from Big Thunder Mountain.

- Sharpen your aim at the Frontierland Shootin' Exposition.
- Walk through the Rancho del Zocalo patio, especially when decorated for Dia de Los Muertos.

Fantasyland

- Go through the Sleeping Beauty Castle walk-through, or watch the alternative experience video.
- Make a wish at Snow White's well in front of the castle, and gaze at her grotto of handcrafted sculptures.
- Cruise Storybook Land Canal Boats or It's a Small World if lines are short.
- Try on some mouse ears in the Mad Hatter chapeau shop.
- Take a break with a vendor treat (such as an ear of corn) on the benches at the old motorboat dock across from the Matterhorn Bobsleds.
- Stick your head in the Fantasy Faire if a show is scheduled, but don't bother with the massive queue to meet a princess.
- The elevated mall near It's a Small World is a convenient spot to stand for the parade or fireworks show.
- Enjoy the stage musical inside Fantasyland Theatre.

Mickey's Toontown

- Play with the interactive doodads dotted around the building facades.
- Take a tour of Mickey's and Minnie's homes, but bail on the meet and greet if the line is out the door.
- Walk though the cleverly decorated children's playgrounds, being wary of bouncing babes.

Tomorrowland

- Take the monorail to Downtown Disney for a bite or a drink, and then return (remember your park ticket!).
- Check the schedule for entertainment on the Tomorrowland Terrace stage.
- Experience the film clips inside the Tomorrowland Theater.
- See the alternative experience at the Finding Nemo Submarine Voyage.
- The line for Buzz Lightyear Astro Blasters moves swiftly, and almost everyone of all ages loves it.
- Browse the *Star Wars* merchandise (including build-your-own light sabers and droid action figures) in The Star Trader with a life-size X-wing overhead.
- Search for imaginatively groomed edible plants along the walkways.
- Explore the Star Wars Launch Bay exhibits.

PART SIX

DISNEY CALIFORNIA ADVENTURE

> *We enjoyed DCA much more than Disneyland Park. More fun, fewer strollers and little kids, more-adventurous people. Just a different feeling all the way around.*
>
> —Mom from Bend, Oregon

A MOST ANTICIPATED SEQUEL

DISNEY CALIFORNIA ADVENTURE held its grand opening on February 8, 2001. Known as DCA among Disneyphiles, the park is a bouquet of contradictions conceived in Fantasyland, starved in utero by corporate Disney, and born into a hostile environment of Disneyland loyalists who believed they'd been handed a second-rate theme park. Its parts are stunningly beautiful yet come together awkwardly, failing to compose a handsome whole. And perhaps most lamentable of all, the California theme is impotent by virtue of being all-encompassing. But after a billion-dollar metamorphosis, DCA overcame its inauspicious debut and emerged as an honorable companion to its storied older sibling across the Esplanade.

The history of the park is another of those convoluted tales found only in Robert Ludlum novels and corporate Disney. Southern California Disney fans began clamoring for a second theme park shortly after Epcot opened at Walt Disney World in 1982. Though there was some element of support within the Walt Disney Company, the Disney loyal had to content themselves with rumors and half-promises for two decades while they watched new Disney parks go up in Tokyo, Paris, and Florida. For years, Disney teasingly floated the Westcot concept, a California version of Epcot that was always just about to break ground. Whether it was a matter of procrastination or simply pursuing better opportunities elsewhere, the Walt Disney Company sat on the sidelines while the sleepy community of Anaheim became a sprawling city and property values skyrocketed. By the time Disney emerged

Disney California Adventure

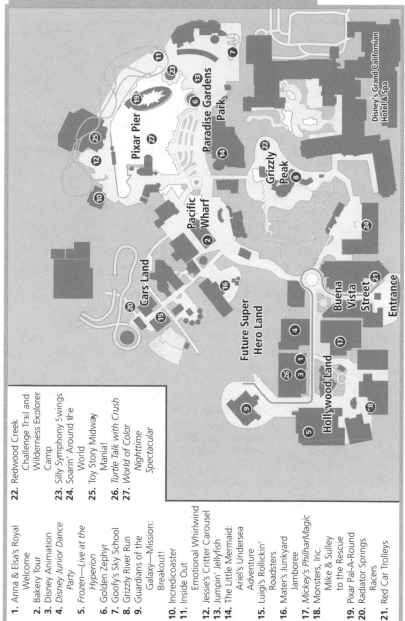

1. Anna & Elsa's Royal Welcome
2. Bakery Tour
3. Disney Animation
4. Disney Junior Dance Party
5. *Frozen—Live at the Hyperion*
6. Golden Zephyr
7. Goofy's Sky School
8. Grizzly River Run
9. Guardians of the Galaxy—Mission: Breakout!
10. Incredicoaster
11. Inside Out Emotional Whirlwind
12. Jessie's Critter Carousel
13. Jumpin' Jellyfish
14. The Little Mermaid: Ariel's Undersea Adventure
15. Luigi's Rollickin' Roadsters
16. Mater's Junkyard Jamboree
17. *Mickey's PhilharMagic*
18. Monsters, Inc. Mike & Sulley to the Rescue
19. Pixar Pal-A-Round
20. Radiator Springs Racers
21. Red Car Trolleys

22. Redwood Creek Challenge Trail and Wilderness Explorer Camp
23. Silly Symphony Swings
24. Soarin' Around the World
25. Toy Story Midway Mania!
26. *Turtle Talk with Crush*
27. *World of Color Nighttime Spectacular*

from its Westcot fantasy and began to get serious about a second California park, the price tag—not to mention the complexity of integrating such a development into a mature city—was mind-boggling.

Westcot had been billed as a $2- to $3 billion, 100-plus-acre project, so that was what the Disney faithful were expecting when DCA was announced. What they got was a park that cost $1.4 billion (slashed from an original budget of about $2.1 billion), built on 55 acres, including a sizable piece carved out for the Grand Californian Hotel. It's quite a small park by modern theme park standards, but $1.4 billion, when lavished on 55 acres, ought to buy a pretty good park.

Then there's the park's theme. Though flexible, California Adventure came off like a default setting, lacking in imagination, weak in concept, and without intrinsic appeal, especially when you stop to consider that two-thirds of Disneyland guests come from Southern California. As further grist for the mill, before the arrival of Cars Land, there was precious little new technology at work in Disney's newest theme park. Of the headliner attractions, only two—Soarin' Over California (now Soarin' Around the World), a simulator ride, and Toy Story Midway Mania!, a virtual dark ride—broke new ground. Most of the rest were recycled, albeit popular, attractions from the Animal Kingdom and Disney's Hollywood Studios. When you move to the smaller-statured second half of the attraction batting order, it gets worse. Most of these attractions are little more than off-the-shelf midway rides spruced up with a Disney story line and facade.

From a competitive perspective, DCA was an underwhelming shot at Disney's three Southern California competitors. The Hollywood section of DCA takes a hopeful poke at Universal Studios Hollywood, while the boardwalk-inspired area offers midway rides à la Six Flags Magic Mountain. Finally, the whole California theme has for years been the eminent domain of Knott's Berry Farm. In short, there's not much originality in DCA, only Disney's now-redundant mantra that "whatever they can do, we can do better."

Finally, after seven years of basically being in denial about DCA, the Walt Disney Company seemed willing to admit that this theme park (which pulled in only about a third of Disneyland's attendance annually) needed some help. On June 15, 2012, the Mouse held a grand reopening to celebrate the completion of a $1.1 billion effort, originally announced in 2007, to address DCA's problems.

Starting at the park entrance, the Imagineers scoured every inch of DCA, injecting charm, character, and ride capacity wherever they could. The current entryway embraces the legacy of Disneyland's founder with a nostalgic re-creation of 1920s Los Angeles. That freshly poured-on theming flowed all the way to the park's pier, where the tacky seaside amusements were softened with new-old Victorian-era stylings. An original family-friendly dark ride based on a popular Piscean princess was added, and the central lagoon now sports a Vegas-quality water show designed to keep crowds in DCA after dark. In 2012 the keystone

DISNEY CALIFORNIA ADVENTURE SERVICES
BABY CARE CENTER In Pacific Wharf, near the Ghirardelli Soda Fountain
BANKING SERVICES/CURRENCY EXCHANGE At the Chamber of Commerce at Buena Vista Street, immediately to your left upon entering
DISNEYLAND AND LOCAL ATTRACTION INFORMATION Information board at Carthay Circle
FIRST AID At the Chamber of Commerce
LIVE ENTERTAINMENT AND PARADE INFORMATION At the Chamber of Commerce
LOST ADULTS AND MESSAGES At the Chamber of Commerce
LOST AND FOUND Lost and Found for the entire resort is located west of the entrance to Disneyland Park.
LOST AND FOUND In Pacific Wharf next to the Baby Care Center
STORAGE LOCKERS Immediately to your right upon entering

of DCA's transformation fell into place with the opening of Cars Land, an entire area dedicated to the best-selling Pixar property.

In 2018, barely half a decade after the first revamp was completed, Disney embarked on yet another makeover of the park. DCA 3.0 ditches the quaint charm of the former Paradise Pier in favor of Pixar Pier, the new home for characters from *The Incredibles, Inside Out,* and *Toy Story.* And A Bug's Land and portions of Hollywood Land have made way for Marvel Super Hero attractions starring Spider-Man and the Avengers, scheduled to open beginning in 2020.

While the park spent its first decade as a punch line, today DCA is a legitimate destination in its own right. Some Disneyholics may never forgive DCA's dire beginnings, dismissing its upgrades as expensive attempts to patch over a flawed foundation. The rest of us will have some fun enjoying the park for what it is: the theme park equivalent of a jukebox musical, featuring a greatest hits collection of attractions also found in Walt Disney World's parks, along with just enough exclusive E-tickets to give DCA a unique personality all its own.

ARRIVING *and*
GETTING ORIENTED

THE ENTRANCE TO DCA faces the entrance to Disneyland Park across a brick-paved pedestrian plaza called the **Esplanade.** If you arrive by tram from one of the Disney parking lots, you'll disembark at the Esplanade. Facing east toward Harbor Boulevard, Disneyland Park will be on your left and DCA will be on your right. In the Esplanade are ticket booths, the group sales office, and resort information.

Seen from overhead, DCA is roughly arrayed in a fan shape around the park's central visual icon, Grizzly Peak. At ground level, however, the park's layout is not so obvious.

NOT TO BE MISSED AT DISNEY CALIFORNIA ADVENTURE
• **CARS LAND** Radiator Springs Racers
• **GRIZZLY PEAK** Grizzly River Run | Soarin' Around the World
• **HOLLYWOOD LAND** *Frozen—Live at the Hyperion* Guardians of the Galaxy—Mission: Breakout!
• **PARADISE GARDENS PARK** *World of Color*
• **PIXAR PIER** Incredicoaster | Toy Story Midway Mania!

There are currently six themed "lands" at DCA, not including **Buena Vista Street.** A left turn at the hub leads you to **Hollywood Land,** celebrating California's history as the film capital of the world. **Grizzly Peak** (which absorbed the former Condor Flats area) is reminiscent of the Pacific Northwest woods, while **Pacific Wharf** nods to Monterey's Cannery Row. You'll find Grizzly Peak by taking the first right as you approach the hub, though you must walk two-thirds of the way around the mountain to reach its namesake raft ride. Pacific Wharf is situated along a kidney-shaped lake and can be accessed by following the walkway emanating from the hub at 7 o'clock and winding around Grizzly Peak. The fourth land, **Pixar Pier,** recalls a seaside amusement park of the Victorian era that's been invaded by computer-generated cartoons. It is situated in the southwest corner of the park, on the far side of the large lake. **Paradise Gardens Park,** on the opposite shore of the lagoon, is the new name for the assortment of remaining ex–Paradise Pier attractions that weren't overtaken by Pixar. **Cars Land** is the sixth land, claiming a former parking lot behind Pacific Wharf, with its primary entrance across from the Golden Vine Winery. A seventh yet-unnamed land dedicated to Marvel's Super Heroes is under construction between Cars Land and Hollywood Land.

SINGLE-RIDER LINES

YOU CAN OFTEN SAVE TIME waiting in line by taking advantage of single-rider lines, a separate line for people who don't mind riding alone or with a stranger. The objective of single-rider lines is to fill odd spaces left by groups who don't quite fill the entire ride vehicle. Because there aren't many singles and most groups aren't willing to split up, single-rider lines are usually much shorter than the regular line. Four attractions at DCA offer single-rider lines: Goofy's Sky School, Grizzly River Run, Incredicoaster, and Radiator Springs Racers. A similar system called Moving Buddy, which is a pass that can be used by small groups of up to two adults plus one lap-seated child, is occasionally available at Toy Story Midway Mania! and Monsters Inc. Mike & Sulley to the Rescue.

PARK-OPENING PROCEDURES

DISNEYLAND RESORT HOTEL GUESTS get a 1-hour jump on the public four mornings each week through the Extra Magic Hours program, which includes access to Cars Land and other select rides around the park (see page 28). You'll be required to show a key card from one of the on-site hotels before being allowed to enjoy early entry. Disneyland Hotel and Paradise Pier guests must go to the park's main entrance; only Grand Californian guests are allowed through that hotel's private entrance into DCA before 11 a.m. The Grand Californian entrance is often overwhelmed, especially on early-entry days, so you may save time by walking to the front gate. All other guests will be allowed through the main entrance onto Buena Vista Street up to 1 hour early and held there until after a brief rope drop musical fanfare at the official opening time. Guests wishing to ride (or retrieve a FastPass for) Radiator Springs Racers first will gather to the right of Carthay Circle, while those headed to Guardians of the Galaxy—Mission: Breakout! line up to the left outside Hollywood Land. The crowd will be walked toward their destination at the appointed hour to avoid a stampede.

BUENA VISTA STREET

FROM THE ESPLANADE, you pass through a Streamline Moderne entrance facade, designed after Los Angeles's fabled Pan-Pacific Auditorium. (If it looks familiar, that's because it can also be recognized as the entrance to Disney's Hollywood Studios park in Florida.)

Once past the turnstiles, you'll find yourself on **Buena Vista Street,** a re-creation of 1920s Hollywood as Walt saw it when he first arrived. Immediately upon entering, to your left you'll find **Oswald's** (a souvenir shop with a snazzy antique car parked outside) and the **Chamber of Commerce.** The street leading to the central plaza is lined on both sides with a variety of shops and eateries with backstories referring to Disney's early biography. Among the shops on the east side is **Elias & Company** (the park's largest shop, named after Walt's father). The west side of the street features an indoor shopping arcade that leads to **Kingswell Camera Shop** (a PhotoPass printing location) and the **Trolley Treats** candy shop (check out the big Rock Candy Mountain model in the window), among others.

The hub area, called Carthay Circle, is home to the *Storytellers* statue (depicting a young Walt Disney with an early version of Mickey Mouse) and a replica of the **Carthay Circle Theater,** where *Snow White and the Seven Dwarfs* premiered in 1937; in this incarnation, it encloses an upscale restaurant and bar.

Winding past the shops and facades, the **Red Car Trolley** transports guests from the park entrance to Mission: Breakout! and back again.

Together, Buena Vista Street and Carthay Circle serve as a point of departure for the park's other various themed areas, as well as bring much-needed charm and warmth to DCA's opening act, forming a fantastic improvement over the flat cartoon-postcard facades that framed the former entryway.

Red Car Trolleys   ★★★

What it is Scenic in-park transportation. **Scope and scale** Minor attraction. **When to go** The first or last 2 hours the park is open. **Duration of ride** About 11 minutes. **Average wait in line per 100 people ahead of you** 12 minutes; assumes both cars in operation. **Loading speed** Very slow.

DESCRIPTION AND COMMENTS Much like the vintage vehicles that travel up and down Main Street, U.S.A., at Disneyland Park, these trolley cars add visual interest to DCA's entrance area but not much entertainment value. Modeled after the Pacific Electric Railway that served the Los Angeles area in the 1920s and 1930s (as seen in *Who Framed Roger Rabbit?*), the trolleys boast authentic details such as narrating conductors who share historical tidbits during your travels, retro-styled interior advertisements, and realistic overhead power lines—unelectrified, as the eco-friendly cars are actually battery-powered. More transportation than attraction, the Red Car Trolleys ferry guests on a one-way trip between Buena Vista Street near the park entrance and Guardians of the Galaxy—Mission: Breakout! (or back the other way), making stops in Carthay Circle and Hollywood Land along the way.

TOURING TIPS It is usually faster to walk the route than to wait for the next Red Car Trolley, but if you wish to experience this nostalgic transportation, do so in the morning. Hop on at the station near the Mission: Breakout! exit; it should be less crowded than the station near the park entrance.

The trolley briefly stops serving guests several times daily, so it can be commandeered as a stage for the Red Car Trolley News Boys show (see show schedule for details). The trolley's ding-ding-ding will be silenced into 2020 due to construction for the upcoming superhero attractions.

HOLLYWOOD LAND

THE ATTRACTIONS AND SHOPPING in Hollywood Land are inspired by California's (and Disney's) contribution to television and cinema. Visually, the land is themed as a studio back lot with sets, including an urban street scene, soundstages, and a central street with shops and restaurants that depict Hollywood's golden age. In 2018 Disney announced the creation of a new land that will be the West Coast headquarters of Spider-Man, Captain Marvel, Black Panther, and their fellow Marvel Super Heroes. The area, which is being built around the existing Guardians of the Galaxy attraction, encompasses the area previously occupied by the kid-centric A Bug's Land (which is now closed), along with portions of Hollywood Land. Early concept art implies that we'll see the land's boxy soundstages replaced with sci-fi architecture evoking Avengers headquarters and Dr. Strange's Sanctum Sanctorum. Precious little information has been officially released so far about the expansion, which is expected to begin opening in 2020. Disney has confirmed that an interactive attraction will allow guests to join Tony Stark's Worldwide Engineering Brigade (WEB) and experience what it's like to have amazing abilities like Spidey—who will wear an exclusive new suit for the occasion—and his friends. From what we've seen, it will be similar to Toy Story Midway Mania! but without the 3-D glasses. Immersive character encounters (such as lessons in the mystic arts from Dr. Strange) and an Ant-Man–inspired microbrewery are also whispered to be in the works, with talk of an Avengers-themed indoor roller coaster rumored for a later addition. The only thing we know you won't find is the Marvel name; the contract with Universal Orlando's Islands of Adventure prohibits Disney's parks from using the comic company's name in the United States.

Anna & Elsa's Royal Welcome ★★★

APPEAL BY AGE PRESCHOOL ★★★★½ GRADE SCHOOL ★★★★½ TEENS ★★★½ YOUNG ADULTS ★★★ OVER 30 ★★★½ SENIORS ★★★

What it is Character greeting with the Frozen sisters. **Scope and scale** Minor attraction. **When to go** Within the first 90 minutes after park opening, or an hour before closing. **Comment** Located inside Disney Animation. **Duration of experience** 3–5 minutes. **Probable waiting time** 20–30 minutes.

DESCRIPTION AND COMMENTS The popular ladies of Arendelle, Queen Elsa and Princess Anna, meet guests within the Disney Animation building. As an added bonus, Kristoff and Olaf sometimes take turns accompanying the sisters. Much like Fantasy Faire's Royal Hall, the Frozen character encounter is richly appointed and has multiple meeting rooms to increase capacity without ruining the magic.

TOURING TIPS In a sure sign that Frozen fever is cooling off, this meet and greet has gone from *requiring* FastPass to manage the maddening crowds to ditching FastPass entirely and still drawing queues of under an hour. Even with the drop-off in demand, the line here isn't particularly efficient, so if your party would like to meet the sisters, you should schedule it early in the day or shortly before closing.

Disney Animation ★★★½

APPEAL BY AGE PRESCHOOL ★★★½ GRADE SCHOOL ★★★★½ TEENS ★★★★ YOUNG ADULTS ★★★★½ OVER 30 ★★★★½ SENIORS ★★★★½

What it is Behind-the-scenes look at Disney animation. **Scope and scale** Major attraction. **When to go** Anytime. **Comment** Quite amusing, though not very educational. **Duration of experience** 40–55 minutes. **Probable waiting time** None.

Thumbs Up for the Whole Family

DESCRIPTION AND COMMENTS The Disney Animation building houses a variety of shows, galleries, and interactive exhibits that collectively provide a sort of crash course in animation. Moving from room to room and exhibit to exhibit, you follow the Disney animation process from concept to finished film, with a peek at each of the steps along the way. Throughout, you are surrounded by animation, and sometimes it's even projected above your head and under your feet!

Because it's not a working studio, the attraction doesn't showcase artists at work on real features, and the interactive exhibits are more whimsical than educational. "Sorcerer's Workshop," for example, is an interactive exhibit where you can use a book-shaped touch screen to discover which Disney character you most resemble.

The Animation Academy, hosted by a Disney cartoonist, teaches you how to draw a Disney character; if you have any artistic inclination, you may consider it DCA's best-kept secret and find yourself taking the class repeatedly, as a Salt Lake City reader suggests:

Animation Academy turned out to be one of my absolute favorite things. I did it four times in a row and would have gone more if I wasn't starving. I plan to devote quite a bit of time to it on my next trip.

And from a Sammamish, Washington, mom:

I took three, and they were the highlight of the trip. I have no drawing ability whatsoever, but following along with the instructor, I was able to make a pretty decent Donald, a passable Mickey, and a Pooh bear, though he looked like he was in a car accident. My 4-year-old loved drawing along, my husband loved it, and my 2-year-old loved scribbling on her paper and drawing board. It was fun for the whole family.

The Animation Academy classes normally rotate during the day through a dozen-odd different classic and current Disney characters, but at times it may be devoted to a single theme. New characters are often added in sync with their film's release.

Both "Sorcerer's Workshop" and Animation Academy provide a good foundation of the animation process and will enhance your appreciation of the other exhibits. Anna & Elsa's Royal Welcome (see page 291) and *Turtle Talk with Crush* (see page 297) are also located here.

TOURING TIPS On entering the Animation building, you'll step into a lobby where signs mark the entrances to the various exhibits. Look up in the lobby for a moment at the ultra-high-definition oversize projections of animations in process, including Disney's and Pixar's latest hits. It takes 40–55 minutes to do all the interactive stuff and see everything. You probably won't experience much of a wait for the Disney Animation offerings except on weekends and holidays. Even then, the Animation building clears out considerably by late afternoon.

Disney Junior Dance Party! ★★★

**APPEAL BY AGE   PRESCHOOL ★★★★½   GRADE SCHOOL ★★★★   TEENS ★★
YOUNG ADULTS ★★½   OVER 30 ★★★   SENIORS ★★**

What it is Live show for children. **Scope and scale** Minor attraction. **When to go** Per the daily entertainment schedule. **Comments** Audience sits on the floor. A must for families with preschoolers. **Duration of show** 24 minutes. **Probable waiting time** 25 minutes.

DESCRIPTION AND COMMENTS Tykes can work out their wiggles as their elders develop tinnitus during this exhaustingly exuberant interactive dance party. Two iPad-wielding live hosts sing and dance their way through a structure that quickly becomes familiar: a large video screen displays a long commercial for a Disney Junior series, then a character from that show appears in the flesh (or fur) for an audience participatory dance-along song. The featured shows include *Mickey and the Roadster Racers*, *Doc McStuffins*, *Vampirina*, and *The Lion Guard*, with Mickey and Minnie themselves arriving in time for the grand finale.

The minimalist story line makes this production seem more like a Disney Cruise Line deck party than a coherent piece of theater, but the production values—from the slickly edited interactive video segments to squeal-inducing bubbles and streamers—are solid enough to satisfy the toddler target audience.

All the jumping, squirming, and high-stepping is facilitated by having the audience sit on the floor, so kids can spontaneously erupt into motion when the mood strikes. Even for adults without children, it's a treat to watch the tykes rev up. However, solo adults might feel creepy amid this extremely youthful exuberance, especially if they lack familiarity with any of the characters. If you have a younger child in your party, all the better: just stand back and let the video roll.

For preschoolers, *Disney Junior* will be the highlight of their day, as a Thomasville, North Carolina, mom attests:

My 3-year-old loved it. The children danced, sang, and had a great time.

TOURING TIPS The show is headquartered to the right of the entrance to Hollywood Land and has an Art Deco marquee. Because the tykes just can't get enough, it has become a hot ticket. Arrive earlier on Sundays, when all showings sometimes fill to capacity. If you arrive to find a line that extends out of the main queuing area and onto the sidewalk, you might not get into the show. Count two palm trees to the left of the theater entrance; if the line extends to the left of the second palm, you probably won't make the cut. If the line hasn't extended past the second palm tree, go ahead and get in line—chances are about 90% that you'll be admitted to the next show. Once inside, pick a spot on the floor and take a breather until the performance begins.

Frozen—Live at the Hyperion ★★★★

APPEAL BY AGE   PRESCHOOL ★★★★½   GRADE SCHOOL ★★★★½   TEENS ★★★★
YOUNG ADULTS ★★★★½   OVER 30 ★★★★½   SENIORS ★★★★½

What it is Live musical show. **Scope and scale** Major attraction. **When to go** After experiencing DCA's rides. **Comments** Great venue; not to be missed. **Duration of show** 65 minutes. **Probable waiting time** 30–60 minutes.

Thumbs Up for the Whole Family

DESCRIPTION AND COMMENTS The 2,000-seat Hyperion Theater is DCA's premier venue for live productions based on Disney animated films. Shows exhibit Broadway quality in every sense (except duration of the show); we rate them as must-see. In 2016 DCA retired the long-running *Disney's Aladdin—A Musical Spectacular,* which spawned a Disney cruise ship show and Broadway production. *Aladdin*'s replacement was the first fully produced stage show based on the blockbuster *Frozen* film, and it arrived in Anaheim two years before a full-length New York version debuted in 2018.

The show is directed by Liesl Tommy, who produced *Eclipsed* on Broadway with Oscar winner Lupita Nyong'o. In addition to all those insistent earworms you know and love from the multiplatinum movie soundtrack, the production features extensive video effects not only on the enormous LED screen that serves as the stage's cyclorama but also on the revolving stage, the "aurora borealis" projection curtain that encircles the audience at key moments, and the actors themselves. Even if you're sick to death of "Let It Go," you'll appreciate the showstopping way it's presented: a huge frosty staircase appears from the back of the stage and then rotates and swings over the audience as Elsa is climbing it and singing, while swirling snow and wind effects fill the entire theater. It's all very impressive.

There's a lot to admire about this adaptation, from the talented multi-ethnic cast to the sumptuous high-tech production values. But *Frozen* has some flaws as a theme park production, principally its hour-plus running time, which will test the patience and potty training of any preschooler. The choreography is busy without being particularly creative, and the script is slavishly faithful to the original screenplay, allowing little room for fresh surprises; without a character like the Genie who is able to improvise, it's hard to imagine ourselves sitting through this show over and over again.

TOURING TIPS The lavish productions at the Hyperion Theater are very popular. Guests start filling the standby queue more than an hour before the curtain rises, so if you want to see it, be prepared to invest a good chunk of your afternoon. When three or four shows are scheduled, the middle performances are the most popular, so arrive up to 1 hour early. The first and last shows of the day are less crowded; show up 30 minutes before.

Another option is the Frozen dinner package, which combines a three-course lunch at Carthay Circle with priority seating at the Hyperion Theater for $89 per adult ($45 for kids ages 3–9). Make reservations at disneyland.disney.go.com/dining/disney-california-adventure/frozen-live-at-hyperion-plus-dining.

Showtimes are listed in the app and on the marquee. The theater is multi-level. Though all seats provide good sight lines, we recommend sitting upstairs for the best view of the staging or on the ground level relatively close to the entrance doors (if possible) for an easy exit after the performance. Finally, be forewarned that the sound volume for Hyperion Theater productions would give heavy metal concerts a good run for their money.

Guardians of the Galaxy—Mission: Breakout! (FastPass) ★★★★½

APPEAL BY AGE   PRESCHOOL ★★½   GRADE SCHOOL ★★★★   TEENS ★★★★★ YOUNG ADULTS ★★★★½   OVER 30 ★★★★½   SENIORS ★★★★

What it is Sci-fi-themed indoor thrill ride. **Scope and scale** Super-headliner. **When to go** The first hour the park is open or use FastPass. **Comments** Not to be missed. Must be 40" tall to ride; switching-off option (see page 147). **Duration of ride** About 2 minutes plus preshow. **Average wait in line per 100 people ahead of you** 4 minutes; assumes 3 elevators operating. **Loading speed** Moderate.

DESCRIPTION AND COMMENTS In 2017 Rod Serling was evicted from DCA's abbreviated adaptation of Disney World's terrific Twilight Zone attraction when Disney gave the once-stately Tower of Terror a gaudy cyberpunk makeover, turning it into the first major foothold of Marvel Cinematic Universe's expansion into Anaheim. What was formerly a once-famous Hollywood hotel gone to ruin is now the pipe-festooned futuristic fortress of Taneleer Tivan, also known as The Collector (played here, as in the films, by Benicio del Toro).

The amoral accumulator has invited park guests inside to tour his museum of arcane artifacts from across the universe, which features a rotating display of weapons and armor from multiple Marvel movies (plus some vintage Disney artifacts) to marvel at while you wait. Tivan's greatest treasures are the Guardians of the Galaxy themselves: Peter "Star-Lord" Quill (Chris Pratt), Gamora (Zoe Saldana), Drax (Dave Bautista), and even Baby Groot have all been captured and suspended in display cases hanging over a vast abyss.

Luckily, the wily Rocket Raccoon (Bradley Cooper) has broken free and is crawling around in the ventilation system overhead. While you're waiting in The Collector's Easter egg–filled office (check out the objects on his desk), Rocket enlists you to help liberate his pals. The life-size Audio-Animatronic of the reckless rodent is among the resort's most realistic figures and is a highlight of the revamp.

For the ride itself, guests board a gantry lift (previously known as Twilight Zone's service elevators) and are propelled up and down the tower, experiencing multiple free falls while immersed in intense visual effects and rockin' tunes ripped right from Star-Lord's *Awesome Mix* tapes. Like Walt Disney World's Tower of Terror, Guardians of the Galaxy—Mission: Breakout! features multiple randomized ride profiles, with different video sequences and drop patterns synchronized to six different songs. Musical options include The Jackson 5, Pat Benatar, and even Elvis (but unfortunately not Blue Swede's "Ooga Chaka/Hooked on a Feeling"), and each soundtrack is accompanied by a different combination of comic vignettes depicting our hapless antiheros' escape. Whichever sequence you get, you can still count on the doors opening at the top of the shaft for a bird's-eye view of the resort.

The hardware behind DCA's tower attraction is very similar to the Walt Disney World version, but they are definitely not clones. Thematic differences in the queues and preshows aside, the two attractions really part company once you are in the ride vehicle. In the Disney World version, the elevator stops at a couple of floors to reveal some eerie visuals, but then actually moves forward out of the shaft and through one of the floors; you don't realize that you've entered the drop shaft until the elevator accelerates vertically. In the DCA attraction, the elevator never leaves the shaft, creating a more straightforward ride experience.

Lacking the eerie atmosphere and lateral disorientation that distinguishes the Florida attraction, DCA instead replaces suspense with non-stop acceleration as soon as the doors close, resulting in a rambunctious ride that's in keeping with the spirit of these comically chaotic characters. As long as the superior original East Coast Tower of Terror remains untouched, we don't object to Disney swapping Serling for Star-Lord, especially since the reimagined attraction's wilder drop patterns are much more dynamic than the original version. Like us, this reader from Calgary, Alberta, went in apprehensive but came out a fan:

I loved the original old-timey Hollywood theme and the creepy Twilight Zone *story line. But I have to say, Guardians of the Galaxy—Mission: Breakout! was by far our favorite ride! The new ride is much faster and more thrilling than before. And the music makes it even more fun! I wasn't a huge fan of the movie, but after riding Mission: Breakout four times, I even bought a T-shirt!*

After 5 p.m. during the Halloween season, a special Monsters After Dark overlay amps up the fear factor even further with startling special effects and original heavy metal music, as you help Rocket rescue Baby Groot from a ferocious fire dragon.

This attraction is a whopper at 13-plus stories tall. As a result, it has great potential for terrifying young children and rattling more mature visitors. If you have teenagers in your party, use them as experimental probes—if they report back that they really, really liked it, run as fast as you can in the opposite direction. Seriously, a senior from Shelton, Connecticut, who tried it in its Tower of Terror incarnation, warns:

I am fine with rides like Matterhorn Bobsleds and Big Thunder Mountain Railroad, but there is NO detail on that ride that is worth the multiple stomach-jolting drops. After the first drop, all I could do was hang on and pray that it would be over soon. My legs were shaking as we walked out.

TOURING TIPS Because of its height, the tower is a veritable beacon, visible from outside the park and luring curious guests as soon as they enter. You can count on a footrace to get there when the park opens. Get a FastPass or try standby during the first or last hour of the day. Mission: Breakout! distributes FastPasses during the early-entry hour, and FastPasses may run out for the day by midmorning. FastPasses go even quicker for the seasonal Monsters After Dark version, which are dispensed as soon as the ride's FastPass return times reach 5 p.m.

To access the attraction, bear left from the park entrance into Hollywood Land. Continue straight to the Hyperion Theater and then turn right. To save time, when you enter the preshow area, stand in the far back corner across from the door where you entered. When the doors to the loading area open, you'll be one of the first admitted.

When one or two of the ride's three elevator shafts stop working (which happens regularly), the FastPass queue slows to a crawl, and the standby line may stop entirely. Ask the attendant if the attraction is fully operational before jumping in line.

Mickey's PhilharMagic ★★★½

**APPEAL BY AGE PRESCHOOL ★★★★½ GRADE SCHOOL ★★★★ TEENS ★★★
YOUNG ADULTS ★★★½ OVER 30 ★★★½ SENIORS ★★★★**

What it is 3-D movie with in-theater effects. **Scope and scale** Major attraction. **When to go** Anytime. **Comment** 3-D effects and loud noises may frighten preschoolers. **Duration of show** 12 minutes. **Probable waiting time** 7 minutes.

DESCRIPTION AND COMMENTS This 3-D movie imported from Walt Disney World's Magic Kingdom features an odd collection of Disney characters, mixing Mickey and Donald with Simba and Ariel as well as Jasmine and Aladdin. Shoehorned into the space originally occupied by Muppet-Vision 3-D, this version substitutes a single standard-size screen instead of the immersive 150-foot-wide triptych used in Florida, but the movie is still augmented by video projections on the walls and an arsenal of special effects built into the theater. The plot involves Mickey, as the conductor of the PhilharMagic, leaving the theater to solve a mystery. In his absence, Donald attempts to take charge, with disastrous results.

Brilliantly conceived, furiously paced, and laugh-out-loud funny, *Mickey's PhilharMagic* will leave you grinning. And while it is loud and in-your-face, this show is softer and cuddlier than some other 3-D films. Things pop out of the screen, but they're really not scary. It's the rare child who is frightened—but there are always exceptions.

TOURING TIPS There's rarely more than a single screening's wait. The theater is large, so don't be alarmed to see a gaggle of people in the lobby.

Monsters, Inc. Mike & Sulley to the Rescue! ★★★½

APPEAL BY AGE PRESCHOOL ★★★★½ GRADE SCHOOL ★★★★ TEENS ★★★½
YOUNG ADULTS ★★★½ OVER 30 ★★★½ SENIORS ★★★★

What it is Dark ride. **Scope and scale** Major attraction. **When to go** Before 11 a.m. **Duration of ride** 3¾ minutes. **Average wait in line per 100 people ahead of you** 4 minutes; assumes 23 cars in operation. **Loading speed** Moderate.

DESCRIPTION AND COMMENTS Based on characters and the story from the Disney-Pixar film *Monsters, Inc.,* the ride takes you through child-phobic Monstropolis as Mike and Sulley try to return baby Boo safely to her bedroom. If you haven't seen the film, the story line won't make much sense. In a nutshell, a human baby gets loose in a sort of parallel universe populated largely by amusing monsters. Good monsters Mike and Sulley try to return Boo to her home before the bad monsters get their hands on her.

The Imagineers did a very good job on the Monsters, Inc. ride, recreating the humor, characters, and setting of the film in great detail. The section of the attraction where you ride through the Door Vault with all of its lifts and conveyors is truly inspired. Special effects are first-rate, and lots of subtle and not-so-subtle jokes are worked into the whole experience. You'll have to ride several times to catch them all. Before disembarking, be sure to banter with sluglike supervisor Roz, an animatronic "living character" that can see and interact with riders.

TOURING TIPS You can usually ride without too much of a wait. Because it's near several theater attractions, the ride is subject to experiencing a sudden deluge of guests when the theaters disgorge their audiences. In a unique twist on the single-rider line operated by other attractions, Monsters, Inc. sometimes offers a Moving Buddy pass. If you are a party of one or two adults, with up to two lap-sitting small children, you can ask the ride's greeter for a Moving Buddy pass, which will permit you to enter through the exit. Because Monsters, Inc.'s ride vehicles have three benches, Moving Buddy pass guests get to fill the otherwise empty back row, resulting in significantly shorter waits.

Monsters, Inc. is an iffy attraction for preschoolers: some love it and some are frightened. Increase your odds for a positive experience by exposing your little ones to the movie before leaving home.

Turtle Talk with Crush ★★★★

APPEAL BY AGE PRESCHOOL ★★★★½ GRADE SCHOOL ★★★★½ TEENS ★★★★
YOUNG ADULTS ★★★★ OVER 30 ★★★★ SENIORS ★★★★

What it is An interactive animated film. **Scope and scale** Minor attraction. **When to go** After you see the other attractions in the Animation building. **Duration of show** 17 minutes. **Probable waiting time** 10–20 minutes.

DESCRIPTION AND COMMENTS *Turtle Talk with Crush* is an interactive theater show starring the 150-year-old surfer-dude turtle from *Finding Nemo.*

Though it starts like a typical Disney theme park movie, *Turtle Talk* quickly turns into a surprise interactive encounter as the on-screen Crush begins to have actual conversations with guests in the audience. Real-time computer graphics are used to accurately move Crush's mouth when forming words. Crush is joined in his tank by son Squirt and Dory the blue tang, along with Destiny the whale shark, Bailey the beluga whale, and Hank the seven-legged octopus from the theatrical sequel *Finding Dory.*

A mom from Henderson, Colorado, has a crush on Crush:

Turtle Talk with Crush *is a must-see. Our 4-year-old was picked out of the crowd by Crush, and we were just amazed by the technology that allowed one-on-one conversation. It was adorable and enjoyed by everyone, from Grammy and Papa to the 4-year-old!*

TOURING TIPS The animation is brilliant, and guests of all ages list *Crush* as their favorite Animation building feature. By late afternoon, the building has usually cleared out. Save this for your last stop there.

PIXAR PIER

WRAPPED AROUND THE SOUTHERN SHORE of the kidney-shaped lake, Pixar Pier (previously known as Paradise Pier) is Disney's headquarters for the nonautomotive computer-animated heroes from Pixar's popular franchises.

The land's original tacky mid-20th-century theme was ironic, and in a perverse way it brought the story of Walt Disney and Disneyland full circle. Walt, you see, created Disneyland Park as an alternative to parks with a carnival atmosphere, simple midway rides, carny games, and amply available alcohol. Amazingly, corporate Disney had made just such a place the centerpiece of Disneyland's sister park. The 2012 refurb's clapboard buildings and retro carnival games gave the area much-needed charm, and in 2018 the area was reimagined yet again, this time as Pixar Pier, DCA's new home for all Pixar characters.

Pixar Pier is subdivided into four neighborhoods. The Incredibles occupy the first quadrant around their new Incredicoaster; Toy Story characters claim the block outside their Midway Mania ride; *Inside Out* has taken over the far end of the boardwalk; and the remaining area around Pixar Pal-A-Round claims a catchall of Pixar characters. Even the existing snack stands have been given new Pixar landlords, like Monsters, Inc.'s Adorable Snowman Frosted Treats; *Inside Out*'s Angry Dogs and Bing Bong's Sweet Stuff, and Señor Buzz Churros and Poultry Palace from Toy Story.

Incidentally, those aforementioned carnival games, which are now all themed around Pixar films like *La Luna* and *A Bug's Life,* aren't as avaricious as their unfair fair ancestors. If you and a companion play together, you can win a stuffed animal for only $5 (less than you'd pay in the park's gift shops). Some games let you combine multiple wins for an impressive prize. The fishing and racehorse games seem easiest.

On your way across the bridge into Pixar Pier, look up at the Luxo Jr. desk lamp atop the archway. The animatronic incarnation of Pixar's longtime mascot nods to guests, and even watches the nightly lagoon show with rapt attention.

Note: Most of the attractions (except Toy Story Midway Mania!) in Pixar Pier close early for *World of Color* performances.

Incredicoaster *(FastPass)* ★★★★

**APPEAL BY AGE   PRESCHOOL ★★½   GRADE SCHOOL ★★★★½   TEENS ★★★★★
YOUNG ADULTS ★★★★★   OVER 30 ★★★★½   SENIORS ★★★★**

What it is Big, bad roller coaster. **Scope and scale** Super-headliner. **When to go** Ride first thing in the morning or use FastPass. **Comments** Not to be missed. Long and smooth; may induce motion sickness. Must be 48" tall to ride; switching-off option (see page 147). **Duration of ride** 2½ minutes. **Average wait in line per 100 people ahead of you** 2½ minutes; assumes 24-passenger trains with 36-second dispatch interval. **Loading speed** Moderate–fast.

Scary

Lose Things

Queasy

Muss Your 'Do

DESCRIPTION AND COMMENTS California Screamin', the opening day E-ticket of Paradise Pier, has been rededicated as Pixar Pier's Incredicoaster, a high-speed adventure starring the superheroic Parr family from The Incredibles franchise. Guests board 24-passenger trains inside a Palm Springs–inspired mid-century modern load building, where they learn that baby Jack-Jack has broken loose from Edna Mode's care and is wreaking havoc with his explosive special powers. Dash, Elastigirl, Mr. Incredible, and Violet all appear in the form of static physical figures inside the coaster's tunnel-covered inclines, attempting to put the incendiary infant down for his nap.

This apparently old-school wooden monster is actually a modern steel coaster, and at 6,072 feet, it's the third longest steel coaster in the United States. The Incredicoaster gets off to a 0-to-55-mph start by launching you up the first hill like a jet fighter plane off the deck of a carrier (albeit with different technology). From here you will experience tight turns, followed by a second launch that sends you over the crest of a 110-foot hill with a 107-foot drop on the far side. Next, you bank and complete an elliptical loop. A diving turn followed by a series of camelbacks brings you back to the station.

We were impressed by the length of the course and the smoothness of the ride. From beginning to end, the ride is about 2½ minutes, with 2 minutes of actual ride time. En route the coaster slows enough on curves and on transition hills to let you take in the nice view. On the scary-o-meter, the Incredicoaster is certainly worse than Space Mountain but doesn't really compare with some of the steel coasters at nearby Magic Mountain. What the Incredicoaster loses in fright potential, however, it makes up for in variety. Along its course, Disney has placed every known curve, hill, dip, and loop in roller coaster design.

A Carlsbad, California, woman found the ride to be a smooth operator:

It was WONDERFUL, and I am a 57-year-old mom, not an adrenaline-crazed young adult! It was my first ever upside-down ride, but it was so smooth and quick that I only felt a gentle pressure pushing me into the seat. It was so fun that I went again! Don't miss this one, at any age!

A Texas woman agrees, writing:

I hate roller coasters, and I loved it. Very smooth.

TOURING TIPS The Incredicoaster is a serious coaster, one that makes Space Mountain look like Dumbo. Secure any hats, cameras, eyeglasses, or anything else that might be ripped from your person during the ride. Stay away completely if you're prone to motion sickness.

Engineered to run several trains at once, the Incredicoaster does a better job than any roller coaster we've seen at handling crowds, at least when the attraction is running at full capacity. The coaster is sometimes shut down two or more times a day for technical problems. Early in the morning, however, it's usually easy to get two or three rides under your belt in about 15 minutes. Ride in the first hour the park is open or use FastPass or the single-rider line (enter up the ramp to the left of the queue).

If you can, try to ride after sunset; the lighting effects inside the tunnels look much better in the dark. Near the exit of Incredicoaster is Jack-Jack Cookie Num Nums, a food cart selling fresh-baked cookies. The cookies are tasty, warm, and chewy. A huge plus is that area smells like fresh cookies. It's intoxicating.

Inside Out Emotional Whirlwind ★★½

APPEAL BY AGE PRESCHOOL ★★★★½ GRADE SCHOOL ★★★½ TEENS ★★★ YOUNG ADULTS ★★★ OVER 30 ★★★ SENIORS ★★★

What it is Kiddie spinning ride. **Scope and scale** Major attraction. **When to go** Before 11 a.m. **Comment** Preschool heaven. **Duration of ride** 90 seconds. **Average wait in line per 100 people ahead of you** 12 minutes. **Loading speed** Slow.

DESCRIPTION AND COMMENTS After the closure of A Bug's Land, Disney relocated Flik's Flyers, a spinning carnival ride, to the western end of the Incredicoaster, on a circular pad once occupied by the long-extinct Maliboomer drop tower. Surrounded by a curved wall of glowing memory balls, with its circling Chinese takeout containers converted into brightly colored gondolas, the repurposed attraction now has an *Inside Out* theme.

TOURING TIPS Though magnetically alluring to the under-8 crowd, this ride is low-capacity, slow-loading, and ridiculously brief. Our advice is to ride before 11 a.m. if you visit on a weekend or during the summer.

Jessie's Critter Carousel ★★★

APPEAL BY AGE PRESCHOOL ★★★★★ GRADE SCHOOL ★★★½ TEENS ★★½ YOUNG ADULTS ★★★ OVER 30 ★★★½ SENIORS ★★★½

What it is Merry-go-round. **Scope and scale** Minor attraction. **When to go** Before noon. **Comment** Yee-haw! **Duration of ride** A little less than 2 minutes. **Average wait in line per 100 people ahead of you** 8 minutes. **Loading speed** Slow.

DESCRIPTION AND COMMENTS Guests can ride atop nine types of cute critters on this merry-go-round fronted by a large statue of Woody's cowgirl companion. The elaborately crafted dolphins and seals from the former King Triton's Carousel have been replaced with cartoonish armadillos, bunnies, buzzards, raccoons, and even adorable skunks, as depicted in "Woody's Roundup" from *Toy Story 2*.

TOURING TIPS Worth a look even if there are no children in your party. If you have kids who want to ride, try to get them on before noon. Jessie's Critter Carousel looks much better at night thanks to the lighting.

Pixar Pal-A-Round ★★½

What it is Ferris wheel. **Scope and scale** Major attraction. **When to go** The first 90 minutes the park is open or just before closing. **Comments** The world's largest chicken coop; may induce motion sickness. **Duration of ride** 9 minutes. **Average wait in line per 100 people ahead of you** 6¼ minutes; assumes all 24 cabins in use. **Loading speed** Slow.

DESCRIPTION AND COMMENTS To the surprise of many, Mickey's face remains on his former Fun Wheel after the pier's transformation, though the ride is now known as Pixar Pal-A-Round and the Plutos and Goofys painted on its gondolas have been replaced with, well, Pixar pals. Higher than the Matterhorn Bobsleds at Disneyland Park, this whopper of a Ferris wheel tops out at 150 feet. Absolutely spectacular in appearance, the wheel offers stunning views in all directions. Unfortunately, however, the view is severely compromised by the steel mesh that completely encloses the passenger compartment. In essence, Disney has created the world's largest revolving chicken coop. As concerns the ride itself, some of the passenger buckets move laterally from side to side across the Ferris wheel in addition to rotating around with the wheel. Because it feels like your bucket has become unattached from the main structure, this lateral movement can be a little disconcerting if you aren't expecting it. If the movement proves too disconcerting, motion sickness bags are thoughtfully provided in each swinging car.

TOURING TIPS Ferris wheels are the slowest loading of all cycle rides, but the Pal-A-Round has a platform that allows three compartments to be loaded at once. The lateral sliding buckets are loaded from the two outside platforms, while the stationary compartments are loaded from the middle platform. Loading the entire wheel takes about 6½ minutes, following which the wheel rotates for a single revolution. And speaking of the ride, the Pal-A-Round rotates so slowly that the wonderful rising and falling sensations of the garden-variety Ferris wheel are completely absent. For our money, Pixar Pal-A-Round is beautiful to behold but terribly boring to ride. If you decide to give it a whirl, ride the first hour the park is open or in the hour before the park closes.

Toy Story Midway Mania! *(FastPass)* ★★★★½

What it is 3-D ride through indoor shooting gallery. **Scope and scale** Headliner. **When to go** First 30 minutes the park is open or use FastPass. **Comment** Not to be missed. **Duration of ride** About 6½ minutes. **Average wait in line per 100 people ahead of you** 4½ minutes; assumes both tracks operating. **Loading speed** Moderate.

DESCRIPTION AND COMMENTS Toy Story Midway Mania! ushered in a whole new generation of Disney attractions: virtual dark rides. Since Disneyland opened in 1955, ride vehicles had moved past two- and three-dimensional sets often populated by Audio-Animatronics (AA); these detailed sets and robotic figures literally defined the Disney creative genius in attractions such as Pirates of the Caribbean, The Haunted Mansion, and

Peter Pan's Flight. Instead, Toy Story Midway Mania! has long corridors, totally empty, covered with reflective material. There's almost nothing there . . . until you put on your 3-D glasses. Instantly, the corridor is full and brimming with color, action, and activity, thanks to projected computer-graphic imagery (CGI).

Conceptually, this is an interactive shooting gallery much like Buzz Lightyear Astro Blasters (see page 255), but in Toy Story Midway Mania!, your ride vehicle passes through a totally virtual midway, with booths offering such games as ring tossing and ball throwing. You use a cannon on your ride vehicle to play as you move along from booth to booth. Unlike the laser guns in Buzz Lightyear, however, Toy Story Midway Mania's pull-string cannons take advantage of CGI technology to toss rings, shoot balls, and even throw eggs and pies. Each game booth is manned by a Toy Story character who is right beside you in 3-D glory cheering you on. In addition to 3-D imagery, you experience various smells, vehicle motion, wind, and water spray. The ride begins with a training round to familiarize you with your cannon and the nature of the games and then continues through a number of "real" games in which you compete against your riding mate. The technology has the ability to self-adjust the level of difficulty so that every rider is challenged, and there are plenty of easy targets for small children to reach. *Tip:* Let the pull string retract all the way back into the cannon before pulling it again. If you don't, the cannon won't fire.

Also of note, a 6-foot-tall Mr. Potato Head interacts with and talks to guests in real time in the preshow queuing area of Toy Story.

TOURING TIPS Much of the queuing area for Toy Story Midway Mania! is covered, which is good, but it's not air-conditioned, which is very bad, with temperatures escalating into the 90s and higher. Not roasting in this oven is a great incentive to experience Toy Story Midway Mania! in the early morning, before it gets crowded.

As you might expect, Toy Story Midway Mania! is addictive, and though it's great fun right off the bat, it takes a couple of rides before you really get the hang of the pull-string cannon and the way the targets are presented. To rack up a high score, you must identify and shoot at high-value targets: high-value targets are small and often moving, while low-value targets are larger and easier to hit. Toward the end of the ride, the top score of the day and the top scores of the month are posted. If you're a newbie and you'd like to ride several times to gain experience and get your skill level up, consider making the attraction your first stop after the park opens.

Disney added FastPass to Toy Story Midway Mania! in conjunction with its MaxPass program, installing the kiosks across the boardwalk from the ride's entrance. We bemoaned this move, after years of praising how much swifter DCA's FastPass-free queue moved in comparison to the molasses-like mess at Disney's Hollywood Studios version, which had to add a third track to tame wait times. Because Anaheim's ride still has only two tracks, it's now essential to either grab a FastPass or ride standby as early in the day as possible. Small parties of up to two adults and one lap-size child should ask an attendant about a Moving Buddy pass, which (when available) allows bearers to bypass the standby queue and fill otherwise empty rows with a much shorter wait. If you're eligible for early entry, the attraction is often a walk-on while everyone else is speeding to Cars Land or Guardians of the Galaxy.

PARADISE GARDENS PARK

LYING ACROSS THE LAGOON from Pixar Pier, Paradise Gardens Park is the new name for the leftover attractions that escaped Paradise Pier's Pixar makeover. It stretches from the western edge of the central lake, along its northern shore, to the *World of Color* viewing terraces.

Golden Zephyr ★★

APPEAL BY AGE	PRESCHOOL ★★★½	GRADE SCHOOL ★★★½	TEENS ★★★
YOUNG ADULTS ★★★½	OVER 30 ★★★	SENIORS ★★★½	

What it is Zephyrs spinning around a central tower. **Scope and scale** Minor attraction. **When to go** Any time it is operating. **Comment** Can't operate on breezy days. **Duration of ride** 2 minutes. **Average wait in line per 100 people ahead of you** 8 minutes. **Loading speed** Slow.

Queasy

DESCRIPTION AND COMMENTS First, a *zephyr* is a term often associated with blimps. On this attraction, the zephyrs look like open-cockpit rockets. In any event, each zephyr holds about a dozen guests and spins around a central axis with enough centrifugal force to lay the zephyr partially on its side. As it turns out, the Golden Zephyrs are very touchy, as zephyrs go: they can't fly in a wind exceeding about 10 miles per hour. Needless to say, the attraction is shut down much of the time. While the Golden Zephyr does not have a height requirement, babies must be able to sit up in order to board, and no lap sitting is allowed.

TOURING TIPS This colorful attraction is another slow-loading cycle ride. Despite its inefficiency, it rarely attracts more than a cycle or two wait to ride, assuming it's even operating (a bold assumption).

Goofy's Sky School *(FastPass)* ★★★

APPEAL BY AGE	PRESCHOOL ★★★½	GRADE SCHOOL ★★★★½	TEENS ★★★★
YOUNG ADULTS ★★★½	OVER 30 ★★★½	SENIORS ★★½	

What it is Disney's version of a Wild (or Mad) Mouse ride. **Scope and scale** Major attraction. **When to go** During the first few hours the park is open. **Comments** Space Mountain with the lights on. May induce motion sickness; must be 42″ tall to ride; switching-off option (see page 147). **Duration of ride** About 1½ minutes. **Average wait in line per 100 people ahead of you** 6¼ minutes; assumes 15-second dispatch interval. **Loading speed** Slow–moderate.

Scary   Lose Things   Queasy   Muss Your 'Do

DESCRIPTION AND COMMENTS Themed as Goofy teaching new pilots how to fly, Goofy's Sky School is a designer Wild Mouse (sometimes also called a Mad Mouse). If you're not familiar with the genre, it's a small, convoluted roller coaster where the track dips and turns unexpectedly, presumably reminding its inventor of a mouse tearing through a maze. To define it more in Disney terms, the ride is similar to Space Mountain, only outdoors and therefore in the light. Goofy's Sky School is an off-the-shelf midway ride in which Disney has invested next to nothing in spiffing up. In other words, fun but nothing special. One Denver, Colorado, woman who otherwise loves the park feels even that middling assessment is too generous, writing:

I think Goofy's Sky School deserves a significant demotion. It doesn't deserve to be called a roller coaster. It jerked us around so much that we were aching afterward.

TOURING TIPS A fun ride but also a slow-loading one, and one that breaks down frequently. Ride during the first few hours the park is open, or use FastPass or the single-rider line (when open).

Jumpin' Jellyfish ★½

APPEAL BY AGE   PRESCHOOL ★★★★   GRADE SCHOOL ★★★½   TEENS ★★½ YOUNG ADULTS ★★½   OVER 30 ★★½   SENIORS ★★½

What it is Parachute ride. **Scope and scale** Minor attraction. **When to go** The first 90 minutes the park is open or just before closing. **Comments** All sizzle, no meat; can't operate on breezy days. Must be 40" tall to ride. **Duration of ride** About 45 seconds. **Average wait in line per 100 people ahead of you** 20 minutes; assumes both towers operating. **Loading speed** Slow.

DESCRIPTION AND COMMENTS On this ride, you're raised on a cable to the top of the tower and then released to gently parachute back to earth. Mostly a children's ride, Jumpin' Jellyfish is paradoxically off-limits to those who would most enjoy it because of its 40-inch minimum-height restriction. For adults, the attraction is a real snore. Oops, make that a real bore—the paltry 45-second duration of the ride is not long enough to fall asleep.

TOURING TIPS The Jellyfish, so called because of a floating jellyfish's resemblance to an open parachute, is another slow-loading ride of very low capacity. Get on early in the morning or prepare for a long wait.

The Little Mermaid: Ariel's Undersea Adventure ★★★½

APPEAL BY AGE   PRESCHOOL ★★★★½   GRADE SCHOOL ★★★★   TEENS ★★★½ YOUNG ADULTS ★★★½   OVER 30 ★★★½   SENIORS ★★★★

What it is Track ride in the dark. **Scope and scale** Headliner. **When to go** Anytime. **Duration of ride** 6¼ minutes. **Average wait in line per 100 people ahead of you** 3 minutes. **Loading speed** Fast.

DESCRIPTION AND COMMENTS The Palace of Fine Arts dome was incorporated into an impressive lagoon-facing facade modeled on early-20th-century aquariums. The seafoam-trimmed building, topped by a statue of King Triton, conceals Disney's 21st-century take on an old-school dark ride. The basics of The Little Mermaid: Ariel's Undersea Adventure are similar to Disneyland's Haunted Mansion: a continuously loading ride system transports you through a series of elaborately themed, darkened scenes with sophisticated special effects. In this case, The Little Mermaid attraction takes you to the bottom of the ocean in clamshell cars, where the ride recaps Ariel's journey from her father's undersea kingdom to her marriage to Prince Eric. After Scuttle the seagull recaps the backstory for you, your vehicle descends backward beneath the simulated sea surface with a spritz of cool air. Assuming that you haven't drowned, you'll then meet a cutting-edge animatronic Ariel (featuring "floating" hair); party down "Under the Sea" with Sebastian the crab; and be menaced by a 12-foot-wide, 7½-foot-tall undulating figure of Ursula, the evil sea witch. The adventure is all set to newly orchestrated versions of Alan Menken and

Howard Ashman's classic songs, and original animator Glen Keane and actress Jodi Benson both returned to lend their talents.

Though the ride is colorful and kinetic, it suffers from shortchanged storytelling, especially in the unsatisfyingly abrupt finale. While it's a welcome addition to DCA's short roster of kid-friendly indoor rides, anyone expecting a modern-day classic to compete with Haunted Mansion and Pirates of the Caribbean may come away somewhat disappointed. But this family from Arvada, Colorado, thinks the ride serves its supporting role well:

Head for The Little Mermaid ride when you need a break. It's well done, and it's air-conditioned.

TOURING TIPS The Little Mermaid has slipped in popularity since the debut of Cars Land and Guardians of the Galaxy. This attraction does not have FastPass, and the Omnimover ride system is capable of efficiently handling more than 2,000 guests per hour, keeping lines moving swiftly even on busy days. If the posted wait is more than 20 minutes, check back in the late afternoon, when you will often be able to walk on with little wait.

Silly Symphony Swings ★★★

| APPEAL BY AGE | PRESCHOOL ★★★½ | GRADE SCHOOL ★★★★ | TEENS ★★★★½ |
| YOUNG ADULTS ★★★★ | OVER 30 ★★★½ | SENIORS ★★★½ | |

What it is Swings rotating around a central tower. **Scope and scale** Minor attraction. **When to go** The first 90 minutes the park is open or just before closing. **Comments** Simple but fun. Must be 40" tall to ride (48" tall to ride solo). **Duration of ride** Less than 1½ minutes. **Average wait in line per 100 people ahead of you** 6¼ minutes. **Loading speed** Slow.

Lose Things   Queasy   Muss Your 'Do

DESCRIPTION AND COMMENTS The theme pays tribute to the 1935 Mickey Mouse cartoon *The Band Concert,* the first color Mickey cartoon released to the public, with guests seated in swings flying around a tower. In the scary department, it's a wilder ride than Dumbo, but SSS is still just swings going in circles. A number of tandem swings are available to allow children 40–48 inches to ride with a parent; look for a separate tandem line to the left as you approach the attraction.

TOURING TIPS This is a fun and visually appealing ride, but it's also one that loads slowly and occasions long waits unless you ride during the first hour or so the park is open. Be aware that it's possible for the swing chairs to collide when the ride comes to a stop—Bob once picked up a nice bruise when an empty swing smacked him during touchdown.

CARS LAND

THE CROWNING CAPSTONE on DCA's 2012 transformation, Cars Land is the first major "land" in an American Disney theme park devoted solely to a single film franchise. Tucked into the park's southeast corner on 12 acres of repurposed parking lot, Cars Land's main entrance is across from the Golden Vine Winery, though there is a secondary gateway in Pacific Wharf (the vista through the stone archway is especially scenic). A massive mountainous backdrop topped with

125-foot-high peaks patterned after 1950s Cadillac tail fins, known as the Cadillac Range, cradles Ornament Valley, home to a screen-accurate re-creation of Radiator Springs. That's the sleepy single-stoplight town along Route 66 populated by Pixar's anthropomorphized automobiles. Along its main drag, in addition to three rides, you'll find eateries themed to the film's minor characters and souvenir shops selling Cars-themed and Route 66 merchandise.

Walking through the aesthetically astounding area is uncannily like stepping into the cinematic universe, and well worth the wait even if you weren't particularly enamored of the merchandise-moving movies. As striking as Cars Land is by daylight, it is even more stunning after sunset; the nightly neon-lighting ceremony set to the doo-wop classic "Life Could Be a Dream" is a magical must-see (showtimes are not publicized but occur promptly at sundown, so ask a Cars Land cast member and arrive early). Finally, a word to the wise from a Dallas, Texas, family:

Tip: *Cars Land has NO shade. Literally none. Wear a hat.*

Luigi's Rollickin' Roadsters ★★★

**APPEAL BY AGE PRESCHOOL ★★★★ GRADE SCHOOL ★★★★ TEENS ★★★½
YOUNG ADULTS ★★★½ OVER 30 ★★★½ SENIORS ★★★★**

What it is Outdoor "dancing" car ride. **Scope and scale** Minor attraction. **When to go** During the first or last hours of the day. **Comment** Must be 32" to ride. **Duration ride** About 1½ minutes. **Average wait in line per 100 people ahead of you** 10 minutes. **Loading speed** Slow.

DESCRIPTION AND COMMENTS When Cars Land opened in 2012, one of its three attractions was Luigi's Flying Tires, a reincarnation of Disneyland Park's Flying Saucers, a Tomorrowland attraction that lasted five years in the early 1960s. Luigi's Flying Tires turned out to be an example of nostalgia being better than reality, so in 2015 Disney shuttered Luigi's to reimagine the attraction, which reopened in 2016 as Luigi's Rollickin' Roadsters.

Guests first queue inside the Casa Della Tires shop (where memorabilia from Luigi's and Guido's careers is on display), and then pass through a garden of automotive-inspired topiaries before approaching the attraction itself, which occupies an outdoor arena. Twenty small open-top faux Fiats (with the franchise's signature cartoon faces) serve as the ride vehicles. Passengers are just along for the ride, as the cars spin and "dance" autonomously around each other in unpredictable patterns, thanks to trackless GPS technology.

With a library of Italian tunes like "Volare" and "Mambo Italiano" for the cars to dance to, each ride experience is a little different (you may even get a solo in the center of the floor while everyone else swirls around you), though each routine ends with a brief but brisk bout of spinning. But the cars' movements are surprisingly jerky, sometimes feeling like a shopping cart with a stuck wheel, and it's impossible to appreciate the choreographic patterns while you're in the middle of it. Much like its predecessor, Rollickin' Roadsters may actually be more fun to watch than to ride, so it's fortunate that benches are provided near the exit.

TOURING TIPS Luigi's capacity is limited. Try to ride during the first or last hours of the day, especially if you are eligible for early entry.

Mater's Junkyard Jamboree ★★★

What it is Midway-type whip ride. **Scope and scale** Minor attraction. **When to go** Before noon. **Comment** Must be 32" tall to ride. **Duration of ride** About 1½ minutes. **Average wait in line per 100 people ahead of you** 10 minutes; assumes both sides operating. **Loading speed** Slow.

Queasy

DESCRIPTION AND COMMENTS On the outskirts of town sits the junkyard home of Mater, the redneck tow truck voiced by Larry the Cable Guy. In his yard sit 22 baby tractors, each towing an open-air two-seater trailer. While Mater's voice emerges from a jury-rigged jukebox singing one of seven specially composed square-dancing tunes (plus one hilarious hidden song that plays only once per hour), the tractors travel in overlapping figure eight patterns along interlocking turntables. The vehicles are transferred from one revolving turntable to another, creating near-miss moments. In addition, Mater's trailers swing freely from side to side, creating a centripetal snapping sensation similar to vintage carnival whip rides. Mater's may look like a simple kiddie ride, but it supplies an unexpected kick that draws us back for repeated spins. This London, Ontario, dad echoed our assessment:

Mater's Junkyard Jamboree was surprisingly good. It doesn't look like much, but you have to ride it. We saw a woman lose her sunglasses because she wasn't prepared for how it swings around. The mechanically inclined adults exiting the ride were impressed with the engineering that allowed for the figure eight movement.

TOURING TIPS Mater is the breakout hit character of the Cars franchise, and his namesake ride is visually attractive but slow loading. Still, it typically has the shortest queue of the three Cars Land attractions.

Radiator Springs Racers *(FastPass)* ★★★★★

What it is Automotive dark ride with high-speed thrills. **Scope and scale** Super-headliner. **When to go** The first 30 minutes the park is open or use FastPass. **Comments** Not to be missed. Must be 40" tall to ride; switching-off option (see page 147). **Duration of ride** About 4 minutes. **Average wait in line per 100 people ahead of you** 4 minutes. **Loading speed** Moderate–fast.

Dark

Scary

Lose Things

Muss Your 'Do

DESCRIPTION AND COMMENTS To the right of the Radiator Springs Courthouse at the end of Route 66 lies the entrance to Cars Land's ambitious headliner attraction. Disney's Imagineers wedded an enhanced version of the high-speed slot cars developed for Epcot's Test Track with immersive sets and elaborate animatronics. The ride, which covers nearly 6 of Cars Land's 12 acres, mixes slow indoor sections with thrilling open-air acceleration in a way that appeals to every demographic.

You begin your road trip by walking through Stanley's Oasis, the town's original 1909 settlement, and end up in a cavernous loading station. There you board a six-passenger convertible, each with a smiling face on its front grille, and you're off on a scenic tour of stunning Ornament Valley, on your way to compete in today's big race.

After a leisurely drive past massive rock formations and a majestic waterfall, you enter the show building for a series of indoor scenes depicting the residents of Radiator Springs. These environments don't quite match the awe-inspiring scale of scenes in Pirates of the Caribbean or Indiana Jones Adventure, but they are a big step up from the old-fashioned Fantasyland dark rides and feature movie-accurate animatronics with impressively expressive eyes and mouths (achieved through a combination of digital projections and practical effects). Along your tour, you'll be side-tracked by a tractor-tipping expedition with Mater, which leads to a run-in with an angry harvester. Before reaching the starting line, you'll need some new tires or a fresh coat of paint. Then it's time to line up alongside another carload of guests as you await Luigi's countdown. The last third of the ride is a flat-out race over camelback hills, under outcrops, and around banked curves, with a randomly chosen car crossing the finish line first. Radiator Springs Racers's top speed of 40 miles per hour falls short of Test Track's 60-plus peak, but the winding turns and airtime-inducing humps supply an exhilarating rush. After a final swing past the glowing stalactites of Tail Light Cavern and some parting praise from Lightning McQueen and Mater, you'll exit your vehicle and inspect your obligatory on-ride photo.

TOURING TIPS While the new Guardians of the Galaxy—Mission: Breakout! has diverted some demand, Radiator Springs Racers is still a massive draw from the minute the park opens every day. With a carrying capacity of about 1,500 riders per hour, the attraction sees standby waits of up to 3 hours during peak season, and FastPasses may all be claimed for the day by noon; even the single-rider queue can run 45 minutes or more. Your best options are to secure a FastPass within the first few hours after park opening, or step into the standby queue shortly before closing. If time permits, try to ride once by day and again after dark; evening illumination makes the outdoor portions especially enchanting.

Note that FastPasses for Radiator Springs Racers are distributed along the pathway to Pacific Wharf that overlooks the ride's finale. You may be tempted to rush to the standby queue at rope drop instead of getting a FastPass, but be warned that the ride regularly opens late due to daily maintenance, potentially wasting your valuable morning touring time. The ride also shuts down for long periods after any substantial rainstorm. Hotel guests using early-entry privileges may retrieve a FastPass for Radiator Springs Racers before regular park hours start. Day guests are currently only allowed into the FastPass queue after official park opening, with guests gathering in a disorganized blob to the right of Carthay Circle before rope drop. This can cause a traffic jam as hundreds of people rush to get in line. Send one member of your party with all the tickets to get FastPasses or use MaxPass, and keep your kids clear of the mob. Don't be scared off by the size of the crowd queuing for FastPasses, says a Superior, Colorado, reader:

The FastPass line for RSR was amazingly efficient. A cast member at every kiosk was shoving tickets in and getting FastPasses out—none of that "which way do I put these in" thing. The line wove down the street, but I was out in less than 5 minutes!

Perhaps the best option is to follow this Suffern, New York, reader's advice and bypass Radiator Springs Racers' FastPass and standby queues:

Don't waste your time waiting to get a Radiator Springs FastPass. It's much faster to just go right to the single-rider line at rope drop.

If you try this technique, be aware that the ride's singles queue often doesn't open until the standby line has built up a bit. You may have time for a quick spin on Luigi's and Mater's and still be among the first into Racers' single-rider entrance.

PACIFIC WHARF

THIS LAND INCORPORATES a Cannery Row–inspired eatery area adjacent to Paradise Bay with a diminutive winery, situated at the base of Grizzly Peak and across from Cars Land, making it the smallest of the Golden State–themed areas. At the base of the winery you'll find **Blue Sky Cellar,** a seldom-used building that is occasionally opened as an annual pass holder lounge or promotional preview center. It would be a stretch to call it an attraction, much less a themed area.

Bakery Tour   ★★½

APPEAL BY AGE	PRESCHOOL ★★½	GRADE SCHOOL ★★★	TEENS ★★½
YOUNG ADULTS ★★★½	OVER 30 ★★★	SENIORS ★★★★	

What it is Free bread! (Plus a short film and walking tour.) **Scope and scale** Diversion. **When to go** Anytime. **Comment** Visitors get a free bite-size sample of fresh sourdough bread. **Duration of tour** 9 minutes. **Probable waiting time** None.

DESCRIPTION AND COMMENTS The Bakery Tour (hosted by Boudin Bakery) is a walk-through attraction featuring hosts Rosie O'Donnell and Colin Mochrie via video. It takes visitors through the history of the Boudin Bakery and also explains how the bread is baked for various restaurants across Disneyland Resort.

TOURING TIPS There's never a wait to enter this attraction, and you get a small bread sample as you walk in. The tour is a great way to kill 10 minutes. See this when you have some downtime, perhaps after a meal, on your way back to Pixar Pier, or before watching *Frozen—Live at the Hyperion.*

If the bread sample whets your appetite, you can buy a full-size loaf (including ones shaped like Mickey) at the café adjoining the exit. Next door is the Ghirardelli Soda Fountain and Chocolate Shop, where you can indulge in diabetes-inducing ice cream sundaes (or snag a free sample of candy) while admiring an animated diorama of San Francisco.

GRIZZLY PEAK

GRIZZLY PEAK, a huge mountain shaped like the head of a bear, is home to **Grizzly River Run,** a whitewater raft ride, and the **Redwood**

Creek Challenge Trail, an outdoor playground that resembles an obstacle course. In 2015 Grizzly Peak absorbed the adjacent area originally known as Condor Flats, rechristening the area around **Soarin' Around the World** as Grizzly Peak Airfield and adding woodsy theming appropriate to a national park in the High Sierras, as opposed to its former desolate desert look.

Grizzly River Run *(FastPass)* ★★★★½

What it is Whitewater raft ride. **Scope and scale** Super-headliner. **When to go** First hour the park is open or use FastPass. **Comments** Not to be missed; you are guaranteed to get wet, and possibly soaked. Must be 42″ tall to ride. **Duration of ride** 5½ minutes. **Average wait in line per 100 people ahead of you** 4½ minutes; assumes 32 rafts operating. **Loading speed** Moderate.

Scary   Wet   Lose Things   Rough

DESCRIPTION AND COMMENTS Whitewater raft rides have been a hot-weather favorite of theme park patrons for decades. The ride consists of an unguided trip down a man-made river in a circular rubber raft, with a platform mounted on top seating six to eight people. The raft essentially floats free in the current and is washed downstream through rapids and waves. Because the river is fairly wide with numerous currents, eddies, and obstacles, there is no telling exactly where the raft will go. Thus, each trip is different and unpredictable. The rafts are a little smaller than those used on most rides of the genre. Because the current can buffet the smaller rafts more effectively, the ride is wilder and wetter.

What distinguishes Grizzly River Run from other theme park raft rides is Disney's trademark attention to visual detail. Where many similar rides essentially plunge down a concrete ditch, Grizzly River Run winds around and through Grizzly Peak, the park's foremost visual icon, with the great rock bear at the summit. Featuring a 50-foot climb and two drops—including a 22-footer where the raft spins as it descends—the ride flows into dark caverns and along the mountain's precipitous side before looping over itself just before the final plunge. Period-appropriate props support the mid-century national park theme.

Grizzly River Run is a heart thumper, one of the best of its genre anywhere. And at 5½ minutes from load to unload, it's also one of the longest. The visuals are outstanding, and the ride is about as good as it gets on a man-made river. While it's true that theme park raft rides have been around a long time, Grizzly River Run has set a new standard, one we don't expect to be equaled for some time.

TOURING TIPS This attraction is hugely popular, especially on hot summer days. Ride the first hour the park is open, after 4:30 p.m., or use FastPass or the single-rider line. Make no mistake—you will certainly get wet on this ride. Our recommendation is to wear shorts to the park and bring along a jumbo-size trash bag, as well as a smaller plastic bag. Before boarding the raft, take off your socks and punch a hole in your jumbo bag for your head. Though you can also cut holes for your arms, you will probably stay drier with your arms inside the bag. Use the smaller plastic bag to wrap around your shoes. If you are worried about mussing your hairdo, bring a third bag for your head.

A Shaker Heights, Ohio, family who adopted our garbage-bag attire, however, discovered that staying dry on a similar attraction at Walt Disney World is not without social consequences:

The Disney cast members and the other people in our raft looked at us like we had just beamed down from Mars. We didn't cut armholes in our trash bags because we thought we'd stay drier. The only problem was that once we sat down, we couldn't fasten our seat belts. The Disney person was quite put out and asked sarcastically whether we needed wet suits and snorkels. After a lot of wiggling and adjusting and helping each other, we finally got belted in and off we went, looking like sacks of fertilizer with little heads perched on top. It was very embarrassing, but I must admit that we stayed nice and dry.

If you forget your plastic bag, ponchos are available at the adjacent Rushin' River Outfitters. If you don't mind walking around in wet underwear, a Vancouver, Washington, reader advises availing yourself of the free short-term lockers found near Grizzly River Run's entrance:

The first time we rode Grizzly River Run, we wore ponchos per your advice. We looked ridiculous and the cast members looked at us like we were aliens. Our last two trips, we left our bags with others in our party, wore flip-flops on the ride, and had a blast! Not having to worry about our stuff getting soaked makes the ride way more enjoyable.

About 50 lockers are located near the bear statue that marks the ride's entrance; use is complimentary for up to 2 hours.

Redwood Creek Challenge Trail and Wilderness Explorer Camp ★★★½

**APPEAL BY AGE   PRESCHOOL ★★★★★   GRADE SCHOOL ★★★★½   TEENS ★★★½
YOUNG ADULTS ★★★½   OVER 30 ★★★½   SENIORS ★★★**

What it is Elaborate playground and obstacle course. **Scope and scale** Minor attraction. **When to go** Anytime. **Comments** Very well done; plan to spend about 20 minutes here. Must be 42" tall.

DESCRIPTION AND COMMENTS An elaborate maze of rope bridges, log towers, and a cave, the Redwood Creek Challenge Trail is a scout camp with a combination of elements from Tarzan's Treehouse and Tom Sawyer Island. Built into and around Grizzly Peak, the trail has eye-popping appeal for young adventurers. A mom from Salt Lake City writes:

Most underrated . . . If this were a city park, it would be packed every day. In Disneyland it seems to be the least popular thing. The kids, young and older, just loved it. The adults were able to run for FastPasses, change diapers, get snacks for all the kids, and sit down while the kids had a great time.

Grab a map near the entrance and complete the self-guided activities to earn your own Wilderness Explorer merit badge sticker.

TOURING TIPS The largest children's play area in the park, and the only one that is dry (for the most part) and relatively shady, the Challenge Trail is the perfect place to let your kids cut loose for a while. Though the Challenge Trail will be crowded, you should not have to wait to get in. Experience it after checking out the better rides and shows. Be aware, however, that the playground is quite large; you will not be able to keep your children in sight unless you tag along with them.

Soarin' Around the World *(FastPass)* ★★★★½

What it is Flight-simulation ride. **Scope and scale** Super-headliner. **When to go** The first 30 minutes the park is open or use FastPass. **Comments** The park's best ride for the whole family; not to be missed. Must be 40" tall to ride; switching-off option (see page 147). **Duration of ride** 4½ minutes. **Average wait in line per 100 people ahead of you** 4½ minutes; assumes 2 concourses operating. **Loading speed** Moderate.

Thumbs Up for the Whole Family

DESCRIPTION AND COMMENTS Soarin' Around the World is a thrill ride for all ages, as exhilarating as a hawk on the wing and as mellow as swinging in a hammock. If you've ever experienced flying dreams, you'll have a sense of how Soarin' feels. Once you enter the main theater, you're secured in a seat not unlike the ones used on inverted roller coasters (in which the coaster is suspended from above). Once everyone is in place, you are suspended with your legs dangling. Thus hung out to dry, you embark on a hang glider tour around the world with IMAX-quality images projected below you, and with the simulator moving your seat in sync with the movie. The immersive images are well chosen and drop-dead beautiful, and special effects include wind, sound, and even smell.

A new ride film debuted at Soarin' in summer 2016, featuring film clips from flights around the world. Instead of being geographically constrained to California, the new film—which was created for the debut of Shanghai Disneyland—glides around the globe from the Matterhorn (the one in Switzerland, not Anaheim) and an arctic glacier to the Taj Mahal and Great Wall of China. Exclusive to DCA is a finale filmed in 2014 over the Disneyland Resort. The visuals are stunningly sharp, thanks to laser IMAX projectors, and computer-animated animals are employed to create clever transitions, an improvement over the original's jarring location changes. Jerry Goldsmith's memorable musical theme returned with updated orchestrations, as did Patrick Warburton's flight attendant preshow, but there's a new trio of scents to inhale along the way; we're growing partial to Eau de Africa. While some of the computer-generated imagery is distractingly artificial, and we still miss the orange-scented original's subtler moments, on balance we feel the updated Soarin' makes a more-than-worthy successor to what was already one of DCA's top-rated rides.

The ride itself is thrilling but also perfectly smooth, exciting, and relaxing. We think Soarin' is a must-experience for guests of any age who meet the height requirement. And yes, seniors we interviewed were crazy about it. But a North Carolina mom says:

Wait a minute! Soarin' was VERY cool but definitely on the scary side for people afraid of heights or who don't like that unsteady feeling. While we were "soaring" up, I was fine, but when we were going down, I had to continually say to myself, "This is only an illusion, I cannot fall out, this is only an illusion."

TOURING TIPS Aside from being a true technological innovation, Soarin' Around the World also happens to be located near the entrance of the park, thus ensuring heavy traffic all day. It should be your very first attraction in the morning after securing FastPasses for Guardians of the Galaxy, or, alternatively, use FastPass. If you arrive later and elect to use FastPass, obtain your FastPass before noon. Later than noon and you're likely to get a return period in the hour before the park closes, or worse, find that the day's supply of FastPasses is gone.

The film features a number of vertical landmarks like the Eiffel Tower that look comically distorted from seats on the far ends. Once directed toward one of the two theaters, politely request to wait an extra cycle for seats in row B1 to have an ideal view.

LIVE ENTERTAINMENT *and* SPECIAL EVENTS

LIKE DISNEYLAND, DISNEY CALIFORNIA ADVENTURE offers a full slate of live entertainment, led by a nightly lagoon show that's worth the proverbial price of admission. The classic Disney characters are still in evidence here, especially around the park's entrance, but you'll also encounter heroes from the Pixar and Marvel universes, as well as original stories exclusive to DCA. And DCA is increasingly highlighting a diversity of flavors and sounds during its festive seasonal events.

Disney's World of Color Nighttime Spectacular (FastPass)
★★★★½

APPEAL BY AGE   PRESCHOOL ★★★★½   GRADE SCHOOL ★★★★½   TEENS ★★★★½
YOUNG ADULTS ★★★★½   OVER 30 ★★★★½   SENIORS ★★★★

What it is Fountain show with special effects. **Scope and scale** Super-headliner. **When to go** Check the app or *Times Guide* for showtimes; FastPass only. If there's only one show, get your FastPass within 30 minutes after park opening. **Comment** Not to be missed. **Duration of show** 28 minutes. **Probable waiting time** Up to an hour for the best view.

Muss Your 'Do   Wet

DESCRIPTION AND COMMENTS The 1,200 high-pressure water nozzles installed under the surface of DCA's Paradise Bay are the infrastructure for Disney's $75 million attempt to keep guests in the park (and spending money) until closing time. If you've seen or heard about the spectacular fountain show at the Bellagio in Las Vegas, *World of Color* is similar but larger, with more special effects and themed to Disney movies. The show includes a musical score and incorporates dozens of Disney films and characters in its 28-minute performance. The show's backdrop includes Pixar Pal-A-Round, which is fitted with special lighting effects for use in the show. Giant projection surfaces sculpted by sprayed water—even larger than those used in *Fantasmic!*—display custom-made animations, and flamethrowers spew almost enough heat to dry off guests standing in the splash zones. What's most remarkable about the show is how the flashing colored lights and pulsating fountains combine to look like low-level fireworks. The effects are astounding, the colors are vibrant and deep, and the music includes some of Disney's best songs without being overloaded by overly sentimental ballads. You can even invest $25 in Made with Magic mouse ear hats, wands, gloves, or headbands that illuminate in sync with the show; better yet, stand toward the rear and freeload by eyeballing others who bought them.

But while *World of Color* is aesthetically entrancing, dramatically speaking it's a bit of a dud. Disney spectacles have never needed especially strong story lines, but *World of Color* is so plotless that it makes *Fantasmic!* next door look like a Russian novel. The show is essentially a 30-minute montage of movie moments with awkwardly edited segues straining to tie them together. Despite the show's titular association with Uncle Walt's 1960s NBC TV show, and the retro theme of DCA's overall rebranding, there's precious little vintage Disney referenced in *World of Color*. Aside from a brief cameo by 1937's *The Old Mill*, almost all the featured films are drawn from the last three decades, with lots of mist-screen time given to modern Pixar heroes such as Buzz Lightyear and Wall-E, and Second Golden Age stalwarts like Aladdin and Ariel, as well as footage from the fourth Pirates of the Caribbean film. There's also a handful of obscurities mysteriously tossed in: was there a fan club somewhere clamoring for more of *Fantasia 2000*'s flying whales? Ultimately, there's enough dazzling eye candy to overwhelm any underlying emotional emptiness in the narrative. Finally, *World of Color* has more false finales than the last Lord of the Rings film, so stay put until you're absolutely sure that the show is over.

During the holiday season, a special "Season of Light" edition of *World of Color* focuses on clips of Disney cartoons with wintery themes—from *Bambi* to *Frozen*—synced with a soundtrack of classy Christmas classics. Highlights include a *Fantasia* ballet backed by the brilliant a cappella ensemble Pentatonix and Goofy's Trans-Siberian Orchestra–fueled lighting display. In the interest of equal time for warmer climes, Hawaii's Stitch and Latin America's Three Amigos even get in on the seasonal action via Bing Crosby's "Mele Kalikimaka" and José Feliciano's "Feliz Navidad." The montage of princesses trying to evade their princes, set to Michael Bublé and Idina Menzel's cover of "Baby, It's Cold Outside," is deliciously ironic, and a skit with *Inside Out*'s Sadness being serenaded by Elvis's "Blue Christmas" draws big laughs. But the stirring climax, featuring soaring hymns sung by Broadway's Heather Headley, is guaranteed to put a lump in your throat. A new "Villainous" edition of the show, highlighting Disney's favorite antagonists, joined DCA's Halloween celebrations in 2019.

TOURING TIPS Entertainment value aside, *World of Color* is an operational nightmare. The effects were expressly designed to be viewed from Paradise Gardens Park, in the tiered area along the lagoon in front of The Little Mermaid attraction. Unfortunately, only about 4,500 people—less than a quarter of the park's average daily attendance—are permitted to stand there for each show. Getting a decent view for *World of Color* requires time, planning, and/or money, and therefore can almost seem to be more trouble to see than it's worth, but we still consider it not to be missed. A couple from San Jose writes:

Though the FastPass line was horrible and waiting for the show was horrible, the show itself was simply amazing.

An Austin, Texas, mom found *World of Color* challenging:

World of Color was fantastic but hard for kids and shorter adults to see unless they are standing right in front facing Pixar Pal-A-Round. My son could not see the preshow at all, and I had to put him on my shoulders for the 28-minute production. My back has not recovered. They need amphitheater reserved seating. We arrived 1½ hours prior to DCA opening to get a FastPass and waited 1½ hours for the show to start when admitted.

If you want anything approaching a decent view of *World of Color*, you'll need a special FastPass, the securing of which can be an annoying adventure in and of itself. Here are your options for obtaining FastPasses, beginning with the easiest (and most expensive) method.

World of Color meal packages are offered by Carthay Circle Restaurant and Wine Country Trattoria. The fixed-price dinner runs $49 per adult ($25 for kids) at Wine Country Trattoria and $74 per adult ($25 for kids) at Carthay Circle Restaurant. Lunch packages are $56 per adult ($25 for kids) at Carthay Circle and $49 per adult ($21 for kids) at Wine Country Trattoria. (The above prices do not include tax or tip.)

All viewing-package meals include an appetizer, your choice of entrée, dessert, and nonalcoholic beverage; selections are from a limited list that is separate from the restaurant's à la carte menu. After your meal, you'll receive special FastPasses for each member of your party, permitting entry into a preferred viewing area reserved for dining-package patrons. Note that you don't actually watch the show from the restaurant, so you'll want to eat early enough to make it to the viewing area. There is also a *World of Color* dessert party for $79 per person (tax and tip included), where you snack on upscale sweets and sip sparkling wine (or nonalcoholic cider) while sitting at tall cocktail tables during the show. Note that in the event *World of Color* is canceled due to technical difficulties or inclement weather, there are no refunds or rain checks for dinner or dessert packages. The viewing sections for premium dining and dessert party patrons are dead center along the waterline. Wine Country Trattoria diners get the second-closest section to the water, standing immediately behind standard Fast-Pass guests who request the splash zone along the front railing, and may catch some spray; Carthay Circle and dessert party guests get the elevated section slightly farther back, which affords a better (and drier) view. To enter the dining FastPass area, look for the illuminated White (Wine Country Trattoria), Green (Carthay Circle), or Purple (dessert party) entrance signs between the Blue and Yellow sections, directly across from The Little Mermaid ride. Though expensive, the dining and dessert packages are the only way to be guaranteed a central viewing spot with minimal crowding, and even then you should arrive up to an hour before showtime if you want to secure a prime spot. On nights when there are multiple *World of Color* performances, early eaters receive passes to the first show, while those eating later get tickets to the later viewing; be sure to confirm when booking your meal which showing you'll be scheduled to attend.

Free FastPasses are distributed on a first-come, first-serve basis from machines located near the entrance to Ariel's Undersea Adventure, starting as soon as the park opens; they can also be reserved using MaxPass. Make sure that you get passes for your whole party at once, or you may end up in different sections or showings. These machines are disconnected from the rest of the park's FastPass system, so your *World of Color* ticket won't interfere with other attractions. On busy days, or if there is only one performance, they may all be claimed before noon. If seeing the first *World of Color* show of the night is a priority for you, we suggest getting a FastPass within the first 30 minutes the park is open. When a second show is scheduled, FastPasses for the late performance can often be had well into the afternoon.

Once you have your FastPass, you'll notice that you've been assigned one of two color-coded sections. Yellow stretches from the right side of the premium viewing section toward the Golden Zephyr, and Blue includes the left side up to the bridge to Pixar Pier. A special section is available by request for disabled guests, and the prime areas in the middle are reserved for VIPs and dining-package purchasers.

Your FastPass also includes a return-time window. You won't be allowed into Paradise Gardens Park's viewing area before the start time, but the best viewing spots will all be claimed shortly after opening, so don't be surprised to see people lining up an hour before the area opens. Once inside the viewing area, try to move to the front of an elevated area. You're best off at the front of an elevated tier farther back, rather than at the rear of a lower section, as these readers from Langley, British Columbia, discovered:

World of Color was great, but it was hard for me to see (wearing flat shoes and being 5'5"). My husband, who is 6'4", also found himself bobbing around trying to see. When we got there, we had good line of sight, but as people stood up and put their kids on their shoulders, it became difficult.

And from a reader in Calgary, Alberta:

Don't trust that a FastPass for World of Color *will guarantee you a good view. Get there as early as you can if seeing the show is important to you. The FastPass said to return 30 minutes prior to showtime, and I assumed that's when they would start allowing people in. Boy, was I wrong! We got there exactly 30 minutes prior, and the FastPass area was already full of people! I spent most of the show staring at the backs of heads.*

If you don't mind getting drenched, ask a cast member about standing front-and-center in the splash zone. On a calm night, you'll be seriously spritzed, and if the wind blows the wrong way, you'll get completely soaked. You have been warned!

If all else fails, it's theoretically possible to view the show from various points around the park, but employees with flashlights will vigorously shoo you away from all the obvious vantage points. The best ticketless viewing spots are on the bridge to Pixar Pier, and next to the Golden Zephyr, to the right of the Yellow section. Unticketed viewing is also available immediately in front of The Little Mermaid attraction. You can see many of the fountain and lighting effects from the opposite side of Paradise Gardens Park and Pixar Pier, near the bases of the Pal-A-Round and Silly Symphony Swings, but the mist projections are illegible from that angle, so we can't recommend it for first-time viewers. On nights when there are multiple performances, you have better odds finding a good spot for the last show.

You can also watch *World of Color* from the upstairs bar of the Lamplight Lounge. The view of the projections is less than ideal, but no reservations are required, and you can sit down with an adult beverage during the show, provided you can secure a perch in this popular watering hole.

While waiting for the show to start, connect your smartphone to the park's free "PierGames" Wi-Fi network and launch any browser to join in the Color Wheel Challenge. Follow the pattern of flashing colored lights on the Pixar Pal-A-Round and duplicate them Simon Says–style on your device; points are awarded for speed and accuracy, with the winner of each round awarded 30 seconds of control over the giant wheel's light display. The game starts 45 minutes prior to the evening's first *World of Color* show and stops about 7 minutes before the performances.

The mass movement toward the exits that immediately follows each performance can be exhausting. Instead, relax and enjoy the musical encore that follows each fountain show; though not as explosive as the main performance, it's a colorful capper to the night, and it's much nicer exiting the park after the initial exodus has subsided. After the show, if you are headed to the hotels or Downtown Disney, you can bypass the crowd at the main entrance by exiting through the Grand Californian Hotel.

GUARDIANS OF THE GALAXY: AWESOME DANCE OFF! This interactive dance show, staged a dozen times during the day outside the Guardians of the Galaxy ride, features three of the attraction's stars. Star-Lord and Gamora arrive on a mission to retrieve Star-Lord's beloved boom box and engage guests in a boogie-off to 1970s disco classics "for the sake of the universe." Stick around until the end or you'll miss the meet and greet with Groot, everyone's favorite anthropomorphic foliage.

HOLLYWOOD BACKLOT STAGE This open-air stage features small productions and Disney characters. During the off-season, visiting school bands, glee clubs, and dance teams frequently use this stage. Check the entertainment schedule to see what's playing.

STREET ENTERTAINMENT You'll frequently find a period-appropriate klezmer, Irish, or other ethnic band playing outside Paradise Garden Grill. On Buena Vista Street, a gang of singing **Red Car Trolley News Boys** (and one newsgirl), loosely inspired by the cult film and Tony-winning Broadway musical *Newsies,* uses the Red Car Trolleys as a roving stage for exuberant song-and-dance performances (look for the high-tech talking Mickey Mouse to make an extended cameo appearance). Also on Buena Vista Street, the **Five and Dime** musical sextet (accompanied by a zoot suit–clad Goofy) sings jazz standards of the 1920s and 1930s, such as "Million Dollar Baby," "I Got Rhythm," and "Bye Bye Blackbird"; this is one of the best street shows in Disney's repertoire. You may also bump into interactive improvisation actors portraying police officers, bicycle messengers, or other eccentric **Citizens of Buena Vista,** a troupe similar to the popular Streetmosphere characters at Disney's Hollywood Studios. Along Cars Land's main drag, **Red the Fire Truck** shows up in the morning with sirens blazing to spray down the crowds. **Mariachi Divas** is a fabulous all-female mariachi musical group that plays sets in the Paradise Gardens Park gazebo. They are probably the only multiple Grammy Award–winning recording artists with a regular theme park gig. We particularly enjoy the Divas' rendition of "It's a Small World." *Operation: Playtime!* in Paradise Gardens Park is a Blue Man Group–esque street show of another color, featuring Toy Story's Green Army Men banging up a storm on improvised drums, and the jovial seven-member **Pixarmonic Orchestra** performs jaunty covers of Pixar soundtrack tunes in a bandshell across from the Pal-A-Round entrance.

DISNEY CHARACTERS Character appearances are listed in the daily entertainment schedule. In addition, Olaf from Frozen, as well as Disney Junior characters, make appearances in Hollywood Land, as do Captain America, Captain Marvel, Black Panther, Spider-Man, and Groot, the talking tree from Guardians of the Galaxy. The "fab five" (plus a couple of obscure old-school Disney characters) can be found around Carthay Circle in dapper roaring twenties duds. Mater and Lightning take turns posing for photos near the Cozy Cone Motel; these life-size vehicles can deliver quips recorded by the original voice actors to grinning guests.

SEASONAL EVENTS Following in Epcot's footsteps, DCA has been expanding its seasonal festival lineup, offering an ever-increasing array of events featuring temporary food kiosks and additional live entertainment. In January the **Lunar New Year** celebration brings a brief processional led by Mulan and Mushu, plus a special 6-minute *World of Color* preshow with music made for Shanghai Disneyland.

The spring **Food & Wine Festival,** which is now held annually on an ever-expanding number of dates in March and April, introduces a taste of the long-running, similarly named Epcot event to Anaheim with a California-focused twist. Vending kiosks are placed throughout the park, mostly along the Pacific Wharf corridor between Carthay Circle and the bridge to Pixar Pier. The booths are comparable to those found at Epcot's events, although far fewer in number, and likewise serve tasty but tiny plates and thimbles of alcohol at indigestion-inducing prices. (Buy a sampler lanyard to save a modest amount, provided you use it up on the more expensive offerings.) Similar seafood and meat menu items can sometimes be found cheaper elsewhere at the resort; your best bet is to stick with the vegetarian offerings, which are filling and fairly priced. Be warned that the festival booths halt sales a full hour before DCA closes, and lines can get long, especially on the weekends; save time by ordering everything you want from one booth, and picking up your selections later by showing your receipt. Also during the festival, Sonoma Terrace and Hollywood Land host free culinary demonstrations and hands-on kids' activities on outdoor stages, as well as extra-fee seminars with celebrity chefs. See disneyland.com/foodandwine for more details.

In the fall, Cars Land's residents celebrate **Haul-O-Ween** with special decorations, custom soundtracks for the Luigi's and Mater's rides, and costumes on the car characters. Starting in 2019, the popular after-hours Halloween events previously held inside Disneyland moved across the Esplanade and became known as the Oogie Boogie Bash, featuring a "Villainous!" version of *World of Color,* a "Frightfully Fun" parade led by the Headless Horseman, a *Descendants*-themed dance party, themed treat trails, and rare character encounters. Parties are held on select Tuesday, Thursday, and Sunday nights in September and October. Tickets start at $110 and include 3–4 hours of admission prior to the park's regular closing time before the Oogie Boogie Bash begins. Visit disneyland.com/HalloweenParty for details.

Cars Land also gets decked out with special decor and attraction music during **Cars Land Christmas.** And **¡Viva Navidad!** honors the holidays with Hispanic flair from November through Three Kings' Day with a festive street celebration, live storytellers, and traditional musicians, all centered on the Paradise Garden Grill area. Visit disneyland .com/events-tours/disney-california-adventure to stay up to date on DCA's seasonal event schedule.

UNHERALDED TREASURES *at* DCA

TREASURE Lamplight Lounge bar | **LOCATION** On the bridge to Pixar Pier

LAMPLIGHT LOUNGE IS A RESTAURANT on the span connecting Pixar Pier to the Pacific Wharf. Instead of heading downstairs to the restaurant from the entrance, though, go around the walkway. There, you'll find the outdoor bar, where you can enjoy a full-service drink menu and a small selection of food. This is also one of the best places to enjoy the view. It's a bit too sunny during the day, but as the sun sets and the evening lights come on, the Lamplight Lounge turns into a mellow hideaway where you can enjoy a beautiful view of Pixar Pier. In the background, you hear music, laughter, and the occasional sounds of a roller coaster, while watching small waves lap against the pier that houses a brightly lit carousel—enough to make you forget that you're sitting in the middle of a completely artificial environment.

TREASURE Redwood Creek Challenge Trail | **LOCATION** Opposite Grizzly Peak

MAYBE A VISIT TO A THEME PARK was your kid's idea, and you prefer a quiet walk in the woods. If you want to take a break from the hectic rush of a trip to DCA, hop over to the Redwood Creek Challenge Trail. You probably assume that this is just a playground designed for kids, but the area is actually a good representation of a wilderness park. OK, so you don't really need to bring your bird-watching book, but there are various nooks and crannies, as well as a few "ranger buildings" that are very well themed (down to the wildlife books on the shelves). You could easily spend a portion of your day just enjoying the decidedly rustic feel of Redwood Creek.

TRAFFIC PATTERNS *at* DCA

AS SOON AS THE PARK OPENS, most guests head straight for Radiator Springs Racers in Cars Land (or the Racers FastPass machines) or to Hollywood Land for Guardians of the Galaxy—Mission: Breakout!

On days of lighter attendance, waits of more than an hour will form within a few minutes at Racers; waits of 2 hours or more appear on holidays and other days of peak attendance. FastPasses for Radiator Springs Racers will typically be gone by midday on most days. FastPasses for Guardians of the Galaxy can disappear almost as quickly, and that ride regularly posts a standby wait of over 2 hours on busy days.

Of the other attractions in Cars Land, waits for Luigi's Rollickin' Roadsters will typically be 15–30 minutes as soon as the park opens, while Mater's Junkyard Jamboree's waits will be low for the first hour or two that DCA is open.

The wait times at the attractions in Cars Land will usually peak 11 a.m.–2 p.m. Radiator Springs Racers will have consistent 75- to 120-minute waits throughout the day, possibly higher if the attraction has to shut down for unscheduled maintenance, a common occurrence. Waits for Mater's Junkyard Jamboree will start to drop by 4 p.m., and lines at Luigi's Rollickin' Roadsters will start to diminish around dinnertime.

For parties of adults and older kids, our advice is to obtain Fast-Passes for Guardians of the Galaxy—Mission: Breakout! immediately at rope drop, then get FastPasses for Radiator Springs Racers as soon as you're eligible. If FastPasses are all gone, consider using the single-rider line for RSR. If possible, wait until the last 2 hours the park is open to try Luigi's and Mater's.

As crowded as Cars Land and Guardians of the Galaxy—Mission: Breakout! get, the good news is that traffic to the rest of DCA is relatively light for the first hour the park is open. When DCA opens before 10 a.m., lines for Soarin' Around the World, the Incredicoaster, and Toy Story Midway Mania! are usually less than 20 minutes, even during holidays.

At Grizzly Peak, Soarin's wait times start to climb about an hour after the park opens and peak 11 a.m.–2 p.m. Once the crowds are in the park, Soarin' will have waits of at least 30–35 minutes for the rest of the day during most times of year. Next door, wait times at Grizzly River Run are relatively low for the first hour the park is open. During summer and warm holidays, lines grow quickly about an hour after the park opens, peaking at around noon. Waits grow more slowly when the weather is cooler but still peak around noon. Expect waits to start dropping around 4 p.m. regardless of the time of year.

In Hollywood Land, waits at Mission: Breakout! and Monsters, Inc. usually peak 11 a.m.–noon. Mission: Breakout!'s waits don't drop off until close to closing time, while the wait times at Monsters, Inc. typically drop off at 4 p.m. most days and 6 p.m. on holidays. *Disney Junior Dance Party!* and *Frozen—Live at the Hyperion* each draw good-size crowds throughout the late morning and afternoon.

Toward the back of the park, long waits develop fastest at Toy Story Midway Mania! and the Incredicoaster—still about an hour after the park opens—and peak by 11 a.m. Like Soarin' Around the World, Toy Story will remain popular for the rest of the day, regardless of season. Secondary attractions, including Goofy's Sky School and Pixar Pal-A-Round, won't usually be too crowded until about 2 hours after the park opens. Like the attractions at Hollywood Land, most lines at B-list Paradise Gardens Park/Pixar Pier attractions start to drop after 4 p.m. Lines at The Little Mermaid seem to be low throughout the day and on any day of the year.

Park departures begin around 3 p.m., when families with small children start heading home. However, 9-to-5 workers with annual passes start coming into the park around 6 p.m. and generally stay for the evening. It's common to see waits hold steady or even rise from early evening until the park closes, undoubtedly because of Cars Land, Guardians of the Galaxy—Mission: Breakout!, and *World of Color*.

World of Color FastPasses are generally available until 11 a.m. or noon most days. Guests with *World of Color* FastPasses will begin queuing in the Pacific Wharf, Grizzly Peak, and Paradise Gardens Park walkways an hour or more before showtime. The largest wave of departing guests occurs at the end of *World of Color*. Just before closing, crowd levels are thin, except, of course, at Cars Land, Soarin' Around the World, and Mission: Breakout!

◀▐■ DCA TOURING PLANS

PRELIMINARY INSTRUCTIONS FOR ALL DISNEY CALIFORNIA ADVENTURE TOURING PLANS

ON DAYS OF MODERATE to heavy attendance, follow the touring plans exactly, deviating only when you do not wish to experience a listed show or ride.

1. Buy your admission in advance (see "Admission Options" on page 17).

2. Call ☎ 714-781-7290 the day before you go for the official opening time.

3. Become familiar with the park-opening procedures (described on pages 288–289) and read over the touring plan of your choice, so you will have a basic understanding of what you are likely to encounter as you enter the park.

DCA ONE-DAY TOURING PLAN FOR ADULTS
(page 382)

FOR Adults without small children. **ASSUMES** Willingness to experience all rides and shows.

Height and age requirements apply to many attractions. If you have kids who aren't eligible to ride, try switching off (see page 147) or use the One-Day Touring Plan for Parents with Small Children. This touring plan includes most of the amusement park rides in Paradise Gardens Park. If you're short on time or wish to allocate more of the day to theatrical attractions, forgo a few of the slow-loading rides in Paradise Gardens Park. This plan prioritizes obtaining FastPasses for Guardians of the Galaxy—Mission: Breakout! over Radiator Springs Racers.

ABOUT EARLY ENTRY If you are eligible for early entry, experience (1) Guardians of the Galaxy—Mission: Breakout!, (2) Toy Story Midway Mania!, and (3) the Incredicoaster, in that order, followed by (4) Soarin' Around the World (time permitting). If you have time, obtain FastPasses for (5) Radiator Springs Racers before official park opening. Pick up the plan after getting your FastPasses, skipping any attractions you've already seen, and return to ride Radiator Springs Racers once your FastPass window starts.

DCA normally hosts early entry on Sunday, Monday, Wednesday, and Friday. Unlike Disneyland, DCA's early entry is for hotel guests only; Magic Morning ticket holders may not enter early. If you are not eligible for early entry, try not to use the plan on an early-entry day. Cars Land may be busy with early-entry guests before you even get past the turnstiles.

DCA ONE-DAY TOURING PLAN FOR ADULTS WITH SMALL CHILDREN *(page 383)*

FOR Adults with small children who wish to experience all major rides and shows. **ASSUMES** Willingness to experience all rides and shows.

Height and age requirements apply to many attractions. If you have kids who aren't eligible to ride, try switching off (see page 147). This touring plan includes most of the amusement park rides in Paradise Gardens Park. This plan prioritizes obtaining FastPasses for Radiator Springs Racers over Guardians of the Galaxy—Mission: Breakout! If your party is more interested in the latter, swap Guardians of the Galaxy for Radiator Springs Racers in the plan.

ABOUT EARLY ENTRY If you are eligible for early entry, experience (1) Guardians of the Galaxy—Mission: Breakout! and then head over to Cars Land to ride (2) Luigi's Rollickin' Roadsters and (3) Mater's Junkyard Jamboree, in that order, followed by (4) Toy Story Midway Mania! If you have time at the end of Magic Morning, ride (5) Soarin' Around the World. If you have time, obtain FastPasses for (6) Radiator Springs Racers before official park opening. Pick up the plan after getting your FastPasses, skipping any attractions you've already seen, and return to ride Radiator Springs Racers once your FastPass window starts.

DCA normally hosts early entry on Sunday, Monday, Wednesday, and Friday. Unlike Disneyland, DCA's early entry is for hotel guests only; Magic Morning ticket holders may not enter early. If you are not eligible for early entry, try not to use the plan on an early-entry day. Cars Land may be busy with early-entry guests before you even get past the turnstiles.

THE BEST OF DISNEYLAND RESORT IN ONE DAY
(pages 369–370)

See page 275 for a description of this plan.

PART SEVEN

UNIVERSAL STUDIOS HOLLYWOOD

UNIVERSAL STUDIOS HOLLYWOOD (USH) was the first film and TV studio to turn part of its facility into a modern theme park. By integrating shows and rides with behind-the-scenes presentations on movie-making, USH created a new genre of theme park, stimulating a number of clone and competitor parks. First came Disney-MGM Studios (now Disney's Hollywood Studios) at Walt Disney World, followed shortly by Universal Studios Florida, also near Orlando. Where USH, however, evolved from an established film and TV venue, its cross-country imitators were launched primarily as theme parks, albeit with some production capability on the side. Disney is also challenging Universal in California with Disney California Adventure (DCA). While DCA does not have production facilities, one of its themed areas focuses on Hollywood and the movies.

Located just off US 101 north of Hollywood, USH operates on a scale and with a quality standard rivaled only by Disney, SeaWorld, and Busch Gardens parks. Unique among American theme parks for its topography, USH is tucked on top of, below, and around a tall hill. The studios consist of an open-access area and a controlled-access area. The latter contains the working soundstages, back lot, wardrobe, scenery, prop shops, postproduction facility, and administration offices. Guests can visit the controlled-access area by taking the Studio Tour. The open-access area, which contains the park's rides, shows, restaurants, and services, is divided into two sections. The main entrance provides access to the upper section, the Upper Lot, on top of the hill. Four theater shows and five rides (including The Wizarding World of Harry Potter), as well as two walk-through attractions and the loading area for the Studio Tour, are located in the Upper Lot. The Lower Lot, at the northeastern base of the hill, is accessible from the Upper Lot via escalators. There are three rides and a couple of meet and greets in the Lower Lot.

On April 7, 2016, USH capped a half-decade of redevelopment with the grand opening of The Wizarding World of Harry Potter, a West Coast annex of the wildly popular Hogsmeade area originally found

Universal Studios Hollywood

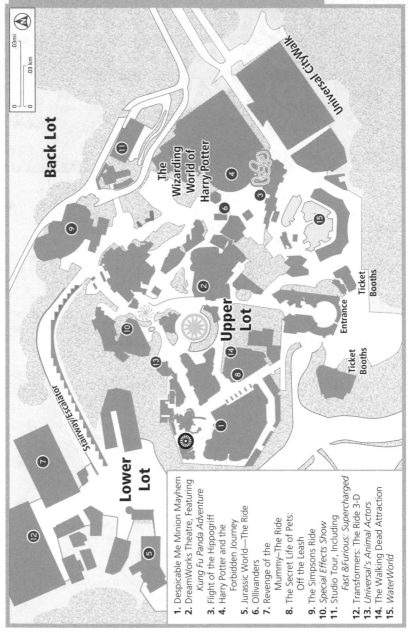

Back Lot

Universal CityWalk

The Wizarding World of Harry Potter

Upper Lot

Lower Lot

Stairway/Escalator

Entrance

Ticket Booths

Ticket Booths

1. Despicable Me Minion Mayhem
2. DreamWorks Theatre, Featuring *Kung Fu Panda Adventure*
3. Flight of the Hippogriff
4. Harry Potter and the Forbidden Journey
5. Jurassic World—The Ride
6. Ollivanders
7. Revenge of the Mummy–The Ride
8. The Secret Life of Pets: Off the Leash
9. The Simpsons Ride
10. Special Effects Show
11. Studio Tour, Including *Fast &Furious: Supercharged*
12. Transformers: The Ride 3-D
13. *Universal's Animal Actors*
14. The Walking Dead Attraction
15. *WaterWorld*

at Universal Orlando's Islands of Adventure. The parapets of Hogwarts Castle that now tower over the Upper Lot, forming a beacon visible for miles around, are merely the most visible effect of Universal's ambitious Evolution expansion plan, which completely overhauled three-quarters of the park in under five years. Casualties of the expansions included the old Wild West arena, *Terminator 2: 3-D*, the tram tour's Mummy tunnel, the Curious George playground, and Gibson Amphitheater. But the extreme makeover has brought USH a beautiful new Art Deco entry corridor and central plaza, upgraded points of interest along the tram tour, and the global attention that comes with The Wizarding World. Universal isn't stopping there in its bid to attract Disneyland guests; two new USH on-site hotels have been proposed, and additional attractions are in the works on both the Upper and Lower Lots.

The park offers all standard services and amenities, including stroller and wheelchair rental, lockers, diaper-changing and nursing facilities, car assistance, and foreign-language assistance. Most of the park is accessible to disabled guests, and TDDs are available for the hearing impaired. Almost all services are in the Upper Lot, just inside the main entrance.

GATHERING INFORMATION

THE MAIN UNIVERSAL STUDIOS information number is ☎ 800-864-8377. Universal Studios' website, universalstudioshollywood.com, is easy to navigate. Once inside the park, use the USH official iPhone or Android app, or visit ushwaittimes.com with your smartphone to see current wait times and show schedules. Incidentally, USH offers free public Wi-Fi (look for SSID "Universal"), but it quickly gets overloaded on busy days, and cell reception can be spotty depending on which side of the hill you're on.

WHAT MAKES UNIVERSAL STUDIOS HOLLYWOOD DIFFERENT

WHAT MAKES USH DIFFERENT is that the attractions, with a couple of exceptions, are designed to minimize long waits in line. The centerpiece of the Universal experience is the Studio Tour. While on the tram, you experience a high-speed car chase and come face-to-face with King Kong, among other things. In other parks, including Universal's sister park in Florida, each of these is presented as an individual attraction with its own long queue. At USH, by contrast, you suffer only one wait to board the tram and then experience all of these events as part of the tour.

In addition to the time saving and convenience provided by the tram tour, most of the live shows at USH are performed in large theaters or stadiums. Instead of standing in line outside, guests are usually invited to enter the theater and wait in seated comfort for the production to begin.

One more distinguishing feature of Universal is that it's *loud*. Unlike Disney's background music, which is carefully curated to create a relaxing ambience, Universal insists on blasting high-energy soundtracks at full volume through every available speaker. When you're lucky, you'll only be exposed to one oppressive score at a time; if you linger too long in spots where competing sound systems overlap, you could quickly lose your sanity. And we haven't even addressed the rides themselves, which typically feature frequent explosions and other earsplitting sound effects played at decibel levels that would make Spinal Tap shudder. As a father from Petaluma, California, put it:

> Universal Studios loves its soundtracks. Every ride had blaring sound effects, and even as we just walked around the park, the music was blaring from various attractions so loud that you had trouble talking to the person next to you. Crowd noise was so loud that you couldn't hear the magical effects in the windows at Hogsmeade! We were frazzled by the end of the day. I highly recommend putting in earplugs when you arrive and keeping them in for the whole day.

A Vancouver, Canada, visitor was even blunter:

> Universal is an assault on the senses. Where Disney is so often quaint and genteel, Universal is brash, loud, and in your face.

TIMING *Your* VISIT

CROWDS ARE LARGEST in the summer (Memorial Day–Labor Day) and during specific holiday periods during the rest of the year. December 25–January 1 is extremely busy, as are Thanksgiving weekend, the week of Presidents' Day, spring break for schools and colleges, and the two weeks bracketing Easter. The least busy time is from after Thanksgiving weekend until the week before Christmas. The next slowest times are late August and September through the weekend preceding Thanksgiving (except for during the popular Halloween Horror Nights event), January 4 through the first week of March, and the week following Easter to Memorial Day weekend. We don't currently maintain a crowd calendar for USH, but you'll find a useful free one at isitpacked.com /crowd-calendars/universal-studios-hollywood.

SELECTING THE DAY OF THE WEEK FOR YOUR VISIT

WEEKENDS ARE MORE CROWDED than weekdays year-round. Saturday is the busiest day. Sunday, particularly Sunday morning, is the best bet if you have to go on a weekend, but it is still extremely busy. During the summer, Friday is very busy; Monday, Wednesday, and Thursday are usually less so; Tuesday is normally the slowest of all. During the off-season (September–May, holidays excepted), Tuesday is usually the least-crowded day, followed by Thursday.

HOW MUCH TIME TO ALLOCATE

THOUGH THERE'S A LOT TO SEE and do at USH, you can (unlike at Disneyland) complete a comprehensive tour in one day. If you follow

UNIVERSAL STUDIOS HOLLYWOOD SMALL-CHILD FRIGHT-POTENTIAL TABLE

DESPICABLE ME MINION MAYHEM Loud with some intense 3-D effects.

DREAMWORKS THEATRE Special effects may frighten preschoolers.

FLIGHT OF THE HIPPOGRIFF Frightens a small percentage of preschoolers.

HARRY POTTER AND THE FORBIDDEN JOURNEY Extremely intense special effects and macabre visuals with wild simulated movement that may frighten and discombobulate guests of any age.

JURASSIC WORLD—THE RIDE Intense water-flume ride. Potentially terrifying for people of any age.

OLLIVANDERS Not frightening in any way.

REVENGE OF THE MUMMY—THE RIDE Scares guests of all ages.

THE SIMPSONS RIDE Motion simulator too intense for many children age 7 and younger tall enough to ride.

SPECIAL EFFECTS SHOW Some intense special effects. Shows how bloody fake wounds are created, and someone is (safely) set on fire.

STUDIO TOUR Parts of the tour are too frightening or intense for many preschoolers.

TRANSFORMERS: THE RIDE 3-D Too intense for children younger than age 7, and potentially terrifying for visitors of any age.

UNIVERSAL'S ANIMAL ACTORS Not frightening in any way.

THE WALKING DEAD ATTRACTION Potentially traumatizing to young children, grown adults, and all sentient creatures. Not appropriate for anyone under age 13 or those afraid of being eaten by zombies.

WATERWORLD Fighting, gunplay, and explosions frighten children age 4 and younger.

our touring plan, which calls for being on hand at park opening, you should be able to check out everything before the park closes, even on a crowded day.

Never mind that USH claims to cover 400 acres; the area you will have to traverse on foot is considerably smaller. In fact, you will do much less walking and, miracle of miracles, much less standing in line at Universal Studios than at Disneyland.

Increased attendance since the opening of the Harry Potter attractions has helped transform USH from a half-day attraction to one that merits a full day's visit. And just as he did in Orlando, Potter has propelled USH's attendance to new peaks; on some peak days the park has had to close its ticket windows and hang SOLD OUT signs as Hogsmeade becomes mobbed from opening until evening.

UNIVERSAL STUDIOS HOLLYWOOD FOR YOUNG CHILDREN

WE DO NOT RECOMMEND USH for preschoolers. Of 14 major attractions, all but 2 (Ollivanders and *Universal's Animal Actors*) have the potential for flipping out sensitive little ones. See the Small-Child Fright-Potential Table above.

All Universal rides with a height requirement offer child switch, which is superior to Disney's rider swap; most attractions allow everyone to wait in line together and have a quiet room where the nonriding parent can wait with the kids while his or her partner rides. Ask the greeter at each attraction's entrance how to take advantage of child switch.

COST

JUST AHEAD OF The Wizarding World's debut, USH did away with its old single-day and annual pass admission structures, instituting its own version of demand-based tiered pricing even before Disneyland did, and sharply increasing prices and blackout dates for pass holders. The new ticket system strongly encourages guests to select the date of their visit in advance. One-day adult tickets are $139 at the gate but can be purchased online for as low as $109 if you select your visit date in advance. Tickets for kids ages 3–9 cost $6 less than adult tickets; children 2 and under are free. In addition to saving you money and time by avoiding the ticket booths, purchasing your admission online also grants you access to early entry, giving you a half-hour head start in The Wizarding World of Harry Potter (see page 339 for details).

A pass that allows you to skip the regular line once at each attraction (including Harry Potter and the Forbidden Journey) using the Universal Express entrance runs $189–$269 (depending on season) for adults or children, including admission. Save $10 by buying online in advance.

The Silver Annual Pass is $199 ($10 less if purchased online) and is good for 12 months after your first visit, with more than 290 valid days, including more than 60 weekend days. The Gold Annual Pass offers 330-plus valid days (including more than 75 weekend days) and costs $329 ($319 online). Finally, the Platinum Annual Pass ($629, $619 online) is the only pass valid 365 days a year with no blackouts. Silver, Gold, and Platinum Passes can be purchased on interest-free monthly installments with FlexPay. The Gold and Platinum Passes include free self-parking before 6 p.m. and also provide 15% discounts on most in-park food and merchandise. The Platinum Pass also throws in a Halloween Horror Nights ticket and priority access to all rides and shows that offer Universal Express, including the Studio Tour. Locals can buy a California Neighbor Pass for only $159 ($149 online) per year, but it's blacked out more often than it's valid and isn't eligible for FlexPay.

For Hollywood-happy high rollers, USH offers a VIP Experience ($359–$410, depending on season; $10 off if ordered online) that includes admission, valet parking, escorted queue-cutting at all attractions, off-tram walking tours of sets and soundstages, light breakfast and gourmet lunch, and amenities such as ponchos and bottled water. The quality of service provided by the VIP touring guides is exceptional, and you'll get to explore places—like Universal's gargantuan prop warehouse or the *War of the Worlds* airliner crash site—that are otherwise inaccessible to guests. Best of all, you travel in style, in a luxury air-conditioned bus that beats the heck out of the standard Studio

Tour trams. If you have the spare dough, it's undoubtedly a better deal than Disney's pay-per-hour VIP guides, and with The Wizarding World included, this service is worth its weight in goblin gold. Reservations are required; call ☎ 818-622-8477 to book or visit universalstudios hollywood.com/tickets/vip-experience for more information.

In addition to the website discounts, admission discounts are sometimes offered in area freebie publications available in hotels. Admission discounts are also periodically offered to AAA members.

While Universal's team members don't have a reputation for the exceptionally sunny service for which their pixie-dusted counterparts at Disneyland are famous, they do excel at guest recovery when things go wrong. For example, when rides at USH break down (as they inevitably seem to do), the operators sometimes hand out free jelly beans to guests stuck in the queue, a policy we wish every park would adopt.

STAYING ON-SITE AT UNIVERSAL STUDIOS HOLLYWOOD

HILTON AND SHERATON both operate hotels on USH's property, but if you've experienced the exceptional perks offered to guests at Universal Orlando's Loews hotels, lower your expectations before booking an on-site room at USH. Both on-property hotels are pricey for the room size and service quality, the parks are a poorly marked 10-minute hike away, and no theme park bonuses—such as front-of-the-line passes or even early entry (unless you purchase a designated vacation package)—are included. You can also walk into Universal from a handful of off-site hotels along Cahuenga Boulevard (we can vouch for The Tilt), though it's a 15-minute hike up an extremely steep slope.

THE SHUTTLE

UNIVERSAL CITY is on the Red Line of **Los Angeles Metro Rail,** which makes it relatively easy to commute by light-rail from downtown LA and many other places, though not from Anaheim. Across the street from the subway station and the bus stop, at Lankershim Boulevard and Universal Hollywood Drive, is a free Universal Studios shuttle bus that will conveniently take you to the main entrances of USH and CityWalk. The bus runs daily, beginning at 7 a.m., with pickups about every 10–15 minutes; service continues until about 2 hours after the theme park closes. Refer to the posted times at each shuttle stop for information on the last departing shuttle. For rail and bus schedules and additional public transportation information, call the Los Angeles Metropolitan Transportation Authority at ☎ 323-466-3876, or visit metro.net.

Alternatively, you can reach USH by taxi, Uber, or bus tours like **Starline Tours** (starlinetours.com), which combine round-trip transportation from Disneyland-area hotels with park admission. Just beware that shuttle services must pick up at multiple hotels and might not get you to the park before rope drop. A reader from Calgary, Alberta, strongly suggests the shuttle option:

I checked Uber prices a couple of times, and they showed about $45 USD one-way. What I didn't factor in was the effect rush hour would have on prices. At the last minute we booked a shuttle and were so glad we did. When I checked Uber prices that morning from the shuttle bus, prices had doubled! It's also much more comfortable to sit through Los Angeles rush hour for 2 hours in a big tour bus than the back seat of someone's car.

ARRIVING *and* GETTING ORIENTED

MOST FOLKS ACCESS Universal Studios by taking US 101, also called the Hollywood Freeway, and following the signs to the park. If the freeway is gridlocked, you can also get to the Studios by taking Cahuenga Boulevard and then turning north toward Lankershim Boulevard. If you are coming from Burbank, take Barham Boulevard toward US 101, and then follow the signs.

Universal Studios has a number of big, multilevel parking garages at the top of the hill, including a massive *E.T.*-inspired facility that opened in 2016. Signs directing you to the garages have improved but can still be a bit confusing, so pay attention as you come up the hill. Even after you have made it to the pay booth and shelled out $25 to park, it is still not exactly clear where you go next. (Preferred parking costs $35, $50 for even closer front-gate parking; parking costs extra if your RV is more than 15 feet long. All parking rates except valet are discounted by $15–$20 after 6 p.m.) Drive slowly, follow other cars proceeding from the pay booths, and avoid turns onto ramps marked EXIT. You may become a bit disoriented, but ultimately you will blunder into the garage. Once parked, make a note of your parking level and the location of your space. Valet parking ($25 for the first 2 hours, $45 for more than 2 hours) is located inside the Frankenstein parking structure and is even more bewildering to navigate to; take the Lankershim exit off US 101 for easier access to valet and the on-site hotels.

Walk toward the opposite end of the garage from where you entered and exit into Universal CityWalk, a shopping, dining, and entertainment complex (no admission required) situated between the parking structure and the main entrance of the park. As an aside, CityWalk is much like Downtown Disney at Disneyland. Some of Universal's better restaurants and more interesting shops are at CityWalk, and it's so close to the theme park entrance that you can conveniently pop out of the park to grab a bite (don't forget to have your hand stamped for reentry). If "riding the movies" at the theme park inspires you to watch one, the 19-screen AMC IMAX Cineplex boasts plush reclining seats, Dolby Atmos surround sound, and razor-sharp Christie RGB laser projectors.

Universal Studios' ticket booths and turnstiles are about 100 yards from the main parking garage. Before approaching the ticket booths and turnstiles, you'll have to pass through an expansive TSA-style security checkpoint; fortunately, Universal's setup is far more efficient than Disneyland's inspections. If you need cash, an ATM is outside and to the right of the main entrance. There are also ATMs inside the park at the Kwik-E-Mart, near the Jurassic Cafe on the Lower Lot, and even a Gringotts money machine in Hogsmeade. Nearby is a guest-services window. As you enter the park, be sure to pick up a park map and check an information board or smartphone app for the daily entertainment schedule.

UNIVERSAL STUDIOS HOLLYWOOD ATTRACTIONS

UPPER LOT

THE UPPER LOT is essentially a large, amorphous pedestrian plaza. In-park signage (which is inordinately confusing) references street names such as New York Street and Baker Street and place names such as Cape Cod and Moulin Rouge, but on foot these theme distinctions are largely lost, and placement of buildings appears almost random. The park's previously utilitarian entry corridor was rejuvenated in 2016 with fresh facades recalling the Golden Age of Hollywood (look for tributes to the studio's past talents, like makeup artist Jack Pierce), and an Art Deco tower serves as a central "weenie" to navigate by, but outside of The Wizarding World of Harry Potter, don't expect Disneyland's dedication to thematic integrity. Universal has announced that **Secret Life of Pets: Off The Leash** will open in 2020 between Despicable Me Minion Mayhem and The Walking Dead Attraction. This animatronic-filled dark ride, featuring Max and his furry friends from the animated Illumination films, casts guests as stray puppies on the streets of New York City, searching for their forever homes. It should provide Universal with a much-needed attraction that the entire family can enjoy together.

Inside the main entrance, stroller and wheelchair rentals are on the right, as are rental lockers. Straight ahead is a TV Audience Ticket Booth, where you can obtain free tickets to join the audience for any TV shows that are taping during your visit (subject to availability).

Attractions in the Upper Lot are situated around the perimeter of the plaza. Near The Simpsons Ride (straight ahead) are the escalators and stairs that lead to the Lower Lot.

Despicable Me Minion Mayhem   ★★★½

**APPEAL BY AGE   PRESCHOOL ★★★★   GRADE SCHOOL ★★★★★   TEENS ★★★★★
YOUNG ADULTS ★★★★   OVER 30 ★★★★   SENIORS ★★★**

What it is Motion simulator ride. **Scope and scale** Major attraction. **When to go** After experiencing the Lower Lot attractions. **Comment** Must be 40" tall to ride. **Duration of ride** 5 minutes, plus 10-minute preshow. **Average wait time per 100 people ahead of you** 3½ minutes. **Loading speed** Moderate–slow.

DESCRIPTION AND COMMENTS Despicable Me Minion Mayhem is a motion simulator ride similar to The Simpsons Ride and Disneyland's Star Tours. You're seated in a ride vehicle that faces a large video screen, on which the attraction's story is projected. When the story calls for you to drop down the side of a mountain, your ride vehicle tilts forward as if you were falling; when you need to swerve left or right, your ride vehicle tilts the same way. The main difference between Minion Mayhem and other simulators is that most other simulators usually provide one video screen per ride vehicle, while Minion Mayhem arranges all of its eight-person vehicles in front of one large IMAX-size video screen. The ride vehicles are set on raised platforms, which get slightly higher toward the back of the theater, affording good views for all guests.

The preshow area is inside the home of adorably evil Gru (voiced by Steve Carell), where you see his unique family tree and other artifacts. The premise of the ride is that you're turned into one of Gru's yellow Minions. Once converted you must navigate the Minion training grounds, where your "speed, strength, and ability not to die" is tested. Something soon goes amiss, though, and your training turns into a frenetic rescue operation.

The ride is a fast-paced series of dives, climbs, and tight turns through Gru's Rube Goldberg–esque machines. Like The Simpsons Ride, there are more sight gags and interesting things to see here than anyone possibly could in a single ride. Guests exit the ride into a colorful carnival-themed gift shop, where they may find the opportunity for a photo with some Minions.

TOURING TIPS Minion Mayhem, a hit import from Universal Studios Florida, features a much more elaborate facade (try ringing doorbells on the homes neighboring the attraction entrance) than the Orlando ride; this version is also blessed with a second theater and preshow, effectively doubling the attraction's capacity. Unfortunately, unlike Orlando's version, Hollywood's ride lacks 3-D visuals and stationary seating, making the attraction less immersive and inaccessible to those who don't meet the height requirement or can't handle the shaking simulators. If the line for Despicable Me exceeds 30 minutes, try late afternoon or the hour before the park closes. Adjacent to the ride's exit, the Super Silly Fun Land area should help small tykes burn off some steam, with wet and dry playgrounds, carnival midway games, and Silly Swirly (★★½), a simple Dumbo-style spinning ride sporting wacky bug-shaped vehicles and Minion-ized disco music.

DreamWorks Theatre, Featuring *Kung Fu Panda Adventure* ★★★★

APPEAL BY AGE PRESCHOOL ★★★★ GRADE SCHOOL ★★★★½ TEENS ★★★★½ YOUNG ADULTS ★★★★ OVER 30 ★★★★ SENIORS ★★★★

What it is Multisensory theater show. **Scope and scale** Headliner. **When to go** The first hour the park is open or after 4 p.m. **Duration of show** About 10 minutes, including 3-minute preshow. **Probable waiting time** About 20 minutes.

DESCRIPTION AND COMMENTS The Art Deco DreamWorks Theatre screens short films featuring franchises from the Universal-owned computer-animation studio; namely, an all-new adventure starring Master Po, the portly protagonist of the Kung Fu Panda series, and his Furious Five friends. After a scene-setting preshow featuring cameos by Shrek (the building's former occupant) and the Trolls, the audience enters what appears to be an ornate theater outfitted with opera boxes and curtains; keep a close eye on those seemingly solid ornamentations. The show incorporates the usual slate of multisensory 4-D effects—water, wind, moving seats, 360-degree surround sound, LED lighting, fog—but instead of 3-D glasses, it uses advanced projection-mapping effects to extend the action beyond the edges of the screen. The plot is inconsequential; this experience is all about kinetic eye candy, interspersed with Jack Black wisecracks, and on that level it certainly succeeds. The venue launched with all-day screenings of *Kung Fu Panda Adventure* but is equipped to rotate programming, perhaps to present seasonal shows themed to Halloween or Christmas.

TOURING TIPS The DreamWorks Theatre holds 224 seats for an hourly capacity of about 1,300 guests. Pop in early, or check back in the late afternoon when wait times should drop below 30 minutes. During the preshow, jockey for a view of both the main door and the trophy case (watch the hammer at the end). In the main show, sit toward the back of the room for the best view of the immersive sidewall imagery. The motion simulation can be quite vigorous, so look for a green stationary seat if you have a sensitive back.

The Simpsons Ride ★★★★

**APPEAL BY AGE   PRESCHOOL ★★★½   GRADE SCHOOL ★★★★   TEENS ★★★★
YOUNG ADULTS ★★★★   OVER 30 ★★★★   SENIORS ★★★½**

What it is Mega-simulator ride. **Scope and scale** Super-headliner. **When to go** Before the Lower Lot opens. **Comment** Must be 40" tall to ride; not recommended for pregnant women or people prone to motion sickness; switching-off option (see page 147). **Duration of ride** 4⅓ minutes, plus preshow. **Average wait time per 100 people ahead of you** 3 minutes. **Loading speed** Moderate.

Queasy

DESCRIPTION AND COMMENTS This ride is based on the Fox animated series that is TV's longest-running sitcom. Featuring the voices of Dan Castellaneta (Homer), Julie Kavner (Marge), Nancy Cartwright (Bart), Yeardley Smith (Lisa), and other cast members, the attraction takes a wild and humorous poke at thrill rides, dark rides, and live shows "that make up a fantasy amusement park dreamed up by the show's cantankerous Krusty the Clown."

Two preshows involve *Simpsons* characters speaking sequentially on different video screens around the line area. Their comments help define the characters for guests who are unfamiliar with the TV show. The attraction is a simulator ride similar to Star Tours at Disneyland Park, but with a larger domed Omnimax-type screen more like that of Soarin' at Disney California Adventure. The interior queue in Hollywood's Simpsons has slightly more breathing room than is found at the same attraction in Orlando, and the ride has been upgraded with 4K projectors and a photo op at the end, but the East and West Coast versions are otherwise indistinguishable.

The story line has the conniving Sideshow Bob secretly arriving at Krustyland, the aforementioned amusement park, and plotting his revenge on Krusty and Bart, who, in a past *Simpsons* episode, revealed that Sideshow Bob had committed a crime for which he'd framed Krusty. Sideshow Bob gets even by making things go wrong with the attractions that the Simpsons (and you) are riding.

Like the show on which it's based, The Simpsons Ride definitely has an edge, and more than a few wild hairs. There will be jokes and visuals that you'll get but will fly over your children's heads—and most assuredly vice versa. A mom from Huntington, New York, had this to say:

The ride is lots of fun and suitable for all guests. I'm not a fan of wild motion simulators, but I was fine on this ride.

TOURING TIPS Expect large crowds all day. We recommend arriving at the park before opening and making the ride your last stop before the Lower Lot attractions open. Though not as rough and jerky as its predecessor, it's a long way from being tame. Several families we interviewed found the humor a little too adult for their younger children. Don't miss the neighboring Simpsonized carnival games and Kwik-E-Mart gift shop for more snarky Simpsons sight gags, as well as an expansive strip of Springfield-inspired shops and eateries (partially patterned after Universal Studios Florida's popular Fast Food Boulevard). Featured destinations include Krusty Burger, Luigi's Pizza, Phineas Q. Butterfat's Ice Cream, Moe's Tavern, and Duff Brewery Beer Garden. You'll also find funny facades of iconic cartoon locations such as Springfield's police station, elementary school, and nuclear power plant; try pressing the button outside Homer's workstation for an explosive surprise.

Special Effects Show ★★★½

APPEAL BY AGE   PRESCHOOL ★★½   GRADE SCHOOL ★★★   TEENS ★★★½
YOUNG ADULTS ★★★½   OVER 30 ★★★½   SENIORS ★★★½

What it is A theater presentation on special effects. **Scope and scale** Major attraction. **When to go** Anytime. **Comments** Predictable but still interesting; may frighten young children. **Duration of show** 30 minutes. **Probable waiting time** 15 minutes.

DESCRIPTION AND COMMENTS Guests view a fast-paced presentation on special effects, with elements borrowed from both the old Special Effects Stages (formerly on the park's Lower Lot) and the *Horror Make-Up Show* found in Universal Studios Florida. Audience members participate in demonstrations of green screens, computer-generated imagery (CGI), and motion capture. For the finale, a volunteer is apparently attached to a flying rig (left over from the short-lived *Creature of the Black Lagoon* musical that once occupied this space) and sent sailing above the crowd. The educational content will already be familiar to anyone who has ever watched a DVD making-of documentary, and the show lacks *Horror Make-Up* humor and spontaneity, but the stunt demonstrations include a spectacular opportunity to watch a full-body fire burn in person.

TOURING TIPS The best seats seem to be in the center of the theater, not directly up front. Or try the seats to the left or right of the center runway.

Studio Tour, Including *Fast & Furious: Supercharged* ★★★★★

APPEAL BY AGE   PRESCHOOL ★★★   GRADE SCHOOL ★★★★   TEENS ★★★★
YOUNG ADULTS ★★★★   OVER 30 ★★★★   SENIORS ★★★★

What it is Indoor-outdoor tram tour of soundstages and back lot. **Scope and scale** Headliner. **When to go** After experiencing the other rides. **Duration of tour** 45–60 minutes, depending on studio productions. **Average wait time per 100 people ahead of you** 2½ minutes. **Loading speed** Fast.

DESCRIPTION AND COMMENTS The Studio Tour is the centerpiece of USH and is one of the longest attractions in American theme parks. The tour departs from the tram boarding facility to the *right* of The Simpsons Ride and down the escalator. (Note that there's also an escalator to the left of The Simpsons Ride, so don't get confused.)

Tonight Show host and former *Saturday Night Live* star Jimmy Fallon is the tour's prerecorded host. All trams are equipped with high-definition monitors showing clips from actual movies that demonstrate how the sets and soundstages were used in creating the films.

The Studio Tour circulates through the various street scenes, lagoons, special effects venues, and storage areas of Universal's back lot. The tram passes several soundstages where current films and TV shows such as *The Voice* are in production, and it actually enters three soundstages where action inspired by *Earthquake, King Kong,* and *The Fast and the Furious* is presented. Other famous sets visited include those from *Psycho, Jaws, War of the Worlds,* and *The Grinch Who Stole Christmas.* A simulated flash flood, long a highlight of the tour, has been enhanced with new sound effects. *Back to the Future* fans may spot the restored Lyon Estates gateway along the tour.

The award-winning *King Kong 360/3-D* is a virtual experience inspired by Peter Jackson's 2005 remake. Guests enter a darkened tunnel where tram-length curved projection screens transform into the jungles of Skull Island. A family of hungry *V. rexes* decides to dine on your tour group, and Kong himself swings to save you, with hydraulic lifts under the cars simulating the sensations of their tug-of-war. The experience is visceral and visually stunning, especially when seen from the middle of a row (sitting on the outside exposes the top of the screen, spoiling the illusion). At only about 90 seconds, *King Kong* is too short to be a satisfying stand-alone attraction (it was substantially expanded for the Orlando incarnation), but it's a terrific addition to the overall tour.

In 2015 Universal debuted *Fast & Furious: Supercharged,* a new finale to the tram tour, featuring Vin Diesel (Dominic "Dom" Toretto), Dwayne Johnson (Luke Hobbs), Michelle Rodriguez (Letty Ortiz), Tyrese Gibson (Roman Pearce), and Luke Evans (Owen Shaw) from the long-running car-racing franchise. Inside a 50,000-square-foot soundstage built on the site of the old avalanche-effect tunnel, the "3D-HD thrill ride" uses hydraulic platforms, 400-foot-long screens, and 34 4K 3-D projectors to make it appear as if your tram is in the midst of a high-stakes car chase, pursuing an international crime cartel at 100-plus miles per hour through the streets of Los Angeles.

The *Fast & Furious* finale begins when your tram driver reveals that a member of your party is a crime witness being sought by both the bad guys and the FBI. Your tram shelters in an industrial warehouse, where a rave is in full swing until the feds crash the party. The F&F crew come to your rescue and escort you on a virtual high-speed highway chase filled with CGI car crashes and simulated explosions. After so much hype, *Supercharged* is frankly somewhat disappointing, failing to advance the *Kong 360* technology in a meaningful way or capture the visceral thrill that made the Fast and Furious films so popular. The dialogue and visual effects are shockingly cheesy (even by theme park standards), but it all goes by in such a nitro-fueled blur that audiences emerge applauding.

The great thing about the Studio Tour is that you see everything without leaving the tram—essentially experiencing four or five major attractions with only one wait.

TOURING TIPS Though the wait to board might appear long, do not be discouraged. Each tram carries several hundred people and departures are frequent, so the line moves quickly. We recommend taking the tram tour after experiencing the rides on the Lower Lot.

Tour trams are four cars long. The front car allows you to see your guide in the flesh; aim for the elevated back row. The third car is the sweet spot for experiencing the 3-D 360 visuals, and the back car bounces around the most from the motion simulation.

Including your wait to board and the duration of the tour, you will easily invest an hour or more at this attraction. Remember to take a restroom break before queuing up. This is one of the few attractions that allows food and beverages to be brought on board. Though the ride as a whole is gentle, some segments may induce vertigo or motion sickness—especially the *Kong* encounter and *Fast & Furious* finale. Finally, be aware that several of the scenes may frighten small children.

Universal's Animal Actors ★★★½

Thumbs Up for the Whole Family

What it is Trained animals stadium performance. **Scope and scale** Major attraction. **When to go** After you have experienced all rides. **Comment** Warm and delightful. **Duration of show** 20 minutes. **Probable waiting time** 15–20 minutes.

DESCRIPTION AND COMMENTS *Universal's Animal Actors* features various critters, including some rescued from shelters, demonstrating behaviors that animals often perform in the making of motion pictures. The live presentation is punctuated by clips from films and TV shows, including *The Secret Life of Pets*. The animals often exhibit an independence that frustrates their trainers while delighting the audience.

TOURING TIPS Presented five or more times daily, the program's schedule is in the smartphone app. Go when it's convenient for you; queue about 20 minutes before showtime. If you purchased front-of-the-line access through a Universal Express or VIP ticket, stick around after select showtimes for a personal audience with some of the furry stars.

The Walking Dead Attraction ★★★½

What it is A fun house–style walk-through of scenes based on AMC's *The Walking Dead*. **Scope and scale** Major attraction. **When to go** After seeing the headliner rides; see daily schedule for operating hours. **Comments** Not suitable for children age 13 and younger. Switching-off option (see page 147). **Duration of experience** About 4 minutes. **Average wait time per 100 people ahead of you** 5 minutes.

Dark   Loud   Scary

DESCRIPTION AND COMMENTS This attraction is an extremely elaborate horror maze inspired by AMC's top-rated zombie drama *The Walking Dead*. Designed in cooperation with series executive producer and horror makeup guru Greg Nicotero, it's a more permanent and elaborate version of the walk-through haunted houses you see around Halloween. Guests walk in the footsteps of Rick Grimes and the show's other survivors, battling through iconic locations such as the Atlanta hospital, the moonshine cabin, and the West Georgia Correctional Facility. As you pick your way through the dark, there are lots of gruesome sights, disorienting devices such as faux fire and lurching animatronics, and, worst of all, live people springing out of dark corners to startle you. If you don't like being startled but really want to see the attraction, follow some teenage girls through. The leaping, growling, menacing ghouls will expend lots of extra energy on the girls and be in a state of relative depletion when you pass through.

TOURING TIPS The Walking Dead is located very near the main entrance to the park. It doesn't take long to tour (as the length of the experience depends on how badly you want out), but once a line builds, it moves very slowly. This attraction operates for limited periods intermittently throughout the day and usually closes before the rest of the park.

WaterWorld ★★★★

APPEAL BY AGE PRESCHOOL ★★★ GRADE SCHOOL ★★★★ TEENS ★★★★
YOUNG ADULTS ★★★★ OVER 30 ★★★½ SENIORS ★★★½

What it is Arena show featuring simulated stunt-scene filming.
Scope and scale Major attraction. **When to go** After experiencing all the rides and the tram tour. **Duration of show** 15 minutes.
Probable waiting time 15–30 minutes.

Thumbs Up for the Whole Family

Loud

DESCRIPTION AND COMMENTS Drawn from the film *WaterWorld,* this outdoor theater presentation features stunts and special effects performed on and around a small man-made lagoon. The action involves various watercraft and, of course, a lot of explosions and falling from high places into the water. Fast-paced and well adapted to the theater, the production is in many ways more compelling than the film that inspired it. The show's climax features stunts and pyrotechnics, making for a rousing finale.

TOURING TIPS Wait until you have experienced all the rides and the tram tour before checking out *WaterWorld.* Because the show is located near the main entrance, most performances are filled to capacity. Arrive at the theater about 30 minutes before the showtime listed in the daily entertainment schedule. Be careful if you sit in on a green bench; when this show says "splash zone," it means it. The stunt team reveals some behind-the-scenes secrets in an interesting show-and-tell seminar for Universal Express and VIP guests after select shows.

The Wizarding World of Harry Potter

Universal Studios Hollywood's Wizarding World of Harry Potter, a close copy of the original "land" at Orlando's Islands of Adventure with some subtle upgrades, is an amalgamation of landmarks, creatures, and themes that are faithful to the films and books. You access the area through its main entrance, an imposing gate adjacent to the DreamWorks Theatre that leads to The Wizarding World's primary shopping and dining area,

Hogsmeade, a village depicted in winter and covered in snow. (A secondary entryway is found between The Simpsons Ride and the Studio Tour escalator, but it may be restricted to exit-only traffic.) The towering castle houses **Hogwarts School of Witchcraft and Wizardry,** flanked by the **Flight of the Hippogriff** kiddie coaster and **Hagrid's Hut.** The grounds and interior of the castle contain part of the queue for the super-headliner **Harry Potter and the Forbidden Journey.** Universal went all out on the castle, with the intention of creating an icon even more beloved and powerful than Sleeping Beauty Castle at Disneyland.

In front of the gate, the **Hogwarts Express** locomotive sits belching steam, and a small station houses a train-themed gift shop. The village is rendered in exquisite detail: stone cottages and shops have steeply pitched slate roofs, bowed multipaned windows, gables, and tall, crooked chimneys. Add cobblestone streets and gas streetlamps, and Hogsmeade is as reminiscent of Sherlock Holmes as it is of Harry Potter. Your first taste—literally—of the Harry Potter universe comes courtesy of **Honeydukes.** Specializing in Potter-themed candy such as Acid Pops (no flashbacks, guaranteed), Tooth Splintering Strong Mints, and Fizzing Whizbees, the sweet shop offers no shortage of snacks that administer an immediate sugar high. The big draw is the elaborately boxed Chocolate Frogs; the packaging looks as if it came straight from a Harry Potter film, complete with wizard trading card. Taking up a small corner of Honeydukes is **Zonko's Joke Shop,** selling toys such as Fanged Flyers (Frisbees with teeth) and adorable Pygmy Puff dolls.

Next door to Honeydukes and set back from the main street is **Three Broomsticks,** a rustic tavern serving English staples such as fish-and-chips, shepherd's pie, bangers and mash, and Guinness stew. To the rear of the tavern is the **Hog's Head** pub, which serves a nice selection of beer and is the quickest place to get The Wizarding World's signature nonalcoholic brew, **Butterbeer** (vanilla soda with butterscotch–marshmallow foam, available cold, frozen, or hot). There's even Butterbeer fudge (tooth-shatteringly sweet) and Butterbeer potted cream (like butterscotch pudding in a jar), and Butterbeer ice cream, sold hard-packed in prepackaged cups. For the adults, exclusive beers are available; we like the Wizard's Brew, a rich chocolate stout. If all that imbibing inspires you to heed nature's call, be warned that Moaning Myrtle haunts both the men's and ladies' sides of the land's only facilities; hearing her cries while you're trying to go can be distracting to say the least.

On the far side of the pub is **Ollivanders,** where young wizards are matched with magic wands (see the full description on pages 343–345) in a brief but charming show. Adjoining the wand shop (where you can browse without queuing for the show) is **Wiseacre's Wizarding Equipment,** where you can buy binoculars or telescopes.

Roughly across the street from the pub, you'll find benches in the shade at the **Owlery,** where animatronic owls (complete with lifelike poop) ruffle and hoot from the rafters. Next to the Owlery is the **Owl Post,** where you can have mail stamped with a Hogsmeade postmark before dropping it off for delivery. The Owl Post also sells stationery, school supplies, and toy owls. Here, once again, a nice selection of owls preens on the timbers overhead. The Owl Post is attached to **Dervish and Banges,** a magic supplies shop selling brooms and Quidditch equipment, and **Gladrags Wizardwear,** ground zero for getting outfitted in fashionable school robes.

Finally, at the exit of Hogwarts Castle is **Filch's Emporium of Confiscated Goods,** which offers all manner of Potter-themed gear, including Marauder's Maps, magical creature toys, film-inspired chess sets, and, of course, Death Eater masks (breath mints extra). In keeping with the stores depicted in the Potter films, the shopping venues in The Wizarding World of Harry Potter–Hogsmeade are small and intimate—so intimate, in fact, that they feel congested when they're serving only 12–20 shoppers. USH also sells most of its Potter merchandise, including wands, at two easily accessible stores near the park entrance.

After a somewhat slow start, Hollywood's Potter attractions have attracted a stampede of interest from locals and tourists alike. Prepare for the land to be packed to the gills if you visit during a peak period. Guests who purchase advance tickets online or book a vacation package, including admission and a room at a designated Preferred Hotel (see universalstudioshollywood.com/hotels for details), are granted early park admission to The Wizarding World 30 minutes before the general public; if you are eligible for this perk, it's your best way to experience the headliner ride and browse the shops with minimal waiting. If the Hogsmeade area reaches maximum capacity (a little more than 6,000 guests), you may need to queue just to enter the land, and then queue again for the individual attractions once inside. If you can't use early entry, your best bet for experiencing Harry Potter may be to bypass the daytime rush and wait until late afternoon, when you should be able to enter without waiting. Crowds flood in after sundown to see the seasonal light show on Hogwarts Castle, but ride wait times are often minimal in the hour before closing.

Flight of the Hippogriff ★★★

APPEAL BY AGE   **PRESCHOOL ★★★½**   **GRADE SCHOOL ★★★★**   **TEENS ★★★**
YOUNG ADULTS ★★½   **OVER 30 ★★★½**   **SENIORS ★★★**

What it is Kiddie roller coaster. **Scope and scale** Minor attraction. **When to go** First 90 minutes the park is open or after 4 p.m. **Comment** Must be 39" tall to ride. Single-rider line. **Duration of ride** 1 minute. **Average wait time per 100 people ahead of you** 6¼ minutes. **Loading speed** Slow.

Lose Things

DESCRIPTION AND COMMENTS Below and to the right of Hogwarts Castle, next to Hagrid's Hut, the Hippogriff is short and sweet but not worth much of a wait. This outdoor, elevated coaster is designed for children old enough to know about Harry Potter but not yet tall enough to ride Forbidden Journey. The ride affords excellent views of the area within Wizarding World and of Hogwarts, and the theming is also very good, considering that this isn't a major attraction. As a children's coaster only slightly taller and longer than Gadget's Go Coaster in

Disneyland, there are no loops, inversions, or rolls: it's just one big hill and some mild turns, and almost half of the 1-minute ride time is spent going up the lift hill. Hollywood's coaster has a layout similar to the Orlando original, but this one is a brand-new model manufactured by Mack (rather than an aging Vekoma) and gives a much smoother and somewhat snappier ride.

For fans of Harry Potter, there are two gorgeous items in this attraction that you will want to see. The first is a faithful re-creation of Hagrid's Hut in the queue (complete with the sound of Fang howling) while the second is an incredible animatronic of Buckbeak that you pass by while on the ride. Remember that when Muggles (also known as humans) encounter hippogriffs like Buckbeak, proper etiquette must always be maintained to avoid any danger. Hippogriffs are extremely proud creatures and must be shown the proper respect by bowing to them and waiting for them to bow in return.

TOURING TIPS If you are eligible for early entry, have your kids ride soon after the park opens while older siblings enjoy Forbidden Journey, or save it for late in the day.

Harry Potter and the Forbidden Journey ★★★★★

What it is Motion-simulator dark ride. **Scope and scale** Super-headliner. **When to go** Immediately after park opening or just before closing. **Comments** Expect long waits in line. Must be 48″ tall to ride; switching-off option (see page 147). Single-rider line. All bags must be placed in a free locker. **Duration of ride** 4¼ minutes. **Average wait time per 100 people ahead of you** 3 minutes. **Loading speed** Fast.

Dark   Loud   Scary   Lose Things   Queasy

DESCRIPTION AND COMMENTS This ride provides the only opportunity at Universal to come close to Harry, Ron, Hermione, and Dumbledore as portrayed by the original actors. Half the attraction is a series of preshows, setting the stage for the main event, a thrilling dark ride. You can get on the ride in only 10–25 minutes using the singles line, but everyone should go through the main queue at least once. The characters are incorporated into the queue and serve as an important element of the overall experience, not merely something to keep you occupied while you wait for the main event.

From Hogsmeade you reach the attraction through the imposing Winged Boar gates and progress along a winding path past the Weasleys' crashed Ford Anglia from *The Chamber of Secrets*. Entering the castle on a lower level, you walk through a sort of dungeon festooned with various icons and prop replicas from the Potter flicks, including the Mirror of Erised from *Harry Potter and the Sorcerer's Stone*. You later emerge back outside and in the Hogwarts greenhouses. The greenhouses compose the larger part of the Forbidden Journey's queuing area, and despite some strategically placed mandrakes, there isn't much here to amuse beyond the majestic view of the mountains. If you're among the first in the park and in the queue, you'll move through this area pretty quickly.

Having finally escaped horticulture purgatory, you reenter the castle, moving along its halls and passageways. One chamber you'll probably remember from the films is a multistory gallery of portraits, many of whose subjects come alive when they take a notion. You'll see for the first time the four founders of Hogwarts: Helga Hufflepuff holding her famous cup, Godric Gryffindor and Rowena Ravenclaw nearby, and the tall, moving portrait of Salazar Slytherin straight ahead. The founders argue about Quidditch and Dumbledore's controversial decision to host an open house at Hogwarts for Muggles (garden-variety mortals). Don't rush through the gallery—the effects are very cool, and the conversation is essential to understanding the rest of the attraction.

Next, after you've navigated more passages, is Dumbledore's office, where the wizard principal appears on a balcony and welcomes you to Hogwarts. The headmaster's appearance is your introduction to Musion Eyeliner technology—a high-definition video-projection system that produces breathtakingly realistic, three-dimensional, life-size moving holograms. After his remarks, Dumbledore dispatches you to the Defence Against the Dark Arts classroom to hear a presentation on the history of Hogwarts.

As you gather to await the lecture, Harry, Ron, and Hermione pop out from beneath an invisibility cloak. They suggest that you ditch the lecture in favor of joining them for a proper tour of Hogwarts, including a Quidditch match. After some repartee among the characters and a couple of special effects surprises, it's off to the Hogwarts Official Attraction Safety Briefing and Boarding Instructions Chamber—OK, it's actually the Gryffindor common room, but you get the picture. The briefing and instructions are presented by animated portraits, including an etiquette teacher. Later, even the famed Sorting Hat gets into the act. All this leads to the Room of Requirement, where hundreds of candles float overhead as you board the ride.

After all the high-tech stuff in your queuing odyssey, you'll naturally expect to be wowed by your ride vehicle. Surely it's a Nimbus 3000 turbo-broom, a phoenix, a hippogriff, or at least the Weasleys' flying car. But no, what you'll ride on the most technologically advanced theme park attraction in America is . . . a bench? Yep, a bench.

A bit anticlimactic, perhaps, but as benches go, this one's a doozy, mounted on a Kuka robotic arm. When not engaged in Quidditch matches, a Kuka arm is a computer-controlled robotic arm similar to the kind used in heavy manufacturing. If you think about pictures you've seen of automotive assembly plants, Kuka arms are those long metal appendages that come in to complete welds, move heavy stuff around, or fasten things. With the right programming, the arms can handle just about any repetitive industrial tasks thrown at them (see kuka.com for more info).

unofficial **TIP**
Even if your child meets the height requirement, consider carefully whether Forbidden Journey is an experience he or she can handle: because the seats on the benches are compartmentalized, kids can't see or touch Mom or Dad if they get frightened.

High-tech high jinks aside, is the attraction itself ultimately worthy of the hype? In a word, yes! Your 4¼-minute adventure is a headlong sprint through the most thrilling moments from the first few Potter books: you'll soar over Hogwarts Castle, narrowly evade an attacking dragon, spar with the Whomping Willow, get tossed into a Quidditch match, and fight off Dementors inside the Chamber of Secrets. Scenes alternate between enormous physical sets (complete with animatronic creatures), elaborate lighting effects, and high-definition video-projection domes that surround your field of view, similar to Soarin' Around the World or The Simpsons Ride. Those Kuka-powered benches really do "levitate" in a manner that feels remarkably like free flight, and while you don't go upside down, the sensation of floating on your back or being slung from side to side is certainly unique.

Forbidden Journey can be a lunch-liberating experience. We recommend that you not ride with a full stomach. If you start getting queasy, fix your gaze on your feet and try to exclude as much from your peripheral vision as possible.

The ride's flat projections have been polished up to 120 frames per second, reducing flicker and motion blur to create a sharper, more lifelike image. Other adjustments from Orlando have also made what was already one of the world's best attractions even better. Interior sets, monumental to begin with, are even more massive in Hollywood, with expanded scenery in the Forbidden Forest and Chamber of Secrets scenes, while lighting and sound effects were amped up to 11 for maximum impact. Of particular note is the expanded army of Dementor animatronics, which regained the outstretched limbs deemed too spooky for Orlando's audiences.

The seamless transitions between screens and sets, and the way the domes appear to remain stationary in front of you while actually moving, serve to blur the boundary between actual and virtual better than any attraction before it. The greatest-hits montage plotline may be a bit muddled, but the ride is enormously effective at leaving you feeling as though you just survived the scariest scrapes from the early educational career of The Boy Who Lived.

To understand the story line and get the most out of the attraction, you really need to see and hear the entire presentation in each of the preshow rooms. This won't happen unless, contrary to the admonishments of the team members, you just park yourself and watch a full run-through of each preshow. Try to find a place to stop where you can let those behind you pass and where you're as far away from any staff as possible. As long as you're not creating a logjam, the team members will likely leave you alone.

Hollywood's Hogwarts has a private secondary queue (complete with its own enchanted portrait gallery) as a Universal Express entrance for guests who paid extra to skip the line. However, if you bring any bags, you may still need to wait in the external queue for an open locker before reaching the Express entrance. The Express queue also doubles as a castle walk tour, providing nonriding guests a way to see the preshow without waiting in line; ask the greeter inside for a ticket that will permit you into the secondary queue.

The dialogue in the preshows is delivered in English accents of varying degrees of intelligibility, and at a very brisk pace. Add an echo effect owing to the cavernous nature of the preshow rooms, and it can be quite difficult for Yanks to decipher what's being said. This is especially evident in the staccato repartee between Harry, Ron, and Hermione in the Defence Against the Dark Arts classroom.

TOURING TIPS The best way to ride Forbidden Journey with a reasonable wait is to be one of the first through the turnstiles in the morning (especially if eligible for early entry) or to visit in the final hours of the evening.

Upon approaching Forbidden Journey's front gates, those who have bags or loose items and therefore require a free locker may be directed into an extended outdoor queue. The Forbidden Journey locker area in Hollywood is much more open and accessible than the one in Orlando, but it can still be crowded and confusing, so send only one member of your party to stow everyone's stuff while the rest of the family waits farther ahead. Alternatively, have one member of your party hold your bags for you in the child swap area.

Universal warns you to secure or leave behind loose objects, which most people interpret to mean eyeglasses, purses, ball caps, and the like. However, the ride makes a couple of moves that will empty your trousers faster than a master pickpocket—ditto and worse for shirt pockets. When these moves occur, your stuff will clatter around like quarters in a slot machine tray.

Whereas on most attractions the wait in the singles line is one-third the wait in the standby line, at Forbidden Journey it can be as much as one-tenth. Because the individual seating separates you from the other riders whether your party stays together or not, the singles line is a great option, as this wife from Edinburgh, Scotland, discovered:

Trust me—sitting next to hubby on Forbidden Journey, romantic though it may be, is not as awesome as having to wait only 15 minutes as a single rider.

To get there, keep left all the way into the castle. Past the locker area, take the first left into the singles line.

If you see a complete iteration of each preshow in the queue and then experience the ride, you'll invest 25–35 minutes even if you don't have to wait. If you elect to skip the preshows (the Gryffindor common room, where you receive safety and loading directions, is mandatory) and use the singles line, you can get on in about 10–25 minutes at any time of day. At a time when the posted wait in the regular line was 2 hours, we rode and were out the door in 15 minutes using the singles line.

USH team members select guests of all sizes "at random" to plop in the test seats near the boarding station, but they're really looking for large people or those who have a certain body shape. Team members handle the situation as diplomatically as possible, but if they suspect you're not the right size, you'll be asked to sit down for a test, so try out the sample seats stationed outside the castle entrance before standing in line. For you to be cleared to ride, the overhead restraint has to click three times; once again, it's body shape rather than weight (unless you're over 300 pounds) that's key. Most team members will let you try a second time if you don't achieve three clicks on the first go. Passing the test by inhaling sharply is not recommended unless you can also hold your breath for the entire 4-plus minutes of the ride.

Ollivanders ★★★★

**APPEAL BY AGE PRESCHOOL ★★★★   GRADE SCHOOL ★★★★★   TEENS ★★★★
YOUNG ADULTS ★★★★   OVER 30 ★★★½   SENIORS ★★★½**

What it is Combination wizarding demonstration and shopping op. **Scope and scale** Major attraction. **When to go** After riding Harry Potter and the Forbidden Journey. **Comments** Audience stands. Enchanting. **Duration of presentation** 6 minutes. **Average wait time per 100 people ahead of you** 18 minutes.

Thumbs Up for the Whole Family

DESCRIPTION AND COMMENTS Ollivanders, located in Diagon Alley in the books and films, somehow sprouted a branch location in Hogsmeade. Potter purists have pointed out this misplacement, but the wand shop was franchised with J. K. Rowling's blessing. Inside this musty store stacked high with dusty boxes, 24 guests at a time can experience the little drama where wands choose a wizard (rather than the other way around). Orlando's original Ollivanders experience became a horrible bottleneck because of its limited capacity, but at USH, the shop has two separate choosing chambers and a blissfully shaded queue, changing it from a popular curiosity into an actual attraction.

Every few minutes, following a script from the Potter books, a wand-selection show takes place in which a random customer (often a child dressed in Potter regalia) is selected to take part in a wand-choosing ceremony. Usually just one person in each group gets to be chosen by a wand, though occasionally siblings are selected together. This is one of the most truly imaginative elements of The Wizarding World: a Wandkeeper sizes you up and presents a wand, inviting you to try it out; your attempted spells produce unintended, unwanted, and highly amusing consequences. Ultimately, a wand chooses its wizard, with all the attendant special effects. The Celtic zodiac-inspired wands ($52) presented in the ceremony interact with shop windows throughout The Wizarding World (see below).

After the presentation, guests exit into a gift shop, where interactive wands are available for purchase, along with noninteractive "famous wizard" replica wands ($46) for a vast variety of characters and toy "learner" wands ($29) for li'l wizards.

TOURING TIPS To increase your odds of being picked, be a cute kid, stand up front, and make eye contact. If your young 'un is selected to test-drive a wand, be forewarned that you'll have to buy it if you want to take it home. You do not need to see the wand-selection show to purchase a wand at Ollivanders—just enter the store directly rather than wait in the long outdoor queue.

INTERACTIVE WANDS AND SPELL-CASTING LOCATIONS Interactive wands ($52) are available in 13 Ollivanders Original styles inspired by the Celtic calendar; interactive wands modeled after those wielded by a variety of characters (including Harry, Hermione, Dumbledore, Sirius Black, and Luna Lovegood) are also available. The widest selection of wands is found in the Ollivanders shop, but stores outside of The Wizarding World at the entrance of the park, as well as at CityWalk's Universal Studios Store, carry a limited variety of interactive and noninteractive wands. Wands can also be ordered from Universal Orlando's merchandise website; wands from Florida or Japan are fully compatible with Hollywood's effects (and vice versa).

Medallions embedded in the ground designate more than a dozen locations around The Wizarding World where hidden cameras in storefront windows can detect the waving of these special wands and respond to the correct motions with special effects both projected and practical. You might use the swish and flick of Wingardium Leviosa to levitate one object or the figure four Locomotor spell to animate another. It can take some practice to get the hang of spell casting, but you'll feel a sense of accomplishment when you unlock a door or make flames erupt from a chimney. Wizards wander around the area to assist novices and demonstrate spells (though they may not loan their wands), but queues to trigger certain effects can grow to a dozen deep at peak times. A map provided with each wand details the location and movement for the effects.

Note that the price of the interactive wands includes unlimited activations of the hidden effects; you don't have to pay to recharge your wand on subsequent visits or even replace a battery. If you encounter a spell-casting location with a sign saying it currently has an anti-jinx in place, just move along to the next one; that's Potter-speak for "it's broken." Damaged wands are cheerfully "repaired" for free at Ollivanders, even without a receipt.

We've received positive feedback so far on the interactive wands, like this praise from a New York, New York, family:

We took our interactive wand and map and explored all the many surprises for well over an hour and had a fantastic time. An interactive wand is highly recommended. Our girls (12 and 14) had a blast making the wand motions and watching the windows come to life.

On the other hand, some guests have found the wands maddeningly difficult to master, as a father from Petaluma, California, warns:

After getting their wands, my boys were soon frustrated to tears that the wands didn't work and that they had wasted their allowance on "a piece of plastic junk," in my oldest son's words. We searched desperately for one of the robed employees to assist us, but it seemed they were all on break somewhere. After a long while we finally located one. He gave a quick tutorial on where to point the wand, how much to move it, where to stand, and so on, and my boys were able to get their wands to work. My best advice is that, after buying the wand, keep it in the box until you find someone helping at one of the magic windows, and get a lesson on how to use it. Many of the magic spells worked the opposite of how you would think, or were so subtle that you weren't sure if the spell had worked or not. The best windows for beginners are (in order) #11 Dominic Maestro's, #2 Three Broomsticks, and #1 Honeydukes.

LOWER LOT

THE LOWER LOT is accessible only via the escalators and stairs descending from the back left section of the Upper Lot. Configured roughly in the shape of the letter *T*, the Lower Lot is home to Transformers, Jurassic World, and Revenge of the Mummy, all headliner attractions at USH. Look for further developments on the Lower Lot in the next few years; construction is already underway on Super Nintendo World, featuring a Mario Kart ride. Be aware that the Lower Lot typically opens 1 hour after the rest of the park, though its attractions remain operating 15 minutes after closing time.

Jurassic World—The Ride ★★★★

What it is Indoor-outdoor adventure ride based on the movie *Jurassic World.* **Scope and scale** Super-headliner. **When to go** The first hour the Lower Lot is open or after 4 p.m. **Comments** Must be 42″ tall to ride; switching-off option (see page 147). Single-rider line. **Duration of ride** 6 minutes. **Average wait time per 100 people ahead of you** 2¼ minutes. **Loading speed** Fast.

Scary Wet Lose Things Queasy Rough

DESCRIPTION AND COMMENTS In late 2018 Universal closed its classic Jurassic Park water ride to retheme it after the recent reboot *Jurassic World* and its sequel, *Fallen Kingdom.* The reimagined attraction remains a boat tour of the dinosaur-filled theme park, which begins tranquilly before turning traumatic. In the new version, a massive Mosasaurus will will snap at you from inside its titanic tank, before you float into a face-off with an angry *Indominus rex.* Instead of the ubiquitous *T. rex* being the bad guy, this time she stomps in to save your bacon at the climactic moment, allowing the boat and its passengers to escape over an 84-foot waterfall.

The new Jurassic World ride still follows the same river path as the original Jurassic Park version, but everything from the scenery and props to sound and lighting have been overhauled, while new animatronics that more accurately resemble the new films' dino designs replace the aging robotic reptiles. The final drop to safety is still a doozy, though it's a foot shorter (and slightly less intense) than its Orlando sibling.

TOURING TIPS You can get very wet on this ride, and extra jets enabled during hot weather practically ensure a soaking. Once the ride is under way, there's a little splashing but nothing major until the big drop at the end. When you hit the bottom, enough water will cascade into the boat to extinguish a three-alarm fire. Bring along an extralarge garbage bag and (cutting holes for your head and arms) wear it like a sack dress. If you forget to bring a garbage bag, you can purchase a poncho at the park for about $10, or rent a locker to stow your stuff for a few bucks less.

Young kids must endure a double whammy. First, they are stalked by giant, salivating reptiles and then are catapulted over the falls. Wait until your kids are fairly stalwart before you spring Jurassic World on them, or let them sit out the ride inside the fossil-themed playground near the entrance.

The reimagined Jurassic World is one of the park's top draws, and the ride will always be jammed on warm days. Ride early in the morning upon arriving on the Lower Lot.

Revenge of the Mummy—The Ride ★★★½

What it is High-tech dark ride. **Scope and scale** Super-headliner. **When to go** The first hour the Lower Lot is open or after 4 p.m. **Comments** Must be 48″ tall to ride; switching-off option (see page 147). Single-rider line. All bags must be placed in a free locker. **Duration of ride** About 2 minutes. **Average wait time per 100 people ahead of you** 7 minutes. **Loading speed** Slow.

DESCRIPTION AND COMMENTS This is an indoor dark ride based on the Mummy flicks, where guests fight off "deadly curses and vengeful creatures" while flying through Egyptian tombs and other spooky places on a high-tech roller coaster.

The queuing area serves to establish the story line: you're in a group touring a 1944 archaeological dig of an Egyptian tomb when evil Imhotep decides to make another comeback. The theming includes authentic hieroglyphics as the queue makes its way to the loading area, where you board a somewhat clunky, jeep-looking vehicle. The ride begins as a slow, elaborate dark ride passing through various chambers, including one where golden treasures are offered in exchange for your soul. Suddenly you're shot at high speed straight forward into a minute of pitch-black hills and tight curves, dead-ending in an encounter with leg-tickling scarab beetles. We don't want to divulge too much, but the roller coaster part of the ride has no barrel rolls or any upside-down stuff.

After an all-too-brief backward section, the attraction anticlimaxes in a darkened dome, where the mummy moans and then blinds you with a strobe. Compared to Universal Studios Florida's ride of the same name, this abbreviated attraction severely disappoints with shorter drops, simpler Audio-Animatronics, and no pyrotechnics.

TOURING TIPS Revenge of the Mummy has a very low riders-per-hour capacity for one of the park's top draws. Your only prayer for a tolerable wait is to be on hand when the park opens and sprint to the Mummy immediately after riding Jurassic World and Transformers. If you can ride Space Mountain without getting sick, you should be fine on this.

Transformers: The Ride 3-D ★★★★½

APPEAL BY AGE PRESCHOOL ★★★ GRADE SCHOOL ★★★★★ TEENS ★★★★★ YOUNG ADULTS ★★★★★ OVER 30 ★★★★★ SENIORS ★★★★

What it is Multisensory 3-D dark ride. **Scope and scale** Super-headliner. **When to go** The first hour the Lower Lot is open or after 4 p.m. **Comments** Must be 40" tall to ride; single-rider line. **Duration of ride** 4½ minutes. **Average wait time per 100 people ahead of you** 3 minutes. **Loading speed** Moderate-fast.

DESCRIPTION AND COMMENTS Transformers—Hasbro's toy robots from the 1980s that you turned and twisted into trucks and planes—have been around long enough to go from commercial to kitsch to cool and back again. Thanks to director Michael Bay's recent movies, "Robots in Disguise" are again a blockbuster global franchise. Recruits to this cybertronic war enlist by entering the N.E.S.T. Base (headquarters of the heroic Autobots and their human allies) beneath a massive dimensional mural depicting Optimus Prime and his nemesis, Megatron, locked in mortal metal combat. Inside an extensive, elaborately detailed queue, video monitors catch you up on the backstory. Basically, the Decepticon baddies are after the AllSpark, source of cybernetic sentience. We're supposed to safeguard the shard by hitching a ride aboard our friendly Autobot ride vehicle Evac, presumably without getting smooshed like a Lincoln in a souvenir penny press when he shifts into android form. Needless to say, Megatron and his pals Starscream and Devastator won't make things easy, but you'll have Sideswipe and Bumblebee (sadly, the modern Camaro version instead of an old-school VW Beetle) backing you up. For the ride's 4½ minutes, you play human Ping-Pong ball in an epic battle between these Made in Japan behemoths. To do justice to this Bay-splosion–packed war of good versus evil, Universal has harnessed the same ride system behind Islands of Adventure's Amazing Adventures of Spider-Man ride, blending motion simulation and live effects with 3-D.

Transformers ups the ante with photo-realistic high-definition imagery, boosted by dichroic 3-D glasses (the same kind used in Star Tours) that produce remarkably sharp, vivid visuals. The plot amounts to little more than a giant game of keep-away, and the uninitiated will likely be unable to tell one meteoric mass of metal from another, but you'll be too dazzled by the debris whizzing by to notice. Fanboys will squeal with delight at hearing original cartoon actors Peter Cullen and Frank Welker voicing the pugilistic protagonists, and then spill into the postride gift shop to purchase armloads of exclusive merchandise, while the rest of us might need a bench on which to take a breather afterward. We'll admit slight disappointment at not getting to see an actual four-story-tall animatronic transform, but the ride's mix of detailed (though largely static) set pieces and video projections was likely a much more maintenance-friendly solution for bringing these colossi to life. Either way, this is one of the most intense, immersive thrill rides found in any theme park.

TOURING TIPS Though the opening of The Wizarding World has taken some of the heat off, Transformers still draws heavy crowds, so ride immediately after Jurassic World upon arriving on the Lower Lot. The single-rider entrance will often let you walk on the attraction, even when the standby wait is an hour, but its queue lacks any theming, so be sure to take at least one trip through the regular line. It can be difficult for your eyes to focus on the fast-moving imagery from the front row; center seats in the second and third rows provide the best perspective. And be sure to say hello to the towering robots posing for photos outside the entrance; they can talk back to you!

LIVE ENTERTAINMENT *at* UNIVERSAL STUDIOS HOLLYWOOD

THE THEATER ATTRACTIONS operate according to the entertainment schedule available in the official park app and on information boards around the park. The number of daily performances of each show varies from as few as 3 a day during less busy times of year to as many as 10 a day during the summer and holiday periods. Characters

like Gru's Minions, The Simpsons, and the Transformers can be spotted hanging out near their respective rides. Characters from DreamWorks films—including the Shrek, Kung Fu Panda, and Madagascar series, as well as *Trolls*—greet guests at designated photo ops around the central Universal Plaza, while Hello Kitty holds court at the Animation Studio Store, and others (SpongeBob SquarePants, Dora the Explorer, Beetlejuice, Dracula, and Scooby-Doo) frequently wander the Upper Lot. Don't miss bantering with the New York apartment dwellers leaning out of the second-story windows above the candy shop. Near the Jurassic World ride, you can take a selfie with a real-life velociraptor (actually an actor inside an impressive full-body puppet) and her wry wrangler.

Two brief street entertainments are staged in a raised outdoor alcove at the Forbidden Journey end of Hogsmeade. Showtimes aren't listed in the park map, but performances usually start every 30 minutes on the hour and half hour.

THE FROG CHOIR (★★★) is composed of four singers, two of whom are holding large amphibian puppets sitting on pillows. Inspired by a brief scene in *Harry Potter and the Prisoner of Azkaban,* the group sings three or four a cappella wizarding-related songs, including "Hedwig's Theme" and "Something Wicked This Way Comes." The 13-minute show concludes with a photo op. Though cute, *The Frog Choir* isn't much more than filler for USH's attraction list and probably not worth going out of your way for.

THE TRIWIZARD SPIRIT RALLY (★★★½) showcases a group of three men performing martial arts–type moves, including jumps, kicks, and simulated battle with sticks, as well as a group of five women performing rhythmic gymnastics. The entire performance lasts about 6 minutes. After each show, the students of Beauxbatons Academy of Magic and the Durmstrang Institute are available for group photos. Hollywood's version of this show is more exciting than Orlando's, with some impressive acrobatics, but is still only a must-do for major Potter fans.

THE DARK ARTS AT HOGWARTS CASTLE (★★★★) is a dazzling digital projection show that transforms The Wizarding World's central icon through magical video mapping effects, synchronized to a newly recorded score of John Williams's symphonic themes. This show explores the scarier side of the Wizarding World, with larger-than-life images of Inferi, Acromantula, Dementors, Death Eaters, and even Lord Voldemort himself appearing to crawl across the castle walls. All appears lost until Harry Potter's powerful Patronus spell—simulated by a synchronized swarm of sparkling drones—gallops in to save the day. There are no pyrotechnics, but the stirring music and spectacular lighting effects make it worth staying late for. The 10-minute performances repeat every 20 minutes after sunset on select evenings; check the park's app for showtimes. People tend to camp out for views of the first two showings of the evening, making it a perfect time to ride the Potter attractions; you should have plenty of elbow room if you stick around for the final runs

of the night. During the holiday season, the standard light show is swapped for one with a Christmas theme, which is a few minutes shorter and lacks drones but features some additional fireworks.

DINING *at* UNIVERSAL STUDIOS HOLLYWOOD

THE COUNTER-SERVICE FOOD at Universal Studios runs the gamut from burgers and hot dogs to pizza, fried chicken, crepes, and Mexican specialties. We rank most selections marginally better than fast food, though executive chef Eric Kopelow has made great strides in creativity and ingredient quality recently. Prices are comparable to those at Disneyland. **The Three Broomsticks** is the best restaurant at USH by far and ranks with the finest quick-service food found in any theme park, but the wait to order during mealtimes can be 30 minutes or more.

Our other favorites in the park outside The Wizarding World are the tacos and margaritas at **Cocina Mexicana** and the soups and salads at **French Street Bistro.** **Mel's Diner** has upgraded its burgers and decor, and **Jurassic Cafe** on the Lower Lot serves Costa Rican–inspired entrées like mojo pork and roasted red snapper. **Gru's Lab Café** (near Despicable Me Minion Mayhem) serves grilled cheese sandwiches with pulled pork, El Macho nachos, fried mac and cheese, and banana-flavored desserts to mollify your Minions' munchies. The Simpsons **Fast Food Boulevard** eateries are a great bet; give Cletus's chicken and waffles, Bumblebee Man's tacos, or a Krusty burger a try, with a Duff beer to wash it down.

For $15.99 (or $13.99 when purchased in pairs; reactivate for $8.99 per day) you get a large Coca-Cola Freestyle souvenir soda sipper cup and one day of unlimited refills from the park's 21 Freestyle fountains, each of which can mix 100-plus varieties of soft drinks; try the Orange Coke!

If you're looking for full-service dining, try **VIVO Italian Kitchen, Antojitos Cocina Mexicana, Buca di Beppo, Dongpo Kitchen,** or the **Hard Rock Cafe** in Universal CityWalk just outside the park entrance. **Jimmy Buffett's Margaritaville,** a longtime crowd-pleaser at Orlando's CityWalk, opened a Hollywood branch in 2017, serving signature laid-back libations and Floribbean bar food. If you prefer counter service, an upstairs food court is full of well-known franchises, with some more-adventuresome eateries like **Voodoo Doughnut, Poke Bar,** and **LudoBird** located on the lower level. If you leave the park for lunch, be sure to have your hand stamped for reentry. To service your caffeine addiction, there are now **Starbucks** outlets on both the Upper and Lower Lots, as well as in CityWalk.

UNIVERSAL STUDIOS HOLLYWOOD ONE-DAY TOURING PLAN *(page 384)*

THIS PLAN IS FOR GROUPS of all sizes and ages and includes thrill rides that may induce motion sickness or get you wet. If the plan calls for you to experience an attraction that does not interest you, proceed to the next step. The plan calls for minimal backtracking.

Before You Go

1. Call ☎ 800-864-8377 the day before your visit for the official opening time.

2. If you have young children in your party, consult the Small-Child Fright-Potential Table on page 327.

ADDITIONAL AREA ATTRACTIONS

FOR THEME PARK ENTHUSIASTS who have exhausted the activities on Universal's and Disney's properties, here are a few other related attractions in the area for you to explore:

THE J. PAUL GETTY MUSEUM AT THE GETTY CENTER (1200 Getty Center Dr., Los Angeles; ☎ 310-440-7300; getty.edu) is like the Disneyland of art museums. An entry plaza welcomes guest with historical multimedia presentations, and easily digestible exhibits and exquisite themed landscaping surround a central hub. There's even a monorail-like tram to ride up the mountain! The Getty's stunning ultramodern architecture actually outshines its second-rate artworks, but the million-dollar views alone are worth the short drive from Hollywood. Best of all, admission is free, and parking is only $20 ($15 after 3 p.m.). Avoid Wednesdays during the school year, when busloads of students are brought in.

BEETLE HOUSE (6356 Hollywood Blvd., Los Angeles; ☎ 929-291-0337; beetlehousela.com) is a nightmare before Christmas come true for fans of director Tim Burton. At this unofficial Burton-inspired bar, drinks fizz and foam, Jack Skellington puppets and Johnny Depp look-alikes roam, and retro music and freak shows fill the evenings. Skip the pricey prix fixe dinner and stick to drinks. Directly across Hollywood Boulevard is the equally unauthorized **SCUM & VILLAINY CANTINA** (6377 Hollywood Blvd.; ☎ 424-501-4229; scumandvillainycantina .com), which looks remarkably like Mos Eisley's notorious watering hole and even serves alcoholic blue milk. Unfortunately, there are no interactive actors or alien musicians, only awful 1980s karaoke. Just be careful; both venues are on the sketchier end of the street, 0.75 mile east of the more tourist-friendly home of Disney's El Capitan Theatre.

KNOTT'S BERRY FARM (8039 Beach Blvd., Buena Park; ☎ 714-220-5200; knotts.com) can credibly lay claim to being America's first true theme park, predating nearby Disneyland by decades. Thrill seekers will love the roller coasters, like GhostRider, Xcelerator, and HangTime; dark ride enthusiasts can enjoy Ghost Town's Calico Mine Ride and Timber Mountain Log Ride, which inspired iconic Disney E-tickets; and little kids get to party with Snoopy and the *Peanuts* gang. Single tickets ($84 adults; $54 ages 3–11 and 62+) and season passes ($98–$218) are significantly cheaper than Disneyland, so Knott's attracts lots of locals. Seasonal events like Knott's Scary Farm during Halloween and the springtime Boysenberry food festival draw big crowds. Food inside the park is pricier than Disneyland, but Mrs. Knott's famous chicken dinner just outside the gates should be on your bucket list.

THE RMS *QUEEN MARY* (1126 Queens Hwy., Long Beach; ☎ 877-342-0738; queenmary.com) has been moored in California for more than 50 years, longer than it sailed the Atlantic, but history buffs and ghost hunters alike should enjoy a visit to the vintage vessel, which is larger than the legendary *Titanic*. Admission options start at $30 per adult ($15 ages 4–11; check Groupon for discounts) and include entrance to a 4-D film and various exhibits (don't miss the ship's massive propeller and engines), plus one or more guided tours focusing on either the naval or paranormal. The old girl has seen better days—as a night in one of the dingy cabins will demonstrate—but you can still appreciate its once-peerless glory beneath the rust and duct tape.

APPENDIX

READERS' QUESTIONS
to the AUTHORS

QUESTION: *When you do your research, are you admitted to the park for free? Do the Disney people know you are there?*

ANSWER: We pay the regular admission, and usually the Disney people do not know we are on-site. Both in and out of Disneyland, we pay for our own meals and lodging.

QUESTION: *How often is* The Unofficial Guide to Disneyland *revised?*

ANSWER: We publish a new edition once a year but make corrections every time we go to press.

QUESTION: *I have an older edition of* The Unofficial Guide to Disneyland. *How much of the information in it is still correct?*

ANSWER: Veteran travel writers will acknowledge that 5%–8% of the information in a guidebook is out-of-date by the time it comes off the press! Disneyland is always changing. If you are using an old edition of *The Unofficial Guide to Disneyland,* the descriptions of attractions existing when the guide was published should still be generally accurate. Many other things, however—particularly the touring plans and the hotel and restaurant reviews—change with every edition. Finally, and obviously, older editions of *The Unofficial Guide to Disneyland* do not include new attractions or developments.

QUESTION: *Do you write each new edition from scratch?*

ANSWER: We do not. With a destination the size of Disneyland, it's hard enough to keep up with what's new. Moreover, we put great effort into communicating the most salient and useful information in the clearest possible language. If an attraction or hotel hasn't changed, we are reluctant to tinker with its coverage for the sake of freshening up the writing.

QUESTION: *Do you stay at Disneyland hotels? If not, where do you stay?*

ANSWER: We do stay at Disneyland-area hotels from time to time, usually after a renovation or management change. Since we began writing about Disneyland in 1984, we have stayed in more than 80 different properties in various locations around Anaheim.

QUESTION: *How are your age-group ratings determined? I am 42 years old. During Star Tours, I was quite worried about hurting my back. If the senior citizens rating is determined only by those brave enough to ride, it will skew the results.*

ANSWER: The reader makes a good point. Unfortunately, it's impossible to develop a rating unless the guest (of any age group) has actually experienced the attraction. So yes, all age-group ratings are derived exclusively from members of that age group who have experienced the attraction. Health problems, such as a bad back, however, can affect guests of any age, and Disney provides more-than-ample warnings on attractions that warrant such admonitions. But if you are in good health, our ratings will give you a sense of how much others your age enjoyed the attraction.

QUESTION: *I have heard that when there are two lines to an attraction, the left line is faster. Is this true?*

ANSWER: In general, no. We have tested this theory many times and usually have not gained an advantage of even 90 seconds by getting in one line versus another. The few rare exceptions are noted in the ride descriptions. What *does* occasionally occur, however, is that after a second line has *just been opened,* guests ignore the new line and persist in standing in the established line. Generally, if you encounter a two-line waiting configuration with no barrier to entry for either and one of the lines is conspicuously less populated than the other, get in it.

AND FINALLY . . .

To end on a high note, consider this compliment from a Redding, California, reader:

> *Thanks to your book, this trip turned out much better than our last, so much in fact that I required only half as much Valium.*

And so it goes . . .

INDEX

Note: Attractions at Disney California Adventure and Universal Studios Hollywood are designated (DCA) and (USH), respectively; all others are Disneyland Park.

celebration pins, 103
cell phone coverage, charging, 102–103
Chamber of Commerce, 289
Cheesecake Factory, The, 198, 210
child swap, 76, 147–148
children
  attraction minimum height requirements, 112
  babysitting, 137
  childproofing your hotel room, 119–120
  Disney characters, meeting or dining with, 77, 151–158
  Disneyland for 4-, 5-, and 6-year-olds, 113–114
  Disneyland for infants, toddlers, 110–113
  Disneyland for teens, 114–115
  inviting your children's friends, 115–117
  lost, 149–151, 217
  preparing to visit Disneyland with, 106–109
  restroom problems, 150
  scary or problematic attractions, 93, 137–145
  and single parents, 118–119
  small, touring plans for, 276, 277–278, 279–280, 322
  small-child fright-potential table, 138–140
  supplies for infants, toddlers, 131–132
  Universal Studios Hollywood for young, 327–328
  waiting-line strategies for adults with small, 145–149
Chip 'n Dale Treehouse, 250–251
Chuck-Bubba Relay, 146–147
Citizens of Buena Vista troupe, 317
CityPass, 19
Cleaver Brothers' Discount Tickets & Tours, 19
clip-out touring plans, 369–384
clothing, 125–126, 162
Club 33, 100
Cocina Cucamonga Mexican Grill, 176
Cocina Mexicana (USH), 350
Columbia Sailing Ship, 238
coolers, mini-fridges, 129
Corn Dog Castle, 176

cost
  admission, 18–23, 328–329
  food, 159–160
  parking, 33, 35, 330
  restaurants, 179
Courtyard Anaheim Theme Park Entrance, 58, 62
Cozy Cone Motel, 176–177
credit cards, 96
Critter Country, 7
  "anti-touring" plan, 282
  Disneyland Park vs. Walt Disney World (WDW), 10–11
  location, 213
  profiled attractions, 225–227
  small-child fright-potential table, 138
CVS, 100

D

Daisy's Diner, 169, 171
Dapper Dans barbershop quartet, 269
Dark Arts at Hogswarts Castle, The (USH), 349–350
Davy Crockett's Explorer Canoes, 225
day packs, 126–127
DCA. *See* Disney California Adventure (DCA)
Del Sol Inn, 58, 62
Denny's, 198
Dervish and Banges (USH), 339
Desert Palms Hotel & Suites, 58, 62–63
Despicable Me Minion Mayhem (USH), 331–332
dietary restrictions, 99
digital cameras, 132
dining
  See also restaurants *or specific restaurant*
  Disney character, 156–158, 164
  at Disneyland Resort, 159–160
  dress, 162
  Fantasmic! packages, 263–264
  fast food in the theme parks, 165–168
  food allergies, special requests, 162–163
  full-service, for families with young kids, 163–164

S

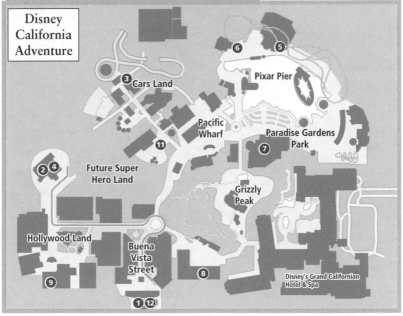

The Best of Disneyland Resort in One Day

Disney California Adventure

Cars Land

Pixar Pier

Pacific Wharf

Paradise Gardens Park

Future Super Hero Land

Grizzly Peak

Hollywood Land

Buena Vista Street

Disney's Grand Californian Hotel & Spa

1. Arrive at the entrance 40 minutes before official opening time.

2. As soon as the park opens, obtain FastPasses for Guardians of the Galaxy—Mission: Breakout! in Hollywood Land.

3. Ride Radiator Springs Racers in Cars Land.

4. Ride Guardians of the Galaxy—Mission: Breakout! in Hollywood Land using the FastPasses obtained earlier.

5. Try Toy Story Midway Mania! in Pixar Pier.

6. Ride the Incredicoaster.

7. Ride The Little Mermaid: Ariel's Undersea Adventure in Paradise Gardens Park.

8. Experience Soarin' Around the World.

9. In Hollywood Land, ride Monsters, Inc. Mike & Sulley to the Rescue! Skip it if the wait exceeds 30 minutes.

10. Eat lunch.

11. If you have time, ride Mater's Junkyard Jamboree in Cars Land.

12. Leave DCA and head to Disneyland Park.

(continued on next page)

The Best of Disneyland Resort in One Day

Mickey's Toontown

Star-Wars: Galaxy's Edge

19

Fantasyland
18

17 28

14

Critter Country
27

20 22

16 Tomorrowland

Frontierland

23

15

26

New Orleans Square

25

24

29

13

Adventureland

21

Main Street U.S.A.

Disneyland Park

13

(continued from previous page)

13. Get FastPasses for Indiana Jones Adventure in Adventureland.
14. Ride Peter Pan's Flight in Fantasyland.
15. Enjoy Star Tours—The Adventures Continue in Tomorrowland.
16. Try Buzz Lightyear Astro Blasters.
17. Experience Alice in Wonderland in Fantasyland.
18. Ride Dumbo the Flying Elephant.
19. See It's a Small World.
20. Obtain FastPasses for Big Thunder Mountain Railroad in Frontierland.
21. Ride Indiana Jones Adventure in Adventureland using the FastPasses obtained earlier.

22. Ride Big Thunder Mountain Railroad in Frontierland using the FastPasses obtained earlier.
23. Watch Disneyland's fireworks show. Find a spot on Main Street or near Sleeping Beauty Castle to watch it.
24. Ride Pirates of the Caribbean in New Orleans Square.
25. Take the Jungle Cruise in Adventureland.
26. See The Haunted Mansion in New Orleans Square.
27. Ride Splash Mountain in Critter Country.
28. Ride the Matterhorn Bobsleds in Fantasyland.
29. Experience Space Mountain in Tomorrowland.
30. Revisit your favorites or see any attractions you missed.

Authors' Select One-Day Plan with Star Wars: Galaxy's Edge

Disneyland Park

1. Arrive at the entrance at least 40 minutes before official opening time.
2. Get FastPasses for Space Mountain in Tomorrowland.
3. Enjoy Star Tours—The Adventures Continue.
4. Try Buzz Lightyear Astro Blasters.
5. Ride It's a Small World in Fantasyland.
6. Experience Space Mountain in Tomorrowland using the FastPasses you obtained earlier.
7. Go to the right of the *Mark Twain* Riverboat dock in Frontierland and get FastPasses for *Fantasmic!*
8. Ride Big Thunder Mountain Railroad in Frontierland.
9. Get FastPasses for Indiana Jones Adventure in Adventureland.
10. Ride Pirates of the Caribbean in New Orleans Square.
11. Experience The Haunted Mansion.
12. Use the Splash Mountain FastPass kiosk to secure Star Wars: Galaxy's Edge boarding passes for the afternoon (if needed), then ride Splash Mountain.

13. Experience Indiana Jones Adventure in Adventureland using the FastPasses obtained earlier.
14. Enjoy an early lunch at the French Market Restaurant in New Orleans Square.
15. Take the Disneyland Railroad from New Orleans Square to Main Street, U.S.A. If the line for the train is too long, skip it and walk.
16. See *The Disneyland Story,* presenting *Great Moments with Mr. Lincoln.*
17. Enter Star Wars: Galaxy's Edge using the boarding passes secured earlier. Ride a) Rise of the Resistance and/or b) *Millennium: Falcon: Smugglers Run.* Use the single-rider line if the standby wait exceeds 90 minutes. Spend time after your rides exploring the land.
18. Eat dinner at a) Docking Bay 7 Food and Cargo. Or, get a snack at b) Ronto Roasters.
19. Watch *Fantasmic!*
20. Watch Disneyland's fireworks from where you watched *Fantasmic!,* or from Main Street, U.S.A.
21. Experience Alice in Wonderland in Fantasyland.
22. Ride Peter Pan's Flight.

Star Wars: Galaxy's Edge and Best of Disneyland for Adults with Children One-Day Plan

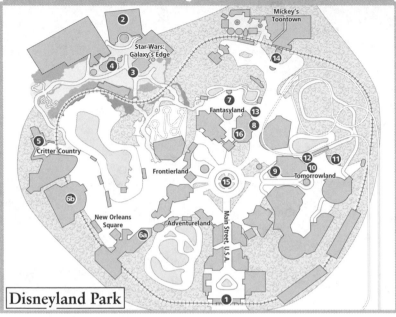

Disneyland Park

1. Arrive at the entrance at least 40 minutes before official opening time. If Disney is distributing tickets to enter Galaxy's Edge, obtain those as soon as possible.

2. Ride *Millennium Falcon:* Smugglers Run in Galaxy's Edge.

3. Get in line for Savi's Workshop, a 20-minute interactive experience where (for an extra cost) you can build your own custom lightsaber.

4. Use this time to explore the nooks and crannies of Galaxy's Edge. If you can, fit in lunch while you wander around Star Wars land.

5. Ride The Many Adventures of Winnie the Pooh in Critter Country.

6. Experience a) Pirates of the Caribbean or b) The Haunted Mansion in New Orleans Square, whichever you prefer or whichever has the shorter wait.

7. Ride Dumbo the Flying Elephant in Fantasyland.

8. Ride Alice in Wonderland.

9. Try Buzz Lightyear Astro Blasters in Tomorrowland.

10. Eat dinner at the Galactic Grill.

11. Ride Autopia.

12. Experience the Finding Nemo Submarine Voyage. If your kids don't want to ride Finding Nemo, head back to Critter Country and ride Splash Mountain.

13. Take a spin on the Mad Tea Party in Fantasyland.

14. See It's a Small World.

15. Watch Disneyland's fireworks show. Find a spot on Main Street or near It's a Small World to watch it.

16. If time permits, ride Peter Pan's Flight.

Star Wars: Galaxy's Edge Complete Plan

Star Wars: Galaxy's Edge

1. Visit disneyland.com at 7 a.m. on the morning of your visit to make reservations for Savi's Workship in late morning and Oga's Cantina in midafternoon. Arrive at the entrance at least 40 minutes before official opening time. If Disney is distributing virtual boarding passes to enter Galaxy's Edge, obtain those as soon as possible.

2. Enter Galaxy's Edge and immediately ride Rise of the Resistance.

3. Ride *Millennium Falcon:* Smugglers Run. Use the single-rider line if the standby wait exceeds 90 minutes.

4. Shop for droids at Mubo's Droid Depot.

5. Arrive at Savi's Workshop 20–60 minutes before your scheduled appointment.

6. Eat lunch inside a working hangar bay at Docking Bay 7 Food and Cargo.

7. When your reservation time comes, grab a drink and listen to DJ R-3X spin some music at Oga's Cantina.

8. Browse Jedi and Sith artifacts at Dok-Ondar's Den of Antiquities.

9. See all the galactic creatures at Creature Stall; look for the snoozing Loth Cat and other ani-matronic critters.

10. If you have little ones, head over to Toydarian Toyshop and take a look at the goods. Keep an eye out for Zabaka the Toydarian.

11. Try some Outpost Mix at a) Kat Saka's Kettle, or grab a sausage that's been grilled by a podracer engine at b) Ronto Roasters.

12. Use any remaining time to explore Star Wars: Galaxy's Edge, interact with the local inhabit-ants, and complete missions in the Play Disney Parks app's Datapad.

13. Watch the evening fireworks (when scheduled) from near the *Millennium Falcon.* The music isn't piped in, so cue up "Yub Nub" on your smartphone for an impromptu Endorian celebration.

One-Day Plan for Adults

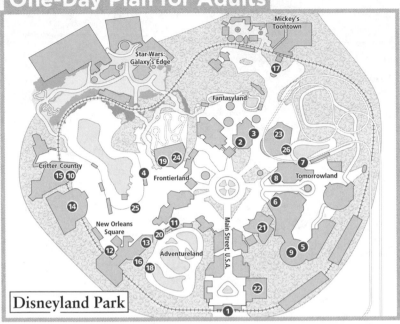

Disneyland Park

1. Arrive at the entrance 40 minutes before official opening time.
2. Ride Peter Pan's Flight in Fantasyland.
3. Ride Alice in Wonderland.
4. Go to the right of the *Mark Twain* Riverboat dock in Frontierland and get FastPasses for *Fantasmic!*
5. Walk to Tomorrowland and obtain a FastPass (or use MaxPass) for Space Mountain.
6. Ride Star Tours—The Adventures Continue.
7. Ride Finding Nemo Submarine Voyage.
8. Try Buzz Lightyear Astro Blasters.
9. Ride Space Mountain using the FastPasses you obtained earlier.
10. In Critter Country get FastPasses for Splash Mountain.
11. Take the Jungle Cruise in Adventureland.
12. Eat lunch at French Market in New Orleans Square.
13. Experience Pirates of the Caribbean.
14. Visit The Haunted Mansion.

15. Return to ride Splash Mountain in Critter Country using the FastPasses obtained earlier.
16. Get FastPasses for Indiana Jones Adventure in Adventureland.
17. Ride It's a Small World in Fantasyland.
18. Experience Indiana Jones Adventure in Adventureland using the FastPasses obtained earlier.
19. Obtain FastPasses for Big Thunder Mountain Railroad in Frontierland.
20. See *Enchanted Tiki Room* in Adventureland.
21. Eat dinner. Try Plaza Inn on Main Street, U.S.A.
22. See *The Disneyland Story,* presenting *Great Moments with Mr. Lincoln.*
23. Obtain FastPasses for Matterhorn Bobsleds in Fantasyland, or or use the single-rider line.
24. Ride Big Thunder Mountain Railroad in Frontierland using the FastPasses obtained earlier.
25. Watch *Fantasmic!*
26. Ride the Matterhorn Bobsleds in Fantasyland using the FastPasses obtained earlier.

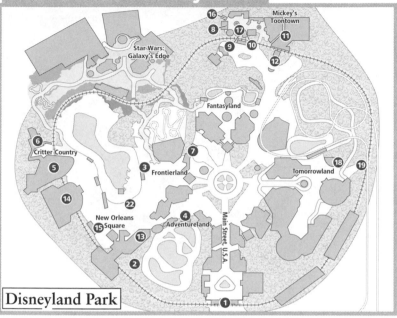

Two-Day Plan for Adults with Children: Day One

Star-Wars: Galaxy's Edge

Mickey's Toontown

16 · 8 · 17 · 11 · 9 · 10 · 12

Fantasyland

6 · Critter Country · 5 · 14 · 3 · Frontierland · 7 · 18 · 19 · Tomorrowland · 22 · New Orleans Square · 15 · 4 · Adventureland · 13 · 2 · Main Street, U.S.A. · 1

Disneyland Park

1. Arrive at the entrance 40 minutes before official opening time.
2. As soon as the park opens, ride Indiana Jones Adventure in Adventureland.
3. Go to the right of the *Mark Twain* Riverboat dock in Frontierland and get FastPasses for *Fantasmic!*
4. Take the Jungle Cruise in Adventureland.
5. Try Splash Mountain in Critter Country.
6. Ride The Many Adventures of Winnie the Pooh.
7. Experience the Royal Hall princess meet and greet in Fantasyland.
8. In Mickey's Toontown, tour Mickey's House.
9. Ride Gadget's Go Coaster.
10. Let the kids blow off some steam at Goofy's Playhouse.
11. Try Roger Rabbit's Car Toon Spin. Obtain FastPasses if the wait exceeds 30 minutes.

12. In Fantasyland, ride It's a Small World.
13. Ride Pirates of the Caribbean in New Orleans Square.
14. See The Haunted Mansion. Obtain FastPasses if the wait exceeds 30 minutes.
15. Eat lunch and take the Disneyland Railroad from New Orleans Square to Mickey's Toontown. If the line for the train is too long, skip it and walk.
16. In Mickey's Toontown, see Minnie's House.
17. Check out *Miss Daisy,* Donald's Boat.
18. Ride Autopia in Tomorrowland.
19. If time permits, take a round-trip on the Disneyland Railroad or Monorail.
20. Eat dinner.
21. Visit any attractions you may have missed earlier.
22. Watch *Fantasmic!*

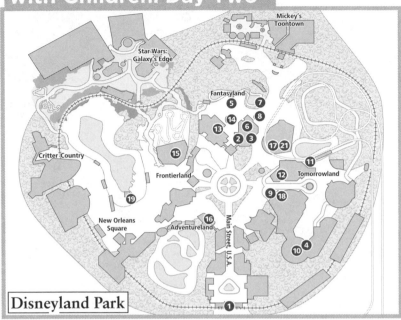

Two-Day Plan for Adults with Children: Day Two

Mickey's Toontown

Star Wars: Galaxy's Edge

Fantasyland

Critter Country

Frontierland

Tomorrowland

New Orleans Square

Adventureland

Main Street U.S.A.

Disneyland Park

1. Arrive at the entrance 40 minutes before official opening time.
2. As soon as the park opens, ride Peter Pan's Flight in Fantasyland.
3. Ride Alice in Wonderland.
4. Send a party member to obtain FastPasses (or use MaxPass) for Space Mountain in Tomorrowland.
5. Experience Dumbo the Flying Elephant.
6. Take Mr. Toad's Wild Ride.
7. Try the Storybook Land Canal Boats.
8. Take a spin on the Mad Tea Party.
9. Obtain FastPasses for Star Tours—The Adventures Continue in Tomorrowland.
10. Ride Space Mountain with the FastPasses you obtained earlier.
11. Take the Finding Nemo Submarine Voyage.
12. Try Buzz Lightyear Astro Blasters.

13. In Fantasyland, ride Pinocchio's Daring Journey.
14. Take a spin on the King Arthur Carrousel.
15. Ride Big Thunder Mountain Railroad in Frontierland.
16. See the *Enchanted Tiki Room* in Adventureland.
17. Obtain a FastPass for Matterhorn Bobsleds in Fantasyland.
18. Ride Star Tours in Tomorrowland using the FastPasses obtained earlier.
19. Take a raft to Tom Sawyer Island, and let the kids run around the island's Pirates Lair.
20. Eat lunch.
21. Return to Matterhorn Bobsleds and use the FastPasses you obtained earlier.
22. Visit any attractions you may have missed earlier.
23. Check the *Times Guide* for parades and fireworks.

Two-Day Plan A: Day One

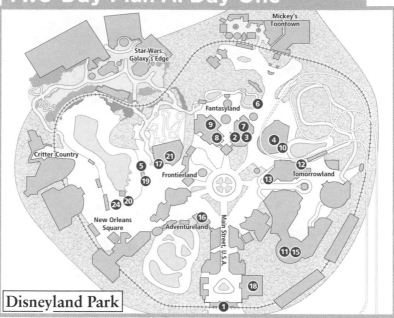

Disneyland Park

1. Arrive at the entrance 40 minutes before official opening time.
2. As soon as the park opens, ride Peter Pan's Flight in Fantasyland.
3. Experience Alice in Wonderland.
4. Obtain FastPasses for Matterhorn Bobsleds.
5. Go to the right of the *Mark Twain* Riverboat dock in Frontierland and get FastPasses for *Fantasmic!*
6. Take a cruise on the Storybook Land Canal Boats.
7. Take Mr. Toad's Wild Ride.
8. Ride Snow White's Scary Adventures.
9. Take Pinocchio's Daring Journey.
10. Ride Matterhorn Bobsleds using the FastPasses obtained earlier.
11. In Tomorrowland obtain FastPasses for Space Mountain.
12. Take the Finding Nemo Submarine Voyage.
13. Ride Buzz Lightyear Astro Blasters.
14. Eat lunch.
15. Ride Space Mountain using the FastPasses obtained earlier.
16. See the *Enchanted Tiki Room* in Adventureland.
17. Obtain FastPasses for Big Thunder Mountain Railroad in Frontierland.
18. See *The Disneyland Story*, presenting *Great Moments with Mr. Lincoln* on Main Street, U.S.A.
19. Ride the Sailing Ship *Columbia* or the *Mark Twain* Riverboat, whichever is boarding first.
20. Take a raft to the Pirate's Lair on Tom Sawyer Island.
21. Ride Big Thunder Mountain Railroad using the FastPasses obtained earlier.
22. Eat dinner.
23. Revisit favorite attractions or visit any attractions you may have missed earlier.
24. Watch *Fantasmic!*

Two-Day Plan A: Day Two

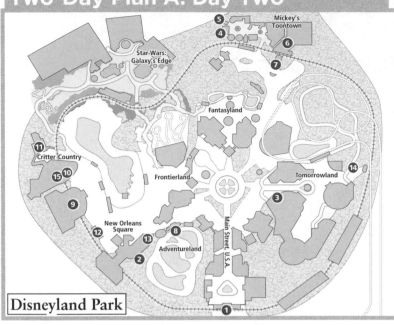

Disneyland Park

1. Arrive at the entrance 40 minutes before official opening time.
2. As soon as the park opens, take the Indiana Jones Adventure in Adventureland.
3. Ride Star Tours—The Adventures Continue in Tomorrowland.
4. In Mickey's Toontown, visit Mickey's House.
5. See Minnie's House.
6. Try Roger Rabbit's Car Toon Spin. Use FastPass if the wait exceeds 30 minutes.
7. Ride It's a Small World in Fantasyland.
8. Take the Jungle Cruise in Adventureland.
9. Ride The Haunted Mansion in New Orleans Square.

10. Obtain FastPasses for Splash Mountain in Critter Country.
11. Ride The Many Adventures of Winnie the Pooh.
12. Take a round-trip on the Disneyland Railroad from the New Orleans Square Station.
13. Ride Pirates of the Caribbean.
14. Take the monorail from Tomorrowland to Downtown Disney, and eat lunch.
15. Ride Splash Mountain in Critter Country using the FastPasses obtained earlier.
16. Revisit any favorite attractions or visit any attractions you may have missed earlier.
17. Check the *Times Guide* for parades and fireworks.

Two-Day Plan B: Day One

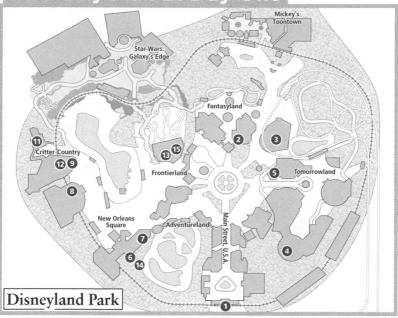

Disneyland Park

1. Arrive at the entrance 40 minutes before official opening time.
2. Ride Peter Pan's Flight in Fantasyland.
3. Ride Matterhorn Bobsleds.
4. In Tomorrowland Ride Space Mountain. Obtain FastPasses if the wait exceeds 30 minutes.
5. Experience Buzz Lightyear Astro Blasters.
6. Go to Adventureland and obtain FastPasses for Indiana Jones Adventure.
7. Ride Pirates of the Caribbean in New Orleans Square.
8. Experience The Haunted Mansion.
9. Go to Critter Country and obtain FastPasses for Splash Mountain.
10. Eat lunch.
11. Ride The Many Adventures of Winnie the Pooh in Critter Country.
12. Ride Splash Mountain using the FastPasses obtained earlier.
13. Walk back to Frontierland and get FastPasses for Big Thunder Mountain Railroad.
14. Ride Indiana Jones Adventure in Adventureland using the FastPasses obtained earlier.
15. Ride Big Thunder Mountain Railroad in Frontierland using the FastPasses obtained earlier.

Two-Day Plan B: Day Two

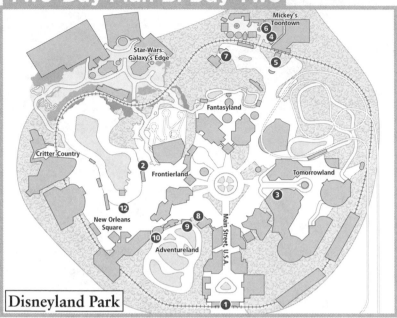

1. Arrive at Disneyland Park around noon.
2. Go to the right of the *Mark Twain* Riverboat dock in Frontierland and get FastPasses for *Fantasmic!*
3. Ride Star Tours—The Adventures Continue in Tomorrowland.
4. Walk to Mickey's Toontown and obtain FastPasses for Roger Rabbit's Car Toon Spin.
5. Ride It's a Small World in Fantasyland.
6. Ride Roger Rabbit's Car Toon Spin using the FastPasses obtained earlier.
7. Check showtimes and see *Mickey and the Magical Map* in Fantasyland.
8. Go to Adventureland and see the *Enchanted Tiki Room.*
9. Take the Jungle Cruise.
10. Experience Tarzan's Treehouse.
11. Revisit any favorite attractions or visit any attractions you may have missed earlier.
12. Watch *Fantasmic!*

Dumbo-or-Die-in-a-Day Plan

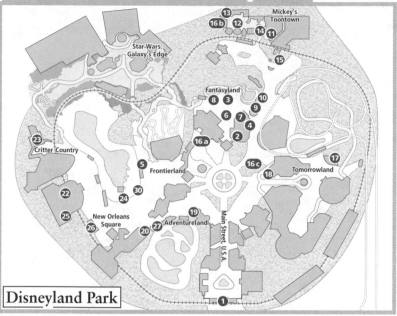

Disneyland Park

1. Arrive at the entrance 40 minutes before official opening time.
2. Ride Peter Pan's Flight in Fantasyland.
3. Ride Dumbo the Flying Elephant.
4. Ride Alice in Wonderland.
5. Send a party member to the right of the *Mark Twain* Riverboat dock in Frontierland (or use MaxPass) to get FastPasses for *Fantasmic!*
6. Ride the King Arthur Carrousel.
7. Take Mr. Toad's Wild Ride.
8. Ride the Casey Jr. Circus Train.
9. Take a spin on the Mad Tea Party.
10. Ride the Storybook Land Canal Boats.
11. In Mickey's Toontown, ride Roger Rabbit's Car Toon Spin. Obtain FastPasses if the wait exceeds 30 minutes.
12. Ride Gadget's Go Coaster.
13. Tour Minnie's House.
14. Let the kids blow off some steam at Goofy's Playhouse.
15. Ride It's a Small World in Fantasyland. Obtain FastPasses if the wait exceeds 30 minutes.
16. Experience the a) Royal Hall princess meet and greet. If your party isn't interested in

princesses, meet b) Mickey at Mickey's House, or c) Tinker Bell and her pixie friends at Pixie Hollow.
17. In Tomorrowland, ride Autopia.
18. Try Buzz Lightyear Astro Blasters.
19. See the *Enchanted Tiki Room* in Adventureland.
20. Ride Pirates of the Caribbean in New Orleans Square.
21. Eat lunch.
22. Obtain FastPasses for The Haunted Mansion.
23. Take The Many Adventures of Winnie the Pooh ride in Critter Country.
24. Take a raft to explore the Pirate's Lair on Tom Sawyer Island.
25. See The Haunted Mansion in New Orleans Square using the FastPasses obtained earlier.
26. Take a round-trip on the Disneyland Railroad from the New Orleans Square Station. Skip the train ride if the line is too long.
27. Explore Tarzan's Treehouse in Adventureland.
28. Eat dinner.
29. Visit any attractions you may have missed earlier.
30. Watch *Fantasmic!*

One-Day Plan for Adults

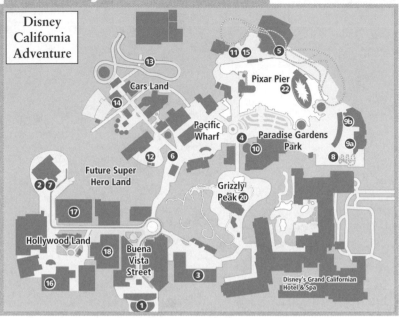

Disney California Adventure

Cars Land

Pixar Pier

Pacific Wharf

Paradise Gardens Park

Future Super Hero Land

Grizzly Peak

Hollywood Land

Buena Vista Street

Disney's Grand Californian Hotel & Spa

1. Arrive at the entrance 40 minutes before official opening time.
2. As soon as the park opens, obtain FastPasses for Guardians of the Galaxy—Mission: Breakout! in Hollywood Land.
3. Ride Soarin' Around the World in Grizzly Peak.
4. Obtain FastPasses for *World of Color.* FastPasses are distributed to the right of the entrance of The Little Mermaid: Ariel's Undersea Adventure in Paradise Gardens Park.
5. Try Toy Story Midway Mania! in Pixar Pier.
6. Obtain FastPasses for Radiator Springs Racers. FastPasses are distributed outside and to the left of Cars Land's main entrance.
7. Ride Guardians of the Galaxy—Mission: Breakout! in Hollywood Land using the FastPasses obtained earlier.
8. Ride Goofy's Sky School in Paradise Gardens Park.
9. Eat lunch. Try a) Paradise Garden Grill or b) Boardwalk Pizza & Pasta.

10. Ride The Little Mermaid: Ariel's Undersea Adventure.
11. Get FastPasses for the Incredicoaster in Pixar Pier.
12. Return to Cars Land and take a spin on Mater's Junkyard Jamboree.
13. Ride Radiator Springs Racers using the FastPasses obtained earlier.
14. If you have time, ride Luigi's Rollickin' Roadsters.
15. Return to Pixar Pier and ride the Incredicoaster using the FastPasses obtained earlier.
16. Ride Monsters, Inc. Mike & Sulley to the Rescue in Hollywood Land.
17. See the Disney Animation exhibit, including Animation Academy and *Turtle Talk with Crush.*
18. Watch *Mickey's PhilharMagic.*
19. Eat dinner.
20. Ride Grizzly River Run in Grizzly Peak.
21. Repeat any favorite attractions or see any missed attractions.
22. Watch *World of Color.*

One-Day Plan for Adults with Small Children

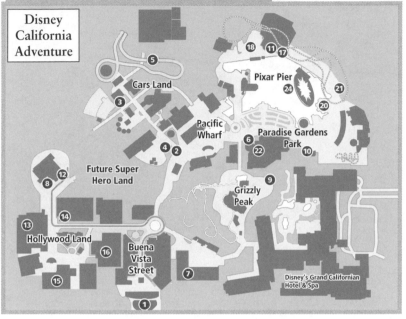

Disney California Adventure

Cars Land

Pixar Pier

Pacific Wharf

Paradise Gardens Park

Future Super Hero Land

Grizzly Peak

Hollywood Land

Buena Vista Street

Disney's Grand Californian Hotel & Spa

1. Arrive at the entrance 40 minutes before official opening time.
2. As soon as the park opens, obtain FastPasses for Radiator Springs Racers in Cars Land. FastPasses are distributed outside and to the left of Cars Land's main entrance.
3. Ride Luigi's Rollickin' Roadsters.
4. Try Mater's Junkyard Jamboree.
5. Ride Radiator Springs Racers using the FastPasses obtained earlier.
6. Obtain FastPasses for World of Color. FastPasses are distributed to the right of the entrance of The Little Mermaid: Ariel's Undersea Adventure in Paradise Gardens Park.
7. Ride Soarin' Around the World in Grizzly Peak.
8. Obtain FastPasses for Guardians of the Galaxy—Mission: Breakout! in Hollywood Land.
9. Explore the Redwood Creek Challenge Trail in Grizzly Peak.
10. Eat lunch. Try the Corndog Castle in Paradise Garden Park.
11. Go to Pixar Pier and get FastPasses for Toy Story Midway Mania!

12. Ride Guardians of the Galaxy—Mission: Breakout! in Hollywood Land using the FastPasses obtained earlier.
13. Check the daily entertainment schedule for the next showing of Frozen—Live at the Hyperion.
14. See the Disney Animation exhibit, including Animation Academy and Turtle Talk with Crush.
15. Ride Monsters, Inc. Mike & Sulley to the Rescue.
16. Watch Mickey's PhilharMagic.
17. Ride Toy Story Midway Mania! in Pixar Pier using the FastPasses obtained earlier.
18. Experience Jessie's Critter Carousel.
19. Eat dinner.
20. Try the Silly Symphony Swings in Paradise Gardens Park.
21. If it's open, experience Inside Out Emotional Whirlwind in Pixar Pier.
22. Ride The Little Mermaid: Ariel's Undersea Adventure in Paradise Gardens Park.
23. Repeat any favorite attractions or see any missed attractions.
24. Watch World of Color.

Universal Studios One-Day Touring Plan

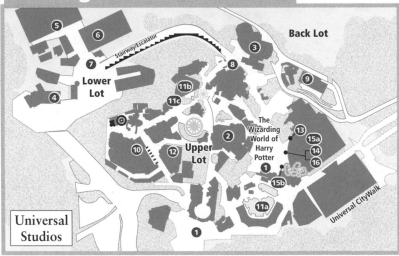

1. If you are eligible for early entry, arrive 1 hour and 20 minutes before official opening time, and enjoy The Wizarding World of Harry Potter until the park opens to the general public. Otherwise, arrive 40 minutes before opening time.
2. In the Upper Lot, see *Kung Fu Panda Adventure* at the DreamWorks Theatre.
3. Experience The Simpsons Ride.
4. As soon as the Lower Lot opens, descend the escalators and ride Jurassic World.
5. Ride Transformers: The Ride 3-D.
6. Check out Revenge of the Mummy—The Ride.
7. Say hello to the velociraptor at the base of the escalators.
8. Return to the Upper Lot and eat an early lunch in Springfield.
9. Take the Studio Tour. Allocate an hour and 10 minutes for the tour.
10. See Despicable Me Minion Mayhem, and explore Super Silly Fun Land if you have small children.
11. Check your daily entertainment schedule for a) *WaterWorld,* b) the *Special Effects Show,* and c) *Universal's Animal Actors* showtimes.
12. Experience The Walking Dead, if you dare.
13. Enter Hogsmeade Village. Explore the shops and experience the wand ceremony in Ollivanders.
14. Check the daily entertainment schedule for *The Frog Choir* and *Triwizard Spirit Rally* shows on the stage outside Hogwarts. Work in the shows around dinner at The Three Broomsticks.
15. Get into line for a) Harry Potter and the Forbidden Journey and/or b) Flight of the Hippogriff during the first two performances of the Hogwarts Castle projection show (performed seasonally).
16. Watch one of the final performances of the Hogwarts Castle show, or revisit your favorites and see any attractions you missed.